G000269136

Further praise for *Speaking for England*:

'A remarkably balanced and objective account, keeping Jack Amery's treason in context ... Racy and readable, modern political history at its best ... *Speaking for England* is crammed with moments of extraordinary drama' *Tatler*

'If you're looking for a good read, pick up a copy of David Faber's first book, *Speaking for England* ... An extraordinary, gripping and moving account' *Vogue*

'The biographical triptych is a difficult genre to realise, but David Faber has succeeded with great technical assurance, exhibiting, as a former MP, a sure understanding of the nuances of parliamentary life, as well as a personal empathy for the life and times of his subjects ... *Speaking for England* is not only an invaluable addition to the political history of the Conservative party, but also an affecting illustration of how, as the proverb says, "a wise son maketh a glad father, but a foolish son is the heaviness of his mother"' D. R. THORPE, *Spectator*

'John does not disappoint ... a bankrupt conman dividing his time between Spain and France [who] at one point was rumoured to be a diamond smuggler, gun runner and, with his marriages to two prostitutes, a bigamist ... Faber does provide some fresh insights' NIGEL FARNDALE, *Sunday Telegraph*

Speaking for
England

Leo, Julian and John Amery –
The Tragedy of a Political Family

DAVID FABER

POCKET
BOOKS

London • New York • Sydney • Toronto

First published in Great Britain by The Free Press in 2005
This edition first published by Pocket Books in 2007
An imprint of Simon & Schuster UK Ltd
A CBS COMPANY

1 3 5 7 9 10 8 6 4 2

Simon & Schuster UK Ltd
Africa House
64–78 Kingsway
London WC2B 6AH

www.simonsays.co.uk

Simon & Schuster Australia
Sydney

A CIP catalogue record for this book is available from the British Library.

ISBN-13: 978-1-4165-2596-7
ISBN-10: 1-4165-2596-3

Typeset by Rowland Phototypesetting Ltd, Bury St Edmunds, Suffolk
Printed and bound in Great Britain by Cox & Wyman Ltd, Reading, Berks

PICTURE CREDITS

Centre for the Study of Cartoons and Caricature, University of Kent: 15
Churchill Archives Centre, Leo Amery Papers, AMEJ 749: 34, 35; AMEL 06/02/04: 24, 26;
AMEL 06/03/15/02: 38; AMEL 10/01/01: 3; AMEL 10/02/01: 1; AMEL 10/34: 17;
AMEL 10/36: 16; AMEL 10/37: 39; AMEL 10/38: 7, 8, 12, 13, 25; AMEL 10/41/01: 2;
AMEL 10/45: 4; AMEL 10/50: 6; AMEL 10/73: 9, 10, 11, 14, 18, 19, 20; AMEL 10/80/01: 28;
AMEL 10/80/02: 33
Empics: 40
Getty Images: 5, 23, 27
Popperfoto: 36
Public Records Office: 29, 30, 31, 32
Sotheby's Picture Library: 41
Summer Fields Archive: 21
The Times: 22
Topfoto: 37

For Sophie

Contents

Acknowledgements

I am extremely grateful to the Amery family for generously allowing me to reproduce family photographs from their grandfather's and father's collections. The voluminous Amery archive is in safe hands at the Churchill Archives Centre, at Churchill College, Cambridge, and I am greatly indebted to Allen Packwood for all his practical help and moral support, and indeed to his team there for their assistance over many months; in particular Katharine Thomson and Ieuan Hopkins who have painstakingly catalogued the Amery papers, and have always been on hand with advice when requested. I also owe a very great debt of gratitude to all the staff at the London Library, especially those in the reading room, for their hospitality and almost daily assistance for the past two years.

Many other archivists at various libraries and archive centres have also kindly welcomed me during my research, and my thanks go to them also; especially Colin Harris in the Modern Papers Reading Room at the Bodleian Library, Christine Penney at the Birmingham University Library, Rita Gibbs at Harrow School, Margaret Pope at the Alpine Club and Eamon Dyas at News International; also to the staff at a number of other collections for their assistance, including the Public Records Office, the British Library, the House of Lords Record Office, the Cambridge University Library, the West Sussex Records Office, the Lambeth Palace Library and All Souls College, Oxford.

I am especially grateful to those few people who gave up often precious time to share their own personal recollections of the Amery family with me: the late Sir Alexander Glen, Katharine Viscountess Macmillan, the Rt Hon. Michael Howard, Sir Clive Bossom and Professor William Rubinstein. I am grateful too to David Nicholson, both for his ongoing advice and encouragement during my work on this book, and also for the legacy bequeathed to future Amery historians by his and John Barnes's magisterial editing, in two volumes, of Leo Amery's diaries. It has been a curious sensation to follow them through the pages of the typewritten, leather-bound diaries which cover fifty years of Leo Amery's life. Many others have helped with a word of advice here, or an anecdote there, which may have seemed insignificant to them at the time, but have often helped me to piece the story together. In particular I am grateful to the late Sir Stephen Hastings, William Massey, Edward Garnier, Dr John Jones, John Hamill, Bruce McCrae, Catherine Faber, Mark Eccles-Williams, Michael Gove, Graham Stewart, Christopher James and David Forbes; also to Dr David Freeman and Dr Richard Grayson, both dedicated Amery scholars.

D. R. Thorpe has been a constant source of inspiration and encouragement from the very first, and a regular contributor of anecdotes and references gleaned in the course of his own research. Nicholas Aldridge has not only provided all possible assistance in his role as archivist at Summer Fields school, but has also kindly read through the manuscript with the careful eye of a classical scholar. And Colin Lee has given incredibly generously of his time to read the manuscript not once, but twice, and has made numerous helpful suggestions, both of style and content, principally but not exclusively in the areas of parliamentary procedure and political history.

Special thanks are due to my agent Michael Sissons for encouraging me to undertake this project in the first place and for then providing much-needed reassurance throughout. And to Andrew Gordon at Simon & Schuster, who not only had the confidence to take me on initially, but has subsequently guided me patiently and expertly through the potential hazards of writing a first book. I am also very grateful to Edwina Barstow for all her tireless help, especially during the editing process, and to my copy-editor John English.

Finally, I am deeply grateful to my family; to my mother for all her support, and to my children, especially my son, for his constant encouragement, and for the interest he has shown, way beyond his years, in the story that is told in these pages. Last, but most important of all, I thank my wife from the bottom of my heart. Without her enthusiastic encouragement this book would never have been started, and without her constant support and occasional cajoling it would most probably never have been completed. She has tolerated my almost permanent state of self-absorption in the lives of Leo, Julian and Jack Amery, and has been forced to endure a level of intimacy with their characters far beyond what is justifiable. She is my rock, and I dedicate this book, with all my love, to her.

Prologue

It was in the early hours of Friday, 20 November 1942, when Leo Amery and his wife, Florence, known as Bryddie, settled down in the splendid L-shaped library of their house in Eaton Square, Belgravia, to listen to the radio. They did so with great reluctance, having already tuned in once, earlier on that evening, to listen for the first time to the very broadcast that they were now about to hear again. This time, however, they were to be joined by their twenty-three-year-old son, Julian, who had just returned from a night out at dinner. For Leo Amery, and indeed the whole family, it had been a hectic and emotional few days. As Secretary of State for India in Winston Churchill's wartime Cabinet, he was closely involved every day with the war effort. Recently there had been almost daily Cabinet meetings to attend, in the wake of 'Operation Torch', the successful Allied landings in North Africa. Leo was himself preoccupied by the search for a new Viceroy for India, in succession to the retiring incumbent, Lord Linlithgow, a task made all the more difficult by the close interest being taken in the new appointment by the Prime Minister himself. Julian, meanwhile, was working at the Baker Street offices of the Special Operations Executive, having already seen service with the organisation in Yugoslavia, Cairo and Jerusalem, although he had spent the afternoon at Conservative Central Office with a view to getting on to the approved list of party candidates for any post-war general election.

'Germany Calling, Germany Calling.' The radio came to life, the announcer intoning the words which were by now all too familiar to those Britons who were regular listeners, whether out of curiosity, amusement or genuine interest, to the output of the German propaganda machine.

> Tonight you will hear an Englishman who is speaking to you at his own request and of his own free will: Mr John Amery, son of the Secretary for India of the British Government, the Right Honourable Leopold Stennett Amery. The German Government bears no responsibility whatever for what Mr Amery is going to say. The German Government has merely sought fit to place its station at the disposal of Mr Amery for what he desires to say, since the world may be interested to hear what an Englishman who looks at his country from the outside has to say. We believe that Mr Amery's observations will be of special interest to you also: Mr John Amery . . .[1]

It was two and a half years since Leo had last seen his eldest son. John Amery, known to his family throughout his life as Jack, was now thirty years old and had been living in France for the past few years. Father and son had spent a few, relatively happy days together in Paris during March 1940, but since the fall of France communication between them had become increasingly difficult and was restricted, by and large, to the occasional telegram. Leo and Bryddie knew that Jack had been living in the unoccupied zone of southern France, and had been dismayed to learn from him that he had, apparently, been suffering from tuberculosis. As he had done throughout Jack's troublesome life, Leo had been generous during the early war years in providing financially for his wayward son, within the restraints posed by the regulations and practical difficulties of dealing with the Vichy regime. Only a week earlier, on 11 November, believing Jack still to be in France, their concern had been heightened by the news of the German occupation of the unoccupied zone.

However, on 17 November, they had heard the news for which, while they could have had no possible forewarning of its precise details, their instincts in relation to their elder son would undoubtedly have prepared them. An American news agency telephoned Leo at home to tell him that the German News Service, Transocean, had been broadcasting advertisements claiming that Jack was now in Berlin, staying at the up-market Adlon Hotel. What was worse, he had supposedly gone there at 'his own request before the Germans marched into unoccupied France'. Shortly afterwards the Press Association called about the same story and, later in the day, a reporter from the *Daily Mirror* succeeded in confronting Leo on the doorstep of his home. The family were in turmoil. There was no possible means of confirming or denying the story, and Leo found himself in the invidious position of hoping, however ghastly the prospect, that Jack had actually been coerced by the Germans into travelling to Berlin. He conceded that all the evidence suggested that 'the Gestapo had got hold of' Jack, and 'were bent on exploiting him in one way or another'. But he could only hope that their purpose was to 'get him to say or do something foolish with the fear of the concentration camp over him'.[2] Incredible as it may now appear, at the time that seemed to be the lesser of two evils.

The news appeared in the press the following morning with varying degrees of prominence. In the course of the previous evening Leo had spoken to the Minister of Information, Brendan Bracken, begging him to do all he could to keep the story quiet, and Bracken's efforts had met some success. But *The Times* ran a short paragraph on the story, while the *Daily Mirror* quoted at length from their ad hoc interview with Leo the previous day, highlighting in gruesome detail his ignorance as to Jack's true intentions. He had last heard of Jack 'through the Red Cross as an invalid' and it was 'just conceivable' that he had asked to go to Berlin 'for treatment for lung trouble'. He could 'not quite credit the German message', but nor could he confirm that Jack was still in the south of France 'because communication is still very difficult'.[3] And the paper backed up its scoop with the still more unpleasant suggestion that Jack was indeed in Berlin with the intention of broadcasting on behalf of Germany.

Later that day Leo was due to go down to visit his old school, Harrow, to attend the School Concert and the annual rendition of the celebrated School Songs. He had, for many years, been a school governor and this year had been invited to travel down to Harrow with the guest of honour for the day and the school's most famous former pupil, the Prime Minister, Winston Churchill. The conversation in the car on the way down centred, as it had done between them for some weeks, on the appointment of a new Viceroy for India, Churchill surprising his Secretary of State with a new name, that of Dick Law, himself the son of a former Conservative Prime Minister. But many years of experience since the days when they had been contemporaries together at Harrow, had taught Leo that visits to their old school were, for Churchill, a welcome opportunity to relax among friends, to reminisce and to enjoy the adulation of the boys. This year was no different. During the singing of the most famous of Harrow Songs, 'Forty Years On', Leo noticed that the Prime Minister 'had tears in his eyes' and at tea afterwards was seen to be enjoying himself enormously, surrounded by a small group of senior boys 'all eagerly listening and smiling as he unbent himself and told them story after story'. On the journey home Churchill spoke kindly to Leo about the news from Berlin. Leo told him that 'if the thing in any way embarrassed him from the point of view of his Government', then he would be only too happy to resign. 'Good God,' replied Churchill, 'I wouldn't hear of such a thing!' Nobody, he thought, perhaps with greater feeling than most, should have to take the blame 'for the aberrations of a grown-up son'.[4]

That evening, any lingering doubts as to Jack's intentions were dispelled by the lead news story on the German News Service. 'When John Amery heard in Berlin of the landings of Americans and British in Algiers and Morocco,' intoned the announcer, 'he decided to approach the Wilhelmstrasse with a request to be permitted to address his compatriots at home over the German wireless.' He had been in Berlin for three weeks, continued the Transocean story, and his 'presence there had been kept a dead secret. At first, he wanted only to have talks and study conditions on the spot', but the 'attack on North Africa prompted him to come into the foreground. He will broadcast on Thursday.'[5] For the family, Bryddie in particular, 'the whole business was nearly unbearable' thought Leo, and he could only hope that it would 'not be too awful' for her or for Julian.[6]

Leo and Bryddie could do nothing but wait for the 'miserable ordeal' of listening to Jack's broadcast at the appointed hour. When they heard it together for the first time, during the early evening, their spirits were briefly lifted. It was immediately 'quite clear' to them both 'that this was not his voice or manner of speaking'. When Julian returned from dinner later that evening, the three of them sat down to listen to the broadcast again.

Listeners will wonder what an Englishman is doing on the German radio tonight. You can imagine that before taking this step I hoped that someone better qualified than me would come forward. I dared to believe that some ray of common sense, some appreciation of our priceless civilisation would guide the counsels of Mr Churchill's government. Unfortunately this has not been the case.

For two years living in a neutral country I have been able through the haze of propaganda to reach something which my conscience tells me is the truth. That is why I come forward tonight without any political label, without any bias, but just simply as an Englishman to say to you: A crime is being committed against Civilisation!

'The priceless heritage of our fathers' and 'of our empire builders', he continued, was 'being thrown away in a war that serves no British interests'. Above all, Britain's 'alliance with the Soviets' was 'morally . . . a stain on our honour', which could 'only lead sooner or later to disaster and communism in Britain, to a disintegration of all the values we cherish most'. The British people must use their 'common sense, to see through the propaganda with which a small group of people try to blind you'. And who were these people?

Look for yourselves! There is not one, not one single great daily paper in London that is not Jewish controlled, not one news reel . . . You are being lied to, your patriotism, your love for our England is being exploited by people who for the most part hardly have any right to be English.

The irony of Jack's outburst was not lost on Leo, himself the son of a Jewish immigrant. In different circumstances, Jack's late Jewish grand-mother might well have been enough to condemn him to a very different kind of a visit to Germany, quite possibly one that could even have ended in a gas chamber. Nevertheless, he continued his talk in the same vein.

The mothers of Britain who had lost sons in the war should know that their boys had died as mercenaries for 'that foul international alliance between New York and Moscow', while, somewhat bizarrely, 'every Sunday English priests are calling on God to help the Bolshevik armies'.

> We have been betrayed, we have been sold out to the inter-national interests of New York and Moscow, who will not hesitate to leave us once they have sucked up all our resources, when the last Englishman has died for their criminal war.[7]

Only at this stage of the broadcast did the quality of the content rise, briefly, above the 'anti-Semitic tripe' that Leo had so far considered it, and began to show some evidence of the hand, as he thought, of the 'German propaganda headquarters'.[8] Appealing to the British people, 'Mr Brown, Mr Jones, you Mrs Smith', Jack urged that they 'decide that this has lasted long enough, that our boys are dying to serve no British interest'. They should ask themselves 'just one question only: is this war really necessary? Who are those men who are urging you to go on and on?' There was 'more than enough room in the world for Germany and Britain'. The British Government claimed that 'Germany seeks world domination', but 'did it ever enter your mind that this is but another trick of that long-planned strategy of Jewish propaganda, expected to thwart Germany's commanding position on the Continent, to which she is after all entitled?' Germany had never 'denied Britain her Imperial position'. It was time for every-one to 'say the word, to come slowly, gradually, but irresistibly back to common sense'.

The remainder of the broadcast sank back, once again, into an almost incoherent anti-Jewish and anti-Communist diatribe. The

British people should be 'ashamed that in London at the Lord Mayor's election there were just two candidates both Jewish', while the German army was the only thing standing between Britain and Communism and 'world-domination by Jewry'. He left his listeners with one thought. It was up to 'the man in the street' to 'overthrow the men who have brought our country so low', while he, John Amery, 'so long as the German Government allows me', would be 'here to help you, to guide you, that we all one day may see again the sun of peace rise over Europe'. He finished by reminding his audience that he was not a defeatist, but a 'patriot whose primary concern is the preservation of the British Empire'.[9]

The turmoil and the pain endured by Leo, Bryddie and Julian while they listened to these words was intense. Their initial reaction was one of confusion. All three tried hard to convince themselves that it had not in fact been Jack's voice to which they had been listening. They knew his voice to be 'low, soft and somewhat slurred', while what they had heard that evening was 'a hard, staccato voice by someone who had evidently done a good deal of speaking and broadcasting'. And, even if Jack had partly sympathised with the views expressed in the broadcast, 'the material and turn of phrase were also clearly not his'. While Bryddie was comforted by Julian, Leo telephoned a message through to the night clerk on duty at Downing Street, informing the Prime Minister that it had not been his son on the radio at all. But while Bryddie continued to plead Jack's innocence, Leo was forced privately to concede that Jack's name was obviously 'a useful asset' to the Germans and that 'to some extent he must have acquiesced in their using it'. It was, he thought, 'all pretty beastly'.[10]

For Leo, in particular, it was a night of turbulent emotions. To what degree had he contributed to his son's behaviour that evening? He had clearly failed hopelessly to introduce Jack even to a basic understanding of his own Jewishness. And as a committed member of Churchill's Government himself, Leo was steadfast in his own determination to prosecute the war until its bitter end, an end that could now only mean one thing for Jack. How was it, wondered Leo, that while Julian was now sitting safely at home in the bosom of his family, and had dedicated himself wholeheartedly to fighting for King and Country, that his elder brother had come to embark on the path he had taken tonight, and that could now only lead inexorably to his own destruction?

Part One

1873–1918

CHAPTER ONE

Pocket Hercules

The picturesque village of Lustleigh nestles snugly in the Coombe Valley, on the eastern edge of Dartmoor, to this day a quintessentially English village. The thirteenth-century church sits proudly at the heart of the village, surrounded by random granite cottages and the wooded hills of Lustleigh Cleave. In 1665 Nicholas Amery acquired a small farm, Middle Coombe, hidden away at the end of a steep, narrow lane and tucked into the side of the valley above the village. With the house came extensive grazing rights on the upper slopes of the Cleave and for a further two hundred years, as his descendants multiplied and expanded their local holdings, the Amery family were to make their living off the land. It was at Middle Coombe that Charles Frederick Amery was born in 1833 and brought up.

Charles Amery came from a long line of Devon farmers and had inherited the family trait, a noticeable lack of stature, albeit in a strong, wiry body. With his farming ancestry, he might have seemed most obviously suited to the outdoor life, but at his father's insistence he was initially destined for a university education and a professional career. In fact, it was his love of the outdoors and a yearning to wander further afield than the surrounding Dartmoor countryside that led him, at the age of just eighteen, to leave home to join the Australian gold rush. It was to be the first of a series of doomed business enterprises, and neither mining nor his subsequent, brief time as a sheep farmer brought him the riches he sought. He soon returned home and signed up as one of the first recruits to the newly formed Indian Forestry Service.

The art of forestry suited him and he quickly rose to the rank of Deputy-Conservator for the North Western Provinces of India. His *Notes on Forestry*[1] became a standard textbook of its day and offers painstaking advice on the correct methods for sowing, planting and felling timber. His career prospects at last looked bright and were enhanced still further by his maternal aunt, Mrs Stennett, a wealthy and childless widow from whom, he was assured, he could look forward to a considerable bequest. When he returned home on leave in 1872, he was careful to pay regular visits to his aunt to safeguard his inheritance and it was perhaps unsurprising that she, in turn, should have wished to find a suitable wife for her increasingly successful nephew. She arranged a meeting with a close friend of hers from London, the young Elisabeth Leitner, and the couple soon became engaged.

Elisabeth came from the far end of Europe, from a world which had little in common with the peace of Lustleigh and the wild Dartmoor landscape. She had been born Elisabeth Johanna Saphir in Pest, the bustling Jewish quarter of Budapest in 1841. The Saphirs were a distinguished and intellectual family of Hungarian Jews, although Elisabeth's father, Leopold Saphir, died when she was a young child. Her eldest uncle, Moritz Saphir, had been born to a Yiddish-speaking, orthodox Jewish family near Budapest but subsequently rejected Judaism, was baptised as a Lutheran and, in later life, came to refer to his Jewish origins as 'a birth deformity, corrected by a baptismal operation'.[2] Elisabeth's widowed mother, Marie Henriette Herzberg, remarried a Johann Moritz Leitner, whereupon Elisabeth and her elder brother, Gottlieb Wilhelm Saphir, assumed their stepfather's surname. Leitner too came from a Hungarian orthodox Jewish family and was reputedly 'destined for the rabbinical chair'. But while practising as a military physician for the Austrian Government in Constantinople, he converted to Protestantism in about 1844 and later became a medical missionary among Turkish Jews and Muslims.[3] It was only after his death in 1861 that Elisabeth and her mother moved to London.

Charles Amery and Elisabeth Leitner were married at St Marylebone Parish Church on 30 January 1873 and, with his leave over, they sailed for India almost immediately. For the next four years the family lived in Gorakhpur, in the United Provinces, and it was there, on 22 November 1873, that Leo Amery was born and named after his Jewish maternal grandfather. Early in 1874 the Reverend Henry Stern, another German-born Jew who had converted to Anglicanism and had been a close friend of Elisabeth's late stepfather, made a special trip out to India to baptise his old friend's new grandchild, Leopold Charles Moritz Stennett Amery.

Leo's earliest memories were few, but they were happy ones. The family was based at his father's forestry headquarters in Gorakhpur, but four or five months of the year were spent on the road visiting the plantations spread across the far-reaching district he controlled, a region which included the head of the Ganges and extended far up into the Himalayas. For Elisabeth, these were the happiest times of the year and life in camp gave the baby Leo his first taste for the great outdoors, a love that was to remain with him throughout his life. He was a precocious child, learning to walk and talk by his first birthday and being fully conversant in Hindustani by the age of three.

When Leo was eighteen months old, his mother gave birth to a brother, Geoffrey, but their idyllic childhood was not to last for long. The Amerys' marriage was not a happy one, and in 1877 Elisabeth Amery returned to England with her two young children. Incredibly Leo, in spite of a subsequent lifetime devoted to worldwide travel and five years spent as Secretary of State for India, was never again to return to the country of his birth. Soon after returning to London, Elisabeth gave birth to a third son, Harold François Saphir Amery, named in part after his true maternal grandfather, and the family settled down to a far from comfortable life in London. Elisabeth's marriage was over and, in the meantime, 'something seems to have upset' Charles Amery's 'balance' and he promptly left for Canada where he tried his hand at farming, then at dictionary publishing in New York and finally at gold mining in British Guiana.

The truth of Charles Amery's sudden departure was rather more prosaic than the 'severe sunstroke' claimed as an excuse by his wife.[4] In

December 1882 Elisabeth finally instituted divorce proceedings against her husband, petitioning that he had 'since the month of November 1879 committed adultery' with a Clara Zupansky and had, since January 1880, lived with her in Vienna and Montreal. He had also, allegedly, 'frequently committed adultery with divers women'. Charles Amery counter-petitioned that Elisabeth had 'connived' at the affair by 'her wilful desertion of the respondent' and had herself 'established an intimacy' with a London barrister named William Fooks.[5] Nevertheless, the decree was granted in 1885, by which time Charles had disappeared. His children were never to see him again and he died, penniless, in British Guiana in 1901, leaving young Leo and his brothers to be brought up by their mother in London.

Elisabeth Amery moved widely among a group of sophisticated and cultured Jews from central Europe, principally Hungary and Germany, many of whom had converted to Protestantism and were now living in London. Her brother, Gottlieb Wilhelm Leitner, was himself one of the most interesting figures of that circle. Born in Budapest and educated in Constantinople, from an early age he had shown a remarkable ability to learn any number of languages. According to his obituary in *The Times*, 'as a linguist he probably had no living rival', and at the age of fifteen he had been appointed as interpreter to the British forces in the Crimea, enjoying the honorary rank of colonel. At the age of nineteen he became a lecturer in Arabic, Turkish and Modern Greek at King's College, London, and at twenty-one its first Professor of Arabic and Dean of the Faculty.[6] He spent most of his adult life in India, where he became well known as an explorer and traveller, returning to England in 1883 and settling in Woking, where he founded the Oriental University Institute, a private college for Indian students, and where he also left his most lasting legacy, Britain's first ever mosque, which remains there to this day.

Elisabeth Amery duly embarked upon a new life in London with her three sons, impoverished but determined that they should succeed, indeed excel at whatever life they chose. She was an attractive woman, dark and petite with fine features. Leo described her as 'deeply religious, and brought up in a somewhat narrowly evangelical circle', yet 'completely unworldly' at the same time. He adored her and recalled her kindness, often of a material kind in spite of her own straitened circumstances, and her keen sense of humour. Laughter played a major part in her young family's upbringing.[7] Her ambition for her children, and for Leo in particular, led her to encourage them to write and to read widely from an early age, while Leo also inherited her natural aptitude for languages.

When his great aunt Stennett died in 1881, she bequeathed her large house on the Brighton seafront to Elisabeth Amery and the family moved there, in the hope of a more comfortable life. For Leo, the main attraction was the huge library, where he spent most of his time reading authors far beyond his tender years, working his way through *Jane Eyre* at the age of six, only for it suddenly to be deemed too adult for him and taken away before he could discover the ending. Unfortunately, the substantial fortune that Mrs Stennett had earmarked for Leo's father before he absconded did not find its way to his family along with the Brighton house. It was to be, all too briefly, the only permanent home Leo would enjoy throughout his childhood as Elisabeth, in order to pay for her sons' education, spent their school years living in lodgings, boarding houses and cheap hotels abroad. At the age of eight Leo was sent as a boarder to a local school in Brighton and, although the youngest and smallest boy in the school, he soon won his first prizes for Latin and French.

But the economies that Elisabeth had already made were still not enough and, after just two terms, the family moved to Cologne, where they were to spend the next two years lodging with an elderly Prussian colonel and his wife, and attending a local day school to learn German. Leo's early memories of the German race were largely unfavourable. He was subjected to regular public beatings at school, often as a result of having been sneaked on by his schoolmates, an activity he soon realised they perceived as their 'joyful duty'. He thus discovered *Schadenfreude*, which he quickly identified as one of the 'less lovable traits of the German character'[8] and, having soon outgrown the teaching on offer, was taught by a private tutor for the last few months of their stay. In 1884, at the age of eleven, Leo accompanied his mother back to England and was enrolled at York House, a prep school for boys in Folkestone. The next three years were happy ones and, while the school failed to prepare the young Leo for the scholarships that lay ahead, there was plenty of outdoor life and ample opportunity for reading. Thackeray was a particular favourite, although the precocious young Leo declared himself to be 'bored' by Dickens.[9] Holidays were spent making trips to France to learn French or under the guidance of a Russian tutor, at whose language Leo soon became proficient.

At the age of thirteen he was taken by his mother to Harrow, to sit the entrance scholarship. The examinations were spread over several days, with the less academic boys, known as the 'half-wits', sent home after the first or second day. It came as a complete surprise to Leo, after the over-tolerant teaching methods at York House, that candidates were required to translate entire passages of English into Latin prose and even to write Latin verses. Not surprisingly, he was weeded out after the first day. However, Elisabeth's financial sacrifices meant that Leo was still able to take up his place at Harrow, albeit without the hoped-for scholarship, and he arrived there in September 1887. By then, he had changed his middle name from his legal name at birth, Moritz, to the less Jewish sounding Maurice. According to one historian, it may be that this was part of a wider strategy, possibly at the instigation of his ambitious mother, 'to do everything possible to bury his Jewish past', although while Harrow 'may well have had an undercurrent of anti-semitism', as an institution 'it was certainly not overtly anti-semitic'. Indeed, a number of his school contemporaries bore famous Jewish names, albeit as scions of families with substantial, self-made fortunes. Having made so many sacrifices to give her brightest child the best possible start in life, Elisabeth Amery may simply have felt that to be Jewish would have been one handicap too many.[10]

She need not have worried. Leo arrived at Harrow with a far wider range of general knowledge than his contemporaries and he soon made up for any lack of classical scholarship. He was placed in the Lower Remove under Mr Stogdon, who began the term by asking a room full of nervous new boys what they considered to have been the most important political event of the summer holidays. As a glum silence descended on the class, the thirteen-year-old Leo, sitting at the very back, timidly suggested that it might have been 'the Nizam of Hyderabad's offer to the Queen to supply money and troops in case of trouble with Russia'.[11] This early appreciation of imperial affairs led to an invitation to tea with Stogdon where, over a bottle of olives, mutual interests such as their common study of Russian were discussed and an invitation issued to join Stogdon's house, West Acre, rather than the Head Master's, for which Leo had been destined. It was to be the beginning of a lifelong friendship with his housemaster, and it was Stogdon, who had been a famous mountaineer in the early days of Alpine climbing, who was first to introduce the young Leo to the pleasures of mountaineering on a climbing party to the Lake District during the Christmas holidays of 1891.

A study of the Harrow broadsheets, the twice-yearly exam results, reveals Leo's meteoric rise through the school's academic hierarchy. He was a regular winner of form prizes, known as Copies, in Classics, Modern Languages and Maths, and for his first five terms he came top of his class, moving up each term from the Lower Remove, through Upper Remove, Fifth Form and into the Lower Sixth.[12] At the end of the summer term of 1889, the Lower Sixth were examined together with the forms above them in the Upper Sixth and, as was the convention, the entire school assembled in the impressive Speech Room to hear the lists read out, starting from the bottom. As the Head Master slowly intoned the names with no mention of Amery, Leo grew increasingly anxious, until finally, after a theatrical pause, he was revealed, in just his sixth term and at the age of fifteen, as the very top scholar in the school.

Leo made the most of every opportunity that Harrow had to offer, and while he maintained his academic pre-eminence as the top scholar throughout his last three years there, he was far from being a 'swot' who paid little attention to other school pursuits. It was at Harrow that his size, or rather, the obvious lack of it, first attracted attention and he never grew to be taller than five foot four. But if his contemporaries thought him a weakling, they were quickly disabused. During his first term he was challenged to a fight by a much older boy in his house, who clearly fancied his chances against the midget new boy. Having at first declined the invitation, Leo quickly realised that his tormentor was not going to be deterred so easily and decided that attack would be the best form of defence. He knocked the older boy out with a single, swinging right hook, an early encounter which understandably gave him what he later described as a 'wholly undeserved reputation for pugnacity', but ensured that he was treated with more respect in the future.[13] It was the first, but by no means the last time that he made sure of getting his retaliation in first.

He soon found more conventional outlets for his strength and tenacity. He became a successful boxer and cross-country runner, and participated enthusiastically in Harrow football. But his most successful sport was gymnastics and for his last two years he was the champion gymnast of the school, revelling in the nickname given to him by the Aldershot colonel who came to judge the school competition, as the 'Pocket Hercules'.[14] In the summer, cricket largely passed him by, although he proved himself to be nearly a hundred years ahead of his time when he suggested that some of the boredom of the game could be eradicated at a stroke by 'so simple a remedy as a fixed time limit for each innings'.[15] And so it was in swimming that he found his solace in the summer, spending long hours at the enormous Harrow pool known as Ducker, 'more like the bend of a river than a bath',[16] practising his diving and swimming underwater.

On one such day in the summer of 1889, at the end of his second year at Harrow, as he was 'standing in a meditative posture on the very brink',[17] Leo was surprised to feel a foot in the small of his back which duly propelled him into the water. His surprise was compounded by the realisation that the perpetrator of this crime was a small 'red-haired, freckled urchin'[18] who had foolishly mistaken him for a fellow new boy on account of his lack of stature. The young Winston Churchill soon realised his mistake. 'I was startled to see a furious face emerge from the foam', he later recalled, 'and a being evidently of enormous strength making its way by fierce strokes to the shore. I fled; but in vain. Swift as the wind my pursuer overtook me, seized me in a ferocious grip and hurled me into the deepest part of the pool.' A swarm of young boys gathered around, regaling Churchill with Leo's many athletic and academic accomplishments, but it was too late. Leo had already gained satisfaction by teaching Churchill some respect for age and authority, and the future Prime Minister was 'convulsed, not only with terror but with the guilt of sacrilege'.

The following day Churchill sought out his target and apologised profusely, claiming as his only excuse that Leo was so small. 'He did not seem at all placated by this; so I added in a most brilliant recovery, "My father, who is a great man, is also small".'[19] This seemed to do the trick and a lifetime's friendship, not always to be a straightforward one, was formed. As with all the best schoolboy anecdotes, the story of Leo's first confrontation with a young Churchill was retold and embellished many times over the years, so much so that forty years later, as Churchill stood on the threshold of the premiership, 'rumour was unsure whether Amery had thrashed Churchill or vice versa'.[20]

Leo's academic career continued to thrive and, by the time he left Harrow, he had at some stage won almost all of the school's most famous prizes and scholarships. Alongside his purely academic knowledge, he had also acquired a passionate love of books, and of the Classics in particular, which were to be a constant source of inspiration to him throughout his life. As editor of the school magazine, the *Harrovian*, Leo claimed another first as Churchill's earliest editor and censor. A highly critical, but anonymous, article by Churchill, ridiculing a recent military display in the gymnasium, caused a rush of correspondence to the magazine and a summons to Leo from the Head Master, Dr Welldon. Although Leo had already censored many of Churchill's most potent criticisms of the school, it was the editor, rather than the author, who was threatened with a good flogging if the libel was repeated. Leo was subsequently joined at Harrow by his two younger brothers, Geoffrey in 1890 and Harold in 1891, although Elisabeth's lack of money meant that they both stayed for only two years. Leo left in the summer of 1892, still top of the school, a senior monitor and with a host of scholarships under his belt. Harrow was to remain of central importance to him throughout his adult life. However, he never did quite overcome his initial dislike of composing Greek and Latin verses and it may have been on account of that reluctance that, somewhat surprisingly, he won a place at Balliol College, Oxford only as a major exhibitioner, rather than with the widely expected scholarship.

▪ ▪ ▪

Leo arrived at Balliol during the tenure of the college's most celebrated Master, the 'cherubic, but awe-inspiring figure' of Benjamin Jowett. Their first encounter was at a regular gathering of freshmen, who had been summoned to read essays to the Master in his lodgings. Scarcely had the young man, whose turn it was before Leo, begun his oration, than Jowett interrupted him with the curt suggestion that he should 'try the next page'. After the same advice had been repeated several times in quick succession, the reading was brought to a premature end, and the student was sent on his way with the observation that he had 'better think before writing next time'. Leo's early efforts to ingratiate himself with Jowett were equally unsuccessful when, alone with him over a glass of wine after dinner, he asked for help in obtaining a career in the Diplomatic Service. 'Wait until I've seen more of you', was the frosty reply.[21] It was said of Jowett that 'he had the power of influencing young men to a degree little short of supernatural', a power which he 'wielded for half a century, turning out a dedicated elite'. Leo was to become part of that elite, the youngest of a group of statesmen who studied under Jowett, which also included Henry Lansdowne, Herbert Asquith, George Curzon, Edward Grey, Alfred Milner and Herbert Samuel.[22]

At his first meeting with his tutor Leo declared himself to be bored by Greek and Latin, referred to his inability to do Latin verse which would rule him out of any of the university's major scholarships, and resolved that he would study science before moving on to history and philosophy. However, after his first successful attempt at composing a set of hexameters, it was decided that he should keep to Classics and, after a year and a half, he duly secured a 'first' in Mods. His initial reservations were justified in that he never did achieve a much coveted Craven scholarship, which would have represented the pinnacle of an undergraduate academic career, and had to satisfy himself instead with a creditable *proxime accessit*. But by working eight hours a day throughout his last year, and in spite of the apparent unorthodoxy of his views on philosophy and economics in the eyes of his examiners, he succeeded in achieving a 'first' in his Greats, the final exams, in the summer of 1896.

His mother's early ambition for him to master languages, and his inherited ability to do so, was to stand him in good stead. For a year after finishing his Mods, Leo turned his hand to learning Sanskrit, while he also resumed his study of Russian, reading Pushkin's *Eugene Onegin* in the original, as well as some Turgenev and Tolstoy. At times throughout his Oxford career his travels gave him the opportunity variously to become fluent in German, French, and Italian, while he improved his Hungarian, Serbian and Bulgarian soon after leaving. In the summer of 1895 he won a scholarship in Turkish at the Imperial Institute, for which he prepared intensively by inviting a young Turkish refugee, who spoke no English, to stay with him and work together for a month. But, as at Harrow, Leo refused to concentrate solely on academic pursuits and played a full part in the sporting, political and social life of the college and university. He took up hockey, which he continued to play after leaving, and won his 'half-blue' for cross-country running, finishing third in the university race of 1896 in a tough field at Cambridge. For Leo and his contemporaries, the social life at Oxford at the time was largely male-orientated, indeed almost monastic, with long evenings spent discussing philosophy and politics in the Balliol quad.

Leo had arrived at Oxford with strongly held political beliefs, but initially it was a life in the Diplomatic Service that appealed more than a political career, and he was an infrequent attender, and still more infrequent speaker, at debates at the Oxford Union, the nursery of so many political careers. Yet it was at Oxford that the political independence of spirit for which he was to be known throughout his career first surfaced. While at heart a Conservative, he was keen too to experiment whenever possible. Always an enthusiastic member of dining clubs, at Oxford he belonged to the Chatham Club, where the toast was 'Church and State', and whose membership was largely Conservative, but not too reactionary. Indeed, he and two friends, his fellow Old Harrovian Nugent Hicks, the future Bishop of Lincoln, and Lionel Curtis, later to become a leading architect of South African union, were threatened with expulsion as closet Socialists. With C. T. Davis, later to be his first Permanent Under Secretary at the Dominions Office, Leo founded an Oxford branch of the Fabian Society and arranged speaking visits to Oxford by such leading lights of the day as the Webbs, Tom Mann, Keir Hardie and Ramsay MacDonald. When the young and idealistic MacDonald visited Oxford, it was Leo's turn to entertain the guest speaker for the evening. They sat up late into the night in Leo's rooms, as MacDonald talked eloquently of a new political party, which would represent fresh ideals and needs. Thirty years later in Parliament, moments before the vote that would install MacDonald as Prime Minister, it fell to Leo to make the last speech from the Government despatch box, during which he reminded MacDonald of their first meeting all those years before in his rooms at Balliol.

It was during the Oxford holidays, in particular the long summer vacation, that Leo first began to develop his lifelong love of travel, especially to the mountains. His first visit to the Alps, in the summer of 1894, set the tone for his family's holidays for the next sixty years. With the warm glow of his 'first' in Mods now somewhat dissipated by a summer term spent largely at play, he packed a large trunk full of books and set out for the small town of Alf, tucked away on a bend of the river Moselle. Here he took a room in the house of a widowed German landlady, within the grounds of an old vineyard, and after an early morning swim he would spend the heat of the day in the cool cellar tackling Plato and Aristotle. He was joined by his brothers, and together they spent the afternoons swimming, rowing or walking in the neighbouring hills. But these walks were no more than training for the main event and when, after five or six weeks, the trunk's contents were finally finished, the three brothers moved on to Switzerland, where Leo was to meet up with an old school friend. On the road from Basle to Lucerne he enjoyed his first sight of a snow-covered peak and, on arriving in Zermatt for the first time, they ran up to the Gornergrat from where 'the wonders of the view held us spell-bound alike with sheer delight and with the wild surmise of youthful ambition'.[23] Before them were stretched out the various peaks that surround Zermatt, the Dent Blanche, the Rothorn, the Weisshorn, the Monte Rosa and, in the foreground most famous of all, the Matterhorn.

Although the heroic era of mountaineering was over, when the great peaks had been scaled for the first time, often by Englishmen, the romance of that period lingered on. In Zermatt famous mountaineers of that generation could be seen around the town or even, in some cases, like the great Whymper, still climbing. It was an inspiring time for a young undergraduate who yearned to be part of the next generation of mountaineers. With the confidence of youth, Leo set about preparing for the climbing ahead. Local guides were employed and the correct equipment acquired usually, in the absence of hard cash, by a mixture of bartering and pleading. After two days of practice on the lower slopes, the Rothorn was the first peak to be successfully scaled, the team setting out by moonlight and finishing with lunch under a burning sun at the summit. Over the next few days, the Weisshorn and the Dent Blanche were also conquered, causing a good deal of grudging admiration among the locals at the nerve of the young beginners. Indeed, the local notoriety achieved by the two young old Harrovians kindled the ambition of another former school colleague, Winston Churchill, who was also on holiday in Zermatt. But his attempt on the Monte Rosa, in spite of its technical success, was a long and painful haul as he suffered from a bad bout of mountain sickness, and he never climbed, nor indeed referred to the experience, again.

In the autumn of 1896, with a first-class degree safely under his belt and a summer of reading in Skye as preparation, Leo returned to Oxford to sit for a Fellowship in History at All Souls. He shared lodgings in the High Street with John Simon, with whom he was to be both political opponent and ally over the next fifty years. Simon considered Leo to be wholly unsuited to political life. 'You are too honest, for one thing,' he told him, 'and you will never settle down to voting straight and claptrap about the claims of the party. You are not very certain about which side is most like you, and in the end you are certain, as it seems to me, to quarrel with them both.'[24] Leo missed out on the All Souls Fellowship, beaten by Cyril Alington, the future Head Master of Eton and Dean of Durham, but he was encouraged to try again the following year and looked instead for a suitable way to spend the intervening time.

A few weeks' holiday over the Christmas of 1896 enabled him to fulfil one of the obligations of his Turkish scholarship at the Imperial Institute by visiting Constantinople. It was a time of considerable unrest and, with perfect timing, he arrived in the city just two days after one of the worst excesses, the massacre of six thousand Christian Armenians, by local 'boatmen and ruffians'. The immediate cause of this foretaste of subsequent Turkish attempts at a 'final solution' had been a sortie by a group of Armenian revolutionaries to blow up the Ottoman bank. Leo wrote home to his mother describing how, while out rowing on the Golden Horn, his boatman had cheerfully told him that the massacre had been carried out on the orders of the Sultan, that he had himself slit the throats of twenty-seven Armenians, and finally showed Leo a fine gold watch which ' "was given me by an Armenian gentleman" he said, with a horrible reminiscent leer'.[25]

On his return, Leo took a small flat in Cheyne Court in Chelsea for his mother and himself and acquired a part-time job as Political Private Secretary to Leonard Courtney, a Liberal Member of Parliament who happened to live around the corner in Cheyne Walk. The post had originally been offered to John Simon, but when he had been unable to take it, Beatrice Webb, Lady Courtney's sister, proposed the 'brilliant Oxford Fabian, Amery' instead.[26] Leo's duties were far from onerous, mitigating the effects of Courtney's blindness by preparing a verbal compilation of the most important stories in the morning papers each day, and preparing him for his parliamentary speeches. While they disagreed fundamentally on most political issues, they still found subjects on which to agree, such as the promotion of proportional representation and women's suffrage, and Leo greatly admired his employer's strength of character, sincerity and personal kindness. A steady stream of political and society figures made their way to the Courtneys' home, and Leo began a lasting friendship there with Sidney and Beatrice Webb. They, in turn, liked the headstrong young graduate who, at the time, shared many of their political views, even if Beatrice found some of them shocking, such as the occasion when Leo gave her an early indication of his anti-appeasing views by advocating 'the sudden destruction of the German fleet, without notice'.[27] Leo was also able, for the first time, to gain access to the inner sanctums of the House of Commons, to the Members' Lobby and the under gallery in the Chamber itself, from where he surveyed the frock coats and top hats of the Victorian Members, and listened to some of the great debates of the post-Gladstone era, admiring in particular Joseph Chamberlain's performance during a debate in July 1897 on the infamous Jameson Raid.

After a summer spent reading and sailing in Burnham-on-Crouch, Leo returned to Oxford for a second attempt at the All Souls Fellowship, once again sharing lodgings with John Simon. One of the essay titles on which they were required to write was 'How small of all that human heart endure, That part which laws or kings can cause or cure', an appropriate subject for two men later destined to play such a substantial role in public life. But neither was confident of success and they were busy consoling each other when they saw a young Fellow from All Souls approaching their house and 'realised one had been elected and each warmly seized the other's hand in congratulations'.[28] In fact, both had been successful.

Leo's election to an All Souls Fellowship, if nothing else, confounded the popular legend that success there depended on being '*bene natus, bene vestitus, mediocriter doctus*'. The attractions of the College for Leo, with its distinctive flavour, were manifest; the intoxicating blend of the interests of the academic world of Oxford with those of the wider political and international world outside; and the social atmosphere, especially at weekends, as politicians, professors, civil servants, bishops, lawyers, journalists and businessmen of all generations came together in the Smoking Room. For Leo, still undecided on a career, and somewhat reluctant to give up the student life, there was also the financial consideration. When asked to provide a statement of means for the College, he suggested that a 'strict working out' of his income 'would probably give somewhat less than £460' a year. The few stocks in his possession were still held in 'trustee securities' for him, and when he came of age he would be 'obliged to reinvest most of it to give sufficient income'.[29] In the meantime, an income from All Souls of £200 per year for the next seven years, the initial period of his Prize Fellowship, made difficult short-term choices seem altogether easier.

The College was presided over at the time by Warden Anson, and Leo met many of the important political figures of the day there: George Curzon, then Under-Secretary at the Foreign Office and soon to be bound for the Viceroyalty of India; George Buckle, the editor of

The Times; Cosmo Lang, to be Archbishop of Canterbury; Arthur Headlam, the Bishop of Gloucester, and Hensley Henson, soon to become the Bishop of Durham. Younger friendships, some to endure for many years, blossomed too, as younger Fellows were elected in turn: Geoffrey Robinson, later as Geoffrey Dawson the editor of *The Times*; Edward Wood, later Lord Halifax; and John Buchan, writer, diplomat and a weekend host to Leo for many years at his home at Elsfield outside Oxford. Years later, when Senior Fellow, John Simon echoed Leo's own feelings when he said that 'apart from domestic happiness, nothing' in his life had meant so much to him as 'the comradeship . . . of the fraternity of All Souls'.[30] In old age, Leo recalled a time of 'bachelor life friendships and of the legendary election for good birth, good dress and modest erudition'.[31]

Bitten by the Levantine bug during his time in Constantinople, Leo decided to return to the near east at the end of his first term at All Souls. The problem was how to finance the trip. His first thought was *The Times* and he turned to the Warden for help. 'It occurs to me', he wrote to Anson, 'that Mr Buckle might have some work for me to do this vacation, either in Austria or Turkey. Could you perhaps make the suggestion to him?'[32] Anson duly arranged for Leo to see Buckle who, although unable to offer anything substantial, agreed that he would gladly consider publishing any letters that Leo sent to him. Leo then telegraphed C. P. Scott, the legendary editor of the *Manchester Guardian*, requesting an interview. He arrived at his office at midnight on the same day and left with a cheque for £100 in his pocket and a mandate to write as much as he could about events from Vienna to Constantinople. The College would require him to be back the following term in time for the Bursar's Dinner, the traditional indication of residency at All Souls. 'If by any fatality I get snowed up in Thessaly or imprisoned by over-zealous Turkish officials,' he wrote, with some prescience, to Anson, 'the college will, I hope not be too severe on me.'[33] The first phase of his career had been decided upon.

▪ ▪ ▪

A few days later he arrived in Vienna and presented himself to William Lavino, the local correspondent for *The Times* and the doyen of the great foreign correspondents across Europe. It was by learning his trade at Lavino's side that Leo became convinced that the world of foreign journalism represented an altogether more enjoyable, and certainly more lucrative, career than the Diplomatic Service. He kept his paymasters at the *Manchester Guardian* happy by providing material, first from Vienna, then Prague and Budapest, and finally Belgrade and Sofia. But it was in Macedonia, the most backward and reluctant outpost of the Ottoman Empire, that Leo found most adventure. He arrived in January 1898, and initially received a warm welcome to the capital, Üsküb (now Skopje), from the *Vali*, Mehmet Pasha, the much feared embodiment of local Turkish rule, 'a Kurd and a rascal'.[34]

It was not long before Leo's natural inquisitiveness and his desire to befriend the oppressed local Bulgars, as well as the Austrian and Russian consuls, led to suspicion that he was spying against the ruling power. A trip across the border into northern Albania, and his openly avowed determination to view the scenes of recent Turkish atrocities aroused further concern and he returned to the capital to find the atmosphere increasingly hostile. The more courageous local Bulgars found their way to his door, and when he tried to prevent the arrest of three Bulgars at the entrance to his hotel, the reaction of the local chief of police, who had been following him for days, was to arrest him also. This was too much for Leo whose unopened umbrella 'somehow broke in two' on the policeman's head, 'while he collapsed on his back in the mud'.[35] Once again, the 'Pocket Hercules' had got his retaliation in first.

He was arrested and ordered to be put on trial, but he refused to comply and instead telegraphed to the Embassy in Constantinople requesting assistance and an apology from the *Vali* for the way he had been treated. He was charged with fostering revolution among the contented subjects of the Ottoman Empire and of an unprovoked assault on the chief of police. Fortunately, the British Consul arrived from Constantinople just in time and arranged for him to be released and accompanied to the Bulgarian border, but not before word of his adventures had reached Oxford. He had already, as he had correctly envisaged, missed the Bursar's dinner and had to write to the Warden asking for an extension to his term. Now, no less a figure than Lord

Salisbury, the Prime Minister and himself a Fellow of the College, wrote to Anson to complain that 'Mr Amery has occupied us a good deal.' It appeared 'to be certain that he struck a policeman, which in those countries is a grave offence'.[36]

Leo was welcomed to Sofia as a champion of the oppressed Bulgars of Macedonia and headed home for Oxford just as he received a worried telegraph of recall from the *Manchester Guardian*, also concerned at the reports which had reached them that he been imprisoned for attacking three policemen. His celebrity status became clear the following winter when, while travelling through the neighbouring Sanjak region, he came across a group of Albanians who recounted to him, in perfect detail, the story of the previous winter's Macedonian insurrection. Miraculously, he was gravely informed, the insurgents had only been saved by the intervention of 'an Englishman of gigantic stature who, single-handed and armed only with a club, had routed two Turkish battalions'.[37]

CHAPTER TWO

——◆——

Reformer

Although now a mature student of twenty-four, Leo had still not yet quenched his youthful thirst for travel. And while he was still considering how best to pursue his now chosen career in journalism, another opportunity presented itself during the spring vacation of 1898. On going up to Oxford in 1892, he had resumed his acquaintance with F. E. Smith, whom he had first met five years earlier at the Harrow scholarship exam. F.E. had arrived at Harrow that day with an extraordinarily high opinion of his own academic abilities. Elisabeth Amery and Mrs Smith had taken tea together, and while Elisabeth, like most mothers, had made a point of seeking out the Head Master and proudly informing him of Leo's academic prowess, F.E. had supposed that no such help was needed on his own behalf, as he felt sure that the school would work it out for themselves. He was therefore appalled, after the first day of exams, to find himself standing alongside Leo, and to discover that neither of their names appeared on the list of those who were required to stay on for the remaining papers. Both of them were to be sent home as 'half-wits'.

Leo attended Harrow anyway, while F.E. went to Birkenhead School, from where he won a scholarship to Wadham. But he was to dwell on his rejection by Harrow for the rest of his life and was never to forgive the Head Master, Bishop Welldon, for having failed to recognise the talent that would produce a Lord Chancellor. Indeed, many years later, by which time, as Lord Birkenhead, he had become the Lord Chancellor, he found himself sitting next to Welldon, by then the Dean of Durham, at dinner with Lady Londonderry. Other guests listened with astonishment as F.E., who had been 'treasuring up for thirty-three years his resentment at having been ploughed, together with Amery, for a Harrow scholarship', launched into a tirade across the dinner table to the effect that it had been his only failure in an otherwise glittering career. Welldon could only reply, somewhat meekly, that it had been Harrow's loss and, indeed, rather his own 'failure', while F.E. later boasted that while thirty-three years had been a long time to wait, 'one always got one's own back in time'.[1]

F.E. enjoyed outstanding success as an undergraduate, excelling on the rugby field alongside the legendary all-rounder C. B. Fry, and shining at the Union, where Leo later recalled his verbal jousting with Hilaire Belloc. In spite of Leo's lack of interest in the Union and his lack of ability on the rugby field, he and F.E. became good friends as undergraduates and saw still more of each other after taking up their Fellowships, Leo at All Souls and F.E. at Merton. Now, fired up by Leo's description of his earlier Balkan wanderings, F.E. agreed to accompany him on a trip together to Greece and, if funds held out, from there on to Asia Minor. They each 'scraped together £100 for the purpose'[2] and made their way to Venice, where Leo chose to visit the art galleries, while F.E. preferred to tour the canals and buildings on foot. Emerging one afternoon from a viewing of Bellini's Madonnas, Leo found his friend 'in a state of great enthusiasm over a little bargain he had picked up',[3] an enormous four-poster bed of ivory-inlaid oak, with accompanying pink brocade hangings, a massive bedroom wardrobe and matching chairs. He had clearly given no thought either as to how this acquisition was to be transported home, or how it was to be accommodated in his modest room at Merton. In spite of F.E.'s satisfaction with the deal he had struck, Leo was more concerned that he had squandered seventy pounds on this bargain and now had almost nothing left for the rest of the trip. Not for the last time, Leo rescued the situation by persuading a suspicious shopkeeper that he was F.E.'s tutor and that the purchase had been wholly dependent on his approval. From then on, he assumed absolute responsibility for F.E.'s spending money, releasing a modest daily allowance.

This opening encounter proved typical of several further student escapades during the trip, Leo always playing the role of the experienced traveller, F.E. that of the great pretender. En route by sea down the Adriatic from Trieste to Corfu, F.E. quickly made the acquaintance of an attractive German girl, winning over her protective mother by portraying himself as a vastly wealthy philanthropist who had rescued Leo from the gutter and was now showing him something of the world before settling him down as a schoolmaster or clergyman. Leo took the mother on one side to explain that it was in fact he who was the doctor and F.E. his mental patient, harmless but certainly not the most suitable match for her precious daughter. From Corfu they travelled on to Patras and up the Gulf of Corinth, 'one of life's unforgettable days'.[4] In a Piraeus café, as Leo attempted, in his rather too classical modern Greek, to secure the hire of a boat, F.E. pretended to be the 'Lord Mayor of Liverpool' and introduced Leo as the 'Regius Professor of Greek at the University of Oxford'. Encouraged by their drinking companion's expression of amazement at the youthful appearance of two such distinguished gentlemen, F.E. went on to claim that he was the 'youngest Lord Mayor in England', while 'Professor Amery' was even younger, but already recognised as 'the greatest living Hellenic scholar in the world, the Porson of our time'.[5] Later, on the train from Smyrna to Ephesus, F.E. again fell into conversation with a fellow traveller, passing himself off as a Roman Catholic to an English parson and launching into a withering attack on the Church of England. Having retreated from his initial position, he expressed admiration for his friend 'Professor Amery . . . the greatest living exponent' of 'that wonderful philosophic faith of Buddhism'. Unfortunately, the parson had spent fourteen years in Japan studying Buddhism, but was only too happy learn more.[6]

After sightseeing in Ephesus, they rode on by donkey into the mountains of central Turkey, but a lack of money, and F.E.'s failing enthusiasm on account of the increasing lack of ˙comfort, forced them to abandon the journey. They made their way home by way of Constantinople and Budapest, where they separated, Leo spending a few further weeks on his own in Budapest and Vienna before returning to Oxford. The holiday was to be 'for both of us ever after, the occasion of endless mutual leg-pulling, a storehouse of happy memories, and an abiding bond of friendship'.[7]

Later that summer Leo joined his former employer, now Lord Courtney, and his family at Cortina for a climbing holiday in the Dolomites. The landlady of their hotel, herself an accomplished climber, operated a strict policy of selection, refusing admittance to any 'foreigners' by which she meant non-English, or any 'frumps', quite shamelessly turning away 'three rusty-looking English maiden ladies who had booked rooms weeks ahead'.[8] Leo hired one of the best-known guides in the town and successfully climbed most of the more challenging local peaks, including his only first ascent of any importance in the Alps. During one particularly treacherous descent in thick mist he suffered his first serious climbing injury when a large rock was dislodged above him and hit him in the eye.

After leaving Cortina, Leo decided to brush up his spoken Serbian and to find out more about the local politics and culture of the Balkans. He travelled first to Agram (now Zagreb), the capital of Croatia, where he marvelled at the enormous statue of the Croat hero Ban Jelacic, recalling the great uprising of 1848 when the Croats drove out the insurgent Magyars. From there he went on to Bosnia, to Banja Luka, where he 'stepped straight into the East',[9] and to Jajce, the ancient capital of Bosnia where the warrior kings had held out for a century and a half against the Turks. From there he travelled by train to the Bosnian capital, Sarajevo, where he noted that the 'Moslems, Catholics and Orthodox enjoyed an impartial tolerant paternal government which had put an end to their ancient feuds', but also identified the 'Serb nationalist agitation' that lurked beneath the surface.[10] In Mostar he took care to photograph the famous bridge, and arrived in Cetinje, the capital of Montenegro, to find a telegram from *The Times* asking him to travel to Crete, to relieve their Balkan correspondent there and to report on the local revolt against Turkish rule.

The ongoing fighting between Cretan insurgents and their Turkish rulers was complicated by a powerful international occupation, backed by warships, of British, Italian, French and Russian troops. While the

European powers were doing their best to evacuate the Turkish forces for their own good, the Turks in turn refused to leave, fearing that they would abandon the Muslim minority to the mercy of the insurgents. The simultaneous Fashoda crisis of 1898 threatened to complicate the situation still further as, for a time, it seemed that war might break out between Britain and France. In fact, the crisis was averted and the Turkish soldiers were successfully evacuated, rather to Leo's disappointment, who arrived to find that 'things were much too peaceful' and the 'chances of a real bombardment had vanished into thin air'.[11] But he had acquired useful experience as a stand-in war correspondent and he returned home to All Souls in time to begin his first academic year as a Fellow. A few weeks later his initial attempt at journalism was rewarded by a letter from the great manager of *The Times*, Moberley Bell, inviting him to join the staff as assistant foreign editor to the newspaper's equally well-known foreign editor, Sir Valentine Chirol. But after three weeks of dealing with foreign telegrams in Chirol's office, Leo was, to his considerable disappointment, thanked for his services and told that he would be contacted again if needed.

Finding himself at a loose end, he was persuaded by John Simon, who had recently started work at the Bar, that he could do far worse than to pursue a career in the law. The next Bar exam was just three weeks away and Simon, who was paying his way by taking on pupils for law exams, told him that 'there was no chance of his passing'.[12] However, incredibly, after 'a disgraceful piece of sheer cramming' for three weeks, twelve hours a day, Leo passed the exams in all subjects.[13] Simon described him as his 'prize pupil' and claimed that his success was due to his 'versatility of mind and endless ingenuity, combined perhaps with some indulgence from the examiners'.[14] While undoubtedly impressive, the exercise was ultimately futile since Leo was never to take up the law and his only subsequent appearances in court of any note were to be as a defendant.

Leo saw a lot of Simon and his Liberal friends, and toyed briefly with a political career in the Liberal Party. He thought a collection of Simon's essays to be 'distinctly good, above the level of ordinary party literature', but stressed that he 'disagreed profoundly with a good deal of the views expressed'.[15] He met a young David Lloyd George for the first time and accompanied Simon to a Liberal conference in Scarborough, where he was introduced as a future Liberal Foreign Secretary and made his one and only speech and public appearance on a Liberal platform. But any aspirations Leo may have had to pursue a career in the law, or as a Liberal politician, were cut short by a change of heart at *The Times*, where he was invited to return as understudy to Chirol who was to spend more time out of the country. An offer of £400 a year, rising by £100 thereafter, was too good to turn down and, early in 1899, Leo began work at Printing House Square, which was destined to be his principal place of employment for the next ten years.

He was first taught the basics of laying out material in the sub-editor's room and watched as the paper was made up each night, learning from the editor, George Buckle, also a Fellow of All Souls. He moved into a room at Toynbee Hall in the East End and spent much of his spare time working for the Children's Country Holiday Fund and visiting local homes, where he was forcefully struck by the 'wretched housing conditions in East London' and commented on the 'steady influx of Jewish immigrants [who] had greatly aggravated the overcrowding and the profiteering'.[16] After a few weeks he was sent to Berlin to relieve the local correspondent there for three months. Although he had fond memories of Germany from childhood and undergraduate visits to Cologne and the Moselle, and was by now fluent in German and widely read in German literature, he still understood little of the country's political aspirations. But his stay in Berlin 'shed a new light on the German attitude' to England,[17] one he found to be of envy, founded on a belief that England's wealth and Empire had been too cheaply won and was too cheaply maintained. He recognised the German Government's encouragement of anti-British sentiment and the accompanying slow, but steady, build-up of military resources. And he had little time for Berlin itself, finding it 'the dull season of a dull capital', as he wrote to Anson, and complaining that 'it would be a great exile living here for any length of time'.[18]

■ ■ ■

Leo returned to London from Berlin at the end of July 1899, to find politicians and journalists alike absorbed by the crisis in South Africa. Peace negotiations had been going on for some time between the British Government and President Kruger's Transvaal Government, over the demands for greater political rights and increased economic opportunities for the *Uitlanders*. Thanks to a new initiative from the Transvaal State Attorney, Jan Smuts, it at last seemed possible that a peaceful settlement might be imminent and Leo was duly despatched by Moberley Bell to cover the outcome in person for *The Times*. He left Southampton on his first ocean voyage on 26 August and, after sixteen days at sea, caught his first sight of South Africa and 'the stupendous wall of Table Mountain, with Cape Town itself nestling' at its foot.[19]

The political situation had deteriorated dramatically while he had been at sea and the war of words between Kruger and the British Colonial Secretary, Joseph Chamberlain, had heightened to the extent that war now seemed inevitable. Leo's first call was to the High Commissioner, Sir Alfred Milner, who received him warmly and thus initiated a close friendship that was to endure for twenty-five years. Milner seemed certain that war was now imminent and privately shared with Leo his fears that the combination of superior troop numbers that were available to the Boers to put into the field, together with their ability to use the local conditions to their advantage, could only lead to defeat for the British forces. At that meeting Milner made a great impression on Leo who was from thenceforth to be 'the devoted disciple'.[20]

His next call was on Cecil Rhodes, the former Prime Minister of Cape Colony, whose views were very different to those of Milner. Leo's first impression of the 'Colossus' was one of profound disappointment, both on account of his 'thin falsetto voice' coming from 'that massive frame and leonine head' and because he seemed to Leo to fail to understand the intensity of feeling of Afrikaner nationalism that had brought the countries to the verge of war.[21] Rhodes believed that if the British Government held firm, with the full weight of its imperial armies behind it, then Kruger would undoubtedly back down. Over a dinner at Rhodes's residence, Groote Schuur, now the home of South Africa's

President, the two men argued late into the night over whether or not the Boers would, indeed, ultimately fight.

While political life in Cape Town was interesting, Leo was impatient to see for himself the situation on the ground and soon left for Bloemfontein where, in the absence of the Orange Free State's President Steyn, he met his right-hand man, Abraham Fisher, 'a venerable figure with a lofty dome-shaped head and a long white beard'.[22] He was initially so moved by Fisher's emotional insistence that Kruger desired peace at any price, that he began to wonder whether his earlier reservations might not have been misplaced, but he later discovered that Fisher had been among the most vociferous of the Boer leaders in urging Kruger to refuse all British concessions. He travelled on to Pretoria, where he met the Transvaal State Secretary, F. W. Reitz, who took him to meet President Kruger. 'Nothing, even in the caricaturists' boldest sallies', had prepared Leo 'for anything quite so massive or quite so ugly'.[23] But he recognised too that he was in the presence of a formidable leader and tried to break the ice in his own broken Afrikaans. Kruger was adamant. There would be no climb-down, too many concessions had already been made, and if war was the only answer, then it was indeed inevitable. Leo was ushered from his presence by the suspicious young State Attorney Jan Smuts, a future Prime Minister of South Africa and who would become a lifelong friend.

With war now inevitable, the mission that seemed most appealing and most advantageous to Leo's career was as *The Times*'s war correspondent attached to the Boer forces. He persuaded a reluctant Reitz to furnish him with a letter of introduction and travelled by troop train to the principal Boer camp at Sandspruit, near the Natal border, where he presented himself, armed with his credentials, to General Piet Joubert, the Boer Commander-in-Chief. The old soldier's initial reaction was suspicious and hostile, but he relented and Leo was billeted in a large tent with a group of soldiers with whom he had travelled from Pretoria. For the next week he shared their lives, keenly observing their preparations for war and finding himself impressed by their determination and efficiency. They reminded him, he wrote to his mother, of a 'Swiss guide on horseback with a rifle over his shoulder instead of rope and axe'.[24]

Unfortunately some of his less sympathetic new colleagues soon made it plain that they believed Leo to be an English spy, and that if official action was not taken, then they would take matters into their own hands. He tried briefly to ride out the storm by moving into a smaller, more discreet tent with the only other journalist in camp, a young Roderick Jones, later to become chairman of Reuters. But with the expiry of the Boer ultimatum to the British that all troops at sea should be stopped immediately, and Joubert's preparations for his advance on Ladysmith, it was made clear to Leo that it was time to move on 'in order to prevent something uncivilised happening'.[25] On his return to Cape Town, by means of one of the last refugee trains before the outbreak of war, Leo found a cable from *The Times* appointing him as chief of their war service, with a free hand to manage the correspondents under his control. Because of the status of *The Times*, he also found himself, at the age of twenty-five, as the chief representative of the press in South Africa in all its dealings with the military authorities.

He decided to visit the front himself and made his way by warship to Durban, and then inland to Pietermaritzburg and Estcourt where the British forces were gathering to launch the relief of Ladysmith. There he was reunited with his old school friend Winston Churchill, now correspondent for the *Morning Post* and, for the first time since leaving Harrow and to his great relief, 'on terms of equality and fraternity'.[26] They shared a tent with the correspondent from the *Manchester Guardian* and went out a number of times on the armoured train provided to conduct reconnaissance trips into Boer territory. After one such sortie they agreed that the exercise was both futile and dangerous and that the train was over-exposed to possible Boer attack, vowing never to go again. Nevertheless, a few days later, when it seemed that the evacuation of Estcourt was likely, they decided to go out on the train the following morning for one last trip. Usually timed to leave at six o'clock, the train had in fact rarely left before eight and they were accustomed to making the most of the opportunity for an extended lie-in. However, on the day in question, Churchill was up and out of bed early and just caught the departing train as it left, for once, on time. Leo had looked out of the tent at the driving rain outside and had decided instead to enjoy another hour of sleep, so missing the train. The outcome is well documented. The train was attacked, Churchill was captured by the Boers, escaped and was widely applauded for his bravery. He later teased Leo that had he not been up early enough that morning to catch the train, he would never have had 'the materials for lectures and a book which brought me in enough money to get into Parliament in 1900 – ten years before you!'[27]

The battle for Ladysmith took place on 30 October 1899 and, a few weeks later, Leo received the first description of the battle and subsequent siege that was to reach the outside world, filed by *The Times*'s correspondent there and smuggled out through enemy lines. By the end of November, the garrison at Estcourt had become increasingly surrounded by the Boer armies and was effectively under siege. With the help of a local farmer Leo escaped through the enemy lines, a 'most excellent adventure', which took them 'all over the country, up steep hills and through innumerable steep ravines and flooded rivers . . . and finally through two Boer camps not 400 yards apart'. Once more back in Cape Town, Leo missed the great battles of what became known as 'Black Week', Lord Methuen's defeat at Magersfontein and Sir Redvers Buller's disastrous defeat at Colenso. Any idea of relieving Mafeking or Kimberley seemed hopeless and Leo began to give more public outlet to his already strongly held views on the mismanagement of the war by the British high command. He wrote to Chirol of the 'incapacity, indecision and timidity displayed by our commanding officers', who were 'always on the point of scuttling out of any position if twenty Boers can be seen'. They were, he thought, 'babies, absolutely helpless, planless and undecided'.[28]

In an effort to stem the tide of dismal news from South Africa the Prime Minister, Lord Salisbury, and the War Secretary, Lord Lansdowne, decided before Christmas that more experienced leadership was required. The supreme command was offered to Lord Roberts, who had spent most of his military career in India, while Lord Kitchener was appointed as his chief of staff. They landed in Cape Town on 10 January 1900, their arrival greeted by Leo as 'a breath of fresh air', while their leadership created a 'new spirit of purpose and energy' within the military organisation in South Africa.[29] British control of the seas had ensured the simultaneous arrival of substantial troop reinforcements and Roberts immediately launched a counter-attack which led to the relief of Kimberley. Desperate not to miss out on the action, Leo travelled to Paardeberg, spending a week with the British forces who laid siege to the town before the surrender of Cronje, the Boer commander. The relief of Ladysmith, and later of Mafeking, followed soon after and, in spite of the guerrilla fighting that was to continue for another two years, for Leo the war was effectively over.

For the next two months he settled down to his job as chief political and war correspondent for *The Times*, living at the newly built Mount Nelson Hotel, the social and working hub of life in Cape Town. During wartime, the Mount Nelson had become home to a 'strange riff-raff of Rand and Kimberley millionaires, army officers, censors, war corres-pondents and dubious women',[30] although the arrival of Rudyard Kipling in Cape Town provided Leo with a new dining companion and a friend for life. However, relations between Leo and Moberley Bell had become increasingly strained, principally on account of Leo's extravagant expenses. While at Paardeberg, Leo had conceived what he considered to be a journalistic innovation by sending a map of the battlefield area, composed of four hundred numbered squares, back to London in a lengthy series of enciphered telegrams. Unfortunately his technological expertise had not allowed for human failings in the telegraph office and the map was completely unintelligible on arrival. Although Leo blamed the local censors – 'all military men especially censors are fools'[31] – Moberley Bell was furious at the unnecessary waste of £1,000, on top of other substantial expenses claims.

In an earlier attempt to placate his manager, and knowing of his enthusiasm for lavish publishing sidelines, Leo had already suggested, almost flippantly, that he might write an encyclopaedic history of the war in South Africa, spread over a number of volumes, 'a good solid standard work with lots of diplomatic and military information, largely embodying what has appeared in *The Times* throughout'. It would be a collector's piece 'which we can recommend in half morocco'.[32] To his surprise, Moberley Bell's greed got the better of him and he gave the project his blessing. For the next few months, while winding up *The*

Times's operations in South Africa, Leo travelled around the country, gathering stories for his regular despatches for the newspaper and material for the first volume of the proposed history. In August he returned home to devote himself full-time to the first volume and found that Moberley Bell had secured the services of specialist contributors for certain chapters and a publishing partner, Sampson Low. However, it was to be Leo, ever the perfectionist, who found that he had to rewrite most of the material with which he was presented and who was to bear the burden of editing the book, as well as researching and writing the great majority of the historical material himself. Six months later, the four-hundred-page first volume of *The Times History of the South African War* was published, to largely favourable reviews. In all, the six volumes were to dominate his life for the next nine years.

For the first time in his life Leo was able to settle down domestically, and he took out a lease on a small set of chambers in 2 Temple Gardens, which enjoyed sweeping views across the Temple garden to St Paul's Cathedral in one direction, and the length of the Thames between Tower Bridge and the Houses of Parliament in the other. He was to live there for eleven years, close to the offices of *The Times* and able to provide a London base for his mother. *The Times* office at Printing House Square was a short walk away, and Leo worked by day on *Volume II* of the *History* and, during the evenings, as colonial editor and stand-in foreign affairs editor for Chirol, who had been posted to the Far East. It was a time of intense Government preoccupation with the state of Anglo-German relations, coupled with anxiety about the British position in the Far East. Russia's aggressive intentions in China had initially led the Colonial Secretary, Joseph Chamberlain, to react warmly to the idea of an Anglo-German alliance, first suggested by von Bülow, the Kaiser's Chancellor. But the general distrust in Germany of all things English, as witnessed by Leo during his time in Berlin a few years earlier, was at its height. The alliance never came about, but Leo used it as a pretext to visit Chamberlain at Highbury, his Birmingham home, to interview him, and to begin a friendship based on admiration that would be crucial to his own early political career.

When he began work on *Volume II* of the *History* in January 1901, he hoped that it would be finished by April. But it was soon obvious, both to Leo and, to his great consternation, to Moberley Bell, that this was to be an altogether lengthier task. Sir Alfred (by now Lord) Milner's return to London in May presented Leo with an immediate dilemma, as Milner began the task of recruiting the team of men with 'youthful energy and unconventional minds'[33] who were to accompany him back to South Africa to begin the work of administrative and business reconstruction there. Milner offered Leo a senior position in his fledgling 'Kindergarten' as his personal secretary, and secured both Leo's agreement to and Chamberlain's approval of the appointment. But Moberley Bell begged Leo to stay and finish the *History*, to which he honourably, albeit reluctantly, agreed. It was a turning point in Leo's career and, in later years, he was often to regret the missed opportunity to join in what he perceived would have been a great adventure. Whether or not he would have subsequently stayed in South Africa, as did some of Milner's other young protégés, and thus missed out on a political career, is debatable. Instead, he put forward his friend John Buchan in his place and helped Milner to recruit another of his old friends from All Souls, Geoffrey Dawson, the future editor of *The Times*, as well as Lionel Curtis who was to be responsible for the reorganisation of Johannesburg.

Moberley Bell urged Leo to publish *Volume II* as soon as possible, while post-war public interest was still at its height, and in the assumption that the description of the war itself was merely a matter of editing the many reports that had been filed by *Times* correspondents from the field. But Leo had other ideas and soon found himself mired down, both with additional material and, editorially, in the more political aspects of the war relating to the inadequacies of army training and organisation. There were too many lessons to be learnt. If the mistakes that had been made before and during the war were not acted upon, then any future conflict would inevitably lead to disaster. Leo decided that 'unflinching frankness in criticism was needed in the public interest'. To Moberley Bell's despair, a history book had been transformed into the mechanism for a full-scale political campaign and, not for the last time in his life, Leo found himself in a battle for a cause into which he had inadvertently stumbled.

The catalyst for his campaign was the announcement, in September 1901, that Sir Redvers Buller, in Leo's eyes the villain of Colenso, was to become Commander-in-Chief at Aldershot. Leo's despatches from South Africa had already been overtly critical of what he believed was Buller's tame surrender at Colenso. He had written of his 'sheer lack of determination and disastrous loss of morale',[34] and now recalled a dinner conversation in Cape Town on the evening of Colenso, when Milner had told him of a telegram that had been sent that day by Buller to Sir George White, the defender of Ladysmith. White had been shocked to receive the message from Buller, whose help he was expecting in the relief of Ladysmith, suggesting that reinforcement was now impossible and that White should surrender to prevent further bloodshed. Now, in the course of his research for the *History*, Leo came across further rumours that appeared to corroborate the telegram's existence.

Deciding to challenge Buller's new appointment, Leo published a letter in *The Times* on 28 September, written by him over the pseudonym 'Reformer', an anonymous signature that he was to use frequently in his campaign for army reform. In the course of a long list of criticisms of Buller, Leo referred to the infamous telegram as if its existence were common knowledge, and waited for a reaction from Buller or the War Office. Sure enough, two weeks later, in a speech to army volunteers, Buller made a weak attempt to defend himself, admitting that he had indeed written 'a telegram that admits partially of that description',[35] but claiming too that he was the victim of a press conspiracy, had suffered from bad luck at Colenso and had in fact been doing White a favour by offering to share the blame for surrender. Leo's attack had hit home. In a stinging reply, 'Reformer' ridiculed Buller's claims, pointing out the disastrous practical results that surrender at Ladysmith would have entailed, and quoting from White's own message, issued to his forces after receiving the telegram, disdainfully rejecting Buller's advice to surrender. Buller, said Leo, was 'unfit to hold high command in the field'.[36] A few days later, citing Buller's ill-advised speech, the War Office confirmed that he had been relieved of the command.

Leo warmed still further to his task, using *Volume II* of the *History* to promote his campaign which now placed him in direct confrontation with the very establishment of which he aspired to become a part. He laid much of the blame for the inefficiency of the army at the door of the former Commander-in-Chief, the Duke of Cambridge, and ridiculed the 'traditions of service', which led to endless ceremonial occasions and parades. He criticised the obsession with 'mathematically straight lines and much other eighteenth century frippery',[37] and described as absurd the idea that the army's red and blue uniforms were an 'attraction for servant maids', and thus a 'stimulus to recruiting'.[38] But he reserved his most scathing criticisms for the army's training methods and its overall administration, which, he wrote, harked back to 'days when kings might use armies . . . or misappropriate the funds for mistresses'.[39]

However, neither Leo's meticulous insistence on accuracy, nor his promotion of a national campaign for army reform, struck a chord with Moberley Bell, whose only interest was in the financial benefits he hoped would accrue to help his ailing newspaper. He wrote repeatedly to Leo urging greater speed and less expense. When Leo replied, enclosing a letter from a senior army officer in which he warmly praised *Volume I* and described how his wife would sit beside his sick bed and read to him from it daily, Moberley Bell's quick-witted rejoinder was to send back a copy of *The Times* from that day with a blue cross marked against the obituary of the aforesaid colonel, who had died 'after long sufferings heroically endured'. [40]

Eventually a new contract was drawn up, under which *The Times* and Leo became joint partners and agreed to share equally in three-quarters of both the profit and loss of the project, while the publishers Sampson Low were to hold the other quarter. Leo's salary of £2,700 was to be debited to the joint account, £200 for the first volume and £500 for each volume thereafter.[41] If Moberley Bell hoped that increased financial responsibility would be an encouragement to Leo, he was to be disappointed, but *Volume II* was eventually published in May 1902 and created a considerable critical sensation on account of its outspokenness. On the whole comment centred on Buller's behaviour at Colenso, and Leo was pleased to be told by Kitchener that he had been 'not at all too severe', and to hear of a letter from

Lord Roberts describing the chapter on Colenso as 'enough to make a dead man turn in his grave, and the worst of it is that every word of it is true'.[42]

CHAPTER THREE

An Imperious Call to Action

In the spring of 1902, with the first two volumes of the *History* safely published, Leo returned to South Africa, both to cover the peace negotiations for *The Times* and to gather further material for future volumes. By the time he arrived, negotiations for the Boer surrender were already well under way. The political landscape had come to be dominated by the British army's introduction of the first concentration camps, built to imprison the families of those Boer guerrillas who had chosen to carry on fighting. Kitchener's decision, at the end of 1901, to call a halt to the policy of rounding up families had, in fact, hastened the end of the war, as many commandos were forced to reassume responsibility for their families. From Pretoria Leo reported on the final terms of surrender, 'satisfactory and explicit', but 'involving no humiliation'.[1] The day following the signing of the treaty, on 31 May 1902, Kitchener travelled to Vereeniging, outside Pretoria, to address the assembled Boer commanders and political delegates. Although reporters were banned from the meeting, Leo alone managed to talk himself on to the train carrying the British staff and, to Kitchener's annoyance, succeeded in reporting on his speech to the conquered Boers.

After a month in Pretoria, Leo took a long-awaited holiday with Geoffrey Dawson and Cecil Rodwell, later to become the Governor of Southern Rhodesia, through the Western Transvaal and on to

Southern Rhodesia, 'an invasion of Southern Central Africa by All Souls'.[2] Travelling by horse-drawn cart, they visited Mafeking and Bulawayo, before climbing up into the Matoppos hills to pay homage at the newly built grave of Cecil Rhodes, who had died in Cape Town in March that year. They travelled deeper into the bush by day, spending the nights in tribal villages, before moving on to the capital, Salisbury, and Umtali, from where Leo caught a boat to Portuguese East Africa. Returning south to Natal, he spent a day on the battlefield at Spion Kop taking photographs for the *History*, before crossing to the Drakensberg, where his successful ascent of the Mont aux Sources range led to one of the peaks later being named Mt Amery by the Mountain Club of Natal.

However, Leo's prolonged absence from Printing House Square had not gone down well with Moberley Bell. In spite of satisfactory sales of the first two volumes of the *History*, with 5,317 combined sets sold out of a print run of 7,500,[3] Moberley Bell bombarded him with correspondence demanding that he return home at once. Leo's flippant replies served only to antagonise Moberley Bell still further. 'Your letter written in sorrow rather than in anger', he wrote from Pretoria, 'about my monstrous behaviour in deserting PHS for so long ... but I don't think I am guilty of the degree of unscrupulousness which you assign to me ... my apologies – not apologetic enough you think, a trifle brazen, perhaps, but you know the wickedness of my ways.'[4] Indeed it was not apologetic enough for Moberley Bell, whose rejoinder was brief and to the point. 'Your continued absence causing utmost inconvenience, has practically killed History and is wholly unwarranted.'[5]

Having finally returned to London in October 1902, Leo spent the next two years working on *Volume III*, devoted primarily to an analysis of the lessons learnt from the defeats of 'Black Week' in December 1899. In *The Times* he resumed his series of 'Reformer' letters, resolving that the time was right for him to become 'in essence a propagandist', and to 'focus all this public dissatisfaction and disquiet into something like a definite programme of Army Reform'.[6] He offered a high profile, yet anonymous outlet for the grievances of senior army officers and, as his confidence grew, so too did his reputation among the senior political and military figures of the day. Early in 1903 he published a series of a dozen articles in *The Times* under the heading 'The Problem of the Army' and later republished them in a book of the same name. And his appearance before the Elgin Commission, set up to investigate the consequences of the war, was described by one of its members, Lord Esher. 'We had the evidence of that clever little fellow – Amery – today,' he recalled, 'who writes the history of the war for the Times. He has seen a good deal, and got a great amount of information from officers, but has often naturally been misled as to facts. He is full of intelligence.'[7]

In the pursuit of his campaign for army reform Leo happily made common cause with opposition politicians who he believed shared his purpose. As a result of the growing esteem in which he was held, in late 1902 he was invited to join a small group of like-minded thinkers assembled by the Fabians Sidney and Beatrice Webb. The Webbs were well known in political circles for their innovative welfare proposals, and set about recruiting a small group of friends who would dine and debate together at regular intervals. The 'Coefficients', as they became known, were carefully chosen for their expertise in the various spheres of political, military and literary life. The members included the future Liberal Cabinet ministers Lord Haldane and Sir Edward Grey, the Fabian economists Professor William Hewins and Pember Reeves, both of whom were later to become Principal of the London School of Economics and the imperialist-minded editor of the *National Review*, Leo Maxse. Philosophy was represented by Bertrand Russell, while Leo recruited Alfred Milner. In her letter of invitation to H. G. Wells to join, Beatrice Webb explained that the 'dining club' was to comprise ten or twelve people and to meet for dinner eight times a year, to discuss 'the aims, policy and methods of Imperial Efficiency at home and abroad'. It was to be 'carefully kept unconnected with any person's name or party allegiance'.

The first meeting was held at the Webbs' home in Westminster in November 1902 and the club continued to meet in members' homes, the Ship Tavern in Whitehall and St Ermin's Hotel until 1910. Its members held varying views as to its importance and influence. The Webbs hoped to create a 'shadow cabinet or brains trust for a new party, standing for strong national leadership, military readiness and a raising of industrial and educational standards'.[8] Leo perceived it as a 'Brains Trust or General Staff', which would meet 'for serious discussion and for the subsequent formulation of policy'.[9] However, Bertrand Russell soon tired of the imperialist beliefs of his fellow members, while Rudyard Kipling declined his invitation for the more mundane reason that attendance was impossible for 'a man who lives three hours down the South Eastern (which for practical purposes is Umtali)'.[10] H. G. Wells was initially attracted by membership in the belief that it would 'give him just the sort of entry into the political world that he was looking for',[11] but he too soon tired of his fellow members and correctly identified himself and Russell as 'by far the most untied and irresponsible members'.[12] He joined the Fabians instead, although the Coefficients appeared in his book *New Machiavelli*, thinly disguised as the Pentagram Circle with Leo portrayed as Crupp, a Tory imperialist.

That Leo was now so widely perceived as an ardent imperialist was almost entirely due to his conversion to the views of Joseph Chamberlain, the Colonial Secretary. Chamberlain had begun his parliamentary career as a Liberal but, along with a number of his colleagues from both the Whig and radical wings of the party, had split from the Liberal Party over Gladstone's proposals for Home Rule in Ireland and resigned from the Cabinet in March 1886. Under the leadership of the then Marquess of Hartington, later the Duke of Devonshire, the dissidents founded the Liberal Unionist party the following month and entered into an electoral pact with the Conservatives ahead of that year's general election, winning seventy-eight seats. For the following nine years the Liberal Unionists gave support to Salisbury, in government and, briefly, in opposition, increasingly uniting on imperial policies as well as Ireland. Although the Liberal Unionists maintained a distinct electoral base, especially in Chamberlain's Birmingham, it was an alliance that soon became known by the all-embracing description 'Unionist Party', and was to govern Britain for seventeen of the next twenty years. In 1895 Chamberlain and Devonshire were finally called to serve in Salisbury's third administration, effectively creating a coalition which was to govern for a further seven years and, although the Liberal Unionists maintained their own party structure until 1912, in reality they had merged with the Conservatives long before that. 'The Unionist Party' declared Salisbury in August 1901, 'is like two men in one pair of trousers.'[13]

Chamberlain had long argued for the need to develop more quickly Britain's vast territories around the world and, in 1902, he first proposed an end to the existing policy of free trade, calling for greater protection for British products. A year later, in May 1903, he made a rousing speech in Birmingham calling for the extension of so-called preferences, or lower rates of payable duty, for all colonial imports and repeated his demand for greater protection for British industry, in the form of retaliatory tariffs against all foreign competition. To the fledgling 'protectionist' movement, of which Leo was now a part, the speech was a rallying call. This was, declared Chamberlain, 'an issue much greater in its consequences than any of our local disputes. You have an opportunity; you will never have it again.'[14] The following morning Leo Maxse burst into Leo's office at *The Times*, 'waltzed' him around the room and 'poured forth a paean of jubilation at the thought that, at last, there was a cause to work for in politics'.[15] Thirty years later Leo described Chamberlain's speech as 'a challenge to free thought as direct and provocative as the theses which Luther nailed to the church door at Wittenberg' and, for younger imperialists like himself, 'a sudden crystallisation of all their ideals in an imperious call to action.'[16]

Although he did not realise it at the time, Leo now embarked on a cause that was to shape his political life for the next forty years and was to prove the most divisive issue within Unionist, and subsequently Conservative, ranks for most of his career. He channelled all his energy into the promotion of Chamberlain's ideas and the policy known as tariff reform. He helped to create the Tariff Reform League and again resorted to the tactic of writing anonymous letters to *The Times*, this time above the pseudonym 'Tariff Reformer'. But Chamberlain's speech, so admired by Leo, had been directly contradicted by one by the Prime Minister, Arthur Balfour, and in the ensuing debate Chamberlain offered his resignation from the Government. By the time, therefore, that Leo attended his first Conservative Conference at Sheffield in early October 1903, he was in a confrontational mood. He protested to Maxse at the 'the auto-castration of the Unionist Party' and the 'cowardice and stupidity of these eunuchs', and promised to 'get together a small band to do some booing and to interrupt AJB with lewd remarks.'[17] Sure enough, at the conclusion of Balfour's speech during which he had reiterated his determination to lead the party from the front, Leo shouted from the back of the hall, 'What about Joe?' The rest of the audience took up the refrain and 'for fully five minutes the hall gave way to cheering and countercheering and the effect of Balfour's speech was largely lost'.[18]

Meanwhile, Leo's dissatisfaction with the refusal of some of his fellow Coefficients to endorse wholeheartedly the cause of tariff reform led him in January 1904, after returning from his first skiing holiday in Switzerland, to assemble a small group of young, like-minded supporters of Chamberlain. They included Leo Maxse, William Hewins, Halford Mackinder, James Garvin, soon to edit the *Observer* for over forty years, F. S. Oliver and H. A. Gwynne, Reuters' chief correspondent in South Africa and later editor of the *Standard* and the *Morning Post*. An initial dinner at Leo's Temple apartment led to the formation of yet another club, the 'Compatriots', described, by one member, John Buchan, as that 'disreputable Imperialist dining club to which I belong'.[19]

While the Compatriots and the Tariff Reform League took Leo ever further down the path of a political career, he remained by day a journalist at *The Times*. Most of 1904 was devoted to completing *Volume III* of the *History* and persuading Moberley Bell that *The Times* should maintain its support for the project, in spite of the now lengthy delays and its lack of financial success. Increasingly forced to choose between a career in journalism and one in politics, he recognised that 'to be more effective than I have been I think it will be necessary for me to become a politician'. There were 'things in the world which I want to see done,' and he was prepared to sacrifice both the increased remuneration and reputation which he was earning with his pen, in order to do his duty in Parliament.[20] In May 1905 his hand was finally forced. Sir Alfred Harmsworth (later Lord Northcliffe) had recently acquired the *Observer* and offered to double Leo's salary, in addition to a tenth share in the ownership of the newspaper, if he would accept the editorship.[21] He promised that he would also have time to stand for Parliament, if he so wished. The offer was a tempting one, but Mober-ley Bell implored him to 'decline the Baronet on any terms',[22] while the editor, Buckle, promised that 'if you stick by The Times, The Times will stick by you'. He flattered Leo that he had always believed that 'if you remained with us, you would come to fill my chair',[23] and Leo finally agreed to stay at *The Times*, while Garvin was appointed at the *Observer*.

Leo's level of political engagement continued to grow and he found himself increasingly in demand as a platform speaker, indeed so frequent and lengthy were his speeches that he suffered badly from laryngitis, a condition which was to afflict him throughout his career, and for which he regularly had to consult a throat specialist and speech coach in an attempt to preserve his voice. Finally, in February 1905, at the age of thirty-one, his name was put forward by Joseph Chamber-lain, as a suitable candidate to contest East Wolverhampton on behalf of the Liberal Unionists. Although Birmingham was by now a bastion of Liberal Unionism, neighbouring Wolverhampton was considered safe Liberal territory and the Liberal Unionists had initially been looking for a local man to oppose the sitting Member of Parliament, Sir Henry Fowler, who had represented the constituency continuously since 1880. However, on 10 April Leo was summoned to a crowded meeting and duly selected as their candidate.

The constituency consisted of part of the city of Wolverhampton itself, and a number of adjoining industrial villages, most notably Willenhall, which Leo thought had 'not changed very noticeably since Disraeli drew a grim picture of it, under the name of Wodgate, in his *Sybil*'. Leo admitted that he 'had never before realized anything quite so dreary or squalid as this then rather decaying bit of the Black Country'. The residents of nearby Wednesfield made their living by 'making steel traps for every animal from mice up to wolves and bears', and Leo, who was never to embrace any form of hunting as a pastime, found it particularly distasteful having to support the commercial interests of these potential constituents. Nor were his own supporters particularly pleased to see him. At his first public meeting, that scourge of politicians throughout the ages, the constituency chairman disclosed that he had 'tried hard to get a respectable local man, but had failed', and had therefore 'searched in the highways and by-ways and at last found a candidate'. Unfortunately, he conceded, 'Mr Amery may not be much to look at.'[24]

Soon after his selection, Leo set sail for a much-needed holiday in Canada, visiting Quebec, Ottawa and Toronto in the east, before heading west to Edmonton, Winnipeg and Calgary and some climbing in the Rockies. From Vancouver he headed back to the east coast by train, spending his last few days in Boston and New York before returning home in the middle of October. When Balfour was eventually forced to resign in December 1905, the Liberal leader, Henry Campbell-Bannerman, initially accepted the task of forming a government. Initial uncertainty as to whether the imperialist wing of the Liberal Party, in particular Asquith, Grey and Haldane, would agree to serve soon proved unfounded and a protracted general election campaign got under way. In the days when elections were commonly long, drawn-out affairs, spread over several weeks, public interest was generally sustained throughout the campaign. However, it soon became clear that the election of 1906 would be wholly one-sided, and that the Unionists were facing a rout. On 15 January 1906 Leo was comfortably defeated in Wolverhampton, polling just 2,745 votes, against the sitting Member's 5,610. Nationally, the Liberals secured 401 seats, with 29 for Labour and 83 Irish Nationalists. The Unionist representation fell from 334 to 157, composed of 132 Conservatives and 25 Liberal Unionists. The Unionist coalition was split between the majority, who supported Chamberlain over tariff reform, and a few who continued to support the compromise on which Balfour had fought the election, even though he had lost his own seat.

For Leo, the election was enlivened by an incident which considerably enhanced his local reputation. Throughout the campaign he was shadowed by a local businessman and councillor called Binks, who became a regular heckler at public meetings. Leo was particularly incensed that Binks repeatedly referred to him as a liar, an accusation he could accept from 'an ordinary working man' in the heat of a political argument, but which he felt 'from a man of his standing and influence could not be allowed to pass unchallenged'. One morning, after Binks had been particularly offensive at a meeting the night before, Leo called at his office to demand an apology. When Binks refused, Leo 'boxed his ears, soundly, to the mingled horror and delight of his head clerk'.[25] Although Leo felt that honour had been restored, Binks, not altogether unsurprisingly, issued a summons for assault, leading to a court case soon after the election. The magistrate expressed surprise that Binks had apparently failed even to attempt to mount any form of self-defence against a much smaller man, but nevertheless fined Leo two pounds plus costs.

The case achieved considerable notoriety, both locally and among Leo's wider circle of friends. 'I clouted a man's head discreetly and quietly in his own office for having called me a liar,' he wrote to Geoffrey Dawson in South Africa. 'He showed no signs of resistance.' A local sympathiser wrote to the *Midland Evening News* congratulating Leo on his actions and enclosing a penny stamp as a contribution towards his fine. The idea caught on and similar local contributions soon allowed him not only to pay off his fine in full, but also to buy a gold watch and chain with the balance of the proceeds. When the watch was later stolen by a pickpocket, during a public meeting at a subsequent election, a further subscription by local people produced yet another, even more splendid, watch. 'Next time,' he told Dawson, 'it will be a nice quiet little murder followed by a silver dinner service.'[26] Binks's own political activities were somewhat hampered thereafter on account of being jeered at by young boys in the street, who would call out 'Look out, Amery's coming', whenever he appeared.[27]

The most significant issues confronting the new Opposition were the future of the Chamberlain policy and Balfour's position as party leader. Leo urged Chamberlain to promote his own leadership credentials, and to force the Conservatives to choose between him and Balfour. But Chamberlain refused, both out of personal loyalty to Balfour and a fear of causing lasting political damage. However, while he declared publicly that he was not a candidate for the Unionist leadership, he nevertheless sought a declaration from the party hierarchy that tariff reform would not be dropped, a concession that was made by Balfour in the exchange of the so-called 'Valentine

Letters' of February 1906. Meanwhile for Leo, the next two years were to be a period of political frustration. Having scented the power of Parliament, he resented the fact that he remained an outsider. During a weekend in Oxford, he listened with admiration, but with envy too, to a full dress rehearsal of his former travelling companion F. E. Smith's legendary maiden speech while the two of them were out walking together on an Oxford towpath.[28]

At *The Times* Leo became a prolific leader writer, occasionally contributing all three leaders in the newspaper on a single night. He continued to oversee the editing of the fourth and fifth volumes of the *History*, whilst writing *Volume VI* himself. A series of addresses to the Compatriots formed the basis of a book, *The Fundamental Fallacies of Free Trade*, Balfour thanking him warmly for a copy, and praising Leo as 'one of the few people from whose writings on the great controversy I anticipate genuine pleasure'.[29] Moberley Bell was less impressed. 'If, instead of bothering yourself with *The Fundamental Fallacies of Free Trade*,' he wrote, 'you had spent that time correcting the fundamental fallacies of free promises, we might by this time have seen the sixth volume, now five years overdue.'[30] Meanwhile, in his social life too, Leo was moving up in the world, attending a constant round of lunches at London clubs such as Boodles and the Carlton, dinner parties in Mayfair and balls at some of London's great private homes. In return, he cultivated friends and political allies with his own small dinner parties at the Savoy. He became a frequent weekend guest at country house parties, and a regular visitor to All Souls, both for quiet week-ends and for more formal occasions such as Encaenia or the Bursar's dinner, as well as to various dining clubs at Balliol.

In August 1906 he returned to the Alps, to Arolla in Switzerland, with his brother Harold, who was home on leave from the Sudan where he was serving as Assistant Director of Intelligence with the Egyptian army, on secondment from the Black Watch. However, the trip was marred when a successful ascent of the Aiguilles Rouges, giving one of the most spectacular views throughout the Alps, almost ended in tragedy. While climbing a vertical rock face one above the other, their guide, at the top of the rope, accidentally dislodged a large rock which crashed down the side of the mountain, breaking his own hand and striking Harold, immediately below him, a glancing blow on the head. It narrowly missed Leo, but the weight as it hit the rope dislodged the guide, already without the use of one hand, from the rock face. He fell head-first past both Harold and Leo, before the rope tightened and Harold too was pulled off the rock face. Leo was forced to take up the strain of the two falling bodies, but fortunately his brother landed beside him on a small ledge, while the guide too came to rest on a lower ledge.

Once they had composed themselves, it became clear that the guide was severely injured and that 'a large piece of the flesh on the top of his head and most of the forehead had been scalped to the bone, and the great flab of scalp hanging down concealed the rest of the features'. However, Harold coolly 'poked about the exposed skull with his fingers and proceeded to put the scalp back into its place and tie it up with a large silk handkerchief'.[31] The guide begged to be left to die in peace, but three hours later they had succeeded in carrying him down the mountain, where a local doctor stitched up his skull, without pain relief and by the light of a paraffin lamp. A few days later, Leo and Harold successfully climbed the Matterhorn by the Zmutt route, a notoriously difficult climb, with, incredibly, the very same guide accompanying them.

▪ ▪ ▪

In July 1906, a few days after his seventieth birthday, Joseph Chamberlain suffered a massive stroke which permanently impaired his speech and movement, and brought to an end his political career. Leo's grief was tempered by the realisation that Chamberlain's succession needed to be quickly secured. He accordingly tried to persuade Milner that he should become Chamberlain's natural successor as leader of the imperial wing of the Unionist Party, and that he should announce his intention to lead the movement. Leo and Milner had, by now, developed a close relationship. Leo was thought of as 'Milner's most competent interpreter'[32] and it was said that 'no one admired Lord Milner more' than he did.[33] To many, theirs was 'a master and pupil relationship'. However, Milner resolutely refused to be dragged into the murky world of party politics or to accept office of any kind, pleading his own weak health as an excuse and that he had merely 'found hospitality in the Unionist camp'.[34] And when Milner gave two speeches at Manchester and Wolverhampton in December 1906, even Leo had to concede that he was 'too utterly sincere and too averse from any kind of personal display for even the very minimum of self-dramatization required by the platform'.[35]

Leo's support for the Unionist leadership, and for Balfour in particular, remained lukewarm. After a speech of Balfour's to a party meeting at the Albert Hall, Leo remarked on 'the shame which many of us felt at . . . the unspeakable piffle of which Balfour delivered himself. Can't he be drowned?'[36] Balfour's private secretary, John Sandars, warned his leader that 'there has been a general weakening of your authority throughout the country. To this weakening Austen [Chamberlain] and [Walter] Long and BL [Bonar Law], Maxse and Amery and others have contributed and are contributing.'[37] In April 1907 an Imperial Conference was held in London, a gathering of the leaders of all the self-governing members of the British Empire. The principal topics for discussion were defence issues and imperial preference. Leo worked hard behind the scenes to further the cause of imperial unity, befriending the Prime Minister of Cape Colony, Dr Jameson, and meeting Alfred Deakin and Sir Wilfred Laurier, respectively the Prime Ministers of Australia and Canada. He also struck up a close friendship with a young member of Laurier's staff, Mackenzie King, himself later to become one of Canada's most celebrated Prime Ministers.

Leo's immediate political ambitions had to be briefly postponed when, after months of ear trouble, he was forced to have two operations in the space of a month, the first to remove some bone from his nose and, when that failed, a more serious mastoid operation at the end of August. To recuperate he sailed again for South Africa, spending a few days with Jameson in Cape Town and visiting Smuts, by now a senior political leader, in the Transvaal. Leaving South Africa by boat, he sailed up the coast to Dar-es-Salaam, Zanzibar and Mombasa, from where he journeyed inland to Nairobi. He looked longingly at the peaks of Mt Kenya and Kilimanjaro, and travelled on to Uganda, where he spent Christmas Day at Lake Victoria, and visited Entebbe and Kampala. Returning to Mombasa, he continued up the East African coast, past Aden and on to Suez, receiving the news en route that *The Times* had been acquired by Lord Northcliffe. After a week's sightseeing in Cairo, Leo visited Luxor and Aswan, before going on to see his brother in Khartoum. They spent a happy week together, after which he returned by boat down the Nile, where, on 6 February 1908, he heard the news of 'the sudden death of a beloved mother, too sudden, happily, for her to realize the absence of all the three sons for whom she lived'.[38]

Over Easter 1908 Leo spent three weeks aboard the yacht of an old friend, Gerald Sellars, lunching with an ailing Joseph Chamberlain in Cannes and receiving a message, in Palermo, that Sir Henry Fowler, the sitting Member of Parliament for Wolverhampton East, who had defeated him at the last election, had accepted a peerage and that a by-election was already under way. He arrived home with less than three weeks to spare before polling day, and to find his new Liberal opponent's campaign in full swing. Nationally, the political climate had improved for the opposition Unionists, who had won a number of recent by-elections, while Leo had by now established himself as a popular local candidate. He fought the election almost exclusively on his record and his support for tariff reform, and his late arrival was more than compensated for by his energy and campaigning drive. On the eve of the poll he spoke at eleven public meetings throughout the constituency and at a rally attended by five thousand people in the local drill hall, but it was to no avail. After three recounts he finally admitted defeat, by just eight votes. Thanking Lord Northcliffe a few days later for the support of the *Daily Mail* during the campaign, Leo indicated that he was considering further scrutiny of the result and was 'investigating quietly into the matter of dead'uns and foreigners whom they managed to poll'.[39] The principal culprit appeared to be a local Catholic priest, Father Darmody, a staunch supporter of Home Rule, who had not only exercised control over his living flock, but had also miraculously enabled some of his late parishioners to vote as well.

Leo was persuaded that an appeal would not reflect well on him and was offered the inducement of contesting the first safe seat that became available. Balfour congratulated him on a defeat that was 'more glorious than many victories' and which would have 'quite as excellent an effect' on Unionist support. While he was not 'able, *as yet*, to count you as an addition to our ranks in the House of Commons', it would not, he hoped 'be long delayed'.[40] In August Leo addressed an audience of forty thousand, the largest of his life, at a celebratory rally, when the gold watch to replace the earlier stolen one was presented to him, together with eight silver goblets, replicas of those used at All Souls, each engraved with a lock and the figure 8 to commemorate the constituency and the narrowness of his defeat.

The remainder of 1908 was spent completing his *History of the South African War*. Soon after taking over *The Times*, Northcliffe sounded Leo out informally as to the possibility of his succeeding Buckle as editor in due course, describing him as one of 'his most valued employees, one of his coming young men'.[41] But Leo's ambitions were, by now, entirely political and he instead suggested his old friend Geoffrey Dawson for the post. Meanwhile, the *History* had to be finished and he spent much of the summer staying with Milner at his Kent home, Sturry Court, trawling through his substantial archive of papers. Moberley Bell, however, remained unimpressed, complaining that 'the matter has become such a public disgrace that we decline to be associated with it any longer'. If Leo 'knew the sort of things that are said openly of you individually and of us as fathering the book you would recognise that we have treated you with culpable tolerance'.[42] Leo was forced to offer to pay £10 for every week that publication was delayed beyond June, and his ultimate share of the loss on the project was £1,000. The enterprise had occupied nine years of his life and it came as a considerable relief that the reviewers, at least, judged the work to be an achievement, while Lord Grey wrote to Northcliffe from Government House in Ottawa that he had 'seen nothing so good or so inspiring'.[43]

With the publication of the final volume and the winding down of his full-time work at *The Times*, Leo was finally in a position to devote himself fully to politics and his search for an elusive seat in Parliament. The vague promises that a safe seat would be found for him proved unfounded, and he continued to nurse East Wolverhampton in expectation of a general election. He helped to found the Trade Union

Tariff Reform Association, which he hoped would constitute 'the nucleus of something in the nature of a Unionist Labour Party', both to provide 'an effective opposition to the Radical-Socialist gang which at present controls the trade union world', and to 'counteract the claim continually made by the present Labour Party that they are the only true representatives of the working man's point of view'.[44]

He was by now one of the more influential young members of his party outside Parliament and he moved effortlessly among his party leaders. His relationship with Balfour was based on grudging mutual admiration and suspicion. When they were fellow guests for a weekend at Belvoir Castle, Leo was frustrated that Balfour ignored his efforts to indulge in political argument, and complained that his party leader was 'not really interested in politics except when in the House . . . The idea of encouraging the young by familiar talk on politics is quite foreign to him.'[45] Leo consoled himself instead by admiring the 'great collection of beauties as far as the ladies were concerned', enjoying animated conversation at dinner with his hostess, the Duchess of Rutland, and Balfour's confidante, Lady Elcho.[46] The house itself he found unimpressive, describing it as 'rather an atrocity externally, in the worst battlement style of the nineteenth century', but containing 'some good pictures'.[47] Indeed, so greatly did Leo enjoy the heady mix of political debate and elegant living at country house parties, that his friends teased him that he had become 'accustomed to staying with Dukes and Marquesses', and now used 'scent into [sic] your bath'.[48]

The Coefficients had fallen into decline, it was said, because George Bernard Shaw 'talked so much that nobody else could get a word in' edgeways,[49] and Leo briefly joined another conspiratorial group, the 'Confederates', formed by supporters of Chamberlain to campaign more actively against those supporting free trade and even, supposedly, plotting to deselect various MPs. They briefly succeeded in creating an atmosphere of 'mistrust, suspicion and animosity', principally because 'no one knew who they were'.[50]

The House of Lords' refusal to pass Lloyd George's infamous 1909 Budget had finally led to an early general election in January 1910. During the summer of 1909 Leo had travelled to the Rockies as a guest of the Canadian Alpine Club, and with the intention, together with his brother Harold, of conquering Mt Robson, at the time still the highest unclimbed peak in the main chain of the Rockies. Although enjoyable, their attempt had been unsuccessful and Leo was returning home across Canada in October when he broke his leg in a riding accident. With an election appearing ever more likely, his supporters at Wolverhampton telegraphed him to express their concern that he might not return home in time. 'Returning immediately,' he replied. 'Have still got a leg to stand on; my opponent has none'.[51] Any sympathy he may have gained from his electors at having to fight the campaign on crutches, was almost certainly outweighed by an inability to canvass properly. The sitting Liberal MP duly increased his majority to 814, while nationally, in spite of losing 105 seats, the Liberals were returned to power with the support of the Irish Nationalists and forty-one Labour MPs. Lord Northcliffe, who had provided Leo with the use of a chauffeur-driven car during the campaign, now urged him to look elsewhere and promised that his own 'views would have some force at headquarters in getting you the right place in future'.[52]

Leo needed little persuasion to move on and informed his supporters in Wolverhampton that he would not be standing again. Over the coming months he considered offers or suggestions from a number of other seats, amongst them East Islington, Plymouth, Leigh, Bootle and South Bristol. He lobbied hard to be selected in South Kensington, and considered South Bedfordshire when he heard that 'the Duke was very anxious to have him there'.[53] But the genuinely safe seat he craved still eluded him, in spite of widespread speculation about his prospects. Meanwhile he planned for the future. While he lived comfortably as a bachelor on his income from *The Times* and other writing, he recognised too that were he to be elected he would need 'some other means of livelihood more easily reconcilable with parliamentary hours than regular work on *The Times*'.[54] He sought additional income in the City, joining the board of a South African colliery, Vaalbank, and becoming involved in the start-up of a number of Canadian investment companies, such as the British and Overseas Company, based in Vancouver, and the Canadian and Empire Trust, while he founded the British Alberta Company from his own rooms.

All were to provide him with much needed additional income over a number of years, although their fortunes waned in the longer term.

▪ ▪ ▪

In May 1910 Leo met Florence Greenwood for the first time at a party and saw her a number of times over the following weeks. It was not long before he gave a small dinner party for her in his chambers at Temple Gardens, his brother Harold realising immediately that he had lost his heart by the look on Leo's face while Florence played the banjo. That it was a match made in heaven is confirmed by the afternoon they spent together at her flat, 'arguing about tariff reform'.[55] In fact Florence was every bit as ardent an imperialist as was Leo. Her father, Hamar Greenwood, had emigrated from Wales to Canada as a boy and had married into a family of American colonists who had settled in Canada after siding with the British during the American War of Independence. Florence had been raised in Whitby, Ontario, within a family fiercely loyal to the United Empire Loyalist tradition, which 'combined a deep suspicion of everything American with an almost exaggerated reverence for the Crown and everything British'.[56] Her brother, a young lawyer also called Hamar, was already a rising Liberal MP in the British Parliament and was to serve as a minister on a number of occasions in the course of Leo's own political career, a cross-party relationship that helped him to build friendships across the political divide. Florence was known to everyone as Bryddie and referred to by Leo, thereafter, simply as B.

In August Leo visited Canada himself for two months and, on his return, proposed to Bryddie on 9 October. The news of their engagement was widely welcomed, by friends, political allies and opponents alike. John Simon, by now a Liberal MP, wrote to Hamar Greenwood assuring him that he knew 'of nothing in the world of friendship more entirely satisfactory than the great news' he had heard.[57] Milner wrote privately to Bryddie, promising her that Leo was 'one of the people in the world that I most value and am most attached to' and praising his 'strength, his simplicity, his kindliness, his utter lack of vanity or pettiness'.[58] They were married on 16 November 1910 at the parliamentary church, St Margaret's, Westminster, the service conducted by two of Leo's oldest friends from All Souls, Canon Henson and Bishop Hicks. They chose Psalm 67, which is said as a prayer at the start of every sitting day in the House of Commons: 'God be merciful unto us and bless us: and show us the light of his countenance, and be merciful unto us.'[59]

Meanwhile, the political climate had changed noticeably during the preceding months. The Irish Nationalists, who now held the balance of power in the new Parliament, were determined to advance the cause of Home Rule, and recognised that reform of the House of Lords was an essential prerequisite if a Bill was to succeed. In March 1910, after months of negotiations, they finally withdrew their objections to Lloyd George's 1909 Budget resolutions, in return for a Liberal commitment to introduce a Parliament Bill to limit the powers of the House of Lords. The new King George V was faced with an immediate constitutional crisis, and Leo was among those who urged compromise, believing that the breakdown of secret talks in June between the Prime Minister, Herbert Asquith, and Balfour was 'a great opportunity tragically thrown away',[60] and urging the Unionist leadership, in a letter to *The Times*, 'to carry through a constitutional settlement in co-operation with their opponents'.[61] But it was too late for compromise. On 15 November Asquith made it clear to the King that he was prepared to dissolve Parliament immediately and to create as many new Liberal peers as would be needed to pass the Parliament Bill.

On the afternoon of 16 November, Asquith paid Leo and Bryddie the compliment of going first to St Margaret's to attend their wedding. He stayed just long enough to sign the register, before slipping away to Buckingham Palace to what he later described as 'the most important political occasion of his life',[62] when the King 'agreed most reluctantly to give the cabinet a secret understanding that in the event of the Government being returned with a majority at the General Election',[63] he would use his prerogative to create the peers demanded by Asquith. Leo, along with the rest of the country, remained in blissful ignorance of the unfolding crisis as he and Bryddie set off to spend their honeymoon in a borrowed cottage in the New Forest. But when they read the news of the impending election the following morning and received a telegram from party headquarters calling him back to London, they left the autumn sunshine behind them to contest the constituency of Bow and Bromley, which had fallen vacant and where Leo was to be installed as candidate.

For the first time Leo campaigned with Bryddie at his side. 'My Press is at your disposal,' Northcliffe told him, 'and I hope Mrs Amery does not mind the photographers who are absolutely essential. To be unknown by democracy is to be damned by them.'[64] The Unionists had previously enjoyed Liberal support in the constituency, and Leo hoped to see off the Labour candidate, George Lansbury. However, amidst rowdy scenes in the East End, Milner was heckled off the stage and Leo was pelted with parsnips. His friends, the Webbs, campaigned surreptitiously against him, ensuring the withdrawal of the Liberal candidate, and Lloyd George sealed Leo's fate by asking the local Liberals to support 'my friend Lansbury'.[65] Leo lost by 700 votes, and immediately set about looking for a by-election to fight, in the hope that Balfour could be persuaded to 'put pressure on one of the older and less useful members of the Party'.[66] Joseph Chamberlain summed up the views of many, advising him not to 'contest another seat where there is really no chance. I do not know who sent you to Bow and Bromley,' he wrote, 'but all your friends would be certain you could not succeed.'[67]

CHAPTER FOUR

Diehard and Inquisitor

It seemed to Leo that he was as far as ever from fulfilling his political ambitions, although he was, at least, free to resume his honeymoon. He and Bryddie spent a few nights in Paris after Christmas, before travelling on to Gstaad, where they spent a fortnight, Leo indulging his newly acquired passion for skiing, while Bryddie learnt to skate. On their return to London, Bryddie moved into his bachelor chambers in the Temple, where they were to remain for a year before finally moving into more suitable family accommodation, a spacious and light Chelsea house, at 9 Embankment Gardens, still just a stone's throw from the river. They were to live there for the next eleven years.

Bryddie was soon 'exhausted by the stress of a strenuous political and social season,'[1] while the summer was one of relatively idle pleasure, spent enjoying exuberant country house parties; at Eaton with 'Bendor', Duke of Westminster, at Sutton Court with Lord Northcliffe, and at Chequers with Sir Arthur Lee; at Cliveden Nancy Astor held a mock 'Parliament' on social reform before dinner to entertain her guests, after which she exhorted them to 'put on their expensive dresses and forget about the poor'.[2] Otherwise weekends were spent in Oxford, enjoying dinners at All Souls, dancing until dawn at college balls and punting on the Cherwell. During August and September, Leo rented a small house near Windsor, at Englefield

Green, where Bryddie could rest and he would swim in the river, walk in the forest and catch up on his reading.

While Leo continued his search for a parliamentary seat, he was first faced with one unpleasant task as a result of the last election he had fought in East Wolverhampton, in January 1910. During the campaign a former British soldier, an ex-Sergeant Major Edmondson, had denounced Leo for a 'damnable libel'[3] against the British army, citing various passages in *The Times History of the South African War*. At the time Leo had decided that such a serious accusation could not go unchallenged and had foolishly chosen a packed public meeting at the end of the campaign, in turn to charge his accuser as having been sent home in disgrace from South Africa for running away in battle. Although at least one eyewitness claimed to support this accusation of cowardice, Edmondson had sued for libel and, a year later, Leo found himself back in court for a case that could well have spelt the end of his political career before it had even started.

Edmondson was represented by the Irish Nationalist MP Tim Healy, who was soon to become a good friend of Leo's and was later to be the first Governor General of the Irish Free State. Leo's old friend F. E. Smith, who had already defended him against Binks, once again acted for the defence. Edmondson had somehow managed to acquire anonymous financial backing for his action, while Leo, to his intense frustration, was expected to foot his own expenses. Nevertheless, Leo's defence assembled an impressive array of witnesses, among them Lord Roberts and a former soldier, Sergeant Morley, who travelled all the way from Canada to testify on Leo's behalf. F. E. Smith used all his formidable powers of advocacy to demolish Edmondson's case in the witness box, Leo performed adequately and, after a week in court, the judge, too, summed up in Leo's favour. When the jury at first failed to reach a unanimous verdict, Leo feared that they might have sided with the rank and file soldier against a defendant who they perceived as being from the officer class, but in the end they found for Leo and disaster was averted, although the issue of his costs, totalling £900, continued to rankle with him until he made a successful plea to the Unionist Party hierarchy for help to the tune of £500.

Leo was becoming increasingly desperate at his continued failure to secure a parliamentary seat and began to lobby more openly, securing a resolution at a meeting of the Tariff Reform League 'to draw the Chief Whip's attention to the fact that neither [William] Hewins nor myself were in the House of Commons'.[4] And he put his now extensive experience of losing elections to good use, sending a nine-page letter to Bonar Law, himself briefly out of Parliament, enclosing numerous suggestions as to how the party's campaigning could be improved. Indeed, the entire party organisation needed rebuilding, 'whatever the row and friction', principally by uniting the Conservative and Liberal Unionist organisations as soon as possible. Worse still was the 'utter badness of the Conservative Central Office' and, in particular, the uselessness of the Chief Whip, Acland Hood, who also fulfilled the key functions of national fundraiser and organiser of the voluntary party throughout the country. Until Hood was 'poisoned or pensioned we shall not get a step forward', he wrote, while the Dickensian nature of the party's headquarters made 'any real efficiency and decency impossible'. Visitors were 'shoved into a little coal hole . . . and kept waiting by the hour', while what was really needed were 'at least two or three tolerable waiting rooms not inferior to those of the ordinary dentist'. Finally, it seemed 'quite absurd that our Party with the enormous reserve of wealth behind it should actually have less money for its election campaign than its opponents'. Leo had been reliably informed that 'the whole of Cadogan Square does not subscribe more than £5 a year to the Unionist party'.

Leo's perceptive suggestion was for Bonar Law to send for his 'friend Max Aitken' (later Lord Beaverbrook), who was 'full of ambition', although Leo doubted whether that 'ambition will ever succeed in carrying him very far' and could not 'conceive his attaining a Cabinet rank for instance'. However, he knew Aitken to have 'really remarkable organising power'.[5] In February 1911 Leo was formally offered the seat of Bedford, with the added incentive that 'the Duke would help with expenses'.[6] It had been narrowly won by the Liberals at the last election and Leo quickly accepted the offer and was formally adopted. However, no sooner had he rented a house locally and begun preparing for a long campaign, than news reached him of the death of Lord Carlisle, which had in turn created a vacancy in South Birmingham where his son Lord Morpeth was the local Member but was now to be elevated to the House of Lords. Both Joseph Chamberlain and his son Neville lobbied strongly on Leo's behalf and, within days, he had visited Birmingham, amicably broken off relations with Bedford and been adopted as the Liberal Unionist candidate for Birmingham South. He had a lucky escape in Bedford where, because of the war, there was to be no vacancy until 1918. Even then, the sitting Member there was one of those Liberal MPs who sided with Lloyd George during the war, and so received the 'coupon' and became immune from Conservative attack. It would have been a long and fruitless candidacy.

At long last Leo had picked a winner. The Birmingham Liberals decided not to contest the by-election and, on 3 May 1911, at the age of thirty-seven, Leo was finally returned to Parliament, unopposed. He was to remain as their Member for thirty-four years. The following day he was introduced to the House of Commons by the Liberal Unionist leader Austen Chamberlain, and was 'well received by all parts of the House'.[7] He was under no illusion as to the opportunity he had finally been granted. It would be 'a great chance', he wrote to Bryddie, 'and I must make use of it. I have got a great deal more reputation than I really deserve for knowledge and I shall have to work hard.' But he lacked neither the courage of his convictions nor belief in his own ability. 'I know I have great weaknesses, but also great strength,' he went on, 'and if fortune is not unkind, I may really play my part in getting big things done.'[8] Certainly he was already well prepared for life in Parliament. Some of his contemporaries had stolen a slight march on him, but he now had a safe seat, was an accomplished and experienced public speaker, and a seasoned and prolific campaigner in the press. He was unquestionably ambitious, but had made few enemies and a rapid rise to the top seemed likely.

He made his maiden speech a fortnight later during the Budget debate and, although he 'got up with great hesitation in face of an almost empty House and with a strong desire to get it over',[9] and spoke, as always, for too long, Lloyd George expressed his 'great delight' at the 'brilliancy of his first appearance in the House' and congratulated 'the party opposite upon having such a valuable accession of strength'.[10] Leo was immediately recruited to join some of the other younger

Members to help in a carefully planned campaign to irritate and disrupt the Government, and he soon became a fully paid-up member of the awkward squad, operating from the second row of seats below the gangway where he sat, somewhat confusingly, in the midst of the Irish Nationalists. Nor was he afraid of tackling difficult issues in his own speeches, as he showed when Lloyd George announced that an insurance fund was to be created for research into the treatment of tuberculosis and Leo recalled his own experience travelling through East Africa, where he had witnessed the ravages of syphilis among the natives, a problem he had subsequently discovered was hardly any less prevalent at home. He tried in vain to find a medical MP to make the case for him, but when no one would agree, 'so unmentionable was the subject in those days', he bravely stood up, with his 'tongue cleaving to the roof of his mouth',[11] and made an impassioned plea that the same consideration should be given to venereal disease. His speech was heard sympathetically and he was warmly congratulated on raising so taboo a subject.

Following the coronation of King George V in June 1911, Parliament returned that summer to the debate, and ensuing confrontation between the Lords and Commons, on the Parliament Bill. The King's promise to Asquith to create new peers, made on the day of Leo's wedding, had remarkably remained secret for eight months, in spite of Kitchener's known reluctance to discuss military operations in Cabinet on the grounds that 'they all tell their wives, except Asquith, who tells other people's wives'.[12] However, once the promise was made public in July, the argument ceased to be one simply between the political parties, but also among the Unionists themselves. Balfour, Lansdowne and the majority of Unionist peers believed that further resistance would be futile, and would drag the House of Lords and, indeed, the King into unnecessary political controversy. But a hard-core group of peers, MPs and some of Leo's fellow 'Compatriot' journalists coalesced around the eighty-seven-year-old former Lord Chancellor, Lord Halsbury, and refused to surrender. Known as the 'diehards', they were determined to continue to oppose the Bill, whatever the consequences for the King or Parliament, and it was to this group that Leo enthusiastically attached himself, regularly attending meetings of the 'No-surrender Committee' and joining in a robust campaign in the press, together with his old friend F. E. Smith.

On 10 August, a stifling hot day, the Bill returned to the House of Lords for the final time, and Leo squeezed into the gallery to hear the last few hours of debate. He listened to the Lord President of the Council, Lord Morley, confirming the King's promise to create sufficient peers to force the Bill through, and to Curzon's 'pompous oration',[13] a speech bitterly resented by the 'diehards' whose cause he had originally supported. The majority of Unionist peers had agreed to follow their leader's instructions and to abstain, but it was thought that as many as one hundred 'diehard' peers were still determined to vote against the Government, enough to defeat the Liberal representation in the Upper House. Early indications suggested that enough 'diehards' had indeed voted to defeat the Bill, but unexpected help arrived for the Government, as twelve bishops, led by the Archbishop of Canterbury, voted to support the Bill. Furthermore the King recorded in his diary that night that 'Rosebery saved the situation by voting for the Government and 20 eminent Unionist peers joined him.'[14] In fact, thirty-seven Unionists voted with the Government, including Curzon to whom the King was particularly grateful. Leo 'went home very angry'.[15]

The battle over the Parliament Bill had left Balfour fatally wounded as Unionist leader, and although Leo thought that the party was 'beginning to show signs of a return to sanity',[16] his friend Leo Maxse's unrelenting campaign in the *National Review*, culminating in his attack under the headline 'Balfour Must Go', was soon to bear fruit.[17] The 'diehards' who had defied Balfour over the Parliament Bill soon formalised their opposition with the creation of another ginger group, the Halsbury Club, in October. Leo was elected to its executive committee and was soon widely perceived as a standard-bearer of the 'BMG' movement. When Balfour suddenly, but not unexpectedly, resigned in November, little had been done to prepare for a successor and while Leo supported Austen Chamberlain's claim as the most obvious and talented successor, his position as a Liberal Unionist angered the Conservative old guard. Having campaigned for Chamberlain, Leo was disappointed when he stood down in the interest of party unity, but broadly welcomed Andrew Bonar Law's subsequent election as the compromise candidate.

With the struggle for Home Rule now dominating the political scene, Leo visited Ireland over the New Year of 1912, where he met members of the 'Provisional Government' in Belfast, set up the previous year, and shared a platform with Edward Carson at Omagh, taking the salute from 20,000 Unionists who marched past to the sound of drums, trumpets and bagpipes. A visit down to Belfast docks to view the newly built *Titanic*, moored serenely awaiting her maiden voyage, left him deeply impressed by the workmen he encountered there, 'determined to shoulder their rifles themselves rather than submit to being governed from Dublin', but concerned by 'the inflexible resolution of the leaders' and their 'complete indifference to the risks involved for themselves or for their flourishing businesses'.[18] After a week spent walking on the Galway coast, and further meetings with both Unionist and Nationalist leaders in Dublin, he returned to London determined to throw himself wholeheartedly into the campaign against Home Rule, publishing a series of articles in the *Morning Post* and contributing regularly to debates in Parliament. He became the master of the parliamentary filibuster and advocated extreme measures to disrupt the Government. 'Don't you think we ought to dig our heels in the ground?' he asked Lord Robert Cecil, and 'refuse to obey the Chairman's ruling until taken out and then be succeeded by another and so on until the whole party are suspended'.[19]

But it was to the issue of tariff reform, and in particular support for taxation on the import of non-imperial goods, including food, that Leo continued to devote most of his energies. The new Unionist leader, Bonar Law, while undoubtedly a 'hawk' in his opposition to Home Rule, held altogether less sound views, in Leo's opinion, on Imperial Preference. Leo bemoaned 'the growing tendency in the party to wobble' over the issue, and when he took a small delegation to see the leader on 14 December 1912, Bonar Law assured them that the idea that 'there could be any change of policy was ridiculous'.[20] Yet just two days later, in a speech in Ashton-under-Lyne, the constituency of another tariff reformer, Max Aitken, he announced severe limitations on the categories of food that would attract duties and the stipulation that they would only do so when specifically demanded by the Dominions themselves. Leo read the speech with alarm and soon found himself at the very heart of a crisis that threatened to engulf the party. Far from clearing the air, Bonar Law's speech had in fact increased the sense of confusion, and everywhere he looked, Leo found formerly supportive MPs and newspapers 'on the scuttle'.[21]

On New Year's Day 1913 Leo hurried about London, visiting first the Chief Whip, then F. E. Smith, and finally Bonar Law himself, who assured him again that there would be no change of policy. However, he also expressed doubt as to whether he could hold the party to this line for long, to which Leo replied, somewhat precociously for one so new to the House, by conveying his 'conviction to B.L. that he had better resign than yield to pressure'.[22] He came away from the meeting confident that Bonar Law would 'stand firm and may refuse to carry on the leadership if the great majority of the party will not come into line'.[23] Leo was only partially right. In fact Bonar Law did not intend to stand firm, indeed he fully intended to give way, but, in a cry for support, he let it be widely known that he was considering resignation. On 7 January Carson drew up a 'memorial' to Bonar Law, in effect an open letter from the party's MPs, appealing to him not to resign and suggesting the postponement of the introduction of any food duties until after a general election. Leo urged his friends not to sign, in spite of Carson and F.E.'s attempts to involve him in its drafting, but he failed to persuade others to join him. Austen Chamberlain encouraged his own supporters to sign, and Bonar Law called Leo to see him again, maintaining that 'it was only the signatures of his Tariff Reform friends that would induce him to stay'. But when Leo went to the Committee Room where the 'memorial' was laid out for signature, he looked at it briefly and left the room, one of only a handful of Unionist MPs who refused to sign. Bonar Law's position had been secured, but Leo recalled Joseph Chamberlain's verdict when Bonar Law had become party leader – 'he is no tariff reformer.'[24]

▪ ▪ ▪

Towards the end of 1912 Leo became involved in what he later described as the 'most unpleasant and exasperating experience' of his political career,[25] with his appointment to an all-party Select Committee set up to investigate the so-called 'Marconi Scandal', a story of insider dealing that went to the very top of the Government. The Imperial Conference of 1911 had endorsed a proposal for a chain of eighteen wireless stations that would link the British Empire, and the Government had subsequently accepted the tender of the Marconi Wireless Telegraph Company to erect the first few stations, in England, Egypt, East Africa and Singapore; Canada, South Africa and Australia would each build their own. Although the contract was only signed in July and approved by Parliament in August, Marconi had, for some time, been publicly talking up its agreement with the British Government, and thus stimulating its share price at the same time.

Marconi was divided into two, supposedly separate, companies in Britain and America, although the British Marconi Company had a holding in the American Company and three British directors, including Godfrey Isaacs, the managing director, sat on the board. Isaacs visited New York soon after the acceptance of the tender and persuaded the American board of Marconi to seize the moment and expand the American business. To finance this expansion, a new issue of American shares was to be launched on the London market in April, with the expectation that they would trade at an immediate, and considerable, premium. The week before the share issue, Godfrey Isaacs had lunch with his two brothers, one of them Sir Rufus Isaacs, the Liberal Attorney General. He offered to sell them a block of these soon to be issued shares, which were already in his possession, at a greatly discounted price of £1.1s.3d, which would guarantee an immediate profit when trading began. Sir Rufus at first wisely declined the offer, in spite of his brother's misleading assurance that the contract with the British Government had already been signed and that there was no connection between American Marconi and the British Company which had secured the contract.

However, a week later, on 17 April, Sir Rufus Isaacs overcame his scruples and purchased 10,000 shares through his other brother, Harry, thus satisfying himself that he was not buying direct from a government contractor and that the new price of £2 a share was a fair market price. In fact, Marconi shares were already exchanging hands at £3. Sir Rufus then persuaded two of his closest political friends, Lloyd George, the Chancellor of the Exchequer, and the Master of Elibank, the Liberal Chief Whip, to buy 1,000 shares each, and a series of complicated purchases and disposals ensued, during which the three ministers sold some of their shares at £3 when trading opened, Lloyd George bought a further tranche of shares himself, and the Master of Elibank bought 2,500 additional shares with Liberal Party funds. While it seems incredible today that three such politically astute men failed to predict the likely reaction to their attempted profiteering, their brazen behaviour would appear to imply that they thought they were doing nothing wrong.

Neither were they very successful at being corrupt. As word of improper trading found its way around the City, the shares soon slumped and all three probably made a loss. It was not long before a clamour developed within the press, and among other financiers who had made a loss, for action to be taken, at which stage the accused ministers should have taken the sensible line of action and owned up to a foolish mistake. Instead, all three, with the full support of Prime Minister Asquith, took the line of guilty politicians down the ages and, in a debate on 11 October, angrily rejected any accusation of insider dealing or wrongdoing of any kind. With masterly use of obfuscating language, all three indignantly denied any dealings in British Marconi shares and the House agreed to set up the Select Committee on which Leo was appointed to serve.

He was under no illusion as to the likely effectiveness of the Committee, recognising only too clearly the obvious shortcomings of a system, as prevalent today as they were then, in which 'the Opposition members are inclined to make the most of the case against Ministers, while the Government supporters are tempted to whitewash.'[26] However, he had been given a chance to shine in a very public setting and he held strong feelings about the basic proprieties of political behaviour. 'I do feel', he wrote to Bonar Law, 'that neither the Attorney-General, and still less the Chancellor of the Exchequer, should have been in a direct inside Stock Exchange ramp', and Rufus Isaacs had been 'well in the know all through.'[27] The Committee was appointed on 25 October, composed of six Liberal, two Irish, one Labour and six Unionist Members, Leo working closely on the Unionist side with Lord Robert Cecil. It immediately became clear that the Liberal chairman, though 'well intentioned', was both 'somewhat deaf and ineffectual', [28] and he soon lost control of the proceedings to the two Liberal stooges on the Committee, James Falconer and Handel Booth, who proceeded to block proceedings at every opportunity.

With the exception of the Chief Secretary of the Post Office, a 'shifty looking fellow and pretty unscrupulous in his statements',[29] Leo found the first few months of evidence tedious, but a campaign by Leo Maxse in the *National Review* reached its climax at his own evidence session before the Committee on 12 February 1913, when he bitterly criticised the ministers concerned. A muddled account of his evidence in the French newspaper *Le Matin* gave Rufus Isaacs the opportunity to instigate libel proceedings and to use his appearance in the witness box, ironically represented by F. E. Smith, to make a partial disclosure of his purchase of American Marconi shares. When he appeared before the Select Committee for three days in March, his evidence was most notable for the acrimonious nature of his exchanges with Leo. Fired by a strong sense of duty, and as tenacious as ever, Leo fired question after question at the Attorney General, who 'grew more and more restive and interrupted constantly', complaining that Leo's questioning was 'offensive'.[30] Leo, in turn, thought Isaacs 'rather too voluble and elaborate for a good witness and too inclined . . . to come out with prepared outbursts of indignation.'[31]

On the second day of evidence the exchanges were particularly heated, as Falconer and Booth did their best to disrupt Leo's questions in a bid to save an increasingly flustered Isaacs, for whom 'it was the only time throughout the proceedings that his customary calm deserted him'.[32] Leo too lost his temper with his fellow Liberal Committee members. 'You want to prevent the truth coming out and you might be decent in doing it,' he shouted at them, complaining that they interrupted 'whenever there seemed at any moment an answer likely to lead to the discovery of anything which seemed unpleasant'.[33] Indeed both Leo and Cecil suspected Booth of having been involved in the purchase of shares himself, so agitated did he become at calls for a declaration of disinterestedness among Committee members.

The third day of Isaacs' cross-examination was conducted almost exclusively by Leo on his own and, in spite of the public compliments that were paid him for his performance, he conceded that cross-examination was an 'art that requires practice', and that Isaacs had 'all the advantage over' him.[34] The Master of Elibank took more drastic action to avoid giving evidence, and left the country for South America in January 1913.

The report of the Unionist Members, drafted by Leo, cleared ministers of corruption but accused them of serious impropriety and criticised them for failing to own up to the House of Commons. It was voted down by the Liberal majority, as was even the chairman's modest effort at mild censure, and the final document, submitted by Booth and Falconer, completely exonerated the ministers as the victims of a conspiracy. However, this was too much, even for the Liberal-supporting press and their own parliamentary party and, in the ensuing debate, expressions of regret made by ministers for their indiscreet and unwise behaviour were duly accepted by the House as a whole. Leo's worst fears had been confirmed. Never, he thought, 'in the whole course of our political history, has there been a worse Select Committee than this one',[35] while the bible of parliamentary procedure, *Erskine May*, later concluded that 'such highly visible failure condemned their successors to a very limited role for almost half a century'.[36]

Although it was an unsatisfactory end to a lengthy episode, Leo emerged with his reputation as a campaigning and eloquent back-bencher greatly enhanced, and a raised profile. 'Mr Amery may have expressed himself the other day with more heat than propriety,' said *The Times*, 'but there is not much doubt that public opinion endorses his complaint that certain members of the Committee have for months past been desirous of preventing unpleasant facts from coming to light.'[37] Others, even on his own side, thought that 'violence like that of Maxse and Amery however well meant can only damage a good cause',[38] and Bonar Law, never one to enjoy personal criticism of friends across the floor of the House (he was a golfing partner of Lloyd George's), was himself reluctant to take a stronger line.

Although formal proceedings on Marconi soon came to an end, the affair rumbled on for a while, Leo observing in the Court News press at Christmas that 'Sir Rufus Isaacs was leaving London for Pontefract', Handel Booth's constituency. 'Is it imaginable', he wondered, 'that the blackmail ministers will have to pay in future will take the form of week-ends with the Handel Booths?'[39] More widespread was the unease expressed about the 'tactful discretion of the Harmsworth press' over Marconi, amid suggestions that Harold Harmsworth had helped to orchestrate the affair from his villa in the south of France, and had 'plunged very heavily in English Marconis not only on his own account but on behalf of Ministers'.[40] In March 1913 Harmsworth had written to his brother, Lord Northcliffe, urging him to 'soft pedal in *The Times* and the *Daily Mail*' over the affair, and assuring him that it would be '*in your interests*' to save Rufus Isaacs' career, given that he was 'destined for high judicial office'. Isaacs later thanked Northcliffe for his 'generous treatment',[41] and was indeed controversially promoted to the post of Lord Chief Justice in October that year. 'I see that Rufus Isaacs has chosen the title of Baron Reading of Earley,' wrote Leo to Maxse, suggesting that 'the full title ought to read Baron Reading of Early Inside Information.'[42] And further proof, for those who sought it, of a corrupt alliance between the Liberal Government and sections of the press came with Harmsworth's conveniently timed elevation to the peerage as Lord Rothermere, in the same New Year's Honours list of 1914.

The mood of regret expressed by ministers during June soon evaporated and on 1 July Lloyd George and Rufus Isaacs were given a banquet in their honour at the National Liberal Club. Lloyd George took the opportunity to deliver a scathing, anti-Tory polemic, denouncing his critics, Leo among them, as 'hungry humbugs steeped in smugness and self-righteousness', while he had been persecuted to the point of 'martyrdom'.[43] This was more than Leo could stomach and he retaliated a week later with a speech 'of slashing invective', launching a bitter personal attack on Lloyd George, who, while he had not been charged with corruption, did nevertheless 'speculate improperly', and did 'for months mislead the House of Commons and the public'. He had not even had the good grace to escape to 'the seclusion of Bogota', like the Master of Elibank, but had instead chosen to 'crow brazen defiance to the public conscience from his own dunghill at the National Liberal Club'.⁴⁴ Leo Maxse published the speech in the *National Review* under the title 'St Sebastian of Limehouse', a reference to Lloyd George's fiery speeches at Limehouse in 1909. The epithet was quickly taken up by the press.

For Leo personally, the Marconi scandal was an exciting, if ultimately depressing, adventure. It is inconceivable to imagine the individuals concerned, perhaps even the Government itself, surviving such a scandal in modern parliamentary times; indeed, Members of Parliament have since gone to prison for considerably more modest examples of insider trading. In many ways Leo was ahead of his time. He believed that a wrong had been done and that Parliament had been brought into disrepute. Throughout his career, it is sometimes possible to consider him as being 'holier than thou' in his upholding of standards and his self-assured propriety. On this occasion, he pursued his quarry relentlessly, but ultimately, although he landed some blows, without success. The tenacity of his interrogation seems to have done him no harm, either professionally or socially, for just three years later he would be serving at Lloyd George's side, and soon after that as a minister in his Government.

▪ ▪ ▪

At the end of the summer of 1913 Leo and Bryddie sailed to Australia with the first ever delegation to one of the Dominions of the Empire Parliamentary Association. The group of fourteen MPs, which included Bryddie's brother Hamar Greenwood, arrived at the beginning of September, and began their visit in Sydney where Leo was able to study Australia's recently introduced system of universal military training and review the newly built Australian fleet in Sydney harbour. In Melbourne the delegation was honoured by a march past of 10,000 young Australian trainees, while Leo visited the Commonwealth Parliament where he met 'Billy' Hughes for the first time, then leader of the Opposition, but later, as Prime Minister of Australia, destined to work closely with Leo for many years. They also travelled out into the countryside, to the vineyards of South Australia and the sugar plantations of Queensland. While Bryddie spent much of the trip staying with friends in the Blue Mountains outside Sydney, Leo ventured on to

Auckland on his own, where he again travelled widely around New Zealand. He met Bryddie again in Hobart and, on 13 November, after nearly three months away, they sailed for home.

By the time they returned to London at the end of 1913, a single issue had come to dominate the political agenda, that of Home Rule and, in particular, the special case of Ulster. Carson's Provisional Government had been formally constituted in September, while the Ulster Volunteers had by now recruited as many as 100,000 men and raised some £1,000,000. Asquith's Government had, in recent months, begun to use increasingly conciliatory language in the search for a compromise solution that would concede a degree of special consideration to Ulster. The Unionist leadership, meanwhile, were only too happy to concentrate almost exclusively on the same aspect of the Home Rule debate, by reiterating their determination to go to whatever lengths were necessary to support Ulster were the Government to attempt to impose a settlement there by force. Leo was unhappy that the Unionist policy now focused so exclusively on the issue of Ulster, believing that his leaders had effectively surrendered over the far greater issue of the supremacy of the Union as a whole. He did not agree with the implication that Government concession over Ulster would be an acceptable solution, but he consented, nonetheless, to become involved in the Unionist campaign.

In January 1914 Leo wrote to Milner, suggesting the concept of a British Covenant, along the lines of Carson's Ulster Covenant, as a means of creating an organisation that would oppose Government attempts at coercion in Ulster. When he put the suggestion to Bonar Law, the following day, the Unionist leader's reaction convinced Leo that he would support the idea of the mass signing of a 'solemn declaration binding the signatories to use every means in their power to prevent the armed forces of the Crown being used against the Ulster people'. Indeed, Bonar Law had 'practically appealed to the Unionist Party to strengthen the hands of its leaders in their pledge to take any measures that may be effective in their support of Ulster'.[45] Leo set about drafting a suitable form of words and encouraging as wide a circle of friends, politicians, writers and academics to sign as he could. But the Covenant's wording was strong meat for some, pledging the signatory, in the event of a Home Rule Bill being passed, to feel 'justified in taking or supporting any action that may be effective to prevent it being put into operation, and more particularly to prevent the armed forces of the Crown being used to deprive the people of Ulster of their rights as Citizens of the United Kingdom'.[46]

Among those who welcomed his initiative was Rudyard Kipling, who not only signed, but also wrote a poem of support, 'The Covenant',[47] and helped Leo and Milner to publish a new magazine, the *Covenanter*, whose somewhat provocative motto was 'Put your trust in God and keep your powder dry'.[48] However, most politicians were deterred by the implication that they might have to support un-constitutional, even illegal, behaviour and were unmoved by Bonar Law's own suggestion that the necessary action might 'involve some-thing more than making speeches'.[49] Austen Chamberlain refused to sign, complaining that 'at one time signatures to parliamentary petitions were no doubt an important political demonstration', but that now they counted 'for little or nothing'.[50] His brother Neville was suspicious of Bonar Law's motives, suggesting that if the Unionist leader wanted a declaration so badly, 'let him draw it up and sign it first himself'.[51] Lord Robert Cecil was concerned only that 'the English hate illegality',[52] while Lord Crawford, a potential recruiting sergeant in the Lords, was honest in his observation that Leo had 'great courage', but that he had always 'distrusted his judgement'.[53] Undeterred, Leo launched the *Covenant* anyway, with a good deal of positive press comment, and campaigned vigorously around the country, and in Ulster itself, to promote it.

The Government began the crucial February 1914 session of Parliament in conciliatory mood. The Unionists at first accepted Asquith's offer of a possible compromise that would lead to an acceptance of the broad principle of Home Rule if Ulster was to be excluded. However, it proved impossible to agree upon the detail of this arrangement and it soon became clear that the necessary con-cessions would not be forthcoming on either side. The Government decided to press on with their original proposals, while simultaneously preparing for possible bloodshed. On 14 March Leo was outraged by the 'provocative and unrestrained'[54] speech in Bradford of the First

Lord of the Admiralty, Winston Churchill, who warned that the Government had made its last concession, and that if Ulster continued to resist, then it could only be because the Unionists 'preferred shooting to voting'.[55] Lloyd George had himself encouraged Churchill to make a speech that would 'ring down the corridors of history',[56] and Churchill duly obliged, counselling that there were 'worse things than bloodshed, even on an extended scale', and that if the Government was to be 'exposed to menace and brutality', then it was time to 'go forward together and put these grave matters to the proof'.[57] Leo was one of those Unionists for whom Churchill's speech was clear evidence that 'the government planned a pogrom against the Unionists of the north',[58] especially when Asquith endorsed it in the Commons the next day.

During the week that followed, Leo's personal involvement in the so-called 'Curragh Mutiny' was peripheral, although his extensive army contacts, built up over many years, often placed him in possession of significant information before his political superiors. When three brigade majors from Aldershot threatened to resign their commissions and leave immediately to join the Ulster volunteers, it was to Leo that they turned, who managed to talk them out of their decision with the help of F. E. Smith. As the crisis unfolded, Leo met daily with the then Major-General Henry Wilson, later to become Chief of Staff, who updated him on the progress of meetings at the War Office between the Secretary of State for War, Jack Seely, and the representatives of the mutinous officers at the British army base at the Curragh in Ireland. Within hours of Brigadier-General Gough, the commanding officer at the Curragh, leaving the War Office on the afternoon of Monday 23 March, Leo was able to brief Bonar Law that Gough had 'received a written assurance to the effect that the troops under his command were "not to be used to coerce Ulster to accept the present Home Rule Bill".'[59] The information enabled Bonar Law to raise the issue in the House later that very afternoon and, the following day, Leo himself was listened to with incredulity by Liberal backbenchers who realised that he knew more of the facts of the case than their own ministers, and who interrupted him with frequent cries of 'Who told you?'[60]

As the parliamentary debate raged over the next few weeks, Leo made himself as unpleasant as possible, using a combination of his inside information from military sources and a sharp tongue to torment Asquith and his ministers at every opportunity. His interjections brought him into regular conflict with the Speaker, as when he accused Churchill of expecting and, indeed, hoping that the Government's Irish policy would 'lead to fighting and bloodshed', a charge that Churchill retorted was a 'hellish insinuation', for which he was in turn forced to apologise by the Speaker.[61] By now Leo conceded that, when he rose to speak in the House, 'the mere sight of me caused a roar of execration to rise' from the benches opposite.[62] On 8 April he succeeded in delaying the Easter Adjournment of the House with a long, rambling speech that bore so little relation to the subject under debate that he was called to order by the Speaker fifteen times. For good measure he called the Prime Minister a liar. And he revelled in his growing reputation as the hatchet man on the Opposition back benches, boasting that he was 'looked upon as the most odious as well as most pertinacious of gadflies', and that even his own leaders thought that the 'studied insolence' of his attacks on Asquith 'went beyond the mark'.[63]

When Asquith finally introduced the Home Rule Bill for its Third Reading on 21 May, Leo once again led the parliamentary opposition, complaining that the country was 'being allowed to drift on into an impossible and appalling situation simply because an old Gentleman cannot make up his mind'. After the Speaker had complained that the expression was 'improper and discourteous',[64] and had then tried to bring Leo to order on several further occasions, the Unionist benches finally tired of compromise and drowned out the subsequent debate with a concerted chant of 'Adjourn, adjourn!' The Speaker foolishly asked Bonar Law whether the demonstration was with his 'assent and approval', to which the Unionist leader replied that he 'would not presume to criticise what you consider your duty, Sir, but I know mine, and that is not to answer any such question'.[65] Leo was greatly heartened by this show of defiance, telling Bonar Law that he could 'have little idea of the enthusiasm and warmth of affection' which his words had 'created right through the Party',[66] although one or two of the older Members were angry that the party leader had been put in such a position in the first place by the behaviour of his backbenchers, and that 'Amery did more than anyone else to promote it'.[67]

When the Bill reached the House of Lords in July, the Unionist majority there amended it to exclude Ulster. A conference at Buckingham Palace, summoned by the King, failed to break the deadlock and on 26 July a group of Irish National Volunteers landed a consignment of rifles and ammunition north of Dublin and engaged in clashes with troops which resulted in dead and wounded. Leo's involvement in the Home Rule Bill was now at an end; symbolically, his hero Joseph Chamberlain died in July, his parting words to Leo that he 'would *fight*' on over Home Rule.[68] But on 28 June the Archduke Franz Ferdinand had been shot in Sarajevo and the Austro-Hungarian ultimatum to Serbia on 23 July had begun the drift to war. For Leo, the parliamentary truce over Home Rule marked the end of his first great battle. He would soon find himself brought in from the outer reaches of rebellious opposition to a position of greater influence, to serve alongside many of those he had hitherto fought so assiduously. Another chapter of his political career was about to begin.

CHAPTER FIVE

———— ◆ ————

Not Overlooked Entirely

Like the rest of the political elite, Leo had been 'all too passion-ately absorbed in the Irish crisis during most of July to realise the imminence of war'.[1] He had devoted much of the past ten years to speaking and writing about the threat of another great war, yet when it came it was as unexpected for him as it was for everyone else. However, he was quicker than most to appreciate the scale of the threat that now faced the country. His contacts within the army, and his friendship with Sir Henry Wilson, by now Director of Military Operations, ensured that he was better briefed than most of his parliamentary colleagues and, possibly, than some of the Cabinet themselves, as to the true nature of the military preparations that had taken place following Sir Edward Grey's negotiations with the French Government over the past few years. Grey's effective com-mitment to the French to come to their aid in the event of invasion had been met with consternation by most of the Liberal Cabinet when it had been revealed to them in 1912. As a result, an exchange of letters between Grey and Paul Cambon, the French Ambassador, in October 1912 had stressed the purely contingent nature of the British commitment, in an attempt both to calm the nerves of the more pacifist Liberal ministers and to reassure the French that the promise would be honoured.

When the House of Commons met on 31 July Leo was concerned at the continuing uncertainty surrounding the Government's intentions. He remained deeply distrustful of Asquith and his anxiety was heightened by a visit that evening from his parliamentary colleague George Lloyd, who reported overhearing a '*sotto voce* aside' from Asquith to the Speaker earlier that day: 'But Sir, this is no concern of ours.'[2] Lloyd had since been to the French Embassy, where he was infuriated to learn that Asquith had justified the inactivity of the British Government on the grounds that he would be unable to achieve cross-party support from the Unionists. Leo and Lloyd agreed to do all they could to lay this falsehood to rest by stiffening the resolve of the Unionist leadership, both writing urgent letters to Austen Chamberlain and contacting friendly newspaper editors.

Saturday 1 August was a day of intense activity. After Henry Wilson had confirmed Leo's worst fears as to the gravity of the situation, Lloyd and Leo Maxse went first to visit Count Alexander Benckendorff, the Russian Ambassador, and then Cambon who told him that the 'French regarded themselves as completely betrayed'. As it was a Bank Holiday weekend, the entire Unionist leadership had left town, although Lloyd managed to persuade Balfour, who had assumed that all was well, reluctantly to forgo his weekend at Hatfield House. Lloyd then travelled himself, by car, down to Wargrave, near Henley, to try to persuade Bonar Law, F. E. Smith and Carson to return to London at once. They too at first proved obstinately reluctant to return to London, F.E. and Bonar Law, in the best traditions of Drake, insisting on finishing their set of tennis while Lloyd waited patiently, and Bonar Law accusing Lloyd of interfering in matters that did not concern him. Eventually, however, they all agreed to go.

Austen Chamberlain, meanwhile, had joined his wife and children for a few days' holiday at Westgate-on-Sea, a fashionable holiday resort in Kent. That same Saturday afternoon he received a telephone call from Leo, who informed him that he would be on the next train to Westgate from Victoria, arriving at 4.50, in time to brief Chamberlain and bring him back to London by the next train. Unfortunately, 'as was only to be expected from the South-Eastern Railway', Leo complained, the engine broke down and he only reached Westgate at about 7.30. Chamberlain was already enjoying his dinner, but recognised the importance of Leo's visit far more quickly than had his Unionist colleagues. By the time the two of them reached Charing Cross it was well past midnight, but they were met there by Lloyd who took them to Chamberlain's house in Egerton Place and briefed them on a meeting that had taken place earlier that evening at Lansdowne House, the home of the Unionist leader in the House of Lords, where Sir Henry Wilson had endeavoured to persuade Lord Lansdowne, Bonar Law, the Duke of Devonshire and Balfour that urgent action was needed. In spite of Wilson's exposé of the threatening military situation, the meeting had broken up without any of the participants showing 'the slightest conception of the fact that war was on or that it signified anything'.[3]

Leo's immediate task was to convince the Unionist leadership that they should make it clear to the Government, beyond any doubt, that they would support them in standing by France. The following morning, Sunday 2 August, Austen Chamberlain met first with Lord Lansdowne at Lansdowne House, where he produced a draft of a letter to be sent to Asquith, and then with Lansdowne and Bonar Law at the latter's house in Edwardes Square. The final text made it clear to the Prime Minister that 'any hesitation in now supporting France and Russia would be fatal to the honour and to the future security of the United Kingdom', and that they offered the Government 'the assurance of the united support of the Opposition in all measures required by England's intervention in the war'. The letter was delivered to Downing Street in time for the Cabinet meeting.[4]

Leo, meanwhile, had breakfasted with Henry Wilson, who told him that 'absolutely nothing was being done at the War Office'. He had then visited the French Embassy with Lloyd and Maxse, where they learnt that Germany had declared war on Russia, and went on to see Chamberlain who recounted the story of the drafting of the letter to Asquith that morning. After dinner, again with Wilson, he visited the editors of *The Times*, *Daily Express* and *Morning Post* in an attempt to stiffen their resolve, before ending the day with another lengthy, late-night meeting with Chamberlain. Yet he still felt a sense of anti-climax. Having spent much of the day 'sitting about feeling pretty miserable', he consoled himself that he and Lloyd 'had done all we could in getting the Unionist leaders to town and bringing them to the scratch of doing something'. Certainly, as lowly backbenchers, they had played a leading role in encouraging their own leaders to stiffen the Government's resolve and, in Chamberlain, they had found a leader who had, in turn, 'taken the situation in hand'.[5] While some historians have since been dismissive of the influence of the Unionist ultimatum to Asquith, it remains a fact that the decision to go to war was taken at the two Cabinet meetings that took place on 2 August, and that the letter had 'provided Grey officially with a plank that had previously been missing from his platform'.[6]

For a brief moment Leo had found himself at the centre of party and national affairs and the next two days were spent following the rapid turn of events as the country moved towards war; the German ultimatum to Belgium; Grey's statement to the House of Commons which Leo thought a 'masterly piece of persuasion';[7] and finally the violation of Belgian neutrality and the expiry of the Government's ultimatum to Germany at 11.00 p.m. on 4 August. And he still had one last pre-war part to play behind the scenes, as rumours circulated at Westminster that the unpopular and supposedly pro-German Lord Haldane was to be reappointed as Secretary of State for War, and that the British Expeditionary Force was not, after all, to be despatched to France. Leo again lobbied his leaders to emphasise opposition to Haldane's appointment and although, on this occasion, Chamberlain feared that Leo was asking too much and risked irritating the Government, it was Lord Kitchener of Khartoum, home on leave from his post as High Commissioner in Egypt, who was 'literally hauled out of his cabin on the steamer at Dover' and confirmed as Secretary of State for War.[8]

Leo had long been a supporter of Lord Roberts's campaign, ignored until then by Government and Opposition alike, for National Service. In the first few days of the war, together with his parliamentary colleague Simon Lovat, he set about drawing up plans for a new recruitment scheme, which would lead to a substantial expansion of the Territorial Army. But when they succeeded in forcing their way in to see Kitchener on his very first day in office, the new War Secretary ignored their proposals for the Territorials and instead appointed them as recruiting officers for his regular army on the spot. Leo concentrated his early efforts in Birmingham, cutting through the red tape that was impeding the recruitment process there and requisitioning the Town Hall, in Kitchener's name, for sole use as the new recruiting office. Overnight he found the equipment and documentation necessary to process the hundreds of men who were trying to sign up, but who had so far done no more than stand in line. So impressed was Kitchener, that the following week Leo was appointed Director of Civilian Recruiting for the Southern Command, with his own room at the War Office, where he was to report to the Director of Recruiting, General Sir Henry Rawlinson.

He soon realised the limitations of his new job as a 'sort of extra secretary to Rawlinson', requiring him to 'go a little gently at first',[9] but he nevertheless travelled extensively around the South and Midlands, bringing together local authorities and existing political organisations in towns and cities to create recruitment committees. Everywhere there was a lack of urgency and it soon became clear that public opinion would have to be won over if progress was to be made. He persuaded several Members of Parliament, including his brother-in-law, to form a Parliamentary Recruiting Committee, encouraging the various party organisations throughout the country to mobilise their resources. One evening, he opened his front door to find that Emmeline Pankhurst and her eldest daughter Christabel had mysteriously appeared on his doorstep, having returned in secret from Brussels, where they had fled to escape arrest for their acts of suffragism. They promised to 'throw themselves whole-heartedly into the recruitment movement, if their past offences were overlooked'.[10] Leo, a longstanding supporter of the suffragettes, took them to see Rawlinson and ensured that their request was met, leading to a suspension of suffragette activities and the creation of the Women's Emergency Corps.

Leo appears to have had the ability, almost uniquely among Kitchener's advisers, whose opinions were generally shouted down, to win the War Secretary over in argument. On one such occasion, Leo did 'what the soldiers did not dare to do, cut his tirade short and patiently explained' his case, whereupon 'Kitchener at once gave way, and all was well'.[11] Another time, Hamar Greenwood recounted to Bryddie how Kitchener had at first been reluctant to accept a particular scheme of Leo's, 'but Amery told him he must, and he has.' This was in spite of the fact that all the soldiers were 'afraid to argue with K. of K. who is not mentally a giant, but he listens to Leo and agrees – though reluctantly – with him.'[12]

But Leo soon realised that the quantity of recruits flooding into the recruitment offices was far beyond that which the army could handle. Too many able men were being turned away and the early enlisters were often those who could least be spared, miners and workers in heavy industry. Leo revived his original idea of using the Territorial Army Associations to take over the work of housing, clothing and training recruits and suggested that men should stay in their jobs until actually called up, while it would be made plain to employers that they should not discharge men, but merely allow them a few hours off to enlist. But Kitchener refused to allow the appeal to employers, arguing that it was his recruitment scheme and he would manage it as he saw fit and, for the first time, Leo failed to win the argument. Recruitment numbers again soared beyond the manageable, as thousands of men left their jobs only to find that they had nothing to live off, to which Kitchener responded by raising the minimum chest and height measurements required to pass the army medical. With no warning Leo was told that his services were no longer needed, he assumed at the instigation of Asquith, who had still not forgiven him for his outspoken attacks during the Home Rule debates.

Leo's former Director of Recruiting, General Sir Henry Rawlinson, had by now been given his own command in Belgium and, at the age of forty-one, Leo crossed over to Ostend in October to join his personal staff. After several days searching, he eventually found Rawlinson in Bruges, where they briefly set up their headquarters in the sitting room of a hotel run by a German landlord. Rawlinson thought that Leo, 'with fluent pen and sharp, clever ways, had helped him greatly'.[13] However, the fall of Antwerp led to a further retreat, initially to Ostend where they were billeted in a splendid local chateau. The family had fled, leaving their cellar of fine wine behind them, but Leo managed to persuade the old butler that it was pointless allowing the wine to fall into German hands and, having enjoyed a good Burgundy over dinner, he filled up all the staff cars when they left the next morning. He later regretted not having taken more, but the butler heeded his advice and sank the remainder of the wine in the lake, where it apparently remained until after the war.

As the German advance continued, Rawlinson fell back further to Ypres, where Leo now began his temporary career as an intelligence officer, responsible for the examination of prisoners of war. His technique was based on his 'knowledge of the German character', which he found 'worked unfailingly with the naturally obedient German private'. He treated them as he believed they would have been treated by one of their officers at their recruitment, probably no more than a few weeks earlier. Having systematically worked through mundane details such as name, age and occupation, he would move on, apparently innocently, to discovering more useful information. Once, as Rawlinson was poised to carry out a pre-ordered attack on a German position, Leo discovered that the captured German soldiers he was questioning were in fact part of a much larger contingent of reinforcements, previously unknown to the British high command. Rawlinson was, at the last moment, able to withdraw from the trap that had been set and to hold the line, marking the beginning of the First Battle of Ypres. But if Leo took professional pleasure in his duties, he also felt acute personal sympathy at the plight of the young German recruits whose letters he had to read. So many of them, he wrote sadly to Bryddie, 'were from mothers and wives and sweethearts, letters full of love and affection and trust in providence'.[14]

Leo continued in his role as intelligence officer for a few weeks, with responsibility for reporting on the progress of French operations further down the line and liaising with the newly re-forming Belgian troops. But with the exception of the occasional visit to the front line, he saw little of the battle itself, although enough to convince him of the terror of coming under sustained bombardment. While visiting a colleague in hospital in Boulogne, he came by chance across his brother Harold in a bed nearby. He had been wounded at the Aisne, had subsequently recovered enough to rejoin his regiment, the Black Watch, but had then suffered further, terrible injuries while leading an attack only the very next day. He was to die of his injuries a year later. And Leo also saw one of his heroes, Lord Roberts, for the last time.

Roberts had come over from England to visit the front for himself, but caught a bad cold while visiting Ypres and died a few days later, Leo attending the old soldier's funeral at St Omer.

While he held strong opinions about the practical rights and wrongs of how war should be waged on the grand scale, both militarily and politically, Leo also remained curiously detached from the daily slaughter on the ground. He refused to forget all that he had found good about Germany before the war, and felt something verging on a sentimental admiration for the enemy at a personal level. 'If we really want to win this war, and win it properly,' he wrote home to his old friend Lord Selborne, 'we had much better announce at once that we want another 3,000,000 men, begin making all the arrangements for equipping, officering and training them now, and call them up in April and May with a view to operations next October.' Yet in the same letter he bemoaned the widespread jingoism that led to so much time being wasted discussing the 'pros and cons of the war and the wickedness of the Germans, and German spies, and boycotting German sausages and Beethoven'.[15]

Leo wrote movingly of the scenes he witnessed on Christmas Day 1914, the 'amazing sight' of the two armies leaving their respective trenches, 'all mixed up on the green strip of no man's land, shaking hands and exchanging souvenirs'. He played in the football matches that took place over the next few days and received a Christmas present in the exchange that took place between the two sides. One unfortunate German soldier, however, was brought to Leo for interrogation, having overstayed his welcome in no man's land and been captured while walking along the front trench distributing cigars. He explained that he wanted to 'repay the lovely presents' that he had himself received, and had 'written home specially for a box of the best'. Leo was pleased to be able to reassure the generous young German by 'painting a rosy picture of the comfort, warmth, and, above all safety of a British prison camp as compared with the discomfort and danger of the trenches'. He promised, too, to write to the young soldier's mother.[16]

In the course of his work, Leo drew up a memorandum for General Rawlinson advocating the opening of a second front to advance into Hungary through Serbia. When he returned home on leave in January

1915, he was summoned by General Callwell, the Head of Intelligence, and told of the Cabinet's decision to send a British and French division to aid the Serbs by way of Salonika. The problem was that the War Office had absolutely no information on Serbia that would help the advancing troops. At Callwell's request, Leo spent a week writing a military handbook on Serbia, its history, politics, economics and topography, using the best collection of books and maps that he could lay his hands on. For good measure, he spent a further three days compiling an English–Serb phrasebook for the troops' most basic needs.

Meanwhile, Asquith's lingering hostility towards Leo resurfaced, as he expressed his disapproval of his serving on Rawlinson's staff. But when Leo tried instead to get himself appointed to the staff of another friend, General Sir Ian Hamilton, who was just about to leave for the Dardanelles, Asquith stepped in again to prevent the appointment. Eventually Leo was forced to appeal to Balfour for help in securing him a posting that would meet with Prime Ministerial approval, and it was eventually agreed that he might serve in any capacity in which his experience could be put to good use, so long as it was not on the personal staff of a senior commander. For a while Leo was left kicking his heels and hoping for a return to more active service, undergoing a course in machine-gun training, watching the first test firings at Shoeburyness of what became known as the 'Stokes gun', and returning for a few days to Belgium where he witnessed the conclusion of the Battle of Neuve Chapelle, which served only to confirm his 'strong conviction of the futility of those trench attacks on the Western Front'.[17]

By March 1915 he had become a permanent member of the Balkan section of military intelligence under General Callwell, and was despatched to the Balkans on a mission to study road, rail and river communications in advance of General Hamilton's expected advance into Hungary. He was also to act as liaison officer between the British military attachés in the various Balkan capitals, a position that would give him diplomatic cover in those countries that were still neutral. It was an important posting. There was still plenty to play for in the Balkans, with the possibility that Greece, Bulgaria and Romania could all be brought into the war to fight alongside Serbia against the common enemies, Turkey and Austria-Hungary. In Athens he renewed his acquaintance with the Greek Prime Minister, Eleftherios Venizelos, whom he had first met in Crete nearly twenty years earlier. He travelled on by sea to Salonika, and then overland to Macedonia and to Nish (now Ñis), where the Serbian Government had relocated itself since the evacuation of Belgrade. He arrived during Orthodox Easter and everywhere he went he heard 'the ceaseless squealing of little pigs', since 'every Serb in the street seemed to be carrying a little black porker . . . protesting with all its might against its prospective contribution to the Easter festivities'.[18] The town was in the grip of a typhus epidemic and he was struck by the squalor of his surroundings. A visit to the front line at the river Danube in Belgrade was, he assured Bryddie, absolutely safe, as it was during the siesta hour. 'Imagine Chelsea and Battersea at war,' he wrote, 'with the Chelsea Bridge blown up, and a mutual understanding between both sides not to shell into the town opposite.'[19]

From Belgrade, Leo went to Bucharest, where the 'very self-conscious imitation of Paris' made him yearn for the 'primitive vigour' of war-torn Belgrade.[20] The main street was packed with an 'animated crowd of highly dressed and highly painted ladies, gorgeously uniformed officers and *flâneurs* of all kinds', the Romanians appearing 'soft and sensual, and mostly concerned with having a good time in the most elementary carnal sense of the term'.[21] In spite of apparent disapproval of the lifestyle in Bucharest, he still found time to spend a drunken evening on board a Russian cruiser moored on the Danube, during which the crew plied him with crème de menthe, slivovitz and vodka. In Sofia he found that the resident minister at the British Legation shared his view that the Foreign Office's scheme to bring Bulgaria into the war was misguided. He had just been ordered, much against his will, to offer parcels of Serbian and Greek territory to Bulgaria as a bribe to enter the war. Not surprisingly, when the offer became known, it caused great offence to those two countries. Leo believed rather that Greece was the most friendly neutral in the region and therefore the most promising ally. Encouragement should be in the form of assistance from a sizeable British force, substantial enough to persuade Romania and possibly Bulgaria to enter the war also, or at least to remain neutral, and the promise of Greek territorial gains at the expense of Turkey. Such a force in the East would, he believed, also help to ease the stalemate on the Western Front. But if the Government failed to commit troops in sufficient numbers, then Hamilton's forces in the Dardanelles were highly unlikely to 'achieve the storming of a few miles of rocky peninsula far more congested and fortified than even Neuve Chapelle or La Bassée'.[22]

Before returning home to persuade his superiors of his proposals, Leo visited the Dardanelles by motor boat. He found a 'none too happy state of affairs'. Hamilton had landed his forces, as ordered by Kitchener, on the rocky tip of the peninsula, from where he had no option but an 'uphill attack on a narrow front over ground seamed with almost endless deep ravines offering ideal positions for the stubborn defence for which the Turkish soldier has always been famous'. Allegedly Hamilton's reports had been withheld from the Cabinet by Kitchener, and he had been starved of ammunition and reinforcements by senior generals on the Western Front who regarded his predicament as a 'futile side-show'.[23] On 4 July Leo watched in horror from the sea one of the last attempts to advance by the left flank of the main force, supported by naval bombardment, as they managed only a short advance at considerable cost. A visit next day to the famous beaches of the original landing left a great impression on him of the heroism of those who had gone ashore there: 'Like the famous charge at Balaclava it was magnificent, even if it was not war.'[24]

But when Leo returned to London, determined to confront the Government over the appalling situation in the East, he found that nobody would listen and that the eastern theatre remained a sideshow. In his absence, Asquith had responded to the early setbacks of the war by reshuffling his Government and attempting to strengthen his position by bringing in the Unionist leaders. Milner, who remained for the moment out of office, but was still active in the House of Lords, had done his best to ensure that Leo himself was not overlooked in his absence abroad. He appealed to Austen Chamberlain that Leo should be given a ministerial role 'on public grounds', and not just because he was a very 'great friend', highlighting Leo's extensive experience of war as a civilian and his abilities as a linguist. 'He may not so far have been very successful in Parliament,' he wrote, acknowledging that he was a 'poor political tactician and no respecter of persons'. But he was 'an absolutely single-minded patriot' and 'his knowledge exceptionally wide and his judgement in *real* things . . . excellent'. And while he had undoubtedly 'made enemies by his zeal and unselfishness', Milner pointedly warned Chamberlain that if his friends did not 'stand up for him, he will continue to be overlooked'.[25] However, when Chamberlain passed the letter on to Bonar Law, he conspicuously failed to endorse Milner's recommendation and Leo would have to wait for a few more years before a ministerial post was to come his way.

Leo criticised the coalition for being 'nothing more than a sop to the growing public disquiet', and regretted that the Unionist leaders had joined it 'because it seemed the right thing to do'. They had won no concessions over policy and, worse still, they had 'abdicated for themselves and their followers the essential function of active and authoritative criticism'.[26] Nevertheless, at Bryddie's suggestion, Leo had 'written a little note to Lloyd George expressing his admiration' of his first speech as the newly appointed Minister of Munitions, although he was not sure how far to go in ingratiating himself. On the one hand he did not want 'any of them to think that I am making up to them with an eye to the odd plum from the coalition cake later on', but he also wanted to dispel his somewhat negative image in the House as 'a rather truculent, rancorous person'. In the case of Lloyd George, it would mean both sides 'forgetting Marconi and other sources of offence'.[27]

In fact, on his return home, Leo found two issues which gave him an excuse to continue his active and authoritative opposition to the Government; conscription and the Government's broken pledge to come to the aid of Serbia. General Callwell recognised that many years of well-informed campaigning in support of universal military service made Leo the perfect advocate to persuade the Cabinet of the merits of conscription. As cover he was given a job in the Balkan section of Callwell's intelligence branch at the War Office, but in reality the next few months were dedicated to a campaign in Parliament, and in the press, in support of conscription. He soon discovered how serious the situation was. After the initial wave of 1,500,000 new recruits at the outset of war, Kitchener's policies, already criticised by Leo, had led to a dramatic fall in both the quantity and quality of many of the latest recruits. The Liberal Government had so far been unable to take any of the difficult decisions necessary for fear of alienating its own backbench support. The problems were, thought Leo, manifold: 'the lack of co-ordination between ministries, the lack of analysis of policies', while 'the complete lack of administrative skill had never been so apparent'.[28]

Throughout the summer and autumn of 1915 Leo worked up the case for conscription, joining forces with a small cross-party group of Members in the House, while also providing written memoranda for members of the Cabinet Committee, under Curzon's chairmanship, which was investigating the issue. It was widely acknowledged that had Kitchener made a direct appeal to the Government to introduce conscription, they would have been forced to defer to the popularity of the Secretary of State for War. But he never did, and instead the Cabinet inched towards the policy in a series of concessions. Asquith's speeches shocked Leo by their apparent complacency and he took great offence at the suggestion that those, like himself, who dared to criticise the war effort were in some way providing encouragement to the enemy. Asquith singled Leo out for particular criticism on account of the huge number of parliamentary questions which he submitted to the War Office. On 28 July Leo replied, telling the House that 'we cannot go on drifting as we have been doing'. He had listened to the Prime Minister eloquently 'bidding us to persevere as we have been doing . . . towards inevitable victory'. But 'if we do persevere in conducting the War in the manner in which we have conducted it hitherto, if we persevere in postponing decisions, if we persevere in waiting and seeing, if we persevere in half-measures, if we persevere with this dogged irresolution on every question of importance, the only end of our perseverance must be inevitable defeat, inevitable failure'.[29]

The debate continued throughout the summer outside Parliament. But it had now become clear to Leo that there was an even greater political prize at stake, the destruction of Asquith and his Government, indeed possibly the eradication of liberalism itself. 'Squiff and

Squiffery must go,' F. S. Oliver told him, summing up the views of Leo's circle of friends that ' "Liberalism" in the worst sense of that vile word is dead, *dead, dead.*' It was like a 'dead foetus in the womb of Government, and more dangerous being dead and putrescent than it would be were it still alive'.[30] 'If only someone would *kill* Squiff,' agreed Sir Henry Wilson.[31] When the House met again in September, Leo returned to the attack, condemning Asquith's 'unanimity in pro-crastination, unanimity in shirking the issues, unanimity in postponing decisions'.[32] He also raised the other major issue confronting the Government, that of the defence of Serbia. The Foreign Secretary, Sir Edward Grey, had warned Bulgaria not to enter the war by invading Serbia, and promised the Serbs all possible support, but Leo ridiculed Asquith's appeal for quiet on the subject. Was 'Bulgaria going to stop mobilizing her troops until the Government had given full and mature consideration' to the matter, and was the 'Government going to tell Germany to postpone their attack upon Serbia until the next Session?'[33] The following morning Leo bumped into Lloyd George in Downing Street, who 'shook him warmly by the hand' and con-gratulated him on his recent speeches.[34]

The last few months of 1915 were disastrous for the war effort. While the Government continued to vacillate and the House of Commons debated the minutiae of conscription, Bulgaria did indeed attack Serbia, with heavy German support, on 11 October. By then the British and French commanders on the Western Front were under-taking the disastrous offensives at Loos, where over 61,000 men lost their lives, and Champagne. The situation in the Dardanelles re-mained deadlocked until the decision to evacuate was finally taken in November and successfully carried out on 18 December. Grey's promise to Serbia went unfulfilled, and the country was overrun. For many, the betrayal of Serbia was the last straw. Edward Carson resigned from the Cabinet, leaving Bonar Law increasingly isolated and excluded from Asquith's inner circle. The new Director of Recruiting, Lord Derby, made one last, vain attempt to secure enough volunteers before Asquith reluctantly announced at the end of the year that compulsory service legislation would be introduced in the New Year. After several months, a Bill was finally passed in May and only

Leo's old friend Sir John Simon resigned from the Cabinet in protest.

Leo made no secret of his desperation about the state of the war, nor his desire to see the back of Asquith. Neville Chamberlain wrote to his sisters about his 'interesting talks with Amery', who was always 'full of information but . . . not of a kind to cheer one up', since he was always in a 'state of gloom about the war'. By December, Chamberlain was weighing up the deluge of bad news from the Balkans that Leo had imparted to him. While he was 'naturally rather pessimistic', Leo's information was 'generally good', and he had 'first hand knowledge' of the region. Sadly, he had also 'just lost his brother to whom he was very much attached'.[35] Harold had indeed recently died, having never recovered from the wounds he had sustained a year earlier. For the last few months of his life, Leo took a conscientious interest in his care and medical treatment, possibly exaggerated by the realisation that he felt 'ashamed [he had] made so little effort to see him sooner'.[36]

As early as the summer of 1915 Leo had suggested to Milner that they should get together an 'effective board of conspirators', prepared to 'get rid of Asquith and Co'.[37] It was now time for action and, 'as so often, the original impetus came from Leo Amery'.[38] He believed that only three men had the ability to lead the country in place of Asquith: Lloyd George, Milner and Carson, and 'that these three men should come together seemed to be an essential condition of victory'. Indeed, he had already urged Lloyd George to 'break away from the existing make believe conduct of the war and claim the leadership for himself'.[39] On 17 January 1916 Leo assembled a small group of trusted friends for dinner; in addition to Lloyd George, Milner and Carson he also invited his old friend Geoffrey Dawson, the editor of *The Times*, Waldorf Astor, who had acquired the *Observer* from Northcliffe in 1911, and F. S. Oliver. The plan was that they would meet monthly for dinner in each other's houses, inviting other guests from time to time.

The sole purpose of the dinners was to 'work for the more effective conduct of the war and, above all, somehow or other, to secure a change of government'. Their only concern was the overthrow of Asquith and his Government, even including Bonar Law, who had refused to follow Carson out of the coalition and had preferred to remain at Asquith's side. Leo wrote again to Lloyd George, urging him to put himself forward as part of a team 'absolutely agreed amongst themselves and capable by their enthusiasm and energy of sustaining the nation'. It was time to put an end to the 'desperate slaughter in the field and hardships at home'.[40] Leo was reticent in later years as to the true extent to which this ginger group was responsible for Asquith's downfall. Milner agreed to participate only if the group was properly organised and its members were of suitable calibre, and it soon achieved notoriety as the 'Monday Night Cabal'. By April 1916 Sir Maurice Hankey, then Secretary to Asquith's War Committee, was warning the Prime Minister that the cabal were orchestrating a 'new plot' against him, led by Leo as the 'very soul of the Unionist War Committee – or rather of all its horrible intrigues against the Government'.[41]

It was a measure of the intimacy of Leo's relationship with senior army officers, and indeed their own disillusionment with Asquith, that his former commanding officer Sir Henry Rawlinson was prepared to do all he could to help. On 17 April Rawlinson wrote to Leo to tell him that all Members of Parliament who were serving under his command would be given leave to vote against Asquith in the House during the debate on conscription. 'I know a lot of them are going over,' he wrote, 'so I hope you will make Squiff sit up even if you don't turn him out neck and crop which would be the best thing.'[42] When Hankey informed Asquith of Leo's involvement in the 'Monday Night Cabal', he suggested at the same time that the Prime Minister should ask the Chief of the Imperial General Staff, Sir William Robertson, 'to send Amery to Salonika or somewhere equally salubrious!'[43] But Hankey would surely not have done so had he known that Robertson had indeed recently sent for Leo and, rather than administer the dressing down which Leo had been expecting, had in fact 'opened his soul' and told Leo of his concern at the 'gravity of the present situation and the complete refusal of Squiff (as he too calls him) to face it'.[44]

The Bill introducing Universal Military Service finally completed all its stages by the end of May and Leo, who had grown tired of office work in London, was relieved when Robertson called him in and told him that he was indeed to be sent to Salonika to take up a post attached to General Milne's staff in the British section of the Salonika army. For the next few months, he made the most of an enjoyable, if undemanding posting, albeit one that began inauspiciously. His immediate commanding officer, the local head of Intelligence, 'surveyed him unfavourably through his eyeglass', and made it clear that he had never asked for Leo to be posted to him and had no time to educate a 'wretched amateur soldier' in either military matters or Balkan affairs. With that, he thrust a handbook across the desk at Leo, suggesting that if he could 'master its contents' he would 'know all there is to be known about this part of the world'. It was, of course, the very handbook which Leo had himself written in such haste barely a year before, causing the officer to have 'his leg badly pulled in the mess'.[45] Leo also found that his Anglo-Serbian phrasebook was in regular use by the soldiers. The army was under the command of the French General Sarrail and consisted of a nucleus of British and French troops from the Dardanelles, reinforced by some Serbs, Italians and Albanians. The allies at Salonika were subsequently reinforced by Greek troops loyal to Venizelos, following his successful revolt against the Greek King's forces at both Salonika and Crete. Leo's job consisted mainly of evaluating intelligence obtained by spies, writing reports and paying occasional visits to the front where the battle was raging against the Bulgarian army.

However, when the opportunity arose to take some leave at home over Christmas, he welcomed the chance to return to the political fray in London. The trip home was the most eventful part of the posting. He set sail on the *Caledonia*, a 9,000-ton ship with a dozen or so officers and two hundred men returning home, either on leave or as invalids. Three days into the voyage the ship was hit by a torpedo from a German submarine. Grabbing what few belongings he could, Leo joined the rest of the ship's company in the lifeboats just in time to look back at the sinking ship. The senior British general pulled rank and insisted that all the officers should stay together in one lifeboat. Leo, however, demonstrating a sound instinct for survival, wisely decided to stay put where he was, in another lifeboat with 'about 20 half naked stokers'.[46] Sure enough, soon afterwards, the flotilla of a dozen boats was pulled up by the submarine which had fired the torpedo and was now looking for prisoners among the survivors. The German crew began searching the lifeboats, but were soon satisfied when they reached the officers' boat from which they duly picked out the captain, the general and several of his senior officers. Leo, feeling 'no false pride', hid himself as best he could at one end of his lifeboat and, 'softly humming "Britannia rules the waves – mais pas ici",' he held his breath until the German sailors lost interest and pointed the remaining survivors towards a hospital ship that was in the area.

The ship took Leo back to Salonika and, having at last secured another passage back to London, he arrived home on 19 December. After working towards it for so long, he had missed the downfall of Asquith's Government. The 'Monday Night Cabal' had achieved its aim: Lloyd George was Prime Minister, and Milner and Carson had both been given important roles in the new administration. From on board the SS *Irania* in the Mediterranean he rejoiced at Asquith's downfall. 'So Humpty Dumpty has fallen off the wall at last,' he wrote to Lady Edward Cecil, although he acknowledged that his 'parallel was bad for H.D.'s balance was precarious, while Squiff's was perfect'.[47] But once again there was to be no ministerial appointment, on account, he was told, of Lloyd George having been obliged to give the plum roles to Unionists and therefore the more junior posts to Liberals. 'I am afraid that I should only be deceiving you,' wrote Austen Chamberlain to Bryddie, 'if I held out any hope that in these circumstances your husband is likely to be offered office.'[48] Leo would have to wait until the end of the war to achieve that goal although in the meantime his mentor, Lord Milner, had ensured that he would not be overlooked entirely.

CHAPTER SIX

A Junior Member of the Government

As soon as Leo arrived back in London, he made his way down to the House of Commons, arriving just in time to hear Lloyd George's first speech as Prime Minister. Leo was delighted to hear that there was going to be a new, smaller War Cabinet and that the Dominion Governments were to be invited to attend an Imperial Conference. Both were ideas which he had espoused for some time. Although he had been denied ministerial office, Milner had arranged for him to be appointed, with his parliamentary colleague Mark Sykes, as one of two political secretaries to the War Cabinet. For administrative purposes he was to be attached to Sir Maurice Hankey, secretary to the Committee of Imperial Defence and now also secretary to the War Cabinet. Leo was pleased with the appointment, which suited him perfectly, especially as his role was 'delightfully vague', his actual military status 'puzzled the War Office for months', and he found himself 'at the centre of government, in touch with its decisions, and in a position to lay his ideas' before those who mattered.[1] Most important of all, he would work closely with Milner, who had been brought into the War Cabinet as minister without portfolio.

The appointment proved controversial. Leo admired Hankey, but the feeling was far from mutual and Hankey was, at first, furious. He resented having Leo 'foisted on him by Milner',[2] and told Lloyd George that while he would agree to the posting 'as Lord Milner insists', he had always suspected Leo of being 'anti-Russian, and would much sooner see him elsewhere'.[3] His fears were not wholly unselfish however, since he 'had a suspicion that [Leo] might be intended to replace' him, a misgiving which was reinforced when, while he was abroad on business with Lloyd George, Hankey 'read in a newspaper that in future Mark Sykes, Amery and he were to be joint secretaries of the War Cabinet'.[4] Leo had presumably been talking up his own prospects among his friends in the press, but Lloyd George quickly dispelled Hankey's feeling of insecurity. Another of Leo's fellow appointees, a young Thomas Jones, who was to go on to serve four Prime Ministers, agreed with Hankey about Leo, who he 'rather avoided as a politician and a pressman'.[5]

Encouraged by Lloyd George's announcement that the Dominions were to be invited to an Imperial Conference, Leo wanted to go one step further, persuading Milner that they should be invited to join the deliberations of the War Cabinet itself. Milner succeeded in convincing his colleagues of the merits of Leo's suggestion, and the revised invitation, drafted by Leo, was duly despatched. However, by promoting his own agenda Leo made further enemies and Hankey soon complained that Leo's 'tactlessness' had caused 'a row with the Colonial Office'.[6] The Colonial Secretary, Walter Long, complained to Hankey over lunch that Leo was 'quite untrustworthy and ought not to be present at meetings, particularly owing to his intimate association with *The Times*.' Hankey was further irritated when Leo demanded a meeting and 'asked to have two assistants to *him* appointed', so that he might 'keep up a regular correspondence with Dominion Prime Ministers', a suggestion that Hankey recorded 'fairly took my breath away'. Leo admitted quite frankly that his 'ultimate idea was to displace the Colonial Office', and while Hankey conceded that the idea had some merit, he concluded that Leo was a 'scheming little devil'.[7]

In fairness to Leo, he threw himself into his work with gusto and, slowly but surely, won Hankey round. He enjoyed his day-to-day role, which involved drawing up the agenda for Cabinet meetings, and then attending to take a full record of the meeting and prepare the subsequent minutes. Hankey's businesslike approach appealed to Leo, insisting as he did that every minute ended with a definite decision before it was circulated. It was then Leo's job to chase up the individual departments to ensure that the decisions were enforced. 'No longer', he boasted, 'was it possible for Ministers to modify, postpone indefinitely or altogether evade Cabinet decisions which were not to their liking.'[8] Hankey soon came to 'appreciate [Leo's] abilities and interests in Imperial affairs',[9] as well as his 'loyalty and erudite and cosmopolitan mind',[10] while Neville Chamberlain thought that his new position gave him 'opportunities of suggestion of which he makes full use'.[11] And, as was to become more familiar still at the end of the twentieth century, departmental ministers and officials soon came to dread the interference of the small group of powerful advisers, housed in a few corrugated-iron buildings in the garden of 10 and 11 Downing Street, known as the 'garden suburb'.

Having won his battle with the Colonial Office, Leo was given the job of drawing up the agenda for the forthcoming Imperial Conference. It was agreed that the Imperial War Cabinet would meet alongside the inner War Cabinet while the premiers were assembled in London for the Conference. All the Dominions, with the exception of Australia, were represented by their Prime Ministers and while the Conference itself achieved only limited success in defining imperial relations between the Dominions, the Imperial War Cabinet, which met fourteen times between the end of March and the beginning of May 1917, was considerably more successful. For Leo it signified 'an immense stride forward in imperial organization', and 'a harbinger of the future – a glowing future of imperial unity'.[12]

Throughout 1917, Leo took advantage of his position to interest himself in as many different contemporary issues as he could. Although he was ostensibly a servant of the War Cabinet, his role frequently gave him a standing that appeared equal, or even superior, to those who were technically very much his seniors. In the face of criticism from some, he used his influence to persuade the Prime Minister to appoint his old friend John Buchan as the Government's propaganda supremo. One evening he spent an hour and a half with Curzon discussing his minutes of a previous meeting of the War Cabinet. Curzon was 'in a fearful state to begin with because he didn't figure sufficiently in the proceedings', and asked Leo if he 'had a personal down on him'.[13] Leo found the episode amusing, and although he eventually calmed Curzon down, he had to remind himself that he was the junior Member of Parliament, and Curzon the former Viceroy of India, Leader of the House of Lords and member of the War Cabinet. On another occasion, the Speaker refused to allow him to speak during a secret session of the House, on the grounds that he was an 'official' of the Government, but Leo insisted that, on the contrary, he should be treated as 'a junior Member of the Government . . . as an Under-Secretary'.[14]

Leo's military status was even more confusing. When, several months after his appointment, the War Office finally acknowledged his position as a 'Personal Assistant Military Secretary to the Secretary of State for War, temporarily lent to the War Cabinet',[15] the War Secretary, Lord Derby, demanded that he should be taken out of uniform. Hankey refused, and responded by recommending that Leo should be promoted from Captain to Lieutenant Colonel, a suggestion that was refused, but he continued to have constant problems with the War Office, most notably in regard to his pay. And when he failed to be promoted to the vacant position of Parliamentary Under-Secretary at the Colonial Office, in spite of Milner's renewed efforts on his behalf, he complained to Leo Maxse that, while his disenchantment with the Government had not quite 'yet reached the point of regretting Squiff . . . recent performances had been well-calculated to sicken the whole country'.[16]

■ ■ ■

For the first time in his political career, Leo now found himself centrally involved in the formation of policy affecting his own Jewish roots. Turkey's entry into the war had raised the prospect of the liberation of vast, Arabic-speaking areas of the Ottoman Empire and had aroused the hopes of Zionist leaders that their dream of a homeland might at last be realised. Leo believed that the British had a unique role to play. Not only did the liberation of Palestine fall directly into the British military sphere of operations but, after America, England was 'the only country where the desire of the Jews to return to their ancient homeland had always been regarded as a natural aspiration which ought not to be denied'. And while Asquith had always been lukewarm in his support for Zionism, both Lloyd George and Balfour, now Foreign Secretary, were more sympathetic.

In spite of his Jewish ancestry, Leo later claimed that until 1917 he had enjoyed only a 'vague knowledge' of Jewish issues, and was 'completely unaware of the Zionist movement'. Even when Mark Sykes won him over to 'active sympathy and interest', that interest was 'at first, largely strategical', believing that there were military benefits of an advance into Palestine and Syria, and of then 'establishing in Palestine a prosperous community bound to Britain by ties of gratitude and interest'.[17] At first glance, such a disclaimer seems disingenuous, given what we know of his Jewish roots and his mother's close-knit circle of Jewish friends while he was growing up. He remained close throughout his life to his cousin Henry Leitner, and it seems unlikely that they had never even discussed their common ancestry and the campaign for a Jewish homeland. And at their first meeting, the charismatic Jewish leader and future President of Israel, Chaim Weizmann, recognised Leo's enthusiasm, his 'larger stature and superior abilities', and that he was the 'most open-minded' of those who offered support. He also appreciated Leo's 'insight into the intrinsic fineness of the Zionist movement'.[18]

Leo liked to portray his support for Zionism as being purely practical. He claimed to understand 'what Jewish energy in every field of thought and action might mean for the regeneration of the whole of that Middle East region which was once the home of the world's most ancient civilizations, and which in the course of centuries had gone derelict beyond hope of recovery by its own unaided resources'.[19] But occasionally we find more thoughtful examples of his philosophical beliefs too, in particular with regard to a Jewish 'National Home'. There was, he told Edward Carson, 'a large body, more particularly of the Jews in Poland and Russia, or those who have recently come from there, who are still in a very real sense a separate nation, not likely to be absorbed without endless friction and suffering into the nations among which they live'. Even those who had 'long ceased to be Jews in the national sense and have become Englishmen or Americans or Frenchmen' were still in sympathy 'with the conditions of their co-religionists elsewhere'. Above all, a national home for the 'Jewish persecuted majority' would help stem the rising tide of 'anti-semitism which is based, partly on the fear of being swamped by hordes of un-desirable aliens from Russia, etc., and partly by an instinctive suspicion against a community which has so many international ramifications'.[20]

Leo's first show of support for Zionism was purely practical. Vladimir Jabotinsky, a Russian Jew based in London, had long supported the idea of forming a Jewish Legion, but had been shunned by official Zionists who feared the repercussions of identifying Zionism so openly with one side in the war, and the possibility of reprisals by Turkey against the Jews in Palestine. Jabotinsky had become friendly with an Ulsterman, Lieutenant Colonel John Patterson, who had created the Zion Mule Corps, an ammunition column in Egypt com-posed of Jewish refugees from Palestine. Patterson wanted to prevent his corps from being disbanded and saw the large numbers of recently arrived Jewish immigrants, especially in the East End of London, as an opportunity to boost recruitment. He had met Leo at Gallipoli, and soon introduced him to Jabotinsky, observing to his delight that there were 'obvious temperamental affinities between' them, and that the 'two men took to one another' at once.[21] Leo took the plan to Milner, who in turn presented it to the War Cabinet, while Leo also acted as intermediary with the War Secretary, Lord Derby, whose support was crucial if the plan was to succeed. Although he had to 'severely water down the political aspects' of Jabotinsky's language,[22] and in spite of Derby's initial reluctance, three Jewish battalions under Patterson's command went on to serve in Palestine. Leo, perhaps a little extrava-gantly, later claimed to have had his 'finger in the pie . . . of the genesis of the present Israel Army'.[23]

Throughout early 1917 Weizmann pressed the Government for a public declaration of British sympathy for the idea of a Jewish state in Palestine. He was pushing at a half-open door. At a dinner with the Astors, also attended by Balfour and Leo, Lloyd George emphasised to Weizmann that he agreed with Leo's view that Palestine should remain under British military control, but that the Zionist movement would have a post-war role to play. On 20 May, at a conference in London, Weizmann declared publicly for the first time that the

Government was ready to support his plans, and on 19 June Balfour invited Weizmann and Lord Rothschild to submit a draft declaration for the War Cabinet's approval. On 18 July Rothschild submitted the text to Balfour, recommending that the Government 'accept the principle that Palestine should be reconstituted as the national home of the Jewish people', and that it would use 'its best endeavours to secure the achievement' of that object.[24]

At a meeting of the War Cabinet on 3 September, from which both Lloyd George and Balfour were absent, Rothschild's draft was considered alongside an amended version of Balfour's and one that had been completely redrafted by Milner, who had removed all reference to the reconstitution of Palestine as a home for the Jewish people and instead suggested the establishment of a home for the Jewish people in Palestine. Edwin Montagu, the Secretary of State for India and spokesman for the Anglo-Jewish community, attended the meeting by invitation and his strong opposition to any declaration which described Palestine as the home of the Jewish people ensured the postponement of a decision. It was agreed to seek the views of President Woodrow Wilson as to the desirability, in principle, of such a declaration, and when the American President ruled out anything beyond a statement of sympathy, provided that it conveyed no real commitment, Leo leaked the reply to Weizmann.

In spite of his distress at Wilson's rebuttal, and his 'scorn for Montagu and all that class of "tame Jew"',[25] Weizmann's personal appeal to Lloyd George ensured, after some weeks, that the subject was restored to the War Cabinet agenda for the meeting on 4 October, at which Leo was present. Half an hour before the meeting, Milner looked into Leo's office from his room next door and showed him one or two alternative drafts, with neither of which he was satisfied. Could Leo draft something which would satisfy the objectors, both Jewish and pro-Arab, without impairing the substance of the proposed declaration? Leo 'sat down and quickly produced the following:

> His Majesty's Government view with favour the establishment in Palestine of a national home for the Jewish race, and will use their best endeavours to facilitate the achievement of this object, it

being clearly understood that nothing shall be done which
may prejudice the civil and religious rights of the existing non-
Jewish communities in Palestine or the rights and political status
enjoyed by Jews in any other country who are contented with
their existing nationality.[26]

Leo felt that he had ensured that there was no suggestion that the
Jews belonged to Palestine, while the 'reference to Jews outside
Palestine was, of course, to satisfy Montagu', and the 'provision about
non-Jewish communities in Palestine was, no doubt, Curzon's',[27] a
recollection borne out by that day's Cabinet minutes. Curzon had
indeed made a spirited defence of Arab rights in Palestine, declaring
that he had 'strong objections on practical grounds' and, with considerable foresight, enquiring how 'it was proposed to get rid of the
existing majority of Mussulman inhabitants and to introduce the Jews
in their place'.[28] There were two further small amendments to Leo's
draft: the substitution of 'people' for 'race', and the removal of the last
seven words. At one stage Weizmann was sent for, but couldn't be
found, even though he was sitting nearby in Leo's office. The text was
again submitted to President Wilson, as well as to Zionist leaders and
Montagu's Anglo-Jewish community, but agreement was held back
for a few more weeks, principally to give Curzon the time to prepare
a memorandum expressing his concerns, based on his experience
in India. Finally, at a meeting of the War Cabinet on 31 October, at
which Leo was not present, the wording was at last agreed and
Weizmann later recalled Mark Sykes emerging from the meeting,
clutching the text in his hand and declaring excitedly, 'It's a boy.'[29] On
2 November Balfour sent to Lord Rothschild the somewhat scruffy
typewritten version, to be known thereafter as the Balfour Declaration.

The significance of Leo's role in the drafting of the Balfour
Declaration became the subject of much historical debate, with
opinions ranging from his absolute authorship to the mere alteration
of a few words. On the sixtieth anniversary of the Declaration,
2 November 1977, an article appeared in *The Times* under the dramatic
headline 'Last Minute Drama that made Leo Amery the brains behind
the Balfour Declaration'. S. J. Goldsmith described an interview with

Leo, shortly before his death in 1955, in which he supposedly claimed to have written the Declaration himself, an assertion which would have conflicted with the description of events in his own memoirs, published just two years earlier. Goldsmith described Leo as 'the real author of the Balfour Declaration, the man who actually wrote the text'. He quoted him as having said that he 'didn't like it very much', but that it had been written by him 'on the back of an old memo . . . in a great hurry', with 'no time for stylistic considerations'. Crucially, Goldsmith suggested that this took place before the War Cabinet meeting on 31 October, while its members were busily assembling around him, and theatrically describes the minutes ticking by as Leo 'kept on composing texts and tearing them up . . . five, possibly six' in all. Suddenly, he 'had a brainwave', and composed a 'new text starting from scratch. Balfour had a look and nodded . . . Milner and Smuts dissolved in smiles.'[30]

Subsequent correspondents to *The Times*, including Milner's biographer, took issue with this description, quoting Leo's memoirs in evidence. Certainly, it seems a fantasy that Leo wrote the Declaration from scratch, not least because the final text is clearly a variation of earlier drafts, and it is more accurately described by other sources as, in effect, 'Milner's formula, re-drafted by Leopold Amery'.[31] Yet given Leo's known intellect and capacity for drafting complex policy documents, it seems entirely likely that Milner would happily have entrusted such a sensitive task to his protégé. Weizmann, for one, had no doubt as to the importance of Leo's contribution, and when he went round to see Leo later that same day, Leo recorded that he 'fell on my neck with gratitude for my efforts on their behalf'.[32] A fortnight later Weizmann and Rothschild held a dinner at the Ritz to thank those who had helped in obtaining the Declaration. 'In this Zionist business', reminisced Leo, 'we juniors who have helped to push it have builded better than we know.'[33]

▪ ▪ ▪

In the course of his daily attendance at War Cabinet meetings, Leo became closely involved in the increasingly antagonistic struggle between Lloyd George and his senior military commanders. Almost the first use Leo had made of the licence afforded him by his new post in January 1917, had been to write a memorandum promoting the idea of greater unity of war policy and that Britain should take over direct command of the conduct of the war. In June Lloyd George endorsed the concept of an inner Cabinet Committee on War Policy, with himself in the chair and Curzon, Bonar Law, Milner and Smuts as the other members. Smuts's addition to the Committee came about as a direct result of Leo's suggestion that his old South African friend should have a greater role in the running of the war. The new Committee's first task was to consider Field Marshal Haig's persistent demands for authority to launch a major attack on the German lines in Flanders at the end of the summer. The result was the disaster of Passchendaele, for Leo a 'symbol of that policy of warfare to exhaustion by mutual massacre against which human nature revolted'.[34] Lloyd George never reconvened the Committee and came to rely instead on advice from another of Leo's close confidants, General Sir Henry Wilson, who had returned from France and offered the Prime Minister an alternative view to that which he received from his now distrusted Commanders-in-Chief and Chief of Staff.

By the end of the summer, Wilson had formulated a proposal for an Inter-Allied Supreme War Council, involving monthly meetings in Paris of the British, French and Italian Prime Ministers, supported by their own advisers, thus sidelining Haig and Robertson. On 7 November, at the Rapallo conference, Lloyd George won backing from the Allies for the Supreme War Council. The staff headquarters were to be based at Versailles to emphasise the Council's official separation from the French military command in Paris itself; Lloyd George and Milner were to be the British representatives and Wilson was appointed as the permanent British military representative, much to Robertson's disgust. Leo received a message from Wilson inviting him to come over to Paris and 'get the Supreme War Council started',[35] although not before the 'difficulties that were raised as to Amery accompanying him . . . were overcome by quiet persistence'.[36]

Leo arrived in Paris with General Sackville-West on 19 November and spent the first few days organising accommodation and preparing the establishment of the Council's affairs. He took advantage of being the first to arrive to scout out the best accommodation available, find-ing it at the magnificent Trianon Palace Hotel, which he immediately commandeered on behalf of the Allies. Although tempted to acquire the best rooms for the British contingent, in the end an equitable arrangement was arrived at whereby the various floors were shared out between the delegations. It was agreed that his own role would be threefold; as political secretary of the British section, personal representative of Lloyd George and Milner, and liaison officer with the War Cabinet. He would remain on Hankey's staff, but Derby still 'flatly declined to make Amery a Lt.Col.',[37] a promotion which was now overdue and the denial of which Leo resented greatly. However, his proximity to the heart of power seems to have gone to his head at the time, suggesting to Milner that he might put forward Leo's 'claim to take Cabinet office if a proper opportunity arose without having gone through the intermediate stage of an Under Secretaryship'.[38]

Opinion was mixed as to his actual importance. On the one hand, although a 'military-affairs busybody', he was one of Lloyd George's 'chief allies' and helped to play a 'key role in attempting to impose a strategy on the army that had the immediate objective of advancing imperialist interests rather than the defeat of the German army'.[39] He certainly enjoyed the Prime Minister's intimate confidence, Lloyd George writing to Bryddie in glowing terms to tell her that he was 'so pleased to have won your brilliant husband's friendship'.[40] Much of the debate at Versailles concerned the issue of manpower and, in par-ticular, whether the British would be able to take over part of the over-extended French front line. Lloyd George was suspicious of the troop numbers which had been supplied to him by the War Office and asked Leo, while on a visit to London, to 'straighten out the figures'.[41] Leo spent the next few days, sometimes working through the night, going over the figures and conducting interviews with relevant officers, deciding eventually that there was clearly a serious flaw in the figures that had been supplied to the War Cabinet. However, not for the first time, he had strayed into territory where he should not have been. Without knowing of Lloyd George's request, Hankey recorded his 'disgust that Amery . . . had been butting in and upsetting or trying to upset the figures . . . and interviewing all sorts of people without his authority'. Leo had 'made a mess of it, and upset many personal and most delicate factors'.[42] Although their relationship was sufficiently improved that the row proved short-lived, the incident demonstrates that Leo still could not shake off the contemporary perception of him as a scheming politician.

In January 1918 Leo was asked by Wilson to draw up a draft Allied plan of campaign for the rest of the year, which could be put to the Supreme War Council as a resolution. In doing so, he restated the case for maintaining a defensive pose on the French and Italian fronts, until the expected German attack had exhausted itself. More controversially, he also suggested making more effective use of those British troops already available in the Middle East to make a concerted push towards Damascus, an initiative which became known as Resolution 12. Once Britain's allies were satisfied that this plan in no way implied diverting troops away from the Western Front, and after some rewriting by Leo, the Council accepted the Resolution, much to the anger of Field Marshal Sir William Robertson, the Chief of the Imperial General Staff (CIGS), known by detractors and admirers alike as 'Wully'. For the next few weeks Robertson and his supporters carried out a press campaign against Lloyd George which only came to an end when the Prime Minister eventually succeeded in bringing about the Field Marshal's resignation.

Having urged Lloyd George for some time to make better use of Smuts in the war effort, Leo had been rewarded when Smuts was appointed as the War Cabinet's personal representative in the Middle East and Leo was himself invited to accompany the South African general on an inspection tour of Palestine. The visit began at the headquarters of General Allenby, the British Commander of the Egyptian Expeditionary Force and they spent three days visiting the front, north of Jerusalem, after which the team adjourned to Luxor, where Leo was closely involved in drawing up plans for the future of the Palestine campaign and, in particular, the advance to Damascus. Leo arrived home from Cairo to witness the climax of the long-standing disagreement between Lloyd George and Robertson over Resolution 12 and, after Robertson's resignation, the appointment of Henry Wilson as CIGS in his place. Leo's former commanding officer Sir Henry

Rawlinson was made permanent military representative at Versailles. Lloyd George was delighted with the victory he had secured over Robertson and warmly praised Leo's role as being worthy of having a statue erected in his honour. Leo too was quietly satisfied that he and 'L.G. found ourselves in very hearty agreement over a very wide field,' and that the Prime Minister had 'expressed his delight at having had an exchange of ideas with someone "who talked sense"!'[43]

At the March meeting of the Supreme War Council, a good deal of deliberation concerned the proposed creation of a central reserve, to be composed of forces from each ally, commanded from Versailles and apportioned to weak positions on the front line as the need arose. When the German offensive began on 21 March, concentrating on the extreme right of the British line, it soon became clear that any mutual assurances about the provision of reserve forces were worthless. Marshal Pétain refused Haig's request to shore up the British line, claiming that all his troops were now needed for the defence of Paris. Certainly Paris was now being regularly shelled by the Germans' 'Big Bertha' gun, from seventy-five miles away, a frightening experience for the Parisians and, indeed, for Leo, who likened it to 'shades of Jules Verne'.[44] However, life in Paris was briefly enlivened by a presidential visit to Paris and the front line by the Minister of Munitions, Winston Churchill. Leo was under strict instructions from Lloyd George that Churchill was to remain in Paris and not to involve himself in directing strategy at Versailles, an assignment he found difficult to discharge. When he went to visit Churchill at the Ritz, they gossiped happily about the war while his host 'wallowed in a hot bath', Leo later noticing that 'Winston was an extraordinary shape' in his 'long night-gown'.[45] Two days later, with 'Bendor', Duke of Westminster, they enjoyed a lunch of a 'dozen huge blue Marennes oysters, a fried sole, roast chicken, Barsac', while the German shells fell around them on the Rue de Rivoli and the Place Vendôme.[46]

The Germans broke through the British lines between Armentières and La Bassée on 9 April 1918 and drove the British back along almost the entire front. On 13 April Haig issued his famous 'backs to the wall' appeal to his forces and Leo renewed his lobbying with Lloyd George on behalf of Milner. Leo had, for some time, insisted that the only remedy for the sustained criticism from within the army was a change of leadership at the War Office. Now, in an uncompromising and self-opinionated letter to the Prime Minister, he warned that unless Lloyd George 'tidy up the Government household pretty drastically in the next week or two, there will be trouble'.[47] It again fell to Leo to persuade Milner, in spite of his natural reluctance, that Lloyd George now considered him the right man for the job and the appointment was approved in April when it was announced that Lord Derby would be going to Paris as Ambassador, to be succeeded by Milner as Secretary of State for War.

Leo accordingly spent more time in London, helping Milner with his new job and attending the House more frequently, although he missed the excitement of Versailles. For the first time he found the confrontational style of domestic politics hard to stomach as the 'contrast between the thought of the men dying in the mud out there and the obscene leers and jests' of Liberal MPs 'made the House seem a pretty intolerable place'.[48] He moved into a small office next to Milner's in the War Office and became assistant secretary to the so-called 'X Committee', an inner policy group composed of just Lloyd George, Milner and Wilson. Throughout the spring and summer months of the German offensive they met daily, sometimes twice a day, before the main War Cabinet meeting, to discuss policy in detail. The meetings often took place on the terrace in the Downing Street garden, the three men walking up and down in line, while Leo tried manfully to take accurate minutes while keeping up with them at the same time.

In June the Imperial War Cabinet and War Conference met for the second time, Leo again acting as Hankey's chief assistant. The meetings were notable for the Canadian Prime Minister, Sir Robert Borden's, stinging criticism of the incompetence of the British army headquarters. In July the participants crossed to Versailles for a meeting of the Supreme War Council, at which Leo appreciated Clemenceau's admiration for the Dominion premiers and his realisation 'for the first time that there is such a thing as the British Empire'.[49] In July, after General Wilson had briefed the Imperial War Cabinet that he could foresee no change in Allied fortunes before 1919, and with the German army continuing their offensive in Europe, Leo was asked by Milner to prepare a memorandum making plans for carrying on the war in the event that both France and Italy were defeated. Although the document was never finished, he concluded that if Britain were forced to evacuate by the Channel ports, they would manage to get away no more than their men and field artillery; if by the western ports, then more heavy artillery could be evacuated, but that vast depots of stores and ammunition would have to be abandoned. Europe would have been lost, but it might have been possible to carry on a war of sorts in the East.

▪ ▪ ▪

As Allied fortunes improved throughout the summer, at the end of August Leo travelled by train to Shrewsbury with Milner and Hankey, where they were met with a car by Sir Bertrand Dawson, the King's physician, and driven on into the Welsh mountains to spend the weekend at Lloyd George's country retreat at Criccieth. While much of the talk concentrated on the terms for post-war settlement, the presence of Dudley Ward, Lloyd George's chief party organiser, ensured that talk also strayed to plans for a now apparently imminent general election. Leo enjoyed the company and the hospitality of his host and his family. The evenings were spent reminiscing, while the days, to Leo's great pleasure, were spent taking long walks in the Welsh hills around Criccieth. On one occasion Lloyd George persuaded the rather more traditional Milner to remove his shoes and socks for a paddle in the river, only for them both to disappear up to their waists in the water. The only sour note was struck by Hankey who wrote to his wife that Leo had 'invited himself, yet settled down as though he were an invited guest',[50] assuming that he was trying just a little too hard for a ministerial role in a new, post-war Government.

As the war moved to its conclusion, both on the Western Front and in the East, Leo became increasingly involved in framing armistice terms for the various theatres of war, principally with Turkey and Austria. By the end of September the Allied army at Salonika had crushed the Bulgarians, and on 1 October the British, with their Arab allies under T. E. Lawrence, took Damascus, a particularly sweet moment for Leo, given his earlier advocacy of such a strategy, while Allenby pushed on to Aleppo and Alexandretta (now Iskenderun). On 24 October Leo went to Versailles to draft the terms for the Turkish armistice, which were subsequently approved by Lloyd George and agreed by the Allies in spite of Clemenceau's concerns. He became peripherally involved in the Allied response to President Wilson's infamous 'Fourteen Points', 'on which old Clemenceau had commented drily that *le bon Dieu* had been content with only Ten Commandments'.[51] And when William Hughes, the Australian Prime Minister, complained that the armistice terms had been agreed with Germany without reference to the Imperial War Cabinet, then technically still in session, it was Leo who was called on to pacify the irate premier. While he agreed with Hughes that in any settlement the British Empire should retain the German colonies it had acquired, by and large Leo was strongly opposed to punitive or vindictive terms against the Germans in Europe. When the armistice terms were finally agreed on 4 November, Leo thought them unnecessarily harsh, as did Lord Milner, who spoke out forcefully against 'gratifying our feelings of anger or indignation against Germany, however justified', and was duly subjected to a series of vitriolic attacks in Northcliffe's *Daily Mail* for being 'pro-German'.[52]

On the morning of 11 November, Leo travelled to Whitehall on the top of a bus, to find the crowd already celebrating the Armistice, and just in time to hear Lloyd George speaking from the steps of Downing Street. He joined in the singing of 'God Save the King', attended the House of Commons and then adjourned across the road with his fellow Members to attend the service of thanksgiving at St Margaret's. Later that evening he attended one of the regular Monday night dinners, whose participants had continued to meet throughout the last three years of the war, in spite of having achieved the original aim of deposing Asquith in 1916. The assembled guests congratulated themselves that they had succeeded both in bringing Lloyd George to power, and in holding the coalition together throughout the intervening years. Leo was also to play a minor role in the introduction of the tradition that a two-minute silence should be observed every year at eleven o'clock on Armistice Day. He remembered that during his time with *The Times* in South Africa, a two-minute silence had been observed every day, as a reminder of the sacrifices being made by those serving at the front. When a friend reminded him of this, he passed the suggestion on to Milner, who in turn secured the approval of the King.

▪ ▪ ▪

The political focus soon shifted back to domestic issues and the prospect of a general election. After the weekend at Criccieth, Leo had been invited to help draft and edit the literature on which the Lloyd George–Bonar Law coalition would fight the election. He played a minor part too in organising a publicity campaign for the coalition, breaking new ground with his suggestion that 'advertising in the Press on modern lines is much better political propaganda than the old business of leaflets and posters.'[53] But, in the course of the press campaign, a lunch that was held with the intention of bringing together Unionist and Liberal press barons in a show of unity proved a disaster. Leo found himself among a 'den of thieves', and took an instant dislike to Lord Rothermere, whom he had never met before, but of whom he thought 'a more perfect specimen of the plutocrat cad it would be hard to imagine.' Irritated by Rothermere's boast that if any one of his editors ever dared to say something of which he disapproved, he would 'have him on the pavement in half an hour', Leo retorted, perhaps unwisely, that it was high time that 'the private ownership of newspapers might have to be effectively limited.' Rothermere was, he decided, 'the kind of creature' who would end up as 'one of the biggest dangers we have got to fight in the future'. [54]

Leo's wartime activities had propelled him to a prominence way beyond that normally associated with a backbench Member of Parliament. When Lord Derby hosted a dinner for Lady Curzon at the British Embassy in Paris on 8 November, the future editor of *The Times*, Henry Wickham Steed, was among the guests. In the course of dinner Wickham Steed launched into an unprovoked attack on Leo, describing him as 'Milner's evil genius with regard to things in Eastern Europe', and went on to give a confused description of Leo's ancestry. Apparently, Leo's father had been a 'Buda Pesth Jew who married a Jewess from some part of Germany' and, after his father's disappearance due to something having 'happened of a disagreeable character', Leo's education had been 'undertaken by his uncle, his mother's brother, another Jew whose name . . . was Lembach'. This uncle was 'a rolling stone and turned up in Demarara where he made money and from there sent Amery to school at Harrow', after which Leo had 'roamed about Austria and the Balkans and had got a smattering of knowledge with regard to those places'. Unfortunately, he now exercised 'a great influence' over Milner, despite not having 'a drop of English blood in his veins and was most untrustworthy'. [55]

In spite of the obvious confusion surrounding Leo's Jewish ancestry, Wickham Steed's remarks demonstrate, not only Leo's new-found political prominence, but also that he had by now been clearly acknowledged as Jewish and was still perceived by the establishment, far from being a natural member of the ruling class, as an outsider. It was a perception that was to last throughout Leo's career, and which makes his almost obsessive devotion to duty on behalf of his country and the Empire all the more difficult to comprehend. The following year his name appeared in a particularly unpleasant publication, *The Jews' Who's Who*, in which he is listed under the heading 'Israelite Finance – Its sinister influence'. Leo is described as the editor of *The Times History of the South African War*, 'which is entirely silent on the subject of the Boer War having been brought about by the International Jew gang of Financiers'. He is also identified as having served as a military intelligence officer in the Balkans, one of a supposedly large 'number of Jews appointed' to such a role during the war. [56]

The dissolution of Parliament was announced on 25 November and the country was soon swept away in a wave of anti-German hysteria, fuelled by the Northcliffe press and their campaign against Milner, and Lloyd George's promise to 'squeeze Germany till the pips squeak'. Even Leo conceded that his own speeches 'lapsed somewhat from their opening level'. When the results were announced on 28 December, the coalition swept back into power, with those like Leo, the so-called 'coupon' candidates supported by the coalition, safely re-elected. It was his first contested election and he won with a healthy majority of 12,211 votes. The Asquithian Liberals were reduced to a rump and the

Labour Party became the official Opposition. For Leo, it was the end of two years that had been 'among the most interesting of my life'. He had enjoyed 'no particular standing or authority', but had been at 'the very heart of great events and in daily touch with great men who did not disdain to listen to my views and, in some measure at least, to be influenced by them'.[57]

Part Two

1919–1938

CHAPTER SEVEN

A Boy of Unusual Character

In many respects the war had been kind to Leo. He was forty years old at its outbreak and, although he had spent the entire war in uniform, he had been spared the worst excesses of serving at the front and the resulting slaughter. It is fair to say that he would have made an unlikely professional, or even full-time conscripted soldier, and in the few photographs taken of him alongside his military colleagues at Versailles, he tends to be standing apart, easily recognisable by his all too obvious lack of height. Nevertheless, during the first two years of hostilities he had faced danger, both in Flanders and the Balkans, and there is every reason to believe that he did so with some relish. But in the second half of the war, in his role as a secretary to the War Cabinet, the Imperial War Cabinet and the Supreme War Council at Versailles, he had come into his own altogether more effectively. His powers of communication, both written and verbal, and his knowledge of politics and military history were already well known and he put them to good effect on behalf of those for whom he worked.

If, at first sight, it appears that Leo had escaped lightly, one has only to scratch a short way beneath the surface to find the evidence of personal tragedy that he shared with almost every family in the land. He had lost both his younger brothers. His youngest brother, Harold, had been gazetted to the Black Watch in 1897 and, after four years in India, had been seconded to the Egyptian Army as Assistant Director of Intelligence for the next ten years. After a spell at Staff College, he had accompanied his regiment to the Western Front with the British Expeditionary Force and commanded a company of his battalion in the retreat from Mons. He had been wounded in the Battle of the Aisne in September 1914, but had rejoined his regiment at Ypres on 1 November, only to be badly wounded again the very next day leading a counter-attack, for which he was mentioned in despatches. It was after this that Leo had stumbled across him in a hospital in Boulogne and, although he fought on bravely for over a year, he was eventually to die of his wounds, after a long and painful illness, on 24 November 1915, at the age of thirty-seven.[1] Leo's sense of guilt that he had seen so little of Harold during the last year of his life, spent in and out of hospital, had been mitigated by the many happy memories of their time growing up together, of staying with him during early visits to the Middle East and of shared mountaineering expeditions in Europe and Canada.

Of Leo's other brother, Geoffrey, we know rather less. A year and a half younger than Leo, he had left Harrow at the same time and gone as an exhibitioner to St John's College, Oxford. In 1898 he was awarded an Eastern cadetship at Kuala Selangor and thereafter had spent much of his life travelling in the Far East. However, he had returned to sign up at the beginning of the war and had been captured, spending most of the war as a prisoner of war in a camp at Ruhleben outside Berlin. He had been due to be part of a prisoner exchange in July 1918 but, according to the British Foreign Office, the Germans had 'kept Mr Amery till he died – as a reprisal' for the British refusal to release six officials from German Protectorates. Geoffrey died of peritonitis in the West End Civilian Hospital in Berlin, still a prisoner of war, on 20 July 1918, less than four months before the Armistice. The Foreign Office official with whom Leo made arrangements for the return of his few possessions promised that they would 'probably have many an opportunity for paying them back and should not forget it'. It was clear that he had died alone and in considerable pain.[2] Leo recorded sadly that it was 'very hard to think that he ought to have got away to Holland and had more than once been told to pack up and then was held back', before he had been captured. As the war had approached its end, Leo and Bryddie had been making plans for him to move to Dartmoor to live with some Amery cousins and 'lead a quiet country life'. But it was not to be. 'Poor little Geoff,' wrote Leo, 'so much of his life was exile, and then to end up with four years of miserable discomfort and die among enemies with not a friendly soul near to hear his last words.'[3]

While Leo had spent some of the war abroad, he had also spent a good deal of it in London and while for long months on end his work kept him too busy even to write up his treasured diary, he was at least able to enjoy life at home with Bryddie. He had returned home late in 1916 to find that she had given up the house in Chelsea at Embankment Gardens and, for the rest of the war they lived out of a suitcase, taking short term lets, both in London and the country, to meet their accommodation needs. In London they took lodgings first in Curzon Street and later in Lord North Street in Westminster, while Bryddie spent some time in Brighton early on during the war, while Leo was abroad. Increasingly, as their son grew older, Bryddie tried to escape London for the perceived greater comforts of life in the country.

John Amery had been born at 9 Embankment Gardens, on 14 March 1912. It had been a difficult pregnancy throughout and he arrived late, after a drawn-out, painful labour for Bryddie, and at the end of 'a long and anxious day'.[4] It was to be the first of many anxious moments that he would cause his parents, and little did Leo appreciate the irony of his words at the time when he confided to his old friend James Garvin, the editor of the *Observer*, that it was a 'wonderful and refreshing thing to have a lad of your own, and a liberal education every day'.[5] Leo was adamant that, 'having suffered under a multitude of names' throughout his own life, his son would have just one. Certainly the simple, English sounding name, John, contrasted strongly with the numerous, more Jewish sounding forenames that Leo had himself been given. And it was not long before even the more conventional John became abbreviated still further and the young boy became known to his family as Jack, the name by which he would be called by all those close to him throughout his life.

Two months later he was christened in the Crypt of the House of

Commons and 'behaved admirably throughout the ceremony'.[6] His godfathers, both old friends and political colleagues of Leo's from Oxford days, could not have been more distinguished and bestowed the added advantage upon their godson of cross-party representation. Sir John Simon had been Leo's fellow candidate at All Souls, was still a Liberal MP and Solicitor-General in 1912, and was soon to serve as Attorney General and Home Secretary during Asquith's wartime administration. Jack's other godfather, F. E. Smith, had known Leo since their first meeting at the Harrow scholarship exam, throughout their days at Oxford together and near-eastern wanderings, and was now a fellow Unionist MP who would also serve as both Solicitor-General and Attorney General during the war years. In due course, both would reach the very pinnacle of the legal profession as Lord Chancellor, and both would find their legal and diplomatic expertise called on, in ways they doubtless never anticipated at the time, in the course of their baby godson's life. His godmothers were Alfred Lyttelton's daughter, Lady Mary Lyttelton, the wife of the Unionist MP, Sir Henry Craik; and Ermine Murray, later the 2nd Viscountess Elibank, and daughter-in-law of Viscount Elibank, the Liberal Chief Whip who, by the end of 1912, was himself being ruthlessly hounded by Leo for his role in the ongoing Marconi scandal.

Jack's early years were unremarkable enough, although there were soon signs of the problems that lay ahead. At the age of just two, his nanny, whom Bryddie recognised as 'an experienced woman', complained to his mother that she found Jack to be 'a very *hard* child', and that unfortunately she really did not 'know quite how to deal with him'.[7] During his infancy he suffered frequently from night-time panic attacks, which in turn led to extreme screaming fits and, between the ages of three and four, to an extended bout of bedwetting. By day he suffered from regular tantrums, from which he needed to be calmed down by either his nanny or his mother. It was possibly on account of this eccentric behaviour that Leo and Bryddie developed an enthusiasm for spending more time in the country, a strategy that involved a good deal of moving around as they relied largely on the hospitality of friends, although they later took on a number of short-term lets of their own. Over the Easter holiday of 1916 Bryddie secured an invitation to stay with Lady Edward Cecil, later to become Lady Milner, at her country house, Great Wigsell, in Kent. The invitation, she admitted, was good news for Jack, a 'dear little boy and of course to me a wonder child', since they were all 'dreading Easter in London' with Leo away in the Balkans.[8] A further extended visit later that summer, to Lord Milner's house at Sturry Court, near Canterbury, resulted in an embarrassed letter of thanks from Bryddie, containing the admission from Jack that she should 'tell Lady Edward I've broken Lord Milner's house'. His mother conceded that he had, indeed, accidentally broken a pane of glass on a rainy day, but that it had been safely mended.[9]

In 1917, at the age of five, Jack went to kindergarten, attending Miss Irene Ironside's private school at Elvaston Place, in London's South Kensington. The school, which remained on the same site for many years, was well known as a nursery for the scions of many of the most illustrious families of that generation; one of Leo's grandchildren was to go there too, over fifty years later. But even here, Jack always endeavoured to be different. As early on as his day of admission, Miss Ironside 'got the impression that he was an extremely abnormal boy'. She soon found that Jack 'always wanted to do the exact opposite of what he was asked to do', not with the normal 'rebellious spirit shown by healthy children', but rather with 'a fixed attitude of an abnormal type'. Everything Jack did was designed to shock. He would turn up at school wearing a long necklace, stretching down to his knees and made of brightly coloured wooden beads. He always insisted on adding ornate decoration to his letters, which he described as 'putting in fantasy', and when he was told that he was not allowed to do so, would take revenge by refusing to write anything but the word 'oxo' on his paper, on the desks and anywhere else he could find. But if such idiosyncrasies seem harmless enough, he was also 'violent and destructive' and 'would bully the other children, twisting their arms'. Interestingly, however, he also showed the first signs of cowardice, always threatening to fight the other children, but never hanging around long enough to allow them to take up the challenge. If a teacher tried to discipline him, he would merely fly off the handle. At all other times he had a 'tendency to shut himself and live inside himself'. All in all, Miss Ironside found him 'unteachable'.[10]

During the summer of 1917, and again in 1918, Leo decided to escape the strain of daily War Cabinet meetings by renting a small house, The Warren, high up on the ridge of the North Downs in Surrey above Woldingham. Bryddie and Jack would spend most of their time there while Leo would drive down for the occasional evening during the week, and at weekends. In the September of both years he rented an old coastguard cottage for Bryddie and Jack on a seaside cliff top at Birchington, near Westgate-on-Sea in Kent. He visited himself when he could, enjoying a day or two relaxing with his son, indulging in Jack's favourite pastime of hunting crabs in the rock pools, and introducing the little boy to his own, that of rock climbing. The peace and quiet was shattered only by the nightly visits of the German aeroplanes and the ensuing fire of the guns at Margate, the little cottage providing front row seats in the 'stalls at a high-class performance of the air raid every evening'.[11]

In January 1918 the family escaped from London again, this time to a rented cottage in the village of Checkendon, near Henley in Oxfordshire. Having initially taken the cottage for two weeks, Leo decided to stay for a year, a source of great excitement for Jack, who spent most of his time exploring in the nearby woods and exhausting his father by building camps and taking him on imaginary hunting expeditions. Leo was delighted, remarking with approval that, at the age of six, Jack was already 'growing very sturdy' and would 'make a good mountaineer some day'.[12] In the meantime, a pony and the accompanying riding lessons would have to suffice. In 1919 there were further seaside holidays in South Devon and at Bembridge, in the Isle of Wight, where Jack had his first, apparently successful experiences of sailing and rowing. Earlier attempts at both rowing and sailing, while on holiday in Exmouth at the age of four, had resulted in another of Jack's uncontrolled panic attacks and an early indication of 'abject physical terror'. Leo recalled how 'a little spray blew over the gunwale', leaving Jack in an 'incontrollable hysterical state', the only solution to which had been to force him to lie, absolutely flat, on the floor of the boat.[13]

It was clear from an early age that the outdoor way of life was one that Leo and Jack could share together. In spite of Jack's problems with his nanny and at school, Leo did not consider him 'in any way exceptionally ill behaved as a child'. But a number of features of Jack's character already caused him disquiet. Like Miss Ironside, he recognised a 'curious unteachability, especially . . . with regard to any physical action'. Repeated instructions as to how something should be done would consistently fall on deaf ears, as though the message had simply failed to get through. He was also concerned about Jack's 'curious secretiveness', in particular when he was asked about school, or what else he had been doing when he was away from home. He appeared to have a 'complete lack of interest in anything done once it was done', living only for the present and remaining 'most uncommunicative' throughout his time at school.[14] In response to this apparently deliberate lack of communication, Leo and Bryddie went to great effort to try to find common ground with their son. By the standards of the period in which Jack was raised they were loving parents, and involved themselves a great deal more in his upbringing than did many parents of a similar class and background. When they were in London, Leo took Jack on regular day trips, when time allowed, to Wimbledon and Clapham Commons, and to Battersea Park in the days when the ponds still froze over hard enough to play games and to skate on the ice. And when the weather was occasionally too severe, even for Leo, then the safe and widely popular attractions of the Science Museum in South Kensington provided many hours of harmless amusement alongside other children of Jack's own age.

Money, or at least a lack of it, was a constant source of concern for Leo. Although he and Bryddie had moved out of their house in Embankment Gardens in 1916, their subsequent lifestyle had been far from frugal. The properties which they had rented in the meantime in London, the country and at the seaside had been expensive and, although Leo was still a backbencher and a mere secretary to the War Cabinet, they led an active and costly social life when in London. While their lifestyle did not compare with some of Leo's more aristocratic political contemporaries, he and Bryddie were keen to maintain appearances and employed a cook and two maids to keep their house running smoothly. At the end of the war, they returned to live in Embankment Gardens again, this time in a house just a few doors away from where they had lived previously. And while they lived expensively, Leo's income was modest. He had done almost no paid journalism during the war to supplement his parliamentary salary, while his few investments had performed badly, to say the least.

He remained a director of the Uitkyk Coal Mining Company in South Africa, but recent borings had suggested that while there was more coal than had originally been thought, its quality was far inferior and the company would need to find fresh coal fields. The prospects for his Canadian interests, meanwhile, principally the British Alberta Company and British and Overseas, were slowly improving. Early in 1918 Leo remarked ironically that he had 'interviewed my Bank Manager as to my overdraft,' and had 'pacified him by dwelling on my odds and ends of property in Canada, my recent legacy (£500 from aunt Jill)', and his expectation of receiving another £5,000 or so of a trust set up by his great aunt, old Mrs Stennett, 'when old Graham dies'.[15] Even his collection of Persian art, lovingly amassed since his first undergraduate travels in the Middle East twenty-five years earlier, was no longer sacrosanct, Christie's offering to find him a wealthy purchaser in New York.

Leo and Bryddie's second son was born at their new house at 3 Embankment Gardens, soon after five o'clock in the afternoon, on 27 March 1919. Bryddie had again endured a terrible pregnancy and, as the birth approached, Leo viewed 'Bryddie's much feared day of trial' with mixed emotions. It was indeed 'a bad business while it lasted', but 'after all the agony all went very normally'. The little boy weighed in at 8lb 2oz, 'a fine sturdy little rascal', all in all 'a great relief after our long anxiety'.[16] It was snowing heavily outside, but after a couple of days the sun shone and the new baby was put outside in his basket in the snow. Sunshine and snow, as they were for his father, were to remain among his chief delights throughout his life. Jack, by then seven years old, had been sent away on holiday to Devon for a few days to give Bryddie some peace and quiet at home, but on his return Leo broke the news to him that he had a new brother. He received it 'with some humorous interest', but on reflection said that 'he would have preferred a cat'.[17]

On 13 June the new baby was christened, like his brother before him, in the Crypt of the House of Commons, and named Harold Julian, after his late uncle, but from henceforward was always known as Julian. Unlike his brother, his godparents were to be of rather less use to him in later life, although through no fault of their own. His godfathers were Sir Robert Borden, the Prime Minister of Canada, whom he was never to see again, and his father's old friend Sir Henry Wilson, then Chief of the Imperial General Staff, who was to be brutally assassinated by Irish gunmen on the steps of his own home just three years later. His godmother was Mrs Muriel Ward, to whom the young Julian seems to have been rather more attached on account of her regular financial generosity on all the right anniversaries.

At the age of three Julian acted as a pageboy at the wedding of Bryddie's sister, his aunt Sadie, to Simon Rodney, an important event for both brothers who were to spend a good deal of time staying with the Rodneys throughout their childhoods. His early relationship with his elder brother was a tempestuous one, on one occasion Jack being caught 'throwing a lighted match into Julian's pram'.[18] Julian's nanny, Caroline Mead, found Jack to be a 'very queer little boy', who could, on the one hand, 'be so loving', but who 'had no self-control'. When he first saw Julian he 'jumped from the table' and 'raved and stormed' from the nursery, scattering his eggs and bread and butter. Such outbursts against Julian's intrusion into his life soon became a frequent occurrence, so much so that he made himself so ill at times that he had to go to bed for several days afterwards. On one occasion, when Julian was six months old, Nanny Mead found his milk bottles floating in the liquid polish that was usually used to clean the silver. Jack had 'clearly wanted to poison the baby', not just out of jealousy, but because he was 'not quite normal'.[19]

In May 1921, having just turned nine, Jack was sent away to a well-known boarding school, West Downs, near Winchester. By and large he enjoyed his time there in the same way as any other boy. His parents, as they always had been, were a good deal more modern in their outlook than were those of many of his contemporaries. In spite of Leo's busy political life, and their still more hectic social life, they were regular visitors to West Downs long before the days when it became fashionable for parents to see their children at boarding school during the term time. Sometimes they would make a weekend of it, staying with friends locally or at the Royal Hotel in Winchester, while on other occasions their visit would be a fleeting one. Jack's appearance in the school play, *A Midsummer Night's Dream*, was followed by an eagerly snatched hour to catch up together afterwards. Bryddie would go to chapel on a Sunday and they would meet for lunch with Leo afterwards, although on one occasion the headmaster vetoed Jack's choice of companion as he considered him unsuitable on account of his being a much more senior boy.

Indeed the headmaster, Kenneth Tindall, noticed Jack at an early stage in his career and kept his eye on him thereafter. From the first moment it was obvious to him that Jack 'was a boy of very unusual character', whose actions throughout his career caused Tindall 'considerable anxiety as they did not appear to be prompted by motives which would actuate a normal, healthy-minded boy'. The headmaster found, in particular, that 'ideas of right and wrong' that would be accepted by any normal boy, 'seemed to mean nothing to him'. Although he appreciated and enjoyed his parents' visits, and 'clearly felt affection' for them, this 'did not prevent him from pursuing a course of action which would be bound to cause anxiety and distress to those for whom he cared'.[20]

Much the same could be said of Jack's relationship with his peers, often a particularly complicated one. Some found him entertaining and his eccentricity amusing. He was '*the* extrovert showman, smoking on the platform at Waterloo until the last minute, and ostentatiously throwing away his stub'. And there was something glamorous about the fact that his father, once he achieved Cabinet status, was always accompanied by personal detectives when he came to visit the school.[21] Even when he attempted to run away from school, it was perceived as an act of bravado, even though he 'got no further than the allotments'.[22] In October 1923, while pacing the touchline at a school football match, Tindall confronted Leo to tell him 'how gravely disquieted he was by [Jack's] complete indifference to the morals of others'.[23] Quite apart from his 'general misbehaviour' that term, he had been 'cheeky and reckless all round'.[24] On one occasion 'his conduct had so enraged other boys that one boy of his own age and size' had asked for permission to fight him. Tindall had given permission on the understanding that the fight would take place under proper boxing conditions, himself being present and other boys there as spectators. But when it was time for both boys to enter the ring, Jack 'lay on the ground and refused to fight, though he cannot have failed to realise the contempt that such an action would arouse in the minds of the other boys'. Tindall was appalled that 'even the ordinary school boy's code of loyalty did not touch him'.[25] Another of his contemporaries at West Downs remembered him as little more than 'a nasty bully, who made poor Matthews follow him around like a dog'.[26]

Leo and Bryddie always tried hard to look on the bright side of their elder son's behaviour. Although Jack was no natural sportsman, he does seem, at the very least, to have taken a shine to cricket, even if he was not particularly proficient at it. One summer's day, Leo arrived to find him batting in a junior game, 'making 30 in quite good style . . . and evidently showing some promise'. He was encouraged that the masters reported Jack to be 'full of keenness, both on his work and his cricket', and that he was 'getting on very well all round'.[27] But this was only a few months before the incident of the abortive boxing match, and even his cricket seems to have suffered from Jack's overall sullenness. When Leo came to watch again two years later, he rather gloomily recounted that he had found Jack 'making a long innings but when he eventually got out he had made only three'.[28] Leo always accentuated the positive. He thought Jack was 'on the whole happy there [West Downs] and did not do too badly. Other boys . . . found him amusing.'[29] His misdemeanours were explained away as a result of coming 'back from his holidays too full of vitality', and even when his son's discipline appeared to have broken down completely, he nevertheless took heart from the fact that 'Jack was certainly in good form'.[30] At the end of his career, Jack was confirmed without protest in the school chapel, finished second in a school swimming race and spoke eloquently at the farewell supper for leavers.

But for Tindall the lingering doubts remained throughout Jack's time at West Downs. His '"naughtiness" could hardly ever be attributed to motives' such as 'a love of adventure or the desire to shine in the eyes of his fellows'. Rather it seemed 'purposeless', causing Tindall to worry deeply, even then, about his future. Not only did he possess no ethical code of his own, 'he had no code of morals at all, but would follow the whim of the moment without any thought of where it was going to lead to or what trouble it was likely to cause to himself or others.' Jack was, sadly, 'undoubtedly an abnormal child'.[31]

For the Christmas holidays of 1920, Leo took Bryddie and Jack on their first family skiing holiday, to Pontresina, high in the Engadine valley near St Moritz. What little skiing Leo had attempted before the war had been, by his own admission, 'of a very primitive kind'. Given that he had been nearer to fifty than forty when he took it up as a pastime, he not surprisingly deprecated many of the modern skiing techniques, in particular the 'speed merchants' who had dispensed with 'uphill skiing altogether', and chose instead to 'ascend a funicular two or three times a day in order to speed down the same hard-beaten track'.[32] With snow almost always guaranteed at Christmas, Pontresina was an ideal resort for a family of mixed skiing ability, and there were other attractions to enjoy as well. For several years the family stayed at the Schloss Hotel, owned by Leo's old friend Sir Henry Lunn, as one of the centres of his now burgeoning winter sports empire. Bryddie, who had always been frail, believed that she was not strong enough to ski, but spent her days instead on the ice rink, becoming an accomplished skater, a talent she shared with a regular fellow guest, Jack's godfather John Simon.

Jack enjoyed skiing and quickly showed that he possessed considerable ability, teaming up with a nephew of Leo's friend Ned Grigg, later Lord Altrincham, who also often stayed at the hotel. He quickly inherited his father's sense of adventure and together they tackled increasingly difficult ski runs, and ever longer cross-country treks, a chance for them to enjoy all too rare moments of shared pleasure between them. At the age of just four, Julian joined the family party for the first time and he too, in due course, became an accomplished skier. The evenings were spent enjoying concerts, dances and fancy dress balls, the number of friends from England who visited together giving the hotel the feel of a country house party. At one such ball the Labour MP Josiah Wedgwood appeared as a Red Indian, while Leo, dressed 'as a mother superior . . . shared first prize with [John] Simon dressed as Dante'. Jack too won a prize 'in the page's suit he was to have worn at [his aunt] Sadie's wedding'.[33]

It was frequently remarked on by Leo's friends that, although in public he could seem austere, in private they knew him to be stimulating and lively company, with a keen sense of humour. And so for a man who managed to convey such a tangible impression of himself as a public figure, these early holidays with the boys provided a welcome respite from the pressures of his parliamentary life, and from the demands which his sense of duty made on himself and his family. They were happy times and, as his career entered its next stage, set against the fevered backdrop of Westminster during the 1920s, and the boys embarked on their very different trajectories towards adulthood, there must have been occasions in later years when he looked back with wonder and regret at what might have become of his family.

CHAPTER EIGHT

A Successful Mutiny

As the war drew towards its conclusion, Leo's thoughts had inevitably turned, once again, towards his own political future. In spite of the prominence he had achieved at Lloyd George's side in the War Cabinet secretariat, ministerial office had continued to elude him and, at the age of forty-five, he knew that he now needed to take his first steps on the ministerial ladder. Remarkably, Leo felt confident enough of his relationship with Lloyd George to offer advice on his post-election Cabinet reshuffle, urging him to appoint a 'Reconstruction Cabinet', with no more than half a dozen ministers, along the lines of the War Cabinet. Bonar Law and Curzon should remain, unless the latter could be replaced by a 'younger and more progressive peer', while he would need 'a good Liberal' and the 'best Labour man you can get' and, above all, it was essential that Lloyd George did not 'put Churchill in the War Office', since the army was 'terrified of the idea'. Finally, Milner was 'clearly much the best man for President of the Council and Minister for the Dominions'.[1]

Leo's unsolicited recommendations were received with little enthusiasm by the Prime Minister. Austen Chamberlain became Chancellor, while Curzon retained his portfolio as Lord President of the Council and Churchill was made Secretary of State for War. And Leo's desperation to see Milner as Colonial Secretary was hampered by his old chief's own reluctance to remain in party politics for a moment longer than was absolutely necessary. The post was offered first to Jack's godfather F. E. Smith, who turned it down – so he told Leo – on the grounds that he could not afford to accept it and was instead, somewhat fortunately, made Lord Chancellor, taking the title Lord Birkenhead. It was finally only 'with the greatest reluctance' that Milner agreed to continue in Government as Colonial Secretary, and then only 'on the express condition that he could have as his Under-Secretary one with whom he was so accustomed to work, and who shared his views so completely'.[2] Even then Leo's appointment met with difficulty. Bonar Law at first refused to help, although he was 'sure there would be an opening for him shortly', and while Lloyd George 'launched forth in high praise' of Leo, he regretted that as he was already 'the sort of person who would be friendly and helpful', he preferred to offer the available ministerial posts to those who were not.[3] Milner duly issued an ultimatum that if Leo was not to be his Under-Secretary, then he would not become Secretary of State and, even when he received his own formal letter of appointment the following day, he refused to accept it until he knew for certain that Leo had been appointed as his deputy also.

So began Leo's ministerial career. The new administration was almost universally condemned by the press. *The Times* spoke of its 'deep disappointment' at the 'lamentably deficient raw material' from which the appointments had been made, and complained that the 'reshuffling of the older hands suggests exactly the same hopeless want of imagination'. F. E. Smith's elevation to the Woolsack, made to accommodate his own financial needs, provoked the 'greatest astonishment', while Churchill's appointment, as Leo had warned Lloyd George, had been to 'the one post where he is calculated to inspire the greatest distrust'. Only Milner's appointment was applauded as the 'one indisputable instance of the right man transferred to the right place' and, to Leo's delight, his own promotion was seen as a 'popular appointment'.[4] He was pleased to learn too that Churchill had also requested him as his Under-Secretary at the War Office, but Leo knew that he would enjoy far greater parliamentary responsibilities serving under a Secretary of State who sat in the House of Lords.

Having got his way over Leo's appointment, Milner set the tone for his stewardship at the Colonial Office by retiring to Sturry Court for a fortnight's holiday, leaving Leo in sole charge of the department. Leo's first task was to win the confidence of Sir George Fiddes, the cautious and somewhat prickly Permanent Under-Secretary, who was already familiar with Leo's reputation and feared that he would try to reform the workings of the office in his first few days in charge. In fact they got on well and at the end of January 1919 Leo was trusted enough to be sent over to Paris, in place of Milner, to attend the Peace Conference and, in particular, to discuss various mandates issues with the other Dominion Prime Ministers. Although it was one of only two visits of note to the Conference, he used the opportunity to renew old acquaintances and, once again, was called on to act as mediator between Lloyd George and the Australian Prime Minister, William Hughes. In doing so, he spent a memorable evening at the Prime Minister's flat, listening to Lloyd George singing 'doleful ... Welsh hymns', and watching him 'cavorting round to the gramophone or the pianola ... being taught various kinds of dances by [his daughter] Megan's young friends'.[5] Leo was amused when Megan pleaded tiredness and retired early to bed, only for him to bump into her again, several hours later, on the dance floor at the Majestic Hotel, the Conference headquarters.

Leo's principal preoccupation at the Colonial Office, indeed a responsibility which he retained even when he moved on to other ministerial duties, was that of Empire migration, in effect the promotion of the settlement of Britons throughout the Dominions. For many years the issue of emigration had been largely ignored, and Leo considered it a source of considerable irritation that, in terms of both quantity and quality, so much of it was to the United States rather than the Dominions. His predecessor as Under-Secretary had introduced an Emigration Bill in 1918 which, although it had failed, had nevertheless provided the impetus for the creation of a small Emigration Office which Leo immediately expanded into a more substantial administrative committee. The word 'emigration', with its connotations of unemployment and forced expatriation, was discarded, and his new policy became known henceforth as 'overseas settlement'. For Leo, the 'development of the population and wealth of the whole British Empire' was 'the key to the problem of post-war reconstruction'. His new policy was designed to bring benefits both to the mother nation, by reducing 'the competition for employment, increasing wages, and raising the standard of living', while the Dominions would reap the benefits of the success of their new settlers and the growth of markets within the Empire.[6] With Milner's help, Leo managed to persuade the Cabinet that a free passage to the Dominions should be made available to every ex-serviceman or woman, an offer which, by the time the scheme ended in May 1924, had been taken up by 86,000 people.

During the summer of 1919 Leo briefly found himself in charge of planning a small war of his own. For the best part of twenty years the so-called Mad Mullah had waged a sporadic war in British Somaliland, now the northern region of Somalia. Britain's other military pre-occupations in recent years had encouraged him to seize yet more territory, but the War Office was only prepared to move against him by building a new railway and deploying two or three divisions in a full-blown military expedition. Leo went to see Churchill and, with the support of Sir Henry Wilson, pointed out that bombing from the air would solve the problem immediately against an enemy with no anti-aircraft defences. Churchill agreed to deploy a squadron from Egypt, on the proviso that Leo would bear full responsibility if the scheme failed. A dozen planes from Cairo, with limited support on the ground, duly dispersed the Mullah's forces in just three weeks in January and February 1920. The total cost was just £77,000, as against War Office estimates of £2,000,000 for their proposed expedition, 'the cheapest war in history' as Leo later boasted.[7]

In August 1919 Milner sent Leo to Malta to investigate the rapidly deteriorating financial and political situation there. Leo and Bryddie sailed from Liverpool on a troop ship bound for Palestine, and during the voyage Leo foolishly allowed himself to be tempted into pulling on a pair of boxing gloves for the first time since leaving Harrow. 'Shorter sight and shorter wind', he later recalled, 'added to the original handicap of short arms', led to a heavy defeat for the now middle-aged minister,[8] although he cheered up on arrival when the Lieutenant Governor expressed his surprise at Leo and Bryddie's comparative youthfulness, joking that they must have come out to Malta for their honeymoon. The visit was a success and when, two years later, Leo's findings were enshrined in a new constitution for Malta, he was rewarded by having 'Amery Street' in the busy and thriving port of Sliema named after him. It is still so-called today.

When Milner left for a four-month visit to Egypt at the end of November, Leo was left in London as acting Secretary of State. He spent a disproportionate amount of time during that period dealing with the arrangements for the Prince of Wales's forthcoming tour to Australia and New Zealand. The Australian Prime Minister, William Hughes, had been offended by the Prince's declared desire to visit New Zealand before Australia, in order to avoid the winter weather in New Zealand, and Leo was forced to draw on all his reserves of diplomacy to resolve the dispute.

The Prince then tried to delay his departure for as long as possible, before attempting to have his Military Secretary, and Leo's old friend Ned Grigg removed from his entourage in favour of his Chief of Staff, Admiral Sir Lionel Halsey. Eventually, having failed to have the tour delayed, the truculent Prince appealed to the Prime Minister for support, but, at a meeting at Downing Street, Lloyd George stepped into the argument in support of Leo. Matters were finally resolved, but not before the Prince's obduracy had forced Leo to appeal directly to the King that 'the Prince of Wales's departure has put me in very great difficulty'.[9]

In August 1920 Leo had his first opportunity since 1912 to re-introduce himself to the joys of the Alps, and chose to visit Macugnaga in Italy, and thus to give himself the opportunity to climb the great Monte Rosa by its challenging south face. But after a few days spent walking with Bryddie and undertaking light training climbs in the company of a group of Italian soldiers, his holiday fell victim to the deteriorating political climate at home. Disorder in some industrial cities had been followed by the threat of strikes by miners, police and railway workers and, just before the House had risen for the summer, a possible general strike. The Government had created an emergency organisation to maintain essential transport and supplies, and Leo had been appointed Regional Commissioner for the North Midlands area. He arrived in Saas Fee in Switzerland to find a telegram from the Chief Regional Commissioner calling on him to return home at once to take up his duties. Conscientious to the last, he left immediately, at one o'clock in the morning, to undertake a route march through the night back to Macugnaga, telegraphing ahead to Bryddie that she should organise a car and train to travel home. But by 5 a.m. he found himself standing on a lower peak, looking up at a new dawn breaking over Monte Rosa. Why 'leave such delights', he mused, just because his chief at home 'had got a fit of nerves?'[10] and he telegraphed home in reply that, in the absence of any further communication, he would be staying for another two weeks and would complete his holiday. His decision was justified when the crisis at home quickly passed.

▪ ▪ ▪

When Lord Milner opened the Empire Conference in January 1921, it was to be the last act of his public life. In spite of a long-held wish to resign, he had reluctantly remained in the job, but had always resolutely refused to play the game of party politics, and had now grown tired and lost all influence with Lloyd George and his Cabinet colleagues. His close relationship with Violet, the widow of Lord Edward Cecil and sister of Leo's old friend Leo Maxse, had been an open secret for years among their closest friends. Now Milner tendered his resignation and wrote to inform Leo, lest he should read it first in the newspapers, that he would be travelling abroad to marry Lady Edward the following day. To the very end, his thoughts were with Leo and his future career, indeed his only regret at resigning was that he would be leaving Leo 'rather alone, among people who have very little real sympathy with the things which we both most care about'. Leo had secretly hoped that he might succeed as Secretary of State, but the job went instead to Churchill. 'I have not the least doubt that you will ultimately get your proper recognition,' continued Milner, 'but I should certainly have been much happier if you had come to your own at this stage.'[11] His departure deprived Leo of the friend and protector to whom he 'owed such political advancement as he had achieved', and of 'the only leader whom I could follow without reservation'.[12]

Leo remained for only a few weeks at the Colonial Office under Churchill's leadership, before accepting Lloyd George's offer, in April, to become Parliamentary and Financial Secretary at the Admiralty, a technical promotion and a return to sole responsibility in the Commons since the First Lord of the Admiralty, Lord Lee of Fareham, also sat in the Lords. He soon warmed to his new job, and was excited to find himself sitting at one end of the long table in the historic Admiralty Board Room, opposite the First Lord, and flanked on either side by the two Sea Lords, including the First Sea Lord, Admiral Beatty. On one of the walls was the mark which, according to folklore, recorded Nelson's height and Leo was relieved to discover that while shorter than Nelson, he was, at least, taller than Napoleon. Inspired by the new Chancellor of the Exchequer, Sir Robert Horne, the prevailing political climate was for the need to make substantial savings in public expenditure, and Leo soon got to work learning the intricacies of the vast Admiralty organisation and preparing a defence against possible spending cuts.

A recent enquiry by the Committee of Imperial Defence had failed to agree on the scale of a new battleship-building programme and, with one eye on the disarmament conference that was then taking place in Washington, Leo presented estimates to the House at the beginning of August, strongly supported by Churchill, to provide for the building of four new capital ships, the so-called 'Super-Hoods'. In the meantime, a committee under the chairmanship of Sir Eric Geddes had been set up with a brief to scrutinise the expenditure of each government department and to wield the axe accordingly. The Admiralty was at first instructed to make savings of £21,000,000, a suggestion initially assumed by the Admirals to be a joke, and there followed a period of claim and counter-claim, with Leo negotiating on behalf of the Admiralty. The Geddes Report was finally published in February 1922, after all departments had been sent a draft copy for comment. However, Leo decided to get his own rebuttal in first and, with the First Lord away in Washington, he and Beatty released the Admiralty's reply to the press on the same day as the Geddes Report itself, strenuously denying the implicit accusations of wastefulness at the Admiralty.

The press was delighted with such overt evidence of a serious rift within the Government and ignored many of the criticisms of the

Admiralty contained in the Geddes Report. But most of the Cabinet were infuriated at Leo's deliberately underhand tactics and there was talk of censure, even dismissal. *The Times* described his behaviour as the 'most striking example of independence' that they could recall, and gleefully described how his memorandum was 'in effect a cry of "Hands Off" both to the Geddes Committee and to the Cabinet'.[13] However, others thought Leo had merely confirmed that he was unfit to hold high office and Austen Chamberlain wrote him a stinging rebuke, although, much to Leo's amusement, he was subsequently forced to defend Leo's actions on the floor of the House as being in accordance with Government policy. As so often when he got himself into a scrape, far from showing remorse, Leo enjoyed the whole furore and seems to have relished being the cause of so much trouble.

Throughout the latter half of 1921 and most of 1922, support for the Lloyd George coalition slowly ebbed away, both among most of its Unionist members, and within the country at large. Like many of his colleagues, Leo was concerned that power had become excessively consolidated in the hands of a small coterie of Lloyd George's most trusted Cabinet colleagues, most of them Unionists. He recognised the 'inherent tendency of all coalitions to coalesce more closely at the top than lower down the scale of party organisation', and believed that Cabinet business was increasingly 'despatched more expeditiously', while those issues that divided members of opposing political parties were 'tacitly sidestepped' to avoid confrontation.[14] Churchill and Birkenhead, friends of Leo's, yet neither of them close intimates, both exercised a profound influence on the Prime Minister, while another of his friends, Austen Chamberlain, by now the leader of the Unionist Party and Deputy Leader of the Commons, was also a member of the inner circle. Edwin Montagu, the Secretary of State for India, described the country as being 'governed by the Prime Minister who has confidence only in Chamberlain, F.E. and [Sir Robert] Horne and carries with him Winston because of the necessity for doing so'. The Cabinet was hardly ever called together, he complained to Lord Reading in India, and 'everything that wants doing is given to one of these people to do . . .'[15]

As the coalition's star waned, so Leo struck up a new friendship with an 'almost unknown Minister', the President of the Board of Trade, Stanley Baldwin, whose distaste for the Government of which he was a member he made abundantly clear to his new friend. Baldwin had been introduced to the top tier of politics by Bonar Law and was 'now left stranded . . . sucking his pencil at Cabinet meetings'. He felt ill at ease with Lloyd George and his style of government, in particular the 'combination of intellectual brilliance with the cynical lack of political or moral principle'.[16] Baldwin and Leo began to walk home together from the House at night, debating the rights and wrongs of their remaining members of the administration. For Baldwin, the danger lay in 'the morally disintegrating effect of Lloyd George on all whom he had to deal with' and, worse still, 'the way in which corrupt practices of every kind were spreading through the higher reaches of Government and the parties'.[17] Leo's concerns, by contrast, were more practical. He disapproved intensely of the central plank of the coalition's platform, the idea that socialism in general, and the Labour Party in particular, had to be defeated at all costs. Such a policy was, he believed, hopelessly short-sighted and would carry no appeal for the vast majority of the electorate and, in particular, the industrial workers, for whose support he especially wanted to appeal. Rather, he urged the Unionist Party to confront socialism by 'dealing effectively with the growing evil of unemployment and wage reductions'.[18] Lloyd George's lack of leadership on economic issues, combined with the free-trade rhetoric of some of the Government's Liberal members, was the true cause of his, and more widespread Unionist, frustration.

Events in Ireland also played their part. The treaty conceding independence to Ireland was signed in the early hours of 6 December 1921, the culmination of almost two years of negotiation and bloodshed. Since the Home Rule Bill had reached the statute book at the end of 1920, Ireland had been subjected to a brutal cycle of arson, torture and murder. Leo, while still retaining his pre-war Unionist zeal, had played a lesser role in Irish affairs since joining the front bench, but he soon found himself intimately involved, on the appointment, in April 1920, of his brother-in-law Hamar Greenwood as Chief Secretary of Ireland. Leo believed him to be a man of decision and courage, but Greenwood's response to the terror, the creation of the notorious 'Black and Tans', so called because of their temporary uniform of military khaki, matched to a black hat and armband, soon aroused widespread controversy on account of their ruthless methods. Leo at first claimed that the ends justified the means, but soon had to concede that the widespread publicity given to their atrocities had led to deep unease among the public and in Parliament.

Just at the moment when it seemed that Greenwood's strong-arm tactics might pay off, in the spring of 1921 the British Government suddenly sued for peace. The Sinn Fein leader Eamon de Valera insisted that any talks should be accompanied by a truce, and Greenwood was summoned to Downing Street and informed by Lloyd George that the Cabinet had decided to negotiate a settlement. Leo felt strong personal resentment at 'the bitter blow' to his brother-in-law, made worse when the Republican military commander Michael Collins later conceded to him that Sinn Fein had been 'dead beat' and 'could not have lasted another three weeks'. He had been 'astounded' by the offer of a truce and assumed that the British Government 'must have gone mad'.[19] Winston Churchill too acknowledged that 'no British Government has ever appeared to make so complete and sudden a reversal of policy'.[20] The truce came into force on 11 July and, after five months of negotiations, a treaty was announced on 6 December. Ireland would enjoy independence, as the 'Irish Free State', with the status and rights of a self-governing Dominion, while Ulster would be given the choice of joining an all-Ireland Parliament or remaining part of the United Kingdom, subject to a boundary commission, should she decide to stand alone outside. Unionist reaction ranged between disquiet and consternation and, although Leo considered resignation and discussed the possibility with Baldwin, he later recalled only the 'sense of shame and indignation' with which he left the House after listening to the announcement.[21]

Lloyd George soon turned his attention towards the possibility of an early general election, in an attempt to rally the coalition. In fact, the suggestion had the opposite effect, concentrating the minds of already restless Unionists, now increasingly describing themselves as Conservatives, most of whom felt that their Liberal allies were the cause, not the solution to their problems. 'Unless we are to become really one

Party with a single policy,' wrote Leo to Austen Chamberlain, 'there must be some way of getting out of the impasse created by one wing putting forward as reasonable demands which the other will regard as monstrous.'[22] He was far from alone in expressing the fears of many of his colleagues that their party was in danger of losing all sense of identity. 'Is there a single item in our present policy', he asked Austen again a few days later, 'which appeals to the instincts or traditions of Unionists?' Their supporters' feelings were of 'despondency and moral unsettlement' and there was 'no elation, only a sinking at heart'. He would not, he warned, continue indefinitely to give speeches 'full of platitudes to apathetic supporters and hungry and bitter opponents'.[23]

Throughout the spring and early summer of 1922 Leo watched as the situation in Ireland continued to deteriorate and a campaign of terror and murder continued unabated. On 22 June the world in general, and Leo in particular, was horrified by the ruthless murder of his old friend, and Julian's godfather, Sir Henry Wilson, in London. Wilson, who had retired as Chief of the Imperial General Staff and had become the Unionist MP for North Down, had been responsible for the reorganisation of the Ulster constabulary. Returning home in his Field-Marshal's uniform after unveiling a war memorial at Liverpool Street Station, he was gunned down in cold blood and broad daylight by two Irish extremists on the steps of his house in Eaton Place. For Leo it was a terrible blow, the loss of 'one of my best friends', raising 'again all the doubts I have felt about the whole hateful Irish business'.[24] Later that evening Lloyd George's inner circle met at Downing Street with the pistols that had been used to kill Wilson laid out before them on the Cabinet table, and the following day Leo found the House 'in a very angry mood'. His friend H. A. Gwynne, the editor of the *Morning Post*, urged him for the second time in as many months to 'break with the Government and lead the Die-hards'; did not Leo ask himself, enquired Gwynne, 'every morning when I was shaving what business I had to stay on?'[25] The greatest opprobrium, however, was reserved for the Unionist coalition leaders. When Austen Chamberlain visited Lady Wilson at Eaton Place to pay his respects, she is reported to have greeted him at the door with the single word, 'Murderer!'[26]

Leo also became peripherally involved in another contemporary scandal, one that is generally acknowledged as having contributed to the demise of the coalition. At the end of May Lloyd George wrote to inform him that he was to be appointed a Privy Counsellor, a recommendation which Austen Chamberlain claimed as his own, although Leo later discovered that Austen had, in fact, been decidedly lukewarm about the appointment behind his back. On 3 June Leo found his name in the Birthday Honours list, 'alongside [that] of J. B. Robinson and some other shockers'.[27] Sir Joseph Robinson, who had been given a peerage, was one of a triumvirate of rich South African businessmen to be honoured, and Leo was intensely embarrassed to find his own name on the list alongside them. Lloyd George's distribution of honours had, he thought, 'gone far beyond the customary discreet sweetening of a claim to recognition of public service by some contribution to party funds, and threatened to bring the whole system into disrepute'.[28] The South African Prime Minister quickly made it clear that he had not been consulted on Robinson's peerage, while the King was 'incensed', telling the Prime Minister that he could not conceal his 'profound concern at the very disagreeable situation which has arisen' and that, while there had been disturbing evidence for some time that the honours system was being abused, the latest peerages were 'an insult to the Crown and to the House of Lords'.[29] Robinson was, reluctantly, persuaded to decline his peerage and Lloyd George finally agreed to set up a Royal Commission to examine the whole issue.

Although Leo, as a junior member of the Government, felt morally obliged to support the coalition and indeed remained on good personal terms with Lloyd George, he recognised that the Unionist Party was now in a state of simmering revolt. On 20 July he attended a meeting of junior Unionist ministers with Austen Chamberlain, after which Chamberlain was forced to acknowledge that they were 'very restless about the continuation of the Coalition under Lloyd George'.[30] He agreed to discuss their concerns with his Cabinet colleagues, but after several days without news, the Under-Secretaries pressed their case and were summoned to a further meeting on the evening of 3 August in the Lord Chancellor's room in the House of Lords, this time with all the Unionist Cabinet members present. There are several published accounts of this dramatic meeting, all of which agree that it marked the moment when the junior ministers finally lost confidence in their Cabinet colleagues.

According to William Bridgeman, proceedings got off to a bad start, Chamberlain arrogantly proclaiming that the meeting was highly irregular but that he and 'his colleagues had decided that they might condescend to hear us'.[31] The Under-Secretaries' case was then introduced 'temperately and fairly' by Sir Robert Sanders, Sir John Gilmour and Sir Ernest Pollock, the Attorney General. Chamberlain invited Birkenhead to reply. Leo listened with incredulity as Birkenhead began by accusing the ministers of 'impertinence in having asked for a meeting at all, when they had already been informed of the Cabinet ministers' views', and then continued 'in the most astonishingly arrogant and offensive manner to lecture them for their silliness and want of loyalty'.[32] He demanded to know the source of their information, 'derided the reports from the country as gossip' and warned them that the 'Conservative Party's only hope was to stick to the Coalition'.[33] Pollock thought Birkenhead's attitude 'unexpected and both hostile and dictatorial as addressed to inferiors who had no right to express opinions',[34] while Baldwin, sitting on the Cabinet side of the table, remained '*more suo*, silent and aloof', although Eddie Winterton detected 'a gleam of sympathy for us in his face'.

The meeting soon degenerated into farce, with one or two ministers tackling Birkenhead, but most, Leo among them, preferring to keep their peace. Balfour made an effort at conciliation, and later admitted that it had not been 'a very happy occasion, nor one that was very tactfully handled on either side'.[35] And Chamberlain conceded privately to his sister that Birkenhead had displayed 'an intellectual arrogance which nearly produced a row there and then and did infinite harm', and that he had, unknown to the Under-Secretaries, subsequently 'remonstrated very courteously but very strongly with him next day'.[36] But the damage had been done. Birkenhead was one of Leo's oldest friends and was Jack's godfather. But Leo realised that 'whatever chances F.E. may have had of the Unionist leadership of the future they are not likely to have survived this unfortunate performance' and compared his old friend to Herodotus's arrogant noble who threw away his chance of marrying the greatest heiress in Greece by insolently dancing on a table.[37]

Leo spent August climbing in Switzerland and enjoying a first taste of summer skiing with his old friend Sir Henry Lunn, the pioneer of the modern-day skiing holiday, at one of his hotels in Mürren. He returned to his office on 12 September, by which time the coalition's downfall had been brought a step closer by Lloyd George's disastrous near-eastern policy. The post-war leader of Turkey, Mustafa Kemal, had refused to accept the terms of the 1920 Treaty of Sèvres, in particular the secession to Greece of large parts of Asia Minor including Smyrna. Lloyd George, who according to Leo had been 'hypnotized by Venizelos's eloquence and by his own anti-Turkish prejudices',[38] had enthusiastically encouraged Greek plans for territorial expansion with disastrous results. At the end of August the Greek army collapsed and, barely a fortnight later, the victorious Turkish army entered Smyrna, burned the city to the ground and massacred over 100,000 of its Christian population. All that now stood between Kemal and Constantinople, even a possible invasion of Europe itself, was a small international force, under the British command of Lieutenant General Sir Charles Harrington, in the neutral zone of the Dardanelles at Chanak.

Harrington stood firm and, on 15 September, the Cabinet met through the day and reaffirmed their determination to defend the neutral zone, if necessary by force. Unfortunately, having sent private telegrams to the Dominion Governments explaining the agreed policy and asking for moral support and reinforcements in the event of war, a communiqué was issued to the public at the same time. Only New Zealand offered assistance, while the warlike tone of the public message scared the British public and further undermined the Government's position. Leo was appalled, reading the latest '*pronunciamento* about the Turkish crisis, with its challenging tone, and its very dubious appeal to the Dominions' with 'stupefaction'. The collapse of Lloyd George's policy could only 'weaken him greatly', and would undoubtedly 'strengthen the movement for independence in the Unionist Party'.[39] During the first few days of October the situation remained tense, as a battle raged at home between those seeking peace, led by Curzon and Baldwin, and the 'fire-eaters and war-mongers',[40] led by Churchill and Birkenhead, with Lloyd George's approval. Baldwin believed that 'W. and L.G. had been all out for war and had schemed to make this country go to war with Turkey so that they should have a "Christian" war *v.* the Mahomedan and turn the Turks out of Europe',[41] while Lord Peel, who had replaced Montagu as Secretary of State for India in March, told Leo that Churchill was 'always intoxicated at the thought of war and was visibly disappointed when the more pacific telegrams came in'.[42]

The crisis was eventually resolved peacefully, thanks largely to Curzon's diplomatic skills. Leo, who was inherently pro-Turk, in spite of his personal regard for Venizelos, had read Bonar Law's celebrated letter to *The Times* on 6 October, in which he warned that he was not prepared to see the country 'alone act as the policeman of the world',[43] as a call to arms. In the midst of the crisis, on 16 September the Cabinet had met at Chequers and resolved to hold an early general election to try to stem the growing tide of Unionist discontent, fearing a likely vote against the coalition at the annual party conference in November. Against the advice of his own party managers, Austen Chamberlain continued to insist that an election be held as soon as possible, even when both the Party Chairman and Chief Whip protested that his own backbenchers would give him 'very little support in the proposed continuation of the Coalition as it is with L.G. as its head'.[44]

On 10 October, the day on which the armistice was signed with Turkey, the Cabinet met in the afternoon and Chamberlain again proposed an early general election, once again in the teeth of fierce opposition from his own Chief Whip, who told him that he would publicly oppose his continued leadership of the party if the policy was forced through without consultation with the party first. When Leo saw Chamberlain that afternoon, his party leader insisted that 'the existing Coalition under Lloyd George was the only one that could save the country from Labour',[45] echoing his words to his sister a fortnight earlier that 'No Govt is possible without coalition', and that 'No Coalition on present lines & *in present conditions* is possible with

Co-Libs except under a Ll.G premiership.'[46] Baldwin had stood out in Cabinet against the decision to call an early election, and when they met for lunch at the Carlton Club two days later, Leo found him in low spirits and talking of resigning immediately. Only Sir Arthur Griffith-Boscawen, the Minister of Agriculture, and, to a lesser degree, Curzon had offered him any support. Although Leo tried hard to talk him out of resignation, by the time Baldwin met his wife off the train at Victoria later that afternoon, his mood had, if anything, blackened further, as he warned her that he would almost certainly have to leave the Cabinet and that his political career might be over.

Chamberlain, meanwhile, had written to Birkenhead, giving the first intimation that it was 'now necessary to call a Party meeting and to tell them bluntly that they must either follow our advice or do without us, in which case they must find their own Chief and form a Government *at once*. They would be in a d—d fix!'[47] The letter appears to show that the genesis of the famous meeting at the Carlton Club the following week lay not in the discontent of the rebels, but rather in the defiance of the coalition's supporters. Leo remarked in despair that Chamberlain seemed to be genuinely unaware of the level of disaffection within Unionist ranks, and historians have subsequently commented that while he demonstrated 'his most noble qualities of loyalty to his Prime Minister and a granitic steadfastness of purpose', Chamberlain also 'displayed the very worst features of his leadership style and the political aloofness and arrogance upon which it was built'.[48] He was 'suffering from the occupational malady which so often besets politicians – the hallucination of indispensability.'[49]

On 13 October Leo visited Bonar Law after breakfast, at his house at 24 Onslow Gardens. Bonar Law had been inundated with letters of support, urging him to take a lead, after his letter to *The Times* of the previous week and was now carefully weighing up his options. Both his loyalty to Chamberlain and his failing health made him reluctant to canvass the party leadership, but he was urged on by his supporters, chief among them his close confidant Lord Beaverbrook, both in private and in his newspapers. Leo found him 'very pessimistic about the Party, convinced that nothing would avert a break up and fearing a long exclusion from office', but also 'very anxious not to be thought to try and queer Austen's pitch', although he would 'obviously take the leadership if he is asked'. Leo lunched at the Carlton with a group of his fellow junior ministers, 'all of them in very intractable mood'. It was agreed that they should get together before the meeting of Unionist ministers the next week, and it was left to Leo to summon them all to the Metropole Hotel for lunch the following Monday. This very action alone marked him out as a ringleader of the revolt in Chamberlain's eyes and in subsequent accounts of the events of that week. But it was only when he read reports in the evening newspapers of a speech by Chamberlain in Birmingham, 'making a big bogey of the Labour peril',[50] that 'any doubts I may have had about my course of action were dispelled . . . somebody had to take the initiative.' It was then, and only then, that Leo sat down and sent telegrams to all his fellow junior ministers inviting them to lunch the following week.[51]

The weekend was a busy one. On Saturday 14 October Leo lunched at the Carlton with Philip Lloyd-Greame, the Parliamentary Secretary at the Overseas Trade Department, and a number of other junior ministers, all furious at Chamberlain's speech. Having told his wife that 'things were beginning to move', Baldwin invited Leo and Lloyd Greame to tea, and Lucy Baldwin rushed home to their house in Eaton Square, 'buying cakes on the way'.[52] Of greater importance still was a speech given that afternoon by Lloyd George in Manchester, during which, against the specific advice of his Foreign Secretary, he had launched into a lengthy diatribe in defence of his Turkish policy, fiercely denouncing the massacre at Smyrna and the part played by the French Government. Curzon, appalled at the potential damage to his peace negotiations, read the speech 'with stupefaction and dismay'. He, too, had by now had enough.[53]

On Sunday morning Leo called on his brother-in-law Hamar Greenwood, still a Cabinet minister and close friend of Lloyd George, who reported that the Prime Minister believed 'the whole thing to be a personal intrigue against him and is determined to fight for all he is worth'.[54] That night Churchill hosted a dinner for the leading coalitionists at his home in Sussex Square in Pimlico. Curzon refused to attend and it was left once again to the Chief Whip, Sir Leslie Wilson, to complain about the decision to hold an early general election. Chamberlain again refused to delay, but offered instead to summon the full body of Unionist MPs to the Carlton Club the following Thursday. Every Member duly received his telegram of invitation from the Chief Whip.

On the morning of Monday 16 October, seventeen Unionist ministers, including Wilson, assembled for lunch at the Metropole Hotel, at Leo's invitation. Leo urged compromise, circulating a draft formula he had devised, by which the two parties that made up the coalition would fight the election separately, and leave the terms of any subsequent alliance to be decided once the election result was known. But his suggestion was rejected as 'too vague' and, instead, a declaration was agreed that the Unionists, 'while welcoming the co-operation . . . of any Party', would fight the election as 'an independent party, and that the leader of the Unionist Party shall be prepared to accept the responsibility of forming a Government if the Unionist Party after the election should be the largest party in the House of Commons'.

The subsequent meeting with Unionist Cabinet ministers, held later that afternoon in a House of Commons conference room at 2 Whitehall Gardens, marked the effective end of Leo's friendship with Austen Chamberlain. After Chamberlain's initial appeal for unity, it was left to Leo to act as spokesman, who found himself in the bizarre position of having to put forward a proposition which was considerably more militant than the compromise he had himself suggested and still supported. But that counted for nothing with Chamberlain, who saw around him only treachery and intrigue. He resented what he perceived as an ultimatum, and took Leo's character-istic loquaciousness as a personal slight, feeling 'hurt that he should have taken the lead at all'.[55] Unfortunately, at least one of those present felt that Leo had summarised the group's revised views 'not very well',[56] while Austen told his sister that Leo was undoubtedly the ring-leader, having 'summoned' the others to lunch that day (as he thought, wrongly, at Leo's house), that he had been 'trucculent [*sic*] and un-compromising', and was only causing trouble because 'he was not made Colonial Sec. in succession to Milner'. He had not 'hesitated to ask first for Cabinet rank & then for a Privy Councillorship', long before Austen thought either to be deserved.[57] As Leo left at the end of the two-hour meeting, Baldwin told him that everything now depended on whether Bonar Law, whose doctor had examined him the previous day and was due to do so again, would be passed fit enough to undertake the leadership.

Bryddie was desperately upset at Leo's falling out with Austen, and wrote begging the party leader not to allow a political difference of opinion to come between them. But in a remarkably curt reply for one known for his unfailing courtesy, Chamberlain complained bitterly that 'nothing could have been more hostile than Leo's opening attitude' at the earlier meeting, 'and nothing more uncompromising than his speech throughout'. Chamberlain felt that he had gone as far as he could down the path of concession and, in a deeply hurtful rebuke, conceded that maybe they had indeed 'come to the parting of the ways' and could 'travel no longer together'.[58] Leo replied immediately, insisting that he felt no lack of personal loyalty towards Chamberlain, but that he felt even more intensely about the future of the party, while Bryddie, realising that she might have done better to have said nothing, conceded that Leo was 'miserable about it all'.[59]

The following morning, 17 October, the junior ministers met again, joined on this occasion by two Cabinet ministers, Baldwin and Boscawen, and the Party Chairman, Sir George Younger. Baldwin 'spoke briefly but with very great feeling to the effect that he could never serve under L.G. again'. Boscawen agreed and the meeting was led to believe that Curzon was of the same mind. The crucial question now focused on Bonar Law's position and his willingness to lead them. When Leo saw Chamberlain again, briefly, that afternoon the gulf between them was as wide as ever. For the first time Leo laid out in detail his differences of principle with the coalition leadership: the Turkish fiasco and the subsequent appeal to the Dominions and, above all, the issue of preference and protection. Never was it more apparent to him that it was he who was the true political heir of Joseph Chamberlain, rather than his hero's own son and, in some distress, he realised that to Austen the fact that Leo 'attached any importance to the policy for which his father had given his life seemed to him an absurd scruple'.[60]

Leo continued to try to find a compromise formula that would satisfy all parties, while Bonar Law continued to consider his own position. He initially told Baldwin that he would not be attending the meeting at the Carlton Club on doctor's orders, while a steady stream of callers at his home tried to persuade him to do otherwise. 'Up to the last moment', he later admitted, 'I was very undecided and if my own family – my sister and children – had not been so strong against my giving up, I believe that is the course I should have adopted.'[61] Meanwhile, the night before the meeting, a group of Under-Secretaries gathered at Baldwin's home after dinner to discuss Leo's compromise proposals. Baldwin 'didn't think it quite straight and would have nothing to do with it'.[62]

A last-minute blow to the fortunes of the coalition appeared in the late editions of the morning newspapers on Thursday 19 October. Alongside Bonar Law's declaration that he would, after all, be attending at the Carlton Club that morning – out of fear that he might change his mind, Beaverbrook had rung to inform the Press Association as soon as he had decided the previous evening – came the news of the coalition's defeat in the by-election at Newport, where the independent Conservative had won by 2,090 votes over Labour, beating the coalition Liberal candidate into third place. Chamberlain had confidently expected the Labour candidate to profit from a split vote and win the seat, thus confirming his anti-socialist rhetoric on the dangers of Unionists standing independently, but instead the result boosted the confidence of those who arrived at the Carlton that cold morning determined to bring down the Coalition Government. To add to the overall atmosphere of a government in decline, Churchill had been rushed to hospital the previous evening with acute appendicitis, and had undergone an emergency operation.

The Carlton Club meeting has achieved almost mythical status in twentieth-century political folklore, described by one historian as 'one of the great turning points of British political life', after which 'the party system was never the same again' and marking 'the end of the Liberal party as a party of government'.[63] A crowd had assembled outside, which booed or cheered in turn as various personalities arrived, yet inside, as the 274 MPs assembled for the meeting at eleven o'clock, the overall mood was 'unexpectedly genial and indeed mirthful'.[64] Leo found the old Tory club 'humming like a bee-hive', while a mischievous backbencher had arranged for two tumblers of brandy to be placed on the top table, Chamberlain discreetly hiding his under his chair, while Birkenhead accepted the libation with alacrity. Bonar Law's entrance was greeted with much the loudest cheer, an early indication of the mood of the meeting.

When Austen Chamberlain opened the meeting, speaking for some thirty minutes, there was no new concession to appease his critics. 'Like Rehoboam of old', thought Leo, he had listened to his advisers and 'now elicited the same reaction of "to your tents, oh Israel"'. His speech restated his oft-repeated argument that the coalition provided the only mechanism for defeating the Labour Party and that it was not for Unionists alone to decide the question of who should be Prime Minister after an election in which they had enjoyed Liberal support. It was 'dictatorial in tone and, in substance, a repetition of the Birmingham speech'. It aroused 'no enthusiasm' and, following a suggestion that there were no policy differences between the two wings of the coalition, 'lively cries of dissent'.[65] Another MP thought it a 'lecture'[66] while its 'school masterish tone grated'. Many were surprised by Chamberlain's 'uncompromising and somewhat aggressive attitude',[67] and it was considered 'ill-judged and received without enthusiasm'.[68]

Chamberlain was followed by Baldwin, who spoke for just eight minutes, but to devastating effect, insisting that the party must rid itself of all association with coalition government in general, and Lloyd George in particular. Two senior backbenchers then proposed the pre-arranged resolution calling for the party to fight the election on an independent platform, before Bonar Law responded to the calls from the floor and rose, somewhat reluctantly, to make the speech which delivered for him the leadership of the party and the premiership. He began diffidently – one of his 'characteristic soliloquizing speeches' thought Leo – but soon made it clear that he too believed that the party should leave the coalition and fight on its own. His remarks were greeted with 'tremendous enthusiasm and settled the business', so much so that Balfour's subsequent 'philosophic analysis' was listened to 'with patience but without conviction'. Leo was himself on the point of getting to his feet but, perhaps fortunately, the Chief Whip, Sir Leslie Wilson, brought the meeting to a close.[69] A card vote confirmed that the motion to leave the coalition was carried, publicly recorded at the time by 187 votes to 87, although ballot records in the papers of John Davidson, Baldwin's Parliamentary Private Secretary, and Austen Chamberlain, show slightly different figures. Leo was one of fourteen Unionist ministers, out of the twenty-four who had voted, who had supported the motion.

Lucy Baldwin, waiting for her husband in a car outside, saw the colourful and wealthy Sir Philip Sassoon, Lloyd George's Parliamentary Private Secretary, rush out of the club with a 'yellowish-white drawn face', and leap into his 'rather unwholesome-looking Rolls-Royce car with a smart but "bookie"-looking chauffeur'.[70] Lloyd George handed in his resignation to the King, who in turn invited Bonar Law, subject to his ratification as the new leader of the Conservative Party, to form a new government. Leo attended a farewell party at the Admiralty given by his chief, Lord Lee, and was irked by Lee's reference in his speech to 'those who had "engineered" the business', but he soon forgot the slight over dinner with a jubilant Lord Milner, ending the day by looking in on a 'very happy' Stanley Baldwin on the way home.[71]

Leo found himself immediately at the heart of Bonar Law's inner circle. The following afternoon he attended a meeting to make arrangements for Bonar Law's nomination as party leader and to discuss issues of policy, primarily Ireland and fiscal policy. As the 'leading Tariff Reformer' present, Leo was asked to put forward his views and surprised everyone by agreeing that while he was as convinced as ever of the need for a policy of tariff reform, he 'felt that this next election would be run really on one issue, a change of Government'.[72] A collective sigh of relief passed around the table, Beaverbrook confessing that the fact that 'Amery, the constant and faithful advocate of Empire, should have agreed to it I own amazed me'.[73] Having made a deliberately friendly gesture in the meeting, Leo still managed to secure a promise afterwards, later to be broken, that the new leader would keep all options open on the future of tariff reform. In the somewhat chaotic atmosphere of Bonar Law's Cabinet making, Leo eventually ended up as First Lord of the Admiralty, in spite of having lobbied hard for the Colonial Office. The Duke of Devonshire had been destined for the Admiralty, but Bonar Law was reluctant to have both the fighting services represented in the House of Lords and, at the last moment, Leo and Devonshire were switched, so late indeed that Leo heard the arrangements being changed on the telephone in Bonar Law's front hall as he arrived for the meeting.

Certainly Leo was a principal beneficiary of Lloyd George's overthrow, but there is no evidence to suggest that this was a prime motivation in deciding his role over the previous few weeks. While he has always been identified as a leading member, if not the senior shop steward, of the so-called 'Revolt of the Under-Secretaries', in fact he urged compromise until the very last moment, and neither his actions nor his motives were as 'revolutionary' as those of some of his colleagues. On the night of the meeting he wrote to Lloyd George from the Carlton Club itself, admitting that he had been 'one of those Unionists who reluctantly came to the conclusion that the present coalition arrangement could not be continued'. But he also thanked Lloyd George for his 'kindness and generous encouragement' during the four years that he had enjoyed 'the privilege of serving under you'.[74] Conceivably this was an attempt to salve his conscience or to keep his options open in the event of a comeback by Lloyd George, but both such motivations appear out of character. Indeed, thirty years later, with nothing left to prove, he described Lloyd George at the time as 'the greatest figure in Europe, as well as in the English speaking world' and admitted that he 'could not help retaining a measure of personal affection' for him, and admiration for his 'imagination and driving power'.[75] Lloyd George, for his part, seems to have borne few grudges either. Admittedly his circular letter of resignation, thanking his former ministers for their 'valuable services', had been modified in Leo's case, and presumably those of some others, to delete the phrase 'and loyal co-operation'.[76] But he and Leo remained close friends throughout the rest of his life, and when he first visited Leo's splendid library at Eaton Square a few years later, his opening remark was 'What a lovely room. I suppose this is where you planned my downfall,' in fact an erroneous assumption.[77]

The coalition Unionists were in less forgiving mood, Chamberlain expressing his outrage at Leo's elevation to the Cabinet, telling his sister that he was 'a poor parliamentarian, very unhandy so far in spite of his brains'.[78] Leo's attempt at an apology, similar to that he had made to Lloyd George, was bluntly rebutted. 'Things are as they are and regret is useless,' wrote Chamberlain, adding meaningfully that he was absolutely satisfied that he, at least, had 'acted rightly as well as consistently'.[79] Churchill, who had seen out the crisis from his hospital bed, was still more publicly outspoken, writing an open letter to his electors in Dundee, who were shortly to throw him out. 'Mr Amery', he thundered, had played 'a leading part in the revolt of the Under-Secretaries', and he viewed 'with disquietude the fact that this Junior Minister has stepped into the shoes of his late Chief – a reward of successful mutiny which is certainly an unwholesome spectacle'. Leo was bemused by this public onslaught, preferring to place greater importance on the ensuing private exchange of letters, the one offering sympathy for Churchill's illness, the other sending a 'kindly letter of good wishes on my promotion'.[80]

If the Chamberlain sisters had grown accustomed to the increasing hostility towards Leo of one of their brothers, they must have been confused by the praise showered on him by their other brother, Neville. Leo, he thought, was 'one of the few men who has constructive ideas' and he hoped that he would be given 'full scope to work out his ideas as the responsible head of a department'. His drawbacks were that 'Austen says he has no judgement', and that 'if only he were half as big again he would before now have reached a much higher place'.[81] He even told Leo that if he were successful in becoming Colonial Secretary, 'he would like to serve under him'.[82] The admiration was mutual. In the aftermath of the Carlton Club meeting, Neville was on board ship returning from Canada, but Leo telegraphed, urging him to make no decisions about his future until his return. Having persuaded Bonar Law to hold back the position of Postmaster General for Neville in the new Cabinet, he went in person to meet the ship and to give him the news. At a painful meeting over breakfast the next day, Austen told his brother that his acceptance of Bonar Law's offer would mean that they would never speak again, as a result of which Neville told Leo that he could not accept it. But when Leo warned that this might be his last chance of office, Neville returned to Austen, who reluctantly accepted the decision, although he conceded that it 'hurt awfully'. In the same letter to his sister, written after the election, he revealed gleefully that he had 'declined the assistance of Amery'.[83]

On 15 November Leo held his seat at Sparkbrook with a majority of 6,043 over the Liberals. The Conservatives won 344 seats, with Labour recording its best result yet with 138, the Asquithian Liberals 60 and the coalition Liberals 57. Churchill and Leo's brother-in-law Hamar Greenwood were among the coalitionist casualties, but Leo was more concerned by Bonar Law's public statement, at one of his election meetings, that there would be no 'fundamental change in fiscal policy *in the new parliament*', not the promise he had made to Leo that there would be no change '*in the near future*'. Bonar Law was already reneging on his promise to keep open the issue of tariff reform.[84]

The new Cabinet differed greatly from the old one and was got together rather more easily than the former coalition Cabinet members had expected, or indeed hoped. Birkenhead derided the new ministers, claiming to be frightened by the Cabinet's intellectual mediocrity, but most of its members already had ministerial experience as Under-Secretaries, and two were destined to spend much of the next twenty years as Prime Minister. Leo was delighted that four of them, Baldwin, Peel, Hoare and Leo himself were old Harrovians, soon to be joined by a fifth, Ronald McNeill, and in a speech to the Harrow Association Baldwin joked that his would be 'a Government of which Harrow should not be ashamed'.[85] As to Birkenhead's criticism that the Cabinet was composed of 'second-class brains', 'three of them had fellowships of All Souls, six had first-class (or double first) degrees, and Amery had both'.[86]

CHAPTER NINE

In and Out of Office

In December 1922, on succeeding to the post of First Lord of the Admiralty, Leo and the family moved from the relatively modest surroundings of Embankment Gardens to the splendour of Admiralty House in Whitehall, still then a single magnificent town house. Leo thought it 'by far the most attractive of the only three ministerial residences, more roomy and better designed than either 10 or 11 Downing Street'.[1] It was certainly the perfect family house, with large entertainment rooms looking over Horse Guards Parade, spacious and comfortable living quarters and plenty of room for Julian and Jack, when he was at home, to play around the house. For Bryddie, it was the perfect venue to hone her skills as a hostess, and it was at Admiralty House that she first began to throw the political parties for which she became renowned during Leo's ministerial career.

While the classicist in Leo admired the house for its high ceilings, fine furniture and paintings, and magnificent fireplaces, Julian's tastes were understandably more childish. With Jack mostly away at boarding school, he had the top floor almost entirely to himself and made of the most of enjoying the run of the house, with its endless opportunities for games. He played with the suits of armour in the front hall, climbed the old cannon in the courtyard and exchanged mutual salutes with the one-armed doorman. From his nursery window he enjoyed a ringside view of the Trooping of the Colour, and could trade pleasantries with the First Sea Lord, Admiral Beatty, whose own office window was at right angles to his. Visitors, however important, were invariably recruited to play Julian's own version of hide and seek, known as 'bears', when he would hide anywhere in the vast mansion and it would be the job of the likes of Baldwin, Chamberlain, Beatty and T. E. Lawrence to find him.

Leo had met Lawrence 'of Arabia' at dinner with Sir Samuel Hoare, now the Secretary of State for Air. He thought Lawrence a 'strange, elusive creature, unsure of himself, alternating between extreme shyness and dislike of publicity, and a no less keen desire that his achievement should be known', but one who nevertheless demonstrated 'a touch of genius'.[2] Lawrence had recently spent six months in the air force, posing as a private by the name of Ross, but had been forced out by the Chief of the Air Staff, owing to the 'awkwardness of the situation *vis à vis* other ranks and junior officers'.[3] Leo took him briefly under his wing, trying to secure him an equally anonymous job in the navy, but the Sea Lords too feared the resultant publicity and Lawrence eventually again became a private aircraftsman, until his early death on a motorcycle. But for several months he acted as Leo's confidant, his knowledge of the Middle East and his advice on the crisis in Iraq often proving invaluable.

Having initially been disappointed at missing out on the Colonial Office, Leo soon threw himself into his new job at the Admiralty with enthusiasm. He got on well with his new neighbour and Julian's 'bear', Admiral Beatty, and spent his first few months in the job visiting naval dockyards and watching the fleet practise war games, while on exercise off northern Spain. He was not directly involved with the major issues that confronted the new administration, although on one occasion, during the London conference designed to break the deadlock with the French Government over Germany's non-payment of war reparations, he was invited to dinner at Downing Street. His ability to speak Italian secured him a place next to the new Italian Prime Minister, Benito Mussolini, who was still basking in the glory of the successful coup which had recently brought him to power. Leo thoroughly enjoyed the evening, gently egging Mussolini on and, although he thought him 'both a braggart and an actor, like that far greater Italian adventurer, Napoleon', he had also to admit that he was a man of 'real ability and of original constructive ideas'.[4] Curzon, on the other hand, was appalled at Mussolini's very presence, urging Bonar Law to have nothing to do with such 'a thoroughly unscrupulous and dangerous demagogue – plausible in manner but without scruple or truth in conduct'. Bonar Law, however, agreed with Leo. 'Look at that man's eyes,' he said. 'You will hear more of him later.'[5]

Curzon was, at the time, engaged in three months of strenuous negotiations with the Turkish representative Ismet Pasha in Lausanne. The powerful British naval presence at Constantinople gave the Admiralty, and thus Leo, a vested interest in the proceedings at Lausanne, as did the continuation of the British mandate in Iraq and, in particular, the oil region of Mosul. Leo worked hard to persuade his new friend Lord Beaverbrook to desist from the aggressive campaign of 'economy at all costs' which he was running in the *Daily Express*, alongside that of Rothermere in the *Daily Mail*, urging the Government to give up its near-eastern interests and typified by Beaverbrook's exhortation that the British should leave the Middle East, 'bag and baggage *and at once*'.[6] While Curzon was successfully persuading the Turks that the issue of the Iraqi border and the status of Mosul should be left to arbitration by the League of Nations, Leo served on the Cabinet Committee which considered the whole issue. In the course of doing so a mutual admiration developed between the two men for the first time, Leo praising Curzon's diplomatic skills, while the Foreign Secretary suggested that Leo be sent to Iraq as the Government's representative, for he was 'capable and experienced' and his 'keen eye would see much'.[7] In fact Leo did not make the trip, but nearly two years later the task was indeed to fall to him to deal with the closing chapter of the Mosul dispute.

At the Admiralty, Leo's two principal concerns were the development of Singapore as a naval base and the future control of the navy's own air service, the forerunner to the modern-day Fleet Air Arm. He voiced his concern at the possible effects of the Washington Treaty on naval strength, and was alarmed by the ever increasing threat from the Japanese to the entire British Empire east of Suez. A new naval dockyard at Singapore would enable the creation of a more mobile fleet, which could be moved around the problem areas of the world with greater speed. His plans were bitterly opposed, both in Parliament, primarily by Asquith, and by the 'economy at all costs' press. His recurring portrayal as a war-monger was taken up with enthusiasm by his former fellow 'Coefficient' H. G. Wells, who depicted him as a perennial juvenile, 'a pleasantly smiling, short, thickset lad of fifteen', who still enjoyed playing with his battleships and cruisers.[8]

Bonar Law's health continued to give cause for concern. His voice had grown increasingly weak, so much so that he was often unable to speak in the House of Commons, and in April 1923 he left for a Mediterranean cruise with his son Dick Law, intending to take a complete rest. But his deteriorating health forced him to abandon the journey at Genoa, from where he travelled with John Davidson, who had become his Parliamentary Private Secretary having previously worked for Baldwin, to Aix-les-Bains. There they met Rudyard Kipling, who was so shocked by Bonar Law's appearance that he immediately telephoned Beaverbrook to join them, who in turn took the Prime Minister to Paris where he would be met by his doctor. Bonar Law booked into the Hotel Crillon, while Beaverbrook stayed at the Ritz.

It was there that Leo found them, two days later on 18 May, as he travelled through Paris en route to Grindelwald for some spring skiing during the parliamentary Whitsun recess. Hearing that Bonar Law was in Paris, Leo duly went round to the Crillon, intending to have dinner with Davidson before continuing on his skiing holiday on the night train to Basle. But Davidson told him that Bonar Law's 'voice was worse, that his throat gave him pain, and that he had entirely lost heart and wanted to resign at once'. He asked Leo to help him to persuade the Prime Minister to take a cure and, at any rate, to keep going in the job until August. Bonar Law invited Leo to stay for dinner and, although he found him 'looking very seedy and miserable', Leo believed that by the time he left he had persuaded him at least to postpone a final decision until he had seen his specialist in London. Crucially for the debate that was to follow, Leo recorded that, in the course of a lengthy conversation about any possible succession, Bonar Law's support was 'on the whole leaning towards Baldwin, but inclined to doubt the possibility of displacing Curzon against his will'. Believing that they had successfully convinced Bonar Law to soldier on, Leo, the Davidsons and Dick Law went to hear the last part of the *Valkyrie* at the Opéra.[9]

What neither Leo, nor the Davidsons, nor indeed it seems Bonar Law's own son knew, was that the previous day his doctor, Sir Thomas Horder, had arrived in Paris and diagnosed the Prime Minister as suffering from incurable throat cancer. He had six months to live at most. He at first confided the news to Beaverbrook alone, who received it like 'the shock of a thunderbolt'. The man whom Beaverbrook had 'loved and revered was doomed to a lingering painful death, his aims unrealized, his ambitions unfulfilled'.[10] Without knowing it, Leo's persuasive rhetoric at dinner had been meaningless. On 19 May he abandoned his skiing holiday and travelled back to London by the same train as Bonar Law and his entourage. That evening, as the Prime Minister was writing his letter of resignation to the King, Leo went round to see Baldwin, who he found 'quite willing to serve under Curzon, though . . . equally willing, if necessary, to become Prime Minister himself'.[11]

The events of the ensuing forty-eight hours have been described many times and in great detail by historians and biographers alike, and while the finer nuances of the motives and behaviour of the key protagonists may vary, the factual details of Baldwin's succession as Prime Minister are now largely accepted as fact. At a time of desperate illness, compounded by deep depression, Bonar Law, having taken the decision to resign, had no desire to give his advice to the King as to the identity of his successor. The British Ambassador in Paris, Lord Crewe, had already assured him that he was under no obligation to offer an opinion, while his family and Beaverbrook asked repeatedly that he should not be required to do so. Leo's dinner conversation with him in Paris provides just one indication that, while his personal preference was almost certainly for Baldwin, he felt that Curzon's claims could and should not be overridden. That suggestion is re-inforced by Bonar Law's letter to Curzon of 20 May, informing him of his decision to resign; the conversation to that effect he had with Baldwin that same Sunday morning, as reported by Beaverbrook and described by his biographer; and a similar conversation with Lord Salisbury the following morning, subsequently described by the King's Private Secretary, Lord Stamfordham. Salisbury, wrote Stamfordham, thought that Bonar Law believed that 'in this very grave and complex situation he would on the whole be disinclined to pass over Curzon'.[12]

Subsequent conspiracy theories focus on the role played that Sunday by John Davidson and Colonel Ronald Waterhouse, Bonar Law's Principal Private Secretary. Waterhouse was deputed, along with Bonar Law's son-in-law Sir Frederick Sykes, to deliver his letter of resignation to the King at Aldershot. In the course of the audience, during which Sykes reiterated that his father-in-law should not be asked for advice on account of his health, Waterhouse handed over either to the King himself or to Stamfordham, a memorandum which did precisely the opposite. The document, written by John Davidson and purporting to express the personal views of Bonar Law, long lay undiscovered in the Royal Archives, but since its discovery has been widely quoted. It presented a 'cogent, vigorous, well-argued, plea for Baldwin'[13] who, it claimed, was popular on all sides of the House of Commons, was trusted in the City and who shared with Bonar Law the attributes of 'honesty, simplicity and balance'. Curzon, on the other hand, did not 'inspire complete confidence in his colleagues, either as to his judgement or as to his ultimate strength of purpose in a crisis', would be a divisive choice representing as he did a 'section of privileged Conservatism' and, as would become the official reason for his rejection, he sat in the House of Lords.[14]

The effect of the memorandum must have been profound on Stamfordham and the King. Intriguingly, a contemporary reference in the diary of Thomas Jones, the Deputy Cabinet Secretary, suggests that the memorandum had been drawn up the night before 'at No 10 by Amery and Davidson', and had been approved by Bonar Law.[15] However, there is not a single suggestion, in Leo's own diary for the evening of 19 May, in his memoirs, nor indeed in any other account of that period, to corroborate such an accusation. Given Leo's fondness in later life for claiming a substantial role in the choice of Baldwin, he would surely have referred to having played such a part. Davidson later claimed that he had written the memorandum at Stamfordham's request, 'simply expressing the views of the normal backbencher on the Government side'.[16] Although the memorandum may have been factually accurate in its representation of Bonar Law's views, Davidson could hardly be considered a neutral observer given his close friendship with Baldwin and his former role as his Parliamentary Private Secretary, while historians have questioned the role and, in particular, 'the ethics of Sir Ronald Waterhouse'.[17]

After spending Sunday in the country, Leo returned to London on the Monday morning and was visited by his fellow minister Willie Bridgeman. Fearing that Curzon's appointment as Prime Minister was imminent, they set out to see Stamfordham themselves, 'in order to let the King know the views of the rank and file of the Cabinet'. They found him leaving his house in St James's Palace, and walked with him across St James's Park towards Buckingham Palace, 'putting to him all the pros and cons', and telling him what Leo understood to be Bonar Law's views from their dinner in Paris.[18] Until his dying day, Leo appears to have believed that the meeting was crucial. Their views, he thought, had been 'quite new' to Stamfordham, who was 'impressed' by what Leo told him of Bonar Law's opinion. According to Leo, Stamfordham 'promised to submit our arguments to the King'. So convinced was he of the significance of his advice that, thirty years later, Leo still applauded Curzon's magnanimity in continuing thereafter to 'show the same unfailing courtesy' to him, 'though well aware of the part which I had played.'[19] Indeed, he believed that Curzon had always regarded him 'rightly, as responsible for Baldwin being chosen'.[20] In fact Leo had been 'deluded',[21] 'deceived by Stamfordham's invariable courtesy', who later recorded that he had already refused a meeting that day with the two ministers, as he 'felt sure that they would be in favour of Mr Baldwin and their advice would not be helpful'.[22]

Events moved quickly. Stamfordham summoned Balfour from a Norfolk house party and the former Prime Minister advised, whatever the individual merits of the two men, that the Prime Minister should sit in the House of Commons. This apparently coincided with the view of the King, who had never liked Curzon anyway, and Balfour returned to Norfolk to be greeted by a fellow house party guest with the plaintive question, 'And will dear George be chosen?', to which he replied, 'No, dear George will not.'[23] Curzon had spent the weekend at one of his country homes, Montacute in Somerset, where there was no telephone and, having received Bonar Law's letter informing him of his resignation, had waited anxiously to be summoned to London to be crowned as Prime Minister. When he received a telegram from Stamfordham inviting him to travel to London, he naturally assumed that the moment he had waited for all his life had indeed arrived. Curzon's biographers have vividly described the long wait for news, the excited train journey to London, all the time making plans for his premiership and the ultimate disappointment of his crushing meeting with Stamfordham. He had, he lamented, been passed over for 'a man of the utmost insignificance'.[24]

The following day Leo visited Baldwin at Downing Street and, on hearing that the new Prime Minister was having trouble deciding on a Chancellor of the Exchequer, told him 'that I should like to do it and believed I could inaugurate the new imperial and fiscal policy better than anyone else'.[25] The press seemed to agree and for a few days it appeared possible that Leo might achieve his ambition. But Baldwin kept the post for himself until August when Neville Chamberlain was finally appointed, to his own surprise but with Leo's approval. Baldwin's attempts to bring Austen back into the fold were not so successful. He only contacted him once the Cabinet was complete and, in the course of an embarrassing meeting at Chequers, then offered him the Embassy in Washington on the rather tactless grounds that he, Baldwin, was the younger man and now had the premiership firmly in his grasp.

Unfortunately for Leo, the Chequers meeting reinforced a perception already enjoyed by Austen that his return had been blocked by other members of the Cabinet, in particular Leo and Salisbury. While it undoubtedly was true of Salisbury, it was not the case with Leo. On 21 June Leo was invited to propose Chamberlain's health at a dinner, and when he asked Baldwin for guidance as to what he should say, received the rather unhelpful advice from the Prime Minister that he thought Chamberlain the 'stupidest fellow he knew', but that he was nevertheless still keen to bring him back into Government in some way and would 'try and persuade Salisbury to acquiesce'.[26] In fact, Leo proposed Austen's health 'in terms which, as he is not a sneak whatever defects he might have', led Austen to 'doubt the report that he had actively opposed my entry into the Govt'. As they drove back to the Commons together after dinner, Austen confronted Leo and asked him outright whether he had indeed campaigned against his return to the Cabinet, a charge Leo vehemently denied. Chamberlain believed him, thinking that while 'in Salisbury it was natural', he had 'disliked the idea that Amery was at fault'.[27] Neville reported a happy outcome all round. Austen 'had had it out with L Amery and had discovered that he had been misinformed', they had 'shaken hands and were once more friends', which Neville thought a good thing as he had always found Leo 'not only perfectly straight but most helpful and suggestive of ideas'.[28]

▪ ▪ ▪

In August Leo took Bryddie, Jack and his French governess Pipette for a family climbing holiday in Chamonix. Now in his fiftieth year, he feared that he might no longer be up to the challenge of the more arduous mountaineering, but he still managed to scale the Grépon, which he thought 'for sheer all round variety and continuity of gymnastic effort on perfect granite it would be hard to beat',[29] while the eleven-year-old Jack accompanied him on some of the more gentle climbs. From Chamonix the family travelled to Marseilles, stopping for two days to visit Stanley Baldwin, who was taking his usual summer holiday with his wife at Aix-les-Bains. Leo attempted to stiffen Baldwin's protectionist sympathies during leisurely walks in the hills, while Jack befriended the new Prime Minister's bodyguards, who would swim at a discreet distance behind him in the lake. At Marseilles the family joined the Admiralty's yacht, the *Bryony*, and sailed first to Malta for three days, where Leo embarked on a round of naval inspections, before continuing on to the Dardanelles to visit battlefield sites and war cemeteries. The highlight of the trip was Leo's official inspection of the Mediterranean fleet, anchored in the Bosphorus off Constantinople, followed by a round of meetings with British military staff and Turkish leaders. He found time too to introduce

Bryddie and Jack to his own favourite sites in old Stamboul, including the Santa Sophia mosque, the bustling bazaars and the Sultans' palace at Seraglio.

In Aix-les-Bains Leo had sensed that Baldwin's approach to the issue of protection was becoming increasingly positive, and he warmly welcomed Neville Chamberlain's belated appointment as Chancellor of the Exchequer. Chamberlain, for his part, was surprised that the job had not gone to Leo. On the evening of 8 October Baldwin invited Leo to visit him at Downing Street to discuss the economic situation. Having been denied a prominent role in the Imperial Economic Conference, which had just opened in London, Leo had been taking an ever more strident line in his recent speeches, openly advocating protection, and as he crossed Horse Guards Parade from the Admiralty, he fully expected a dressing down from the Prime Minister. He had even mentally prepared himself for the possibility of offering his resignation and fighting his own campaign in the country. But to his astonishment, Baldwin told him that he 'had come to the conclusion that nothing but protection could deal with the unemployment situation' and invited him to Chequers for the weekend to help draw up the new policy. It was, thought Leo, the 'best news I had heard for years'.[30]

That weekend at Chequers, on 13 and 14 October, has been identified by some as the moment when Baldwin arrived at the decision, 'widely condemned at the time as an act of gratuitous folly',[31] to fight the disastrous 'tariff' election of that autumn. Visiting Chequers over a year later, by which time Baldwin was back in power, Thomas Jones found Leo's name in the visitors' book, alongside those of Philip Lloyd-Greame, Neville Chamberlain, William Ormsby-Gore, and the Prime Ministers of Canada and Australia, and could 'readily believe that such a gathering precipitated the disaster which followed'.[32] Leo recorded that the conclusion reached was that Baldwin should 'announce a whole-hearted policy of protection and preference', while, crucially, also giving 'the country a chance of understanding what it is all about by postponing the election until after the middle of January'.[33] Baldwin's subsequent change of heart, and his sudden decision to call an early election, may best be explained by the fact that Lloyd George was shortly due to return from a lecture tour in the United States and Canada, and that Baldwin 'had information that he was going protectionist and had to get in quick'. Rather than welcoming the conversion of a previously self-avowed free-trader, Baldwin was worried that tariff reform was 'the one issue which would pull the party together including the Lloyd George malcontents',[34] and that the former Prime Minister would regain his influence over his old Unionist Coalition partners, and thus over the Conservative Party as a whole. In spite of Baldwin's own admission, years later, that there was 'no truth' in the suggestion that he had been 'pushed by Amery and the cabal',[34] Leo's critics, such as John Davidson, always 'suspected the influence of Amery'[35] in the Prime Minister's decision.

Leo now found himself as part of an inner core of Cabinet members advising Baldwin on the formulation of a policy of protection. On 25 October he accompanied the Prime Minister by train to the Conservative Party Conference at Plymouth, where the new policy was warmly welcomed by the majority of delegates. He also became involved in an attempt to persuade the former Unionist coalitionists, Austen Chamberlain and Birkenhead in particular, back into the fold. Austen wrote to his old friend that he hoped 'with you that the new developments are going to re-unite us', and that he 'promised Baldwin support to the end if he meant business', although he remained 'concerned by the vagueness and uncertainty of touch with which he is opening his campaign'.[36] Leo reassured him that Baldwin was 'set on a definite policy and means to go right through with it',[37] but in the end the negotiations with both men came to nothing. The Prime Minister refused to bow to their demand for immediate Cabinet status, while Jack's godfather Birkenhead was blocked by the 'almost unanimous' objection of the wives of the party's MPs. 'The women of England', reflected Leo, 'want either political or moral respectability (if they can't get both!) and F.E. was too much all round for them.'[38]

While delighted with the party's new protectionist policy, Leo remained deeply apprehensive lest an election should be fought without adequate preparation and favoured a lengthy campaign to educate both the party's own supporters and the wider electorate. Years later he reflected bitterly that 'the two keenest protectionists in the Cabinet

and those most freely criticized for having forced a rush election',
namely Neville Chamberlain and himself, were in fact 'the most anxious to secure more time for educating our public'.[39] But at a Cabinet
meeting on 9 November his proposals were again overruled by the
party managers, who feared a lengthy campaign through the autumn
and winter. Baldwin announced the dissolution on 13 November, and
Leo again drafted his election address, before spending most of the
campaign helping in other constituencies and leaving Bryddie to fight
on alone in Birmingham. As Leo had feared, the Conservatives were
immediately thrown on the defensive over the minutiae of the protection policy, and while he increased his own majority to 7,555, the
party lost 88 seats across the country, reducing their representation in
Parliament to 258. The Labour Party improved from 144 seats to 191,
and the Liberals from 117 to 158, leaving the Conservatives in a
minority against a combined Opposition, including Irish Nationalists,
of 352.

Leo was appalled to hear that Baldwin was thinking of resigning
both the premiership and the party leadership and wrote assuring the
Prime Minister that he 'stood head and shoulders above any man in
the country and that if he now threw up the sponge he would cart all
of us who had pinned our faith to him and would smash the Party'.
He urged Baldwin to meet the House of Commons and 'force the
Liberals to face the necessity of supporting Labour which is bound to
mean their eventual break-up and disappearance as a Party'. And
while Birkenhead and his fellow former coalitionists were still hoping
to create a new, 'anti-socialist' administration under Derby, Austen
Chamberlain, or even Asquith, Leo thought they were 'born idiots' if
they were seriously considering giving support to an Asquith government. 'One of the three parties has to disappear,' thought Leo, 'and
the one that is spiritually dead and has been so for thirty years or more
is the natural victim.'[40]

The following day Leo and Bryddie travelled down to Chequers,
where it was agreed over lunch that Baldwin should stay on, present a
King's Speech to Parliament and force the other parties to decide on
their own course of action. Neville Chamberlain and his wife, Annie,
arrived for tea and Leo left at the end of the day 'feeling we belonged

to a true band of friends', and that even if he had to give up the Admiralty, which he 'had grown so fond of', and Admiralty House, 'which would be a sad heartbreak for Bryddie, that all will turn out right in the end'.[41] He took the family skiing in Pontresina for Christmas, Julian's first visit to the Alps, and returned in time to help complete the drafting of the King's Speech and for the opening of Parliament on 15 January 1924. Two days later the Labour Party moved a motion of no confidence and Asquith made it clear that he would not deprive Labour of their legitimate claim to office. On 21 January Leo made a final, brief intervention in the House, to give details of the Admiralty's proposed cruiser building programme, and as he looked across the despatch box, reminded the Labour leader, Ramsay MacDonald, of their first meeting thirty years earlier in his rooms at Balliol. Leo had 'listened till a late hour of the night', as MacDonald had 'expounded with all the fervour of youth his conviction that the old historical parties . . . had outlived their useful-ness'. Now he was to be congratulated on having given a 'life's work' to achieve his 'daring dream', as the following day he would be 'called to the greatest and most responsible political office in the world'.[42] Sure enough, that night the vote of no confidence in Baldwin's government was carried by a majority of seventy-seven, ushering in the country's first ever Labour Government, under Ramsay MacDonald.

▪ ▪ ▪

The effects of opposition were more immediate and more severe for the Amery family than for most of Leo's Cabinet colleagues, already safely ensconced in their splendid London houses and fine country estates. Having relied on the grace and favour grandeur of Admiralty House for the past year, the family was now homeless. The expectation of a change of government since the election had at least given Leo a chance to prepare, and the search for a new home had already begun. However, his prospects were far from rosy and while most political analysts did not believe that the new Labour Government would survive for long, Leo was facing, for the time being at any rate, a substantial cut in income. He decided, once again, to rent temporary accommodation and, to the dismay of the young Julian, the family was 'driven from the splendours of Admiralty House to dark and dingy apartments in Cadogan Gardens' in Chelsea.[43]

The political goodbyes were equally desultory. The Cabinet met for the last time the morning after the vote of confidence, after which Leo handed in his seals of office to the King, who thanked him generously for his services as First Lord. According to Lord Derby, Leo's demeanour at the Palace was 'very gloomy'.[44] His fellow Admiralty Board members also gave him a warm send-off, although a greater cause of satisfaction was the farewell comment of the office messenger that, whoever might succeed Leo as First Lord, 'we could not beat this one and we could not have a worse one than Mr Winston Churchill'. In fact Leo and Bryddie took great care to invite his successor, Lord Chelmsford, the recently returned Viceroy of India, to dinner at Admiralty House, both to brief him on a number of Admiralty matters and to introduce Lady Chelmsford to her new accommodation. And at a final meeting of ex-Cabinet ministers in Leo's library at Admiralty House, the decision was taken both to create a 'Shadow Cabinet' secretariat, the forerunner of the Conservative Research Department, and that 'we had better invite both Austen and [Sir Robert] Horne back and swallow F.E.'.[45]

Leo was determined that the family's enforced temporary housing arrangement should not last long and while Bryddie did her best to make the house at 7 Cadogan Gardens a comfortable home, carefully unpacking and arranging Leo's now substantial library, he devoted all his spare time to the search for a new house. Properties throughout Mayfair and Belgravia were viewed, considered and discarded. Most, he thought, were thoroughly 'unprepossessing', Eaton Place in its entirety was 'too dull',[46] while a house in Eaton Square was 'decorated in villainous taste'.[47] Eventually, however, the choice was narrowed down to a few houses, all in Eaton Square within walking distance of the homes of both Stanley Baldwin and Neville Chamberlain. By the end of March, the choice had been made and, on 16 June 1924, the family moved into their new home, accompanied by the decorators. Number 112 Eaton Square was to be his and his family's home for the remainder of his life and, indeed, that of his younger son also.

With his family safely settled at last, Leo could turn his attention to strengthening Baldwin's resolve over the issue of protection. But when the Shadow Cabinet met at Baldwin's home on 7 February, it was to Austen Chamberlain that the new Leader of the Opposition turned to lead the policy discussion. Austen seized the chance with enthusiasm, insisting, with Curzon's support, that a promise of protection should be put on hold for the foreseeable future. So delighted was the avowed free-trader Lord Derby at this 'splendid' performance, that he thought an outsider who had happened to stumble in on the meeting 'would have thought that it was Austen Chamberlain and not Baldwin who was leader of the Party'.[48] When his own chance came, Leo spoke for ten minutes, 'very earnestly but I think without any touch of resentment', in support of maintaining the existing policy and embarking on the programme of public education which he had previously suggested. But it soon became clear that 'all but Amery were in agreement' with Austen,[49] and Leo left the meeting resolved to create a non-party organisation outside Parliament to continue the work.

When Baldwin later went out of his way to reiterate that he would not commit the party to support a general tariff unless public opinion clearly demanded it, Leo wrote publicly to his leader emphasising his own difference with party policy and reasserting his support for the full policy of protection. 'I think it is only fair to you and to our other colleagues, as well as to myself,' he wrote, 'that I should make my position clear at the first possible moment.'[50] And when Austen Chamberlain was chosen to speak from the front bench during a debate on preference, Leo was furious, complaining that Austen's behaviour had put him 'in an intolerable position, and I must have the matter cleared up'.[51] Austen in turn blamed Baldwin, while Neville sided with Leo, accusing his brother of being prejudiced because of his 'personal dislike of Amery',[52] and did what he could to support Leo in his attempts to keep the policy alive. Both took evident delight at being summoned by their fellow former ministers, according to Neville, 'to discuss the misdeeds of Amery and myself'.[53]

Leo managed to fall out with the party leadership over another important issue of the day. While he believed that the new Labour Government provided an ideal opportunity to destroy the Liberal Party once and for all, and hoped that some right-wing Liberals, such as his brother-in-law Hamar Greenwood, might defect to the Conservatives, the former coalitionists hoped that by dropping the party's commitment to protection, the appeal would be greater to the Liberal free-traders, of whom the most high profile was Winston Churchill. In February 1924 Churchill put his name forward as an independent 'Constitutionalist' candidate to fight a by-election in the Abbey division of Westminster against the official Conservative candidate, Otto Nicholson. Even Baldwin, while unable to endorse him officially, conceded the importance of 'getting Winston over'.[54] But Leo warned that it was a 'mistake on our part to encourage it and foolishness on his part to want to do it',[55] and while it was not true that he 'had detested Churchill since the Boer War',[56] Leo did consider Churchill's behaviour to be 'true to type', and that he was only too happy to 'desert his Liberal colleagues with the same swift decision that led him to climb over the railings at Pretoria and escape without Haldane and Le Mesurier 25 years ago'.[57]

Neville Chamberlain shared Leo's mistrust of Churchill's motives in his attempt at political rehabilitation to the party he had deserted twenty years earlier, and both were furious when Baldwin imposed a ban on former Cabinet ministers even speaking on behalf of the official Conservative candidate. But after several failed attempts to persuade Baldwin publicly to support the Conservative candidate, Leo decided to do so himself and, on the Saturday before polling day, a few innocuous lines appeared in *The Times*, to the effect that Leo had written a letter of support to Nicholson in which he expressed 'the hope that all who care for the unity of the Conservative party will do all in their power to secure his return by an overwhelming majority'.[58] Baldwin was horrified, admitting that while he was 'responsible technically' for Leo's action, he had still 'never dreamed he would be such a fool'.[59] The problem was further exacerbated by Balfour's subsequent release of an open letter which he had written in support of Churchill, but which he had initially suppressed at Baldwin's request. The release of the two conflicting letters laid bare the obvious divisions within the party and gave the press a field day. However, although Churchill's candidacy very nearly let in the Labour candidate, Nicholson scraped home by just forty-eight votes and Churchill was subsequently elected at Epping Forest that October, rejoining the Conservative Party a year later.

Although Leo missed the responsibilities of ministerial office, he soon came to enjoy the novelty of opposition and was a regular attender and speaker in the House. He resumed his pre-war habit of provoking the Government benches whenever possible and, as the House was preparing to rise late one evening, he intervened during a debate on evictions to complain at the ' "sob stuff" which we have heard in this House'. This proved too much for the Member for Glasgow Gorbals, Geordie Buchanan, who denounced Leo as 'a little swine – a guttersnipe'[60] and, as they both got up to leave the Chamber, blocked his path 'rather excitedly and truculently' with a number of his fellow Clydesiders. Leo enquired if Buchanan had used such unparliamentary language deliberately, 'and as he said "Yes" rather aggressively I discovered that I had hit him a good punch on the jaw'. As a general scuffle threatened to break out, peace was restored by the intervention of other Members, and Leo was able to 'retrieve the remnants of his eyeglasses which had fallen off, before quietly retreating'.[61] He discovered the next day that Buchanan had gone round to the Bath Club, spoiling for a fight, at one o'clock in the morning, but after both had received a mild rebuke from the Speaker about the growing use of abusive language in the Chamber, they apologised to each other on the floor of the House. The episode earned Leo 'a good deal of undeserved popularity with the rank and file of our Party', but also marked the 'beginning of a lasting friendship with one of the best of good fellows, Geordie Buchanan, the victim of my momentary loss of control'.[62]

▪ ▪ ▪

During the summer of 1924 Leo took the family, including Julian for the first time, to Mürren, where he secured the services of one of the most respected guides in the Alps, Josef Pollinger, who had climbed with the leading mountaineers of his day. Although the weather forced them to abandon Mürren, Leo went instead with Pollinger to his home in Zermatt, where they successfully climbed the Dufourspitze, at 15,297 feet the highest peak conquered by Leo during his mountaineering career. He returned from holiday to find a rejuvenated Conservative Opposition and a crumbling Government. MacDonald was coming under increasing political pressure over his controversial attempt, in an effort to please the left wing of his party, to hold out the hand of friendship to Soviet Russia in the form of two Anglo-Russian Treaties. The situation was made worse by the publication of an allegedly seditious article in the *Workers Weekly* by a well-known Communist journalist, J. R. Campbell, in which he urged troops to refuse to attack fellow workers in either the class war or a military one. The resulting furore over the failed proceedings against Campbell, instituted by the Attorney General, but dropped at MacDonald's behest, ended with the Prime Minister rashly lying about his own involvement. His position was further undermined by the subsequent release of papers showing that he had compounded his original lie on the floor of the House and the Conservatives joined forces with the Liberals to defeat the Government, forcing MacDonald to call for an immediate dissolution.

For the third time Leo drafted the party's manifesto, and while it contained no proposal for a general tariff, the passage on protection was left deliberately vague. The young Conservative candidate in Stockton, Harold Macmillan, himself a keen supporter of protection and poised to enter Parliament for the first time, welcomed Leo's skill in leaving 'Baldwin in a fairly free position by adopting those ambiguities so familiar in election manifestos'. But he regretted Baldwin's later promises not to impose a general system of tariffs, once 'Amery's guiding and persistent hand was temporarily removed from him'.[63] The tide was already flowing strongly in the Conservatives' favour when, on top of the existing strength of feeling about the Russian Treaties and the Campbell case, they were given added and unexpected impetus by the notorious affair of the Zinoviev letter. The text of a confidential letter purporting to come from Zinoviev, the President of the Soviet Comintern, urging the British Communist Party to campaign for the ratification of the Russian Treaties and to work for revolution by means of the creation of subversive cells in the armed forces, had fallen into the hands of the Foreign Office. On 24 October, the Foreign Office released the letter with an accompanying note of protest to the Russians and, in spite of MacDonald's mumbled excuses in the latter days of the campaign and protests that the letter was a fake, the damage had already been done.

Leo's majority fell slightly to 5,959, but the Conservatives were returned with 412 MPs, a majority of 211, while the Liberals were reduced to just 40 seats. After his own count, Leo and Bryddie went to support Neville Chamberlain in the neighbouring constituency of Birmingham Ladywood, where, after several recounts, Neville triumphed over the Labour candidate Oswald Mosley by just 77 votes. The long night was made worse for the Amerys and the Chamberlains by the 'offensive attitude of Mosley's supporters',[64] while Leo thought that Mosley, who accused everyone else of cheating, 'behaved very badly' and was a thoroughly 'hairy heeled fellow'.[65]

This time there was never any doubt but that Leo would go to the Colonial Office as Secretary of State. When Austen Chamberlain suggested Churchill for the post, Baldwin 'replied that this was reserved for Amery',[66] in spite of Chamberlain's reservations. Baldwin's only concern had been that Leo might have been 'in bad odour as a "diehard" among the Irish',[67] but Leo assured him that he would build bridges with the Taoiseach, William Cosgrave, as soon as possible. In his favour, the Prime Minister recognised that he was 'a hard worker, keen on the Colonies and on Empire settlement'.[68] Leo welcomed Austen Chamberlain's appointment to the Foreign Office, and even Birkenhead's rehabilitation as Secretary of State for India, but shared the widespread consternation at Churchill's promotion to become Chancellor of the Exchequer. Indeed, so great was the general shock at the appointment that it was said that Churchill himself initially assumed he was being offered the post of Chancellor of the Duchy of Lancaster, and Leo was foremost 'amongst those prominent figures who showed the least delight in welcoming [Churchill] back into the fold'.[69] His mood was further soured when he ran into the new Chancellor looking 'very cheerful', having achieved 'in the shape of the fatted calf what he had failed to get for all his effort while sojourning with his former depraved associates'.[70]

Leo's own appointment, on the other hand, was widely welcomed among his parliamentary colleagues and the press alike, and there was very little that could dampen his enthusiasm for the challenges that now lay ahead. He had at last achieved a significant lifetime goal: a senior Cabinet post, of his own choosing, in a Conservative Government with a large majority.

CHAPTER TEN

Conform or be Kicked

During the last few months of opposition, Bryddie had been busy transforming the new family home at 112 Eaton Square into a house fit for a Cabinet minister. It boasted a 'spacious double drawing-room in an otherwise moderate-sized house'[1], a description which might raise eyebrows today, but provided Leo with what he most needed, a substantial library for his collection of books, and a suitable environment for working and entertaining. There was also enough wall space to hang his by now substantial collection of Persian art, built up over many years but which had, until then, remained in storage. Julian, too, was happy again, enjoying the run of an entire nursery floor with his faithful governess Pipette, who was to play an important role in the upbringing of both Jack and Julian. The orphaned daughter of a deep sea trawler fisherman from Finistère in Brittany, she had been raised in an old-fashioned, strictly Catholic convent and had come to England as a refugee at the beginning of the First World War.

Pipette made a considerable impression on both boys, with her dark flowing hair, so long that she could sit on it, and her endless repertoire of colourful stories about her own upbringing, French history and France's heroes. In spite of that strict upbringing, she was broad-minded and possessed a rebellious streak which greatly appealed to the boys in their different ways. When, at an early age, Jack took to drawing obscene pictures of naked women, which he had disfigured with a male organ and then left lying around the house for Pipette to find, she simply paid no attention and ignored them. Perhaps her greatest attribute, however, was that she spoke not a word of English, with the result that both boys were fluent in French from an early age, frequently annoying other children and their nannies by refusing to communicate with each other in anything other than French when they went out for tea.

Julian's childhood tastes were altogether more academic than his brother's. He was, by and large, a serious child who enjoyed grown-up conversation, whether with Pipette or his parents. History and politics were already his favoured subjects. He debated the finer points of the French Revolution or the ambitions of Napoleon with Pipette, and never missed an opportunity to impress his parents with his linguistic skills, his latest discovery at school or the most recent book he had read. Like his father, he read voraciously from an early age. On one occasion Leo, tiring of his six-year-old son's ceaseless chatter in fluent French, sarcastically asked if he knew the correct French word for 'chatterbox'. 'Rather offended', Julian replied 'gravely that it would be *bavard* or *loquace* but if the chatterbox was repetitive it should be *radoteur*'. Having thus silenced his father, Julian retired to his nursery, 'satisfied that I had got the better of that particular debate'. It was not just his family who found themselves on the receiving end of this precocious self-assuredness. Like Jack before him, he went first to Miss Ironside's school in Kensington, but when the family moved to Eaton Square he too moved to Mr Gladstone's school in nearby Cliveden Place, still a well-known London pre-preparatory school for boys today. The master who taught French there seemed to Julian 'singularly ignorant of the language', and failed to see the humorous side of his young charge's frequent attempts, in front of the rest of the form, to 'put him right both as to syntax and pronunciation'.[2]

With Jack away at West Downs, Julian enjoyed a comparatively solitary childhood at the top of the large house in Eaton Square. And yet, as with his brother before him, his parents made a considerably greater effort to spend time with their young son than did many other similar parents of their generation. Although he had by now reached the peak of his political career, Leo succeeded in striking up a close and loving relationship with Julian from the very outset, striking a balance, whenever possible, between childish play and indulging his son's more adult interests. Julian's schoolwork was a source of pride, whether by identifying every country in the world by its place on the map, or by following up a perfect rendition of the 'Marseillaise' with a lengthy debate on the true Republican instincts of its composer. As he had with Jack before, Leo made regular visits with Julian, sometimes to the zoo, a favourite destination, or to a succession of museums, the Imperial War, Science and Natural History, although the Elgin Marbles at the British Museum made the greatest impression. Trips to the park, and the tiger hunts that took place there, were greatly enhanced by the presence of Leo's ever-present and faithful personal detective, McLeod, who was always willing to play the role of the hunted tiger. And when they ventured further afield, to Paris, the more routine sights such as the Arc de Triomphe and Notre Dame were eclipsed by the Invalides, leading to Julian's life-long fascination with Napoleon.

▪ ▪ ▪

As Jack approached the end of his less than glorious career at West Downs, Leo's mind focused increasingly on his son's future schooling. His own career at Harrow had been enjoyable and distinguished, and he had maintained strong links with the school over the intervening years, speaking frequently when invited to do so at school events. It seemed only natural to him that his eldest son should follow in his footsteps. Bryddie was not so sure. Many of her friends were Old Etonians and had later sent their own sons to Eton. Having been initially introduced to the school by the late Lord Roberts, she had subsequently visited it on a number of occasions over the years and she insisted that Leo now visit Eton for the first time in his life to consider it for Jack. His initial impression was a favourable one. It was a beautiful day, and Leo was 'much impressed by the beauty of Eton but still on the whole inclined to send Jack to Harrow'.[3] A few weeks later, he proudly joked to an audience of Harrow boys that there would be no more 'leakage into the Thames Valley'.[4]

By the summer of 1924, Jack's penultimate year at West Downs,

Leo had become increasingly involved in Harrow school life and friendly with the Head Master, the Reverend Lionel Ford. Bryddie persuaded him to make one last visit to Eton in an effort to change his mind, but he decided that it 'didn't appeal for the boys', and was far more excited by a visit a few days earlier to Harrow with Stanley Baldwin, when the two of them were fêted and flattered by the Head Master, and invited to carve their names in a space especially found for them on the wall of the Old Fourth Form classroom.[5] The following year, Leo's mind was finally made up for him. He was first invited to sit on the school's Rothschild Scholarship Committee, before being formally invited to become a Governor of Harrow, acting as the Masters' Governor, responsible for representing the interests of the teaching body on the Board. He was delighted to learn that he had been proposed for the post by the Head Master and Assistant Masters, and he attended his first Governors' meeting in February 1925. There was now no question of Jack going anywhere other than Harrow.

The following month, he duly went up to Harrow from West Downs to sit the scholarship exam. Although he failed to win an award, he did well enough to pass into the school with some ease and immediately started to take a greater interest in Harrow and, in particular, in his fellow West Downs pupils who would be going on there with him. That summer, the family went as usual to Switzerland, this time to Maloja in the Engadine valley. With Jack growing up fast, and Julian already showing an interest in mountain pursuits, Leo chose Maloja for its suitability as a family venue and its 'exhilarating air and the exquisite beauty of the landscape' as well as the 'widest choice for every taste and capacity'.[6] Jack took little interest in the varied pastimes on offer: tennis, golf, boating, even swimming in the icy lake. But he had, by now, taken to mountaineering and, together with the tutor whom Leo had employed to look after him for the summer, made a number of ascents with his father up Piz Margna and Corvatsch, as well as enjoying some high-altitude summer skiing. The highlight of the holiday for the whole family seems to have been the moment when Leo's detective, the ever-present Sergeant McLeod, fell down a small crevasse and briefly disappeared from view.

In September 1925 Jack followed in his father's footsteps by going to

Harrow, enrolling at the Head Master's House. Ford was approaching the end of his fifteen-year reign as Head Master at the school, initially characterised by his 'reputation for discipline, athleticism, and devout Christian faith'.[7] A radical reformer in his early years, he had presided over dramatic changes to the curriculum and a rapid increase in the number of boys at the school. However, by the mid 1920s he had badly lost control of both the teaching staff and the boys, and when, in 1924, he took his second sabbatical in just a few years, the Governors too began to lose patience.

Jack duly arrived at Harrow at the end of one of the most controversial years in the school's history, the Easter term of 1925 marking 'a low point in Harrow's reputation'. In March 1925 a group of seven senior boys were stopped by the police while travelling by car to visit a nightclub in London. A wave of hostile publicity rained down on the school, not least because one member of the party was the Head of School, and two of the others were monitors. Those three were immediately withdrawn from the school by their parents, while the remaining four left at various times during the following year. Ford now cut 'an increasingly pathetic figure, weighed down by family tragedy (his son had just died suddenly at Eton) and . . . the prospect of professional failure'.[8] He reacted inadequately to the nightclub scandal, attempting to shake off the resulting bad publicity by appearing superficially unconcerned and expressing surprise that there had been 'only seven out that night!'

As it happened, the presence of Harrovians at London nightclubs should hardly have caused a stir. John Betjeman recalled that 'whenever the police raided the Hypocrites Club or the Coconut Club, the '43 or the Blue Lantern there would always be Harrovians there. They used to go down on the Metropolitan Line.'[9] But the publicity surrounding the affair added to the general air of decadence that had spread throughout the school. Betjeman had in fact himself been at Marlborough but, according to his daughter, rather curiously had 'always favoured Harrow . . . partly for its impressive list of old boys, partly for its suburban location and partly for its old school songs'. He would often wear the 'Harrow School straw hat and talked about "my old school" ', and admired the fact that Harrow, at the time, was 'rich and slack'.[10] Certainly the fees were extremely expensive, even in comparison with other schools, although the rising numbers had led to severely cramped conditions in the boarding houses and school rooms.

Those in authority turned a blind eye to the persistent bullying, while the beating of boys by other boys was encouraged. During the decade prior to Jack's arrival, the school had 'witnessed heightened sexual activity',[11] and he arrived at the school during a period when the 'vice was incredible', and there was regular 'ferocious buggery'.[12] To Graham Greene, the school seemed 'to combine extraordinary barbarity in discipline with a really civilised attitude of trust'.[13] Cecil Beaton, who had just left the school and had somehow got away with wearing make-up and, by his own admission, being 'rather effeminate' during his time there, recalled how 'one boy found himself in another's bed on his first night at the school, while another crossed the hill from West Acre to the Grove for the same purpose. The situation varied from house to house. In some there was "open naughtiness", in others very little.'[14] The future playwright Terence Rattigan arrived the term before Jack and was himself 'not averse to a little "naughtiness", as the school always styled it'. One of Rattigan's friends boasted that 'we were all homosexual for a while at Harrow'.[15]

As a new Governor at Harrow, Leo must not only have been aware of the general poor state of discipline at the school at the time, but must indeed have known all of the more gruesome details too. It seems extraordinary that, given Jack's already disturbed childhood, his obvious early sexual awareness, and his well-documented propensity for individualism and rebellion at West Downs, Leo did not even apparently consider that the vices on offer at Harrow would be sorely tempting and the school way of life severely restricting. What makes his decision still more astonishing is the knowledge that the Head Master's House, where Jack was enrolled, was considered to be among the worst offenders. The future writer Giles Playfair, a year or two older than Jack, later described how the Head Master's was going through a particularly shocking period in its history. He recalled that 'vice was prevalent' and that the 'system allowed viciousness to go unchecked'. Indeed he had the scars to prove it, having been stabbed by another boy in his house for daring to write a rather half-hearted socialist tract during the 1924 General Election. His housemaster, C. W. M. Moorsom, initially threatened dire retribution on the perpetrator, only to waive all punishment on being told the nature of Playfair's provocation.[16] In the same Easter term of 1925, with the help of his father, the actor Sir Nigel Playfair, young Giles had also been instrumental in persuading first an incredulous Moorsom, and then a more sympathetic Head Master, of the existence of a widespread homosexual ring in the Head Master's House. Several culprits were expelled, but Leo can scarcely have felt comfortable arriving there with Jack to begin his public school career just a few months later.

During his first term Jack initially settled in well. He was intelligent, bilingual in French thanks to Pipette, and his summer climbing holiday with Leo and the family had ensured that he was reasonably fit. There is no record as to whether his father's elevated status as a Cabinet minister and school Governor either gave Jack an enhanced status himself, or indeed made him a target for the older boys in his house. When Leo first found an excuse to visit the school, only a few weeks after the beginning of term, he found that Jack was 'in best of spirits and obviously thinks Harrow a good deal better fun than West Downs'. His chief interests were reading and, ominously, politics.[17] At the end of his first term he came fifth in the 2nd Fourth Form, the form for new boys, and was duly moved up.[18] But it was not to last for long. In almost no time at all, Jack's behaviour began to deteriorate rapidly, made worse by the stifling atmosphere of public school life as he perceived it.

Leo later recalled that 'from the first' Jack had 'resented the tighter discipline of public school and above all fagging and the authority of senior boys generally'. He enjoyed neither games nor work and, crucially, 'scoffed at house patriotism and all the current schoolboy conventions'.[19] In understanding Jack's almost instant rebellion on arrival at Harrow, it is important to appreciate the overwhelming schoolboy code of conduct by which 'compulsory games were considered equally, if not preferentially, with compulsory lessons'.[20] The future Prime Minister of India, Jawaharlal Nehru, who had been at Harrow a few years earlier, complained of his time there 'how dull most of the English boys were as they could never talk about anything but their games'. He also commented on the 'background of anti-Semitic feeling' at the school, noting that Jewish boys were known as 'the damned Jews',[21] although there is no evidence that Jack was ever subjected to such abuse, nor indeed that his Jewish ancestry was ever discussed or even discovered.

Cyril Norwood, who succeeded Ford as Head Master, was obsessed by the 'Danger from Individualism'. Central to a public school education was his 'ideal of physical fitness and bodily prowess, beauty and the service of beauty, courage and self-sacrifice, honour and honesty . . . knighthood and chivalry'. These could only be achieved by a greater reliance upon 'games and open-air prowess, where these involve corporate effort'.[22] Jack was particularly unimpressed by the overt militarism of the school and the ensuing compulsory attendance at Corps; 'slacking at Corps' was an all-embracing charge levelled at 'so-called aesthetes, punishable by inevitable beating'.[23] In 1913 Arnold Lunn, the inventor of the modern skiing slalom, had published his novel *The Harrovians*, a damning critique of life at the school, which had aroused widespread outrage, especially among old boys. 'Conform or be kicked' was his school motto, and he described in detail the tedium and violence of compulsory house football, the anti-Semitism and the endless cycle of bullying, usually by those who were good at games, which led in turn to an 'aristocracy of muscle' and 'muscleworship'.[24] Lunn's father, Sir Henry Lunn, had opened up large parts of Switzerland to English tourists and was a close friend of Leo's. It was he who had first introduced Leo to the delights of skiing and with whom the family stayed from time to time in Mürren. It is inconceivable that Leo would not have read *The Harrovians* and not paused for a moment to consider whether Harrow was indeed the right school for Jack.

While he may not have enjoyed the more regimented aspects of school sport, Jack had, by now, become an accomplished skier, and he won his first boys' race during the Christmas holidays, when the family again returned to Pontresina in the Alps. Shortly after going back to Harrow the following term he contracted measles and, after a spell in the school sanatorium, he was allowed home for a month to recuperate. The break was, in many ways, disastrous. He relished, in common with any boy of his age, not only the opportunity of being able to miss lessons, but also the physical absence from boarding school too. When the moment came to return he became desperately homesick, explaining to Leo that what he hated most about school was 'the having to do something continuously, whether it is work or play'. As it transpired, 'footer in the rain' was, for Jack, 'a very real grievance'.[25] It was at this time, as he approached his fourteenth birthday, that he also began to develop what was to be a lifetime's obsession with cars and motor cycles. During the Christmas holidays he pestered Leo, at first to buy him a motor car or, when that seemed a hopeless cause, even a scooter of some kind. Leo stood firm on this occasion, but it was a theme to which Jack would return.

The Head Master's House had by now been taken over by a new housemaster, A. P. Boissier, in whose appointment as Head Master, fourteen years later, Leo was destined to play a controversial role as the Masters' Governor. Boissier began to take an increasing interest in Jack's behaviour. He noted that 'in a peculiar way', Jack 'sought notoriety and limelight', but in the absence of any skill at the recognised means of acquiring it, such as sport, he tried instead to do so 'by holding "ultra" views on many subjects, and expressing them openly on every occasion'. What was worse, in an obvious echo of his time at West Downs, he 'seemed to revel in the fact that so many of his companions thought him mad'. He was increasingly in trouble with both masters and his fellow pupils because, in a criticism that was by now increasingly familiar, he believed that 'rules and regulations did not exist'. The reaction to him of masters and boys alike simply 'gave him a still further "jaundiced" outlook on life and added considerably to his abnormality'.[26]

Leo, too, was becoming increasingly concerned, not least because after just a few months Jack was already expressing a desire to leave. At the conclusion of a visit to Harrow with Bryddie, Leo wearily conceded that he had found Jack 'still hankering very much after the idea of private tuition at home, with late dinner every night, plenty of opportunities for the cinema and no doubt a motor cycle to buzz about on in between'.[27] He had again stood firm against the proposal to acquire a motor cycle but, within a few months, he had given in and Jack was indeed happily 'buzzing' around London during the holidays, at the age of just fourteen, on his very own scooter. In some desperation, Leo cornered the Head Master at a reception at the House of Commons, to ask what more could be done to improve Jack's enjoyment of Harrow. The problem, thought Norwood, was that his 'general outlook was much beyond his years'. To be blunt, 'his contemporaries were not interesting enough'.[28] Jack's main problem was that he was quite incapable of being what was, in Harrovian parlance, more important than anything else, namely a 'useful member of the House'.

By the spring of 1926 there had been a further marked deterioration in Jack's general behaviour and, in particular, his behaviour towards others. He began to indulge in petty stealing from local shops and from other boys. Once again, his indifference to public opinion or the moral judgements of others was palpable. He hired a private room of his own in Harrow, where he and one or two other boys would go to drink and smoke whenever they could find the time to get away. He began to emulate the previous year's Head Boy, and took to climbing out of his house at night to visit night clubs in London. In particular, he regularly frequented Mrs Meyrick's club in the West End, for whom he soon 'constituted himself as a sort of tout', earning commission by encouraging as many of his older, rich friends as he could to do likewise. Leo was upset that in 'a curious sort of way he seemed to think that a fine position'.[29]

In June Leo visited the school with his fellow old Harrovian, the Prime Minister, Stanley Baldwin, for the consecration of the Harrow War Memorial. He found that Jack's habitual misbehaviour had been temporarily interrupted for a few weeks by another visit to the sanatorium, this time with a bout of mumps. But it was not long before Jack returned to his more customary way of life, and on 4 July 1926 he recorded what is, perhaps surprisingly, his only entry in the Head Master's notorious Punishment Book at Harrow. For 'shop stealing, moral breakdown and unsatisfactory work' he and an older boy were 'severely warned' by Boissier. Jack might well have considered himself lucky. A few days earlier, another boy had been given a beating by Norwood for the high crime of 'shiftiness'.[30]

A few days later, Leo seized the opportunity of a day out at the annual cricket match against Eton at Lord's to have a 'good talk with Jack about school life'.[31] But, whatever he said, it seems to have had little effect. When, two weeks later, he collected Jack from school at the end of term, he found him 'looking more disreputable than it is possible to imagine', with a 'large piece bitten out of a broken down hat', and wearing 'shoes that a tramp might have worn'. He also noticed a marked 'absence of washing' and thought his son looked 'exactly like the son of the gentleman in the Pears Soap advertisement'.[32]

For the summer holiday of 1926, the family returned again to St Moritz. It was to be a summer of initiation for Jack. The first few days were spent relaxing and walking by the lake, while Leo, Jack and Bryddie even attempted a three-ball at golf for the first time. Jack's golf seems to have come on well, while Leo, who had always considered golf to be a dreary pursuit, was hardly able to complete a hole in single figures. On 16 and 17 August, Leo took Jack 'to do his first big mountain', setting off at 3 a.m. after a night spent in the overcrowded base camp hut with a group of German tourists. The climb was 'a good test of beginner's nerve', but Jack 'never turned a hair and showed no sign of undue fatigue'. Tired out on the way down, Leo and Jack allowed their guide to tow them down the mountain for much of the descent, sliding hundreds of feet at a time in a sitting position.[33]

For the rest of the holiday, while his father left for a week's more professional climbing at Zermatt with Josef Pollinger, Jack was left largely to his own devices, his brother Julian still being in the care of the long-suffering Pipette. When he returned to England he was able to boast, both to his school friends and, extraordinarily, to his family, that while in St Moritz he had met and succeeded in seducing a young Dutch girl, thus losing his virginity at the age of fourteen. And by the time the family returned to the Alps at Christmas, Jack had clearly outgrown the cosy hotel life of skiing, skating and fancy dress parties. The Schloss Hotel in Pontresina, where the family had always stayed, had become 'too cosmopolitan and unsuitable for Jack'. To Leo's intense embarrassment, while Jack's skiing improved still further, so too his behaviour deteriorated. He 'spent too much time in the hotel', and his deliberate attempts to annoy their fellow guests, many of whom were old friends of Leo's, eventually led to the whole family moving to another hotel.[34]

As the beginning of the new term approached, Jack once again became increasingly reluctant to return to Harrow. On the morning of 25 January 1927, Bryddie got up early and discovered to her horror that he had 'decamped' during the night. He had taken a small suitcase, and both Leo's wallet and his service revolver, and had then broken into the pantry at Eaton Square from where he had made his escape by means of a skylight. A scribbled note revealed that his destination was Lausanne in Switzerland, where he intended to 'make his career' as a garage mechanic. His obsession with cars remained as strong as ever, and he had recently learnt to drive while spending a few days on holiday with Pipette in Brittany, en route from the family holiday in the Alps. Leo thought it more likely that Brittany was his true destination, and Bryddie and the loyal Sergeant McLeod were despatched to Southampton in pursuit while Leo went straight down to Harrow to see Norwood.

The Head Master was remarkably understanding, advising against Jack's return to Harrow in the short term and suggesting that a tutor at home would be better for both his health and academic progress. However, he said that he would be happy to have Jack back at Harrow in due course, when he could resume his school career in the normal way. Meanwhile, in Southampton, the resourceful McLeod, with a little local help, had tracked Jack's suitcase down to a local hotel and discovered that the runaway was in fact whiling away his time at the cinema. When Jack emerged later that evening, McLeod 'put his arm round his neck and gently conveyed to him that the escapade was over'. Jack was relieved and 'rather surprised that he did not get another caning'.[35] In spite of the agreement that he should remain at home for the time being, he did, however, have to return briefly to Harrow for a showdown with the Head Master. Norwood pointed out, reasonably enough, that Jack was 'letting his parents down badly and sacrificing all the splendid future that might have been his'. But Jack remained unimpressed. 'In the position of a garage hand', he attempted to reassure his Head Master, 'he would be his own master, would not be driven, and need not do more than he liked.' He was not really worried about either his parents or his prospects, indeed 'he did not seem to feel that any consideration was due to his father or to his mother'.[36]

At the same time his parents took Jack to see Dr Maurice Wright, a renowned psychiatrist, for an examination. Nearly twenty years later, and even in the absence of his contemporary notes, Dr Wright remembered the hour's consultation well. He had come to the firm conviction that Jack had 'no moral sense of right and wrong', an incurable condition he believed, and also 'no sense of remorse or shame' and 'no ambition to make a career for himself'. He strongly urged Leo and Bryddie to get Jack a tutor, both 'for his own protection and for the protection of the public in general'.[37] One can only imagine the feelings that such a report must have aroused in the minds of his loving, and hitherto trusting, parents. Boissier too looked back on his brief time as Jack's housemaster with similar emotions. He had been a schoolmaster at Harrow for almost twenty-four years, and remembered Jack as 'without doubt, the most difficult boy I have ever tried to manage'. Boissier too found him 'abnormal' in the sense that he was 'unable to distinguish right from wrong' and that he believed that 'every rule and regulation that bound others did not apply to him'.[38]

The new tutor engaged by Leo to look after Jack was Leander Jameson, 'a nice youth' who, after a few days, 'Jack had already taken to quite keenly'.[39] However, Jack's initial enthusiasm for his new tutor was, at first, far from mutual. On only the second day of Jameson's employment, they were travelling together on a London bus, when Jack took out a packet of cigarettes and began to smoke. His tutor politely pointed out that this was against both his and his father's wishes and, when Jack refused to put the cigarette out, Jameson took it from his mouth and threw it out of the window. Jack calmly got off the bus, and made for the nearest policeman, brazenly informing Jameson that he planned to report him for indecent assault. But when he reached the policeman he merely asked him the time, and then behaved for the rest of the day as if nothing had happened.

Jameson's attempt to organise riding lessons for Jack also failed abysmally, when he had to be removed from the riding school after just three lessons because he refused to be taught and abused the instructors, using obscene language, in front of the other children. Leo's initial plan had been to rent a house in a peaceful setting at Wentworth, where Jameson could go to stay with Jack to continue with his studies, but the arrangement fell through. Instead they were packed off to stay in the more familiar surroundings of Jack's uncle and aunt, Simon and Sadie Rodney, at their home at Bury Green in Hertfordshire. By and large the arrangement was a success. Although Jack's academic work was far from accomplished, Jameson was largely satisfied with Jack's behaviour at Bury Green and Leo even dared to hope that he was 'beginning to understand a little how silly he has been'.[40] Like others before him, Jameson noticed Jack's lack of physical courage and his dislike of any form of physical exercise, especially in the winter. His incompetence when he did attempt one of the physical activities that Jameson organised for him would usually lead to a childish and extreme loss of temper. On one such occasion, Jack's smouldering resentment became so violent that he drew a knife and attacked his tutor. Jameson swiftly disarmed him and gave him a good caning, after which Jack behaved more respectfully. What Jameson found most astonishing was that in spite of the unpredictability of Jack's behaviour and the frequent arguments between them, Jack still managed to keep their relationship on an entirely friendly footing.

By the spring, Leo was urging Norwood to accept Jack back to Harrow. But Jameson felt that he needed more time with his charge and asked if he might stay on and give up the alternative job which Leo had already found for him in South Africa. For a while Leo considered the idea of sending Jack to stay with his old friend George Lloyd and his wife in Cairo, but he wisely decided that the distractions of Egypt, even if he were staying with the British High Commissioner, would be too great for Jack. In July Leo and Bryddie embarked on their world tour of the Dominions and Jameson was left in sole charge. By now, at the age of fifteen, Jack had amazingly managed to secure from his father his first car, a Morgan two-seater. During the summer he drove Jameson to Scotland for a motoring holiday, giving his tutor the opportunity to observe at first hand his impatience when obstructed in any way on the road. 'For a boy of fifteen', observed Jameson, 'he was fantastically arrogant and rude to strangers.' That autumn they went to Dartmoor, a day out with the South Devon hunt ending with Jack escaping to the local pub, getting 'drunk and extremely abusive', before bolting on his horse down a tarmac road.[41] Jameson had two major complaints about travel with Jack. One was his obsession with sleeping with the windows firmly shut, rendering the bedroom hermetically sealed. And as he insisted on being accompanied to bed by his large Irish setter, the smell was often overpowering, although in fairness this was a habit almost certainly acquired in earlier childhood from Pipette, who had a phobia about fresh air. Jack's other preoccupation, even when sent on the simplest errand, was to 'get in touch with a girl, usually of the least desirable type'.[42]

Leo and Bryddie were away on their Dominions tour for seven months. When they returned in February 1928, Jack seemed genuinely pleased to see them, questioning them closely about the trip and giving the impression that he wanted to make a completely fresh start. It was eventually agreed that he should return to Harrow the following term, for a year at the very least, and that, if he was successful in passing his exams, his father would allow him to spend some time in France before going up to Oxford. It was also agreed with Norwood and Boissier that it was best that he should not return to the Head Master's, but should go instead to one of Harrow's so-called 'small houses', housing just two or three boys at a time, in this instance to one run by W. H. Barrett, the senior science master.

Before returning to Harrow, he went on one last trip with Jameson, this time to Norway, marred only by his theft of a coat from a fellow guest in their hotel. Jack duly sold the coat on, and used the proceeds to buy a present for the hotel receptionist, showing no remorse whatsoever when his crime was discovered. The hapless Jameson, at last coming to the end of his time in charge, managed to smooth matters over, but noted once again that 'at no time did John have any sense of guilt over the incident'.[43] At the end of April Jack returned to Harrow, enthusiastic to 'concentrate on the role of the model schoolboy', but nervous at the reception he was likely to receive from masters and boys alike.[44] He was particularly looking forward to playing cricket, doing some acting and attempting to ingratiate himself with the teaching staff.

Less than a month had passed before bad news reached home. While watching a cricket match from a distance, Boissier had noticed 'two boys walking a bye instead of running it', thus committing that cardinal Harrow offence of 'deliberately slacking at cricket'. Rather than just letting the incident pass, especially given Jack's recent history, Boissier made a point of reporting it to the school captain of cricket, Lindsey, in the certain knowledge that retribution would be dire. The next morning, Jack was hauled before this embodiment of schoolboy heroism, known at Harrow as 'Bloods', and, in spite of his protestations that the accusation was unjust, warned that he would inevitably be beaten. Matters were made worse still by his house cricket captain, 'a boy called Nigel Jones', who told him with great glee that he was 'going to get it really hot'.[45] At this moment, perhaps not altogether unsurprisingly, his 'terror of physical discomfort and pain overcame him'.[46] Quite simply, he had no intention of loitering around at school to find out what might happen next. That night he waited up until the rest of the school was soundly asleep, quietly let himself out of the house and made his way back to London, arriving at Eaton Square early the next morning by bus.

His housemaster, Barrett, came to London immediately. Jack's escape appeared to have been entirely unplanned; he was still in his school clothes and had hidden his school boater under a hedge. But Barrett had little sympathy for Jack who was an 'extremely unusual type of boy', with a 'complete lack of mental balance', and was 'entirely unsuited to the discipline of school life.' He had '*never* had to deal with anyone just like him' during his entire teaching career.[47] Above all, he told Bryddie, the Head Master didn't want him back. But Leo was not to be so easily defeated. Visiting Norwood, he acted as defence counsel for Jack, putting his own side of the story and forcing the Head Master to concede that he had run away in a moment of panic rather than in deliberate defiance of the school rules. A compromise could be reached. Jack could indeed return to school, 'save only for a slight swiping from Lindsey to preserve the authority of the cricket captain'. Not surprisingly, Jack was 'very upset'[48] at this attempt to spare Lindsey's reputation among his fellow 'aristocrats of muscle', and not remotely convinced by the Head Master's assurance that the caning would be 'purely formal'. Jack accompanied Leo down to Harrow that evening to see Barrett, but the school absolutely refused to back down on the issue of the caning. By now, Leo's sympathies were well and truly with his son, and he assured him that he would not compel him to return to Harrow. Indeed, Jack's 'state of mind at the idea of going back was such that we could only have taken him by force'.[49]

So ended Jack's ill-fated career at Harrow, with a whimper rather than a bang. Norwood and Barrett were duly informed and Jack left quietly for the last time. Many years later at the end of Jack's life, Boissier, who was to go on to become one of only two Head Masters at Harrow appointed from within the school, vehemently regretted that his efforts with Jack had been to 'no avail'. Jack's failure to run a crucial bye and his own reaction were, by now, long forgotten. Boissier had, he maintained, 'tried every means in his power' to help Jack and, in the intervening years, had 'often felt guilty that I did not do more for him'. He had, unfortunately, been 'beaten by a unique character'.[50]

The year that followed proved to be an unsettled time of private tutors and travel for Jack. He spent the summer in London, enjoying his new-found freedom at sixteen, making new friends and accompanying his mother to various balls and other social events of the summer 'season'. A new tutor, Kingsley Walton, was employed to prepare him for his Oxford Responsions exams. Remarkably, after their first meeting, Walton was congratulating himself that he 'could not have found a more charming, gentlemanly or accommodating boy'. Walton's qualifications at Latin and Greek were, by his own admission, 'nil', but he was the master of Jack at maths and his pupil's natural ability at languages was promising. But on the very first evening they were out together, with no warning, Jack suddenly 'turned into a West End hotel and . . . ordered drinks in the lounge'. Walton insisted that they leave immediately and could only control Jack by threatening, as he did throughout his time at Eaton Square, that he would leave if his pupil did not do as he was told. This seems to have always had the desired effect whenever Jack, 'against his own interests', attempted to 'upset the apple cart'.[51]

In August 1928 the two of them went to Iceland for a month together, the plan being to enjoy the outdoor life, sleeping in a tent and catching fresh fish for their food. En route to catch the boat for Reykjavik, they spent a night in Edinburgh staying with an old friend of Walton's. Among their luggage for the camping trip was a portable gramophone and a case of a dozen records, only three of which really mattered to Jack, 'Old Man River', 'Tea for Two' and 'I'm a Lucky Boy'. These were his pride and joy, and he guarded them zealously, carrying them himself to ensure that they could not be broken by any careless loading of their luggage. On the way to the docks by taxi, 'full of excitement at our immediate prospects', Jack, with no warning and 'apropos of absolutely nothing', got up, put the records on the seat and 'jumped up and down and smashed them'. Fortunately there was time for the taxi to stop at a record shop in Leith and the records were duly replaced. Jack, 'without one word or one flicker of an eyelash' about his actions, once again insisted on carrying them himself to ensure that they would not be broken by a careless porter.[52]

The ensuing camping holiday was not altogether a success. Although Jack showed considerable initial enthusiasm for sleeping under the stars, ostentatiously refusing the offer of more comfortable accommodation, and went out of his way at first to humour Walton, 'counting on a good report' from his tutor to his father, he was unable to hold out for long. Once again, with no warning, 'as if he had a blackout', he disappeared from the camp. For a week he enjoyed the bright lights of Reykjavik, Walton keeping watch from a discreet distance, before returning 'with all his usual charm as if nothing whatsoever had happened'.[53]

By the end of 1928, Leo decided that Jack, with a brief stint at a London crammer now under his belt, would never pass his Oxford exams while distracted by the bright lights of London. He was sent instead to Château d'Oex, a Swiss school for English boys run by a Mr King. In the meantime Leo paid Alexander Lindsay, the Master of Balliol, a discreet visit to sound out Jack's likely prospects there. To his intense disappointment, Lindsay had clearly received word about Jack from an unknown source, and told Leo that while he might get in to Oxford, 'maybe it would not be Balliol'.[54] Meanwhile in Switzerland, while Jack's prowess at skiing continued to increase rapidly, at Easter 1929 Mr King politely invited Leo to come over and take Jack away. Unfortunately, he 'didn't quite fit in'. Thankfully there had been 'no serious crimes but a certain general free and easiness which had upset the respectable British community.'[55] Jack had found the other boys dull beyond belief, and his 'bar loafing and his approaches to girls were calculated to give the school a bad name'.[56] With a general election on the horizon at home, Leo collected Jack and took him on to Zermatt, where he left him for a few weeks in the care of his ever dependable old friend and guide Josef Pollinger. Leo returned to London to search for a new tutor, finding a suitable candidate in the person of one G. C. Nock, a young and temporarily unemployed schoolmaster.

At the end of April, Nock set off for Switzerland with Jack, this time to spend the three summer months on the shores of Lake Geneva, although from the first he seems to 'have been utterly overawed' by his charge's 'baleful egoism'. The relationship appears to have been a disaster. His recollection of his time with Jack reads as one long, formal indictment. Jack 'fancied himself as the lone wolf' among a society made up of sheep, and 'openly wanted to reach great heights by dishonest means'. He had no sense of obligation, even to 'a gangster's code' and had 'all sorts of cunning schemes for raising money'. However, in one perceptive observation, Nock also recognised that Jack's behaviour was largely about gaining his parents' attention. Jack thought Leo a 'fool not to have been dishonest and taken advantage of his position', and that it was 'absurd that his father was comparatively poor'. Most intriguingly, Nock made reference, the only one of its kind, to Jack's attempts to corrupt Julian, trying to 'seduce his brother to misbehaviour', although the only evidence for this was the gift of a roulette wheel, accompanied by some lessons as to how to use it. Jack got his own back by insisting on climbing the Jungfrau, the mountain so beloved by his father, in his bedroom slippers.

When Jack decided that it was time to return home, he simply set off for Boulogne on his own, and eventually fetched up at Eaton Square having lost his passport and car registration documents, and having spent two days in getting to London from Dover. Unfortunately for Nock, Jack returned from Switzerland with a complaint that was to plague him for many years. He had contracted syphilis. Nock already viewed Jack's sexual behaviour as 'precocious',[57] but was now even more concerned at Jack's claim, admittedly unproven, that he had been 'playing the passive role in a homosexual relationship and said it was a good way to make money.'[58] Leo and Bryddie were appalled, but sensible enough to send Jack to a leading specialist, Dr Osmond, who treated him, on and off, for the next nine years. Their pain was intensified by Jack's apparent indifference to having caught this terrible disease and to being treated for it, finding it difficult to persuade him to continue with the course of treatment. In July Jack went to Oxford to sit his Responsions exams and, amazingly, succeeded in passing. However, his father's pleasure and pride were soon dashed by his declaration that he would not be taking up his place there after all. Instead, he had decided to make his name in the film business. His academic career, such as it had been, was now well and truly at an end.

CHAPTER ELEVEN

Father of the Commonwealth

Leo, meanwhile, had set about his work at the Colonial Office with enthusiasm. The enormous room occupied by his predecessors was very much as it had been left by his hero Joseph Chamberlain. The minister enjoyed the advantage of sitting behind a large desk, with the light behind him and looking across at his visitor in an armchair which was just slightly lower than his own. The carpet in front of his desk was threadbare, supposedly worn out 'by the shuffling feet of nervous but persistent applicants for promotion or honours'.[1] At the far end of the room, a large walnut map case and accompanying globe spelled out the extent of the Empire still governed from that very room while, curiously, a portrait of George Washington beside the fireplace reminded Lord North's successors of potential pitfalls.

In accepting the position, Leo had insisted that he should be allowed to carry out his long-advocated reform of the Colonial Office, namely that the department should be divided into two. A new, entirely separate office, with its own civil servants and ministers, would take on responsibility for the Dominions, a reorganisation which had long been requested by the Dominion Governments themselves, as recognition that their relationship with the mother country was one of diplomatic equality, as opposed to the administrative dependence of the Colonies. Leo quickly won the approval of Baldwin, although the new Chancellor of the Exchequer, himself a former Colonial

Secretary, was not so happy. Churchill, under pressure from his Treasury officials to save on additional salaries, 'was not at all sympathetic' and told Leo that in his day the 'CO was lightly worked and that he had never had any difficulty doing it all'. Leo resisted the temptation to reply that, in his opinion, Churchill 'had largely neglected the work' anyway,[2] but he won the argument, and in July 1925 he assumed the joint role of Secretary of State for the Dominions and Colonies.

Leo played a peripheral role in the negotiations that led, in October 1925, to the signing of the Locarno Treaties. Austen Chamberlain had been 'less than enthusiastic about Amery's nomination to the Colonial Office', and Leo's dogged representation of the views of the Dominion Governments was to endear him still less to the new Foreign Secretary as the months passed. MacDonald's outgoing government had initially given its approval to the 1924 Geneva Protocol, under which security for France was to be automatically guaranteed by the League of Nations. But Leo, together with Churchill and Birkenhead, believed that the League's principal function should be one of conciliation rather than military coercion and he vigorously opposed the notion that there should be an open-ended commitment to join a conflict in defence of France. As Chamberlain conducted negotiations with Aristide Briand, the Prime Minister of France, and Gustav Stresemann, the Chancellor of Germany, Leo once again found himself cast in the role of troublemaker, a 'formidable Cabinet critic' of Austen,[3] giving voice to the fears of the Dominions, who were unhappy at the prospect of being drawn into any future European dispute.

After one Cabinet meeting in March 1925, the Permanent Under-Secretary at the Foreign Office, Sir Eyre Crowe, wrote to Chamberlain in Geneva that he had never heard 'such utter rubbish as Mr Amery poured forth'.[4] And when the Duke of Portland, who was responsible for organising travel arrangements for the British delegation to Geneva, placed Chamberlain and Leo in the same train compartment in the expectation that 'they would be happy gossiping together', he received a 'sharp message that Amery was to be placed elsewhere'.[5] When the pact was finally agreed by the Cabinet, Maurice Hankey recorded that Leo 'accepts it, only because he is certain the French won't take it – a bad reason'.[6] And, at the moment of Chamberlain's greatest diplomatic triumph at Locarno in October, it is doubtful that he agreed with Leo's private claim to 'a very real share in the paternity of Locarno'.[7] However, Leo made up for earlier criticism by offering Chamberlain 'a thousand congratulations' and, in an eerie pre-echo of Austen's brother on his return from Munich in 1938, declared that he had brought back 'Peace with honour all round'.[8]

Leo's own departmental concerns throughout 1925 were focused principally on the Middle East. The situation in Egypt had been deteriorating for several years and Leo was soon required to deal with the aftermath of the assassination of Sir Lee Stack, the commander of the Egyptian army, and the ensuing overreaction of the British High Commissioner, Lord Allenby, which was to cost him his job later that year. Equally pressing was the issue of Colonial Office responsibility for administering the League of Nations' 'mandated' territories, in particular Palestine and Iraq. The Treaty of Lausanne had referred Turkey's claim to the fertile and oil-rich Mosul province of Iraq to the Council of the League of Nations, who had in turn sent a Commission of Inquiry to Iraq in early 1925. Leo decided to visit Iraq for himself, accompanied by Sir Samuel Hoare, the Secretary of State for Air, and they flew first to Amman where they were warmly welcomed by the Emir, later King Abdullah of Jordan, cementing a friendship that was to endure for more than twenty-five years until Abdullah's assassination in 1951.

Leo arrived in Baghdad amid great publicity, soon after the League of Nations inspectors had left, and was encouraged to hear that the Commission seemed ready to recommend the retention of Mosul by Iraq, provided that Britain would guarantee to maintain the protection of Iraq. For four days the two Cabinet ministers held meetings in Baghdad with King Faisal, Iraqi government ministers and their predominantly British advisers, including Gertrude Bell, a seasoned traveller and experienced archaeologist, well known throughout the Arab world. Having been recruited as a major by British Intelligence during the First World War, she had gone on to serve successive High Commissioners in Baghdad and to become a de facto kingmaker in the new state of Iraq, and close confidante of King Faisal. Leo and Bell shared a mutual admiration, based on a shared interest in Middle Eastern affairs and a love of mountaineering. Bell's 'fifty-seven hours' ascent of the Finsteraarhorn' was, according to Leo, 'one of the supreme stories of Alpine adventure',[9] while Bell admired Leo's 'sense of great sympathy and consideration' and 'earnest desire to do the best thing possible', in spite of his being 'rather overweighted with brains', with an 'encyclopaedic' knowledge.[10]

With his business concluded, Leo took a brief sightseeing tour of the country, visiting Mosul itself, the ancient sites at Nineveh and Hatra, and military installations at Kirkuk and Basra. On the way home he stopped off for a few days in Jerusalem to stay with the High Commissioner, Sir Herbert Samuel. The level of British military strength in Palestine, and the maintenance of internal order there, was a controversial topic. With Churchill calling for increased efficiency savings, Palestine was policed on a limited budget and Leo found himself treading a fine, but apparently successful, line between the wishes of the Jewish and Arab populations. He told local Jewish leaders that he recognised the 'necessity of making special provision to enable the Jews of Palestine to provide for their cultural and social needs', but emphasised too that the Jewish 'National Home' had to learn to 'exist in Palestine side by side with an Arab "National Home", the whole forming a Palestinian national entity'.[11] Such enlightened views may seem strange given his Jewish ancestry, although he still publicly expressed his admiration for the Jewish farmer settlers he met and their achievement in cultivating a previously barren landscape. As if to provide deliberate balance, he held meetings too with Arab leaders, to whom he also provided assurances that he was sympathetic to their cause, to the accompanying dismay of the Jewish leadership.

Leo and Hoare flew home by way of Rome, where Leo found Mussolini suffering from ulcers, and looking 'dreadfully ill . . . and altogether changed from the rather bombastic theatrical person' he had sat next to at Downing Street two years before. This time he thought Mussolini to be 'quiet, humorous, wise and very attractive'.[12] Back in London, he awaited the report of the League of Nations' Commission, which in July recommended that Mosul province should indeed be incorporated into Iraq, but only on condition that

British mandate control continued for another twenty-five years. In September Leo introduced the British case before the Council of the League in Geneva, believing that he 'made a very great impression on the Council', and claiming that his performance had been described to him as the 'best and clearest exposition of a case that had ever been put before them'.[13] But the decision was referred back, yet again, to a further sub-committee and at home Leo was forced to endure a sustained attack from the Beaverbrook and Rothermere newspapers, who intensified their calls for a British withdrawal from the Middle East. 'For weeks on end,' he recalled, 'Amery the spend-thrift, the wrecker, the warmonger, was the theme of leading articles and cartoons.'[14] As the clamour grew for the League to avoid war by finding in Turkey's favour, Leo's hand was strengthened by reports from Iraq that the Turks had crossed the frontier and brutalised the Christian inhabitants of the Assyrian border villages and the League eventually endorsed Leo's case. The Anglo-Iraqi Treaty was approved by Parliament the following year, and Leo was later to look back on his securing of the Mosul oilfields for Britain as one of his greatest achievements.

▪ ▪ ▪

Having already visited all of the existing Dominions and got to know their leading politicians personally, Leo prepared for the Imperial Conference of 1926 by visiting the newest Dominion, the Irish Free State. Well known as an adversary of Home Rule, he knew that there would be fences to mend, and was helped in doing so by his friendship with Tim Healy, now the Governor General. Determined to prove that he accepted the new political reality with goodwill, in August 1925 he and Bryddie visited Dublin, ostensibly to attend the Dublin Horse Show, where he made a point of rejecting his security advice and travelling around the city, and the show itself, in an open-topped car. Indeed, he was positively amused when Sergeant McLeod, who over-saw the security arrangements jointly with Healy's own bodyguards, informed him that they were 'among some of the worst gangsters that he had to look after for Scotland Yard in old days'.[15]

Leo was only peripherally involved in the events of early 1926 that led to the General Strike of that year. Together with Churchill, he represented a minority dissenting voice in Cabinet against the Government's decision to accept the findings, known as the Samuel Report, of the Royal Commission appointed to consider wages, conditions and management in the coal industry, both men objecting strongly to the proposed nationalisation of mineral rights. With the rest of the Cabinet he sat through a series of emergency meetings on 2 May, a Sunday, in response to the trade unions' vote in favour of a strike the previous day. The strike lasted eight days, and seems to have left Leo thoroughly underwhelmed, although he admired the sense of fighting spirit and English common sense demonstrated by the public, and appreciated the opportunity to catch up on his paperwork in the absence of postal deliveries to his department. It had been, he later wrote, the 'mildest-mannered revolution that ever tried to coerce a constitutional government'.[16]

The Imperial Conference of 1926 was destined to reshape the constitution of the Empire and Leo prepared for it meticulously for over a year. Although he had attended previous Conferences as an adviser, this was to be the first at which he would actively participate, and he laid the ground by entering into a steady stream of correspondence with the Dominion Prime Ministers before their arrival in London, and regular meetings with them once the Conference was under way. He briefed his Cabinet colleagues exhaustively in advance and created an inner Committee of Inter Imperial Relations, to be composed of the Prime Ministers alone, and to be chaired by Balfour, whom he knew to be 'entirely in sympathy with the newer conception of Commonwealth equality'.[17] Leo's personal ambitions for the Conference have subsequently at times been misrepresented, some historians claiming that a reluctant British Government was dragged, against its will, to an acceptance of equality within the Commonwealth by a group of Dominions, led by South Africa and Ireland, who were desperate for ultimate independence. But this analysis completely misrepresents Leo's own conviction that the principal purpose of the Conference was to 'get rid of every last vestige, not only of substance, but also of mere historical form, which might be thought to limit the complete independence and equality of the Dominion Governments'.[18]

Certainly he understood the strength of feeling and recognised that of all the leaders, General Hertzog of South Africa would arrive in London most determined to fight for the principle of equal status. Not surprisingly, Bryddie was asked to prepare an intimate dinner at Eaton Square, also attended by the Baldwins, at which Leo reassured the South African premier that his sole intention was to achieve for the Dominions, in a new Commonwealth, 'equality as sovereign states' and 'unity under a common crown', dual goals which he would 'pursue with the same relentless energy'.[19] When the Conference opened in October, Balfour laid out his own views on the concept of Commonwealth: the coexistence of seven autonomous communities, their equality of status and the two characteristics that they shared with each other, but with no one else, namely the common Crown and the common citizenship of their inhabitants. In reply, Hertzog insisted that a precise definition of the relationship between the Dominions was essential before any other decisions could be reached and produced his own formula, suggesting a public declaration by all the Dominions of their constitutional rights as independent nations, equal in status and entitled to international recognition.

When, the following day, Hertzog tabled a formal draft embodying his proposed declaration of independent status, Balfour responded with an alternative draft of his own and a series of meetings ensued over the next five days in an effort to find an acceptable form of words. There was unanimous agreement that a written constitution for the British Empire was not the ambition, but a number of stumbling blocks remained. The Canadian Prime Minister, Mackenzie King, objected to the use of the word 'independent', on account of its negative connotations for the Canadian people of American secession. The Irish delegation wanted to know more about the practical applications of so-called equality, while Hertzog tried to eradicate all reference to the word 'Empire' and its suggestion of centralised authority. In direct contrast, the Prime Minister of New Zealand, Gordon Coates, refused to accept a formula which contained no mention of the word 'Empire', until Leo, with the aid of an *Encyclopaedia Britannica*, managed to convince them both that the word implied only a complex political structure, rather than a specific form of government.

The text finally agreed upon described the relationship between the United Kingdom and the Dominions as one of '*Autonomous communities within the British Empire, equal in status, in no way subordinate one to another in any aspect of their domestic or external relations, though united by a common allegiance to the Crown, and freely associated as members of the British Commonwealth of Nations.*'[20] To Leo's annoyance, in the final report the paragraph was mistakenly printed in italics, as if emphasising that it had been added at a later date and he tried unsuccessfully to have the public copies altered. Nevertheless, the work which he had set in motion and had managed throughout was to lead directly to the 1931 Statute of Westminster and, at the time of Balfour's death in 1930, *The Times* described the declaration as a 'landmark of the first importance in the constitutional evolution of the British Commonwealth'.[21] Leo's preparation for the Conference at home and abroad, his nursing of Hertzog, and his eye for detail had all been crucial to its success. 'To ascribe,' wrote one historian, 'as some authorities have seemed to do, the principal result of the Imperial Conference of 1926 to the forces of Dominion "nationalism" under the determined leadership of Hertzog, Mackenzie King and the Irish is to leave Hamlet out of the play.'[22]

Yet not everyone was impressed by Leo's handling of the Conference. His old feud with Austen Chamberlain resurfaced, Austen complaining bitterly that Leo, 'with all his ability and intense zeal, fails completely for lack of any sense of preparation or judgement'. The charge lacks foundation, for while the accusation that Leo lacked judgement was made from time to time throughout his career, the suggestion that he was ever ill-prepared for anything is bizarre. Austen cited one meeting when Balfour could 'hardly keep from screaming' on account of Leo's behaviour, but there is no other evidence for his assertion that Leo 'irritated the Dominion Prime Ministers as much as he worries his colleagues'.[23] Maurice Hankey, acting as secretary to the Conference, put the opposing view, having long since overcome his earlier suspicions of Leo. He now found him to be a 'powerful ally' in his 'endeavours to strengthen the ties between the Mother Country and the self-governing Dominions'; of the incorporation of the famous paragraph into Balfour's report, he later confirmed that he 'would not like to deny Amery's claim to have suggested the idea'.[24]

Leo was always to look back on the success of the Balfour Report as 'one of the big things I have worked for most of my life',[25] the fulfilment of ideas for which he had worked for many years and for which purpose he had created the office of Dominions Secretary. But even then he remained concerned that the positive aspects of the Conference had not been adequately emphasised and he was eager, as soon as possible, to calm the anxieties of those who viewed the decisions reached in London as symbolic of a general weakening of ties between Dominions and mother country. His suggested solution was to undertake a world tour of all the Dominions, in a single trip which would last several months. Baldwin's initial reaction was unfavourable, fearing that Leo would be away for too long, but he agreed to discuss it with the King. Leo urged him to sanction the trip as 'an essential act of Imperial policy', which would help to allay the 'deep rooted suspicion' among the Dominion Governments that the 'old centralist conception of an Empire governed, or at any rate bossed, from London' still existed.[26]

While waiting for Baldwin's decision, Leo played an active role in international and domestic politics throughout the early months of 1927. Foreign affairs were dominated by the threat to British interests in China and the resulting prospect of military intervention during the Shanghai crisis. On both the issue of defending the threatened British settlements in China, and during the ensuing potential diplomatic break with Russia, he was one of the Cabinet hawks, again lining up alongside Birkenhead and Churchill against Austen Chamberlain's more conciliatory approach. In the field of home affairs, Leo found himself on the other side of the fence, strongly supporting Government plans for two of his most long-espoused causes, reform of the House of Lords and extending the franchise for women. Baldwin's plans for Lords' reform were ultimately dropped, but not before Leo made it clear to his Cabinet colleagues, in words that still hold true today, that 'the key to the whole question' was a solution which would 'prevent future swamping' and would 'justify in the public eye any subsequent increase of powers'.[27] He was more successful with his support for giving the vote to women aged twenty-one, although 'Winston led the opposition with great vehemence' and was 'very unhappy indeed' at the outcome, 'as indeed was also F. E.'.[28]

In the meantime, Leo continued to harass the Prime Minister about his favourite subject, namely protection, a further cause of antagonism with Churchill. He complained regularly to Baldwin at the slow pace of progress and the lack of a bold policy, and on one occasion went so far as to threaten resignation if the issue was not given greater prominence. He bitterly criticised the contents of Churchill's April Budget, and aroused a collective groan around the Cabinet table whenever he raised the topic. His most natural ally, Neville Chamberlain, thought that Churchill was, in fact, 'coming along nicely', and would be altogether more amenable if Leo 'could be prevented from nagging at him'.[29] Leo even had the nerve to write to Baldwin, suggesting that Churchill be 'put in charge of defence in replacement of Balfour', while 'proposing himself for the Exchequer'.[30]

Matters came to a head over an essentially trivial, but symbolic issue. In his ongoing quest for savings, Churchill identified over half a million pounds of unspent funds in the coffers of the Empire Marketing Board, the organisation responsible for marketing Dominion goods throughout the Empire. He proposed to inform each Dominion Government, by telegram, of his intention to annex the funds. The Board had been one of Leo's proudest creations and he was incensed by Churchill's aggressive attempt to seize his unspent imperial assets, which he perceived as typical of the Chancellor's hostile attitude to the interests of the Empire. Having thought that he had secured Baldwin's support and a promise that the threat would be dropped, Leo was appalled when the issue unexpectedly came up at Cabinet ten days later. Churchill 'weighed in very sarcastically', informing Leo that it was no business of his if the Prime Minister chose to send a telegram to the Dominions, since 'the Dominions Secretary was only a post office in these matters'.[31] Leo reacted furiously, disowning Cabinet responsibility and making another thinly veiled threat to resign. The meeting was temporarily suspended while Neville Chamberlain stepped in to act as the reluctant peacemaker, although he thought Leo's demeanour was 'overwrought', and the argument a 'very tiresome episode' and an 'absurd quarrel'.[32] However, when the meeting resumed Leo apologised and the Empire Marketing Board's funds were declared to be safe. Leo's statement of justification to the Cabinet was, typically, as long as his expression of gratitude for Neville's efforts was short. 'My Dear Neville,' he wrote, '*Thank you*.'[33]

Baldwin's initial scepticism at Leo's proposal to make a six-month tour of the Dominions had been endorsed by the King, who objected to the principle of his ministers travelling at all. It is important to remember nowadays, in the era of the political 'junket', that in the days before air travel such a trip would have been arduous in the extreme, involving long and far from comfortable ocean voyages, and lengthy journeys around vast continents, often in rudimentary conditions. Leo justified making the trip in a single journey on the grounds that it would save both the additional time and expense of making a number of sea voyages back and forth to various parts of the world. And in a display of self-confidence that would be unheard of in a modern-day politician, he was only too happy to leave ministerial affairs at home in the hands of his Under-Secretary, Billy Ormsby-Gore. Baldwin eventually not only agreed to Leo's proposal, but himself accepted an invitation to visit Canada. It was therefore agreed that Leo would travel first to South Africa, so as not to overlap with the Prime Minister, and then continue on eastwards around the world.

▪ ▪ ▪

On 22 July 1927 Leo, Bryddie and a small staff set sail for Cape Town on the *Arundel Castle*, Neville and Annie Chamberlain waving them off from the quay. The results of the Imperial Conference had been well received in South Africa, but Leo arrived to find Hertzog in the midst of a political crisis concerning the new South African flag. The opposition, under Smuts, had been ready to accept any flag which included the Union Jack in part, but the hardliners in Hertzog's Cabinet, especially Dr Malan, were determined that the flag should be based exclusively on the colours of the old House of Orange. So serious had the crisis become that Leo was warned by some against making the trip at all, for fear of his becoming too closely embroiled personally. But he was never likely to be put off by such a consideration, and was soon holding meetings with the respective leaders, finding his old friend Smuts in an 'anxious' frame of mind and looking 'thin and rather older', while Malan he thought 'very much the fanatic to judge from his eye and rat trap jaw'.[34]

From Pretoria he travelled further north, across the Limpopo river to Salisbury in Southern Rhodesia and Bulawayo in the North, where he discussed the issue of land rights – he insisted, in the face of ministerial opposition, that at least half of the 17 million acres of unallotted land should be disposed of to local natives – and the possible future amalgamation of Northern and Southern Rhodesia. Formal business was combined with the more enjoyable *indaba* meetings with local chieftains, of the Mashona in the South and Matabele in the North. They came in their hundreds, sitting in a semi-circle around the Secretary of State, and bringing with them their complaints, ranging from a lack of education to a lack of beer. Leo promised to do what he could about the former, but managed to solve the latter immediately, in return for which Bryddie was presented with a python skin for her birthday, from which she was urged to fashion herself a pair of shoes.

After sightseeing at the ruined temple at Zimbabwe and Victoria Falls, the party travelled to the three Protectorates still directly under Colonial Office jurisdiction. At a village feast in Bechuanaland Leo was presented with three fur rugs, made from a black-maned lion, a leopard and a golden jackal. After a brief stop for talks with Sir Ernest Oppenheimer in Kimberley, and another birthday present for Bryddie, this time a diamond, they continued to Basutoland, where Leo was granted an audience with the ninety-year-old Chief Jonathan. Fearing that he was to be regaled with a catalogue of grievances against the local administration, Leo enquired apprehensively after the old man's health. 'My heart has been sore', was the grave reply, 'ever since my dear Queen Victoria died.'[35] When Hertzog subsequently demanded that the Protectorates should be transferred to the Union for administrative purposes, Leo's private thoughts provide an interesting insight into his views on colonial government. Having visited for himself, he felt ashamed at how little his predecessors had done for the Protectorates, and that 'instead of spending money and thought on developing their resources and, still more important, raising the general standard of their peoples', the British Government had for years been 'content to protect them from outside interference, leaving them to carry on under a very unprogressive form of indirect tribal rule as museum pieces, human Whipsnades, in an Africa that was being transformed at a breathless pace'.[36]

After a few days' holiday, spent climbing in the Drakensberg mountains, including a visit to Mt Amery, the remainder of Leo's time in South Africa was spent visiting Johannesburg, Bloemfontein, Durban and the Eastern Cape, while he held several days of talks with Hertzog in Pretoria. His suggestion that, for a time, the Union Jack should be flown on certain buildings alongside the new South African flag, met with a cautious welcome from both sides of the argument. He addressed British and Nationalist audiences alike, telling an audience in Durban that the British Empire was 'not something superimposed on its nations but, like the Kingdom of Heaven, was something within each of them',[37] while he gave a lecture to students at Stellenbosch University in near-fluent Afrikaans. The press, which had initially been deeply sceptical about his visit, congratulated him on its success by the time he left, and he set sail for Australia at the end of September with the words of Jan Smuts ringing in his ears. 'Your visit here', he told Leo, 'did untold good.'[38]

Leo and Bryddie arrived in Western Australia on 10 October and, after a round of civic receptions and meetings in Perth, he travelled by train to Adelaide. Throughout his time in Australia the principal topics for discussion were the issue of migration, the work of the Empire Marketing Board and help for the farmer settlers, many of whom he met during his visit. Everything he saw convinced him still further of the need for a system of imperial preference and support for the Empire markets. In Melbourne he stayed with the Governor General, his former parliamentary colleague Johnny Baird, by now Lord Stonehaven, and held a series of meetings with the Australian Prime Minister, Stanley Bruce. A short visit to Tasmania without Bryddie afforded him the sole climbing opportunity of the Australian leg of his tour, an ascent of the 4,700-foot Mt Wellington before breakfast, while a visit to the Melbourne Cup caused him to remark that the English Derby was, by comparison, 'a very primitive and simple affair', although he was forced to admit that he 'knew nothing about racing and never bet'.[39] Nevertheless, his chosen horse won the big race at

5-1, to the general delight of the local racing fraternity and press.

Leo had last visited Canberra when it had been a mere drawing on an architect's desk, but he now held meetings there with Bruce's Cabinet, made a radio address to the nation and gave a *tour d'horizon* of British foreign policy to the House of Commons, sitting in secret session. In Sydney he and Bryddie relaxed for a few days at Government House, overlooking the harbour, before travelling on to Queensland and concluding his tour in Brisbane. The pace of the visit had been frenetic throughout and he left Australia with happy memories, writing proudly to Baldwin from on board ship that he had 'been immensely impressed by the usefulness' of his tour so far. In Australia he had addressed meetings of seven different Cabinets, had got to know intimately most of the corresponding ministers and had the opportunity of addressing thousands of Australians directly. Tens of thousands more had heard him on the radio. For many Australians, their concept of the British Government was no longer 'something purely abstract about which they occasionally read short cables, but something living and concrete represented by somebody they have seen or heard'.[40]

In New Zealand they were greeted by the Prime Minister in Auckland, before undertaking official engagements in Parliament in Wellington. But he had a chance to relax too, addressing a group of settlers at Ashburton on the joys of Dartmoor, and proving a popular guest at Christchurch College, where one of the younger boys was moved to write home to his father: 'Dear Dad, A man called Amery has just been here making a speach (*sic*). It was the finest speach I ever heard. It lasted five minutes and he asked for a whole holiday.'[41] Leo had also carefully managed to plan the New Zealand leg of his trip to ensure that it would last for four weeks, while the official engagements could be fulfilled in three. His party dispersed for the week, and Leo hired a local guide to spend the time mountaineering, including an attempt on the 12,349-foot Mt Cook, which proved ultimately fruitless on account of the weather. Christmas 1927 and the New Year were spent at sea, although the ship stopped briefly en route at Fiji, which Leo enjoyed, and Hawaii, which he thought too American.

They arrived at Victoria Island on 6 January 1928 and immediately embarked on yet another round of dinners and receptions, rallies and meetings with ministers. It became clear immediately that Bryddie would be equally in demand as a guest in her own right in Canada. Leaving Vancouver by train, they stopped for a day's skiing at Banff, before undertaking more engagements at Edmonton and Calgary, including sumptuous dinners with the Ranchmen's Club and the Mounted Police, and then to Winnipeg, where Leo addressed a meeting of a thousand members of the Canadian Club. In Toronto, where pro-Empire sentiment was at its strongest, they were more warmly received than ever, and Leo accompanied Bryddie on a visit to her childhood home, 'the pleasant little old-world town of Whitby, a few miles out on the lake shore'.[42] Welcomed back as an international celebrity returning to her roots, almost the entire population turned out to greet Bryddie, including many of her old school friends and her eighty-seven-year-old former teacher. Although they were accompanied for most of the day by two carloads of photographers, Bryddie still managed to spend a few quiet minutes at her parents' grave and to see her old home. Leo welcomed for once not being the centre of attention and found it 'altogether a rather moving, happy and tearful occasion'.[43]

At Ottawa they stayed with the Governor General, Lord Willingdon, at the magnificent Rideau Hall, before travelling on to Montreal for a day, to Quebec, where Leo was again able to spend some time skiing and impressed his hosts by delivering his speeches in fluent French, and finally to New Brunswick and Newfoundland. They arrived back in Liverpool on 12 February, to be met later that evening in London, on the station platform, by Julian and Jack, both of whom had grown considerably. They had been away in all for seven months and, in making the trip, Leo had fulfilled one of his life's great ambitions, one that he had inherited from Joseph Chamberlain who had never managed to achieve it. His 'original purpose had been to counteract the centrifugal forces then at work in the empire', and he felt that he had been completely successful in explaining and reinforcing the new constitutional concept of Commonwealth status. In South Africa he had helped the Government out of a critical deadlock and had furthered the cause of migration and Empire trade in Australia and New Zealand.

But for Leo personally there was an added bonus. He had discovered, to his pleasure, that the governments and people of all the countries he had visited strongly shared his views on imperial preference. He had been encouraged to continue his campaign at home and had, he believed, been granted a 'moral mandate' to press for greater action.[44] He and Bryddie had travelled over 55,000 miles and, in addition to his more intimate meetings with ministers and their advisers, he had delivered an extraordinary 300 speeches, a selection of which he subsequently published in a volume entitled *The Empire in the New Era*, the foreword written by Balfour shortly before his death. He knew too that he had succeeded in strengthening his personal contacts throughout the Dominions. However, subsequent events would prove that he was wrong to assume, as he did at the time, that this position of strength within the Empire would necessarily improve the esteem in which he was held by his colleagues at home, as he set out to 'tackle the really big job', the country's 'conversion to the idea of economic co-operation and preference'.[45]

▪ ▪ ▪

It was not long before Leo realised that, in his absence, the political tide had turned against him and his position had been weakened rather than strengthened. His colleagues, far from having their interest in his causes reawakened by his efforts overseas, had been too busy with the day-to-day affairs of state even to pay much attention. His comparison with Joseph Chamberlain was apt, for he now found himself in the same position as his predecessor on his return from South Africa in 1903. Seven months away had merely emphasised the distance between him and some of his colleagues, and even natural allies such as Neville Chamberlain had been partially won over by Churchill, who had used the time to reinforce his own policies in Cabinet. As the world drifted towards the Great Depression, Britain faced a mounting economic crisis and rising unemployment. Leo could only complain bitterly about the inaction and timidity of his fellow ministers, although his personal relations with both Baldwin and

Churchill remained cordial. Although the Cabinet was still divided, there was widespread support for Leo among the rank and file of Conservative MPs. After a backbench meeting broke up in disarray when the President of the Board of Trade ruled out all food duties, Leo took the opportunity to write to Baldwin, warning him that he intended to fight on if that was the line to be taken. 'I do trust you understand I am in earnest,' he wrote, somewhat ominously.[46]

Leo spent the Easter of 1928 quietly with the family on his beloved Dartmoor before returning to London determined to have it out with Baldwin. On 7 May they spent an hour alone together, an opportunity for a 'long deferred blowing off of steam on the general position' and to tell the Prime Minister that it was time for him to 'choose between Winston and myself'. Either Churchill had to be moved or he, Leo, should be placed in a post with greater economic responsibility, preferably the Board of Trade, where he could enforce his own safeguarding policies. Baldwin was 'as usual, silent, sympathetic and friendly', but gave no hint as to how he was thinking.[47] By now the party was in a state of almost open mutiny and Leo became increasingly reckless, privately threatening that he would have to 'proceed to extreme measures in the autumn'. 'I am no Joseph Chamberlain, I know,' he wrote to Leo Maxse, but the 'unripe fruit which resisted his plucking 25 years ago is ripe'.[48]

In public Leo continued to maintain his discretion, unlike the Home Secretary, William Joynson-Hicks, who responded to one of Churchill's increasingly frequent tirades in favour of free trade by breaking ranks and calling for bolder action on tariffs. Not only did he lay bare for the first time the full extent of the Cabinet rift on the issue, but Neville Chamberlain thought the most damaging aspect of the speech was that it 'accentuated the feeling of bitterness already existing between Winston and Leo'. The situation was only exacerbated when Leo poked fun at Churchill during a Cabinet meeting, to the amusement of his colleagues, but not the Prime Minister who issued a stern call for discipline. On 2 August Baldwin called a further Cabinet to agree a statement, which he now thought essential, to explain the Government's policy towards safeguarding. Leo and Neville walked to the meeting together from Eaton Square, and agreed that Leo would open the discussion, expressing his own support for safeguarding, while Neville would support him at a suitable moment. Chamberlain was by now the 'only member of the Cabinet who has any influence'[49] over Leo, and succeeded in brokering a compromise whereby Leo conceded that it was now too late to introduce food taxes or a general tariff before the election, while Churchill agreed to an enquiry into the general conditions of the iron and steel industries, and acknowledged that its findings might lead to some variety of safeguarding measures.

The crisis was, for the moment, averted and Baldwin made a point of thanking Leo 'very warmly for the way he had expressed himself at Cabinet and had helped to contribute to an agreed solution'.[50] But when Leo opened his Sunday newspapers that weekend, he was furious to read the description of the agreed policy which had been altered considerably. The pledge not to introduce a general tariff had been emphasised, while the proposed enquiry into safeguarding was given little prominence. Leo sensed the hand of Churchill and wrote to Baldwin immediately to distance himself from the declaration.

Ever since returning from his Dominions tour, Leo had privately prepared himself for the possibility that he might have to offer his resignation. As the months passed, the idea developed and, when he looked back over twenty years later, he believed that he had made the biggest mistake of his political career by not resigning in July 1928. His resignation at that moment would have been dramatic and would have enjoyed the overwhelming support of Conservative back-benchers. His authority and standing within the party would have been greatly enhanced, and he would have had the opportunity to campaign actively for his preferred policy during a general election campaign. He had not done so out of loyalty, personal friendship and optimism that things might improve. He had no desire at the time to break away from colleagues, nor deliberately to weaken the party on the eve of an election. Neville Chamberlain remained a close friend, while he felt a genuine affection too for Baldwin with whom he had no wish to fall out. He was tired and almost certainly deeply worried by Jack's untimely departure from Harrow that very summer. He reflected ruefully on Robert Browning's lines:

> Next day passed, and next day yet
> With still fresh cause to wait one day more.[51]

By the time he arrived in St Moritz in August his anger and frustration had subsided somewhat and, with Jack left behind in London with his new tutor, Leo was able to devote most of the holiday to encouraging Julian's mountaineering ambitions, before moving on for a few days of more serious climbing in Saas Fee and Zermatt with the Pollingers. When he returned to London in September, it was as though nothing had changed. At the annual party conference in Yarmouth a motion was passed overwhelmingly in favour of more widespread safeguarding, but Baldwin chose to ignore much of the speech which he had invited Leo to draft for him on the issue. When the King's Speech made no mention of safeguarding in November, morale on the Conservative benches fell still further and, by the end of the year, Leo was badly depressed and had never felt so 'estranged from most of my colleagues in the Cabinet'.[52] He would have been even more unhappy had he known that Baldwin was secretly planning a pre-election reshuffle and that, far from offering Leo his hoped-for promotion to the Board of Trade or even the Treasury, the Prime Minister had already offered half of his portfolio, responsibility for the Colonies, to Neville Chamberlain, hoping that he 'might get over his difficulty with Leo by leaving him with the Dominions'.[53] Chamberlain was delighted by the offer.

Although he knew nothing of Baldwin's plans, Leo too had concluded that the Government could only be saved by making changes at the top. He discussed his ideas with Neville Chamberlain, who unsurprisingly failed to tell him about Baldwin's offer, but agreed with Leo that a reshuffle was essential, nowhere more so than at the Treasury. Leo suggested moving Churchill to become Lord President of the Council, a role that would put him in charge of co-ordinating defence matters, where he could be 'kept busy planning wars in Afghanistan and elsewhere', and one which he had 'hankered after all his life'.[54] Neville should himself go to the Treasury, failing which Leo would like the job himself, in which case he would suggest Neville for the Dominions and Colonies Office, ironically the very job he had already been offered by the Prime Minister. But when Leo wrote to Baldwin proposing these changes, he could have had no idea of the detrimental effect that his letter would have on his own prospects. Baldwin thought the letter a 'melancholy grouse about some squabble with Winston', insisted that there was no chance of Leo going to the Treasury and, in his most damning criticism of all, added that Leo did not 'add a gram to the influence of the Government'.[55] Chamberlain had not been altogether honest with Leo, since he was able gleefully to report to his sister that Baldwin had 'decided to give him the office he desired, or rather the two offices', but that 'what he will do with the present holder I don't know and nor does he'.[56]

In a mood of increasing complacency the Conservatives drifted towards electoral defeat as, according to the editor of *The Times*, 'the doom of the Baldwin Administration could clearly be foreseen . . . by all save those whom it most directly concerned'.[57] Certainly Leo's mind was elsewhere, as he was increasingly marginalised professionally and forced to make an unscheduled trip to Switzerland to remove Jack from his school at Château d'Oex and take him to Zermatt. Yet he too shared in the general mood of misplaced optimism, writing to Leo Maxse, that he did 'not think we will come to grief somehow at the election'.[58] He tried to influence Baldwin's manifesto, and was scathing about the disastrous campaign slogan, 'Safety First', chosen, he assumed, because 'there was really nothing else left for him to say either about his past record or his programme for the future'.[59] Once again Bryddie ran his campaign in Sparkbrook where the majority of 2,992 was his smallest yet, while the Unionist stranglehold on Birmingham was broken for the first time in a generation. Although Lloyd George was the undoubted star of the campaign, the benefit of his oratory went to the Labour Party, who secured 287 seats to the Conservatives' 261, with the Liberals increasing their representation from 43 to just 59.

The Conservatives' shock at losing confirmed their earlier over-confidence. As in 1923, the immediate dilemma was whether to resign immediately or to meet Parliament and see what the Liberals would do. At a Cabinet meeting on 3 June 'everyone was very cheery' and even Churchill was 'most affectionate' to Leo, congratulating him on his success against the tide in Birmingham. Although Chamberlain favoured an agreement with Lloyd George, and Leo wanted to force the Liberals to put Labour into power, Baldwin was adamant that he must resign at once. The meeting broke up with everyone parting 'very happily, voting ourselves the best government there has ever been and full of genuine affection for SB'.[60] Leo's successor at the Dominions and Colonial Office was his old friend from Coefficient days, Sidney Webb, who was dragged out of retirement to sit in the House of Lords as Lord Passfield, a title which his wife refused to use. She thought it characteristic of Leo, and indeed 'of English political life' that, on hearing of Webb's appointment, he 'followed him from Cheyne Walk to Grosvenor Road (at 3.00 a.m.!) in order to put him au fait of the personalities of the office'.[61]

CHAPTER TWELVE

A Statesman in Embryo

In early 1928, with Julian's ninth birthday fast approaching, it was time for him to follow his brother's example and to go away to boarding school. However, Jack's experiences at West Downs had adversely coloured Leo's opinion of the school and he decided to look elsewhere for Julian. At the suggestion of a number of his Oxford friends at All Souls, Leo's interest alighted instead on Summer Fields, a boys' preparatory school off the Banbury Road, in North Oxford. In March he visited the school for the first time and wrote to Bryddie from All Souls to admit that he was 'much taken with the place'. The headmaster Cyril Williams was 'a parson, but shows no external signs of it except a black tie with his brown tweed suit'. He was 'manly and keen-looking', while his wife, Hermione, was 'youngish and nice-looking'. The school facilities were good, the dormitories cosy and the playing fields extensive, although there was 'no warmed swimming bath'. There was, however, a 'farm with ten yielding sterilised cows'.

Perhaps recalling Jack's time at West Downs, he stressed that the prefects were appointed by the headmaster by virtue of their '*position* in the school', and that there was 'no sort of *election* and no exercise of authority'. The standard of work was 'obviously high' and, although there was 'no cramming', the school had 'a wonderful list of scholarships'. After a further visit with Bryddie, Leo's mind was made up. What appealed to him above all was that the school's syllabus was firmly grounded in the Classics and the Bible, and it prided itself on providing the best preparation possible for scholarships, usually of the classical variety, to Eton. Leo was delighted to hear that Homer was widely read, and 'saw a Latin prose by a boy of 11½ which was miles beyond anything Jack has attained to'.¹ Ever the classical scholar himself, an added bonus was that the school still 'used the old Latin pronunciation'.² Although the school was technically full, Leo's determination ensured that Julian was enrolled for the beginning of the summer term.

One of the school's most celebrated masters, the future Poet Laureate Cecil Day Lewis, arrived to teach there the same year as Julian. He later recalled his time at Summer Fields in affectionate terms; it was 'an exceptionally good school of its kind'. As 'a nursery for Eton, where every year it won a number of scholarships', Summer Fields 'conveyed to the newcomer a sense of prestige and privilege'. The boys were, by and large, 'quick witted and attractive . . . with an easy manner and a charming touch of independence'. His fellow masters were intelligent and hard-working, and welcoming towards Lewis as a newcomer. 'The climate and accommodation', on the other hand, 'left something to be desired.' There were, at the time, three families who owned the school, all of whom were equal partners, and all of whom withdrew their own dividend. The result was that for twenty-five years there had been little investment in the facilities to complement the increasing numbers of boys. And the spartan classrooms were made more inhospitable still by the 'icy damp of the North Oxford winter' which 'gripped us for weeks on end'.³

It was into this environment that Julian was introduced by his father on a reconnaissance trip to the school during the term before he was due to start. The presence of the little Cabinet minister, with his even tinier son and ever-present bodyguard, caused quite a stir among the boys as they toured the school with the headmaster. Julian was unusually quiet all day, but when he returned home that evening he announced to Pipette, with typical gravity, that 'J'adore Summer Fields.'⁴ In fact, as well as looking forward to making friends and playing cricket, the principal attraction of the school appears to have been the smart, grey flannel suit he would now be required to wear and, in particular, the excitement of owning his own waistcoat. On the appointed day, Julian enjoyed a last lunch at home, and his first glass of port alone with his father, before being driven to Oxford, with his nervous parents, in a large and old-fashioned chauffeur-driven Daimler.

It is a feature of Julian's career at Summer Fields, whatever his successes or failures there, that individual moments were vividly remembered, often many years later, by several of his contemporaries. Even when he arrived with his parents for his first day, in the splendid Daimler, he again immediately caught the eye of the other boys. One of the school's prefects, later to become Sir Kennedy Trevaskis, a distinguished diplomat, recalled the first appearance at the school of the eminent, but diminutive, Cabinet minister and his 'very small son'.[5] Julian's early impressions of the school probably differed little from those of hundreds of other boys of his generation but, in truth, he was appallingly badly prepared for the privations of boarding school life. With Jack away at West Downs, he had effectively been brought up as an only child. He had not been spoiled by his parents in the sense of being over-indulged or loosely disciplined, but he had enjoyed great comfort, in both the material, as well the emotional, sense of the word. He had always had his own space and privacy at home, and had 'rather enjoyed being alone'. He had spent considerably more time in the company of adults than of other children, and had little experience of having to share, or indeed of the 'rough and tumble of collective life'. Pipette had been his constant companion while his mother had 'surrounded him with love'. Now he found himself in a world of freezing dormitories and crowded schoolrooms, with hard benches; compulsory cold baths ('I had had cold baths for fun in very hot weather'); and lumpy porridge for breakfast in the enormous, austere dining hall, where the idea of eating '*en grand comité*' and 'the noise of a hundred small children breakfasting together seemed appalling.' He hated milk, and had never been made to drink it, even in tea. As a result he flatly refused to drink the tea which was provided by the school in large urns, with the milk already mixed in.

The tears soon came and flowed freely. Above all, it was the lack of privacy, the absence of a 'place of refuge' that hurt. But worse was still to come. In a desperate search for peace and solitude he made his way to the school lavatory, known as the Vinery, only to find to his consternation a row of 'earth closets without plugs', or even doors, in 'a kind of garden' where 'the stench was appalling'.⁶ He took up the story on his third day, in his first letter home to his parents, a missive which must rate highly as being among the most heartbreaking and soul-destroying ever received by a mother who has just sent her child away to boarding school for the first time. 'I have seen the lavatories', he wrote to the adoring Bryddie, and they were 'most awful with no plug and I've never been but pleas (*sic*) write an (*sic*) ask if I can have one for myself'.⁷ He continued on the same theme the very next day. 'This letter is rather important,' he wrote, 'it is about the Vinery. I am getting on *very* badly and have not been for two days.'⁸ The effect on Bryddie, already beside herself with worry, was predictable, and it is unlikely that she would have agreed with Leo's overly sanguine description of the 'rather sad little letter from Julian which made her unhappy'.⁹

Unfortunately, Bryddie's distress was further compounded by Julian's description, in the same letter, of the result of his first, ill-fated visit to the Vinery. Making his way back to his form room, with the tears coursing down his cheeks, he was confronted by an older boy who accused him of being a 'rotten little cry-baby'. This was too much for Julian and, although the boy was twice his size, he took a leaf out of his father's book and threw the first punch, splitting the boy's lip. Although he 'got much the worse of the subsequent fighting' and was comforted by the same prefect who had noticed him on arrival, Trevaskis, school opinion quickly hardened against this aggressive new boy. 'The world seems very different here,' he mused to Bryddie. 'I have already made a few friends and I am sorry to say a few enmesy (*sic*).' What was worse, 'most of the boys are bullys (*sic*) and kick.'¹⁰

By his own admission, Julian was often his own worst enemy and conceded that some of the bullying he suffered, during his first year in particular, was probably in part as a result of his own behaviour. He refused to conform to the customs or routine of school life, and exuded a self-confidence which could only have been interpreted as a form of provocation by the other boys. He held strong opinions, many of them acquired from Pipette, which ran quite contrary to normal school-boy ethics. In particular, he had 'developed a point of honour which would have been excessive in a sixteenth-century Castilian grandee'. He took offence at the smallest affront and was 'determined to leave no injury unrevenged'.[11] The headmaster warned Leo that Julian was a 'very fastidious little fellow, far too inclined to criticise and, I fancy, has a very good opinion of himself'. On one occasion, the boys in his dormitory were comparing their respective heights, and Julian was found to be much the smallest. 'Ah,' he replied, 'but I make up for size in intelligence.' He was also 'rather old-fashioned and a trifle fussy for a boy of his age'. The result, inevitably, was that he had been 'taken down a peg or two'.[12]

He was 'bullied mercilessly' remembered another boy. 'Amery baiting' became a popular sport at the school, frequently led by a 'large, swarthy boy' who, many years later, sat 'well behind Julian on the benches of the House of Commons'. The baits were 'cruel, unequal affairs, as cruel and unequal as bull-fights and scarcely less noisy', and almost always 'ended in blood and tears'.[13] Another contemporary remembered Julian as a 'diminutive but very aggressive little boy', whom he and a group of friends had 'teased into a white heat of frenzy' one afternoon, before leaving him 'upside down in a tall litter basket in the playing field, into which he fitted precisely'.[14] Even the gentle Mrs Williams had to admit to Bryddie that 'when Julian comes up against other boys it is his own fault'. He had a 'quick wit and a very ready tongue', and should not 'pull the legs of older boys'. While he could 'always come off best in any war of words, the bigger and stupider boys had no means of retaliating except with physical force'.[15]

Among other fellow pupils, who later recalled in vivid detail his time with Julian at Summer Fields, was the future Sir Nicholas Henderson, British Ambassador to Washington. The problem for Julian was that he insisted on being 'provocative, uncompromising and combative'. In an eerie reminder of Kenneth Tindall's description of Jack at West Downs, Julian refused to 'temper his beliefs or behaviour to the accepted codes of boys or masters, and was prepared to do battle in support of his own'.[16] But there the similarity with his brother ended. Julian 'had great moral courage' and won the respect of his peers for that, however foolhardy it may have seemed at times. He never merely yielded to superior force, but met it head on, seemingly 'oblivious of Queensberry rules' and with 'no inhibitions about losing his temper'. Above all, 'though of limited physique, he never resorted to higher authority for protection', but relied instead upon the 'fury of his tongue, the length of his nails, and the lowness of his punches', none of which, it must be said, was ever enough to protect him from a good beating.[17]

Although he never sought out the protection of masters, in one respect he was fortunate. Like many other unhappy boys, he came under the care and protection of the headmaster's kind-hearted and popular wife, Hermione Williams. Her husband, Cyril Williams, 'though by nature genial, had a rather hectoring manner and had ruffled some feathers'.[18] His parents, from whom he had taken over the school, wanted him to be at once stern and feared, but popular at the same time, an almost impossible balancing act for a headmaster. He initially had little sympathy for Julian, writing to Leo that he was 'too assertive for his age', that his 'superiority complex was much in evidence' and that he was concerned lest Julian 'developed into a buffoon'.[19] His report at the end of Julian's first term warned that 'occasionally the smartness of his tongue brings upon him the wrath of his equals', and by Christmas Julian had still not apparently learnt his lesson, since his 'caustic tongue has often brought him into trouble with his peers'. He needed to be 'more circumspect in future'.[20]

Hermione, on the other hand, was much loved both by the children and, in particular, by the parents. Although she had settled down to life in such a quintessentially English environment, she was in fact, like Leo's mother, an immigrant from Eastern Europe. Indeed, during the First World War she had often been mistaken for a German on account of her strong accent. It may be that Leo had been attracted to the school as a result, but in any case she soon became close friends with Bryddie, and they kept up a regular correspondence throughout Julian's career. During his first few terms at Summer Fields especially, Hermione would write often to reassure Bryddie that all was well and, when he was ill or in trouble, she would write almost daily. She found Julian a 'most amusing little chap' and, after his first experience in the

Vinery, wrote that as he 'seemed such a tiny little man', she and Matron had 'decided that it will be better if he uses the inside lavatory'.[21] When Bryddie asked politely if Julian might have his own pot of tea at meal times, Hermione at first agreed, and then abandoned the old tea urns completely and ensured that each table in the dining room had its own teapot and separate milk jug from then on.

Julian's relationship with the older boys finally came to a head at the beginning of his third term. He was standing in his classroom 'innocently' sharpening a pencil with a new scout knife, when one of them confronted him as to why he was sporting a red silk handkerchief in his breast pocket. Julian, 'in the memorable words of the Welsh Attorney . . . "took the high line and told him to bugger off".' But this time it was he who felt the force of the first blow across his face. Seeing red, Julian struck back, but claimed to have forgotten that he was still holding the penknife in his hand, and left a deep cut above his assailant's eye from which blood soon began to pour. His victim was carried off, screaming, to the sanatorium, while Julian, having been at first confronted by an angry crowd of his peers, was summoned to the headmaster's study.

Julian feared the worse, but for once Williams failed to act upon his normally disciplinarian instincts, apparently because, 'by a miraculous coincidence', he had done the same thing himself when a boy. Instead, he took the opportunity to have a long, friendly talk with Julian about skiing and mountaineering, as well as the 'importance of turning away wrath with a soft answer and of showing some regard to public opinion as well as the letter of the law'. It was advice that Julian was never to forget. And when he subsequently left the study, he was able to issue his own 'communiqué' to the throng now eagerly assembled outside, that there would be no punishment 'or any rot like that'. He and Dr Williams had enjoyed a 'cordial exchange of views', they had both understood each other's point of view, and they now 'looked forward to close co-operation in future'. Julian was happy too to shake hands with his victim, by now stitched up, when he returned from the sanatorium. Any other potential bullies were discouraged by the subsequent scar and the headmaster's attitude, while Julian, for his part, 'learned to keep his temper and his tongue under closer control'.[22]

From that moment on he made new friends and began to find school life altogether more pleasant.

Not only did Julian not expect the masters to get him out of trouble, 'he scarcely seemed to expect anything of them at all',[23] and by his own admission had a 'rather over-developed sense of justice and what are nowadays called "Human Rights".' He was constantly arguing with masters about the levels of discipline at the school, especially with 'a rather formidable senior master', Geoffrey Bolton, 'a tall, austere, bony classicist and cricketer, who hated foreigners'. Matters came to a head one day when 'G.B.', as he was known, told him that he was making too much noise at lunch and to stop talking so much. Springing to his feet, Julian replied, 'Sir, that is an outrageous statement, I have not spoken for five minutes.' While Bolton backed down on this occasion, Julian was now plainly a marked man and, sure enough, the next time that he was caught stepping even slightly out of line, Bolton gleefully administered a good beating.

Julian decided that he must retaliate for this injustice and became the founder and chairman of the school's 'Anti-Authority League'. Having set up cells in the various classes, he went about the school addressing 'public' meetings of the boys when there were no masters about. There was no great incitement to violence, he simply 'aired our grievances, unmasked current examples of injustice and advised my fellows to adopt an attitude of coldness and sullenness towards the masters'.[24] Within a few days a third of the school had joined, his timing having proved impeccable. There was indeed a debate going on among the masters themselves as to the suitable level of discipline at the school, and Julian's liberal views found favour with some of his more progressive teachers. Strangely, one of his least favourite teachers was one who shared his views and who also later went on to achieve recognition in his field, the novelist L. A. G. Strong. He thought the discipline at Summer Fields was 'rigid to the point of harshness', while 'beatings were common, and the high standard of classical scholarship derived almost as much from fear as it did from the system of teaching'.[25] Such an apparently enlightened attitude towards the harsh regime he encountered at the school made him popular with most boys, but not, it would seem, with Julian, who only remembered his 'sarcastic and, at times, almost sadistic turn of mind'.[26]

If the micro-politics of boarding school life were a favourite interest, then the altogether more substantial world outside of national and international politics was already the main business of Julian's life. To his contemporaries, he was destined from an early age to be Prime Minister. His manner earned him the nickname 'Pompo', a recognition that he was 'so much more serious and self-assured' than the rest of the boys, and was already in many ways what he aspired to be, 'a real, forthright, mature politician who was already of seasoned Cabinet timber'.[27] To a future parliamentary colleague, Nigel Nicolson, he was 'the most glamorous of all' his friends, 'already a statesman in embryo', who 'read *The Times* daily and smoothed his hair with brilliantine'.[28] His fastidious personal appearance was widely commented on, in particular the 'hair brushed straight back without a parting',[29] and the 'perfectly arranged handkerchief in his breast pocket', which had already landed him in so much trouble. Such was the 'pristine state of this cotton construction that the rest of us assumed that he never blew his nose'.

That was the assumption of another contemporary, the future actor Patrick Macnee, who found Julian 'the most dominating presence and hypnotic personality' in the school. However, he also thought that there was one serious obstacle to Julian's immediate political ambition, namely that 'he perched precariously on a political seesaw of indecision, his views veered from left to right from term to term'.[30] For a while he was a passionate supporter of Lloyd George, an admiration that failed to endear him to many of the more conservative masters, and which had almost certainly been brought about in part by Bolton's loathing of the Liberal statesman. After several requests from Julian, and lengthy correspondence between Bryddie and Hermione Williams, a signed copy of Lloyd George's *We Can Conquer Unemployment* was eventually procured for him, which he would rather ostentatiously carry around the school clutched to his chest. He also kept a biography of his great hero, Napoleon, close at hand and would frequently demonstrate to his friends how the great man would have thrust his right arm into his coat across his chest. He spoke of 'Winston' with the same familiarity as his cricketing friends would speak of 'Gubby' (Allen), an old Summerfieldian who had recently played in his first Test match for England.

Many of his speeches were impromptu affairs. Hermione recalled how he would 'stand on his desk in Lower School and harangue the other eight-year-olds on politics',[31] while on another occasion, a contemporary remembered a 'diminutive figure, dressed immaculately in green tweed plus-eights, standing on the lockers, haranguing a none too respectful audience on the iniquities of the Tory party. His hair was brilliantined and his gestures were both menacing and majestic.'[32] But it was in the more formal surroundings of the school's debating society that he found his rightful forum. In November 1930 he opposed the motion that 'The best way to keep peace is to prepare for war', speaking 'vividly of the horrors of war and quoting Xenophon'.[33] The following year he opposed Government funding for the Schneider Trophy, 'amidst gesticulations reminiscent of the Salvation Army' and also, presumably in his role as chairman of the 'Anti-Authority League', supported the abolition of fagging in public schools.[34] At Julian's suggestion, the society also staged mock parliaments, including debates on capital punishment, the Locarno Treaty, negotiations with Russia and English intervention in the Sino-Japanese war, during which 'Mr Amery ranted so shrilly that it was impossible to follow his arguments, if he had any'.[35] And in a chilling premonition of a future, real-life tragedy, he played the judge in a mock trial of a man charged with his wife's murder. 'Mr Justice Amery' reported the school magazine gleefully, 'put on his black cap . . .'[36]

However, without doubt his finest hour came at the age of eleven, during a debate on conscription, at a time when pacifism was '*de rigueur* in the schools and universities of England'. Several of the more senior, popular and athletic boys had already confidently put the case for 'pacifism or at any rate, for "voluntariness" ', and clearly enjoyed the overwhelming and vocal support of their audience. Then it was Julian's turn. Nicholas Henderson later recalled the 'small, pale and most unmilitary looking' figure, his hair shining with brilliantine in the lights of the debating chamber. 'With one hand on the lapel of his jacket and the other clutching his notes, he began his speech in a voice quavering with age rather than youth.' 'Mr President,' he began,

'I am in favour of conscription. I have been in favour of conscription all my life . . .'[37]

Julian's precocity and individualism at school is important, not only for what it tells us about him as a boy, growing into a young man, but also as an insight into the way the Amery family lived at home and in the holidays. He enjoyed an exceptionally close relationship with his adoring parents, his mother in particular being 'a creature of pure tenderness and gentle radiance' for him.[38] Any sense of awe he may have felt at his father's importance as a Cabinet minister was tempered by the use of the nickname 'Coco', which both Julian and Jack used for Leo well beyond their childhoods. He kept up a frequent correspondence with his father on affairs of state, about which Leo would write to him on terms of equality. Bryddie was known as 'Porick' and frequently referred to in letters as 'My Sweetheart' or 'My Angel', terms of endearment that must have been unusual from a young boy to his mother, even then. Some of his friends found such an obvious display of affection embarrassing, but not Julian, who was 'uninhibitedly devoted to his parents in a demonstrative, scarcely English way'.

Summer Fields had, of course, been chosen largely because of its position on the outskirts of Oxford, where Leo still spent a good deal of his time at All Souls or, with Bryddie, staying with their many local friends. The regular opportunities to visit Julian were too good to miss. While many of his friends' parents would come to collect their children in large, expensive cars, Leo's extravagance on Julian's first day at the school had been a one-off. He and Bryddie would arrive by local taxi, from the station or a house in Oxford, and while other boys would cringe at any public display of affection from their parents in front of their peers, Julian would be waiting for them, and his friends would look on as Leo and Bryddie alighted from the taxi and they all hugged each other, 'all more or less the same size'. Julian was always 'uniquely unashamed' of his parents, and was 'quite unabashed to be seen kissing them and being kissed by them in public'.[39]

Indeed, he was intensely and visibly proud of them, especially his father's political success and, of course, much of his historical and political knowledge was received wisdom. He believed 'that he, his mother and father were all equals, all in it together, and indeed from a distance the three of them did look extremely equal physically.'[40] In his mother, Julian recognised 'the steel of her will-power and the tribal intensity of her loyalties', qualities which she was to retain throughout her life and demonstrate in the face of the worst possible adversity. Julian wrote home commiserating that the Labour Party had won the Battersea by-election, that 'Coco got rather a bad time with Mr Churchill in Parliament'[41] and, after the 1929 general election, that 'The Cabinet is not nice'.[42] When Leo was succeeded as Colonial Secretary by his old friend from 'Coefficient' days, Sidney Webb, Julian could not help poking fun at 'the man who is taking Coco's place', best known for his splendid beard which had supposedly once caused him to be interrupted during a speech with the rejoinder to 'shut up, you nanny goat'.[43]

As they had been with Jack at West Downs, Leo and Bryddie were frequent visitors to Summer Fields. Whenever possible they would take Julian out, to see friends locally or sightseeing round the Oxford colleges, followed by a much-needed lunch at a smart hotel, or sometimes further afield. Leo became a familiar face at Summer Fields, watching school matches even though Julian was rarely taking part and going to school plays, in which invariably he did play the starring role. On one such occasion, Julian wrote, directed and starred in a play written and produced entirely in French. Leo also took to entertaining some of the senior masters to dinner at All Souls and once gave a well-received lecture to the school, accompanied by an innovative slide show, on mountaineering in general, the Rocky Mountains and his ascent of Mt Amery in particular. Julian took the opportunity to ask his father to request a half holiday for the school, a proposition that was turned down, although Leo realised that 'frankly he regards me as rather a useful asset'.[44] In the summer there were regular punting trips on the Cherwell in fine weather and long discussions in the cricket pavilion watching the rain pouring down outside. After one such lengthy debate about the merits of Napoleon, Leo was forced to admit that even his own extensive 'knowledge of history was not always adequate to Julian's searching questions'.[45]

However, it was during the holidays that Julian's relationship with his father blossomed and his education continued apace. Nicholas

Henderson recalled being invited to spend the first day of the Christmas holidays with Julian in London. While most of the other boys spent the train journey discussing which West End shows they were hoping to see over the holidays, Julian briefed himself for lunch with his parents by reading *The Times*. Bryddie met them off the train with a porter and a taxi at the ready, and quickly transferred them all to Eaton Square for Henderson's 'first experience of a Cabinet meeting' in the enormous, dark dining room, while the butler hovered discreetly, serving lunch. Once the pleasantries about school and Julian's new friend were safely disposed of, the four of them got down to sorting out 'together the burning problems facing England and the Empire'. Although by now out of office, Leo 'spoke authoritatively and at some length' about such matters as the Locarno Treaty, and 'gave the impression of really being in control of events, as if the others had merely managed to usurp temporarily the seats of power'. When Henderson was asked for his own views, he correctly realised that he was there 'not to sing, but to listen for his supper' and wisely took it as his cue to pass 'the ball rapidly to Julian who . . . took it gratefully and made off at a steady, confident pace'. He seemed not to be arguing against his father, but it was more 'as though he was combining with him in the face of some unmentionable enemy', and was 'completely *au fait* with the problems'.[46]

Julian met many of the great contemporary figures of national politics, indeed international politics, both at home in Eaton Square and while travelling with his parents. It was hardly surprising, there-fore, that in such a 'climate of people and ideas', he should have 'developed a precocious interest in politics and especially in Imperial questions'.[47] Politics mattered to him and represented real life. His god-father had been murdered for political reasons and he saw at first hand both his father's and his uncle's bodyguards. He was a regular visitor with his father to the House of Commons, and the debates to which he listened were then analysed and dissected for their significance. On one such occasion, in the spring of 1930, he met Lloyd George in the Lobby with Leo. When asked what he hoped to do when he grew up, he gave what was then for him the stock answer that he intended to go into the navy. 'There are much greater storms in politics,' replied

Lloyd George with a frown. 'If it's piracy you want with broadsides, boarding parties, walking the plank and blood on the deck,' he continued, then 'this is the place'.[48] From that moment on, it would be politics for the young Julian.

School holidays were invariably spent abroad and gave Julian what his school friends saw as 'a faint aura of "foreignness" about' him. He spoke fluent French, which annoyed the other boys only a little more than, as it had done at his previous school, it did the French master. And, as if to rub it in, he scorned anyone who used a French–English dictionary, insisting on using a Larousse himself. His 'spiritual home seemed to be the Balkans', and he 'gave the impression that his holidays were spent in Wagons-Lits'.[49] Certainly the holidays were spent mostly in the mountains, climbing in the summer and skiing in the winter, and Julian became proficient at both from an early age. Although Leo, by now approaching sixty, was taking his mountaineering more gently, he was still strong and Julian was able to accompany him on his training walks at the beginning of each climbing holiday. In 1930, at the age of eleven, Julian climbed the 10,000-foot Monte Forno in St Moritz and, a few days later and in appalling weather, the Corvatsch, both no more than a brisk walk for the accomplished climber, but a considerable feat for a young boy.

The Easter holidays of 1931 gave Leo a welcome opportunity to escape from the ongoing political crisis at home for a week's holiday alone with Julian, now aged twelve. Jack had seen the Mediterranean at the same age and the two of them set off alone for the south of France and the Pyrenees. The first few days were spent sightseeing, in Carcassonne, Narbonne and Perpignan before crossing by train to spend some time walking in the foothills of the Pyrenees. However, the sight of the snow-covered Mt Canigou, towering above them at 9,200 feet, proved too tempting both for the seasoned mountaineer and the novice schoolboy. The locals warned that it was impossible to climb the mountain outside the summer months, so deep was the soft spring snow on the upper reaches. But Leo, naturally, knew better and having found a local driver who was prepared to take them up the first 3,000 feet, he and Julian duly scampered to the summit. He later reflected that it had not been entirely 'prudent allowing a small boy to climb unroped and with only a walking-stick up so high and narrow a ridge', but the climb left a lasting impression on the young Julian.[50]

Soon it was time for Julian to move on from Summer Fields. While clearly an intelligent boy, he had not excelled in the academic hot-house atmosphere there, and his reports over his final two years demonstrate that he had little interest in working hard for exams. The senior master recommended that he should follow his brother to Harrow and Leo took the opportunity of a Governors' meeting at his old school to prepare the ground. After Jack, there was no question of Julian going to the Head Master's House, but the housemaster at Leo's own former house, West Acre, a 'devoted and quietly loyal Old Harrovian'[51] by the name of F. A. Leaf, assured Leo that there would be a place for Julian there. However, a mere change of house was not going to be enough for Bryddie. Jack's experience at Harrow had left her with 'deep misgivings' about Julian going there at all, and it was she who persuaded Leo that he should be sent to Eton instead.[52]

Julian's last two terms at Summer Fields were difficult ones. The deputy headmaster warned that he had become increasingly strident in his political opinions, particularly in his criticism of the National Government, and that he had got into trouble as a result. He 'fiercely resented any injustice and would fight against it to his last breath', which was a problem given that he 'tended to consider personal criticism as an injustice'.[53] He joined the other boys who made their way to Eton in the summer of 1932 to sit the scholarship exam, but the headmaster had warned that he was unlikely to win an award, and so it proved, although he passed into the school easily. Julian was bitterly disappointed, but the deputy headmaster thought that 'this non-success will not do him any harm in the long run'.[54] He only hoped that he would maintain his sense of humour, learn to curb his pride, and that 'the increased freedom at Eton will not go to his head'.[55]

CHAPTER THIRTEEN

Who is for the Empire?

If Julian left Summer Fields with an exalted opinion of his own abilities and achievements, it seems likely that it was a trait he had inherited from his father. On his departure from office in June 1929, Leo looked back on his time as Dominions Secretary with considerable satisfaction; indeed, with a minority Labour Government now in power, he could be forgiven for assuming that it was only a matter of time before he would be back behind his old desk. But it was to be another eleven years before he was again to enjoy the trappings of office. He had held the post for longer than any incumbent since Joseph Chamberlain. His separation of responsibilities within the department had been a success and had been warmly welcomed by the Dominion Governments, who appreciated the more direct line of communication that they now enjoyed with the British administration. Above all, Leo and Bryddie's Dominions tour in 1927, the first of its kind, had cemented his relationship with the leaders and, indeed, the people of those countries.

The new definition of Commonwealth status, hammered out with Balfour at the 1926 Imperial Conference, had already proved to be of fundamental importance to the future of that institution, and Leo knew that the Dominions would now never again accept a further loss of sovereignty as they moved towards nationhood of their own. Yet he was less interested in the concept of the Commonwealth as a political structure than he was by the possibilities it offered as a single economic unit. At the heart of both his beliefs and his achievements lay his advocacy of a far-reaching scheme of imperial development, with Britain providing the manpower and the wealth, while trading with the rest of the Empire, to their mutual benefit.

Leo has been praised by one historian for having given 'the greatest impetus to Colonial development between the world wars'.[1] He oversaw a period of fundamental change and, in spite of his long-running battle over budgets with Churchill at the Treasury, he still managed to initiate a successful policy of colonial development. The creation of the Empire Marketing Board was Britain's first venture into overseas aid, culminating in the Colonial Development Act of 1929, the first example of western economic assistance to the non-developed world ever to be enshrined in legislation. He was 'one of the moving figures in the building of the institutions of the British Empire', instituting widespread reforms in the fields of healthcare, education and agricultural research, all of which greatly improved standards of living in the countries concerned. He supervised a programme of substantial investment, presiding over the building of roads, bridges and hydro-electric installations. In Treasury circles he was known as the 'Mad Mullah',[2] a pejorative reference by which he was doubtless personally flattered, while future Chancellors of the Exchequer would have cause to thank him for a further achievement, the securing of the Mosul oilfields in 1925 for the British protectorate of Iraq.

It is all too easy to view Leo Amery as an unreconstructed imperialist, dedicated, as was Churchill, to maintaining the supremacy of British rule throughout the Empire. Certainly he had failures, most notably his unsuccessful attempt to persuade East African countries to join in federation to create a single, larger bloc to be ruled by the white settlers. Conversely, in Palestine, he supported settler-led development, insisting on equal rights for all communities. But his imperialism was 'more ethical than strategic, more visionary than calculating'.[3] Another historian considered Leo to be 'one of the two or three best informed Colonial Secretaries Britain has ever had', and that to his admirers he was 'a man of imaginative vision and fearless determination, alive to the demands of a new time, a dynamo of energy and a passionate believer in England's imperial mission'.[4] Above all he was known for his love of the job, and the boundless energy and enthusiasm that he brought to it, sometimes a little too much for the liking of his Cabinet colleagues. 'I love office,' he wrote to Baldwin in 1927, 'I love the sense of getting things done, I love the comradeship of Cabinet.'[5]

During Leo's tenure as Colonial Secretary, the house in Eaton Square became an extended home for hundreds of Colonial and Dominion officials on leave, and other visitors from around the world. Julian later recalled that Bryddie's receptions at Eaton Square were 'attended by at least 150 guests every week, drawn partly from overseas and partly from British public life'.[6] And yet, when it came to an end, he still regretted that in Cabinet his four and a half years in office 'had been an uphill and largely unsuccessful struggle'.[7] With the exception of Churchill, most of his colleagues, including Baldwin himself, shared Leo's belief that some form of imperial protectionism was the solution to unemployment and Empire development. But no other minister was 'so doctrinaire . . . and none trusted Amery's judgement',[8] a constantly recurring accusation during his time in office. He also talked too much, both in Cabinet and outside.

'Why will Leo insist', asked one anonymous colleague, 'on answering every speaker at Cabinet? Why does someone not pull his coat and stop him?'[9] He 'allowed his powerful mind to range over the whole of Cabinet business', a habit which failed to endear him to most other ministers, and was simply unable to stop himself becoming increasingly garrulous and aggressive in his advocacy of imperial preference. Nothing better illustrates the effect of this loquacity than the deterioration of his political relationship with two of his closest friends and potential allies, Austen and Neville Chamberlain, the sons of his hero. With Neville, Leo's 'relations cooled almost imperceptibly' and, although Chamberlain 'believed that what Amery stood for was in substance right', the problem was that Leo 'often exaggerated his case'.[10] It made it difficult to support him in Cabinet, but easier for those opposed to him on principle to speak out more publicly. Neville remained 'an old friend, but he felt no enduring confidence in his judgement'.[11] They continued to spend time together, socialising

together in London with their wives and, as Members for neighbouring Birmingham constituencies, frequently travelling together by train
and attending joint political meetings. But in Cabinet, wrote Neville,
Leo came to be 'listened to with almost undisguised impatience and in
the House he does not seem to carry much weight'. What was worse,
he had 'no sense of proportion and insists on little points with the same
exasperating pertinacity as on big ones'.[12]

Neville's brother Austen held similar views. During the crucial
sessions of the subcommittee on Inter Imperial Relations at the 1926
Imperial Conference, Chamberlain would sit to the right of Balfour,
Leo to his left. After one such meeting, Austen complained bitterly that
Leo had 'jumped with both feet into the thorniest bush in the
Conference thicket, & only last night I begged him to avoid it!' He had
been 'utterly unaware that anything was wrong and had . . . naively
explained that Balfour did not know what to do so he had gone to his
rescue!' If the worst came to the worst, Austen was quite prepared to
'kick his shins as I understand one colleague was already obliged to do
at a Conference by way of conveying to him that he was saying the
wrong thing . . . Funny isn't it!'[13] While his supposedly good friends
were cracking jokes at his expense, it is entirely symptomatic of Leo's
trusting innocence that his memory of the same incident was that
Balfour had 'dozed off', but had nonetheless 'rarely missed a point'.[14]

There was also an element of jealousy, even of intellectual fear,
among some of Leo's colleagues. It was Balfour who was supposed
to have described him as 'the cleverest bloody fool alive', someone
who was 'frequently most devastatingly right, but never knew how to
play his cards in the game of politics'.[15] He was considerably more
cosmopolitan than most, a lifetime of travel having given him a 'wider
knowledge of the world' than most of his fellow Cabinet members,
which he combined with 'enthusiasm and . . . a powerful mind'. He
also refused 'to be soured by rebuffs' and had a remarkable 'capacity to
get much done with little money'.[16] But his frequent trips abroad
aroused resentment too, and his Dominions tour of 1927 was, with
hindsight, a mistake in domestic political terms, further weakening his
position at home. He was also the victim of snobbery, some senior
Conservatives looking down on him as "a funny heavy-handed little

person . . . almost a fanatic'. The Earl of Crawford and Balcarres was delighted when he 'tackled F.E. at the Carlton about ministers being so much abroad', and was told that 'it was an excellent thing on general grounds that a tiresome bore like Amery should spend a long time abroad'.[17]

But it was the length of Leo's speeches that proved his ultimate undoing. Even Julian later admitted that 'the scholar in him and his training on *The Times* led him to pack too many points into his speeches', a defect which, 'with his lack of theatre, diminished his immediate oratorical impact'.[18] His well-known pugnacity, attributed to his strength as a mountaineer, often made matters worse. He would rarely surrender on even the most trivial point of debate, and was obsessed with the minutiae of policy. One backbencher recalled a 'dull day in the House', listening to Leo's speech on the Imperial Conference. He was, he thought, without doubt 'one of the most boring, ponderous and long-winded of speakers', although he grudgingly conceded that Leo was also 'one of the best informed and ablest of our ministers'.[19] During one of his statements to the House, 'Balfour was asleep and Hankey thought the votes would have gone through from sheer boredom.'[20] Yet an old friend, Lionel Curtis, once wrote to tell Bryddie that he had heard Leo make 'the most brilliant and witty after-dinner speech at All Souls', and despairingly asked, 'why on earth does he not treat his public audiences now and then to this sort of thing if he can do it so well?'[21] However, the majority verdict was that he 'never quite carried sufficient weight among his cabinet colleagues to secure easy implementation of his policies. Perhaps he talked too much: it is always fatal.'[22]

▪ ▪ ▪

In the immediate aftermath of election defeat, Leo's first preoccupation in 1929 was, as it had been six years before, with his own finances. His ministerial salary had been augmented by the rental income from a number of properties in Southwark, which had been left in trust to Bryddie, and on which increased rents were now falling due. However, the houses needed upgrading and he had been forced to go to the bank to borrow £2,000 to pay for the modernisation.

Although for once his account was in credit, he knew that if he was to have a prolonged spell out of power or even on the backbenches, he would need an additional income. An invitation to speak at a lunch given by the Incorporated Society of British Advertisers gave him the double opportunity to criticise the recent Conservative campaign and to solicit work. He was approached about possible non-executive directorships at Barclays Bank and Rio Tinto, but turned down an offer to become chairman of the Sugar Federation, a trifle optimistically, in case he should have 'to weigh their claims as Colonial Secretary or Chancellor of the Exchequer'.[23] A particular source of jealousy was Churchill's revelation that, throughout his time in office, he had continued to contribute articles to *Cosmopolitan* magazine at the generous rate of £500 a time.

The complacent attitude of the Conservative leadership at their electoral defeat was not shared in the constituencies, where Baldwin's timid support for protection had gone down badly. Leo shared the frustration of the rank and file that there had still been no change in the direction of policy and, on 9 July 1929, speaking from the front bench during the debate on the King's Speech, he launched a 'long-suppressed tirade against Churchill's free trade obstructionism'. He blamed the party's defeat squarely on the lack of a bold imperial policy and called for a comprehensive system of tariffs and imperial preference.[24] Reaction was polarised. Leo thought the speech had gone well, and he was warmly applauded by his own backbenches, but he realised also that his remarks had been greeted with horror by his front bench colleagues. Austen Chamberlain was furious, insisting that Leo must now 'conform or leave the front bench as the party will not stand an independent policy from one of the front bench leaders'.[25] Neville, on the other hand, broadly agreed with Leo, having himself declared publicly that the time was ripe for a new imperial policy. However, he was still moved to regret that it had been 'an uncomfortable week in the House', and that Leo's 'exposure of differences had shocked the party'. Churchill, in particular, was 'going about like a bear with a sore head'.[26]

At the first meeting of the new Shadow Cabinet on 11 July, Baldwin again stressed that there would be no change of policy, while Austen Chamberlain renewed his call for an alliance with the Liberals to defeat the new Socialist Government. Leo spoke vigorously in opposition to such an idea, before Neville 'made a somewhat half-hearted attempt' to support him and Churchill again sided with Austen. It was evident to Leo that Churchill had been 'colloguing vigorously with Lloyd George since the election', and was 'heading straight for a coalition in which no doubt everything I have ever worked for is definitely to be thrown over'.[27] As they left the meeting, Leo warned Neville that he was 'so disgusted that he should retire to a back bench', and although Chamberlain talked him out of committing 'self murder', the idea privately appealed to him, 'for with the best intentions he ruins any cause in which he is interested'.[28]

Three weeks later Churchill and Leo found themselves making a joint crossing of the Atlantic, one on a speaking tour and the other to go on a climbing expedition in the Rockies. The relief among their colleagues was palpable. Baldwin told his Private Secretary that 'Winston is off to America in one ship and Amery in another, and peace reigns in the land.'[29] He was wrong, as they were in fact on the same ship and, far from complaining, both of them appear to have welcomed the opportunity for a lengthy debate on a whole range of topics. One evening, having talked late into the night in Churchill's cabin, Leo got up to leave as his host began to dress for bed, 'putting on a long silk nightshirt and a woolly tummy bund over it'. Churchill asked why Leo was smiling. 'Free Trade, mid-Victorian statesmanship and the old-fashioned nightshirt,' he replied, 'how appropriate a combination.'[30] Nevertheless, Baldwin's relief was understandable. Throughout his premiership, the often rowdy disputes between Leo and Churchill within Cabinet had been the source of endless problems and Baldwin had never enjoyed acting as peacemaker. His Principal Private Secretary, Sir Robert Vansittart, whose own office backed on to the Cabinet room, recalled that whenever he heard raised voices, the 'most frequent vocalists were Winston and Amery'. Baldwin was a 'poor hand at keeping order', principally because Leo's 'alpinizing energy resented the more abounding energy of the Chancellor with overtime for other men's departments.'[31]

The relationship between Churchill and Leo was, throughout their long political careers, a complex one. The time they had spent at school together bestowed a common bond on them, about which Churchill was fond of reminiscing. He would frequently regale guests at dinner parties with accounts of their first encounter beside the Harrow swimming pool, or the morning in South Africa when Leo had missed the armoured train on which Churchill was subsequently taken prisoner. But in spite of that schoolboy friendship and a shared social life, they were never intimates and although they united on some aspects of policy, their differences over protectionism were never overcome. One of Churchill's biographers perceptively recognised that 'there was always a definite restraint in their relationship, a lack of warmth, a noticeable caution and reserve'.[32] Baldwin would often comment, only half in jest, that more than half of the Cabinet's time was taken up with the dialogue between the two of them, and everyone was well aware of the 'continuous battle between' them, a series of 'day-to-day differences in Cabinet and in the conduct of inter-departmental business'. Leo only hoped that theirs had been a 'friendly variance'.[33]

When the Earl of Crawford gleefully recorded his conversation with Birkenhead at the Carlton Club about the amount of time Leo spent abroad, F.E. claimed to enjoy the support of Churchill in his criticism. According to Crawford, Churchill felt 'small affection for Amery' and, when 'asked about the travelling allowances, he said that for every week Amery was absent from the country, the weekly rate of allowance was to rise, and to do so handsomely'. It is impossible to tell whether or not the quote is accurate, but it is worth noting that it is third-hand and out of the mouth of a man whose diaries are scattered with disparaging remarks about Leo. When Crawford visited Sandringham in 1923, he complained that he could not imagine 'anything more middle class than a very long greenhouse with small pink begonias, and with a looking glass at one end to create the illusion of greater length'.[34] If the King was 'middle class', Leo must have been beyond the pale.

Leo had not visited the Rocky Mountains for twenty years, but he had often thought of returning and electoral defeat had given him the opportunity to do so. In fact, his vanity had got the better of him. Mountains are generally either named after the first person to climb them, or after 'more or less eminent elderly gentlemen who have never seen them'. Leo had already enjoyed the former honour in South

Africa, and had achieved the latter during his Dominions tour of 1927, when a 10,940-foot peak in the Rockies had been named Mt Amery in his honour. The 'challenge was obvious', to prove himself 'as a mountaineer and not merely as a politician, justified of the appellation.'[35] The plan was to trek through the wilderness peaks of the Columbia Icefield, climbing Mt Amery and a number of other prominent peaks along the way. He was accompanied by two well-known local climbers, a sizeable pack convoy to carry the provisions and a renowned Swiss-born guide, Edward Feuz, who had come to the Rockies as a child and was to achieve seventy-eight 'first climbs' in the course of a legendary career.

Several days after leaving Lake Louise they enjoyed their first view of Mt Amery, 'a steep snow-crowned tower soaring gracefully into the sky', and a few miles later the mountain was revealed in all its glory, 'an immense four-square bastion of solid rock towering, in alternate steep-pitched slopes and bands of vertical cliff, over 6000 ft. sheer above the main valley'.[36] They climbed for four hours before the weather deteriorated and Feuz suggested they turn back, but Leo insisted they carry on and, by mid-afternoon, as the blizzard raged around them, they reached the summit. Leo had 'made good his claim to Mt Amery in the mountaineering sense',[37] indeed the ascent was one of the great achievements of Leo's mountaineering career. The weather had been so bad at the summit that he still needed to be convinced that they had been successful, but his fears were allayed over the next few days when the party successfully climbed two nearby peaks, Mt Bryce at 11,560 feet, and the 10,964-foot Mt Saskatchewan, from where they could see the stone cairn which they had built on the summit of Mt Amery. 'I do not think I have ever felt so keenly', wrote Leo, 'the emotion of being in a world never yet touched or even seen by man as that evening.' It was equivalent to the 'thrill that Keats attributed to the first glimpse of the Pacific or the first reading of Homer'.[38] The trip was completed with a first ascent of a smaller, as yet unnamed peak, for which Leo suggested the name Mt Julian, 'to encourage my ten-year-old boy's mountaineering ambitions'.[39] The mountain remains so-called to this day.

▪ ▪ ▪

Before leaving for Canada, Leo had held a series of meetings with Lord Beaverbrook to discuss how they might work together to promote Empire trade. Beaverbrook had been greatly impressed by Leo's speech during the debate on the Address and, in a repentant article in his *Sunday Express*, entitled 'Who is for the Empire?', he had taken himself to task for his previous neglect of Empire policy and pledged himself to campaign for greater Empire unity in the future. The result was his so-called 'Empire Crusade' and Leo quickly recognised the importance of such revitalised support for his own long-held views. He visited Beaverbrook on a number of occasions at Cherkley, his home near Leatherhead in Surrey, and soon discovered that he had 'all the fervour of an evangelist', and had developed into a 'speaker of revivalist eloquence'. However, he was concerned too that the campaign's slogan, 'Empire Free Trade', would confuse the public and be unacceptable to the Dominion Governments. Beaverbrook showed his journalistic mettle by conceding Leo's point, but reassuring him 'that the appeal of a slogan was more important than its accuracy'.[40]

The effect on the Conservative rank and file was immediate. The party's candidate at a by-election in Twickenham, in August 1929, came out in support of Beaverbrook's campaign, and was promptly disowned by Baldwin, against Leo's strong advice. Instead, he hoped to persuade Baldwin and Beaverbrook to work together, and recognised that Empire Free Trade would not 'come in one flash anyway', but would have 'to be built up by a series of slow processes'.[41] But while Leo, in spite of his concerns, remained a loyal member of the Shadow Cabinet, Beaverbrook disliked Baldwin intensely and saw his 'Crusade' as a means of deposing him. Baldwin's suspicions were increased by Beaverbrook's threat to run a candidate of his own against the official Conservative at every by-election, as well as by his burgeoning alliance with his fellow press baron Lord Rothermere, who had carried a personal grudge against Baldwin since 1923, when he was refused a coveted earldom and the accompanying political promotion for his son.

Samuel Hoare, a close friend of both Beaverbrook and Baldwin, temporarily brought about a truce between the two men, but if Leo shared Beaverbrook's ultimate aim, he continued to have doubts about his methods. At a public meeting he noticed that Beaverbrook was 'tremendously worked up', and there was 'something in the glint of his eye' that made Leo wonder whether he was not 'really near the edge of his balance'.[42] A few days later, Beaverbrook invited Leo to dinner at Cherkley and told him that although he had originally been inspired by Leo's sense of purpose, he could now not understand why he was not prepared to speak out as strongly as Beaverbrook did himself. He urged Leo to appoint himself leader of the whole movement, but Leo could only mutter apologetically that, while his views remained as forthright as ever, he believed that opinion within the party was moving in the right direction and he had no wish to alienate those who were still considering their position.

The family went skiing in St Moritz over Christmas 1929, Leo feeling more than usually depressed at both his lack of political success and, worse still, his inability to make 'progress with the necessary though unpleasant task of earning something to live on'.[43] He returned to London determined to resort to stronger action, and found that Beaverbrook and Rothermere were in the process of putting their alliance on a more formal footing, attacking Baldwin in their papers on an almost daily basis. On 27 January Leo warned Baldwin privately that if the door were not left open to the possibility of food taxes, then he would have to voice his opposition more publicly. A week later Baldwin made a widely reported keynote speech at the Coliseum Theatre in London, claiming that the safeguarding of industry was now a central plank of Conservative policy, but ruling out any taxation of food. This time Beaverbrook seemed satisfied, but Leo was not. Two days later he made an outspoken speech in his Birmingham constituency, condemning Baldwin's remarks and flatly stating that he could not 'accept as meeting the urgency of the situation at home and in the Empire a flat negative pledge of so sweeping and unqualified a character'.[44]

Reaction was immediate. The Deputy Cabinet Secretary, Tom Jones, commented privately that Leo had 'proclaimed aloud his dissatisfaction with S.B.'s "milk and water" policy' and assumed that he would 'no longer be allowed to sit on the Front Opposition Bench'.[45] Neville Chamberlain confided to his sister that Leo 'had claimed his freedom',[46] while Lord Linlithgow was the first to break ranks publicly, demanding Leo's immediate sacking from the Shadow Cabinet in a letter to *The Times*. If Leo insisted on advocating a policy other than 'that laid down by the Leader and accepted by the party as a whole', then Baldwin should 'make it plain that he must do so from outside the official ranks of the party'. Writing in his capacity as chairman of his local West Lothian Unionist Association, Linlithgow went on to echo the complaint of the voluntary party down the ages, that when there is 'indiscipline at headquarters it is idle to expect either staunchness or zeal among the rank and file'.[47]

The letter caused Rothermere, writing in the *Daily Mail*, to call for Baldwin's replacement as leader by Beaverbrook. As a result Baldwin wrote 'a rather sad note' to Leo, expressing his disappointment that he had 'felt constrained to act' as he had, and complaining that he could not see 'what possible good it can do'.[48] The following morning he sent for Leo, and asked him to mitigate the mischief he had caused, although Leo rightly pointed out that Rothermere's reaction had been to Linlithgow's letter rather than to his Birmingham speech. The agreed solution was an open exchange of anodyne letters, in which Leo maintained his policy position and publicly reaffirmed his loyalty to his leader, while Baldwin meekly penned a brief reply at Leo's dictation, acknowledging that he had always appreciated Leo's point of view and knew that he could count on his cooperation in future. This contrivance suited Leo well since it gave him a clear mandate to pursue his own line, while making it clear that he remained an indispensable and loyal member of the Shadow Cabinet. Beaverbrook was unhappy at the news and tried to stop the publication of the letters in the following day's *Times*.

Baldwin refused to afford Beaverbrook the same latitude as he had Leo; it was personal and could not be extended to Beaverbrook himself, or to any other members of his Shadow Cabinet. Leo considered that to be an untenable position, but still urged Beaverbrook to desist from initiating a vendetta against party leaders or candidates who disagreed with him. But it was too late and Beaverbrook went ahead and converted the Empire Free Trade Movement into a new political party, the United Empire Party, with himself as its leader. Rothermere was delighted, comparing the movement to 'a prairie fire ... bigger than you, me and all the Conservative Party put together'.[49] Leo was not so pleased. 'I am sorry you have done this,' he wrote, 'as it makes the situation much more difficult for all who were sympathising with you.' Beaverbrook had been making 'excellent progress . . . However, there it is.'[50] But Beaverbrook was unrepentant. He had done nothing wrong, had tried his best to work in collaboration with the Conservative Party and had finally been swayed by Rothermere's offer of support.

The new party enjoyed considerable early success, enrolling 173,000 members and collecting over 100,000 subscriptions in the first fortnight. But when Beaverbrook announced that he would contest fifty Conservative seats across the south of England, Leo's fears were confirmed, while the pace of recruitment slowed. That, and his growing disenchantment at having Rothermere as a partner, led Beaverbrook once again to seek a compromise with Baldwin. He was 'already finding Rothermere a bad bedfellow and wants to come to terms with you' wrote Leo to Baldwin, adding that the moment was now ripe to 'make the Party position stronger than it has ever been and to leave Rothermere in outer darkness and returning to his favourite vomit, i.e. Lloyd George'.[51] Leo continued to act as peacemaker and Beaverbrook and Baldwin agreed a compromise that were any new food duties to be proposed at a future Imperial Conference, the issue would become the subject of a national referendum. Leo did not much like the idea, 'dreading S.B.'s molluscous inertia', but he 'could not very well see how I could object'.[52] The deal was broadly welcomed by the rest of the Shadow Cabinet, and when Rothermere confirmed that he would indeed support Lloyd George henceforth, as Leo had predicted, Beaverbrook resigned the leadership of the United Empire Party.

Once again the truce did not last long, and Beaverbrook soon dropped the idea of the referendum and decided to oppose Baldwin wholeheartedly, again allying himself with Rothermere. To his own amazement Leo continued to be cast in the unlikely role of moderator. 'The Conservative Party is an obstinate creature', he told Beaverbrook, 'which cannot be beaten over the head too much. An occasional cut with the whip' might be all right, but the party would not tolerate his continuing aggressive tactics.[53] But neither Beaverbrook nor Baldwin would take a more conciliatory line, and in a rousing speech to a meeting of MPs and party candidates at Caxton Hall on 24 June, Baldwin attacked the two press barons and warned them that he was no longer prepared to allow them to 'dictate the policy to a big Party, to choose a leader, to impose Ministers on the Crown . . . a more preposterous and insolent demand was never made on the leader of any political party.'[54]

Unfortunately for Leo, his attempts at mediation had left him on the wrong side of everyone. Baldwin could not understand why their personal friendship did not extend to Leo's support for his policies in the face of press criticism, while Beaverbrook believed that Leo had shown a lack of nerve in failing to support more wholeheartedly his attacks on Baldwin, when he might well have been the ultimate beneficiary of Baldwin's overthrow. In the aftermath of the Caxton Hall meeting, Lord Derby affirmed that 'of course to my mind the man at the bottom of the whole thing is a man I have always disliked and distrusted – Amery.'[55] But Leo believed that he had acted with honour. He had supported Baldwin loyally and had done all he could to prevent the divisions within the party becoming a chasm.

Throughout the summer the tide of opinion continued to move in the direction of the tariff reformers. Leo spent the summer at Chamonix, writing a short book, *Empire and Prosperity*, during an otherwise energetic climbing holiday. The problems at home seemed 'all very futile' from beneath the towering presence of Mont Blanc.[56] On his return to England Leo became still more outspoken in public, criticising Baldwin strongly in a speech in his constituency at the end of September and complaining to Beaverbrook that the *Daily Express* had failed to report it, in spite of it having been 'a considerable advance on anything I have said before'. Beaverbrook replied that he had given an immediate order that Leo's speeches were to be more fully reported and confided that 'the Editor of a newspaper is only useful so long as he works honestly and earnestly in furtherance of the political programme. The moment he shows the slightest tendency to "stall" he can do incredible injury.'[57] He also repeated his offer to serve in a Conservative Cabinet under Leo's leadership, a suggestion which led Leo to assume that 'Max both overrates my personal ambition and underrates my judgement of the situation.'[58]

Leo now quietly stopped attending Shadow Cabinet meetings, although he continued to speak from the front bench on Colonial and Dominion affairs. Baldwin's position remained critical throughout the autumn, and he survived another vote of confidence on 30 October. A few days later several of his former Cabinet colleagues held a private meeting in Lord Salisbury's room, with a view to strengthening their leader's hand by making it clear publicly that none of them claimed any divine right to be consulted on policy or to sit in any future Cabinet. Leo thought the proceedings rather too serious and came up with his own alternative for them to sign, that 'We the undersigned old gangsters, keenly alive to each other's senility, wish to make it quite clear that we shall be only too delighted to see any of the others bumped off should you wish to do so.'[59] Churchill, who was himself considering resignation from the Shadow Cabinet, promised that he, at any rate, would stick to Leo 'with all the loyalty of a leech'.[60]

▪ ▪ ▪

Having broken his leg skiing on New Year's Eve 1930, Leo spent the rest of his holiday in his hotel bed, once again left to ponder another disappointing year. Baldwin appeared to be as unpopular as ever, and Leo's efforts to be loyal to his old friend had been largely thrown back in his face. He felt happy that the policies he supported were gaining in popularity and credibility, but wished that he had been brave enough to take a more striking and controversial line. Above all, he was deeply concerned at his lack of income. He had hoped to write something 'of permanent value (and immediate lucrativeness)' during the year but nothing had materialised and such articles as he had written had 'done very little to keep the wolf employed'.[61] He had already been forced to give his bank a charge over what securities he still owned to cover his now substantial overdraft.

The early months of 1931 were dominated by Churchill's split with the party over India and the ongoing whispering about Baldwin's leadership. Leo quietly returned to the Shadow Cabinet just as Churchill was leaving. 'I imagine his game', thought Leo, was 'to be a lonely and formidable figure available as a possible Prime Minister in a confused situation later on.'[62] Sam Hoare reported to both Leo and Neville Chamberlain that the question of Baldwin's leadership was 'again growing acute'. Neville felt uncomfortable that he was seen by many as the one person who could bring about Baldwin's retirement, but could 'not act when my action might put me in his place'.[63] However, he admitted to Leo that he had been approached by a number of people who wished to see him take over the leadership, while his brother believed that Baldwin should be 'told squarely what the position is and invited to consider it', and that 'poor Neville has to do the job'.[64]

Matters came to a head in March when an independent Conservative mounted a direct challenge to Baldwin's leadership in a by-election in St George's in Westminster. When at first no Conservative could be found to contest the election, Baldwin considered resigning his own seat at Bewdley to fight the constituency himself and force a vote of confidence in his leadership. Leo helped to talk him out of what he thought an absurd gesture, and eventually Duff Cooper successfully defended the seat. On 25 March Baldwin asked to see Leo and, having conceded that several members of the front bench no longer supported him, they discussed possible successors, agreeing that Neville was the most suitable. But Leo told Baldwin that if he could see his way through his current troubles, then he 'would stand by him', although he stopped short of advising Baldwin not to resign. On his way home he mused that Baldwin was 'really a much bigger man than the others', and realised that he felt 'very fond of him'. He 'dreaded the change' and when he got home that night Bryddie had to reassure him that he had said the right thing and sent a note round herself urging Baldwin not to resign.[65]

At Shadow Cabinet the following morning, Baldwin finally agreed that future Conservative policy should include the protection of British agriculture by means of duties on foreign foodstuffs. He thus 'retained the leadership of the Conservative party but in return accepted the full Tariff Reform programme'.[66] Meanwhile, by the summer of 1931, the economic crisis was reaching a climax. Escalating levels of unemployment and a widening balance of payments deficit had led the Bank of England to warn Ramsay MacDonald bluntly that the problem lay in a lack of political confidence in the Government, and the prospect of a coalition was being openly discussed. Leo sensed 'an undercurrent of mutual sympathy' between Baldwin and Ramsay MacDonald, 'based on a common shrinking from definite policies and decisions'.[67] However, he continued to believe that coalition was neither likely nor desirable and in early August set off for his annual climbing holiday at Campo Carlo Magno in the Italian Dolomites, a region he had not visited for twenty years. For ten days he prepared to climb the Guglia di Brenta, a peak which had long tempted him and which he knew if he failed to conquer before his fast-approaching sixtieth birthday might be lost to him for ever.

Julian and Bryddie joined him a week later, but on 24 August, the very morning he was to undertake the climb, he was woken early by two telegrams, urging him to call home. He had already seen a Milan newspaper the night before, containing the news that the King had returned to London from Balmoral and Baldwin from his own holiday in Aix. By eight o'clock he had got through to Neville Chamberlain by telephone who, in reply to Leo's enquiry as to whether he should return home immediately, replied 'yes though somewhat indefinitely', his tone suggesting to Leo that 'they had been doing things which they knew I should not approve of'.[68] Leo left immediately, settling Bryddie and Julian into a hotel on the shores of Lake Garda, where he found Duff and Diana Cooper enjoying lunch. 'He might have finished his holiday,' remarked Cooper, who was destined for a junior ministerial post in the new Government, 'for he was not to get office again for nine years.'[69] At Le Bourget airport in Paris, the European edition of the *Daily Mail* confirmed that a new National Government was indeed to be formed under Ramsay MacDonald. The 'Old Gangs had coalesced after all', and 'under the most futile of the old gangsters'.[70]

Leo felt let down, especially by those who had previously opposed the idea of coalition. Baldwin asked to see him at the earliest opportunity, only to cancel the meeting twice, 'like a schoolboy feeling rather guilty and afraid of a talking to'. The Cabinet list, published on the day of his return, did not impress him either and he reluctantly resolved that he would 'find himself compelled to criticise a great deal from the outset'.[71] He wondered whether, had he been in London, he might have talked his colleagues out of joining a coalition under

Ramsay MacDonald, but refused to reproach himself. He wrote to *The Times*, warning that the coalition would face difficulties and seriously considered voting against the unanimous acceptance of the proposals at a party meeting a few days later. Nor did he believe Baldwin's promises that it would be a short-term solution, urging instead that there should be an early general election.

Nearly two weeks later, Baldwin finally agreed to see Leo. Although he had told his friends that he was 'glad to think that they had the grace not to ask me whether I should like to join in their Tom Cobley show', Leo had been forced to concede also that 'after all the years bingeing up Baldwin it was pretty disheartening to find him slipping back out of everything in a fortnight.'[72] Now he gave vent to the hurt and frustration that had been mounting since his return. He told Baldwin 'very frankly that he had behaved very badly' in leaving him for a fortnight with no explanation. Why, he asked, had others, 'definitely my inferiors in claims or authority with the Party' been preferred to him, and why had he not at least been given the opportunity of joining the new Cabinet? Baldwin affected surprise that Leo should be so upset, and excused himself on the grounds of having been 'overwhelmed with work'. But he then 'realised that he had behaved badly and asked forgiveness with such sincerity' that Leo let the matter drop.[73]

When the House met the following day Leo arrived early and, for the first time since the war, put in a prayer card, the parliamentary mechanism for reserving a seat. Finding the new Government benches already overflowing, he chose the corner seat on the third row back below the gangway, traditionally occupied by independent back-benchers or retired former ministers. He was to share it for many years with Austen Chamberlain, while Churchill chose the matching seat in the front row below the gangway. Having listened to others criticise the coalition, when it came to his turn to speak Leo remained loyal, reluctantly urging the House to support the new Government. He was congratulated for his selflessness by a number of Labour Members, and by Churchill, who compared his behaviour to 'the real mother in the judgement of Solomon; complete indifference to his own personal part, if only he were sure of the victory of the policy.'[74]

Leo did not enjoy campaigning during the ensuing election of October 1931, but he retained his seat with his largest ever majority. Nationally the coalition won with a majority of 558, to which the Conservatives contributed 471 seats, a result which convinced Leo that they could easily have won a majority on their own. Immediately after the election, Austen Chamberlain offered Baldwin his place in any new Cabinet to make way for younger men, an action which drew widespread praise and brought a melancholy letter of congratulation from Leo. 'We haven't always agreed,' he admitted, 'though I know you have long since forgiven our difference.' He only hoped that he might be 'one of the juniors who may benefit by your action', but recognised that 'probably I shall find myself excluded for having too definite views and being too impatient to get things done.'[75] He was to be proved right.

He hoped to reclaim his former position as Colonial Secretary and wrote to Baldwin asking that he might be allowed to do so, but there were to be only eleven Conservatives in a Cabinet of twenty, and the new Chancellor, Philip Snowden, complained that the protectionists were already over-represented. Although Leo claimed that he would have 'had the gravest doubts about' serving in the Cabinet, and that his feeling at being passed over was 'one of relief rather than distress', he was unhappy at the manner in which he had been treated. Bryddie took it 'very bravely', while Baldwin appeared to be genuinely upset, claiming that he had 'fought hard' for Leo 'up to the end'.[76] Of those omitted, Leo 'alone could have had a grievance' and, when they met a few days later, Baldwin told him 'much about the misery the whole thing has been to him' and how he appreciated Leo's stoicism. Ramsay MacDonald had objected to him on the grounds that his views were 'too uncompromising' and that he lacked 'a national outlook'. Leo thought Baldwin was 'anything but happy over the situation and inclined to think it would not last', hoping, optimistically, that 'it would not be very many months before' they were colleagues again.[77]

Leo was the object of widespread sympathy on all sides of the House, and from ministers and backbenchers alike. Harold Macmillan consoled him with the opinion that 'the second eleven were better than the first and due to replace it shortly.'[78] On his fifty-eighth birthday later that month, Leo commiserated with himself that he was 'rather fat, out of condition and out of office',[79] a set of circumstances he shared, in part at least, with both Churchill and Lloyd George. However, he might have consoled himself had he known of the judgement, many years later, of a Prime Minister, by then retired, who looked back on the National Government of 1931 as 'a collection of the most respectable mediocrities of all parties'.[80] In spite of that, Leo was to remain in the political wilderness for the remainder of the decade.

CHAPTER FOURTEEN

Let Justice Be Done Though the Heavens Fall

When Parliament assembled on 10 November 1931, Leo kept his interventions, especially those of a critical nature, to a minimum. He spoke out strongly in favour of the Statute of Westminster, which implemented the new definition of Commonwealth, agreed during his time as Secretary of State, but again found himself opposed by Churchill, who criticised the attempt to end legislative control over the old Dominions, Ireland and probably, at some stage in the future, India as well. The irony was not lost on the House, one backbench colleague noting that as Churchill had 'surrendered Ireland', at a time when Leo had been 'opposed to him very properly, the change of viewpoint is amusing'.[1] During the debate on the Address, however, Leo launched a powerful assault on the National Government in general, and Ramsay MacDonald in particular, which went down well with the House as a whole. It was not so popular with Neville Chamberlain, who believed that Leo had 'begun to show his resentment at being left out by increasingly sharp attacks', but 'perhaps he thinks he has no chance of office now.' He told his sister that, when he came to reply, he had avoided mentioning Leo by name as 'I don't want to be the first to begin personalities.'[2]

From the back benches Leo continued to lead the campaign for tariffs, although the new Government initially gave no indication that it was thinking likewise. However, on 19 January 1932, a Cabinet committee under Chamberlain's chairmanship recommended a general revenue tariff of 10 per cent. The free-trade Liberals within the Cabinet at first threatened to destroy the coalition, but a peace deal was brokered by which they were allowed to speak out publicly against the policy rather than resign from the Government. Leo was appalled that the arrangement was accepted so willingly by politicians and the press alike, and did his best to speak out against what he considered to be a constitutional departure. And when Chamberlain introduced the measure in the House, in the form of the Import Duties Bill, Leo could only muse that, although he was himself now out of office, the policy for which he had fought for the past thirty years was, at last, to be implemented by the son of his hero, under whose influence he had joined the campaign in the first place.

While Leo concentrated on building up his portfolio of business interests for much of the early part of 1932, the Government was making plans for the Imperial Economic Conference, to be held in Ottawa that summer. Initially Leo had hoped that he might be invited to attend the conference in an official capacity as part of the British delegation. However, no such invitation was forthcoming, and when he read the list of the official team who were to attend, he remarked that, while 'quite an army were going', he did not think 'any of them could handle the business as well as I could'.[3] Such an attitude had almost certainly contributed to the absence of an official invitation in the first place. However, an old friend, the Australian financier W. S. Robinson, offered to pay for his passage if he would accompany him instead, and Leo also accepted invitations from the Empire Sugar Federation, of which he was president, and the Central Chamber of Agriculture, to represent their interests in Ottawa.

Beaverbrook, who had for some time been encouraging Leo to act as a catalyst for the destruction of the coalition, strongly advised him against making the trip, warning that he would invariably be 'tainted with any possible failure of the Government', and so weaken his own 'position from the point of view of the formation of an alternative Government'.[4] But Leo's mind was made up for him when Richard Bennett, the Canadian Prime Minister, publicly welcomed the news that he was to attend. Unfortunately, Bennett's action only heightened the sense of mistrust felt by the official British delegation, led by Baldwin, with whom Leo set sail on board the *Empress of Britain* on 13 July. The voyage passed without incident as Leo mixed freely with his former colleagues, and he felt encouraged by the lengthy talks he had with Baldwin as they paced the deck together. He was amused too to see that a pamphlet he had written in advance of the conference had become essential reading for his fellow passengers.

On arrival in Ottawa, however, it soon became clear that any ambition Leo may have had to play a leading role was not to be fulfilled. At the opening ceremony in the House of Commons, he found it 'a little strange sitting up in a gallery among minor unofficial advisers, and thinking of the speech which I might have made'.[5] His lack of official status caused immediate problems. Most of the Dominion premiers agreed with Bennett, and were only too enthusiastic to seek Leo's advice and to work his ideas into their speeches. He was even invited to chair some of the subcommittees and to draft the ensuing reports, which were in turn sent on to the British delegation for consideration. But as the relationship between the British and Dominion Governments cooled, accusations soon followed that Leo was deliberately trying to sabotage the conference behind the scenes. It was certainly true that he wanted to achieve more than Baldwin and Chamberlain were prepared to concede, and he supported the demands of the Dominions that the Commonwealth should develop common agricultural and industrial policies among its member countries. When negotiations foundered over a proposal to impose duties on meat, it was to Leo that the Dominion Prime Ministers turned, asking him to intervene with Baldwin and Chamberlain on their behalf.

Chamberlain reacted with fury. Not only had 'well-meaning articles in the press' represented Leo as 'the single intellect who truly understood the complexity of the economic issues',[6] but he now appeared to be colluding with the Dominion representatives against those of his own Government. Chamberlain accused him 'of wrecking the Conference by inciting the Dominions to make impossible requests', an allegation which mortified Leo. If only Chamberlain understood 'how little "inciting" ' he had actually done, 'and how meekly I have hung about in the hope that I might be useful'. With the conference in crisis, Leo was being lined up as the fall guy and portrayed as 'the devil in the whole business, the mysterious schemer who has been working things up to a deadlock', and was on the 'side of the "enemy"'.[7] In reply he told Chamberlain that his only ambition had been to contribute to the success of the conference, and of his 'distress' that he 'should have formed so entirely wrong a mental picture of my activities here'.[8] Privately, however, he recognised 'how embarrassing it must have been' for Baldwin and Chamberlain 'to have on the spot someone who was on much more intimate personal terms with all the Dominion delegates, who carried more weight with them than they did, and whom they knew to share none of their own scruples about "breaking up the national Government".'[9]

The damage had been done. At home Chamberlain's brother Austen was busy complaining about 'the amazingly disloyal action of Amery at Ottawa'.[10] The Colonial Secretary, Jimmy Thomas, warned Leo that 'nothing would induce the Tory Ministers ever to include him in any Government again',[11] a threat that both Baldwin and Chamberlain were indeed later able to carry out. On his return to London he tried to play down the accusations of disloyalty and publicly supported the agreements reached in Ottawa. 'I am unwilling to say more just now,' he wrote in response to a request from Lady Milner to write an article, 'as I do not wish to appear critical or captious.' His position in Ottawa had been a 'difficult one', he confessed wearily, as the British delegation had looked on him throughout 'with suspicion'.[12] And when the free-trade Liberals eventually resigned from the Cabinet in September, in protest at the Ottawa agreements and took Philip Snowden with them, there was no question of Leo being offered a post in the ensuing reshuffle. Instead, Leo was increasingly turning his mind to another issue, one he described at the time as the 'pacifist delusion' and, many years later, as the 'growing menace in the world outside, and the strange and sorry story of national aberration and political ineptitude with which we, first, ignored and then aggravated the menace, before finally drifting once more into war'.[13]

Leo was outspoken in his views on the Disarmament Conference, which had assembled in Geneva in February 1932. He blamed the increasing support for disarmament at home on 'a pacifist Prime Minister intent upon retrieving his credit' and, to his great dismay, 'the natural temptation of Conservative Ministers to pay lip service to the prevailing current of opinion'.[14] For five months Leo watched as the delegates in Geneva indulged in what he saw as a futile discussion on the merits of a so-called 'proportionate' versus 'qualitative' reduction in arsenals, in effect the proposed elimination of the more offensive heavy weapons. France, keeping a watchful eye on her increasingly hostile neighbour, was reluctant to agree to any military reductions, while Germany, still subject to the limitations imposed at Versailles, now demanded the equality of status that she believed had been promised in 1919. If the world would not disarm to the German level, then Germany would achieve military parity by rearming herself.

At home Leo watched as the disarmament lobby grew in strength and reputation. In October the Archbishop of Canterbury led a deputation to urge the Prime Minister to speed up the pace of disarmament and to accept the principle of equality of status with Germany. In the same month Leo debated with Lord Robert Cecil at the Cambridge Union, on a motion that Britain should disarm to the German level. He was heavily defeated, but was less distressed by the result than the noisy hostility of the undergraduates which meant he could hardly be heard. Leo had never believed that armaments were the cause of war. 'I know of no instance in history', he later told the House of Commons, 'where the competition of armaments has of itself played any serious part in bringing about a war.' Wars were the result of 'causes far deeper than disarmament'.[15] While disarmament might, in certain cases, diminish wider international suspicion, it could also have the opposite, and devastating, effect of strengthening the relative position of a nation that sought to overturn the world order. However, he believed too that while the disarmament of Germany in 1919 had been justified, it had also contained too great an element of punishment and that Germany's ensuing lack of military equality was a crucial grievance that must be tackled.

By the end of 1932 Leo had become resigned to 'occupying my

corner seat' in the House for a further three years, and then, 'when these people have given the Socialists a fat majority, exchanging it for an Opposition back bench'. If only he had 'any power of parliamentary oratory comparable to Winston's', then he could have done 'things single handed'.[16] In February 1933, after Leo had contributed to a debate on the Manchurian crisis and the subsequent Japanese invasion of northern China, his friend John Simon, by now the Foreign Secretary, invited him to chair the Commission of Inquiry which the League of Nations was to send to the region to investigate. Leo declined the offer, principally because of his growing business interests at home, but when the issue was again raised in the House he took the opportunity, to the consternation of many of his colleagues, to defend Japan's actions and to launch a bitter attack on the League of Nations. 'I am afraid that there is a good deal of conscious or unconscious hypocrisy,' he concluded, 'when we talk about the League of Nations, about disarmament and about peace. I have endured it for a good long time. At any rate I have freed my soul this afternoon.'[17]

His severest criticism, however, was reserved for Baldwin's declaration that he had been 'impressed with the appalling consequences of a future war conducted from the air', and his subsequent suggestion, fashionable at the time, that 'if the nations were serious on the question of Disarmament they ought to agree to scrap all military and naval aviation.'[18] Leo was not even impressed by the proposed exemption for so-called 'police' bombing in 'outlying' areas of the Empire, something he had himself used successfully while Colonial Secretary. On 10 November 1932 Baldwin had told the House that it was important for 'the man in the street to realise that there is no power on earth that can protect him from being bombed. Whatever people may tell him, the bomber will always get through.' The only defence against widespread civilian bombing was 'offence, which means that you have to kill more women and children more quickly than the enemy if you want to save yourselves'.[19] Leo was appalled by this outburst and two weeks later warned the House that the Government's suggestion that disarmament by itself would provide 'a foundation for lasting peace' was 'based upon a profound delusion'. They had created a 'Frankenstein's monster in the shape of a sincere, well-meaning, unintelligent public opinion, hypnotised' into believing, 'in its genuine and admirable love of peace, that peace must somehow be secured by disarmament, the more sweeping the better, the more impracticable and the more foolish the better'.[20]

Leo returned to the issue in March the following year, this time with support from Churchill. The Government had formally tabled its proposals at Geneva for abolishing all air forces except those for 'police purposes in outlying places'. Churchill criticised Baldwin for 'causing alarm without giving guidance', while Leo, who had been secretly briefed by the Permanent Secretary to the Air Ministry, Sir Christopher Bullock, concentrated on the specific proposals put forward at Geneva. It was, he asserted sarcastically, typical of the 'conscious hypocrisy' with which the question of disarmament was approached, that the Government 'now proposed the abolition of aeroplanes that could bomb us, but reserved the right to bomb Kurds or Pathans, a right, no doubt, essential to the maintenance of civilization in "outlying places".'[21] His only regret was that, once again, his thunder had been stolen by Churchill who had 'said all the kind of things I wanted to say and probably said them much better'. Not for the first time his own speech was, he thought, 'rather heavy and ineffective'.[22]

On 14 October 1933 Germany, by now under the leadership of Adolf Hitler, withdrew from the Geneva Conference and the League of Nations, an action which Leo hoped might give the Government cause to reconsider its policy. But the tide of pacifism, epitomised by the loss of the East Fulham by-election to Labour, was too strong to swim against. When the House debated the progress of the Geneva Conference on 7 November, Leo recorded that Simon's contribution was 'long and lucid as usual', Austen Chamberlain 'put all the blame on the Germans, Lloyd George all on the French', while Eden was 'suave and highly official'.[23] When Leo rose to speak, he made his point bluntly. 'Germany wants to rearm. Germany means to rearm. Germany is going to rearm and nobody is going to stop her,' he told the House. 'The Disarmament Convention is dead and no one is going to be able to galvanize it into life,' he continued and, comparing himself to the child in the Hans Christian Andersen fairy tale who dares to ask why the Emperor is wearing no clothes, he urged the Government to 'stop this wild-goose chase after mechanical, reach-me-down schemes of world disarmament and peace, and leave Europe to settle her own affairs.'[24]

There was, however, one policy over which Leo was in full agreement with Baldwin and the National Government, namely India. Having been born there, he had always taken a keen interest in Indian affairs, despite having never returned to the country since leaving at the age of three, and he felt considerable pride in the story of the British Raj. And while his knowledge of India was not on a par with his experience of the Dominions, he had always followed Indian political affairs closely. The Conservative leadership was committed to a liberal attitude to the question of Indian self-government and Leo, although often portrayed as a diehard imperialist, held equally progressive views. As long ago as October 1929, his former colleague from All Souls, Edward Wood, by then, as Lord Irwin, the Viceroy of India, had declared that the attainment of Dominion status should be India's ultimate goal. Leo had not always been a supporter of Wood, once describing him as a 'dignified exterior who says nothing',[25] but on this occasion he agreed with him wholeheartedly, to the horror of most of his Shadow Cabinet colleagues. Now, four years later, having been responsible for the successful transition of the Dominions to equal status, Leo believed that the same principle should apply to India and that the ultimate aim of responsible British rule there should be Dominion status. It was, he thought, 'far wiser to meet the demand for self-government half way than to keep the safety valve screwed down'.[26]

During the Indian Round Table Conferences of 1930 and 1931, and subsequent parliamentary debates, Leo had continued to defend Government policy on India, in the face of mounting opposition from Churchill and his fellow Conservative diehards. It was a source of particular anxiety for Leo that he should find himself so publicly in disagreement with many of his old friends. In the House of Lords, for example, the opposition was led by George Lloyd, a former governor in India and recently deposed as High Commissioner in Egypt by the Labour Government. He and Leo had fought many battles together and were old friends, but in February 1931 he had written to Leo that 'if India goes, everything goes; our honour, our wealth, our strategic security and our prestige.' Leo replied that he could not even bring himself to put pen to paper in response, 'for that might put an end to all friendship'.[27] Leo welcomed the appointment of another friend, Sam Hoare, as Secretary of State for India in the National Government, applauding his 'genuine goodwill towards Indian aspirations', and did his best to shore up support for the Government's policy from the backbenches. Week after week he attended the Conservative India Committee, throwing himself 'into the breach to prevent its being stampeded by Churchill'.

Leo enjoyed an unusual standing in the party during debates on India. As a former diehard, no one could accuse him of being 'week-kneed on Imperial issues or of merely advocating a Front Bench view',[28] a position that considerably enhanced his influence. In March 1933, after three Round Table Conferences and three special commissions to India, the Government eventually presented a White Paper to Parliament, embodying a draft scheme for provincial self-government there. A joint Select Committee of both Houses was created, on which Churchill and a number of other diehards refused to serve, instead launching increasingly personal attacks on Baldwin. A year later, in April 1934, Churchill shocked the Commons by claiming that Hoare and Lord Derby had colluded to tamper with evidence which had been submitted to the Select Committee by the Manchester Chamber of Commerce, and demanded that the matter be referred to the Committee of Privileges. To Hoare's great relief the Committee cleared him of any wrongdoing and Churchill was advised to let the matter drop. However, on 13 June, when the Committee's report was presented to the House, Churchill seized the opportunity to launch another attack on both Hoare and the Committee of Privileges itself.

For once his speech fell flat, and when a dramatic attempt to expose new-found evidence of malpractice was greeted with laughter, he lost his stride completely. It was to give Leo the opportunity to achieve 'his greatest oratorical victory over Churchill'.[29] Having endured Churchill's hour-long philippic, Leo rose to defend Hoare. He confessed that he 'had hoped for a very different speech' from Churchill, since there was 'no one in this House who knows better how to conduct a skilful and good-humoured retreat from an untenable position', and no one 'to whom, as an old favourite in difficult circumstances' the House would be 'more willing to extend its fullest consideration'. He attacked Churchill's Lutheran conviction that 'personal considerations must not affect the faithful and uncompromising discharge of public duties by members of the House.' The law must take its course, however powerful were those whom it brought down. He had 'at all costs been faithful to his chosen motto: "Fiat justicia, ruat caelum".' Quick as a flash, Churchill swung round and demanded that Leo translate. Leo knew his Roman proverbs well, and that the literal translation was 'Let justice be done though the heavens fall.' But the vernacular translation, he told Churchill, was that 'If I can trip up Sam, the Government's bust.'[30]

Churchill had walked straight into the trap carefully laid by Leo, who had 'scarcely dared to hope that the fish would swallow my fly so greedily'. So successfully had he highlighted the contrast between Churchill's pose and his true intention, that the House fell about laughing and it was some time before order could be restored. Leo went to bed that night 'having given Winston the best ducking he has had since he first pushed me into Ducker in 1889. But he remains unsinkable and will no doubt bob up again after a bit.'[31] Leo's speech had, he thought, been 'one of the most successful from the purely parliamentary point of view' that he had ever delivered,[32] while Hoare was relieved and grateful that he had 'torn Churchill's charges to pieces'.[33] But when, two days later, Leo found himself the centre of attention and the recipient of 'whispered congratulations' at a dinner, Churchill greeted him 'with a broad grin' and asked whether the translation had been impromptu. Leo had to concede that it had not been, and Churchill admitted that for thirty years 'he had always said to himself when he entered the House "never interrupt", but has always been let down again and again by his impetuosity.'[34] It was to be a source of great personal regret to Leo that, at a time when he and Churchill were in strong agreement over the issue of disarmament, 'our difference over India prevented a closer and more continuous co-operation'.[35]

While Leo continued to harbour hopes that he might once again serve at the heart of Government, in the summer of 1934 he was informally approached by his friend John Buchan to enquire whether he might be interested in succeeding Lord Hugh Cecil as the Member for the Oxford University constituency. He was initially attracted by the offer, as it would entail 'a great saving not only of money but even more of drudgery, especially for B'. After thirty years of 'strenuous fighting in purely industrial seats', he thought he would be justified in 'falling back upon the essentially more congenial atmosphere of a University seat'. After a good deal of thought, however, he turned down Buchan's offer on the grounds that it would have been too great a 'wrench' to leave Birmingham.[36]

The decision was also made easier by the impressive portfolio of business interests which he had now accumulated, so much so that he was increasingly in two minds as to whether he could afford to accept ministerial office, even if were offered. There had been mutterings that he might be invited to rejoin the Cabinet as part of a reshuffle timed to coincide with the the King's Silver Jubilee celebrations of May 1935, but when Baldwin succeeded Ramsay MacDonald as Prime Minister on 7 June, Leo was once again excluded. While relieved that he could hold on to his newly acquired business income, he was once again disappointed by Baldwin's 'tongue-tied and furtive' manner when informing him, deliberately avoiding all eye contact in the lobby. Leo felt bitter at Baldwin that he had not only 'made him PM in 1923', but had more recently 'averted a landslide against him' over India. Now, sadly, he was probably 'out of it for good' and would 'most probably have to leave it to others, possibly Julian, to see through what I have begun'.[37]

▪ ▪ ▪

Since Hitler's rise to power in 1933, Leo had begun to take an increasingly close interest in events in Nazi Germany and in the Chancellor himself, commenting as early as October 1932 on his 'absurd personality'.[38] Leo's business interests took him to Germany and Austria regularly, where he came into contact with a large number of businessmen, many of them Jewish, and was deeply impressed by the testimony of those who feared for their lives. And he expressed his strong disapproval, in September 1933, when George Lloyd returned from meeting Hitler, whom he had found 'extremely simple and modest', and shared with Leo his enjoyment of 'a cheery dinner party with Goering and some of his ruffians'.[39] The following month he received a call from a fellow director of the Hirsch Copper Company who had been forced to resign his position as chairman of a leading German aluminium company, on account of being Jewish. Equally distressing were the first-hand accounts which reached him of conditions in Germany, 'nobody daring to speak even to members of their own family', and 'large numbers of people, not only Jews but Liberals and Socialists literally likely to starve in the next few months'.[40]

In February 1934 Leo visited Vienna for a few days, ostensibly to address a pan-European gathering on the effects of the Ottawa Conference, although the pill was sweetened by the prospect of two weeks skiing in Kitzbühel beforehand. He arrived there in the aftermath of the suppression of the socialist uprising against the Dollfuss regime, and he held meetings with all the political factions, including Dollfuss himself, by whom, 'far from finding him a bigoted reactionary', he was 'greatly impressed by his engaging simplicity, cheerful confidence and essential moderation'. During his talks with the British Minister, he was disturbed to discover that the Foreign Office 'had not even yet realised the gravity of the Nazi menace or made sufficient allowance for Dollfuss's difficulties'.[41] Within a few months, the Austrian leader had been murdered.

In May, during a visit to Berlin, the cancellation of a business meeting on a wet afternoon enabled Leo to sit down to read *Mein Kampf*, 'in the original unexpurgated German'. He finished the book on the journey home, finding it 'very interesting and stimulating', and being particularly impressed by Hitler's 'intense sincerity and clear thinking on some points'. On the other hand, he was clearly 'quite insane about Jews and Socialists', and Leo doubted whether 'he will really settle down to ordinary statesmanship for long'. Above all, he believed, Hitler's success might well prove to 'be a great danger'.[42] At home, the talk among Conservative colleagues was of the 'brutality shown at Mosley's meetings' and Leo hoped that the 'Government will be prompt in suppressing the whole blackshirt movement'.[43] And when, in January 1935, the family chose the Black Forest for their annual skiing holiday, they listened to the radio in their hotel broadcasting the results of the plebiscite in the Saar region. Leo was unimpressed by Hitler's speech, especially by his 'husky and undistinguished' delivery, and noted that his 'diction was equally undistinguished and noteworthy for several non-German words which his followers are so busy eradicating'.[44] Goebbels, on the other hand, 'spoke beautiful German in a fine clear voice' and there could be 'no doubt of his quality as an orator'.[45] After listening to Nazi songs on the radio, the few British residents in the hotel got together surreptitiously for their own impromptu rendition of 'Rule Britannia'.

In August 1935 Leo decided to try a new destination for the family climbing holiday and settled on a hotel on the shores of the Königssee, a mountain lake at the foot of the Watzmann, a mountain in the Bavarian Alps he had long wanted to climb. Although only 9,000 feet high, it was renowned for having the highest unbroken rock face in the Alps, a sheer east face of 6,000 feet, towering above the Königssee below. After meeting Leo in London, the German Ambassador, Joachim von Ribbentrop, had alerted Hitler to his likely presence in the area, just a few miles from his retreat at Berchtesgaden. One of Hitler's ADCs soon arrived at the hotel with an invitation to visit and, the following day, Hitler's large black limousine turned up to whisk Leo away in the company of Hitler's chief interpreter. The drive took them through Berchtesgaden and Obersalzburg, and up a winding road crowded with tourists trying to catch a glimpse of Hitler's country house. Eventually they arrived at the bungalow at Rosenheim, which enjoyed a spectacular view across the valley to Austria, and was at the time Hitler's favoured home in the days before he moved to the mountain retreat which became more familiar in later years.

Hitler greeted Leo on the veranda, wearing a plain grey flannel suit, and showed him into a large room which was lined with tapestries and had 'an immense plate-glass window occupying the whole of one side', a concept that Leo later discovered was copied by Lloyd George in his library at Churt, as a result of his own subsequent visit there. Leo's first impression of Hitler was that 'both his appearance and his manner were those of a shop-walker', an echo of Lord Halifax's visit, two years later, when he famously mistook Hitler for a footman and made to offer him his coat. They wasted little time on pleasantries, but quickly moved on to politics and talked for two hours. For an hour or so Leo kept up with the pace, but during the second hour Hitler 'gave himself a clear run on the theme of all he had achieved for Germany',[46] and how unanimous was the support he enjoyed save for 'the infinitesimal section of political fanatics, international Jews and actual criminals who were against him'. It was an interesting speech, thought Leo, 'as an indication of his platform oratory and of the kind of moral fervour which he can generate'.

However, Leo's opinion of Hitler was far from wholly negative. While he 'did not find the hypnotic charm' he had heard of, he appreciated Hitler's 'directness and eagerness to let his hearer know all his mind'. On European economic issues, he found himself in broad agreement with much of what Hitler proposed. 'Intellectually', thought Leo, he had 'a grip on economic essentials and on many political ones, too,' even if his views were 'crude at times and coloured by deep personal prejudice'. All in all, Hitler was 'a bigger man' than he had expected and they got on well together, largely due to 'the fundamental similarity of many of our ideas'. But Leo had also to admit that they 'didn't discuss some controversial subjects like Austria, constitutional liberty, Jews or Colonies'.[47] Although such an omission now seems extraordinary given the contemporary importance of such issues, Leo's strongly held views and, indeed, his own Jewishness, he later explained it away by claiming that he had deliberately sought to avoid confrontation. Julian, along with a school friend, had accompanied Leo in the car as far as the gate house, where the two boys sat drinking coffee with some of Hitler's aides. He later recalled only that his father had thought Hitler 'rather dull but much less extreme in his views than he had expected'.[48]

■ ■ ■

Leo returned from his summer holiday and his meeting with Hitler to play a significant, if controversial, role in the developing crisis between Mussolini's Italy and Abyssinia. Although he had taken some comfort from Sam Hoare's appointment as Foreign Secretary, he nevertheless quickly established himself as 'the leader of Conservative dissent' in relation to Abyssinia, possibly, as one historian has suggested, as a result of being again passed over for office, although he undoubtedly 'saw no reason to restrain indefinitely the expression of opinions he would have held in any case'.[49] He had already been dismissive of the agreements reached at the Stresa Conference in April 1935, had long since ceased to trust the League of Nations as a vehicle for preventing war in Europe, and was scathing about Eden's attempts to advance the cause of 'collective security' in Geneva. He believed too that the Government was wholly culpable for allowing the inexorable growth of the peace movement at home.

From his earlier contacts with Mussolini and his Ambassador in London, Count Grandi, Leo knew that the mere threat of sanctions would do little to calm the Italian leader's arrogant determination to wage war on Abyssinia, and believed that the Government was merely driving Mussolini into Hitler's arms. 'For electioneering purposes and largely through Eden's insistence,' he thought, 'Italy was being made an enemy where the German problem demanded that she remain a friend.'[50] Baldwin, meanwhile, was cynically trying 'to outbid the combined Oppositions and sail back to office on a wave of virtuous indignation as the true champion of collective responsibility.'[51] Leo initially hoped that Hoare would win the battle in Cabinet against the imposition of sanctions, but when the Foreign Secretary spoke in support of collective security and the League of Nations, in Geneva on 12 September, he decided that the time had come to act. On the 24th he saw Hoare at the Foreign Office and 'made it plain that I regarded the Government policy with profound misgivings, and thought that it could only lead to disaster; at the worst war, at the best humiliation before the world of having tried to stop Italy and failed.'[52]

On 3 October 1935 Mussolini invaded Abyssinia and, two days later, Baldwin branded as isolationists those who refused to support the League. Leo responded with a furious speech of his own in Birmingham, insisting that economic sanctions were futile so long as the United States, Germany and Japan all stood outside the League, and that the only way to prevent war in Abyssinia was by 'declaring war on Italy ourselves'. While that might have been the wish of the Government, he doubted whether it was that of the British people, and concluded that he 'at any rate . . . was not prepared to send a single Birmingham lad to his death for the sake of Abyssinia'. The speech caused a widespread stir, and earned Leo a 'scathing rebuke' from Neville Chamberlain, who described it as a 'mischievous distortion of realities'.[53]

Twelve days after the invasion Leo took a deputation of MPs to see Baldwin to lobby against military sanctions, a policy which Hoare ruled out anyway a few days later. Leo's speech in the same debate was poorly received by a hostile House, and even those who agreed with him in private wished that he had held his counsel. His only consolation was a quiet word from Churchill who, while once again finding himself in profound disagreement on the substance of Leo's speech, congratulated him on being the 'straightest man in public life'.[54] During the ensuing election campaign Leo, Churchill and Neville Chamberlain were labelled 'fire-eaters' and 'militarists' by Herbert Morrison,[55] but Baldwin was safely returned to power with a majority of 258 and a clear mandate to pursue his policies, while Leo was returned in Birmingham with an only slightly reduced majority.

In December Leo supported the so-called Hoare–Laval Pact which ceded two large areas of Abyssinia to Italy, while retaining a region in the centre of the country which was contemptuously christened 'A Corridor for Camels' by *The Times*. Although Mussolini accepted the plan, Government supporters of the League of Nations felt betrayed by the apparent volte-face and, while Hoare was away taking a short holiday in Switzerland, the Government backed down and the Foreign Secretary was forced to resign. Leo was outraged that Baldwin had withdrawn his support from Hoare without offering him the opportunity to explain his agreement with Laval to the House, believing that he could have successfully done so. Hoare eventually made a dignified and restrained personal statement, explaining his resignation, with Leo sitting at his side on the backbenches.

Baldwin's fall from grace during the six months following the 1935 election was spectacular. By February 1936 the rumblings of discontent with his leadership were growing more audible and, by early March, Leo 'found the atmosphere of dissatisfaction with the Government very strong'.[56] His own star, by contrast, was once again on the rise, as the Government's policy of sanctions against Italy unravelled. On 6 March Hitler ordered his troops into the demilitarised zone of the Rhineland, 'a most adroitly timed stroke', thought Leo, 'and an interesting commentary on the folly of a policy which has broken up the Anglo-French-Italian understanding.' However, he thought that the 'one good thing that might come out of it is a dropping of sanctions against Italy'[57] and, sure enough, by June Neville Chamberlain was describing sanctions as the 'midsummer of madness' and in July they were finally abandoned.

The previous December *The Times* had called for the creation of a new Ministry of Defence and the appointment of a new ministerial defence supremo. The campaign had been the brainchild of the military historian Basil Liddell Hart, and although his personal choice for the job would have been Churchill, both his editor, Geoffrey Dawson, and the deputy editor had favoured Leo, 'either as Minister or as permanent non-political chairman' of a new defence organisation. Liddell Hart conceded that if Churchill was to be ruled out, Leo would be a 'fitting choice'.[58] It seemed possible that either Churchill or Leo would be offered the job and, on 10 March, a backbencher approached Leo in the smoking room and urged him to 'take the lead and call the Conservative Party out of Coalition.'[59] However, three days later came the 'world shaking announcement', in reply to Hitler's invasion of the Rhineland, that Sir Thomas Inskip, the Attorney General, was to be appointed 'Minister for the Co-ordination of Defence'. Churchill subsequently described the appointment as 'the most remarkable since Caligula made his horse Consul', although Leo had to concede that there was ample precedent for Baldwin appointing someone so well 'equipped with an amiable disposition and with the impartiality of ignorance'.[60] Until then Inskip's principal claim to fame had been his fierce opposition to the introduction of a new prayer book in the 1920s, and Leo could only imagine that 'Baldwin must have mixed up the revision of the War Book with the revision of the Prayer-book.'[61]

During 1936 Leo increasingly allied himself with a small group of backbenchers who coalesced around Churchill and Austen

Chamberlain, and who began to campaign for an increase in the pace of rearmament. In July he was one of thirteen MPs who formed a deputation to Baldwin on the issue and, in particular, the relative weakness of the RAF in contrast to the Luftwaffe. Baldwin and Inskip were polite but vague, and promised more detail in the autumn. However, when the delegation returned in November, the replies they received left Leo profoundly worried. In the House, while Churchill concentrated his fire on the poor quality of Britain's air defences and a lack of munitions, Leo returned to the subject which had been his speciality thirty years earlier, that of the readiness of the army and, in particular, its rapidly shrinking size. In October a group was established under his chairmanship, consisting of fellow politicians, businessmen and senior soldiers, to look into the question of army reform and, once their proposals were published in 1937, the group formalised its activities by creating an Army League, giving support to the War Office in its struggles with the Treasury.

Leo played only a small role in the other great political drama of the latter half of 1936, the abdication of King Edward VIII. He had enjoyed a close working relationship with George V during his time as Dominions Secretary and had equally high hopes for the new King. The day after George V's death in January, Leo was one of more than a hundred Privy Counsellors summoned to St James's Palace to hear the new King Edward make a short speech. He had high hopes for the new reign but, as the year wore on, the gossip surrounding the King's affair with the American divorcée Mrs Wallis Simpson dominated the conversation in both the smoking room at All Souls and the drawing rooms of Belgravia. Once the story became public, Leo gave his full support to Baldwin's handling of the crisis, once again finding himself in the opposing camp to Churchill who made a passionate defence of the King's right to marry and still retain his throne. 'It was curious', remarked Churchill sarcastically, 'that whenever a big issue had arisen', he and Leo had always 'taken different points of view.'

On 4 December, after Baldwin's statement in the House of Commons, Leo found Churchill in the smoking room, 'completely on the rampage, saying that he was for the King and was not going to have him strangled in the dark by Ministers'. Churchill 'was never so excited', thought Leo, 'as when he is doing a ramp for his own private ends',[62] although he subsequently modified his views, coming to understand that Churchill's motives were not purely to work up an anti-Baldwin campaign, but that he was in fact 'personally very fond of the King'. Nevertheless, Leo still believed that the 'country was getting progressively more shocked at the idea that the King could hesitate between his duty to the throne and his affection for a second rate woman'.[63] After introducing the Abdication Bill in the House of Commons, Baldwin told Leo that he 'still really loved "the little man", but did not think him quite sane', while Mrs Simpson was 'a really wicked woman'.[64] Leo and Bryddie listened to the King's abdication speech together in a Birmingham hotel the following day, and while Leo was 'strangely moved by the voice I knew so well', Bryddie, ever the Empire Loyalist, 'had little use for the speech and still less for the reference to a woman who is still legally another man's wife'.[65]

In May 1937 Baldwin resigned as Prime Minister and was succeeded by Neville Chamberlain, just two months after the death of his brother Austen. Leo had already spoken to Baldwin privately about the possibility of his own inclusion in Chamberlain's first Cabinet. He recognised that it would be a serious financial blow to him to give up his directorships, but he had always put his duty before his personal affairs anyway, and would be happy to do so again. Baldwin promised to speak up on his behalf and Leo privately hoped that he might be offered the Board of Trade, the War Office, or even the Treasury. But it soon became clear that he had never featured in Chamberlain's plans at all and, when he saw the list, he was disappointed, but far from downcast, at being excluded. Far more hurtful was the muddled letter he received from Chamberlain, attempting to explain his omission. 'I am afraid you may have felt disappointed', wrote the new Prime Minister, 'that I did not ask you to join the new Government although that would have meant a sacrifice of income. But you will have realised that, as Asquith said I believe, there are always more horses than oats.'[66] Leo replied that he had indeed been 'disappointed, deeply disappointed, though certainly not for the reason which the closing sentence of your note would seem to suggest'. He had not sought office for the sake of it, but in the hope of being part of 'something more than a mere reshuffle or réchauffé', and of playing a full role in 'a new and lively policy in national and Imperial affairs'.[67] Chamberlain's reply once again missed the point, implying that Leo had mistakenly taken offence at an accusation of selfishness. The mutual distrust and antipathy between the two former friends had now put their relationship beyond repair.

CHAPTER FIFTEEN

———◆— ◆—

An Accomplished Chancer

By the early 1930s Leo's career was at its lowest ebb. Although ostensibly a supporter of the National Government, he was in the political wilderness and facing serious financial difficulties, soon to be made worse by Jack's increasingly erratic behaviour. During the decade that followed, Leo's frustration at being out of office and out of favour were compounded by Jack's waywardness. Yet in spite of his disappointment at Jack's refusal to take up the offer of a place at Oxford in 1929, Leo was still determined to do all he could to give him the best possible start in his chosen career, the film industry. Leo contacted a Mr Bruce Woolfe of British Instructional Films, who had done work for the Colonial Office during his tenure as Secretary of State. Based in Welwyn, north of London, it was agreed that Jack would start work there, with the intention of gaining experience of working in a studio environment and, ultimately, of going into the business of film production himself. Unfortunately the arrangement lasted no more than a few months. Although Jack did nothing specific to disgrace himself, he soon tired of the job, and Leo was contacted by Woolfe on a number of occasions to express his concerns at Jack's absenteeism. It was not helped that he suffered a bad bout of measles early on during his time in Welwyn. Eventually he left, tempted by the offer of joining a small, travelling film company with the extravagant title of Assistant Film Director.

Given that Leo was by now out of office and was desperately casting around for additional sources of income with which to supplement his meagre parliamentary salary, the last thing he needed was for Jack to become a drain on his limited resources. Initially, there was cause for hope that Jack's new career would prove a success. After a few months in his new job, he received his first dividend of almost £100, as his share of the proceeds from a film called *Guilt*. He prudently put away £60 towards opening a bank account and spent the rest on 'an enormous Renault' which he subsequently 'spent most of the day repainting'.[1] Contemplating Jack's future on New Year's Eve 1930, from his hotel bed in St Moritz where he was laid up having broken his leg skiing, Leo was cautiously optimistic. Even if the business was 'not that impressive', Jack was at least 'working hard' and 'acquiring the rudiments of sense and responsibility'.[2] Sadly, it was not to last.

Although still a few weeks short of his nineteenth birthday, Jack was now determined to fulfil his 'ambition of being the youngest living film director'. He somehow persuaded friends and family to part with enough money for him to begin production of a new film, *Jungle Skies*, to be shot in Africa on a budget of £100,000. Leo and the rest of the family were told little about the project, other than that it involved Jack directing 'aeroplane crashes, war dances of native tribes etc. – a remarkable enterprise in many ways' for a boy of his age.[3] At the same time, Jack took the ill-fated decision to support the production of *Jungle Skies* by branching out into the world of management, setting up a new agency, with the strikingly original name of 'Managements', supposedly to supply producers, actors, props and transport to the film industry. His share of the company and resulting profits would be 51 per cent, and he set up another agency, 'Tomorrow's Advertising', with the same two fellow co-directors. Again Leo expressed cautious optimism that the company might succeed, but less than two months later it was in financial trouble and Jack came to see his father, pleading for money with which he could buy out his none too reputable associates. Not for the first time, and certainly not for the last, the Amery family's lawyer Mr Mead was called in to negotiate an arrangement with a creditor and to extend a further line of credit to Jack. For good measure, a Mr Hamilton, the owner of Moon's Garage from whom Jack had acquired his second-hand Renault, also put in a claim against him for unpaid bills.

In early 1932, a 'tiresome letter from the Inland Revenue clamouring for arrears of surtax' was accompanied in the post by 'others about various doings of Jack's, not very serious but annoying'.[4] Leo was summoned to regular meetings at his bank, the National Provincial, before his requests for further increases in his overdraft facility were referred to head office. Eventually, the general manager, Sir Alfred Lewis, agreed to raise his maximum overdraft limit to £7,000, on the strict understanding that it could go no higher. Although Leo was still a high-profile politician, with a successful Cabinet career only recently behind him, he found it difficult approaching friends for help. Nevertheless, over the course of the first few months of 1932, he managed to secure for himself a number of directorships which contributed significantly to his salary. None were sinecures, and for a while he spent as much time conducting business as he did in the House of Commons.

Several times a week Leo attended meetings at the offices of Southern Railways, and from time to time accompanied his fellow directors on tours of the region to monitor the track, stations and rolling stock of the company. At the company's Annual General Meeting in February he narrowly survived an attempt to vote him off the board for lacking the necessary technical background in railways. Another railway company, the Gloucester Wagon Company, builders of trains and carriages, also invited him to join its board, which involved extensive travel around the south-west. His South African connections brought him a directorship at the South West Africa Company, with a promised share of the annual profits of around £600 a year, while Sir Edmund Davis, 'a South African financier with a rather Napoleonic profile, who was opening up the Copper Belt in Northern Rhodesia',[5] invited him to join the board of the Fanti Consolidated Mining Company for £500 a year. In June he became a director of the shipbuilders Cammell Laird, which was worth £300 a year and necessitated regular visits to Liverpool, while, most lucrative of all, the directors of the Iraq Currency Board invited the former Secretary of State to be their chairman at an annual income of

£1,000. Most audacious of all, he suggested to Sir Alfred Lewis, who had only recently made available to him an overdraft facility of £7,000, that he might be a suitable candidate to join the board of his own bank, the National Provincial, but the offer was politely declined on the grounds that he was still regarded in the City as too much of a politician rather than a businessman.

Jack continued to live at Eaton Square when he was in London, much to Bryddie's delight. In spite of his frequent troubles, the family lived happily together, Leo working increasingly hard to pay the mounting bills and Bryddie forgiving her eldest son almost anything he did. He knew how to flatter his parents, and enjoyed playing the part of the loving son, for instance by offering his car for them to visit Julian at Summer Fields, or by sitting in the gallery of the House of Commons to listen to his father speak. He would accompany them too to the great London parties of the day, often as Bryddie's escort when Leo was unable to attend due to parliamentary duties. Even Leo took pleasure at witnessing Jack's performance at a ball at Canada House, watching as the now accomplished charmer 'got away with a charming little bit of Turkish delight in the shape of the Turkish Ambassador's daughter'.[6]

Increasingly, however, Jack had begun to drift away from the bosom of the family. The occasional quiet night at home, over a family rubber of bridge, imperceptibly became more infrequent. He spent long periods abroad, primarily in Tanganyika, where he was engaged in the production and filming of *Jungle Skies*, although this enterprise too soon became immersed in controversy. Leo was embarrassed to receive a visit one day from Oliver Baldwin, the estranged son of the former Prime Minister, and himself recently elected as a Labour MP. A friend of his, Miles Mander, was in dispute with Jack over a script he had been asked to produce for *Jungle Skies*. Jack claimed that he had already paid for certain corrections to be made, and when Mander had failed to make them, had stopped the cheque accordingly. After two meetings, Leo quickly reached the conclusion that Jack was in the wrong and Mander was entitled to have his cheque cleared at once. Then on 7 July Jack appeared at Bow Street Magistrates Court on a charge of causing an obstruction with his car in Long Acre, Covent

Garden, the month before. The court was told that he had simply abandoned his car in the middle of the road while he went to a local bar for over three hours, and had refused the subsequent orders of a policeman to move it. He was fined £5, at which point the magistrate revealed that he already had seventy-three previous driving-related convictions, almost half of them for obstruction.

For much of the summer of 1932 Leo was in Ottawa for the Imperial Conference and, on 22 August, he returned to his hotel to receive three urgent cables. The first was from Jack, informing him that he intended to get married that morning, although he failed to reveal to whom, while the other two were from Bryddie and her sister, Sadie Rodney, urging Leo to refuse to give his consent to the marriage. Jack's sudden decision to marry had taken everyone by surprise, including, it seemed, the intended object of his affection, one Una Eveline Wing. Una was a twenty-two-year-old 'actress', already known, however, to the London police as a 'common prostitute who frequented the West End'.[7] The previous June she had been fined 40 shillings at Marlborough Street Police Court for soliciting, which was presumably how Jack had met her in the first place. He had told her that he was twenty-eight years old and had no family, his parents having died when he was young. They had only met on two or three occasions when he rather bizarrely informed her of their impending marriage by issuing a press release containing the news. He told her that he was 'in serious financial difficulties', and hoped that he would 'give his creditors confidence at having married a rich woman'.[8]

Unfortunately there was a major flaw in Jack's plan. He was still under twenty-one and so needed parental consent to get married in England. He had initially gone to Chelsea Registry Office to apply for a licence to marry and had lied about his age. But the publicity resulting from his press release had alerted the authorities and it appears that Bryddie had persuaded her brother Hamar Greenwood to tip off the Registry Office as well. The Deputy Superintendent Registrar refused to marry them, while the office of the Director of Public Prosecutions ordered the police to call at Eaton Square to interview Bryddie and to warn Jack under caution that he might have committed perjury. When the officer called, Bryddie confirmed that

Jack was indeed under twenty-one but told him that the couple had left for France the night before. Una had had a new passport, valid for three months, issued to her on the day of travel. In Leo's absence in Canada, Bryddie again called on Hamar, who wired ahead to the British Embassy in Paris to alert them to the situation and asked that the British consulates throughout France could be prevailed upon to help. Later the same day, Leo was rung up in Toronto by the *Evening News*, to be told that Jack and Una had appeared before the press in Paris to announce that they intended to marry on the Continent somewhere, apparently 'on the Latvia-Soviet border!'⁹ Although Bryddie urged Leo not to alter his plans, which were to travel on to New York for a few more weeks, he reluctantly decided that he must come home as soon as possible and booked himself to return two days later on the *Australia*.

He arrived at Southampton on 1 September 1932 to be met by a barrage of reporters and photographers. It was worse still at Waterloo where he reluctantly posed for photographs, but refused to say anything at all about Jack. His brother-in-law's experience as a former Home Office minister proved valuable and, on his advice, Leo retained the services of a new lawyer, a Mr Davies of Lewis and Lewis, whose father was also a Member of Parliament, and who specialised 'in dealing with dubious people and queer cases'. Jack now returned, somewhat shamefaced, from the Continent, to confront the 'whole tangle of Una Wing, *Jungle Skies* and motor offences',¹⁰ while Leo and Bryddie were, for the first time, confronted with some of Jack's more disreputable partners.

Chief among these was a character who became known to Leo as Johnston-Noad, and was already known to the police as Johnson Noad, 'otherwise known as Count Noad, a shady solicitor'. Noad was Jack's partner and fellow shareholder in an array of business ventures: John Amery Allied Distributors Ltd, John Amery Productions Ltd, A & H Productions Ltd, Jane Developments Ltd, John Amery Corporation Ltd, Amery Hudson & Murray Ltd and, curiously, Maidstone Airport Ltd. Among those who had suffered at their hands was a young man called Amis, the son of an Essex pub landlord and retired policeman. Amis had tragically lost his leg in a car accident and had received a generous compensation payment. Noad and Jack had 'cultivated a friendship' with the father and son, persuading them to purchase two debentures of £250 each in another company, J & D Productions Ltd, with which they had then undertaken various visits to Africa. However, the police had eventually decided that there was insufficient evidence to mount a prosecution for fraud.[11]

Jack and Noad had recently fallen out, but Noad now met his match and the mere mention by Leo of the involvement of Messrs Lewis and Lewis proved enough to frighten off the disreputable solicitor. Similarly, an unpleasant looking American by the name of Greig, who had also enjoyed a loose business arrangement with Jack in his film interests, was also shown the door by Mr Davies. Other problems were not so easily dismissed. A summons served on Leo for non-payment for another car had to be settled promptly and, most serious of all, Jack was due back in court a few days later to face his latest motoring charge. Earlier that month he had been seen by a policeman, in the King's Road in Chelsea, driving with an out-of-date tax disc. When the officer had held up his hand to stop the car, Jack had driven straight at him, before swerving out of the way at the last moment, mounting the pavement and attempting to escape down a side street. He now faced charges of dangerous driving, failing to stop and failing to produce a valid driving licence or certificate of insurance. Davies was alarmed to hear that this was now roughly Jack's eightieth motoring summons and, although he advised a spell abroad again as soon as possible, thought that Jack should dispose of the court case first and not put himself in the position of a fugitive, with a warrant out for his arrest.

The following day Leo sought advice over lunch at Bucks Club in Mayfair from a friend who was also an eminent King's Counsel, St John Hutchinson, who in turn agreed to 'sound out the police authorities'. He returned with the advice that they were 'not disposed to be vindictive' towards Jack, but that it would be best for him to 'appear and face the music' in person or, at the very least, to be represented in court. Jack, not surprisingly, chose the latter option and fled to Paris on 9 September, Leo making no effort to prevent Una accompanying him as they would 'soon get tired of each other' there anyway.[12] Even this departure was not without incident, with the news-papers, by now intrigued by Jack's story, reporting that they had missed their scheduled sailing and had privately chartered a boat to take them across the Channel. A few days later Jack was represented by Davies at Bow Street Magistrates Court, was fined £50 and disqualified from driving for five years. Leo, meanwhile, settled an allowance on Jack to help him survive in Paris and sat back to wait to see what would happen next.

He did not have long to wait. Ten days later Jack telegraphed home, asking Leo to send more money urgently while Una contacted Bryddie to say that he was critically ill. For the first time, Leo turned to his old friend from All Souls, Jack's godfather John Simon, by now the Foreign Secretary in the National Government. It was to prove a wise decision over the coming months. The doctor at the British Embassy in Paris was despatched to examine Jack, reporting that he was suffer-ing from nothing worse than nervous fatigue. Leo once again agreed to pay off Jack and Una's outstanding debts, but warned that he would no longer do so thereafter. Simon offered to stop off to see his godson on his way back from diplomatic business in Geneva, while a family friend who had seen the couple in Paris reported that Una could almost certainly be persuaded to leave Jack for the right price.

Leo now made the first of many visits to see his son in Paris, stop-ping off en route to a conference in Basle, and finding that the couple were living far beyond their means and talking of moving to Spain where the cost of living would be cheaper. When he returned a few days later, on his journey home, he visited them at their lodgings at the Hotel Terrass in Montmartre. He offered Una a free ticket back to London with him, if Jack would go on by himself to Spain, but realised that they were determined to remain together, and merely ended up by paying to redeem Jack's car which had been impounded by the local garage. On a further trip to Paris in November, Leo invited Jack for lunch at the Hotel Bristol, where Leo was staying, and found that 'boredom and hard-upness have made him think a good deal'.[13] His latest plan was to try to find work at a film studio in Nice and, after lunch, Leo once again broke his own resolution and accom-panied Jack to the local pawnshop to retrieve some of his possessions.

By any standards, 1932 had been a disastrous year for Leo. While he had endured endless political frustrations, he had at least 'tried to do something to mend a completely derelict financial situation', and had 'scraped together an income' which, but for Jack's behaviour, might well have been enough to see the family through. As it was, 'Jack has cost us both much, of which the money has been the smallest item.'[14] And while there was a good deal of sympathy among Leo's friends and political colleagues for the problems he faced with his wayward son, he must have been all too aware also that Jack provided a plentiful source of gossip which kept them amused. 'If you had ever set eyes on that little gutter snipe,' wrote Neville Chamberlain to his sister, 'you would feel no surprise at anything he might do.'[15] After a year in which he had taken less exercise than usual, Leo felt old and out of shape, especially in his beloved mountains. Jack's troubles had knocked much of the old flair and enthusiasm out of him, and he was comforted only that Julian 'promises well' and was 'growing in mind and stature'.[16] Little did he know that the worst was still to come.

For the Christmas holidays of 1932 Leo and Bryddie rented a small house on the South Downs at Rottingdean, near the home of his old friend Sir Roderick Jones, with whom he had shared a tent as fellow journalists in South Africa over thirty years before, and who was now the chairman of Reuters news agency. Jones generously agreed to give Jack a chance, offering him a job working for the chief of the Reuters bureau in Shanghai. In early February Leo travelled to Marseilles to try to persuade his son to accept the offer. He was met by Jack in yet another large but ramshackle old car and together they motored to Aix where, over lunch at the Casino, Leo tried to impress upon him that this was a wonderful opportunity to make a fresh start. Una would not accompany him at first, but would be welcome to do so, and to marry him, if Jack could prove that he could successfully hold down the job and earn his own way. In the meantime, Leo would pay Una an allowance. Jack seemed keen to go but was still reluctant to leave without Una.

The following day Leo lunched alone with Una. Since the day of their first meeting, he had been under no illusion as to her true calling in life. He glanced nervously around the dining room, fervently hoping that 'the one English couple in the room did not recognise me for Miss W's appearance leaves no doubt as to her normal profession', which she would 'no doubt resume when Jack leaves'. However, he had also seen a kinder, gentler side to her which encouraged him. Over lunch she was 'perfectly reasonable about it all and made no attempt to bargain for herself'. She was 'evidently fond'[17] of Jack, but her principal concern was that he was quite incapable of lasting for any length of time in a steady job. However, it was eventually agreed that Jack would indeed take up the job and he was booked to sail from Marseilles on 24 February. Leo returned to London for a few days to make the various arrangements for booking tickets and transferring money to Shanghai. Roderick Jones was not the only old family friend to be asked to do Jack a favour. In response to an enquiry as to his progress from his godfather John Simon, Bryddie asked if the Foreign Secretary would be so kind as to 'send a line to our Consul General' in Shanghai, asking him 'to keep an eye on him when he gets out'. Jack was going out, she wrote, 'with a genuine desire to make a fresh start'.[18]

Leo returned to Marseilles in time to see Jack off on 24 February. His suspicions should have been aroused immediately, since there was no sign of his son at the railway station to meet him as agreed and, when Leo took a tour around the steamer he was booked on and introduced himself to the captain, no one on board had heard of Jack's booking. The two finally met up and, about half an hour before the boat was due to leave, Jack casually told his father that 'there was a cocktail party of his film friends on board, anxious to have a farewell carouse and that he did not think that I would care to meet them.'[19] Jack's story was, of course, a fabrication, although his gullible father even climbed to the top of the harbour tower to wave farewell to the departing ship. Jack, unsurprisingly, was not on board. Nearly a month was to pass before Leo and Bryddie discovered the truth, and then they were to do so in dramatic fashion.

Jack had, in fact, never gone near the steamer bound for China but had sold his ticket, met up again with Una, and used the proceeds to take them both to Athens. On 21 March Leo received a message from the Foreign Office informing him that Jack and Una were attempting to get married in the Greek capital, but that the British Consul had refused to marry them as Jack was still, by just a few weeks, under age. Sir Roderick Jones generously offered to hold Jack's job for him in Shanghai, but it was now clear that there was little prospect of Jack ever taking up his offer. By 31 March the newspapers were full of stories confirming that Jack and Una had, indeed, got married. Frustrated by the refusal of the British Consul to marry them, the Athens *Morning Post* reported that, instead, the 'ceremony took place in the private chapel of an Athens villa and was performed by the Greek Archimandrite, who had previously baptised the bride and bridegroom according to the rites of the Greek Orthodox Church'.[20]

Leo and Bryddie were not the only interested parties to be shocked. Canon John Douglas, a senior Church of England representative who was in Greece at the time on an Anglo-Catholic pilgrimage, complained bitterly to the Archbishop of the Greek Orthodox Church that the baptism, and therefore the marriage, was unlawful and against the teachings of the respective churches in relation to conversion from one to the other. Archbishop Chrysostom replied that the couple had not, in fact, been baptised, but 'chrismated according to the prescribed methods of receiving converts'. Both Jack and Una had, he claimed, 'a genuine desire to adhere to Orthodoxy', and their claim 'could not have been rejected'. While the Greek Church would never set out actively to lure converts away from other faiths, they were 'mutually free and bound to receive adherents who came to them *sponte sua*'.[21] By now Jack had reached twenty-one anyway and, having achieved minor celebrity status as Leo's son and by his controversial marriage, he decided to live it up publicly in Athens, staying at the best hotel in the city and entertaining freely with money he did not have.

Six weeks later there was worse news still. Jack telephoned from Paris to say that he faced imminent arrest, on a warrant issued in Athens, in connection with an allegedly fraudulent purchase of diamonds. He urgently needed his father to telegraph money, to enable him to escape as soon as possible to Luxembourg, a country with no formal extradition understanding with Greece. Leo refused, but when a Reuters telegram from Athens confirmed the news, he once again consulted his lawyers and caught the night train to Paris by way of Newhaven. The following day Jack came to see his father at the

Hotel Bristol and poured out his story. He had, he claimed, been put up to the purchase by some 'Russian crooks' and had spent £850 on the diamonds, only for his cheque to prove worthless and the Russians to relieve him of the diamonds for £150. The jeweller had, understandably, gone straight to the police. Leo was rightly suspicious; Jack had in fact bought the diamonds for Una shortly before leaving Athens, knowing full well that the cheque was worthless. Leo nevertheless went into action, recruiting the help of two officials at the British Embassy and retaining a Parisian lawyer, Maître Frank, with the help of his London solicitors. Frank's first two suggestions 'were not very helpful', namely that Jack should either avoid the charge by being voluntarily interned for mental deficiency, or should immediately join the French Foreign Legion. However, he did confirm that Jack was liable for extradition to Greece if he remained in Paris or, indeed, if he returned to London where the resulting publicity would be much worse. It was agreed that negotiations should be opened up with the Greek Government to see if 'the jeweller could be squared', and that Jack should be kept in Paris for as long as possible. Leo even thought of going to Athens himself, but instead returned to London to make arrangements there, passing the journey by reading the second Lord Birkenhead's biography of his late father, F. E. Smith, one of Leo's oldest friends and Jack's godfather.[22]

A few days later Leo and Bryddie returned together to Paris and, at their first attempt to visit Jack, by now languishing in a cell at the Dépôt de Préfecture, were refused admittance by a suspicious duty guard, who refused to believe their protestations that they were not English journalists using a cunning ruse to obtain a story about the now well-known young Englishman under his care. The following day they returned and were allowed to talk to Jack, separated by a double metal grating, a yard apart. He 'looked pretty well pulled down ... both mentally and physically', and had 'had a real lesson'. From there they went to Jack and Una's apartment in the Hotel Terrass in the Rue de Maistre in Montmartre which they were surprised to find was clean and well kept, and looked after by a landlady who 'spoke well of them'.[23]

The full force of the legal and diplomatic firepower available to Leo now rolled into action. On the advice of a local political friend, a leading French attorney, George Picot, was retained to represent Jack in court, and duly advised that bail could well be granted if Jack was seen to have the support of both the local embassy and the Foreign Office at home. Leo therefore again contacted the Foreign Secretary, John Simon, who agreed to help his godson in any way he could, in particular by enlisting the support of Foreign Office officials in Athens to try to encourage a settlement with the Greek jeweller. Meanwhile, British Embassy officials in Paris contacted their counterparts at the Greek Legation, who agreed to do all they could to persuade their superiors in Athens that Jack should be allowed out on bail. In addition, the British Embassy staff agreed to suggest to local French officials that, when the arrest warrant arrived from Athens for processing at the Greek Legation, they might be prepared to delay extradition proceedings by suggesting some technical objection or requesting further information.

Leo again returned to London, this time to try to raise the money both for Jack's bail and, more importantly, to pay off the jeweller in Athens. Clearly he did not have access to that kind of money himself, but two old friends, Hugo Hirst and the South African financier Abe Bailey, immediately agreed to help. Leo's dismay and embarrassment at having to ask for such a favour was all too apparent. It was 'not a pleasant thing' for him 'to have to borrow from one's friends in these emergencies', but he was fortunate to have friends to whom he could talk frankly. He visited Simon at the Foreign Office, who showed him a telegram from his Greek counterpart suggesting that the jeweller should be paid in full, a suggestion to which he had replied 'demurring'. Later the same day he heard that Jack had appeared in court and, thanks to a 'wonderful' performance by Picot, had been granted bail for 'the very satisfactory sum of 10,000 francs'. Indeed Picot had generously paid the sum himself so that Jack could be freed immediately, and he was now safely back at the Hotel Terrasse with Bryddie, who agreed with Leo that it 'would never have done paying off the jeweller without giving Jack a real fright' and that, having 'looked into the abyss', he now had 'the chance of a fresh start'.[24]

The focus of attention now shifted to Athens and the need to pay off the jeweller. Using a local Greek lawyer as an intermediary, Davies at first tried to bluff the jeweller that Leo was 'under no obligation to buy out the boy', and was 'not so anxious about saving him from prison as to wish to pay the full £850'. Leo hoped that such a subterfuge would save him 'a few hundreds that will be spent to retrieve Jack's folly'. He was further embarrassed when another rich friend, Peter Perry, insisted on offering an additional loan, recognising that he would 'get through the Jack business but with a good load of debt round my neck'.²⁵ He returned to Paris to join Jack, Bryddie and Sadie Rodney, who had travelled out to be with her sister.

The next fortnight was spent anxiously awaiting news from Athens while Leo and Bryddie settled down in Paris, both to keep an eye on Jack and to get to know his new wife. Bryddie's brother, Hamar (by now Lord) Greenwood, again offered his help. A paint manufacturing company, Berger Paints, of which he was chairman, had a factory in Paris and he suggested the idea of temporary work there for Jack, initially in the manufacturing department and, if all went well, later on in sales. Leo was left alone with Jack and Una in Paris for a few days, while Bryddie returned to England to spend the 'Fourth of June', the school's speech day, at Eton with Julian. They spent the time together, visiting Versailles, having dinner in the open air in the Bois de Boulogne and driving out of Paris for picnics in the forest of Fontainebleau. In spite of everything that had been done for him, Jack remained reluctant to compromise his own pleasure in any way. He had no wish to face the drudgery of work in a paint factory, but hankered after retrieving his unfinished film, now entitled *It's a Lion*, or, failing that, a return to Nice, where he hoped to work as a secretary-cum-chauffeur for a Mr Hall, who owned cafeterias and dance halls on the Côte d'Azur. The reason Jack gave was that nothing would induce him to accept a favour from his uncle and, as the day approached that he was due to start work, he began complaining violently about having to go to Bergers. After three days of quiet persuasion, Leo was, for once, furious.

Jack did, eventually, agree to try the job at Bergers, although he continued to spend a good deal of his time around Paris with his parents. When Leo returned again to London, Bryddie stayed behind and wrote to John Simon from the Hotel Terrass, thanking him for all that he had done for his godson and describing in detail the time they were spending together in Paris. Jack, she acknowledged, had had a 'terribly severe lesson', but he had 'profited by it' and, with his new job, the old 'daredevil and work dodger had given way to the old' Jack, with an 'earnest desire to do right and do well'. Her presence in the hotel where he and Una lived, 'on the top of Paris', had, she believed, given Jack renewed stability and he looked 'less ill and miserable' than when they had arrived. Above all, familiarity had bred friendship in the case of Una, whom Bryddie now conceded was 'not unwise', and 'kind and nice' to Jack. She believed that they genuinely 'cared for each other' and that this was now a turning point in Jack's life. He was 'so young' and the 'world had seemed so easy to conquer'.[26]

The Greek jeweller, meanwhile, refused to back down over the terms he demanded for a settlement of the case. Not only did he want the full price for the lost diamonds, but he insisted that his costs should be covered and a public apology made for the defamation he claimed he had suffered when Picot had presented Jack's case in court. Leo's case was further undermined by his own realisation, at long last, that Jack's Russian conmen had been a fabrication and that he had in fact taken the diamonds out of Greece with him and almost certainly pawned them in Paris. But Jack continued to lie about what he had done with them, and Leo found himself in an embarrassing position with the various officials in London, Paris and Athens to whom the story had already been spun. He finally decided that the only way to prevent extradition proceedings against Jack was to pay up in full and he duly arranged for £900 to be transferred to Athens, £500 down at once and the rest to be payable over twelve months. When the whole sorry saga finally came to an end, one way or another Jack's 'escapade' had cost Leo in the region of £1,400. With remarkable equanimity, he decided to 'look upon the expense as equivalent to an unforeseen general election'.[27] He and Bryddie returned to London in the forlorn hope that their elder son would, at last, settle down to a more responsible existence.

However, Jack lasted barely two months in the job at Bergers before once again leaving Paris for Nice to seek his fortune in the film business. By Christmas he was back in London. Although he had not stayed long in Nice, his return to England gave Leo renewed hope that he and Una might finally settle down. They rented a small house, Ditton Lodge, in Lower Cookham Road, Maidenhead, while Leo gave Jack a weekly allowance of £10, a generous sum at the time. On one occasion Jack even suggested to his unimpressed father that he thought he might like to train as a solicitor, presumably as a means of making a saving on his own legal fees. But his father's allowance was never going to be enough for Jack and Una to live off, and an all too familiar way of life soon unfolded, as Jack once again turned his hand to various shady business ventures, while Leo tried to earn enough from his company directorships to pay the outstanding bills. More embarrassing still, Jack's creditors were often friends or the sons of friends of Leo's, whom he had somehow managed to persuade to invest in one or other of his schemes. Leo felt little sympathy for the son of a Lady Georgiana Mure, who came to see him to complain that her son had invested his entire life savings in one of Jack's hare-brained schemes for smuggling silk stockings into England by air.

Una, at least, recognised his obvious business flaws from an early stage in their marriage. He had 'a terror of being without money', about which he would 'worry to an uncontrollable extent'. He would never sit still, walking up and down for hours on end while he planned his next great business endeavour. He was happiest when 'scheming and laying plans for big financial coups, but never had the patience or self-control to carry them out'. Most worrying for his father, he had no concept of proportion or the value of money, and 'would spend large sums on schemes whose prospects were always doubtful' and whose profits would never have added up to much anyway.[28]

If life in a cottage in Maidenhead sounds like a rural idyll, it was in fact anything but. Jack was, by now, constantly on the move and was beginning to lead the nomadic existence around Europe that was to characterise his life for the remaining pre-war years. In spite of everything that they had been through together, Una continued to demonstrate a remarkable tolerance of Jack's idiosyncratic nature. Many of his behavioural characteristics were relatively trivial in nature, but nevertheless conformed to the observations made about him by others in earlier life. His pet nickname for Una was 'Teddy Bear', although he already had his own, real teddy bear, to which he had been attached since childhood. In a curious pre-echo of the character Sebastian Flyte in Evelyn Waugh's *Brideshead Revisited,* not to be published for another ten years, Jack would carry the bear around with him wherever he went, taking it with him 'to cafes and restaurants, sitting it beside him and buying it drinks and comic newspapers'. He had an equally strange obsession with his overcoat, buying an extra seat for it at the theatre or cinema, and demanding to take it with him into a restaurant or hotel. 'If the staff insisted on placing his overcoat in the cloakroom', he would refuse to eat there and storm out.[29]

Other complexes were more sinister. Leo had already noticed that 'from quite a boy' Jack had always gone around with a revolver. He suffered from 'sudden panic attacks about people after him', especially 'creditors and others he had injured' who he assumed were trying to beat him up.[30] Una, too, noticed that he was paranoid about being attacked and always kept a gun with him. When they returned home to their house in Maidenhead after a night out, he would refuse to get out of the car until Una had looked around first and unless his revolver was to hand. On one occasion, when Una was driving and their car was forced off the road by another driver, Jack leapt out and smashed the windscreen of the offending vehicle with the butt of his revolver.

However, most disturbing for Una was their sexual relationship, Jack's tastes seeming bizarre even to an experienced prostitute. She considered him a 'sexual pervert', who continued to practise homosexuality throughout their marriage, often in return for large sums of money. He also used prostitutes regularly, paying them to tie him up and beat him with such force that Una 'had seen the fresh scars'. He was a 'sexual exhibitionist', enjoying having Una watch while he had sex with another woman, and occasionally enjoying sex with a woman immediately after she had had sex with another man. When they were out in public together, he would encourage her to give the impression to others that she was his mistress or a prostitute, rather than his wife, or even a 'rich mistress who had made large sums of money by blackmail'. On one occasion, when they were in a cocktail bar together, she foolishly let it be known that she was, in fact, his wife. Jack flew into a 'white rage' and beat her. His sexual habits were symptomatic of a more widespread lack of interest in his personal hygiene. He was 'dirty in his habits' and would 'sleep for days on end', getting up only to 'eat and perform his functions'.[31]

■ ■ ■

Throughout 1934 and 1935, Jack continued to subsist alternately by travelling around Europe in an effort to keep his film career going, and by indulging in small-scale, unsuccessful business ventures from their home in Maidenhead. In February 1934 he suddenly turned up in Vienna, where Leo was attending a conference in the aftermath of the Socialist uprising there. Jack was full of stories about how he had run into trouble with a group of Communists he had met in Budapest, and spent a few days touring the city with his father, after which he returned to Budapest in June, telling Leo that he had to go there to see 'his chief as their last film was rejected by Fox on the grounds that it might be too controversial' in London, 'dealing as it does with the Nazi movement in Germany'.[32] Early in 1935 he broke his arm when he drove his car off the road in Innsbruck, fell down a ravine and had to be cut out of the wreckage. Leo wired out the money for the necessary medical expenses. And he began increasingly to undertake film work for a German producer, Merz, which involved regular visits to Berlin throughout 1935, broken only by the offer of a four-month contract in Hollywood, which appears not to have been taken up. And all the while he attempted to keep his business interests in England going too, usually at Leo's expense.

By early 1936 Leo was at last beginning to approach some kind of financial stability. Although he had recently rejected as unsuitable a number of company directorships, worth as much as £3,000 a year, he had also been offered several which he had taken on and, as a result, was now spending less and less time in the House of Commons during the normal working day. He worried that he had become 'so drawn in by finance and freedom from incessant money worries as to lose courage to risk it all if the critical moment should come for me in politics',[33] but such doubts were quickly dispelled by the realisation that whenever he had 'a little in hand I suddenly discover that more than all of it is owing to the Chancellor of the Exchequer'.[34] Nevertheless, the directorships that did come his way were lucrative. He spent a good deal of time at Youanmi, a South African gold mining concern, and somehow managed to get away with becoming chairman of one of their potential competitors, the Gold Exploration and Finance Corporation, at a salary of £1,000 a year. Sir Edmund Davis placed him on another of his subsidiary boards, a tungsten producer, the St Swithin's Ore Company, and he also joined the board of the Trust and Loan Company and the fledgling Palestine Airways, organising flights between Palestine and Cyprus.

In January 1936 came the most exciting invitation yet, over lunch at the Savoy with Simon Marks, to join the board of Marks and Spencer. After an introductory tour of the company offices in Baker Street and an intimate family lunch, again at the Savoy – 'the most purely Jewish function I think I have ever attended'[35] – he extended his overdraft to allow him to invest in the company's shares and was elected to the board. The work was often tedious, for example spending an evening signing a thousand Marks and Spencer share certificates, but extremely well paid, and he was soon in a position to pay off all his outstanding tax arrears. He also became a director of the Goodyear Tyre Company in Wolverhampton and was soon able to record that his earnings for the previous twelve months had reached £10,500, a considerable achievement given that he had left office with no savings in the bank, a substantial overdraft and a sizeable tax demand pending. However, much still depended on the behaviour of his elder son. 'If only Jack behaves,' he mused, 'I might be able to work my way back towards reasonable solvency.'[36] But Jack's circumstances showed no sign of improving, and by late 1936 his life was poised to enter a new period of crisis.

With his film-making ventures in abeyance, Jack had embarked on a number of new projects at home. Remarkably, Leo had convinced Sir Roderick Jones to give him one last chance at Reuters, this time in London, and he worked there intermittently for a number of months in 1936. However, of more immediate interest was a new venture, an off-licence in Maidenhead, opened in partnership with a new partner, one James Dixon, who ran an informal nightclub, the

Boulters, from his own home. The Parade Wine Stores was soon sold, only for Jack to open a similar business adjoining the Hungaria Club, another well-known local nightclub. Trading as Thames Wine Stores, the shop effectively provided a steady supply of alcohol for parties at local nightclubs, and was frequently mentioned in contemporary police reports. The end of Jack's business career was now imminent. As his creditors circled, he made one last appeal to his father to bail him out. But this time, even for Leo, the price was too high. On 2 November 1936 a court in Windsor declared Jack bankrupt, to the tune of £5,081, with no assets to show. It was to mark the beginning of a new phase of his life.

■ ■ ■

It is difficult to confirm, with any great accuracy, Jack's exact movements over the next two years. Certainly he spent the great majority of his time travelling throughout Europe, leaving Una at home in Maidenhead. But it is not strictly true, as has since been suggested, not least by Leo himself, that he left England for good, 'to settle abroad and make a new start',[37] never to return. Indeed, he continued to be a frequent visitor both to Maidenhead and to Eaton Square throughout 1937 and 1938. Leo later claimed that he had spent those two years 'engaged in working for the Franco cause in Spain', engaged primarily in 'sabotage and gun-running work in Germany and France', although also apparently seeing active service with Italian troops.[38] It is true that he came to see Leo on two occasions in October 1936 to say that he intended to 'attach himself to the insurgents' in Spain, although Leo had 'strongly advised him to stay with Reuters if they will still have him'.[39] In January 1936 he was still working at Reuters, although bored by the job, and was considering a further offer of work from his uncle Lord Greenwood.

Considerable emphasis has been placed on the proof provided by entries in Jack's passport as to his true movements during this period. It is true that, in the words of one historian, 'his passport reveals no period longer than a few weeks, apart from five months at the end of 1936 and the beginning of 1937, when his movements are unaccounted for.'[40] However, with the added benefit of Leo's diaries covering the same period, it becomes impossible to rely on the stamps in his passport as being in any way accurate evidence of his true movements. For example, his passport shows him to have been in France between 30 May and 2 August 1936, whereas in fact Jack looked in at Eaton Square a number of times between those dates, on one occasion on 5 June, together with Una for lunch with his parents. On 4 July Leo went down to Maidenhead to visit the couple in their home, a 'little country house', which he thought an 'attractive little place with quite a good garden within half a mile of the river'.[41] Jack's passport further suggests that he was in Germany, without a break, between the end of August 1936 and the beginning of March 1937. In fact we know that he travelled a good deal during that period, was a frequent visitor to Eaton Square and was even working, however half-heartedly, for Reuters for some of that time. The only conclusion to be drawn is either that he had a second passport which he used on some of his travels and no longer survives or, more likely, that some customs officials around Europe were simply more zealous in stamping it than others.[42]

The month of March 1937 was to be a crucial one. Jack's brother Julian was later to assemble evidence purporting to show that on 15 March Jack joined the Spanish Foreign Legion and was accordingly granted Spanish citizenship. In fact, Jack's passport shows that he left Lisbon on 9 March on a Dutch merchant ship, the *Titus*, arriving in Genoa ten days later. The ship's log shows that Jack was the only passenger on board and that the *Titus* made no other stops en route, lying off the Algarve in bad weather for three days between 12 and 14 March. Members of the crew later swore that no one could possibly have left the ship during the voyage.[43]

It has been further suggested that Jack's claim to have seen combat during the Spanish Civil War was 'either a fantasy or a straightforward lie to his family'.[44] However, the claim that he was involved in gun-running was Leo's, and appears to have been made as a result of his own investigations, rather than on the basis of Jack's word alone. After the *Titus* reached Genoa, Jack's passport appears to show that he spent the period between 24 March and 14 August, without a break, in France. In fact he merely passed through France en route for London and, on 25 March, he looked in on Leo at Eaton Square to describe the 'complete Odyssey' he had recently made 'round Portugal, Spain and Morocco to Genoa'. He initially told his father that he had managed to get some more film work in Berlin, but Leo later 'discovered he was still trying to deliver a cargo of munitions he had sent from Berlin last autumn'. They were now awaiting shipment at Melilla in North Africa, where Jack had 'spent a night in gaol, being suspected of trying to take them to Valencia'. During a lengthy conversation with Leo about the Civil War, Jack further reported 'complete tranquillity in the Franco area, but Valencia in chaos and dead bodies, both of old and recent murders, lying about openly.'[45]

It is, of course, quite possible that Jack made up the entire story, and was a sufficiently good liar to sustain it in the course of a long, face-to-face conversation with his father. But the fact that he initially tried to conceal what he had really been doing, and that Leo then discovered it for himself, by independent verification, does lend an air of authenticity to the gun-running story and possibly suggests that Jack had, indeed, visited Spain in secret. The description of the scenes in Valencia may have been the basis for, or further confirmation of, Leo's later assertion that what Jack had witnessed, 'at the taking of Barcelona, of the Communist torture chambers there,' had 'greatly intensified his horror of the prospect of the spread of Communism in Europe'.[46]

Incredibly, even at this late stage, Leo was still hoping to keep Jack in England and to find him a job. At the end of June 1937 Jack and Una's landlord in Maidenhead, an insurance broker called Leslie Brewer, demanded repossession of the house by the beginning of August. Brewer later claimed that he had always disliked Jack because of the way he and Una had treated Ditton Lodge as tenants, and Leo was once again forced to come to Jack's financial aid, settling out of court a claim made by Brewer against Una for the damage that had been done to the house. Jack and Una duly moved back to London, to a small house at 11 Cheltenham Terrace, off the King's Road in Chelsea, while Leo tried yet again to persuade his friends to find Jack a reputable job. One offered to get him started in the advertising industry, but by the time Jack joined his family for a few days at Sir Edmund

Davis's villa in Cap Ferrat in September 1937, he had again found himself work in the south of France, this time as a 'secretary-interpreter-chauffeur to an inventor called Rigby', who was trying to 'dispose of a patent to the Italian Government'.[47] This work may or may not have existed, or it may have been a cover story for his gun-running exploits, not that his father was by now under any illusions about that aspect of his life. However, it does go some way to explaining the frequency of the border crossings, as recorded in his passport, that he apparently made between Italy and France at this time.

Unfortunately his passport entries once again provide an incomplete history of his movements for this period. Julian had been taken ill at the end of the holiday in the south of France, and Jack agreed to drive his car back to London for him, delivering it to Eaton Square on 1 October, when he told his father that he would be returning to Nice to carry on his employment with Rigby. In the course of his peripatetic wanderings around Europe, he returned to London on a number of occasions during 1938, staying with Una at Cheltenham Terrace and visiting his parents, probably to ask for money, at Eaton Square. Leo, by now perhaps sensing from his conversations with him that Jack was increasingly being seduced into a dangerous political world on the Continent, valiantly continued to try to find suitable work for him in London. In September Leo visited him at his flat at the Hotel Terrass in Paris and was encouraged to find him looking better and apparently earning a little money.

Leo's instincts were right. What is beyond doubt is that at some stage in the mid-1930s, Jack met and fell under the spell of the 'forceful and eloquent personality' of Jacques Doriot. Having served in the French army with distinction during the First World War, winning the Croix de Guerre, Doriot had gone on to join the Communist Party and been elected mayor of the Parisian suburb of Saint-Denis. In 1934 he had 'revolted against Moscow control', calling for the Communists to go into partnership with other socialist organisations in order to create a united front against the new threat of fascism. Disowned by the Communists and impressed with the success of the Nazi Party in Germany, he subsequently crossed the political spectrum from one extreme to the other and became the 'head of a violent anti-Communist popular organization in France' and, in 1936, formed the fascist Parti Populaire Français.[48] At about this time Jack met Doriot, joined his movement and, under his tutelage, 'extensively studied Communism' which 'led me to Austria, Czechoslovakia and various other countries, including Italy and Germany'.[49]

In January 1939 Leo was again in Paris, returning from a skiing holiday in Klosters, and invited Jack to lunch at the Hotel Bristol where he was staying. Jack was 'not looking too well' and had recently 'lost a short lived job as a film director'. Worse still, he was involved once again in a legal dispute. The previous November his assistant on the film, 'a youth called O'Connor', had become involved in a fight, 'nearly killing a Frenchman in a bar in Nice' who had insulted the wife of the Jewish financier who was backing the film.[50] The financier had been forced to settle the case out of court, pawning his wife's jewels in the process, and had then turned to Jack, blaming him for O'Connor's behaviour and seeking financial redress. For the first time, Jack complained openly to Leo about the influence of the rich Jews with whom he did business in the film world. The episode would appear to be the source of Leo's claim, several years later, that Jack's 'failure in the film world and his unfortunate experience with money lenders', had 'inclined him to the current Nazi and Fascist doctrine of the Jews as the prime instigators of Communism as well as of the evils of international high finance.'[51] Leo's solution was to try to persuade Jack to join the family skiing holiday in Klosters, where Leo had already taken his skis and skiing clothes in the hope that he might turn up, but he never did.

The Spanish Civil War ended on 1 April 1939 and Leo was again in Paris on 29 April, having a long discussion with Jack about his future over lunch at the Trianon Palace Hotel and again, later that afternoon, during a walk around the grounds of the Palace of Versailles in the pouring rain. But Jack was already making plans to return to Spain and he entered the country on 22 August, making his home at the Hotel Derbi in Madrid. His immediate concern was to get to Burgos in order to locate Julian's car, which had been abandoned there. Julian had last been in Burgos in April of that year, returning home from his spell as a war correspondent, covering the aftermath of the fall of Madrid, for the *News Chronicle*. Unfortunately the car's camshaft had broken and he had been forced to leave it behind when he returned to Oxford for the summer term. In early August, en route for a summer of reading on the Dalmatian Coast, Julian had stopped off in Paris for lunch with his brother. After the years Jack had spent living abroad, Julian was 'anxious to know his views'. Jack was 'sure there would be war' and, given the demoralisation suffered by the French after Munich, equally 'sure that France would collapse'.[52]

At the end of lunch, Julian promised Jack that if he could collect the car from Burgos and have it repaired, then he could happily benefit from any money that he might raise by selling it. This Jack duly did, bringing it back to Madrid where he sold it for 17,000 pesetas. The rest of his time in Spain was spent travelling around the country, especially to San Sebastián in the north, transporting and selling oil and other black market commodities in a series of small-time deals. In a bar in Madrid he foolishly chose to confide about himself at length to a waiter who, at the outbreak of war, became a spy for the Germans, only to be subsequently turned by the British and run as a double agent, BATICON, by MI6.[53] In spite of his friendship with Doriot, and his later claims to have closely followed European politics of the era, Jack appears to have been taken by surprise by the outbreak of war. He was in San Sebastián at the time and, although he was eventually successful in securing an exit visa and crossing the border into Portugal on 13 December, it would be another three months before he was either allowed or chose to leave Portugal and return to Paris. There was still, as yet, absolutely no indication of the dramatic and tragic role he was soon to play in the war.

CHAPTER SIXTEEN

Love and Adventure

While relations between the two brothers remained warm, contact between them had been sporadic at best in the years before their lunch in Paris in August 1939. While Jack had been drifting aimlessly round Europe, Julian's ambitious mind was turning increasingly towards his own future. In early August 1932 Leo wrote to him from Ottawa, congratulating him on his achievements at the end of his career at Summer Fields, and 'looking forward confidently to doing yourself credit at Eton'. Acutely aware of Jack's downward spiral, and mindful of his own absence in Canada, Leo urged Julian to assume responsibility for looking after Bryddie, by making her 'feel that one of her men can take the place of the other'.[1]

Just two weeks later Leo heard the news of Jack and Una's attempted elopement, forcing him to return home early from Ottawa. One small benefit was that he was able to accompany Julian and Bryddie back to Eton for the start of Julian's first term there, and to meet his housemaster, Hugh Howson, a renowned mountaineer himself, whom Leo had last met while climbing the Grépon in the Alps. The house matron, Miss Owen, hailed from Wolverhampton, and had helped Leo at his unsuccessful attempts at election there over twenty years earlier. Leo was reassured to find that 'Eton certainly welcomed the new boys in a kindlier fashion than Harrow did,'[2] and that Julian accordingly settled happily into his new surroundings.

Hugh Howson, known to the boys as 'Huggie', had appealed to Leo as both a fellow mountaineer and an Old Harrovian. Julian, however, found him 'austere in standards and a purist in style', while he was also 'shy and tongue-tied'. Although Julian was no longer quite as precocious as he had been during his time at Summer Fields, he still found that Howson's shyness, and his reluctance to discuss openly any matter of potential discomfort, was a barrier between them, and that Howson accordingly had 'little influence' on him.[3] His house, Jourdelay's, was large, with decent sized rooms, a garden and its own squash court. But it was also the lowest lying house in Eton and, when the Thames flooded, so too did the local sewers and the boys were, on a number of occasions, duly sent home. Perhaps most suitably from Julian's point of view, Howson had a reputation for running a house 'composed of a literate and predominantly intelligent selection of boys', but which was, 'from an athletic viewpoint totally undistinguished'.[4]

Although still outspoken in his views and eccentric in his dress, many of the sharper edges of Julian's character had been rounded off by the time he left Summer Fields, and at Eton he made friends more easily. Among the first, and subsequently most enduring, was his fag master Nicholas Elliott, later to enjoy a distinguished career in intelligence, both during and after the Second World War. The usual duties expected of a fag were mundane, if time-consuming: tidying the senior boy's room, making and lighting his fire, preparing tea and running errands to other houses. But Julian and Elliott struck up an altogether more mutually profitable partnership. One Sunday evening, Julian went to Elliott's room to tidy up, only to find the older boy struggling with his weekend essays, which were known as 'Sunday Questions' and generally embraced a moral or religious theme. Julian rose to the occasion, pacing up and down the room in true Napoleonic fashion, while dictating, at length, a series of essays for Elliott to hand in the following morning. The work was deemed a considerable improvement on previous efforts by Elliott's master, and this first transaction soon led to a more permanent arrangement whereby Julian was spared all fagging duties in return for a weekly essay.

Only once was the hoax almost discovered. One Sunday, Elliott had returned to school too late for Julian to dictate the essay. Instead, he wrote it out himself on the Sunday night, and gave the text to Elliott the following morning, just in time for him to take it with him to his class, but without being able to check it through first. The title was 'Does the end justify the means?' and, as his theme, Julian had taken the life of the great Turkish President Atatürk, whose biography Leo had recently given him to read. Not only did Elliott know nothing whatsoever about Atatürk, unfortunately it also happened to be his turn to read his essay out aloud to the class that morning. According to Julian, Atatürk 'was generally hailed as a great and progressive states-man', yet it was well known that his public conduct and private morals had left much to be desired. Had 'murder, cruelty' and 'repeated breach of faith and atheism' really all been essential to his success? And was it significant that he had chosen for his relaxation 'drunken orgies and lechery'? The essay was liberally illustrated with anecdotes of how Atatürk had been 'besotted by drink and enfeebled by venereal disease'.[5] Once he had begun reading, Elliott had no choice but to carry on, much to his fellow pupils' amusement and the obvious concern of his master, increasingly shocked at the anarchic message of his previously mild-mannered pupil's work. Thankfully for both boys, Elliott's eloquence was sufficient to carry off the deception, and their arrangement survived unscathed.

If Julian had arrived at Eton rather more mild-mannered than he had been during his time at Summer Fields, he still retained his grudging dislike of authority and a strong anti-establishmentarian streak. He had little time for the school's ancient traditions, not least the 'absurd' school uniform of tailcoats and stiff collars which he thought made the boys look like 'undertakers or footmen'.[6] He failed to shine at games, and loathed being made to play the school's own version of football, the Eton Field Game. Instead, in a move reminiscent of Jack during his time at Harrow, he filled his spare time by renting a private sitting room above a shop in the High Street, known as Lower Rowlands, and already much frequented by other boys. Here he could escape the boredom of house life, and would embark on regular trips to Windsor, one such illegal visit to the cinema there earning him the only beating of his school career. And, by cunningly opening a bank account and thus obtaining a line of credit at all the major banks in Eton, he managed to fund his increasingly extravagant lifestyle.

▪ ▪ ▪

As they had at Summer Fields, Leo and Bryddie took a close interest in Julian's school career, and were regular visitors to Eton. By now, Leo was out of office and, in spite of his burgeoning commercial interests, had more time to devote to his younger son. Julian's first year at Eton coincided with some of Jack's worst excesses, not least his arrest in Paris, and it was Bryddie who was sent down to Eton, from time to time, to explain the current state of affairs to Jack's younger brother. By and large Julian was 'very sensible about the Jack business',[7] although Leo did put his foot down when Julian sent him a draft article that he was proposing to have published entitled 'Thank God for the Crisis'. Julian's theme was that it took a 'crisis to produce a great man and that great men alone rarely matter', and while Leo thought it well written, he was 'not prepared to let him start using my name for the stunt press, above all at this time'.[8]

Leo's visits to Eton became more frequent still in 1933, when Nicholas Elliott's father, Claude Elliott, succeeded Dr Cyril Alington as Head Master. Elliott was another friend of Leo's with whom he climbed, a fellow member of the Alpine Club, whose 'appearance was impressive' and, although a tall man, who shared with Leo the 'strong physique of the mountaineer'. The first Head Master of Eton not to have taken holy orders, he was to go on to 'prove himself a headmaster of the highest quality'.[9] Elliott had been appointed to the headmastership from Jesus College, Cambridge, and Julian thought him 'more a Don than a schoolmaster', and lacking the 'histrionic touch which boys rather need'.[10] Nevertheless, Leo and Elliott knew each other well from holidays spent together in the Alps, and Leo soon became a regular visitor to the Head Master's Eton lodgings. It proved a difficult arrangement, both for Julian and, indeed, for Nicholas Elliott, who 'was always rather in awe' of Leo.[11]

In the summer of 1933, shortly before Elliott was due to take up his appointment, a further change occurred in Julian's school life. In August Leo had returned alone to Chamonix with the intention of revisiting certain climbs, for which he had lacked the time during previous visits. But on the day of his first climb of the season, he heard the news that Julian's housemaster, Hugh Howson, along with three other fellow Eton masters, had died attempting a climb of the Piz Roseg, in the Bernina Alps. Reluctantly Leo decided that to carry on climbing himself, 'while B. and Julian were under the shadow of a tragedy touching them so nearly',[12] would only cause Bryddie in particular further anxiety. He therefore abandoned his climbing holiday, and went instead to spend a few days walking and swimming with Stanley Baldwin in Aix-les-Bains.

Howson's death was a blow to Claude Elliott, who had been counting on the support of his mountaineering friends when he took over the headmastership in September. It also radically changed the atmosphere in Julian's house. Howson was succeeded by Dick Routh, a historian who had previously enjoyed political ambitions of his own. While most boys appreciated the fact that he was a more energetic housemaster than Howson had been, and that he was determined to improve the standing of the house in the school as a whole, Julian's alternative views did not always sit easily with the more disciplined atmosphere. Julian, and his behaviour, became a regular source of irritation for his new housemaster.

During the late summer of 1933, Julian and Bryddie joined Leo for a family holiday at La Fiorentina, the home of the South African financier Sir Edmund Davis at St Jean Cap Ferrat. Davis had already taken Leo under his wing, generously employing him as a director of more than one of his mining companies, and the holiday in the south of France was to become an annual visit for the Amery family until the outbreak of war and their host's early death. Davis had made his fortune in South and South West Africa, and in Northern Rhodesia, leaving the development of gold and diamond mining to others, and concentrating instead on the development of previously neglected metals such as copper, vanadium and asbestos. In England he lived at Chilham Castle, near Canterbury, which he had restored at great expense and was well known as an accomplished art collector and generous patron of the arts. He had no children of his own and was only too happy to lavish his generous hospitality on Leo and his family.

La Fiorentina was a large Italian villa, with views across the bay at Beaulieu towards Monaco, and terraced gardens leading down to the sea and its own swimming pool. Fellow guests included Leo's old friend Lord Lloyd, the former High Commissioner in Egypt, the artist's widow Laura Anning Bell, herself a painter, and Marshal Caviglia of the Italian army. Guests could swim from a raft moored out at sea, and both Julian and Leo learnt to water ski, Julian soon becoming proficient and maintaining his interest in the sport well into comparative old age. Otherwise the days were spent enjoying the Davis's renowned hospitality, or visiting the local sights in Monte Carlo, Nice and Cannes. Davis was especially kind to Julian and frequently invited him to spend shooting weekends at Chilham Castle during the school holidays.

Following his beating for the visit to the cinema in Windsor, Julian became increasingly frustrated with the drudgery of school life. In disciplinary terms he was now on a last warning, and could find no outlet for his energies in sport. He tried hardest at cricket, playing intermittently for his house side and even going to the trouble of having cricket coaching at Lord's during the Easter holidays, but it was clear to Leo on the occasions when he went to watch that such early promise as Julian may have shown was not to be fulfilled. Nor did he find academic work any more agreeable, constrained as he was for the first three years of his career by the necessity of sitting the School Certificate exam at the age of sixteen. So bored had Julian become by school life that he once wrote to the Ethiopian Minister in London, volunteering to fight against the Italian invasion, but he received a polite letter of refusal on the grounds that he was unable to speak the language. He did, however, put in for a prize donated by the author André Maurois for an essay written in French on the influence of France on European civilisation. Although he was still a few weeks short of his sixteenth birthday and was competing with boys two years older than he was, he carried off the prize and became a private pupil of the senior French master at Eton. With his School Certificate safely out of the way, he went on to specialise in history which he was to study for the remainder of his school career.

Politics was never far from Julian's mind, and he was elected to the school's Political Society in time to attend a meeting addressed by his father on the current political situation. He had left Summer Fields as an avowed supporter of Lloyd George and an outspoken critic of Baldwin's National Government, inspired no doubt in part by Leo's exclusion from it. He made a study of the Russian Revolution and was 'for a time rather attracted to Communism', before giving that up for a study of fascism and the Nazi movement in Germany. However, when his research took him to a public meeting addressed by Oswald Mosley, he found that 'the Anti-Semitism repelled and the black shirt and Roman salute seemed rather ridiculous in London.' Through his father he met both of his great idols Lloyd George and Churchill, and, by the time he left Eton, he had decided that 'there was not much wrong with the British Constitution but only with the men who ran it', and that he would become a Conservative, albeit one who was out of sympathy with the leadership of the day.[13]

Leo's influence on his younger son was considerable, and the holidays were a time to step up Julian's political education. He accompanied his father to the major political events at which he spoke; a rally at the Albert Hall in memory of Joseph Chamberlain and a commemoration of Magna Carta at Runnymede. During the Easter holidays of 1934 they travelled together to the First World War battle-fields on the Western Front, and then on to Waterloo. At Ypres Leo showed Julian where he had interrogated German prisoners during his time on General Rawlinson's staff, and tracked down several of the civilians still living whom he had known at the time. Holidays were largely spent abroad, skiing at Christmas and climbing in the summer, although Leo had by now deserted St Moritz and experimented by visiting a new skiing destination each year: the Tyrol in 1933, followed by the Black Forest, Innsbruck, Zermatt and Kitzbühel in successive years.

By the summer of 1936 many of Julian's closest friends had already left Eton and he was keen to follow them. He suggested to Leo that he might spend the few remaining months before he was due to go up to Oxford studying a language abroad. But Routh convinced Leo that Julian stood a good chance of winning the prestigious Brackenbury history scholarship at Balliol and his father insisted that he stay at Eton and see out his time there. When Routh had first taken over his house, he had found Julian's eccentricities, both of opinions and of dress, tiresome in the extreme. 'Twenty years hence, when he is a great man,' he wrote to Leo, 'he may look upon his own follies only as a reincarnation of the extravagancies of Disraeli himself.' But by the time Julian left Eton, Routh had warmed to some of those eccentricities and praised him as 'the best historian in the best division that I have met for ten years or more'.[14] But it was still not enough to win the coveted Brackenbury scholarship in January 1937. Although Julian's French was the best of all the candidates and his History paper was also strong, like his father before him he was let down by his Latin and Greek.

Julian eventually left Eton at Easter 1937 and his father agreed that he should spend the summer learning German. Baron Franckenstein, the Austrian Minister in London, arranged for Julian to spend a few months at an academy near Vienna, and he set off, with a school friend to accompany him as far as Germany, in a newly acquired Humber car. Enjoying their first taste of freedom and, thanks to Leo, with a budget to match, they took their time making their way across Europe. Having crossed over to Ostend, they enjoyed a leisurely stay in Brussels where they made the most of the cuisine and local nightlife, before making their way slowly to Cologne and Bonn. After a further few days in Munich and Salzburg, they went their separate ways, Julian eventually arriving at the Schloss which was to be his summer home several days late. There was a further complication. Baron Franckenstein's efficient preparations had not warned that the school was for girls only, and Julian arrived during lunch one day to find himself the only man in the dining room. However, the owners needed the income, the girls seemed happy and Julian could see little in the way of a problem. Over the next few weeks, his experience of learning German was greatly enhanced by the added pleasures of accompanying his fellow students around the busy Viennese social season.

Julian went up to Balliol in October 1937 to read Modern Greats, otherwise known as philosophy, politics and economics, under the tutelage of another of his father's friends, Humphrey Sumner, later to become Warden of All Souls. After his stay in Austria, Julian had driven down to the south of France to join his parents for their annual visit to La Fiorentina, but had been taken seriously ill there with inflammation of the gall bladder and had spent much of the holiday in a hospital in San Remo. As a result, he arrived at Oxford having lost a lot of weight and was still very much in a state of recuperation. His father was concerned that he would miss out on almost all college activities during his first term, while Bryddie accompanied him back to Balliol and made a great fuss of settling him into his new accommodation. Julian, however, was unconcerned at the state of his health. After the constraints of Summer Fields and Eton, the sudden absence of school rules and regulations brought with it a new-found freedom.

Julian arrived at Oxford at the same time as a group of Old Etonian friends, many of whom were to play important roles in his life thereafter. Simon Wardell, whose father worked for Lord Beaverbrook, had been one of his closest friends at Eton and had joined him at Balliol. Alan Hare and Sandy Hope also arrived at Oxford from Eton, while he soon became acquainted with the somewhat disreputable Ranbir Singh, the son of an old school friend of Leo's, Sir Maharaj Singh. He also befriended Maurice Macmillan and Hugh Fraser, both to be future colleagues in the House of Commons, and the former his brother-in-law. Politics began to dominate their lives almost immediately. Julian joined the Oxford Union, which brought him into contact with contemporaries such as Ted Heath, also at Balliol, and Denis Healey. And, as he had at Eton, he made a point of joining all the political societies and attending as many meetings as he could, even those organised by the university's fascist and communist groups.

He was fortunate too to have Leo on hand to effect introductions to his own extensive circle of Oxford friends. Julian would dine frequently with his father at All Souls on a Sunday night, where he met many of the university's leading figures across the dining table. Sandy Lindsay was the Master of Balliol, where Leo was still a regular visitor, while H. A. L. Fisher, formerly the President of the Board of Education in Lloyd George's Cabinet, and now the revered Warden of New College, encouraged Julian's interest in Napoleon, in whom he was himself a renowned expert. At Christ Church Julian met Professor Lindemann, later to become, as Lord Cherwell, a senior adviser to Churchill. And at All Souls he met many of Leo's closest academic and political friends, Lionel Curtis, Geoffrey Dawson, Lord Halifax, John Simon and A. L. Rowse. It was a source of great pride to Leo that Julian, unlike many of his contemporaries who were still schoolboys at heart, was 'able to talk with everybody of every age about anything'.[15]

Undergraduate life revolved primarily around his political circle of friends and the clubs to which they belonged. As Leo had before him, Julian joined the Carlton Club, conveniently close to Balliol, became secretary of the Chatham Club and joined the French Club, which introduced him to many of the French undergraduates then at Oxford. He helped to found a weekly newspaper, the *Oxford Comment*, successfully persuading an aspiring young journalist at Worcester College called Woodrow Wyatt to agree to edit it. As one of its star reporters, Julian arranged interviews with Harry Pollitt, the leader of the Communist Party of Great Britain, Oswald Mosley, the pacifist MP George Lansbury and Leo's old sparring partner from 'Coefficient' days, H. G. Wells. The *Oxford Comment* provided Julian and his friends with a few weeks of amusing entertainment, until their financial backer pulled the plug and the paper folded. Oxford was still, for the most part, a male-dominated institution, and Julian and his friends relied largely for female company on friends visiting from outside. One such visitor to Oxford was to provide him with his first experience of true love, while he, in turn, was to provide her with a source of literary inspiration for many years to come.

On 3 December 1937, towards the end of Julian's first term at Oxford, he was having lunch in a local restaurant, when he spotted a friend sharing a nearby table with a pretty, slightly older woman. Her name was Barbara Pym and she was in fact twenty-four, six years older than Julian. Formerly an undergraduate at St Hilda's College, on leaving Oxford she had returned to live at her family home in Oswestry in Shropshire and had embarked optimistically on her chosen career as a novelist. She had written her first book while still at Oxford, dedicated to the man with whom she had enjoyed a passionate love affair as an undergraduate. However, they had recently separated and, when she first met Julian, she had just heard that her former lover was soon to be married to a Finnish girl. To take her mind off the news, she had decided to revisit some of her friends in Oxford and now, having been to a pre-lunch sherry party in one of the colleges, she was noisily putting on a mock Finnish accent to amuse her lunch companion.

Barbara noticed Julian immediately. He was about the same height as her, 'slight and dark with a quizzical monkey face'. He was wearing a 'camel hair coat and a spotted tie and looked sleek and neat'. Their mutual friend introduced her as Päävikki Olafsson, and she carried on pretending to be a Finn after Julian had sat down at her table. Once their mutual friend had left them alone together, they discussed her writing for a while before she accepted his invitation to go back to his rooms at Balliol. They were situated on one of the furthest staircases away from the main gate, with a view out over St Giles' and the Randolph Hotel, and she immediately noticed the lack of tidiness, and the prominently displayed copy of the *Statesman's Year Book* on the table. She refused a drink, but accepted a Camel cigarette and they sat silently for a while on the sofa. Then Julian took her hand, pretended to read her palm and suddenly kissed her. She was initially startled. It was the first time anyone so much younger than her had done such a thing, yet he 'had so much charm and a kind of childish simplicity, combined with Continental polish that was most appealing'. They listened to German and Hungarian records on his gramophone and, when it was time for her to leave, he insisted on keeping her handkerchief and walking her down to the bus stop in the street below his window. She 'went home happy next day'. Their first meeting had lasted some two hours.[16]

For Christmas, Julian was going to Kitzbühel with Simon Wardell, Sandy Hope and Ranbir Singh. It was to be his first skiing holiday alone with friends rather than his family, and Leo wished 'he had chosen better company', fearing that they would 'do not much skiing and too much sitting up late and fooling about'.[17] At the end of term Barbara had written, wishing him well for his Pass Moderation exams and Julian replied, addressing her as 'Liebe Vicki' and enclosing a replacement handkerchief so that she might 'dry your tears when you read Werther'. He described for her the ball he had been to at the

Austrian Legation in London, where everyone had worn peasant dress or uniform, and 'occasionally swarthy Hungarians had smashed their glasses against the wall'. Still flushed with the initial excitement of their romance, he promised to send her 'a postcard of some mountains and some peasants', and begged to see her again in London. Would she be 'a Shropshire spinster? a Finnish student? or just a novelist up to see her publisher?'[18] His letter offered her 'a glimpse of another world and Barbara was fascinated and . . . enchanted by the glamour' of Julian's life.[19]

When he returned to Oxford in the New Year, Julian wrote again to complain that Barbara had been on his mind 'all day and stopped me concentrating on Louis XVI. I simply can't believe', he continued, that 'I've only seen you once for an hour and a half.' He had been listening to Hungarian songs from Budapest on the wireless, which had made him feel 'very melancholic' and 'very Hungarian', presumably a reference to his paternal grandmother's roots.[20] Barbara was flattered and excited by Julian's attention, coming, as it did, so soon after the end of her previous attachment. Even the reference to Hungary struck a chord with her. In 1935 she and her sister Hilary had enjoyed a visit to Budapest with a group from the National Union of Students and she had subsequently used it as the location for the climax of her second novel *Civil to Strangers*, which she had written in 1936.

In February Barbara was back in Oxford, unsure whether or not she should look up Julian again but, having tossed a coin, deciding to leave a note for him at Balliol. When she returned later to her lodgings in St John's Street, she found him waiting there for her and at first 'scarcely knew him'. But he was soon busy telling her about the *Oxford Comment* and his planned trip to Spain, during the Easter vacation, to cover the Civil War. She was initially worried that they were both disappointed at meeting each other again, but 'soon we had our arms around each other and I knew it wasn't so.'[21] The next morning he came round to see her, wearing a 'nice rough brown suit' and 'square toed Austrian suede shoes'. That evening she went to his rooms at Balliol again, momentarily losing her composure when she found 'three old Etonians like teddy bears there', but once they had left Julian 'embraced me with such force that he hurt my nose and made it crooked'. After seeing a depressing play at the Oxford Playhouse, they cheered themselves up with a bottle of Niersteiner from the bar at Balliol. Barbara recorded how Julian would 'take hold of my hand and kiss my fingers in the middle of dinner and pay me the most charming compliments'. They talked about her latest book, her past loves and Julian's ambitions. He told her that 'he couldn't bear to die without having done something by which he could be remembered.'[22] They had spent about five and a half hours together during this, their fourth meeting.

Over the course of the next few days, they spent as much time as possible together. Barbara went with a group of her socialist friends to a pacifist meeting at the Town Hall, to be addressed by George Lansbury, and was surprised, but excited, to find Julian standing in the front row. He had not seen her and, when the meeting ended, she had to chase after him down the street before she could catch up with him. He grasped her tightly by the hand, and all her 'unhappiness vanished'. Back in his rooms they drank more Niersteiner, bought from the Randolph Hotel, and 'talked and loved'. He read some of her latest novel and she made a 'half hearted attempt to convert him to Pacifism'. But Julian thought that 'there were worse things than war, and that if he thought all beauty was going out of his life he would simply shoot himself.'[23]

They visited the Ashmolean together, feeling like 'two people having a coltish flirtation'. He bought her violets, and she gave him half a dozen in return, 'one for every occasion we had met', and she wrote a poem for him in her favourite style, that of John Betjeman.[24] They had lunch in Julian's rooms in Balliol, 'eggs with cream on top, chicken and chocolate mousse. And Niersteiner, of course.' And afterwards they spent the afternoon in the Botanical Gardens, lying side by side on the grass, while Julian told her about Jack, who he said 'was more charming and more cruel than he was'. He kissed her in the hothouse, by the orchids, and stole a spray of three for her, 'pinky mauve with purple centres like velvet', while she 'tried to capture and hold the happiness of that moment'. The smell of the orchids evoked, for Julian, the image of a tomb and they wished that they could share a marble vault together, although she quoted Marvell to him:

> The grave's a fine and private place
> But none I think do there embrace.

After she kissed him goodbye in the quad at Balliol, leaving a 'smear of lipstick on his forehead', she 'went home feeling terribly happy and thankful'.[25]

On 11 March Barbara went to lunch again in Balliol. It was a fine, sunny day and they ate 'fish, duck and green peas, peaches and cream, sherry, Niersteiner and port.' Julian was wearing his 'East end style suit from Savile Row, slate blue with padded shoulders and trousers with no turn-ups'. Barbara thought the afternoon that they spent together 'so lovely that I would gladly have died there and then', but as evening fell she was 'suddenly filled with fear and sadness' because she knew instinctively 'it would have to be goodbye.' Julian stood in front of the mirror, calmly combing his hair and putting on his coat. He came up behind her, kissed her one last time, and then he was gone, leaving her alone in his rooms. She inscribed a card of Boecklin's *Die Insel der Toten* with their initials and the dates of their first and last meetings, and added a line from her favourite poem by Heine, a 'leitmotif' of her friendship with him, '*Neuer Frühling gibt zuruck . . .*' (New Spring gives back . . .) She took a red anemone from her buttonhole and placed it on Julian's neatly laid out blue pyjamas, and left Balliol for the last time 'in a happy daze'. When she went back to her lodgings to change for dinner, she found two dozen daffodils from him with a card, written in German, saying that 'although he had to go away I knew that he had thought of me.' For Barbara, it was 'a perfect ending to what had been one of the happiest episodes' of her life. She was relieved that she 'didn't see him again in Oxford'.[26]

▪ ▪ ▪

By the time Julian arrived at Oxford in 1937, the Spanish Civil War had been raging for a year and had become the dominant issue in student politics. He quickly developed a fascination with the war, pinning a map of the war zones to his wall and following the progress of the fighting every day. All that was missing was the chance to visit Spain for himself and to witness something of the war at first hand. He saw it as an opportunity to enhance his reputation among his fellow undergraduates by writing some articles which he might then succeed in having published at home. A chance meeting at Eaton Square over lunch with the Duke of Alba, then Franco's representative in London, gave him the opportunity he needed to request a visa for himself and two friends, Sandy Hope and Michael Lyle, to attach themselves to the Nationalist forces as neutral observers, a role that had hitherto been forbidden by Franco's commanders. The Duke readily agreed and it was decided that they would leave for Spain at the beginning of the Easter holidays. Bryddie was 'rather anxious about it all', while Leo, in spite of his initial scepticism, saw 'no harm in a little mild adventure'.[27]

The three undergraduates left for France on 19 March. Barbara had written to Julian wishing him luck in his end-of-term exams and he replied from the Lord Warden Hotel in Dover, while waiting for his boat. The gloomy hotel reminded him of the Randolph and their time together in Oxford. 'If I never come back,' he wrote, 'you can remember that at least I cared.' He asked her to think of him on his nineteenth birthday the following week and to drink his health with a bottle of Niersteiner. Meeting her had been 'one of the big pieces of luck in my life', but he could not promise that he would 'always be faithful to my little Finn', although it would take someone special 'to gain my heart now that I have at least your memory'.[28] And in a passing remark he mentioned casually that he had forgotten to attend the French Unseen paper for his Pass Moderations, an admission which so upset Barbara that, on receiving the letter, she immediately went round to check with his tutor at Balliol whether anything could be done to remedy the situation.

For the first time since she had known him, Barbara gave vent to the frustration she felt at the one-sided nature of their relationship. Perhaps it was the arrogance of his 'oh-so-calm' admission that he had 'forgotten to go to the Schools' to sit one of his exams that made her so angry, 'you have no idea how angry' she wrote to a friend. 'How will Mr J. become oh so celebrated and famous', she went on, 'if he is doing silly things like this?' Possibly too she was upset by the equally casual manner in which he had made it clear in his letter that he already considered their affair effectively to be over, and that it was a relationship in which he could not possibly promise to be faithful to her anyway. Although she felt 'broken' by the turn of events, she recognised that Julian was far from feeling sorrowful, indeed was probably by now 'in Paris, kissing people's hands and paying nice compliments and being charming'.[29]

Julian and his friends crossed the border into Spain at the end of March 1938 and spent their first night in San Sebastián. But when they presented their credentials to the local governor the following morning, even the personal recommendation of the Duke of Alba had little effect, and it seemed initially as if their journey might have been in vain. Not for the first time, however, fate intervened in the form of an old friend of Leo's. Staying in the same hotel was the aged Marquis Merry del Val, for many years the Spanish Ambassador in London and a regular visitor to Eaton Square, where he had met Julian in the past. He agreed with Alba that the three young undergraduates should indeed be encouraged to see something of the war zone, and made the necessary arrangements with both the governor of San Sebastián and his own son Pablo, who was head of the press department in Burgos, Franco's capital. The local governor, annoyed at being overruled, decided that if the young Englishmen were really so desperate to see the realities of war, then he would show them war in its most gruesome detail. They duly spent their first two days in San Sebastián visiting the local hospitals and orphanage, where they were treated to lengthy tours of the plastic surgery wards, the shell shock wards and, indeed, the operating theatres themselves. 'For boys of nineteen', admitted Julian, 'this was strong meat.'[30]

Having been issued with safe conduct passes, they drove first from San Sebastián to Burgos, where they found themselves at the very heart of the Nationalist war effort. The town was a military melting pot, brimming with a varied assortment of soldiers of different nationalities, and the young Englishmen had their first experience of mixing with the Nationalist officers who spent their evenings, in spite of the cold, parading in the main street or drinking coffee in the pavement cafes. Some wore the red berets of the Carlist Militia, the *Requetés*, others the dark blue of the *Falangist* party uniform. German Air Force officers mixed with Italian infantrymen and soldiers of the Spanish

Foreign Legion, the infamous *Tercio de Extranjeros*, wearing their distinctive grey-and-green uniforms. Most easily recognised were the Moorish cavalry, in their white turbans and ankle length cloaks. But Julian was impatient to move closer still to the fighting and, after an uncomfortable night in a local hotel, he secured a meeting the next day with the young Merry del Val and, with his help, the offer of passes to the battle areas and further assistance from his officials on arrival there.

They left for Saragossa on 28 March, taking with them a Major Bauer, the military correspondent for the *Journal de Genève*, and by evening were mixing with the international press corps already assembled there in the Hotel Europa y Inglaterra. They had arrived at a defining moment of the war on the Aragon Front. The Nationalist forces had recently launched a major offensive and had succeeded in advancing nearly a hundred kilometres in just a few days, driving the Republican troops back to the rivers Cinca and Ebro. If they could now continue the advance, their prize would be to reach the sea and to cut Barcelona off from Valencia, Madrid and the rest of the Republican areas. The following morning, on Bauer's advice, Julian's party, together with a military escort, broke away from the rest of the press corps, who were waiting to accompany the final Nationalist push, and drove instead to the towns of Huesca and Barbastro, on the extreme edge of the advancing front.

In Huesca the young students came across a walled cemetery where the advancing Republican forces had earlier set up a position just outside the town, only to be cut off from their supply lines and later shelled and starved into submission by the Nationalists holding the town. In their desperation, they had created a scene of 'apocalyptic horror', tearing open the graves, removing skeletons and decomposing bodies, and displaying them in 'grotesque or indecent postures'. Some were sitting around a table playing cards, a bottle of wine in one hand and a glass in the other. Others had been forced together in obscene erotic embraces, while another had been crucified against the cemetery wall.[31] From Huesca they pushed on towards Barbastro and the front at the river Cinca, passing the artillery and infantry columns alongside which they were now advancing, and crossing the Cinca with the first Nationalist troops to do so. When they returned to the hotel in Saragossa that evening, they were able to boast of their scoop to the journalists who had waited all day to accompany the main body of the advance which had failed to materialise. The following morning Julian attached himself to the press corps at a briefing given by General Yagüe, the commanding officer of the advancing forces, whose notorious exploits earlier in the war had earned him the sobriquet of the 'Butcher of Badajoz'.

Four days later, on 3 April, Julian and his friends were allowed to join the main advance across the river Cinca, into the town of Fraga, and on towards Lérida. In the course of the advance he came under sustained enemy fire for the first time in his life, and was later chastised by his Spanish military escort for lying down in the road as the bullets flew above their heads. Indeed, all three narrowly escaped death when a defensive position, in which they had taken shelter, received a direct hit from a shell only moments after they had vacated it. And, in the course of the sustained bombardment which followed, Julian took cover in a shell hole with an officer of the Foreign Legion who turned out to be Peter Kemp, one of the few Englishmen fighting with the Nationalist forces at the time and a future friend and colleague of Julian's in the Balkans during the Second World War. Eventually he accompanied the victorious Nationalist forces into Lérida where the young Englishmen looked on cautiously at the drunken celebrations taking place in the midst of the scenes of destruction and slaughter in the town.

The young Merry del Val now warned that there would be a temporary lull in the fighting and, still together with his friends, Julian drove south through Valladolid, Salamanca and eventually to Seville, where they met General Queipo de Llano, who had captured the city and was now Franco's acting governor of Andalucia. For a few days they were shown around the city, visiting some of Queipo's organisations by day, while enjoying the traditional night-time hospitality of the Holy Week fiesta. But after a few days admiring the flamenco, bullfights and religious processions, and having even received an invitation to a party on board a German U-boat anchored in the Guadalquivir, it was time to head back for the summer term at Oxford. Sandy Hope and Michael Lyle took the car home by way of a boat out of Gibraltar, while Julian made his way home by air to Paris, where he stopped off en route to spend a day with Jack.

Julian returned to Oxford to find himself 'something of a lion'. As he had intended, his exploits in Spain had set him apart from many of his contemporaries who had spent the Easter vacation engaged in considerably more mundane activities. He was soon in demand as a speaker at various societies and dining clubs, while Leo used his influence to help him place three articles about the Civil War in the *Daily Telegraph*. Leo was more proud than ever of his younger son, and thought that he might well have a future in journalism if he could only 'prune the exuberance of his early literary style'.[32] But Julian was already making plans for the summer vacation, and was busy considering various schemes, including visits to Hungary, Kashmir, or a return to Spain. Leo 'urged him not to forget either finance or the needs of work', but was pleased to hear that Julian had made his maiden speech at the Oxford Union, albeit 'to a rather empty House' and was 'busy inventing a new policy for the Conservatives' which he intended 'somehow or other to plant on Oxford'.[33]

Also waiting for Julian at Balliol was a letter from Barbara. She had been 'praying every day' while he was in Spain, and had written him 'a beautiful poem for his birthday . . . in heroic couplets', the first letter of each line spelling his name down the page. Yet she harboured no illusions as to his feelings for her. She pictured him opening the letter in his room, reading the poem 'through once and then it will be lying on his table with all the letters from his admirers'. She imagined him sharing its contents with his 'charming French' friends, or joking about it with his 'rich Indian friends' as they listened to Josephine Baker on his gramophone; not the 'sad German record, or the funny Russian one, or the *romantisch* Hungarian one', which might have reminded him of her.[34] Julian replied a few weeks later, wishing her a happy birthday in return. 'May you have as many more', he wrote, 'as you gave me minutes of happiness, and contrary to the normal rule may they make you, if it is possible, more beautiful.' He had no present for her other than his love, but he was at least 'back from Spain unhurt', although his hair was 'perhaps a bit greyer' and his 'brow more wrinkled'. He hoped

that she would visit him in London. 'Just walk up to the front door of
112 Eaton Square', he suggested, 'bang twice with each brazen knocker
and walk down the long marble corridors to where Julian walks end-
lessly dictating to a battery of tired secretaries.'[35] It was an image that
Barbara was later to use more than once in her books.

Julian had done remarkably little work during his first year at
Oxford. The term time had been largely spent embarking on his
fledgling careers in student politics and journalism, while simultaneously finding his way around the hectic social life that Oxford and
London had to offer in those pre-war years. When not travelling
abroad, he had spent the holidays enjoying a never-ending succession
of parties and debutante balls; Leo remarked wryly in July 1938 that
Julian had been 'after a different flame every evening', and had once
had 'to fit in an extra one at a farewell breakfast' before leaving for his
summer holiday. In spite of his protestations of love in his letters
to her, Barbara no longer featured in Julian's romantic plans. The
holiday in question was supposed to go some way towards making up
for his lack of academic endeavour during his first year. Julian and
his old school friend Alan Hare decided to spend the first few weeks of
the long vacation on a reading holiday in the south of France. Bryddie
was not keen on the idea. Having already visited Oxford during the
previous term to clean and tidy his rooms for him, she was now concerned that there would be 'bad food and too much hot weather'. She
would have preferred them to go to Scotland.[36]

Nevertheless, Julian and Hare drove down to the south of France,
where they rented a small villa on the outskirts of Toulon and, for six
weeks, studied their books by day and enjoyed the night life on the
Riviera. But by the beginning of September Hare had to return to
London, and Julian pushed on with his earlier plan to return to Spain.
He had followed the progress of the Civil War closely throughout the
summer, and had noticed that few of the national newspapers had
correspondents attached to the Nationalist forces. His articles in the
Daily Telegraph had been well received and, after approaching a
number of newspapers, the *Daily Express* agreed that, while they could
not put him on their full-time payroll, they would accredit him as their
correspondent. They would pay him modest expenses and a fee

for any articles which he might submit and which they subsequently used. Julian duly returned to Burgos and set himself up in the Hotel Condestable with the rest of the international press corps.

For a time he contented himself with filing copy from the interviews he managed to conduct with various Nationalist leaders in Burgos, including the Commander-in-Chief of the navy and General Jordana, the Minister for War. He also met a former Chief of the Imperial General Staff, Field Marshal Sir Philip Chetwode, who was in Burgos as the head of a neutral commission, to try to arrange an exchange of prisoners between the two sides and facilitate a mutual withdrawal of foreign 'volunteers'. The mission was not a success, not least because having been assured by the Nationalists that there were just a few foreign volunteers fighting with their army, principally Germans and Italians, Chetwode found himself billeted on the same floor of the Condestable as the entire Portuguese military mission. Julian wrote a satirical article on Chetwode's visit which failed to get past the censors, but which he subsequently smuggled out of Spain with the help of a Red Cross worker returning home on leave.

From Burgos Julian also visited the Madrid front, stopping en route in Ávila and subsequently spending a few days with a battalion of the Foreign Legion near Talavera. As well as visiting the front line on the river Tagus, he witnessed Franco addressing a review of the Italian Littorio Division and heard the Foreign Legion's founder, the notorious General Millán Astray, giving a powerful recruiting speech. At the end of the ceremony Julian met both Astray and Franco, the latter politely refusing his request for an interview. Julian thought him 'not impressive to look at, nor in any way magnetic', but he had never met a man 'who radiated such complete self confidence'.[37] Unfortunately, the deteriorating political situation in the rest of Europe was keeping the war in Spain off the front pages at home, especially those of the *Daily Express*. He was back in Burgos when news reached him of the Munich agreement and he decided that, with the term in Oxford already under way, it was time once again to return home. He arrived home two weeks late for the beginning of term, 'looking very well' according to Leo, but needing 'to be contrite with the Dons for being late'.[38]

Julian returned to find Oxford in the throes of a celebrated by-election. The Conservative Party was deeply divided between the official candidate, Quintin Hogg, an ardent supporter of Neville Chamberlain and what he had accomplished at Munich, and the Master of Balliol, Sandy Lindsay, who stood against him as an 'anti-Appeasement' candidate. Julian viewed Munich as a defeat for Britain, a belief which had been reinforced in Burgos by the gloating of a senior German officer with whom he had become acquainted. Back home, a briefing from his father only increased his indignation and, alongside Ted Heath and a number of other student Conservatives, he threw himself into the campaign in support of Lindsay. Twenty-five years later, by then a prominent supporter of Hogg's failed bid for the leadership of the Conservative Party, Julian was embarrassed to recall the slogan he used throughout the by-election campaign, that '*A vote for Hogg is a vote for Hitler.*'[39] Although Hogg won the seat comfortably, the campaign crystallised Julian's political beliefs and, together with Hugh Fraser and Maurice Macmillan (whose father Harold Macmillan had spoken for Lindsay during the by-election), he mounted a successful campaign to assume the leadership of the Oxford University Conservative Association. Fraser became President and Julian its Secretary, later succeeding to the presidency himself, when he invited his father, among a number of other prominent opponents of Chamberlain, to address the association.

In contrast with Leo's low-key interest in student politics during his own time at Oxford, Julian soon began to play an increasingly high-profile role in the Oxford Union. On 23 February 1939 the Union held a debate, not for the first time, on the issue of conscription and Leo agreed to speak in favour of conscription alongside Julian's friend Hugh Fraser, soon to be elected President for the following term. Although they lost the vote, Leo recalled an enjoyable dinner before the debate with the President, who was in the chair for the evening, 'Heath of Balliol, a very nice youth,'[40] while Julian took the opportunity of speaking to Vernon Bartlett, the editor of the *News Chronicle*, who was debating in opposition to his father that evening. Julian asked whether there might be an opening with his newspaper to return to Spain once again and report on the impending fall of

Madrid. A few days later Bartlett contacted Julian. The Spanish authorities had refused entry to an official correspondent from the *News Chronicle* on the grounds that it was an unfriendly paper, and asked if Julian would go quietly instead.

He left immediately for San Sebastián and secured a lift on to Madrid, arriving in the capital just a few hours after Franco's advance troops. He booked into the Ritz, but the hotel had no heat and there was little food in the city, while hundreds of people were sleeping rough on the streets. The soldiers of the defeated Republican army had been ordered to leave the city and were, in many cases, quite literally walking home. Meanwhile officers on the 'wanted' list were being hunted down and executed. One evening Julian had a drink at the Ritz with a Spanish officer he had befriended previously in Burgos. The soldier made his excuses early to go for a last dinner with his girlfriend, to whom he had become engaged before the war. They had fought on opposing sides, he with Franco and she as a Communist youth leader. The reunion was to be their first since the end of the war and would almost certainly be their last. She was to be arrested the following day and was certain to face lengthy imprisonment and possibly even a death sentence.

Julian filed a number of articles for the *News Chronicle* in which he suggested that, in the now increasingly likely event of a more wide-spread European war, the new Spanish regime and the majority of the population would be openly supportive of Germany. But he also believed that Spain was 'too exhausted to take an active part in a European War', and lacked the necessary supplies of food or munitions. Rather, he thought, in the event of war 'Spain would maintain a hostile neutrality towards the Entente.' In later years Julian would look back on the significance of his visits to Spain from the perspective of his own political development. While his initial sympathies had been with Franco, a closer understanding of Nationalist propaganda had, by the end of the war, led him to a more balanced view. Above all, both sides had been 'guilty of unspeakable cruelties, individual and collective'.[41] But as events unfolded throughout the rest of Europe in 1938, he had ceased to judge the war on its own merits and had begun to place it in its wider international context. By the time he returned to Oxford for

1. The 'Pocket Hercules'. Leo as champion gymnast at Harrow in 1891.

3. Captain Leopold Amery, intelligence officer, in 1915.

2. In August 1908, after failing to win a by-election by eight votes, Leo addressed an audience of forty thousand in Wolverhampton, when he was presented with a gold watch and eight silver goblets.

4. The Imperial War Cabinet at Downing Street in 1917. Leo is standing on the far left of the back row, alongside (from left to right) Admiral Jellicoe, Sir Edward Carson, Lord Derby, Major General Maurice and Sir Maurice Hankey. Austen Chamberlain and Lord Robert Cecil are standing fourth and fifth from left in the middle row. Sitting in the front row are (from left to right): the Labour Party leader, Arthur Henderson; Leo's mentor, Lord Milner; Lord Curzon; Andrew Bonar Law; Lloyd George; the Prime Minister of Canada and Julian's godfather, Sir Robert Borden; the Prime Minister of New Zealand, William Massey and General Smuts.

5. Lloyd George and Leo out walking at Criccieth, the former's Welsh home, in August 1918.

6. 'The comradeship of Cabinet'. Leo (right), in 1923 when First Lord of the Admiralty, with Neville Chamberlain, Stanley Baldwin and Austen Chamberlain.

7. Jack, aged three, with Bryddie in 1915.

8. Nanny Mead, who found Jack 'a very queer little boy', holding the baby Julian, while Jack sits alongside his ever-faithful French governess, Pipette, in 1920.

9. Jack, aged eleven, on board the Admiralty yacht, the *Bryony*, in August 1923 during Leo's inspection of the British fleet in the Mediterranean.

10. Jack and Julian skiing in Pontresina, Christmas 1924.

11. Jack, aged fourteen, on his first motorbike in 1926.

12. The Prince of Wales (later Edward VIII) at the Cenotaph on Armistice Day 1921. Looking on in the front row alongside Leo (far left) are (from left to right) Lord Curzon, Winston Churchill, Arthur Balfour and Austen Chamberlain. Lord Robert Cecil is standing behind Leo and Neville Chamberlain is partially hidden by Balfour.

13. Leo, when Secretary of State for the Dominions and Colonies, with Sir Samuel Hoare during their visit to Baghdad in April 1925.

14. Leo speaking in the shadow of Cecil Rhodes, the 'Colossus', in Bulawayo during his Empire Tour in August 1927.

15. 'Tales of the Dominions' by the contemporary cartoonist Low, from the *Evening Standard* of 14 February 1928. Leo tries, unsuccessfully, to convince Lord Birkenhead, Stanley Baldwin and Winston Churchill of the benefits of Imperial Preference.

16. Leo equipped for mountaineering in the New Zealand Alps, during his Empire Tour in December 1927.

17. 'Victory'. Leo (right) and his guide, Edward Feuz, on the summit of Mt Amery in the Canadian Rockies on 20 August 1929.

18. Leo and Julian beside the river Cherwell during Julian's first year at Summer Fields in 1928.

19. 'All equals, all in it together'. Leo, Bryddie, Jack (aged fifteen) and Julian (aged seven) at the Rodneys' home, Bury Green, in 1927.

20. Bryddie with Jack, aged sixteen, at Bury Green in 1928.

21. 'The Chairman of the Anti-Authority League'. Julian at Summer Fields in 1931.

22. Jack and his wife, the 'actress' Una Wing, in London before their elopement to Athens in 1932.

23. Jack, with Una close behind, under arrest in Paris in May 1933, following his fraudulent purchase of diamonds in Athens.

24. & 25. Leo (above) and Julian (below) skiing in St Moritz.

26. Bryddie skating in Klosters, during Leo's last skiing holiday in January 1939.

27. Julian addressing the Oxford Union during a debate on conscription on 27 April 1939. It was this photograph that Barbara Pym cut out of the *Oxford Mail* and kept on her mantelpiece beside a bunch of red roses.

28. Leo (centre), a Governor at Harrow for thirty years, with Winston Churchill and Arthur Boissier, the Head Master and Jack's former housemaster (far left), at Harrow School Songs in December 1940.

29. Jack's second 'wife'. Jeanine Barde's *Fremdenpass*, the passport issued to foreigners by the Nazi authorities.

30. 'Rather a sensation'. Jack's *Fremdenpass*.

31. Jack addressing a Nazi meeting in Antwerp in March 1944. The local commissioner of police, who attended the meeting, later appeared at Jack's pre-trial hearing to give evidence against him.

32. Jack (second from left) with collaborationist Flemish officials and German officers in Antwerp in March 1944.

33. Leo with the newly appointed Viceroy of India, Sir Archie Wavell, at the India Office in 1943.

34. 'At the head of a Turkoman horde'. David Smiley and Julian (centre right) with Tajik and Kazakh deserters in the mountains of Albania in September 1944.

35. Billy McLean (centre) and Julian discussing policy with the Albanian Zogist leader, Abas Kupi (front left), in the summer of 1944.

36. 'Thank God you're here'. Jack and his third 'wife', Michelle Thomas, being taken into custody in Milan by Captain Alan Whicker in May 1945.

37. Crowds gathering to read a notice announcing Jack's execution for treason outside Wandsworth prison, on 19 December 1945.

38. 'All is over'. Julian and Leo with Michelle Thomas soon after Jack's execution in 1946. Michelle married and moved to Switzerland, where Julian continued to visit her until her death.

39. 'To encourage filial respect'. Leo and Julian on a visit to Canada, and to Mt Amery in particular, in June 1949.

40. Julian marrying Catherine Macmillan at St Margaret's, Westminster on 26 January 1950.

41. Cecil Beaton took this photograph of Leo and Bryddie in the library of their home at Eaton Square. It was said of Bryddie that after Jack's death she 'never smiled again'.

the summer term of 1939, he had concluded that a Republican victory would probably have been the best tactical outcome for Britain, but that at least Franco's regime was now too exhausted to play a role of any significance in support of Germany.

On 27 April 1939 the Oxford Union once again debated conscription on the motion that '*In view of this country's commitments and the gravity of the general situation in Europe, this House welcomes conscription.*' Julian was selected to propose the motion. Two days earlier Leo had again been defeated on the same subject at the Cambridge Union, on this occasion by the military historian Basil Liddell Hart, who was to oppose the motion again at Oxford. Liddell Hart was supported by the then undergraduate and later Tory MP John Biggs-Davison, while Julian was seconded by Randolph Churchill. There were police posted outside to keep order and the hall itself was full to overflowing. Julian opened the debate by welcoming Liddell Hart, who had 'come hot foot from his triumph at the Cambridge Union, his hands still reeking with my father's blood'. He was glad to have such an early opportunity to 'carry out a filial vengeance'.[42] It was reported back to Leo that Julian had spoken 'most convincingly, with distinction both of argument and manner', and that he had 'certainly made a good start in his career as a politician, if that is to be his career'.[43] The *Oxford Mail* described the debate as 'one of the most outstanding' in the Union's history and printed a photograph of Julian standing at the despatch box. 'Attendance was a record. Every available space was occupied in the gallery, on the floor, the window sills, and even the President's rostrum.' Including those in the gallery there had been 'over a thousand people present', and when the vote was taken, Julian and Churchill had won the day by 423 votes to 326.[44]

Julian's success at the Union brought him plenty of publicity and, together with Hugh Fraser and another senior member of the university Conservative Association, Patrick O'Donovan, he decided to capitalise on all the attention. They issued a seventeen-point political manifesto, a *Statement of the Principles of a New Conservatism*, which was widely distributed to Members of Parliament and the press. 'The people of England', it began extravagantly, 'demand a National policy, clear cut and constructive.' Reviews were mixed. The radicalism of the manifesto's economic section aroused the greatest interest, Beaver-brook condemning their ideas as 'too totalitarian', while socialist Members of Parliament applauded the young Conservatives' 'flirtation with nationalisation'.[45] While the manifesto was 'an attempt to bring the fundamental ideas of Disraeli and Joseph Chamberlain up to date', the *Daily Express* regretted that 'in economic policy the authors advocate a state control which would have shocked Mr Disraeli and Mr Chamberlain, and which smacks of the totalitarianism which they have shown themselves eager to resist abroad.'[46] Leo, however, was delighted. 'It is a great comfort to me', he wrote of Julian, 'that with all his originality his general ideas are essentially in line with my own.' He was hopeful that his younger son might now 'be able to continue my work and be luckier than I have been'.[47]

■ ■ ■

With the prospect of war looming ever larger, Julian was determined to be prepared with a role to play should war break out and, early in 1939, he joined the Oxford University Air Squadron. What he had seen for himself in Spain and read about life in the infantry during the First World War had convinced him that, if he 'had to fight, the sky seemed the best place', and he undertook his initial tuition in an Avro Tutor at Abingdon, before attending a training camp at Lympne Airport in Kent at the end of June. He enjoyed learning to fly, but was a far from model pupil in the eyes of his instructors. The Wing Commander in charge of his squadron complained that 'attendance at lectures you treat as something quite unimportant', and that 'you appear to have joined this Squadron under the misapprehension that you were joining a flying club!'[48]

Julian had not yet completely forgotten Barbara and on 2 June he wrote to wish her 'many happy returns', promising that he had 'never forgotten you and . . . never will'. He described to her his adventures in Spain, his flying lessons and his 'boring speeches' at the Union. 'Sometimes I wonder why I do all these things,' he complained. 'I expect it's because I can't do anything else.'[49] And on 4 July he saw her again for the first time in a year, coming face to face with her at a set of traffic lights in Portman Square. Possibly she had been encouraged by his letter and had engineered the meeting. She had recently walked past the house in Eaton Square on a number of occasions, 'newly painted in cream and royal blue' with the smell of 'Sunday dinner coming up from the basement', in the hope that she might see him. At home she kept 'the photograph of him at the Union', from the *Oxford Mail*, 'on the mantelpiece and in front of it a spray of red roses'. Now, once again, she 'met one I had loved and had not seen for more than a year' and, for the first and only time, Julian invited her back to 'that curious house . . . with its oil paintings and smell of incense'. And while she was there with him, she met his mother, 'a splendid character for a novel'.[50]

True to her word, Barbara Pym included Bryddie in several of her novels, while Julian appears, in one guise or another, in almost every one she wrote thereafter, as well as in her private correspondence and diary. He became 'one of her richest sources of inspiration' and, according to her biographer and best friend, she 'thought about Julian for most of her life', in spite of their having known each other for such a short time. For Barbara, the 'power of the memory and the feeling she had deliberately generated from it was simply *because* the incident had been so brief, so perfectly rounded.' There was 'no pain, only a pleasurable memory'; Julian had been her creation and she could therefore enjoy 'the freedom to have these deep and continuing feelings about him, the sort of feelings she could not have had for a real person.'[51] 'I don't think I have ever thanked God for any happiness more sincerely,' wrote Barbara, 'than I do for the approximately twenty hours I spent with Julian Amery in the winter of 1937 and spring of 1938.' Even were she never to see him again, nothing could 'take away what has been'.[52]

In *Crampton Hodnet*, written in 1939 and 1940, but only published posthumously in 1985, Pym recreates the intertwined academic and ecclesiastical worlds of North Oxford in the pre-war years. She describes three contemporary love affairs and draws heavily on the Amery family, based on her single visit to Eaton Square in the summer of 1939. Simon Beddoes is a young, dashing and ambitious under-graduate, the son of the late Sir Lyall Beddoes, the former British Ambassador to Warsaw. Barely an hour after meeting Anthea

Cleveland, the daughter of an Oxford don, Simon kisses her in the library of her house and declares his undying love for her. He is 'dark and thin', with a 'young, lively face and charming manners'. His widowed mother lives in a large house in Belgravia, he spends his holidays skiing in Kitzbühel and speaks regularly at the Union. And while Anthea lies awake at night thinking about him and 'solemnly blowing kisses' in the perceived direction of his college, Simon's only concern is for the speech he will make the following day at the Union. 'Of course he adored Anthea', wrote Pym, 'but "Man's love is of man's life a thing apart", especially when he is only twenty and has the ambition to become Prime Minister.'

Bryddie appears in *Crampton Hodnet* as the widowed Lady Beddoes, a 'charming' but 'rather pathetic' woman, 'lost, as if her life were without purpose'. She has endured a loveless marriage with her successful husband and talks of having grown fond of him in the same way as she might have of a cherished piece of furniture. In an echo of Leo's own mother's Hungarian roots, Lady Beddoes had 'been nothing at all, just the daughter of an English Professor teaching in Warsaw', and her son was always remarking 'how unwise it was to let his mother travel anywhere alone because she always began telling her life story to the most impossible people.' When called on to open a garden fete at the North Oxford vicarage, Simon worries that she will forget what she is meant to say in her speech as she is so 'hopelessly vague'.

Pym describes her own brief affair with Julian in great detail. Inevitably Simon soon tires of Anthea, but not before she has visited him at Randolph College (Pym's name for Balliol), where the entrance would often be blocked by 'a group of rich young men newly arrived from town. Suede shoes, pin-striped flannels, teddy-bear coats and check caps – Anthea knew the uniform so well.' She describes intimate lunches, washed down with Niersteiner, in his rooms, his suddenly 'taking hold of your hand while you were eating, and kissing your fingers', and how 'compliments flowed so easily from his lips.' She is always trying to think of something intelligent to discuss with him politically and writes long letters, to which he never replies. His final letter to her, ending their brief affair because he has met someone else, is written in 'sprawling, childish writing' and is littered with 'curious parliamentary phraseology', as befits a young man who one day will be 'Secretary of State for Something, answering questions in the House.'[53]

▪ ▪ ▪

Like the rest of his generation, Julian found that life in both Oxford and London was soon overshadowed by unfolding events in Europe, although he continued to enjoy the social season throughout the summer of 1939. He also regularly accompanied Leo to political gatherings, where the talk was dominated by the ever-growing prospect of war. At a party at 11 Downing Street, hosted by Jack's godfather John Simon, Julian met Neville Chamberlain for the only time, the Prime Minister joking that he was 'sorry to see that' Julian 'was following in his father's footsteps and making speeches critical of the Government'.[54] The Master of Balliol wrote to Leo to say that Julian had a good chance of obtaining a 'first' in his Modern Greats if he was really determined to work hard for it, but Leo recognised that it was 'very difficult for a boy like him to settle down to his Greats work at a moment like this'.[55]

Julian too was thinking ahead. If he was to put in the amount of work required to succeed in his exams, then he would go somewhere warm for a reading holiday during the summer holidays and work intensively at his weakest subjects. He first considered France or Italy, but if war were to break out while he was away, he had no desire to be called up to serve with the Royal Air Force on the home front. However, if he was to ensure that he was further east, he would be prevented from returning home immediately, and might be called up to serve with the Polish or Egyptian air forces; he would be one of only a handful of Englishmen in eastern Europe at the outbreak of war. At lunch one day with his father and the Yugoslav Minister in London he met Mabel Gruitch, the American widow of a Yugoslav diplomat. She owned a holiday home on the Dalmatian coast and invited Julian to spend the summer holidays with her, an offer he accepted with alacrity.

Julian's car was still in Burgos with its broken camshaft, but he managed to buy a second-hand Ford for £12 and, having loaded it up with as many books and personal possessions as he could manage, he set off from London leaving a tearful Bryddie behind. He stopped off in Paris to see Jack, the last time he was to do so for six years, and drove on through Strasbourg, the Rhine Valley and on to Munich and Salzburg, everywhere he went witnessing Germany's preparations for war. He drove on south into Yugoslavia and to the Dalmatian Coast where he set up home for several weeks in Mabel Gruitch's villa outside Crikvenica, after which he moved to a flat in the town and spent the next few weeks immersed in his books. But on the last day of August he received a telegram from Leo warning him that the Air Ministry had ordered him to report to the Middle East Command in Egypt and advising him to begin the journey there immediately. The next morning, in a café in the main square of Crikvenica, Julian joined a crowd of Yugoslavs and Germans to listen to Hitler's broadcast announcing the invasion of Poland.

That evening Julian packed up his belongings and prepared to begin his journey to Egypt by way of Bosnia and Belgrade. At home his father was preparing his own damning indictment of Neville Chamberlain, which he would deliver the following day in the House of Commons. Julian wrote home to tell Leo and Bryddie of his plans, 'a fine manly and thoughtful letter'.[56] While he shared Leo's belief that war could have been averted had the Government stood up to Germany sooner, he felt relieved too 'that the issue with Germany had at last come to a head'. He would never return to Oxford and his previous life there, and there would be no 'first' and no presidency of the Union. But he felt 'no regrets', only relief that he would be 'spared the gloomy prospect of having to climb the ladder of the bar or journalism from the bottom rung'. Instead, 'war would provide adventure', and 'all previous bets were off'.[57] On 2 September he left Crikvenitsa, offering Mabel Gruitch a lift as far as Belgrade, his car draped in a Union Jack. They drove through Bosnia by way of Bihač and Banja Luka, where they heard the news of Britain's declaration of war. From there they crossed the border into Serbia at the river Drina and drove on straight to Belgrade. Julian was now twenty years old and, for him, the war was about to begin in earnest.

Part Three

1938–1955

CHAPTER SEVENTEEN

In the Name of God, Go

The news of the Austrian Anschluss in March 1938 'came as a terrible blow' to Leo, and marked a turning point for his hopes of European unity in the face of the increasing Nazi threat. Czechoslovakia's vulnerability was clear for all to see and Leo believed that 'the best hope of peace now lies in telling Germany that if she touches Czechoslovakia we are in it too.'[1] In a letter to *The Times* he emphasised that 'clearly there is an end of all discussion for a settlement with Germany.' Instead, Britain should 'read the writing on the wall, press on with even greater determination with rearmament', and 'stand close to France.'[2] Two days later, Neville and Annie Chamberlain cancelled a lunch appointment with Leo and Bryddie at Eaton Square to participate in the emergency debate on the fall of Austria. Privately Leo found Chamberlain's statement too restrained, and wished that the Prime Minister had been more outspoken in his support for the Czechs and his condemnation of Hitler. But when it came to his own opportunity to participate in the debate, he confined his criticism to calls for an end to indecision and for the creation of a policy cabinet or, better still, a National Government. 'We must no longer go on drifting or halting between inconsistent policies,' he told the House, for without 'a clear-cut policy one way or the other, we shall certainly end in war.' It was time for the Government to stop 'havering, half encouraging Czechoslovakia, half encouraging France with the idea that we stand behind her, half encouraging Germany to think that we shall run out.' Britain should either make it clear that she would indeed 'stand out' or, alternatively, that 'the first German soldier or aeroplane to cross the Czech border will bring the whole might of this country against Germany.'[3]

By the time Chamberlain addressed the House again, ten days later on 24 March, he had largely calmed the fears of Leo and his fellow critics. While he rejected the idea of giving a cast-iron guarantee to Czechoslovakia, he strongly implied that if German interference there led to a general war in which France was involved, then Britain would almost certainly become involved also, whatever her legal obligation. The pace of rearmament was to quicken too, and Leo was broadly 'satisfied at the time', later conceding that he did not have a definitive reply to his own earlier rhetorical question as to precisely where Britain should stand. Indeed, he was 'still very uncertain whether we could do anything for Czechoslovakia, and whether we might not have to resign ourselves to falling back, with Italian support, on holding Yugoslavia and the Balkans, and letting Germany find her elbow room in the rest of the Danubian area and in Eastern Europe.'[4]

Leo agreed with the Government that Italy could be persuaded back into the position of providing a useful counter-balance to German influence and, with the blessing of Lord Halifax, the new Foreign Secretary, he arranged to spend the Easter recess in Rome to assess the situation for himself. He arrived just as the negotiations between the British Ambassador, Lord Perth, and the Italian Foreign Minister, Count Ciano, were reaching their successful conclusion. Leo was encouraged by what he found. There was a real desire, he thought, among Italian politicians and people alike, for Britain and Italy to 'be friends again and let bygones be bygones'. Mussolini greeted Leo 'warmly and even affectionately as a tried friend of Italy', and assured him that he would abide by the new agreement and would work towards political stability in Europe. Leo thought that Mussolini had 'grown greatly in personality' since their last meeting, and remarked how 'impressive' were his 'dark eyes with the whites showing all round, set in his powerful brown face'. Most noticeable of all, however, was the fact that the Italian leader was 'now completely bald'.[5]

For the next few months Leo watched from the sidelines as the crisis in Czechoslovakia unfolded. In May, as Chamberlain prepared a limited reshuffle of his senior team, there was once again speculation that Leo was to be brought back into the Government, although Beaverbrook's strident demand in the *Evening Standard* that he should be reappointed Colonial Secretary probably did him more harm than good. Leo charitably put his failure to gain preferment under Chamberlain down to the Prime Minister's wish to promote from within his existing team and, once again, felt on the whole relieved to be excluded. In fact, given the deterioration in their relationship over recent years, there were by now almost no circumstances under which Chamberlain would have countenanced having Leo in the Cabinet again. On 24 April came the demand from Konrad Henlein, the leader of the Sudeten German Party, for greater autonomy for the Sudeten Germans, which was followed by organised disturbances in the Sudetenland, the ensuing response of the Czech police and Hitler's mobilisation of troops on the Czech border. On 21 May Chamberlain finally joined France and Russia in warning Hitler that he could not count on British abstention in the event of a wider European war and, although the warning had the desired effect in the short term, an infuriated Hitler resolved to march into Czechoslovakia at the beginning of October.

Leo Amery is rightly acknowledged as a leading critic of Chamberlain's policy of appeasement towards Germany during the summer and early autumn of 1938. However, it is important to recognise that it was only in the immediate aftermath of Munich that he became truly outspoken. Until then he gave cautious backing to Chamberlain and chose to concentrate, in his public statements at least, on calling for rearmament, National Service and reform of the administrative machinery of government by the creation of an inner policy cabinet and a National Government to include all parties. He did not agree with Chamberlain's off-the-record remarks, made at a lunch given by Nancy Astor and reported in the *New York Times*, that he would be prepared to consider the 'separation of the German districts from the body of the Czech republic' and their annexation to Germany.[6] However, Leo accepted that the smaller German regions in Czechoslovakia could not be prevented from coalescing under orders from Berlin, a compromise he might have been willing to accept had 'Hitler and his associates been ordinary sane men'. Unfortunately, as he had now come to realise, the world was in fact 'dealing, not with ordinary human beings, but with a dangerous monomaniac and a gang of servile thugs'.[7]

Throughout the spring and summer of 1938 Leo began to attend meetings of a group of Conservative backbenchers loosely assembled around Anthony Eden, who had resigned as Foreign Secretary in February over foreign policy disagreements with Chamberlain, in particular in relation to Italy. Known simply as 'The Group', they met informally to discuss foreign affairs and had 'no fixed membership, organization, or officers'. However, they were significant enough to come to the attention of the Whips Office, who 'sneeringly' referred to them as 'the Glamour Boys', an unlikely epithet for Leo.[8] In common with the few MPs who were also meeting at the time under Churchill's leadership, all the twenty or so members of 'The Group' were bound together by a common belief that 'nothing but a firm and determined policy could prevent the Dictators from practising aggression.' Nor were they 'under any illusion as to the real nature of the Nazi regime'.[9] However, there was no formal system of policy-making, nor was any member bound by a collective decision. Indeed Eden himself described their deliberations as 'entirely free-for-all and not bounded by the prolix or the tedious'.[10]

In July, Halifax asked the Liberal peer, Lord Runciman, to travel to Prague in an attempt to mediate between the rival claims of the Czech Government of Eduard Beneš and the Sudeten Germans, under Konrad Henlein. It was therefore against the background of the Runciman commission's unsuccessful negotiations that, in August, Leo set out for what was to be his last great mountaineering holiday. He and Bryddie went first to Davos where he practised short climbs and spent time with his old friend Count Coudenhove-Kalergi, the founder of the *Pan Europa* movement and, for many, the instigator of the first grass-roots campaign for European unity. From Davos Leo went on to Zermatt where he met a number of his climbing friends, including Claude Elliott from Eton. Now in his sixty-fifth year, he found that climbs which he had made with ease when younger were now increasingly beyond his physical capacity, and he had to abandon any thought of an ascent of the Matterhorn. From Zermatt he met Bryddie and Julian at Sir Edmund Davis's villa, La Fiorentina, in the south of France, spending a day with his host inspecting the French defensive fortifications on the Italian border. On the way home, he stopped off in Paris to see both Jack and the British Ambassador, Eric Phipps.

The wider national and international events of the following weeks, including Chamberlain's three visits to Germany, are well documented. Leo returned to London on 14 September, to be greeted by the news that the Prime Minister was planning to fly to Munich, and on to Berchtesgaden to see Hitler, 'a bold stroke', thought Leo, 'and one which might just conceivably save the situation.'[11] Chamberlain himself had high hopes for his plan. He described it as being 'so unconventional and daring that it rather took Halifax's breath away', and expressed the optimistic hope that 'if it came off, it would go far beyond the present crisis, and might prove the opportunity for bringing about a complete change in the international situation.'[12] Leo's initial reaction to the news was one of cautious optimism and he continued to offer the Prime Minister guarded support in the hope that war could still be averted, however unlikely he personally believed that to be. When he met Annie Chamberlain in Whitehall on 16 September, he congratulated her on her husband's action, and he wrote to Chamberlain the following day. 'You have done a great thing and, if the peace of the world is going to be saved, yours will have been the outstanding contribution.'[13]

The qualified nature of Leo's support for Chamberlain was exemplified by a meeting he attended with Halifax at the Foreign Office on 16 September. He made two suggestions to the Foreign Secretary, 'firstly that Czechoslovakia should declare itself neutral and be guaranteed, and secondly, that a plebiscite is quite unworkable, but that it might be possible to make a definite cession of the north-west corner which Masaryk had wanted in 1919.' Halifax 'rather boggled at the idea of a British guarantee but otherwise was inclined to agree.'[14] However, when Chamberlain returned from Berchtesgaden, and details of Hitler's demand that the Sudeten Germans be returned to the Reich forthwith began to emerge, Leo's sense of unease intensified. He accepted that the proposals were not so very far removed from those he had himself put forward to Halifax, namely 'a territorial concession plus neutrality and a guarantee'. But when he dwelt on the 'outrageous conduct of Germany', he could 'not help seeing red', and had little confidence in a permanent settlement 'won by sheer threat of violence'.[15] He was equally annoyed that Chamberlain had gone to Germany so ill-prepared as to have been surprised by Hitler's obvious determination to make war at once, and nor was he happy that the Prime Minister had expressed the personal opinion that he 'didn't care two hoots whether the Sudetens were in the Reich, or out of it, according to their own wishes'.[16] And when the French Government – and the Czech leadership also, in the face of Anglo-French insistence – agreed to Chamberlain's proposals, Leo foresaw nothing less than Czechoslovakia's 'destruction as an independent state'.[17]

Chamberlain returned to see Hitler again at Godesberg on 22 September, and was greeted with a new set of demands. The Anglo-French proposal for an ordered cession of German-speaking territories was peremptorily dismissed by Hitler, who insisted that nothing short of the immediate occupation of all German-speaking areas by German troops would suffice, the final deadline to be 1 October. The seriousness of the situation was brought home to Leo on the morning of 24 September as he, Bryddie and their servants went to be fitted for their gasmasks. Leo returned home and settled down to write a strong letter to Halifax, in which he deplored the idea that pressure should be applied to the Czechs to accept Hitler's ultimatum. 'Almost everyone I have met', he wrote, 'has been horrified by the so-called "peace" we have forced upon the Czechs.'[18] Halifax was himself already deeply troubled by the news from Godesberg, Hitler's 'un-adulterated blackmail' marking the 'turning-point in his attitude towards Hitler and Nazism'. Leo's letter was just one of a number with which he had been 'inundated',[19] but the influence of an old and trusted friend undoubtedly contributed to Halifax's own conversion later that night.

If the twenty-four-hour period following Chamberlain's return from Godesberg was critical for Halifax, it also represented the moment

when Leo finally came down firmly on the side of those opposed to
the Prime Minister and any further negotiations with Germany.
Hitler's intransigence at Godesberg and Chamberlain's meek acceptance of his demands now proved too much, even for Leo. The change
in mood was almost instantaneous. Halifax's Private Secretary, Oliver
Harvey, himself a noted anti-appeaser, remarked on 25 September
that 'Winston, A.E. [Anthony Eden], and Amery are horrified at the
possibility of our urging Czechoslovakia to accept.'[20] Unable to sleep,
Leo had got up that morning at six o'clock to write a long letter to
Chamberlain, urging him not to 'shirk the responsibility' of standing
up to Hitler, and insisting that he should refuse to pass on Hitler's
ultimatum to the Czechs without expressing the British Government's
own condemnation of it first, 'namely that it was unacceptable and
that we could not ask the Czechs to accept it.' He showed the letter to
Bryddie at breakfast and, on her advice, 'toned it down considerably,
so far at least as strong language is concerned',[21] although the message
it contained remained equally forthright.

How, demanded Leo, in respect of Hitler's insistence that the
Czechs should hand over all German-speaking areas immediately,
could Chamberlain 'expect them to commit such an act of folly and
cowardice'? And how could the Prime Minister have 'forwarded
Hitler's arrogant demand without comment'? Surely, he remonstrated,
'after all the responsibilities which we – and you in person – have
assumed by our intervention, we must take up *some* attitude towards
it.' Chamberlain should inform Hitler that the demand was 'un-
reasonable', and that if he invaded Czechoslovakia then 'he must
realize the consequences'. Any other course would make Britain look
'so ridiculous as well as contemptible in the eyes of the world', that
he could 'hardly conceive the idea being seriously considered'. He
had supported Chamberlain's first visit to Berchtesgaden, but Hitler
had now gone too far, and Leo concluded with the warning that if
the 'country or the House should once suppose that you were prepared
to acquiesce in or even endorse this latest demand, there would be
a tremendous revulsion of feeling against you'.[22]

Leo had decided on his chosen path, and wasted little time in promoting himself to the forefront of opposition to Chamberlain. Having

delivered his letter to Downing Street in time for the morning Cabinet meeting, he telephoned Eden to warn him that the Cabinet were considering recommending Hitler's new terms. It was a symbolic telephone call. Leo had never been close to Eden, of whom he was reportedly 'intellectually contemptuous',[23] and with whom he had often disagreed in the past. But he now recognised the importance of a united front. Eden too had been playing a waiting game, gathering supporters around him in private, but refusing to criticise Chamberlain in public. Now, possibly encouraged by Leo's call, he in turn called Halifax to advocate that the Government should refuse to endorse Hitler's new proposals. Meanwhile, in a letter to the former Australian Prime Minister, Billy Hughes, Leo described 'Hitler's incredible ultimatum asking the Czechs to put their necks in his halter as a preliminary to further business', and questioned whether 'our empty sacks can muster up sufficient courage to stand on end and say "NO".' If they could not, he predicted 'a terrific row in the House and probably the break up of the Government'.[24]

That night Leo wrote to *The Times*, the letter appearing the following morning to widespread approval. The crucial issue, he observed, was no longer 'the merits of the Sudeten claim to autonomy or secession', about which he acknowledged there to be strong arguments on both sides. The principal concern was 'whether the now openly avowed object of destroying utterly the Czechoslovak State shall be achieved with our acquiescence'. The Czechs had reluctantly accepted Hitler's initial, one-sided ultimatum, as put to them by the British Government, but 'of discussion of how the transfer of territory might be carried out in order and decency', there had been 'not a word'. Instead, they were faced with a second ultimatum which would deprive them 'of all power of resistance, in order that the rest of the business of dismembering their country shall be carried out at Germany's will and pleasure'. The issue was, therefore, straightforward. 'Are we to surrender to ruthless brutality a free people whose cause we have espoused, but are now to throw to the wolves to save our own skins,' asked Leo, 'or are we still able to stand up to a bully?'[25]

Three days earlier Leo had, for the first time, attended a meeting at the house of his friend and parliamentary colleague Sir Edward

Spears, where he had found a number of MPs, including Harold Macmillan, discussing the international situation. Now, on 26 September, he attended a similar meeting in Spears' office at which he strongly objected to the suggestion of a number of those present that they should make a public declaration in support of cooperation with Russia. From there, the Spears group went on to a further meeting in Churchill's flat in Morpeth Mansions, where Leo found a 'queer collection' assembled, including Robert Cecil, Brendan Bracken, Bob Boothby, Dick Law, George Lloyd, Ned Grigg, Harold Nicolson, Macmillan and the Liberal Archie Sinclair. Churchill soon arrived, fresh from a meeting with Chamberlain, whom he described as a 'very exhausted and broken man'. Leo's sympathy was heavily laced with sarcasm. 'The poor fellow,' he mused, 'he has done his best valiantly, but he should never have attempted such a task with such slender qualifications for it.' By contrast, however, he was delighted that 'Winston and I are now once more working together in the third war.'[26] According to Nicolson, the meeting agreed that if 'Chamberlain rats again', they would form 'a united block against him', and that they would anyway 'press for a Coalition Government and the immediate application of war measures'.[27]

That evening Leo listened to Hitler's broadcast from the Sportspalast in Berlin, 'the most horrible thing I have ever heard, more like the snarling of a wild animal than the utterance of a human being.' The 'venom and vulgarity' of Hitler's attack on 'Beneš the liar' made Leo feel physically sick, and he found 'something terrifyingly and obscenely sinister in this outpouring of sheer hatred'. However, he consoled himself too. 'Thank God we are not Germany,' he wrote, 'and capable of being led by a man like Hitler.'[28] Earlier that day Chamberlain's special envoy Sir Horace Wilson had delivered a final appeal to Hitler that a German-Czech commission should be appointed to implement the original proposals for partial German occupation of the Sudetenland, as agreed at Berchtesgaden. The following morning Wilson delivered Chamberlain's accompanying private message to Hitler, warning that if this suggestion was rejected, France would undoubtedly go to war and Britain would be sure to follow. Hitler was furious, threatening to annihilate the Czechs if they refused to agree to the Godesberg terms, while Wilson controversially endorsed the ultimatum on his return to London, counselling that 'the only thing to do now was to advise the Czechs to evacuate the territory'.[29]

That evening Leo, along with the rest of the country, again listened to the wireless, this time to Chamberlain's broadcast, best known for its reference to the horror that he felt that 'we should be digging trenches and trying on gasmasks here because of a quarrel in a far-away country between people of whom we know nothing.' He was, he promised, 'a man of peace to the depths of my soul'.[30] Leo listened carefully to the speech of one of his longest-standing colleagues in politics, 'the utterance of a very weary and heartbroken man'. 'Poor Neville,' he mused. While Chamberlain's words might well 'help to unite the whole country and the Empire in sympathy with his efforts for peace', they would also only 'encourage the Germans to go ahead'. The Prime Minister had described himself as 'a man of peace to the inmost of his being', something Leo believed he 'assuredly' was. But he was also, thought Leo, an 'essential civilian' and 'quite incapable of thinking in terms of force, or strategy or diplomacy'.[31]

The German ultimatum to Czechoslovakia was due to expire at two o'clock the following day, 28 September. During the morning Chamberlain drafted messages to Hitler and Mussolini offering to visit Berlin for a five-power conference in one final attempt to resolve the crisis. Leo went first to a meeting at Churchill's flat, before going down to a packed House for Chamberlain's statement that afternoon. As a lacklustre speech, outlining the basic historical narrative of the crisis, was drawing to a close, Chamberlain's Parliamentary Private Secretary, Lord Dunglass (later to become Prime Minister himself as Lord Home), slipped into the chamber behind the Speaker's chair. He handed two typewritten sheets of paper to Sam Hoare who, in turn, passed them on to John Simon, who put them in front of the Prime Minister. At first Chamberlain ignored them, but Simon picked up one of the notes and pushed it into Chamberlain's hand. Only then did he pause to read them and, after nervously asking Simon if he should read them out loud immediately, Chamberlain announced to the House that Hitler had accepted his suggestion and, as a 'last, last word for peace', he would be going to meet Hitler, Mussolini and Daladier in Munich the following day.

The reaction, recorded Leo, was 'tremendous', as the House rose to its feet in applause for the Prime Minister and 'cheered him tumultuously'. Leo's first reaction was that it was a 'curious moment, immense relief, tinged with the uncertainty whether it was more than a few hours respite'.[32] As the Government benches stood, some Members threw their order papers in the air and one cried out 'Thank God for the Prime Minister.' Even the Opposition benches joined in, 'cheering the Prime Minister enthusiastically'. However, only 'Churchill, Eden and Amery remained seated.'[33] Another observer in the chamber at the time, himself an experienced commentator on Czech affairs, enjoyed an uninterrupted view of the Conservative benches. He watched as Members cheered and waved their order papers, 'some actually weeping with emotion and relief'. But he would 'never forget the grim, set faces of three men, who held aloof from the demonstration, realizing the dire consequences which the House was preparing for itself: they were Mr Churchill, Mr Eden and Mr Amery.'[34]

In spite of Leo's reservations and his assumption, along with many others, that the delivery of the note had been carefully stage-managed, he reluctantly had to acknowledge that Chamberlain had pulled off a dramatic coup. He was even bold enough to speculate that a peaceful outcome to the crisis was now a real possibility, believing that Mussolini would realise that he had everything to lose in the event of war, and would be desperate to broker a peaceful resolution between Britain and Germany. But his optimism did not last long. Chamberlain returned from Munich on 30 September, having accepted the compromise proposals put to him, ostensibly by Mussolini, although they had been telephoned through to Rome from Berlin the night before. There was to be an international commission, comprising the British Ambassador in Berlin, a German and a Czech, which would agree the precise definition of the plebiscite areas and the final borders, as well as what military equipment could be removed by the Czech government. Hitler achieved a propaganda coup with the agreement that his troops could march into Czechoslovakia within twenty-four hours rather than the week agreed at Godesberg. And the Czechs were also offered a guarantee against external aggression which, like everything else agreed at Munich, was to prove meaningless.

It was 'a pretty ignoble result', thought Leo, 'and we shall all be looking down our noses presently'. Eden, too, was 'pretty gloomy about it'. Leo sought out Halifax who made an effort to allay Leo's misgivings but 'obviously wasn't very proud of the result'. That evening Leo travelled to Birmingham to attend a long-standing constituency function, and was met off the train by Bryddie. The scenes of rejoicing which had greeted Chamberlain at Heston, where he had famously waved the piece of paper on which was written his 'agreement' with Hitler, and later outside Buckingham Palace, had spread to the Midlands. Birmingham, Bryddie told him, was 'delirious with enthusiasm and gratitude to Neville', and it would be quite hopeless for Leo to make a 'critical speech'. He accordingly 'scrapped most of what he had intended to say',[35] but allowed himself to express some misgivings, nevertheless. It would be their duty, he warned his audience, 'when our first rejoicings are over, and when we realize the immediate danger we have escaped, to be honest with ourselves and without any self-delusion probe the question of what kind of peace we have secured and the price we have paid for it.'[36]

Even at this late stage, the various dissenting groups were unable effectively 'to work together, formulate a common policy, or decide a clear line of action'. They made no attempt to 'draw up a statement of their views and present it to the Government', relying instead on 'feverish activity' to 'work off their frustration'. Leo was one of those who 'hurried round, encouraging wavering Cabinet Ministers to resist the Prime Minister's policy'.[37] Bob Boothby later remembered the chaos of those days, 'a confused and interminable nightmare', and the frequent meetings of three distinct groups of dissidents, 'a Churchill group, an Eden group, and an Amery group'. Only once did the three groups meet together and, even then, they were unable to agree on a common line as to how they should vote. Leo, however, had by now not only made up his own mind but was actively encouraging others to follow his lead. Boothby would 'never forget the cool courage with which Amery marshalled the facts and presented the arguments in favour of resolute action on our part'. Leo 'had no doubt that there would be war and that we would win'.[38] In particular, Leo appears to have acted as a calming influence on some of the younger Members, and when he found Macmillan, 'very wild, clamouring for an immediate pogrom to get rid of Neville and make Winston Prime Minister', he managed to 'pour cold water on that sort of talk'.[39]

Boothby's recollection is partially contradicted by an exchange of correspondence that took place between Leo and another MP from the same group, Paul Emrys-Evans, over fifteen years later. While preparing his memoirs Leo tried to recall whether Churchill had been deliberately excluded from the Eden group because 'we thought he would dominate our proceedings or because we did not want to be identified with him.' It could even have been because Churchill 'did not wish to be bothered with us'.[40] Emrys-Evans remembered with certainty that the reason had been both because Churchill 'would have dominated', and because there had been a feeling that he 'would bring in Bob Boothby who, it was felt, was not to be trusted'. As late as 1954 Churchill still 'greatly resented his exclusion from the Group and has never forgotten it'. Indeed, he had recently accused one of its surviving members of 'keeping him and Anthony apart'.[41]

The debate on Munich opened on 3 October, with Duff Cooper's personal statement explaining his resignation, followed by Chamberlain in what Leo thought a poor speech. Leo spoke the following day, describing the cession of the Sudetenland as 'a triumph of sheer, naked force, exercised in the most blatant and brutal fashion'.[42] On 3 and 5 October he attended meetings of the Churchill group at Brendan Bracken's house in Lord North Street, called to decide whether the group should vote against the Government or abstain. Although Churchill was enthusiastic to register his vote against the Government, Leo was one of those who helped to persuade the others that a block abstention would be more effective, a decision which was endorsed on 6 October, the day of the vote. Even then, both Leo and Eden almost changed their minds at the last moment. Chamberlain's speech winding up the debate impressed Leo greatly by its sincerity and restraint, and when the division was called, both he and Eden went out into the Lobby to discuss the possibility of supporting the Government after all with other members of the group. But Macmillan and his younger colleagues were adamant that they would not change their mind, and so it was that Leo was one of a group of twenty-two Conservatives in receipt of the Government whip who abstained, ostentatiously remaining in their seats. Churchill, Eden, Macmillan and Cooper were among their number, and Nicolson boasted that it was 'not our numbers that matter but our reputation'. The House understood that most of those who had abstained 'knew far more about the real issue than they do', and it was 'clear that the Government were rattled by this'.[43]

That evening Leo wrote to Chamberlain in contrite terms. 'Your speech moved me deeply,' he confessed, 'and very, very nearly persuaded both myself and Anthony Eden to vote. I only hope, most sincerely, that the misgivings which even you could not dispel today, will be disproved by the events of the near future.' If so, Leo would 'not hesitate to admit it' but, in the meantime, he conceded that he had 'hated differing from you at the moment of your keenest anxieties and greatest triumph'.[44] This letter could be interpreted, and indeed probably was by Chamberlain at the time, as a craven attempt by Leo to ingratiate himself with a Prime Minister whom he had, only hours earlier, conspired to wound mortally. Just a few weeks later Leo was one of more than two hundred MPs who signed a Commons motion assuring Chamberlain of their 'unqualified support for his successful efforts to preserve peace and his determination to strengthen the defences and improve the standard of living of the Nation.'[45] Yet in reality Leo by now had no political need to find favour with Chamberlain. Rather, his letter is an example of a particular naivety which he demonstrated throughout his career, a genuine belief that political ideology, and the confrontations that inevitably arose from differences of opinion, could and should be kept wholly separate from personal friendships. He could never understand why nobody else ever felt the same way.

In the aftermath of Munich, there was some realignment of the groups which had hitherto coalesced around Churchill and Eden. Leo had attended a number of meetings of the Churchill group prior to, and during, the Munich debate. But he was to have little contact with them from now on, possibly, in the view of one historian, because he was 'wooden about Collective Security and Russia and too willing to hedge his bets about Chamberlain'.[46] Certainly Leo's well-known and frequently expressed opposition to cooperation with Russia would have set him apart from the other members of Churchill's group, although another historian has noted that in this respect, at least, 'Amery's sense of proportion on both occasions was probably better than [that of] his colleagues.'[47] Instead Leo continued to ally himself to Eden, both of them contributing a number of articles to newspapers outlining the concept of a national policy, and soon finding themselves as the nucleus of a group of like-minded Conservatives who began to meet regularly to discuss the situation. The two groups ran in parallel, although from time to time there was some overlapping.

By 8 November meetings were taking place at the home of Jim Thomas, Eden's former Parliamentary Private Secretary, in Great College Street (appropriately enough for Leo, the former home of Lord Milner). The following day Nicolson recorded a 'hush-hush meeting with Anthony Eden', also attended by Leo, Macmillan, Cranborne, Cooper and a number of other Munich rebels, 'all good Tories and sensible men'. They decided not to advertise themselves as a formal group but to 'meet together from time to time, exchange views, and organise ourselves for a revolt if needed'. Nicolson was encouraged that Leo and Eden were 'wise people' and did 'not mean to do anything rash or violent', while the group's members, unlike those attached to Churchill, did not give the 'impression of being more bitter than determined'.[48] The group also met occasionally at the home of another Conservative MP, Ronnie Tree, in Queen Anne's Gate. An indication of the seriousness with which their meetings were regarded by the Government came a few years later when Sir Joseph Ball, a 'dislikeable man with a reputation for doing some of Chamberlain's "behind-the-scenes" work', cheerfully confessed to Tree 'that he himself had been responsible for having my telephone tapped' at the time.[49] In fact it was well known that Ball worked for the twin masters of the Conservative Party and MI5 for many years.

▪ ▪ ▪

Over the next few months Leo busied himself with his two principal political preoccupations of the time; vigorous opposition to the suggestion that some of Germany's former colonies should be returned, and a campaign in favour of the introduction of some form of National Service. Throughout his tenure as Colonial Secretary, Leo had been obsessed with resisting any territorial concessions to Germany in respect of her former African colonies. There were rumours that Chamberlain had given a verbal assurance to Hitler at Munich that certain former colonies might be considered suitable for restitution and, on 15 November, Leo was one of thirty-seven MPs who signed a parliamentary motion urging that 'no agreement should be made under which any British colonies or mandated territory should be transferred without the consent of the people of Great Britain.'[50] So passionately did Leo feel, that he settled down to write a book on the subject, *The German Colonial Claim*, which was published in 1939 and came to be regarded as a definitive text on the issue.

Leo then wrote to Chamberlain suggesting that he should 'bring in some of the Opposition in order to enquire into the whole defence situation, and if possible secure an agreement on National Service'. When, not surprisingly, Chamberlain refused, Leo began himself 'informally to try to get in touch with the other side with a view to starting something in the nature of a National Service League'.[51] He began by inviting Clement Attlee to lunch, but the Labour leader would have nothing to do with the proposal so long as Chamberlain remained Prime Minister, while Lloyd George also rebuffed Leo's approach, on the grounds that he had long since refused to sign open letters to the press of any kind. Undeterred, Leo launched the manifesto anyway, calling for the immediate creation of a national register which would cover the entire population. In December he led the attack in the House against the Government's own proposals for a voluntary register and, in January 1939, he helped to launch the Citizens Service League, an offshoot of the old Army League. And although he failed to persuade either Churchill or Eden to become directly associated with his movement, he was largely responsible for the high parliamentary profile which the issue of National Service was soon to achieve.

In spite of the impending international crisis, Leo and Bryddie still found time to take their annual skiing holiday in the Alps over Christmas and New Year. For the first time in his life Leo took no books, no papers, indeed no work of any kind with him. The fortnight they spent at Klosters was to be Leo's last experience of skiing, and was memorable for him in that it 'marked a sad relapse from all his principles and past practice'. For the first time, rather than walking up the mountain, he used 'one of those new-fangled ski hoists in which you hang on to an overhead wire and are pulled up the practice slopes'. His only excuse was 'growing laziness and short-windedness', while he consoled himself with the thought that 'the old age pension qualification was also a moral qualification for skiing by funicular.'[52] They returned to London by way of Paris where, as usual, they looked in on Jack on their way home.

In much the same way as Leo had been absorbed with the crisis in Ireland in the months preceding the outbreak of the First World War, so now he became increasingly distracted by events in Palestine in early 1939. He had so far been happy to justify his opposition to Munich on the grounds which he had publicly explained, namely that the British Government had failed to take a definite line in support of the Czechs and then to stick to it. Chamberlain should either have told them 'to make their own terms with Germany', he wrote to Beaverbrook, or assured them from the outset that the Government 'stood behind them Horse, Foot and Artillery'. Instead the Prime Minister had encouraged 'the poor devils to rely on us up to the last moment, never even hinting to them that we might expect them to cede territory'.[53] Now, however, while the Government wrestled with the aftermath of Munich and Hitler's territorial ambitions, Leo began to concentrate increasingly on a different, albeit related threat: that which Hitler now so obviously posed to the Jews of Europe.

Nothing reassured Leo more conclusively that he had been right to rebel over Munich than 'the orgy of terrorism and economic destruction with which in November Hitler visited the hapless Jews of Germany'.[54] In December 1938, attending as the official Conservative spokesman, he had addressed a mass rally at the Albert Hall, held in protest against the racial and religious persecution in Germany. Yet even now he made no reference in public, or indeed in the privacy of his own diary, to his own Jewish ancestry. Number 112 Eaton Square became an informal meeting-place for Jewish leaders and a hospitable drop-in centre for Jewish refugees from central Europe. In May 1939 he recorded a visit from an Austrian artist from whom, in spite of the dire nature of his own financial circumstances, Leo bought several pictures, while he also made him a generous loan in the hope that it might help to secure his brother's release from a concentration camp. Chaim Weizmann, the leader of the international Zionist movement, was a frequent visitor, sometimes in the company of Churchill, and was later to thank Leo warmly for the 'unstinted encouragement and support' he gave during those months.[55]

For some time Leo had become increasingly critical of what he considered to be the Government's policy of reneging on the commitments made to the Jews of Palestine in the Balfour Declaration, laying the blame on the 'anti-Zionist hostility of the Foreign Office and its anxiety to appease Arab sentiment in the Middle East'.[56] In May 1939, while most of Leo's fellow Conservative dissidents were concentrating on the deteriorating situation in Europe, Malcolm MacDonald, the Colonial Secretary, issued a White Paper on Palestine. The Government's long-term aim was the creation of an independent Palestine within ten years, but the more substantive part of the White Paper concerned future immigration levels into Palestine. The key proposal was that 75,000 more Jews were to be admitted over the next five years, after which all Jewish immigration could be halted if that was to be the majority decision of the local Arab population. As far as Leo, Churchill and a few other Zionist supporters were concerned, this proposal was a direct repudiation of the promises made in the Balfour Declaration, the terms of the British Mandate and the pledge made by Churchill in 1922 that, subject to 'economic absorptive capacity', the Jews were in Palestine by right and not on sufferance.

On 22 May Leo rose in the House to answer MacDonald's 'disingenuous' introduction of his proposals. 'I have myself rarely risen', he later wrote, 'with a greater sense of indignation and shame or made a speech which I am more content to look back on.'[57] He began with a staunch defence of the Balfour Declaration, claiming that its authors had demonstrated 'British statesmanship' at its best by showing the foresight to plan the 'framework of a Home, a City of Refuge, which might, if it were allowed, be at this moment affording immeasurable relief, spiritual as well as material, to the agony of the Jews'. MacDonald's proposals were, he claimed, 'a direct invitation to Arabs to continue to make trouble', while the Jews were to be calmly informed that 'all the hopes they have been encouraged to hold for twenty years are to be dashed to the ground, all the pledges and promises that have been given to them, broken'. Leo could no longer 'divest himself of a definite personal responsibility in this matter'. He had, at all times, 'worked whole-heartedly for what he believed to be the interests of all the peoples of those countries, of every race', and now 'enjoyed the good will and the respect of both Jews and Arabs'.[58]

The speech was a resounding success and, although Churchill spoke powerfully in support of him the following day, Bryddie, who had been in the gallery, told Leo that his had been 'as good as any speech he had made in the House', while Harold Nicolson went so far as to describe it as 'the best speech he had ever heard in the House'.[59] The Government's majority was drastically cut as many supporters followed Leo and Churchill into the Opposition lobby. After the war Leo was to reflect bitterly on what he considered to be the 'immediate consequences' of the White Paper, 'on the doors of mercy shut on the hapless refugees from Hitler's torture chambers, or on the growth, intelligible, though not excusable, of Jewish terrorism'.[60]

As Hitler's intentions towards Poland became increasingly obvious throughout the summer, Leo continued to make clear his opposition to Government policy. Nicolson recorded that the Government Whips 'were terribly rattled by the existence and secrecy' of the Eden group, although they 'respected Eden, Duff Cooper, Amery and the big bugs'.[61] On 2 August Chamberlain moved that the Commons should adjourn for the summer recess until 3 October, subject to an earlier recall only if the public interest should necessitate it. Arthur Greenwood, standing in as acting leader of the Opposition due to Attlee's illness, proposed an amendment that the House should in fact meet again on 21 August, ostensibly in view of the seriousness of the international situation, but with the obvious implication that Chamberlain could not be trusted. As the debate became increasingly bad-tempered, the amendment was supported by Archie Sinclair for the Liberals and by a number of Conservatives, including Churchill. Leo, who had intended to remain quiet, rose shortly before Chamberlain's reply and urged the Prime Minister to 'give a lead in expressing the sense of national unity which animated all sections of the House', and to give 'serious consideration to any responsible representations' which might be made to him in support of a recall of Parliament. Chamberlain, however, treated the amendment as a vote of confidence in both the Government and himself, and called on Conservative Members to defeat it.

Leo could sense the 'dismay on all sides of the House' at the Prime Minister's 'complete misjudgement of the atmosphere',[62] and the Government won the vote only after a lengthy debate and with a greatly reduced majority. Most memorable was the speech made by Ronald Cartland, a young Conservative MP who had been a frequent participant at meetings of the so-called Eden group. He had been 'profoundly disturbed by the speech of the Prime Minister', and appealed to him to consider Leo's suggestion that the debate should be viewed in the context of national unity. 'We are in the situation', he told the House, 'that within a month we may be going to fight, and we may be going to die.' In the face of sustained barracking from Chamberlain's supporters, he reminded the House of the 'thousands of young men at the moment in training in camps', and warned the Prime Minister that the time had come 'to get the whole country behind you rather than make jeering, pettifogging party speeches which divide the nation'. A fellow Birmingham MP and enthusiastic supporter of Chamberlain, Sir Patrick Hannon, later apologised to the House for having been 'partly responsible for getting him in his present seat', and for the 'poisonous quality of the speech' Cartland had delivered.[63] A month later Cartland joined his army unit and was killed in May 1940, during the retreat to Dunkirk, the day before his younger brother died in the same action. His life was later immortalised in a biography written by his sister, the novelist Barbara Cartland. When Leo read it, he thought it 'not at all badly done', although it was 'of course very feminine' and he had 'no doubt poor Ronnie would have winced at a good many passages'.[64]

As events turned out, the House had to be recalled anyway on 24 August, the day after the signing of the Nazi-Soviet non-aggression pact. All Leo's worst fears were confirmed. After weeks of ultimately futile negotiation and prevarication, Germany invaded Poland at dawn on 1 September. The Eden group met that evening to be told that certain ministers had resigned and a War Cabinet was to be formed; Churchill was to join and Eden would be brought back into the Government, albeit not as a member of the War Cabinet. The following day, 2 September, the House met to rush through the Military Service Bill that would introduce conscription. Churchill tried to cheer Leo up by saying that he had no great desire to join the War Cabinet and that he would have preferred it had Leo been there too. The House waited, 'a long, and most unfortunate wait', until almost eight o'clock, for Chamberlain to make his statement. Chips Channon noted that a good number of Members, 'genuinely distressed' by the delay, had 'quenched their thirst in the Smoking Room', and by the time Chamberlain stood up they 'were full of "Dutch Courage"'.[65] When Chamberlain did finally address the House, he merely described the bare facts of the situation in a flat, almost embarrassed voice. Mussolini's last-minute suggestion of a Five Power conference had come too late; Sir Neville Henderson, the British Ambassador in Berlin, had received no reply to his final ultimatum; and the British and French Governments were now discussing how much longer they would give Hitler to reply. But the anticipated declaration of war never came.

'The House', noted Leo, 'was aghast. For two whole days the wretched Poles had been bombed and massacred, and we were still considering within what time limit Hitler should be invited to tell us whether he felt like relinquishing his prey!' Chamberlain's statement deserved to be met with a 'universal howl of execration'.[66] In fact, the Prime Minister sat down in near silence. Hugh Dalton, who thought that a free vote at that moment might have overthrown the Government, sensed the 'consternation and anger through the House', and noticed that 'Amery and Duff Cooper, in particular, were red-faced and almost speechless with fury.'[67] In Attlee's continued absence, Arthur Greenwood rose to reply for the Labour Party. Leo now realised that it was 'essential that someone should do what Chamberlain had failed to do', and his fear that the deputy Labour leader might be tempted to make 'a purely partisan speech'[68] was heightened when Greenwood began by announcing that he would be speaking for the Labour Party. Leo 'could not help' himself. 'Speak for England,'[69] he cried out across the chamber, implying that the Prime Minister had notably failed to do so. Churchill recalled that Leo's intervention was 'received with loud cheers',[70] while Chamberlain's 'head whipped around as if he had been stung'. There was 'a storm from both sides of the House', and Conservative backbenchers in particular 'were almost speechless with fury'. Greenwood rose to the occasion and made 'the speech of his life'.[71]

Leo's intervention was, without doubt, one of the two best-known moments of his parliamentary career, and has since come to be acknowledged as one of the most memorable parliamentary quotations of all time. Indeed, so celebrated did those three words subsequently become that Bob Boothby later claimed them as his own, when shown a copy of the relevant passage by Harold Nicolson in the course of preparing his own diaries for publication in 1965. However, there is no other source of support for this claim, even from Boothby's own biographer, who merely notes that 'it does not particularly matter' which of them made the remark.[72] Every other contemporary account attributes the remark to Leo, including that in his own diary, written up the following morning before the intervention had achieved its later notoriety. Sir Edward Spears noted that Leo was sitting in his usual 'corner seat of the third bench below the gangway on the Government side', and that he had 'voiced in three words his own pent-up anguish and fury, as well as the repudiation by the whole House of a policy of surrender.'[73] Duff Cooper recalled that he was sitting just one seat away from Leo, with Eden between them, while Macmillan remembered it as a 'moment which stands out vividly in my own memory'.[74]

The House broke up in confusion as Greenwood followed an ashen-faced Chamberlain back to his room and told him that, unless an ultimatum was made to Germany the following day, the Prime Minister would lose all remaining support in the House. Leo felt 'too moved to speak', while Spears later claimed that two Members had actually been sick. But in one respect, at least, Leo was able to make an accurate prediction that night. 'I expect my intervention', he mused, 'has anyhow killed all chances of Neville asking me to join his Government. The sooner he drops out the better.'[75] Churchill, after first meeting with his supporters that evening to consider an attempt to overthrow Chamberlain immediately, accepted the offer of a return to the Cabinet as First Lord of the Admiralty, while Eden was offered the post of Dominions Secretary. But as far as Leo was concerned, Chamberlain remained, hardly surprisingly, in unforgiving mood. 'The House of Commons was out of hand,' he reported to his sister a week later, 'torn with suspicions and ready (some of them, including, particularly, Amery, the most insulting of all) to believe the Government guilty of any cowardice or treachery.'[76]

On the morning of Sunday 3 September, Leo attended a meeting of the Eden group at Ronnie Tree's house in Queen Anne's Gate. Eden informed them that, at the Cabinet's insistence, Chamberlain had agreed to the delivery of the ultimatum to Germany at nine o'clock that morning, to expire after two hours. He was then questioned as to whether he intended to accept the offer of Dominions Secretary, at which he 'rather writhed and wriggled'. Tree did not own a wireless, but luckily one of his housemaids produced one and the group duly listened to Chamberlain's broadcast, announcing that war had been declared at 11.15. As Leo then started walking back towards the House, with Eden, Cooper and Nicolson, the first air raid siren of the war rang out across Whitehall. At first affecting nonchalance, they were soon forced to make greater haste by a nearby policeman, and to 'tumble into' Edward Spears' passing car, Nicolson complaining loudly that he was forced to 'sit on Amery's knee and Anthony sit on mine'.[77] At noon Chamberlain addressed the House, 'good, but not the speech of a war leader', thought Leo. 'I think I see Winston emerging as PM out of it all by the end of the year.'

He was desperate for a role. 'This is now the third war in whose opening I have participated,' he mused, and 'I wonder much what my

part in it may be.'[78] To his old friend Geoffrey Dawson, the editor of
The Times, he vented his frustration at being excluded. He had not
given a second thought to being out of office in recent years, a time of
'indecision, half-measures and make believe'. But it was now 'absurd'
that he 'should not be made use of today'. After all, 'next to Winston
and Hankey I know more about the conduct of war than any of them,
not to speak of my greater knowledge of European affairs and my
authority with the Dominions.' And if he was 'just senior to Winston
in actual years, I am, I think, a good deal his junior in body, and
not yet fossilized in mind.'[79] Nevertheless he was not too proud to ask
for Churchill's help, and consoled himself that in Churchill, Eden and
Hankey, all of whom spoke to Chamberlain on his behalf, he had
'some friends inside the fort who may help me to get over the wall.
Once inside I can do the rest.' Officially Chamberlain replied that
there would be 'some difficulty about fitting in one who had held such
high offices',[80] although the truth was almost certainly more prosaic.
When the idea of Leo and Duff Cooper rejoining the Government was
raised, a month later, at a meeting of the War Cabinet, Chamberlain
rejected it 'with an irritated snort'.[81]

Although frustrated by his exclusion from the main events of the
war, Leo had time over the next few weeks to put his own affairs
in order. He ensured first that Eaton Square was prepared for air
raids and had a bedroom made up in the basement. He removed his
voluminous collection of diaries and personal papers from the house
and arranged for them to be stored at two separate sites: the more
contemporary ones at a cottage in Turville Heath, near Henley, which
he and Bryddie had rented to get away from London when they could,
and those papers for which he had no immediate use, in the cellars
of All Souls, where they were to remain throughout the war. Most
bizarrely, for some reason Leo chose this moment of his life to have
his first driving lessons, in and around Henley, although he gives no
indication as to what prompted such a bold step at the age of sixty-five,
with the outbreak of war imminent.

He turned down Chamberlain's half-hearted offer of the chairmanship of a Select Committee and, with Eden back in government,
assumed instead the unofficial chairmanship of the group that had

previously borne Eden's name. The new, so-called Amery group was 'merely the Edenites sailing under a flag of convenience',[82] but they still continued to meet every Wednesday evening for dinner, sitting at a round table in a back room of the restaurant at the Carlton Hotel. After initially keeping a low profile and their public criticisms to a minimum, the group soon decided that 'their function was to harass the government until it conducted the war as though it meant it.'[83] Both Eden's and Churchill's Parliamentary Private Secretaries, Jim Thomas and Brendan Bracken, continued to attend the meetings and briefed their masters on the levels of backbench dissent. Leo also became involved with a more significant, all-party parliamentary group, chaired by Clement Davies, later to be Liberal leader. He was invited to participate largely as a result of his friendship with the Independent MP Eleanor Rathbone, who supported Leo's campaign for family allowances and acted as the group's secretary. This, in turn, brought him into regular contact with Sinclair, Attlee and Greenwood, all of whom were to play prominent roles in the fall of Chamberlain.

Leo's discontent at the manner in which the war was being pursued soon turned to anger. On 5 September the Polish Air Attaché in London took a message to the Air Ministry asking that British bombers launch immediate raids against German airports and industrial areas to relieve the pressure on Poland. The Air Secretary, Kingsley Wood, was asked by a number of senior MPs to accede to the request. Hugh Dalton was appalled at the failure of the RAF 'to do anything except drop leaflets', and when he suggested that the Black Forest be set alight with incendiary bombs, Wood replied that it 'would be contrary to the Hague Convention', and that the Air Force should 'concentrate on military targets'.[84] Leo knew the Black Forest well, and that it was the site of substantial ammunition stores. It had been a dry summer and incendiary bombs would do their work quickly, but Wood again turned down the suggestion. 'Are you aware it is private property?' he asked. 'Why, you will be asking me to bomb Essen next!'[85] Indeed, Wood did not intend even to bomb the munitions works at Essen for fear of alienating American opinion. Leo left the meeting in a fury. While 'the hapless Polish Army was being overrun . . . by the overwhelming German Air Force, which had no scruples about bombing Polish civilians', the British Government was sending 'bombers to drop leaflets telling the Germans how misguided they were to be at war!'[86]

After spending a quiet Christmas and New Year in Wales, Leo returned to London determined somehow to play a greater role in the conduct of the war. Chamberlain carried out a limited reshuffle in early January 1940, as a result of sacking the War Secretary, Leslie Hore-Belisha, an act of which Leo strongly disapproved. But in spite of Churchill's assurance that he was continuing to press Chamberlain for a job for Leo that was worthy of his abilities and his seniority, he remained on the backbenches. Finally, he reluctantly accepted the chairmanship of a Government committee tasked with bringing aid to Finland, which had been invaded by Russia in November 1939. Although it did not sound much, Leo took on the role, not least because his love of mountaineering and skiing had long caused him to take an interest in mountain warfare. Indeed, he managed to persuade General Ironside, the Chief of the Imperial General Staff, to create a section at the War Office dedicated to mountaineering and winter warfare.

In January the Cabinet agreed to send an international volunteer force of some 500 men to Finland, and Leo set himself up with a small secretariat in borrowed offices to coordinate the expedition. Bryddie assembled a group of her friends to knit socks for the soldiers, while Leo used his contacts at Marks and Spencer to produce white overalls. The expedition soon turned into a further excuse to attack the Government. Leo invited his favourite protégé Harold Macmillan to join his committee and to go on a fact-finding mission to Finland. It was to be Macmillan's 'first big break'.[87] Finland surrendered on 14 March and, in a debate in the House a few days later, Chamberlain opened by 'making a great deal of the proposed really hypothetical expeditionary force', and of the 'list of materials actually sent to the Finns'. In doing so, he 'successfully slurred over the delays and hesitations in sending anything and the inadequacy of what was sent compared with what the Finns asked for'.[88] Macmillan, however, used the expertise he had acquired on his trip to launch a scathing assault on Government policy. In a brave speech, which gave heart to the various groups of MPs opposed to its war policy, he effectively destroyed the Government's defence.

The fall of Finland only added to the increasing discontent among many Members, while Leo was 'beginning to come round to the idea that Winston with all his failings is the one man with real war drive and love of battle'.[89] At an Amery group dinner at the Carlton in January, Viscount Cranborne had suggested that 'a very small committee should be created of very respectable Conservatives', on which their group would 'be represented by Amery'. The committee's role would be to 'exercise pressure on the Cabinet'.[90] At the end of March Cranborne's idea was taken up by his father, the Marquess of Salisbury. 'A small Committee of influential members of both Houses' was to be formed, 'to watch the conduct of the war' and to 'make representations to the Government where they consider there is a risk of mistakes being made or where it seems that the trend of public opinion is not appreciated.'[91] The organisation soon came to be known as the Watching Committee and, although it shared many members in common with both the Amery and Davies groups, it was 'far more dangerous for the Prime Minister'. While one historian has interpreted its role as 'not to embarrass the Government but to press for changes in policy',[92] another has written, more bluntly, that it was 'committed to the destruction of Neville Chamberlain'.[93]

The Watching Committee met for the first time on 4 April at Salisbury's home at 21 Arlington Street. Paul Emrys-Evans acted as secretary, and its membership marked a departure from other groups, composed as it was not purely of Chamberlain's critics, but of those with a broad range of opinion and expertise. A balance was struck between membership of the Lords and the Commons, and between old and young. There were nine former Cabinet ministers. A number of its members were supporters of Chamberlain, while others were recruited for their technical expertise in some aspect of warfare. The 'blend of critics and loyalists was deliberately created so that all sides of party opinion would be represented'.[94] The fact that so many of its members were senior political figures gave the committee a direct line to ministers, and Salisbury himself called on Chamberlain regularly to push for changes in war policy, in particular the creation of an inner War Cabinet.

On 9 April, only a few days after Chamberlain had famously talked of 'Hitler having missed the bus', the Germans invaded Denmark and Norway. Once again the Government was bitterly criticised for its failure to react quickly enough to the crisis and for its failure adequately to supply the British Expeditionary Force sent to liberate the Norwegians. Leo summed up the frustrations of many in a letter to Dawson at *The Times*, regretting the 'tacit truce against bombing any objective on land even of the most obvious military character while the Germans are deliberately bombing defenceless towns in Norway and hunting the hapless Norwegian Royal family.'[95] As the Norway campaign lurched from disaster to disaster, culminating with the ignominious evacuation of British troops on 2 May, Chamberlain's critics continued to look for an opportunity to get rid of him once and for all. Their chance came on 7 May, when the House began a two-day debate on the Norway campaign.

Leo spent the morning preparing his speech carefully. The era of Cromwell was one of his favourite historical topics and he looked up a number of his favourite Cromwellian quotations, including one which he thought might be 'too strong meat' for the debate ahead, but which he kept to hand 'in case the spirit should move' him. The House was in a sombre and anxious mood, and Chamberlain opened the debate with a 'dull exposition of the whole business which was a very obvious flop'.[96] The speech had misjudged the mood of the majority of Members, most of whom already knew the details of the Norway fiasco and were more interested in 'the character and structure of the Government of which that failure was only an illustration'. Leo felt emboldened. After listening to Attlee reply for the Opposition, he settled down on his bench for 'two hours of that agonized discomfort which only members of the House know, divided between perfunctory listening to unimportant speeches which never seem to end, and vainly trying to remember the all-important points of the all-important speech one hopes to make oneself.' This time, he knew that 'what he had to say mattered'.[97]

As a Privy Counsellor Leo had the right to be called to speak, but it was at the discretion of the Speaker as to when that would be, and it soon became clear that it was his intention to sideline Leo by forcing him to speak during the dinner hour, when the chamber traditionally empties. The one diversion in the meantime was a speech by Sir Roger Keyes, who had come to the House dressed in his full dress uniform as Admiral of the Fleet, complete with six rows of medal ribbons, to speak for 'some officers and men of the fighting, sea-going Navy who are very unhappy'.[98] At eight o'clock in the evening, when he was on the point of postponing his contribution until the following day, Leo was finally called to speak. There were barely a dozen Members left in the House, but Clement Davies quietly urged him to make the case against the Government, and went off to recruit an audience from the smoking room and dining rooms. He need not have worried. Members soon 'streamed in pretty rapidly, a tribute less perhaps to my eloquence', thought Leo, 'than to the thought that I might be saying something of moment'.[99]

Leo began his speech as he intended to go on, criticising Chamberlain for giving the House 'a reasoned, argumentative case for our failure', when in reality 'wars are won, not by explanations after the event but by foresight, by clear decision and by swift action.' Nothing in the Prime Minister's speech had convinced him that Chamberlain possessed those qualities. He went on to criticise the Government for its lack of foresight in Norway, for the manner in which the operation had been carried out and, in particular, for the Prime Minister's misplaced self-satisfaction that it had been a job successfully carried out. By now, Leo had the full attention of a crowded House and was encouraged by the growing murmurs of approval around him. Warming to his theme, he moved on to the main substance of his speech, calling for a complete overhaul of the Government and the immediate creation of a National Government, supported by a small War Cabinet, free of departmental responsibilities and able to prosecute the war efficiently. 'We cannot go on as we are. There must be a change,' he continued and, while he refused to be 'drawn into a discussion on personalities', personally he wished to see a leader with the qualities of 'vision, daring, swiftness and consistency of decision'.

By now the atmosphere in the chamber was tense, but noisily

supportive. 'Somehow or other', Leo went on, 'we must get into the Government men who can match our enemies in fighting spirit, in daring, in resolution and in thirst for victory.' He recalled a favourite quotation, that of Cromwell to John Hampden in the face of heavy Roundhead losses at the hands of Prince Rupert's Cavalry.

'I said to him, "Your troops are most of them old, decayed serving men and tapsters and such kind fellows." ... You must get men of a spirit that are likely to go as far as they will go, or you will be beaten still.'

Having quoted Cromwell, Leo admitted that it might 'not be easy to find these men', but that the country was 'fighting today for our life, for our liberty, for our all; we cannot go on being led as we are'.[100] At this point he paused, and looked around him. He knew that he 'could only dare to go as far' as he could carry the House with him, and that to 'go beyond the feeling of my own friends, would be not only an anti-climax, but a fatal error of judgement'. His purpose was not a 'dramatic finish', but a practical one, 'to bring down the Government if I could'. Across the chamber he caught the eye of Lloyd George and the look of 'admiring appreciation' on his face. He felt himself 'swept forward' by those around him and knew that he had to finish the job.[101]

I have quoted certain words of Oliver Cromwell. I will quote certain other words. I do it with great reluctance, because I am speaking of those who are old friends and associates of mine, but they are words which, I think, are applicable to the present situation. This is what Cromwell said to the Long Parliament when he thought it was no longer fit to conduct the affairs of the nation:

'You have sat too long here for any good you have been doing. Depart, I say, and let us have done with you. In the name of God, go.'[102]

They were, thought Churchill, 'terrible words coming from [Chamberlain's] friend and colleague of many years, a fellow Birmingham

Member, and a Privy Councillor of distinction and experience.'[103] And Leo knew that while he might have made 'better speeches before', he had 'never made one that was so effective both at the moment and in its consequences.' Lloyd George told him that it was 'one of the best speeches he had ever heard in the House' during fifty years there, and that he had never heard one with 'so dramatic a climax'.[104] Acclaim was almost universal. 'Diminutive in size but filled with fire', Leo had 'made the speech of his life', thought Tree,[105] while Spears remarked that the House had 'remained still and strained as it watched the redoubtable small squat figure of Amery smash the Government'.[106] Macmillan described it as 'the most formidable philippic' that he had 'ever heard delivered by a former Minister against a lifelong friend and colleague.' It had been 'decisive' in destroying Chamberlain. 'Point after point was hammered home', recalled Macmillan later, 'with ruthless iteration and almost ferocity.' Leo, so often 'prolix or monotonous', had delivered a speech 'far beyond his usual form', mixing 'clarity, indignation, anger; but all clothed in simple and compelling language.'[107]

The Davies and Amery groups held a joint meeting later that evening to decide on a plan of action for the following day and, at Boothby's suggestion, Leo was invited to take the chair. Although no decision was taken as to whether or not to force a division, so powerful had Leo's speech been that a number of Members were now urging that the group should vote en bloc against the Government. The Watching Committee convened at Arlington Street at eleven o'clock the following morning and the majority view, in spite of Salisbury's objection, was that its members should not abstain in the vote, but should try to force the Government out. Herbert Morrison led off for the Opposition, warning the House that the Labour Party would indeed seek to force a division. Chamberlain reacted foolishly, leaping to his feet to boast that he still had friends in the House, to whom he would look for support in the division lobby later, but he only succeeded in giving the impression that he was attempting to turn a subject of national importance into a party, even a personal, issue.

The vote, when it finally came, was the most dramatic in which Leo had ever taken part. All evening the Government Whips and

Chamberlain's Parliamentary Private Secretary, Lord Dunglass, had been trying to buy off some of the waverers with promises that Chamberlain would listen to their concerns and even carry out a reconstruction of his Government. Leo chaired a further meeting of dissidents in a committee room while the debate carried on downstairs and the decision was finally reached by the majority to vote against the Government. Not a single Conservative had voted against the Government over Munich. Now, Leo was one of forty-two Conservatives who did so, with a further thirty-six abstaining, many ostentatiously remaining in their seats. Many of the rebels wore uniform. When the vote was read out, Chamberlain 'blanched, but quickly recovered himself'.[108] The Government had won by by 281 votes to 200, but he knew that the greatly reduced majority would be devastating for him personally. Harold Macmillan reportedly tried, but failed, to strike up a rendition of 'Rule Britannia', and Leo felt little pleasure at Chamberlain's discomfort. When the vote was announced there were shouts of 'resign, resign' and, as the Prime Minister left the chamber past the Speaker's chair, 'erect, unyielding, sardonic', the Labour benches echoed Leo's words, 'Go, in God's name go.' It was not, thought Leo, a 'pleasant moment' and he went home 'musing on the cruelty of politics'.[109] Chamberlain later reflected that the debate had been 'a very painful affair' and that the 'Amerys, Duff Coopers, and their lot are consciously, or unconsciously, swayed by a sense of frustration because they can only look on.'[110]

The next two days were notable principally for their confusion. The Watching Committee met again on the morning of 9 May, when Leo made it clear that 'the Prime Minister cannot really survive for more than a week or two', and there was general agreement that he should be replaced by either Churchill or Halifax. Later that afternoon the combined Amery and Davies groups met, again with Leo in the chair, and with their numbers considerably swelled after the events of the night before. Leo knew that he was personally shouldering much of the official opprobrium for what had happened, and that Chamberlain was still attempting to buy off the rebels, probably by sacrificing Simon and Hoare. Indeed, at some stage on 9 May Chamberlain appears to have considered the idea, at the suggestion of Sir Horace Wilson, of sending for Leo and offering him office. Dalton went so far as to record that 'at the instigation of Sir H. Quisling [Wilson]', Chamberlain had decided to 'send for Amery and offer him free choice of any office, other than the Premiership itself, if he would bring his rebels in. This was refused.'[111] Halifax's biographer believes that 'Chamberlain saw Amery and offered him the choice of either the Chancellorship of the Exchequer or the Foreign Secretaryship', adding that 'it is not known what Halifax thought of his job being hawked around' in this way.[112] Leo himself only refers to the idea as a rumour and gives no details of any actual meeting, but clearly would have refused the offer if indeed it had been made.

Incredible as it may seem with hindsight, there appears also to have been a movement afoot for a brief time in favour of installing Leo himself as Prime Minister. Clement Davies told him that he had discussed the matter with the Labour front bench who had suggested that 'the Tory whom they would soonest serve under' was Leo. Leslie Hore-Belisha told Leo that he had discussed the matter with Beaverbrook and they were agreed that 'what was really wanted was a clean sweep eliminating the old Conservative gang as far as possible', and that the best way of doing so was to make Leo Prime Minister 'as the man who had turned out the Government and also as best qualified all round'. Hore-Belisha later claimed that he had also secured Duff Cooper's approval for the idea. In fairness to Leo, he does not seem to have taken the proposal very seriously himself. It was 'rather sudden' and he 'discouraged the idea' so long as it seemed likely that Churchill or Halifax would succeed.[113]

On 10 May Britain woke up to the news that Germany had attacked Belgium and Holland during the night. Incredibly, Chamberlain appears initially to have believed that this strengthened his claim to remain in office and telephoned Attlee, assembled with other Labour leaders in Bournemouth, to say so. But by now both the Watching Committee and, more importantly, the Labour leadership, had decided that Churchill should be Prime Minister and Chamberlain resigned that evening. In the early afternoon Leo had gone round to see Churchill at the Admiralty to urge him to form a small War Cabinet immediately. Churchill asked Leo 'if he would like [the Ministry of]

Supply', to which Leo replied that 'he was willing to take on any task', but suggested that he could be 'of most help to him in dealing with the co-ordination of defence or of economic policy'. Leo left the meeting realising that Churchill 'meant to keep defence entirely in his own hands and had no idea that economic policy mattered'.[114] Later that evening the King sent for Churchill and invited him to become Prime Minister.

CHAPTER EIGHTEEN

—◆——◆—

When You Lose India,
Don't Blame Me

Leo was made to wait several days by Churchill before discovering
his own fate, while speculation was rife among his supporters that he
would be given a senior War Cabinet position. Amidst the confusion
he hoped initially to be made Chancellor of the Exchequer, and was
bitterly disappointed when that post was given to Kingsley Wood, a
survivor of the Chamberlain regime. He could only listen on the wireless as other appointments were made, but not his own. Macmillan
urged Bracken that Leo should be made Churchill's deputy for
defence, but Bracken replied that a return to the Dominions Office
was more likely. What was abundantly clear, however, was that while
just a few days earlier Leo and Churchill had been equals, there was
now no longer any doubt as to who was in charge. The new Prime
Minister would make his appointments without reference to those who
had helped him to achieve his own position. On 13 May Leo was
finally summoned to Downing Street.

Churchill greeted him warmly, pacing confidently up and down
the room. 'I've nothing to offer you', he began, 'except blood and toil,
tears and sweat',[1] upon which he offered Leo the position of Secretary
of State for India. He would sit in the Cabinet, but would not be a
member of the inner War Cabinet. Leo tried briefly to persuade him
that he might be more use at the Dominions Office, but Churchill
flattered him, emphasising the important military contribution that

India would have to make to the war effort and the likelihood of the war moving further east. Reluctantly, Leo accepted the offer, but told Churchill that he felt he 'was being side-tracked from the main conduct of the war'.[2] Before leaving, and with typical selflessness, Leo endorsed the claims to office of his 'young men'. He secured a promise that Harold Macmillan, Bob Boothby and Dick Law would all become junior ministers, but was disappointed that Churchill could find nothing for Clement Davies, who had contributed so significantly to the fall of Chamberlain. In the waiting room outside he met Malcolm MacDonald, who had been made Minister of Health, and who had been greeted by Churchill with the same curious form of words.

Walking home, Leo 'almost regretted acceptance and thought seriously for a moment of telephoning back to cancel it.' He was particularly upset that 'the old gang, and Neville in particular, had succeeded in keeping him not only out of the War Cabinet, but out of any real part in things.'[3] But after talking to Bryddie, Greenwood and Macmillan, he decided that he must 'accept whatever public duty was assigned' to him. Churchill was 'the right man to conduct the war, with or without' Leo's direct help.[4] In the House of Commons that evening there was widespread pleasure at Leo's appointment, tinged with disappointment that he had not been given a more significant post. He and MacDonald soon understood the motive behind Churchill's well-rehearsed opening remarks to them both earlier that day. 'I would say to the House,' he told a packed chamber, 'as I said to those who have joined this Government: "I have nothing to offer but blood, toil, tears and sweat."'[5]

While Leo may have initially considered his appointment to the India Office, in the words of one historian, to be a 'stunning and almost humiliating blow',[6] he did not take long to settle down to his new role and was even able to shrug off a deliberate snub from a bruised Chamberlain when they met two days later at Buckingham Palace. After eleven years in exile he was once again back in government, albeit as a result of a political coalition. It was a step in the right direction, and he wondered whether it was to be 'only a belated splutter of his political candle or the beginning of a real second innings'. His only, by now familiar, concern was that he could 'not see quite how he would survive it financially'.[7] Certainly it was a curious appointment. Churchill obviously wished to keep Leo away from the main business of the war, yet he had given him control of the one area of policy over which they had argued fiercely for many years. And once he had accepted the role, Leo put aside any disappointment he may have felt and threw himself into the work with his usual zeal. 'He is a real war leader', he wrote of Churchill, 'and one whom it is worth while serving under.'[8] And when the Cabinet met on 28 May, and Churchill promised to 'fight it out', Dalton reported that 'there was a murmur of approval round the table, in which I think Amery, Lord Lloyd and I were the loudest.'[9]

If Leo felt side-tracked from the main business of the war, he soon made up for it by becoming a constant presence in the War Room at the War Office, monitoring every detail of the evacuation from Dunkirk, the continuing battle for France and the potential threat of a German invasion of Britain. On 14 June Leo circulated a paper to the War Cabinet in which he set out four key objectives: to keep France in the war, to secure what French resources could still be saved to be used in another theatre, to do everything possible to prevent an invasion of Britain and, most controversially for Leo in view of his long-standing distrust of America, to bring in the United States as soon as possible. The following evening Macmillan was among a group, including Halifax, Robert Vansittart, the former Permanent Under-Secretary at the Foreign Office, and the French Ambassador, who gathered at the Reform Club to hear Leo's 'bold and revolutionary plan, by which France's remaining strength, moral and material, might be rallied to a determined resistance'. It involved, realised Macmillan, nothing less 'than a complete union between France and Britain'.[10] But although Leo's ideas were endorsed by the Cabinet and by De Gaulle, they had come too late to prevent the French surrender to the Germans.

In spite of Leo's admiration for Churchill's leadership, it was not long before an opportunity arose for him to cause trouble. The fall of France provided an excuse for some of the younger Under-Secretaries to express their discontent at the way in which the Government was being run, and they looked to Leo, as their mentor, to support them.

At the Reform Club dinner Leo had found Macmillan 'rather excited and convinced that we ought to have an immediate revolution from below to sweep away the whole old governing powers'.[11] Two days later Macmillan called on Leo and between them they agreed on a three-point plan for reform of the Government: first, there needed to be 'greater power of Ministers to deal with their civil servants, even to the point of sacking them without Treasury permission'; second, 'that members of the War Cabinet should have some sort of definite responsibility for groups of departments'; and lastly, that it should be 'put to Winston that there were still too many of the old gang' in positions of power, especially Chamberlain and Halifax in the War Cabinet itself.

Having agreed that Leo should put forward these proposals in a letter to Churchill, they were joined at Eaton Square by Bob Boothby, the Independent Liberal MPs, Clement Davies, Arthur Salter and Thomas Horabin, and the one man whom Leo still believed could add weight to the War Cabinet, Lloyd George. The former premier was by now seventy-six years old, and had already turned down an invitation to join Churchill's War Cabinet at the end of May, on the grounds that the offer had been conditional on Chamberlain's approval. Churchill had eventually persuaded Chamberlain to accede to his request, and had written to Lloyd George to tell him so. But, on 17 June, Leo later recalled the former Prime Minister 'prancing up and down the room, waving the invitation from Winston and snorting at the idea of being allowed back by permission of "that pin-head".'[12] From Eaton Square Leo went on to lunch at White's Club where he found Salisbury and Duff Cooper, both of whom opposed the idea of sending the letter. The conspirators later assumed that it was Cooper, in a bid to prove his loyalty, who had stolen a copy of the letter at lunch and taken it straight round to Downing Street.

The following day Leo asked to see Churchill who, at first, refused. 'He is very tiresome,' Churchill told his Private Secretary, John Colville, 'always wanting to air his views about how to win the war, on behalf of the Junior Ministers, instead of getting on with his work at the India Office.'[13] But having made him wait a while, Churchill finally relented and Leo was ushered in. The Prime Minister's opening words did not bode well for the interview ahead. Holding out his hand, he said simply, 'I want the letter.'[14] He then rejected Leo's suggestions, and admitted that Chamberlain had warned him to beware of an 'intrigue' by Leo and the Colonial Secretary, George Lloyd, 'to get the Cabinet changed'. Leo protested that they were both 'wholeheartedly interested in the work of their departments and wanted nothing else', save that the some of the junior ministers should have a greater say. But Churchill was having none of it. Macmillan and the others should 'stick to the job he had given them', and if anyone within the Government 'wished to criticise its working or its composition they should resign and criticise from outside'. There would be no changes. Somehow the interview still 'ended in friendly fashion', although Leo went away with his tail between his legs, accepting that they had 'all better resign themselves for the time being to doing their work'.[15]

Although the so-called 'Under-Secretaries' Plot' descended into farce, its repercussions were more long-term. Churchill never forgot what had happened, later reminding Colville of how 'a number of Tories had tried to break up the Government and to engineer the formation of a kind of dictatorial triumvirate', to consist of Churchill, Lloyd George and Ernest Bevin, the Minister of Labour. The key 'instigators had been Amery, Harold Macmillan, Boothby and P. J. Grigg'.[16] The day after Leo's meeting with Churchill, Boothby, in a grave error of judgement, wrote at length to the Prime Minister suggesting almost all of Leo's ideas. He too was summoned to Downing Street, where Churchill went through the letter 'sentence by sentence, and scorched it'. The following day Boothby received a 'red ink minute' from Churchill to the effect that it would be better if he 'confined himself to the work he had undertaken to do', while Churchill later complained that he had been 'intriguing against Neville' with Leo.[17] It was a message that Macmillan too 'took to heart and learnt well'. He realised that while Leo had been an able mentor in the past, Churchill was now 'the only patron worth having'.[18]

Barely had Leo managed to repair his relationship with Churchill following one argument, than he contrived to fall out with the Prime Minister again, this time over his own ministerial portfolio and the constitutional future of India. Leo had wasted no time in immersing himself fully in Indian affairs and began by striking up a cautious, if friendly, relationship with the Viceroy, Lord Linlithgow. Leo knew that his proposals for India's future were controversial, and would be considered radical, and possibly dangerous, by Linlithgow, Churchill and, indeed, probably the Cabinet as a whole. Yet Churchill had curiously appointed Leo in the full knowledge of his views, which he had often expressed in Parliament, namely that India should become an independent nation within the British Commonwealth. Leo now wished to make a promise to the Indians, as soon as possible, that they would be allowed to frame their own constitution the moment that hostilities were over. It was a policy which Churchill viewed as 'heretical', believing that there were no circumstances whatsoever under which British sovereignty should be ceded.

As soon as he took up office Leo began to sound out Linlithgow, conducting a regular, direct line of correspondence by means of secret telegrams. It was a form of communication which he had used to good effect at the Colonial Office, but under Churchill's leadership it was to prove his first major mistake. 'We are always being pressed', he told Linlithgow as early as 2 June, 'for a date for inaugurating Dominion Status.'[19] And in view of the 'improved attitude of Gandhi and Nehru', he suggested a British initiative to 'get together an informal conference to consider methods of approach to the constitutional problem'.[20] Linlithgow was unhappy with the suggestion, believing that the suggested participants for such a conference were wholly unsuitable, but Leo soon felt justified when he made his first appearance at the despatch box, as Secretary of State, on 26 June. He was given a warm welcome, but was left in no doubt that the issue of constitutional reform would be raised at every opportunity, while Attlee encouraged him to confront the Cabinet with his proposals as soon as possible, and suggested that he should travel to India himself to study the situation. The idea appealed to Leo, principally as an opportunity to overcome misrepresentation of his proposals by senior British officials there, whom he knew to be inexorably opposed to his radical ideas. He could give the Indians assurances as to his future policy in person. The Viceroy, once famously described by Nehru as 'heavy of body and slow of mind, solid as a rock and with almost a rock's lack of awareness',[21] was appalled. He had no desire to see the alert and intellectual Secretary of State interfering in his personal domain.

On 13 June 1940, Leo complained to Linlithgow that there was 'a risk of our missing the moment for action'. He wanted the Viceroy to make it clear that the Government were 'out for whole-hearted co-operation and were prepared in large measure to accept Indian views as to how the defence of India is to be conducted'. He suggested too that Linlithgow should appoint an Indian Minister of Defence, but again the Viceroy disagreed. Four days later, on the same day as he had spent the morning with Macmillan preparing his controversial letter to Churchill, Leo still found time to urge Linlithgow towards an acceptance of more significant constitutional reform. Even were it to remain necessary to 'continue to govern India autocratically', it would surely be easier to do so if one of them could only 'announce clearly the future stages towards Indian self-government'. Under an onslaught of telegrams from Leo, Linlithgow finally agreed to put the proposals to the Indian leaders and, on 19 June, held meetings with Gandhi and Jinnah, finding the latter forthcoming, but the former somewhat intransigent.

Leo believed that the fall of France had created sympathy for Britain among the leaders of the Congress Party, and that the time was ripe to make a bold promise of post-war independence for India. After weeks of trying unsuccessfully to persuade Linlithgow to accept his ideas, Leo was amused to discover that the Viceroy now put the policy to Gandhi as his own, while Gandhi's replies imitated those which Linlithgow had originally given Leo. In an effort to find agreement over a timetable for constitutional reform and to ensure Congress participation, Linlithgow offered two concessions to test the water: first, that the Government would 'abide by conclusions of any representative body of Indians on which various political parties could agree', and, second, that they would 'spare no effort to bring about Dominion Status within a year after conclusion of war'. Crucially, in the context of the events of the following three weeks, Linlithgow emphasised that he was making the offer personally and not formally on behalf of the Government, but Gandhi rejected it anyway, insisting on immediate independence. However, the Viceroy was sufficiently encouraged to express to Leo the hope that the Cabinet might be 'prepared to go so far as the rough sketch which I suggested', and, in an admission which would have been inconceivable a few weeks earlier, conceded that their secret correspondence by telegram now showed that 'we are so closely in agreement both as to the line to be taken and as to tactics.'[22]

Leo was now desperate to earn Indian goodwill for the British war effort, and redrafted Linlithgow's offer as a more formal proposal, albeit one which still embodied the two crucial concessions of Indian political appointments to the Viceroy's Executive Council, and the promise of immediate post-war Dominion Status. He began to lobby a number of his Cabinet colleagues, securing the support, as he believed, of Halifax, Simon and Attlee. On 12 July he was finally given the opportunity to put his proposals to the Cabinet, where they were discussed for an hour and a half. The meeting was a disaster. Churchill was positively hostile, interrupting Leo throughout his presentation, while the Colonial Secretary, George Lloyd, although personally a close friend of Leo's, took his usual hard line over India. Only Attlee gave lightweight support to the policy, but still criticised the actual draft proposal.

That evening Leo summed up his frustrations in a letter to his only ally, Halifax, who had unfortunately been absent from Cabinet that day, inspecting his family pile in Yorkshire. 'My dear Edward, where oh where were you this morning?' he grumbled. It had been an 'uphill battle with very little backing from anybody'. Churchill had been 'full of eloquence', while Simon had 'left him in the lurch'. In future, he pleaded, 'I shall need all yr help.' Halifax was entirely sympathetic to Leo's predicament and offered to do all he could, but warned Leo to remember that Churchill's stance on Indian policy was 'not a matter of argument but instinct, which, in turn, is affected a good deal by his own past on the subject'.[23] Leo tried writing a lengthy justification of his policy to the Prime Minister, but Churchill brushed it aside with a shameless appeal to Leo's well-known patriotism, with which he intended to suppress all argument once and for all. 'I hope you will not press me unduly', wrote Churchill, 'at a time when all our thoughts should be devoted to the defence of the Island and to the victory of our cause.' Leo hardly knew what to say. 'How can I fail to be moved by an appeal such as you make in your letter?' he replied the same day.[24]

Although Linlithgow had acknowledged, in his letter to Leo of 1 July, that Cabinet approval would be needed for the proposals he had put to Gandhi, the Viceroy soon panicked and tried to distance himself from the policy. He telegraphed Leo twice, in quick succession, to complain that he had been pressed too hard by him into accepting Leo's ideas. Linlithgow had 'assumed you had taken prior soundings of the Cabinet', and claimed only now to realise that the declaration 'so arbitrarily urged upon me had not any backing from Cabinet either in principle or in form'.[25] To make matters worse, Churchill now intervened personally, sending a telegram of his own to Linlithgow in which he questioned the Viceroy closely as to the true level of his support for the declaration, and urged him to disown the entire policy. And he repeated the patriotic blackmail he had used on Leo, gently enquiring whether it was really wise to be issuing a 'new constitutional declaration', at a time 'when invasion appears imminent, when the life of the Mother-country is obviously at stake?'[26]

Linlithgow's reply proved disastrous for Leo. In a bid to clear his name, he conveniently forgot that it was he who had first put the proposed declaration to Gandhi, and claimed that he had only agreed to the idea under pressure from Leo and in the belief that the Cabinet was already fully in support of the proposals. Of course, given the Prime Minister's opposition, he would be only too happy to make whatever changes were necessary. Most damaging for Leo, he offered to make available to Churchill copies of the entire secret correspondence by telegram which had passed between himself and Leo in recent weeks. As a result, at the Cabinet meeting on 25 July, Leo endured 'a thoroughly bad morning'. Churchill began with 'a tremendous onslaught' against his Secretary of State for 'having misled the Cabinet as to Linlithgow's original attitude'. Again, Halifax was Leo's only supporter, while, in spite of having promised their support beforehand, Attlee 'was no use and Greenwood wouldn't even open his mouth'. Churchill announced that he would redraft the declaration himself, once he had studied the telegrams. It was, mused Leo, 'all very difficult' and made it 'extraordinarily hard for Winston and myself to continue working together'.[27] The Permanent Under-Secretary at the Foreign Office, Sir Alexander Cadogan, remarked that he found it all 'rather embarrassing, so I came away!'[28]

The following day Leo was summoned to see Churchill at Downing Street. In the immediate aftermath of the previous day's meeting, Colville could tell that there had been a 'blood row', and assumed that 'Amery will resign.'[29] In fact Leo mounted a staunch defence of his position. He insisted that there was no question of his having misled the Cabinet as to Linlithgow's attitude, or of having pressed the Viceroy too hard. In 'ordinary times it might have been the simplest thing' for him to resign, but if he did so 'it could only raise trouble here and in India'. He then, in spite of some embarrassment, went through the telegrams with Churchill, who became increasingly 'perturbed' as he realised that they 'reflected freely upon him'. However, thought Leo, 'he had asked for it and I was not going to be in a position of having kept back a single word.' Churchill was furious. He would 'sooner give up political life at once, or rather go out into the wilderness and fight, than to admit a revolution which meant the end of the Imperial Crown in India.' It was a disgrace that within a few weeks of gaining office, Leo had 'attempted to initiate a revolutionary policy' of his own. Leo managed to keep his temper and the interview was 'quiet and not unfriendly', but Leo correctly guessed that, after he had left, Churchill would 'read and re-read the telegrams and get more and more angry as he does so.'[30]

Churchill did not enjoy reading the 'ill-advised references to himself' in the telegrams, but Colville's prediction that 'as far as Amery is concerned, the fat is in the fire', proved unfounded.[31] In fact, it was Halifax who managed to calm Churchill down by persuading him that Leo had been 'more fool than knave' in his behaviour.[32] Churchill contented himself instead with delegating Colville to open up a private line of correspondence with Linlithgow behind Leo's back, using a secret cipher of his own, and also recruited P. J. Grigg, then the Permanent Under-Secretary at the War Office, and gave him the additional job of spying on Leo. Grigg was to scrutinise all telegrams between Leo and Linlithgow to ensure that neither of them 'strayed from the straight and narrow path of firm resistance to Indian Nationalist pretensions',[33] a role he performed successfully until, after the fall of Singapore in February 1942, Churchill unexpectedly appointed him as Secretary of State for War.

Churchill's redrafted declaration was a greatly watered-down version of Leo's original proposals. There would be no guarantee that a purely Indian body would frame any post-war constitution, while the earlier suggested timescale for the granting of Dominion status, to have been a year after the end of hostilities, was removed. However, the Viceroy was to be allowed to appoint more Indians both to his Executive Council and to a newly formed War Advisory Committee. And the Muslims were to be given an effective veto over any transfer of power that would be detrimental to them. The Viceroy made the so-called 'August Offer' on 8 August but, although the proposals were warmly welcomed when Leo introduced them in the Commons, in India the Congress Party dismissed them out of hand, and reaffirmed its commitment to absolute independence. Leo felt that the revised declaration was too imprecise, and was disappointed that an opportunity had been missed to send a clear signal to India. In private he disclaimed any responsibility for the 'August Offer', always preferring his own original wording. But it did lead to an improvement in his relations with Churchill, and he was relieved when, after an enjoyable dinner at Downing Street with Bryddie, during which the two old Harrovians had reminisced about their time together at school, the Prime Minister wrote, 'Pray think no more of this incident, which is now ended satisfactorily to all parties concerned.'[34]

Although the Congress Party rejected the 'August Offer', the Muslim League, under the leadership of Mohamed Ali Jinnah, took more time to consider the offer. Leo held mixed views about Jinnah and the League. While he believed the unity of India to be of paramount importance, and indeed had some sympathy with broader Muslim claims, he was horrified by their specific proposals for partition and what he believed would be the ensuing 'balkanisation' of India. 'A complete break up of India, on Ulster and Eire lines,' he told Linlithgow, 'seems a disastrous solution.' He was convinced too that 'one of the essentials for internal liberty' was 'reasonable external security and definite boundaries.' India currently enjoyed the benefits of a strong external frontier, but partition would bring that to an end. The north-west region of Pakistan would 'include a formidable Sikh minority', while the north-east part, now Bangladesh, then enjoyed a 'Muslim majority so narrow that its setting up as a Muslim state, or part of a wider Muslim state, seems absurd'. 'In fact,' he concluded with some prescience, 'an all out Pakistan scheme seems to be the prelude to continuous internal warfare in India.'[35]

Nor did he warm to Jinnah as an individual, describing him in a further letter to Linlithgow as 'the miserable Jinnah . . . eaten up with vanity and only prepared to cooperate if he felt that he was to be the shadow behind the throne in future.'[36] However, in spite of these concerns, his sympathy for Muslim claims gradually grew stronger, especially after Congress's rejection of the 'August Offer', and, little by little, he began to take Jinnah more seriously. He encouraged Linlithgow to do whatever he could to win Muslim acceptance for the 'August Offer', and to find sufficient representative Muslims to serve on the enlarged Viceroy's Council. But he was eventually forced to conclude that the new declaration had now become so watered down that to make any further concessions would be perceived as an admission that Congress and the Muslim League could effectively veto any constitutional reforms between them and the declaration was, for the time being at least, quietly shelved.

■ ■ ■

During the autumn of 1940 Leo again came into conflict with Linlithgow, this time over the Viceroy's efforts to ban the activities of Congress, by proscribing the party and all its members. He had already written to all governors in India affirming that 'the only possible answer to a "declaration of war" by any section of Congress . . . must be declared determination to crush the organization as a whole,'[37] a pronouncement which became known as the 'Revolutionary Movement Ordinance'. Leo, however, was far from happy, believing that outlawing Congress would serve only to give the party credibility and that, in propaganda terms, it was essential that any action against them appeared to be because it was 'their anti-war policy and not their general political outlook to which we are objecting.'[38] He also suggested that Linlithgow should take action against individual members of Congress rather than the party as a whole.

On 15 September Gandhi presented an ultimatum to the Viceroy, insisting that Indians should be given freedom of speech to protest against the war, failing which there would be a campaign of civil disobedience. Linlithgow refused, and Congress launched the *satyagraha* campaign, during which selected individuals, chosen by Gandhi, shouted anti-war slogans or made anti-war speeches, leading to their inevitable arrest. On 25 October Leo approved the arrest of his fellow old Harrovian, Jawaharlal Nehru, who, to the shock of politicians in both London and India, was subsequently sentenced to four years' imprisonment by a local court. By the summer of 1941 almost 23,000 people had been arrested under the Defence of India Act, of whom over 5,000 were actually imprisoned, but the campaign achieved, even in the judgement of its own protagonists, only moderate success. In June 1941, nearly eleven months after he had made the 'August Offer', and in spite of the refusal of Congress to cooperate and opposition from Churchill, Linlithgow decided to go ahead anyway with the expansion of his Executive Council. For the first time the balance of power lay with its eight Indian, rather than its four British, members.

Japan's entry into the war, at Pearl Harbor on 7 December 1941, radically altered the importance of India to the overall war effort. Leo was Secretary of State, not only for India, but for Burma also, and Japan's obvious ambition to conquer Burma, finally achieved in May 1942, left India herself badly exposed to possible Japanese invasion. In October 1941 the Burmese leader, U Saw, had visited London on a goodwill mission and had seized the opportunity to demand immediate self-government. However, Leo was intensely distrustful of U Saw, believing that his only real aim was to promote his own ambitions to become 'a dictator in Burma', and Leo's confidential briefing informed him that the Burmese leader's 'chief interests in life were drink, pretty ladies and, above all, U Saw'.[39] The sinking of two British battleships, the *Prince of Wales* and the *Repulse*, a few days later, left Japan with virtually the freedom of the seas in the Far East.

It was fortunate for Leo that a decision to release all of the *satyagrahi*

prisoners had been announced by Linlithgow a few days before Pearl
Harbor, and that there could therefore be no suggestion that their
release had been in response to the declaration of war with Japan.
Churchill had, as usual, strongly opposed the plans, designed by Leo
and Linlithgow both to demonstrate clemency, and as a show of
support for the newly expanded Executive Council, all of whose members, both Hindu and Muslim, had supported the release. However,
when Leo persuaded the Cabinet to accept the proposals Churchill
reluctantly fell into line, albeit with a whispered aside to Leo that
'When you lose India, don't blame me.'[40] But the need for full Indian
cooperation in the war was now greater than ever, and the fall of
Singapore in February 1942 merely emphasised India's strategic
importance. 'I am carrying here, almost single-handed, an immense
responsibility,' reported Linlithgow, never one to play down his own
importance. 'Indeed, I do not think I exaggerate to affirm that the key
to success in this war is very largely in my hands.'[41]

The pressure for constitutional reform in India again gathered
pace. Leo was proud of the contribution made to the war effort by
over 400,000 Indian troops around the world, but there was still a
widespread feeling that India's war potential was not being exploited
to the full, due to the continuing refusal of the nationalist leadership
to participate. Churchill and Leo came under renewed pressure to
launch a new initiative, both from the American President Roosevelt,
and from the Labour members of the War Cabinet at home. On
2 January 1942 encouragement came from a third source. The moderate Indian leader Sir Tej Bahadur Sapru, along with twelve colleagues,
sent Churchill their suggestions for breaking the constitutional
deadlock, demanding that he make a 'bold stroke of far-sighted statesmanship . . . to enlist India's whole hearted active co-operation in
intensifying the war effort.' Their demands included the immediate
granting of Dominion status and the expansion of the Executive
Council into an all-Indian government.[42]

Both Leo and Linlithgow reacted by standing firm and repeating
the terms of the 1940 offer. But there the agreement between the two
men ended, their views of Indian claims to self-government differing
widely. On 21 February Linlithgow sent Leo a telegram that was to

become notorious. 'India and Burma have no natural association
with the Empire', he wrote, 'from which they are alien by race, history
and religion, and for which as such neither of them have any natural
affection.' Both were only within the 'Empire because they are conquered countries which had been brought there by force, kept there by
our controls, and which hitherto it has suited to remain under our
protection.' If Britain was to 'take a bad knock' or, heaven forbid, lose
the war, he had no doubt that the Indian leaders' only concern would
be 'to make terms with the victor at our expense'.[43] Leo, whose guiding
principle of duty led him firmly to believe that the British had an
honourable mission to perform in India, found 'one or two things in
Linlithgow's letter not altogether to my liking'.[44]

Attlee was even more appalled, describing the Viceroy's language
as 'crude imperialism' and an 'astonishing statement to be made by
a Viceroy'. He called Linlithgow's judgement into question and enquired of Leo 'whether someone should be charged with a mission
to try and bring the political leaders together'.[45] At Cabinet two
weeks earlier Attlee had already bluntly told Churchill that the
Viceroy lacked the required statesmanship to negotiate adequately,
and that a special envoy should therefore be sent to India to do so in
his place. The Prime Minister now responded by producing his own
policy statement, proposing the creation of an elected Defence Council
to oversee the running of the war, which would in due course frame a
new constitution for India at the cessation of hostilities. However, the
executive and legislative framework in India would remain largely
unchanged. Initially Churchill intended to fly out to India to present
his proposals in person, but after the fall of Singapore it was suggested
that a radio broadcast might be more suitable. Linlithgow complained
bitterly to Leo that he was, 'for the first time in my life, really cross
with you all over this business', and begged Leo that he should be
'in some way cushioned by you and your Office from the full impact
of these explosions in the Prime Minister's mind'.[46]

Churchill had, by now, created an India Committee of the War
Cabinet, with Attlee, recently appointed Deputy Prime Minister, as
chairman. However, Churchill decided to preside over the first meeting himself, and Leo recorded that the discussion was 'killed by

Winston's complete inability to grasp even the most elementary points'. He seemed 'quite incapable of listening or taking in even the simplest point but goes off at a tangent on a word and then rambles on inconsecutively'. He was not merely 'unbusinesslike', but 'overtired and really losing his grip altogether'. Stafford Cripps, who had recently returned from his post as Ambassador in Moscow and was now Leader of the House of Commons, told Leo that Churchill had behaved similarly at a meeting the previous day. Leo noted that 'a complete outsider coming to the meeting and knowing nothing' of Churchill's reputation would have thought the Prime Minister 'a rather amusing but quite gaga old gentleman who could not understand what people were talking about.'

At subsequent meetings the committee made better progress towards drafting, and then agreeing, a new declaration to be put to the Indian leadership. It described the procedure for setting up a newly elected assembly at the end of the war and for framing the constitution of the new Dominion thereafter. Leo's most significant contribution was in persuading the committee, and Cripps in particular, to include the so-called 'local option' clause, by which any 'dissident province' which was unhappy could 'stand out but not prevent the others framing a constitution'.[47] This would, admitted Leo, give 'the Moslems the power to have their Pakistan if Congress is not prepared to meet them'.[48] Although he conceded that 'most of the Hindus will set up a howl of protest against the thought of dividing Mother India',[49] Leo was thus prepared to risk such a break-up, the very thing he most feared, as a necessary evil for gaining Jinnah's support. And while he hoped that such an outcome would never come about, his insistence at the time on the inclusion of the so-called 'option clause' was to have far-reaching consequences in paving the way for partition in 1947.

In spite of the promise that there would be post-war reform, the declaration stressed that, for the duration of the war, the British Government would 'bear the full responsibility for, and retain the control and direction of, the defence of India as part of their world war effort.' At the same time, the 'task of organising the military, moral and material resources of India' must remain the responsibility of India herself, while the British Government 'desired, and invited, the immediate and effective participation' of India's leaders and her people.[50] Controversially, the declaration also contained a clause, which Leo vigorously opposed, allowing India the right to secede from the Commonwealth at any time in the future, should an independent government decide to do so. It soon became clear to Leo that the document was not nearly self-explanatory enough, and he duly resurrected the idea of sending an emissary to India to explain it. Over the weekend of 7 and 8 March it was agreed, in the face of Leo's initial opposition, that the emissary should be Stafford Cripps.

Leo's original intention had been to go to India himself and, although he 'took a natural liking to Cripps', he distrusted him over India, believing him to be both 'endearingly simple in character' and, 'for all his ability, naive in his outlook on politics in general and on Indian affairs in particular'. At a more directly practical level, he thought that Cripps had 'swallowed all Nehru's views', and 'believed unquestionably in the unfailing virtue of arithmetical democracy and the sacred right of majorities and could only regard ninety million Moslems as a tiresome opposition.'[51] Not only was he concerned that 'the Moslems regarded Cripps as an out and out Congress man', he was also, rightly as it turned out, worried as to how Cripps would get on with Linlithgow. There was also, undoubtedly, an element of professional jealousy in his opposition to Cripps, but when Churchill insisted on the appointment, Leo quickly fell into line and invited Cripps and his wife to dinner at Eaton Square. Cripps's dietary requirements left the more conventional Leo and Bryddie confused. 'Do you include fish and eggs in your diet (when procurable?),' Leo enquired, 'or are you a vegetarian of the straiter sect?'[52]

The Cripps Mission to India has been extensively chronicled and analysed by historians of Indian independence, not least thanks to the voluminous original paperwork that exists. In advance of his departure Leo's principal involvement was in smoothing Linlithgow's already ruffled feathers. Cripps arrived in Delhi on 23 March, and his first meeting with the Viceroy did not augur well. He showed Linlithgow a list, detailing his own proposals for a reformed Executive Council. Linlithgow studied it, noted that all its members were to be Indian except for the Viceroy himself and the Commander-in-Chief, and brusquely informed Cripps: 'That's my affair.'[53] Yet two days later Cripps felt able to assure the moderate president of the Congress Party, Abul Kalam Azad, that the Council's current members would resign en bloc and be replaced with names from lists to be provided by the Indian parties. Leo believed Cripps's ambition to be the complete 'Indianisation' of the Viceroy's Executive and the replacement of Linlithgow himself.

Within a few days of Cripps's arrival the contents of the declaration had been widely leaked and it soon became obvious that Congress would reject it, Gandhi famously describing it as a 'post-dated cheque on a bank which is obviously going broke'.[54] Cripps, however, supported Azad's more moderate request to have an Indian appointed to a prominent defence role, warning Churchill that anti-British feeling was running high, that the defeats in Burma and Singapore had led to a serious diminution in British prestige, and that it was essential to persuade Indian leaders to cooperate before matters got out of hand. Leo supported Cripps's suggestion and it was agreed that discussions on that basis could proceed with Congress leaders, so long as any final decision was ratified by the Cabinet, rather than on the ground in India.

Linlithgow, however, felt sidelined and on 2 April asked that he and Sir Archie Wavell, the Commander-in-Chief, be allowed to telegram their own views to the Cabinet separately from Cripps. He reported that Congress was divided, and that while the Gandhi faction would not accept the new proposals in any form and refused absolutely to contribute to the war effort, the majority of Congress, and Nehru in particular, 'was anxious to collaborate in the defence of India'.[55] Cripps duly suggested three alternatives: to make no further concessions at all; to hand over the Defence Ministry to an Indian, subject to a written understanding that no policy would be followed contrary to that of the British Government as communicated by Wavell; or to create a new portfolio for an Indian minister, who would be given control over any defence-related functions which the Commander-in-Chief might be happy to assign. Cripps favoured the second option, while both Linlithgow and Wavell made it clear that they would only accept option three.

By Easter Sunday, 5 April, Leo had begun to have serious doubts about the mission. He found Cripps's thinking muddled and, while anxious to avoid the breakdown of the talks, he suspected Congress of putting up a smokescreen for their more general demand for immediate independence. On 6 April the War Cabinet endorsed the third of Cripps's options, but insisted that he make it clear to the Indian leadership that the pre-eminent position of the Viceroy would remain. Over the Easter weekend Cripps had been helped by the arrival in Delhi of Roosevelt's 'personal representative', Colonel Louis Johnson. Although ostensibly in India to look into war production, he soon became involved in the negotiations and it was Johnson who suggested modifications to the proposal in an effort to win over Congress. For two hectic days he acted as an intermediary between Cripps, Linlithgow and Wavell on the one hand, and Nehru and the Congress leaders on the other. By 8 April he had drafted a formula detailing the functions to be ascribed to an Indian defence member, and Cripps cabled Churchill, praising Johnson, and urging the War Cabinet to accept it. But Linlithgow again complained that he and Wavell had been ignored and cabled Leo, expressing his 'strong sense of grievance', and warning that 'the latest Congress manoeuvres might well be designed to drive a wedge between His Majesty's Government and USA.'⁵⁶

Leo received Linlithgow's warning on 9 April, six days after Johnson had first become involved, and complained that it was the first he had heard of the American's intervention. 'I neither liked this', he recorded, 'nor Cripps's conduct nor the alternative version.'⁵⁷ Churchill too was becoming more concerned and, almost for the first time, Leo found himself making common cause with the Prime Minister over India. Two events over the next two days sealed the fate of Cripps's mission. When Roosevelt's Special Adviser, Harry Hopkins, arrived in London to discuss wider war issues, he assured Churchill that Johnson had no authority from the President to mediate in India. Churchill cabled Cripps immediately, instructing him that Johnson was to play no part in Indian affairs outside his specific mission dealing with munitions, and pointing out that the American President had no desire to be drawn into the Indian constitutional issue. And when Cripps promised Nehru that the Congress leaders would play a leading part in a new 'National Government', following a drastic reduction in the Viceroy's role, Churchill, and indeed the Cabinet as a whole, decided that enough was enough.

On 9 April the War Cabinet sent Cripps two telegrams, one objecting to the Cripps–Johnson defence formula, and the other rebuking him for having negotiated behind Linlithgow's back and asking for clarification of the term 'National Government'. The next morning Cripps offered to resign, and later that evening Congress's letter of rejection arrived, expressing regret that they had been misled as to the type of Cabinet government which Cripps had been proposing. On the same day, in London, the India Committee, with Churchill in the chair, drafted a cable to Linlithgow, copied to Cripps, confirming that 'there can be no question of any convention limiting in any way your powers under the existing constitution.' If Congress leaders had been given that impression by Cripps, it 'should be definitely removed'.[58] His mission was at an end.

Blame for the breakdown of the Cripps mission has been variously apportioned by historians: to Cripps himself, for being over-ambitious in his attempts to 'Indianise' government in India and for making promises to Congress he could not keep; to Churchill, for undermining Cripps at crucial moments; and to Linlithgow, for his intransigence and the secret telegrams which did so much to damage Cripps's negotiations. Cripps himself placed the blame on Gandhi, in particular on a two-hour telephone conversation he was reported to have had with the other Congress leaders on the morning of 9 April, during which he apparently persuaded them to change their minds and reject the Cripps–Johnson proposals. Certainly the last-minute rejection of the proposals by Congress allowed the British Government to divert much of the attention away from the failed constitutional negotiations, and to place the blame on the shoulders of the nationalists. In particular, it did much to convert public opinion in America to a more sympathetic view of the British position in India.

Criticism of Leo's role, meanwhile, has tended to concentrate on two conflicting accusations: on the one hand, on a perceived 'weakness' in failing to support Linlithgow adequately, and an 'inability to protect [Linlithgow] from having a vital constitutional pronouncement thrust upon him by the War cabinet';[59] and, on the other hand, that his 'reflective, almost academic mind' was 'baffled and blown about by the storms of policy battlefields', at one moment 'floating an idea towards Delhi, only to pull it back hastily if Linlithgow frowns', and the next moment acting in London 'as if he is the Viceroy's agent at head-quarters, cushioning the nagging of Cripps and trying to smother the erratic explosions of the P.M.'[60] In truth, Leo was relieved when the negotiations finally broke down, and admitted to sharing the feelings of 'someone who has proposed for family or financial reasons to a particularly unprepossessing damsel and finds himself lucky enough to be rejected.'[61]

One result of Cripps's failure was a brief rapprochement between Leo and Churchill, the Prime Minister even beginning to look upon his Secretary of State 'as a steady and supporting influence and not as a dangerous innovator'.[62] But in India the vacuum left by Cripps's failure was soon filled by the celebrated 'Quit India' campaign. At the end of April Gandhi declared that only immediate independence from Britain could prevent a Japanese invasion and, even if India were invaded, she would defend herself with a policy of non-violence. 'Let them entrust India to God', wrote Gandhi, 'or, in another parlance, to anarchy. Then all the parties will fight one another like dogs.'[63] The leaders of Congress were concerned that Gandhi's rhetoric could be interpreted as favouring alliance with Japan, and they persuaded him to drop his call for British troops to leave India. But at a meet-ing of the Congress Working Committee from 6 to 14 July, he still managed to persuade them to accept a resolution demanding the immediate end of British rule and the 'starting of a mass struggle on non-violent lines'.[64]

Leo knew immediately what this would entail. On 13 July he sent a number of telegrams to Linlithgow suggesting that he arrest Gandhi and the Working Committee at once, while he urged Churchill to 'act promptly now: "Twice armed is he that has his quarrel just; But thrice armed he who gets his blow in fust." '[65] In fact it was decided to wait until the full meeting of the All-India Congress Committee (A-ICC), to be held in Bombay the following month. Public and press opinion in Britain had hardened against the Congress stance, and Leo hoped that the full party meeting might refuse to ratify Gandhi's resolution. The Muslim League warned of riots if Congress succeeded in 'coercing the British Government into handing over power to a Hindu oligarchy',[66] but Leo assured his fellow minister Lord Woolton that India could only move forward 'on the basis of a constitution arrived at by agreement between its various elements', and that there would be no 'surrender to the demands of the little totalitarian handful who control Congress'.[67] Nevertheless, after two days of debate in Bombay, the A-ICC ratified Gandhi's resolution.

Leo was pleasantly surprised that, even in Churchill's absence, the entire Cabinet, including Cripps and Bevin, supported his firm stand, and early on the morning of 9 August the police in Bombay began arresting Congress leaders. For the next few months Leo monitored the uprising carefully. The spontaneous rioting, and the systematic destruction of railways, post offices and means of communication throughout India, led Linlithgow to confess to Churchill that he was 'engaged here in meeting by far the most serious rebellion since that of 1857, the gravity and extent of which we have so far concealed from the world for reasons of military security'.[68] Leo concentrated his efforts, by and large successfully, on maintaining Cabinet and public support, appearing regularly in the press and on the radio. George Orwell, then working at the BBC's Indian service, and no supporter of Leo's Indian policies, recalled a 'ghastly speech of Amery's, speaking of Nehru and Co. as "wicked men", "saboteurs" etc'. Interestingly, given Leo's now considerable experience of broadcasting, Orwell also had 'some difficulty getting Amery to talk in a way suitable for the microphone rather than a public hall'. In the end, it was decided that 'there was nothing for it but to record him exactly as God and Harrow made him.'[69]

The Government had long considered how best to deal with the prospect of Gandhi undertaking a hunger strike. On 4 January 1943 Leo drafted a memorandum for the War Cabinet suggesting that, in such an eventuality, the 'Government would not interfere.' The governor of Bombay, Sir Roger Lumley, who had custody of Gandhi, disagreed on the grounds that reaction to his death from fasting would be 'be so formidable that it should not be allowed to happen', and that it would inevitably lead to 'very serious demonstrations in the Province'. In spite of this advice, both Leo and Linlithgow wanted to take 'a firm line with Gandhi'.[70] The Cabinet decided to leave the final decision to Linlithgow and, on 29 January, after refusing the Viceroy's request to repudiate the 'Quit India' resolution, Gandhi announced that he was to undertake a twenty-one-day fast. The Viceroy's Council in India supported Lumley's release of Gandhi for the duration of the fast, in spite of Cabinet opposition, but Gandhi turned down Linlithgow's offer anyway. Leo subsequently reported, somewhat frivolously, that 'the fast seems to have begun in a most amiable mood on the part of Gandhi and all concerned.'[71]

In fact Leo had little time for Gandhi and agreed with the view of Linlithgow's successor as Viceroy, Lord Wavell, who assessed Gandhi's character as '70 per cent extremely astute politician, 15 per cent saint, and 15 per cent charlatan'.[72] 'What I have never been able to discover', mused Leo, was why Gandhi was 'so universally accepted as a great man even by those who think his politics unpracticable.' Leo viewed him as a 'very woolly pacifist, simple, a life preacher with no ideas of any particular distinction who has combined a reputation for holiness most successfully with a political dictatorship exercised in a wrecking and negative sense'. He was, in fact, 'an astute politician who had assumed mysticism for political purposes and may end by being forgotten as a mischievous politician and only remembered as a real saint'.[73] Indeed Leo, supported by Churchill, would have allowed Gandhi to starve to death, albeit in the face of considerable alarm at such a prospect from America and China in particular. Gandhi's health reached its nadir in the middle of February, after which Leo suspected that he began to take glucose and his condition improved. On 5 March Leo reported that 'the old fraud's life is spared',[74] and recalled Byron's experience: 'My mother-in-law has been dangerously ill. She is now dangerously well.'[75]

▪ ▪ ▪

One of the most drawn-out sagas of Leo's tenure as Secretary of State for India concerned the appointment of Linlithgow's successor as Viceroy. He had held the post since 1936 and, in August 1942, he gave

Leo early warning that his term of office would be coming to an end, and that he and Churchill should give consideration to his replacement. But the Prime Minister was unable to reach a decision in the autumn of 1942 and, so lengthy were the subsequent deliberations, that Linlithgow was forced to extend his own term by six months to fill the gap. In late 1942 Churchill's eye alighted on Sir Miles Lampson, then Ambassador in Egypt, who had, in the Prime Minister's view, provided there 'an admirable example of the way Britain's position of Imperial supremacy should be asserted'. He was a diplomat of the old school, a 'relic of a previous age', who 'believed in the pomp and ceremony of the British Empire'.[76] Leo, however, in spite of personal friendship with Lampson, was wholly opposed to the appointment of a 'middle-aged diplomat, with no knowledge of the Empire or positive Imperial zeal'.

Instead, in a moment of desperation, Leo suggested himself for the position. Having first spoken to Churchill, he followed up his verbal offer with a letter the following day asking the Prime Minister to give 'serious consideration to the proposal'. However, having claimed to have the 'essential qualification' for the job, he had also to admit that what he was most interested in was 'the immediate post-war situation in this country'. His ambition was 'to wean this country, or at any rate the Conservative Party, from the internationalist tripe which has, of necessity perhaps, been talked during the war, back to a healthy and constructive Empire policy'. He could see no one, 'least of all Anthony [Eden], who can give the kind of lead . . . that I shall hope to try and give if I am here'. Churchill, however, was having none of it. He appreciated Leo's 'public-spirited motive' in making such an offer, but Lampson was 'far more than a diplomat', and anyway, if Leo did not think himself, at '69 too old, how can you cavil at 61?'[77]

A number of other candidates emerged over the course of the next few weeks. Sir Roger Lumley, the former governor of Bombay, was considered to have acted weakly over Gandhi. Lord Cranborne's doctors vetoed his going, in spite of Leo's promise that 'Delhi was now beautifully air conditioned, and that it was not obligatory for Viceroys to go tiger shooting', while the sons of two former Prime Ministers, Dick Law and Gwilym Lloyd George, were considered unsuitable.

The Labour Party could not spare its leader, Clement Attlee, although he claimed anyway that he lacked the private means to accept, while Churchill turned down the possible appointment of the Liberal leader Sir Archie Sinclair for fear that he would have to invite his likely successor, Herbert Samuel, into the Government. Nor could he spare the Lord President, Sir John Anderson, from his War Cabinet, nor John Colville. Harold Macmillan was considered briefly but was, thought Churchill, 'too unstable'.[78] Leo lobbied hard, over a period of several months, for the appointment of his old friend Sam Hoare, then pining away unhappily at the British Embassy in Madrid. Hoare made no secret, when writing to Leo, of the fact that he coveted the position, but Churchill had never forgiven him for their disagreement over the India Act in 1935, and claimed that the public had not forgiven him for the Hoare–Laval pact and Munich.

The most serious candidate, and one on whom both Leo and Churchill agreed, was Anthony Eden. When he first broached the idea with Eden in February 1943, Leo was delighted to find that the Foreign Secretary was 'quite willing to do it if it is thought the best thing', while Leo admitted that he would 'jump at the chance of sending him for I think he has courage', and his 'ease of manner and quickness of wit' would be a welcome contrast to Linlithgow.[79] Eden's Private Secretary summed up the conflicting pressures faced by Eden in trying to make a decision: 'for A.E. to go would be to lose all he has now gained – to miss the Premiership, to miss the vital peace-making years, to confound his friends and confirm his critics.'[80] Certainly it was commonly acknowledged that Eden was Churchill's natural heir, a position reinforced by a letter of recommendation along those lines from Churchill to the King. Leo, however, believed not only that Eden was the right man for the job in India, but that he was 'really better fitted for that task than for leading the nation here', on account of his lacking 'constructive imagination or understanding of social and economic problems'. He thought that he and Eden between them 'might just possibly do a big thing'.[81]

Both Leo and Churchill returned to the fray with Eden over a period of several months and Leo wrote at length to the Foreign Secretary on 9 May. The letter was fair and balanced and, as usual,

Leo offered sound advice and showed considerable political pre-science. He asked Eden to consider what he believed to be the strong likelihood that the Conservatives would lose a post-war election, and that Eden might therefore be more gainfully employed bringing democracy to India than languishing on the Opposition front bench. But the Foreign Secretary was eventually swayed by advice from a number of different quarters, including the King, who believed him to be an essential counter-balance to Churchill, and Baldwin, who advised him that 'when in doubt between two duties, it is wise to choose the most unpleasant.' Ultimately, however, he listened most closely to the advice of his friends, who warned him that to leave domestic British politics at that moment would undoubtedly have disastrous consequences for his political future. His decision was indeed, according to Eden's biographer, 'one of those watershed moments that come in so many careers'.[82]

The choice of Viceroy eventually alighted on Field Marshal Sir Archie Wavell. In much the same way as Churchill's appointment of Leo as Secretary of State had been a curious one, given their strong differences of opinion over India, so too was his agreement that Wavell should become Viceroy. Churchill's motive, thought Leo, had been to 'dispense with Wavell' from active military duties, 'who he thinks is tired and lacking drive'. The Prime Minister hoped that Wavell would want a quiet life in India and would shrink from any dramatic constitutional reform. Leo, on the other hand, thought that Churchill had 'greatly underestimated' Wavell,[83] and that the simple act of appointing a serving soldier to the role did not necessarily guarantee that he would be any less radical than a serving politician. Leo compared the case of Allenby in Egypt, the second volume of whose biography Wavell had just finished writing. Churchill had clearly not yet read it. 'I am not sure', mused Leo, 'whether Winston would have been so keen about Wavell as Viceroy if he had realised how thoroughly Wavell backs up Allenby's policy of sympathy with Egyptian nationalism.'[84]

Leo was proved correct. Even before Wavell left for India, it was quite obvious to Churchill that he had indeed made a mistake. Wavell took the opportunity afforded him at Cabinet meetings, in the India

Committee and even in his public speeches to make it clear that he
intended to be a reforming Viceroy, and that his sole goal was to bring
independence to India. He soon launched an initiative of his own,
around which all future policy was to be based, suggesting a forum
for bringing together Gandhi, Nehru and Jinnah, with various other
Indian representatives, and making them the offer of self-government
for India as soon as possible after the end of the war. Although he
supported the intention behind Wavell's proposals, Leo at first thought
them muddled, but the two men soon found common ground on
which they could work together. Wavell admired Leo, noting that he
generally had 'an interesting and up-to-date point of view on any
question and is always well-informed'. Above all, he was 'certainly not
the obstinate Tory die-hard that Indian, and some British, papers and
politicians are fond of depicting. He has usually very liberal views
about India.' Leo, for his part, warned Wavell that Churchill knew
'as much of the Indian problem as George III did of the American
colonies'.[85]

Matters came to a head shortly before Wavell's departure for
India. Churchill was so angry at the new Viceroy's proposals for
Indian independence that he almost refused to attend the official
dinner, held in his honour at Claridges. He then reacted with fury to
Wavell's speech, in which the Viceroy clearly set out his own views, in
direct contradiction of the Prime Minister's speech just a few minutes
earlier. As usual Leo took the blame, and Bryddie even found herself
on the receiving end of a ticking off from Mrs Churchill. At Cabinet
the next day Leo tried to get his own point across, and put the case for
Wavell's proposals at the same time, believing that he had done so
successfully. Unfortunately Wavell thought that Leo 'did his best but
talked too long and allowed himself to get tied up on points of detail
by the P.M.', who 'waved the bogey of Gandhi at everyone'. The
Prime Minister harangued both Leo and Wavell at length, and refused
absolutely to countenance any form of government in India that
included Gandhi. As he did so often, he eventually fell back on an
appeal to the patriotism of those present that nothing should be done
to put the overall war effort at risk. The next day, at an ill-tempered
meeting, Churchill produced a Cabinet instruction for Wavell which

ordered him to give priority to the defence of India but did not rule out constitutional reform. On reading it later, Leo remarked that Wavell would be 'wafted to India on a wave of hot air'.[86]

■ ■ ■

With Wavell now in India, and his time largely taken up during his first few months there with the effects of the Bengal famine, Leo continued to put forward his own ideas for Indian independence, most notably that India should be granted Dominion status either on VE or VJ Day. From now until the end of the war, his relationship with Churchill over India was to sink to its absolute nadir. It was as a result of his frequent disagreements with Churchill during this period that Leo is wrongly portrayed by some contemporary commentators as having not stood up sufficiently to Churchill, a Prime Minister who 'so dominated Cabinet proceedings that members were cowed into silence'.[87] Certainly Churchill was well known for his reluctance to brook criticism, either personal or political, in Cabinet. Linlithgow, who 'admired [Leo's] qualities', nevertheless thought that he 'was quite unable to get his stuff across in Cabinet, or I think in Parliament'. Wavell thought that Leo supported his own causes 'manfully and quite skilfully', but also echoed a familiar complaint about Leo's performance, that he could 'never make a point and leave it at that, he always over-elaborates', and that all too often 'no one paid any attention and the P.M. interrupted and stopped him before he had finished.'[88] Chips Channon thought that Leo was 'terrified of Winston', constantly fearing 'that his job may be in jeopardy'.[89]

Whatever other failings Leo may have had, moral or physical cowardice in the face of frequent, and often noisy, attacks from Churchill was not one of them. There is no contemporary evidence whatsoever that the prospect of losing his job held any great terror for him. On the contrary, he appears to have been virtually the only member of Cabinet who regularly stood up to the Prime Minister, and was not afraid to become embroiled in an argument with him. In August 1944, in the course of one particularly long tirade from Churchill on one of his pet subjects, the issue of India's Sterling Balances, Leo lost his patience and told Churchill that he 'didn't see much difference between his outlook and Hitler's which annoyed him no little'. Indeed, Leo was 'by no means sure whether on this subject of India he is really quite sane'. Later on during the same meeting Churchill asked 'indignantly' why Leo was smiling. When Leo had finished putting his case, he noticed that the other members of the Cabinet had clearly 'enjoyed the fun' and were 'partly shocked and partly delighted that Winston should be spoken to in plain terms'.[90]

As Leo became more strident in his continued support for his own, and Wavell's, proposals for post-war Indian independence, so his relationship with Churchill deteriorated further. Hugh Dalton recorded that 'many outside would be surprised to find' that Leo was 'always in Cabinet the warmest advocate of a "sympathetic" and a "constructive" policy on India, but is overborne by the PM.' Leo always stood up for 'India and the Indians' and, as a result, 'Amery and the PM shouted at one another quite a lot.'[91] On 6 November 1944 Leo had 'the worst open row with Winston that I have yet had'. Once again the subject was Sterling Balances, Churchill denouncing Wavell 'for betraying this country's interests in order to curry favour with the Indians'. Leo bit his tongue for a while, but 'could not help in the end exploding violently and telling him to stop talking damned nonsense. So the sparks flew for some minutes before he subsided and business continued.'[92] Leo's own plans for Indian independence came to nothing, not least because he could not manage to persuade even Wavell to support them in Cabinet, and because they were seen to hand over to the Indian parties too much of the initiative for taking independence forward. He therefore supported Wavell when he returned to London to put forward his own proposals for a joint conference of Indian leaders.

In spite of their battles in Cabinet, Leo's and Churchill's personal relationship appears, incredibly, to have survived intact. Indeed they both had a shared, albeit among politicians all too rare, capacity to separate the personal from the political. They continued to dine together with their wives throughout the war and, from time to time, visited Harrow together for important events there. And throughout Leo and Bryddie's long ordeal and anguish over Jack's behaviour, Churchill showed them both great kindness and compassion. In spite of regular gossip that Leo was on the point of losing his job because of his arguments with Churchill, the latter seems to have spared him precisely because of their tempestuous relationship. At times he might have liked to get rid of Leo, but refused to do so purely because it seemed the obvious thing to do. Leo, for his part, came close to resigning on a number of occasions, most notably during the Washington Loan negotiations, but always pulled back from the brink for fear of causing damage to Churchill's Government. The Prime Minister's attitude to Leo was, he thought, a mixture of 'respect for the persistence of his views', and 'resentment over their many past differences, with an underlying good humoured affection going back to school days'.[93] As the war drew to a close, Wavell felt sure that he at any rate understood the secret of Leo's success in dealing with Churchill: 'What a gallant, loyal, straight little man he is.'[94]

CHAPTER NINETEEN

Sons of the Eagle

When Julian arrived in Belgrade early in September 1939, he still had every intention of obeying his orders from the Air Ministry, and of continuing on his way to report to the Middle East Command in Egypt, or of joining the British mission attached to the Polish forces. He arrived armed with a letter of introduction to the British Minister in Belgrade, Sir Ronald Campbell, an old friend of his father's, and, after two days spent exploring the city and participating in the celebrations for the King's birthday, he duly reported to the Legation to present his credentials and introduce himself to the Air Attaché. By now, however, Warsaw had fallen and there seemed to be little chance of his seeing active service in Poland. Campbell therefore suggested that he might like to stay in Belgrade for the foreseeable future and, given his recent journalistic experience in Spain, act as deputy to the Press Attaché, Stephen Childs, enjoying the rank of Assistant Attaché.

For the first few weeks Julian's duties were relatively mundane. Every morning and afternoon he would listen to the BBC broadcast and then convert what he had heard into a short news bulletin with an accompanying commentary. The bulletins were subsequently despatched to a number of influential people in Belgrade, as well as to the local newspapers, to whose editors Julian would deliver his work personally. He soon built up a strong rapport with the editors of the three principal newspapers: the *Politika*, the oldest newspaper in

Belgrade, owned and edited by a well-known local Communist; the *Vreme*, a government-owned paper which, although technically neutral, frequently favoured the Germans; and the *Pravda*, owned by seven brothers who took a pro-Allies line but would do anything for money. Most days Julian also visited the press section of the Yugoslav Foreign Ministry, where he again made a number of good contacts.

It was not long before Julian had settled into the rhythm of diplomatic life in the Balkans. Leo saw Campbell in Paris at the end of October, and was relieved to hear that his son had already become an invaluable member of the Legation's staff, while a friend from Belgrade, passing through London, called on Leo and Bryddie at Eaton Square to report that Julian was 'on the top of his form and immensely enjoying the Ruritanian atmosphere' there.[1] Childs too visited the Amerys for dinner during a trip to London and spoke warmly of the contribution Julian was making. In particular his arrival had been welcomed by the small group of British correspondents based in Belgrade, who were grateful for the increased stock of useful information supplied by Julian, although most of them had been working and living in the Balkans for many years and were often of more use to Julian, especially in introducing him to the social life of Belgrade, than he was to them.

Julian soon discovered that the majority of Yugoslav journalists were broadly supportive of the Allies, but they complained that much of the information they received from the press office at the Legation was deemed, by their editors at least, to lack objectivity. He decided to counter this by suggesting to Childs that the Legation should set up its own 'independent' news agency, supplying its bulletins to the local press from a supposedly neutral source. The idea was approved by the Ministry of Information who sent a journalist out from London to coordinate the setting up of the Britanova News Agency, which in turn began to disseminate bulletins culled from the BBC and British press. Julian also created a fortnightly magazine, the *Britannia*, whose sole purpose was also to circulate as much pro-British propaganda as could be got past the local censors. Only once did he overstep the mark, when he tried to help two Yugoslav journalists who were visiting London by giving them letters of introduction to, among others, his father, Harold Macmillan, and his old school friend Simon Wardell, whose father was at the *Daily Express*. Wardell, he promised them, would 'act as an unofficial bureau for giving the right sort of information and introductions', since all he had to do was to ring up his father every afternoon, 'getting what is considered inside dope and retailing it to the gentlemen in question'.² Unfortunately his superiors were not amused. Such flagrant bypassing of official channels was 'most undesirable', and might well lead the Yugoslav journalists 'to believe that the opinions were authoritative'. Julian had meant well, but his behaviour had been 'tactless' and 'misguided', and earned him a strict reprimand from Campbell in Belgrade.³

Leo offered to help with the new magazine, writing articles himself and soliciting contributions from his friends in London. 'You may remember my introducing to you some years ago', he wrote to Lloyd George, 'a bright little boy who cherished a great political admiration for you.'⁴ That boy was now doing his bit for the war effort in Belgrade, and wondered if his childhood hero could provide an article for his magazine. Lloyd George willingly acquiesced, supplying an article entitled 'Why the Jew is persecuted'. Julian thanked him warmly, pointing out that it was well suited to Yugoslavia on account of the 'large colony of Spanish Jews' there and praised it as a 'good example of the constructive response the Jews can make to humane treatment'.⁵ Further contributions from Lloyd George soon followed, including a copy of the speech he had made at the 1937 National Honey Show, 'The Morals of Bee Keeping'. Julian was equally delighted with this article, in spite of its less obvious political content, assuring Lloyd George that *Britannia* aimed to 'keep the Yugoslav public in touch with British political life and thought', but that 'nothing polemical' would get past the censors anyway.⁶

Once firmly established as a member of the Legation, Julian was able to travel more widely and to cultivate his political contacts. Government ministers tended to deal with his superiors, but he soon became acquainted with a number of opposition politicians. He was already concerned that Campbell's sole diplomatic ambition appeared to be to damp down pro-Allied sentiment, for fear of provoking German military action in the region. Campbell urged Julian to exert extreme caution in the course of his dealings with opposition leaders. British policy was to work closely with Prince Paul and his ministers, while Julian's job was to ensure that British propaganda was disseminated in the right places and that any negative publicity was rebutted at the first opportunity. In this respect, Julian was largely successful. His hard-won contacts at the Yugoslav Foreign Ministry enabled him to publish an immediate refutation of a German-inspired, front-page article in *Vreme*, which had falsely suggested that large numbers of British ships were being sunk in the Atlantic, earning him congratulations from Campbell for 'performing his delicate mission with conspicuous success'.[7] Julian also made an equally practical, if rather more controversial, contribution to the cold war in Belgrade, by stealing the briefcase of a German whom he found himself sitting next to at lunch one day in a local hotel. Having persuaded the front desk to call the German away to take an urgent telephone call, Julian walked out with the briefcase, to the delight of the Legation's Naval Attaché.

In January 1940 Julian's life changed with the arrival in Belgrade of a new Assistant Naval Attaché, Sandy Glen. Like Julian he had been at Balliol, where he had developed a love of exploration that had already taken him on expeditions to the Arctic. Although he had been a banker before the war, it was soon clear to Julian that Glen's professional duties in Belgrade 'had little to do with the Navy and were by no means as blamelessly "diplomatic" ' as his own. Glen was, in fact, the Legation's naval intelligence officer and the two young men soon became close friends, pooling their resources by renting a spacious flat together near the Legation, in the heart of Belgrade. They employed a Slovene cook, whom they later discovered to be an Italian spy, and a Croatian housemaid, and it was not long before the flat became the centre of diplomatic social life in the city. Glen recalled that there was a party almost every night, after which the guests would adjourn until the early hours to a local club such as the 'Russki Czar' or, Julian's favourite, the 'Cazbek'. Most memorable was Julian's twenty-first birthday party on 27 March, at which 'some gypsy players were imported from a neighbouring café, the wine flowed freely, and several glasses were shattered against the wall.'[8] The last guests left long after dawn.

Glen was soon visited in Belgrade by his immediate superior, the chief of the Balkan Unit of 'D' Section, Julius Hanau. 'D' Section had been the creation of Major Lawrence Grand, who had been seconded from the regular army to MI6 in 1938 with orders to create a new section within the Secret Intelligence Service (SIS), whose object was to subvert the enemy's war effort in its own and in neutral countries. As the war progressed, 'D' Section grew to become the Special Operations Executive (SOE), but in 1940 it was still a relatively small and intimate organisation, and its work was kept so secret that even Campbell was not fully aware of Hanau's and Glen's activities. Before the war Hanau had been a successful arms dealer and, as an agent for Vickers, had been responsible for negotiating the construction of the Yugoslav navy's first two destroyers in 1926. Glen described him as 'an early guide to all things a bit slippery'.[9]

On this occasion Hanau had come to Belgrade to investigate the potential for organising an uprising in neighbouring Albania against the Italian occupation, and Glen asked Julian how much he knew about the country. The truthful answer was almost nothing, but Julian quickly showed the same resourcefulness as his father had done twenty-five years earlier, when he too had hastily turned himself into a Balkan expert. Within a few hours, and with the help of two Albanian friends of *The Times* correspondent in Belgrade, Ralph Parker, Julian had assembled an authoritative dossier on the political situation in Albania. Hanau was impressed by the hurriedly compiled briefing and, eager to impress on the Foreign Office that 'D' Section had itself 'discovered a real expert on Albania', he wrote to Grand that their staff in Belgrade would be 'greatly strengthened by the co-option of Julian Amery, whose expert knowledge of Albanian affairs would be an invaluable asset to the organisation'. Julian duly became a member of the local 'D' Section team, continuing with his work as assistant Press Attaché while being simultaneously charged with fomenting revolt in Albania. The 'dreams of childhood', he realised, 'were coming true with a vengeance.'[10]

The flat in Belgrade was transformed from a centre of social life to a centre of intrigue, as the two young men built up a network to carry out 'D' Section's plans for Albania. While their numbers were reinforced to a degree from London, Julian also recruited some local people, including Ralph Parker, who had been so helpful in compiling the Albanian dossier. He was sent to join the Consulate in Skopje, the nearest Yugoslav city to the border, while 'D' Section also strengthened its representation in Athens and Salonika. The former leader of the Yugoslav Republican Party, Yovan Djonovitch, became a regular visitor to the flat and a tutor to Julian in all things Albanian, while the two Albanian exiles whom he had met previously with Parker were also recruited. The Kryeziu brothers, Gani and Said, came from a prominent Kosovan family which had been exiled from Albania as a result of a long-running feud with King Zog. However, once the King had fled the country at the time of the Italian invasion the previous year, they were willing to put aside all earlier disagreements to help free Albania from Italian occupation.

On the advice of the Kryeziu brothers, another Albanian exile was invited to Belgrade to help with the operation. Abas Kupi was a former guerrilla leader who had fought against King Zog but had then changed sides to become one of the King's highest ranking commanders. He could neither read nor write, was a man of few words and, to Julian's delight, bore a strong physical resemblance to Napoleon. He was a staunch monarchist who had fought a rearguard resistance to the Italian invasion, allowing the King time to escape, before fleeing to Istanbul himself. Now the three Albanians helped Julian and his team to set up a courier network, bringing intelligence from within Albania to Belgrade, while supplies and arms were returned by the same method. Glen shared his basement offices at the Legation with the other military attachés, and later recalled that their rooms there were stacked to the ceiling with plastic explosive, bomb-making equipment and large piles of hard currency. The reports from inside Albania convinced Julian that, given the right level of support from outside, there was sufficient evidence that enough tribes could be persuaded to rise up under Abas Kupi's leadership.

The united front was reinforced by a successful approach to the Albanian Communist leader Mustafa Djinishi, who also agreed to put aside past differences and work with Kupi and the Kryeziu brothers. The three groups met frequently, in secret locations throughout Belgrade, under Julian's chairmanship, and everything seemed to be in place for 'D' Section's plans to be implemented. But Italy had still not entered the war, and it remained a major objective of Allied policy to keep her neutral. The prospect of an uprising in Albania was considered too great a risk to that neutrality and the plan was vetoed by Julian's superiors. Nevertheless, when Italy did attack Greece in October 1940, the groundwork that had already been done proved invaluable in setting up the Albanian resistance movement with which Julian was again to come into contact four years later. In the meantime, by May 1940 Hanau's activities in the Balkans had been largely exposed and led to a German demand that he be expelled from Yugoslavia. He returned to London and was succeeded in Belgrade by Bill Bailey, a stocky metallurgist who had worked before the war for the mining magnate Chester Beatty, and somehow reminded Julian of Al Capone.

The fall of France radically altered the situation in the Balkans and transformed life for the British mission in Belgrade. The German Legation became the dominant power, and the local press began to pursue a uniquely pro-German line, closing down all the sources of British propaganda which Julian had so carefully nurtured. For the first time the Yugoslav Government, and its people, came to accept that German victory in Europe was now inevitable. Julian, however, continued to strengthen his relationships with opposition leaders, most notably with the leader of the Serbian Peasant Party, numerically the strongest opposition grouping in Yugoslavia. Milan Gavrilovitch had created a loose federation of the four Southern Slav ethnic groups, the Serbs, Croats, Slovenes and Bulgars, and now took Julian under his wing and gave him 'at least a glimpse of what young Communists were up to'.[11] Julian, who Sandy Glen remembered at the time as 'an exceptionally attractive and elegant young man', who was also 'very good company and great fun',[12] enjoyed regular hospitality at the Gavrilovitch household, largely because of the affectionate hope of the peasant leader's wife that the handsome young Englishman would marry one of her three teenage daughters.

Julian had become increasingly disillusioned with official Foreign Office support for Prince Paul and, on being approached by his old friend Djonovitch with proposals for organising a coup against the

Prince, accepted the invitation with alacrity. Djonovitch warned Julian that Prince Paul was already effectively acting as an unconscious agent of the Germans and would soon do so more willingly, and urged that Britain should withdraw her support for the regime and strike first before the Germans overran Yugoslavia and, possibly, the whole of the Balkans. Djonovitch had already initiated talks with opposition leaders in Bulgaria, where King Boris was, if anything, viewed with even greater hostility on account of his pro-German sympathies. Julian discussed the proposal with Ronald Campbell, the new Legation Minister who, rather confusingly, shared the same name as his predecessor. The advice from the Foreign Office was that Julian should maintain contact with the conspirators, but assess more accurately the true level of support in the country for Djonovitch's proposals. Julian accordingly conducted his own survey of various groups within Yugoslavia, discovering that there was widespread backing for Djonovitch among other opposition leaders and Church elders. Military opinion was represented by Draža Mihailovic, then Chief of the Operations Bureau of the General Staff, who, over dinner with Julian, described his plans for fighting a guerrilla war against likely German occupation.

Julian reported his findings back to his 'D' Section colleagues and to Campbell, but he failed to convince the Minister that the policy was worthy of British support. Official policy continued to insist on support for Prince Paul at all costs, and Campbell viewed Julian's support for the proposed coup as the immature intriguing of a young adventurer. Julian should have accepted the judgement of his superior, but he had by now convinced himself that the overthrow of Prince Paul was essential to British interests in the region, and that only he was in a position to take the necessary action to safeguard British interests and to change the entire course of the war. With the agreement of his colleagues in 'D' Section, he decided to take a few days' leave in Istanbul where he would brief Hanau, who was then on a visit there from London, and if necessary use his father's influence to get through to a higher authority than Campbell.

En route to Istanbul Julian stopped off in Sofia, where he met the local leaders of the Peasant Party, including George Dimitrov, to whom he had previously been introduced by Gavrilovitch; Dimitrov was later to be smuggled out of Bulgaria to Istanbul in a coffin. As was the case in Yugoslavia, they had no wish to see their country aligned with Germany, nor to fight a war against either their neighbours or Britain. Like their Yugoslav brothers, they supported the removal of their own, pro-German King Boris, and the creation of some form of southern Slav federation with Yugoslavia. Before leaving for Istanbul, Julian foolishly confided his own views, and those of the Bulgarians he had met, to the British Ambassador, Sir George Rendel. Unfortunately for Julian, Rendel shared the enthusiasm of his counterpart in Belgrade for royal rule. More unfortunately still, Julian made the mistake of also divulging his plans to the local 'D' Section officer in Sofia. He left Bulgaria still confident that, with British help, first Yugoslavia and, in turn, Bulgaria, could be persuaded to rise up against their rulers and thus slow down the inevitable German advance into the Balkans. Hanau agreed with his conclusions and returned to London determined to raise them at the highest level.

As soon as Julian left Sofia, the 'D' Section officer there, whether intentionally or not, gave Rendel the impression that Julian's sole purpose in visiting Bulgaria had been to encourage the overthrow of King Boris. Enraged by what he believed to be the subversive activities of a young upstart, Rendel contacted Campbell to warn that Julian had obviously been doing the same thing under his own nose in Belgrade. Rendel also sent a 'contemptuous' telegram to the Foreign Office in London, complaining at Julian's behaviour and dismissing him as a young man driven by 'the easy philosophy of action for action's sake'.[13] Opinion was fiercely divided. Julian managed to convince Campbell that he had said nothing in public which contradicted official policy, but he had also to admit that he had continued to collect information with a view to getting that policy changed, and had done so while officially a member of Campbell's staff. He was no longer, Campbell told him bluntly, welcome to enjoy Legation cover if he was going to use it to undermine his chief. He was not to return to Belgrade. Julian later accepted that he had been insubordinate, but felt that his loyalty lay increasingly with his 'D' Section superiors, and that his actions would soon be justified by the turn of events. Glen thought that Julian had shown 'exceptional political sagacity, coupled with an initiative and daring' which was 'unusual, but all the more commendable' in a twenty-one-year-old.[14]

The incident seemed trivial to Julian at the time, and the future minister responsible for SOE, Lord Selborne, was later to dismiss it as a case of 'friction with George Rendel', and to describe it as a 'trivial matter about some dinner conversation', to which he 'did not attach any importance'.[15] Leo, too, on first being told what had happened, thought that 'Rendel and Ronald Campbell must have been rather absurdly stuffy over a comparatively slight error of judgement',[16] but later conceded that Julian's 'conception of what should be done in the Balkans' was, 'of course tremendously realist', and that he had indeed given 'Campbell cause for complaint by going on with his D work when told not to'.[17] Whatever the rights and wrongs of the case, the criticism of two senior British diplomats was to remain on Julian's file throughout the war, and was to prove a major obstacle to his seeing active service on a number of subsequent occasions.

Although he had fallen out of favour with the Foreign Office, his colleagues at 'D' Section rallied round and Julian spent the next few months in Istanbul, acting as chief assistant to Bill Bailey, now the head of Balkan affairs. He divided his time between exploring the city and carrying out his relatively mundane duties, principally drafting telegrams and reports for Bailey, and briefing and debriefing agents between their assignments in the field. He also assumed responsibility for liaising with members of other intelligence organisations such as MI6, while a representative of Czech intelligence made contact with Julian, in a number of the great mosques of Istanbul, on behalf of a Russian intelligence officer who was keen to acquire British advice and expertise as to how best to plan acts of sabotage against the Germans in the Balkans. In September Bailey sent Julian to Bucharest to liaise with the local 'D' Section officer there on preparations for armed resistance to what seemed likely to be an imminent German occupation. In October Mussolini's invasion of Greece suddenly brought the Balkan theatre of operations into the mainstream of the war, and Bailey decided that Julian's knowledge of the region might be of more use at home.

He travelled first to Cairo where he found himself among old friends, including Francis Fisher, a friend from days at both Summer Fields and Eton, who was acting as ADC to Sir Archie Wavell. Julian was invited to put his thoughts on the situation in the Balkans to both Wavell and Anthony Eden, who was on a mission to Cairo at the time, assessing at first hand the state of affairs in Egypt and North Africa. Eden showed some interest in Julian's views on Albania, but brushed aside further talk about Yugoslavia and Bulgaria with the excuse that these were matters for the Foreign Secretary, not the Secretary of State for War. In his impatience to get things done, Julian felt annoyed by such a bureaucratic approach, but he enjoyed equally modest success with Wavell, whom he found intimidating and even less interested in his pleas for Allied intervention in the Balkans. Wavell did, however, invite Julian to join him for dinner with his family, before his onward journey to London by the necessarily circuitous route of the Sudan, Nigeria and the Gambia.

▪ ▪ ▪

Julian arrived home to find that much had changed. Churchill was now Prime Minister and had appointed Leo as his Secretary of State for India. 'D' Section was housed in ever-expanding offices in Baker Street, while Hugh Dalton had been made the Minister for Economic Warfare and had been placed in command of 'D' Section's 'Scarlet Pimpernel work',[18] as Leo described it, with the celebrated exhortation from Churchill to 'set Europe ablaze'. In an effort to secure support for his Balkan policies, Julian visited the new head of the Balkan and Middle Eastern sections, George Taylor, and persuaded him to take up the cudgels with the Foreign Office. This Taylor did, with mixed success. The Foreign Office rejected both the idea of supporting King Zog as leader of an exile movement in Albania, and the recommendation to support direct action in Yugoslavia and Bulgaria against Prince Paul and King Boris. However, it was agreed that contact should be maintained and Taylor suggested that Julian should return to Belgrade. But the Foreign Office would not agree to this nor, indeed, that he should go instead to Istanbul. Julian had become a 'bone of contention between two powerful departments' and it was reluctantly decided that he should return to the RAF.[19]

Leo had already decided to do what he could to help. Bryddie had little desire to see Julian subjected to the dangers of fighting the Luftwaffe in the skies above England, and reluctantly agreed that the Middle East was the right place for him. Leo went first to see Archie Sinclair, the Secretary of State for Air, to ask if Julian could be released from his RAF duties for 'D' Section work, and then saw Julius Hanau to confirm that there would still be a role available for him. He even made a point of checking with Lord Halifax, the Foreign Secretary, that there was no hidden black mark against Julian at the Foreign Office. Finally he approached Dalton himself, who had 'heard well of Julian but that he had been a bit injudicious'.[20] At lunch with the Amerys one day, Bryddie proudly showed Dalton 'a photograph of their handsome looking son Julian, who has been getting into some trouble for indiscretion in the Balkans and the Middle East'. Dalton agreed to see Julian, in the knowledge that he would 'win the heart of Mrs Amery for ever if I could make some arrangement to use him'. And when Julian was finally summoned into the minister's presence, Dalton agreed with his assessment of the political situation in the Balkans. He thought that Julian made 'an excellent impression' and had 'shown much energy, initiative and resource', and that same evening he wrote to his chief executive Gladwyn Jebb, suggesting that Julian should be 'effectively used somewhere'.[21]

Hanau added his own letter of recommendation, confirming that Julian had demonstrated 'a political flair very exceptional in most Englishmen', and had a quality, 'so rare in Englishmen, of being able to ingratiate himself with foreigners of all races and convictions'. He hoped that everything possible would be done to keep Julian in 'D' Section, adding that he 'would be one of the first men selected by me as a collaborator on any new mission'.[22] But in spite of Dalton's intervention with both Halifax and Sinclair, at the end of November Julian was ordered to report to the RAF training centre at Torquay. While sympathising with Julian's disappointment, Leo privately thought that a period of routine work would do him no harm, and that a 'short spell of physical training will do him a world of good'.[23] For the next few months Julian duly suffered the privations of undertaking training, in the freezing cold, with a group of raw recruits who had not yet even learnt to fly. His desperation was alleviated only marginally by frequent visits from his concerned mother and, by the New Year, Hanau was writing to tell him that the 'Amery case has become quite a *cause célèbre*'.[24] Eventually Dalton proved true to his word and Julian was released from the RAF and returned to London.

There had been further changes during his absence. 'D' Section had been transformed into the Special Operations Executive, known initially as SO2, before becoming the better-known SOE. Julian was formally enrolled on SOE's books at the rank of captain, made to sign the Official Secrets Act, and given the code name AHA. Dalton promised that after two months of desk work in London he would be sent back to the Balkans to carry on where he had left off. Unfortunately, an unforeseen obstacle was to present itself in the shape of Julian's appallingly neglected teeth. In need of a major operation to remove a wisdom tooth, he went into hospital on the day of a particularly heavy German bombing raid. The anaesthetist was knocked over by the force of a bomb blast, the operation went disastrously wrong, and Julian ended up with a broken jaw and serious infection. A lengthy period of enforced recuperation was spent first at the Hertfordshire home of Randolph and Pamela Churchill and afterwards back at Eaton Square, from where Julian was forced to watch the deteriorating situation in the Balkans with envy.

Julian had always looked up to his father as a schoolboy and undergraduate with a sense of awe, but their relationship now entered a new phase. He felt that his time in Spain had already narrowed the 'gulf' in experience between them, while his setback in the Balkans had taught him 'some humility', and he finally began to 'appreciate fully the breadth of [his father's] vision and the vigour and audacity of his thinking'.[25] Leo, for his part, found that Julian had 'certainly matured enormously in the last year', and that 'his judgement on political matters' was now 'remarkable'.[26] For instance, in Bulgaria, Julian's old friends in the Peasant Party were waging a successful campaign of sabotage in expectation of the German invasion, and it seemed possible that King Boris might indeed be overthrown. Given Julian's 'real knowledge' and 'unlimited realism' on the subject, Leo duly took his advice and wrote to both Churchill and Eden suggesting that Britain should 'urge Turkey and Yugoslavia to force Bulgaria into line at once, giving them a definite promise of the whole of Wavell's Army and further reinforcements if they did so.'[27] He even offered to go out to the Balkans himself to negotiate the terms, but it proved too late. With King Boris's encouragement, the Germans entered Bulgaria and the opposition leaders, with whom Julian had negotiated, were forced to flee.

In Yugoslavia too Prince Paul was preparing to come to terms with the Germans. Gavrilovitch's Peasant Party withdrew its support for the Government in Belgrade, while Djonovitch encouraged his military friends to make plans for a coup. At Julian's suggestion, as the only member of the British Government who spoke Serbian, Leo delivered an impassioned broadcast to the Yugoslavs on the evening of 25 March 1941. Although some aspects of the content had to be approved by Churchill himself, after a last-minute disagreement between SOE and the Foreign Office, the broadcast was most memorable for Leo's appeal to the Yugoslavs to 'remember that on the field of Kosovo King Lazar had chosen the heavenly crown rather than the earthly one of subjection to Ottoman rule.'[28] The following day, 26 March, Prince Paul went ahead and signed his pact with Hitler anyway, only for a *coup d'état* led by a group of army and air force officers to depose him that very night.

Leo was quietly satisfied with the apparent success of his performance, and was delighted by the gentle chaffing of his parliamentary colleagues that he was 'now bringing down Governments at long range', and that he had said 'In God's Name, Go to Regent Paul'.[29] Julian discovered at the time that 'the speech was widely heard in Belgrade and may have contributed to the general spirit of resistance', while the officers who organised the coup later confirmed to him that they had taken the broadcast as a sign of British support and 'were strengthened in their determination to act'.[30] Retribution, however, was swift and on 6 April Germany invaded Yugoslavia and swept all before them. The Yugoslav Government escaped, but whole divisions of the army were taken prisoner, while Campbell, Glen and the rest of the British Legation fled to the coast and were evacuated by sea. The German forces subsequently overwhelmed the Greek army too, leaving the Balkans firmly under Hitler's control.

Hugh Dalton found that Bryddie was 'still all over [him] by reason of her son',[31] and it was agreed that Julian should return to Istanbul to work for Bill Bailey. However, after the fall of Yugoslavia, it was decided that he should only go as far as Cairo, where he rented a spacious flat for himself on the banks of the Nile, overlooking the Pyramids. It was to provide a base from which he would embark on a number of missions around the Middle East over the next twelve months. He was sent first to Jerusalem, to lay the foundations for future cooperation with the Yugoslav King Peter and his government in exile there (it later moved to London). The Balkan section of SOE had also made their headquarters there and, for much of the summer of 1941, Julian lived at the King David Hotel. The principal aim of Julian's work was to bring together the Yugoslav, Greek and Bulgarian Governments, all now in exile, with a view to agreeing a uniform plan of action throughout the Balkans. His success in forging a tripartite agreement between his old Bulgarian friend Dimitrov, and Simovitch and Tsouderos, the Yugoslav and Greek Prime Ministers, had the added bonus for Julian and his colleagues that all three governments gave authority for SOE to work underground in their respective countries.

Those members of SOE's Belgrade mission who had escaped capture after the fall of Yugoslavia had now settled in Cairo, together with a number of exiled Yugoslav leaders. Yovan Djonovitch proposed to SOE that the British should help to build up resistance within Yugoslavia by providing money, arms and political guidance. First, however, it would be necessary to reopen communications with those leaders still left behind. Resistance to the German occupation had been taken up by two distinct groups of Yugoslavs. One of these, the Partisans, had evolved almost spontaneously into a dynamic and well-supported organisation under the command of the Communist Josip Broz, the self-styled Tito. In the other camp was the better organised and planned movement, the *Chetniks*, loyal to King Peter and largely composed of former regular soldiers under the command of Colonel

Mihailovic. Most had returned to their homes after the fall of Yugoslavia, and were now living as civilians, while their numbers increased, in preparation for an organised revolt against the Germans. In July 1941, with large numbers of German troops redeployed from Yugoslavia to the new Russian front, a general uprising broke out in Montenegro which quickly spread to Serbia and Bosnia. The question for SOE was how best to support it.

Djonovitch confirmed that Mihailovic had established a headquarters at Suvobor, high on a Serbian plateau, where he had amassed a hundred thousand men. He now asked for liaison officers to be parachuted in with wireless sets to establish a line of communication. But in Cairo Julian found it impossible to get permission for such a venture. Bailey had been replaced and the new overall chief of the Balkan and Middle Eastern sections, Terence Maxwell, had no interest in the plan. The turf wars between various organisations were as bitter as ever and, in desperation, Julian eventually wrote to his father asking for help. He soon heard that both Churchill and Dalton had given their agreement that a British mission should be sent to support Mihailovic, and 'Operation Bullseye' was duly approved. Unfortunately, it soon became clear that an aerial drop was out of the question. There was no suitable airfield available, nor could enough planes be spared to allow a crash landing, while a parachute drop was deemed too dangerous.

Julian decided instead to take a team in by submarine and a British officer with 'D' Section experience of Yugoslavia, Bill Hudson, was chosen to lead the mission. He spoke fluent Serbo-Croat but did not know enough about broader SOE policy to be of value to the Germans should he fall into enemy hands. The two Serbian volunteers whom Djonovitch had initially proposed for the mission refused to travel when they heard that they were to be put ashore in Montenegro, rather than dropped into Serbia as they had expected. But at the last moment Julian found two Montenegrin air force officers to join Hudson, while Julian was to accompany them himself by flying with them as far as Malta. The journey was eventful, the pilot being unable to find Malta in the dark and being forced to put down in the open sea until daylight, and from Malta Julian wrote a carefully worded letter to his father, from which Leo correctly guessed the nature of the mission. He was delighted that Julian was finally to see action and that the policy he had himself advocated, that of encouraging Yugoslav resistance, finally appeared to be coming to fruition. Leo thought him 'fully conscious of the danger he was about to run and thrilled by the thought of it and his responsibility'.[32]

The team spent a few days in Malta, Julian lodging, appropriately enough, on Amery Street in Valetta, named after his father in the 1920s. Although he was under orders to go no further, his enthusiasm for adventure and his desire to experience a submarine landing for the first time, proved too great a temptation. On the afternoon of 13 September the team embarked on their submarine, the *Triumph*. So rushed had been the preparation for the mission, that the ship's log recorded that while 'Captain Hudson and his three Serbs (*sic*)' were 'in great heart, their equipment had to be substantially supplemented from ship's resources.'[33] They travelled by day under water and on the surface at night and, two days into the voyage, they torpedoed and sank a 6,000-ton Italian tanker, only to find themselves attacked in turn by a destroyer, forcing them to lie motionless for several hours while depth charges exploded around the submarine. Their radio reported news of the successful uprising in Yugoslavia and, on 16 September, they were the first Allied submarine to enter the Adriatic by the Straits of Otranto since the fall of Yugoslavia. That night they approached the shoreline in Perisicadol Bay, a small inlet just north of the town of Petrovatz, near the border between Montenegro and Albania. The team were ferried ashore in relays with their equipment, Julian accompanying them in the dinghy to ensure that the landing had been successful. The submarine set off up the coast, stopping briefly off Dubrovnik the following morning and, from there, making its way across to the Italian coast and back down into the Mediterranean and on to Alexandria.

'Operation Bullseye' had been a great success and Julian had carried out his own part in it with distinction. Hudson and his team established contact with a group of Tito's Partisans in Montenegro and later reached Mihailovic's headquarters, although not until the spring of 1942. To his frustration Julian had no further involvement in the

Yugoslav resistance of that autumn and winter nor, indeed, in the growing antagonism between Tito and Mihailovic which allowed the Germans to regain their lost territory. With Russian interest in the Balkans on the increase, Julian was already thinking about what might happen after the war, and believed strongly that Britain should give its principal support to Mihailovic as the more likely long-term friend. However, he also acknowledged Tito's success at fighting a more successful guerrilla war, one that was more akin to SOE operations, and believed that Britain should send missions to both groups. But for the time being SOE leaders decided to support Mihailovic alone, a policy which was initially made difficult in the absence of any further drops into Yugoslavia after 'Operation Bullseye'.

For the next few months Julian returned to staff duties in Cairo. Although he found the desk job tedious, he enjoyed life in Cairo, then at the crossroads of the Allied war effort in the Middle East. General Auchinleck had succeeded Wavell as Commander-in-Chief and, soon after meeting Julian, suggested that he should attend the Staff College in Haifa, with a view to joining his personal staff. Julian admired Auchinleck greatly and welcomed the change from Wavell, but although flattered by the invitation, his sole aim was to break away from staff duties and to find a job in the field. The Balkans remained his best hope. He soon befriended both the newly appointed Resident Minister in the Middle East, Oliver Lyttelton, and the British Ambassador, Sir Miles Lampson, and was often called on to entertain the regular stream of VIPs whose travels took them through Cairo, Randolph Churchill and Duff Cooper's wife, Diana, being among those who reported back favourably to Leo. In his spare time Julian explored the local sights, both in Cairo itself and, when he took his first few days' leave of the war during the winter of 1941, at Luxor, Edfu and Aswan.

■ ■ ■

By the summer of 1942 Rommel had reached El Alamein and was threatening both Alexandria and Cairo itself. The prospect of the fall of Cairo presented SOE with a number of problems throughout the region and Julian was ordered back to London. His task was to explain in person to his superiors at Baker Street plans for the possible dispersal of SOE operatives for future operations in the event of Egypt falling to the Germans. After a forty-four-hour journey, Julian arrived home on the day that the House of Commons was debating the conduct of the war on a vote of censure. As the officer with the most recent first-hand information from Egypt, he believed that he had a responsibility far beyond his mission for SOE, and went at once to see his father at the India Office, giving him 'a very depressing account of the morale of the troops in Egypt', and their 'lack of confidence in any officers above the rank of Major'. While there was no time to achieve the necessary numerical reinforcement of the troops on the ground, 'the one thing that could be increased in a few hours was morale.'[34] He suggested that Churchill himself should fly out and visit the troops there.

Leo telephoned Downing Street immediately, where the call was taken by John Martin, one of Churchill's Private Secretaries. The Prime Minister was in a meeting of the War Cabinet at the time, but Martin prepared a memo for him to the effect that Julian, who was 'in the Intelligence in Cairo', had 'much of interest to say about the general position and particularly the morale of the Army'. Leo was anxious that Churchill 'should see Julian some time today'.[35] Over lunch at Eaton Square, Harold Macmillan encouraged Leo to try again, which he did, only to be told that Churchill was now having his afternoon rest and would be leaving later for Chequers; Julian should present his thoughts in the form of a written memorandum. It was not until Julian had arrived at Baker Street some hours later that his father finally got through to Churchill himself, and Julian was summoned, at a few minutes' notice, to see the Prime Minister at Downing Street.

On arrival he was shown into the Cabinet Room, where he found Churchill dressed 'in Air Force-blue siren suit, with a white silk shirt open at the neck', and the trademark cigar and glass of whisky in his hand. His face was 'very white', his 'eyes a watery blue' and, as an initial greeting, Churchill 'flashed a smile of welcome'. Sir Alan Brooke, the Chief of the Imperial General Staff, sat at Churchill's side and, after a few pleasantries, Julian was invited to speak his mind. He told Churchill frankly of the low morale of the troops in Egypt, especially among the armoured units. Churchill's face 'remained a mask' throughout, while Brooke 'frowned, as if resenting the comments on morale'. The only way to alleviate the problem, urged Julian, was for Churchill himself to visit the troops there, which would, in itself, 'have an electric effect'.[36] After answering a number of practical questions from both men, the interview was terminated after twenty minutes and Churchill once again became friendly, asking after Randolph and as to whether Leo agreed with his son's analysis.

Leo was extremely proud of Julian. It had 'certainly required some nerve . . . for a very young Captain' to describe the army as 'defeatist in front of the CIGS'.[37] Little did he in fact realise just how much nerve had indeed been required. Brooke was furious. He sat in silence while Julian, a 'most objectionable young pup', calmly described the twin problems of lack of equipment and poor morale in Egypt. 'The cheek of the young brute was almost more than I could bear,' he recalled that evening, and was further enraged to discover that most of Julian's ideas were 'based on conversations with a few officers in the bar of Shepheard's Hotel in Cairo'. Brooke was particularly annoyed that, in spite of Julian's 'bumptious manner . . . sitting there and lecturing' the two of them, he had nevertheless successfully 'impressed Winston because he had flattered him'. Churchill was delighted at the 'wonderful message that young man has brought back for me from the Middle East', to which Brooke had replied that it was wonderful only if the Prime Minister was 'prepared to listen to a bar lounger'.[38] Churchill pretended either not to hear or understand.

A month later Julian heard that Churchill had indeed arrived in Egypt to visit the troops there, and felt vindicated when John Martin told him that his 'intervention had been in a sense decisive' in Churchill's decision to make the trip.[39] Leo, meanwhile, was equally concerned by what Julian had told him of the SOE operation in Cairo. Not only had Julian upset those who were now in command by a demonstrable show of loyalty to their predecessors, they were also upset, Leo realised, that 'Winston had taken up some suggestion' which Julian had made to him, and 'objected very strongly to his being in touch through me with high quarters'. His letters had been censored, their methods were 'Byzantine' and he had received no thanks for his part in Operation Bullseye.[40] Worse still, both Leo and Bryddie were appalled at the state of Julian's health. Not only was he thin and sallow, but a specialist soon diagnosed a lung infection and it transpired that he had contracted a mild form of tuberculosis. So while he was supposed to report for office work at Baker Street, Julian in fact spent much of the summer recuperating, under his mother's care, in the small cottage the family had rented for the summer months at Turville Heath in the Chilterns.

And when a lack of finance forced Leo to give up the cottage at Turville at the end of the summer, they enjoyed a remarkable stroke of good fortune when they were offered the use of an altogether more substantial country house, Bailiffscourt, near Littlehampton in Sussex. The house belonged to an old friend of Leo's, Lord Moyne, formerly Walter Guinness, who had acquired the ruins of an old abbey in the 1920s and, to gratify his wife's love of the Tudor period, had converted them into a magnificent mock Tudor mansion. The conversion was a blend of the old and the new. While every one of the thirty or so bedrooms had its own bathroom, an extraordinary luxury for the time, the house was also decorated throughout with both original and reproduction Tudor furnishings and fittings, right down to the pewter plates, two-pronged forks, and the servants' period costume. In the grounds, Moyne had built a chapel and planted hundreds of trees, which had been especially imported from France. Chips Channon described it as a 'rich man's folly . . . a Norman feudal monster entirely created overnight' by Moyne. It was extremely comfortable, but the 'gadgets, the bible boxes, the wrought iron and other feudalities were faintly ridiculous'.

That was of little consequence to Leo. In August 1942 Lord Moyne was appointed Deputy Minister of State in Cairo and offered the house to Leo, subject only to its being maintained during his absence. Leo and Bryddie made the Tudor mansion their home for two years, spending weekends there and entertaining a host of politicians and visiting dignitaries. For Leo there was the added bonus of long walks, both around the immediate estate, and further afield. Duff and Diana Cooper lived nearby at Bognor Regis, and Sir Roderick Jones at Rottingdean, where Leo had rented a house previously. For Julian

too it became a second home, where he could stay and entertain
friends while he was in England. Channon enjoyed his stays there,
remembering the Amerys as 'a kindly, cosy gentle family, Angels
all.'[41] Their tenancy continued after Moyne's promotion to the post of
Minister Resident in the Middle East, and only came to a sad end
when he was assassinated by Jewish extremists in Cairo in November
1944.

On Christmas Day 1942 Julian's former chief, Bill Bailey, was
parachuted into the mountains of Montenegro to join Mihailovic. The
following March he asked that Julian be sent to join him, but the
request was flatly refused by his superiors in the SOE office in Cairo,
who were apparently 'frightened of his joining Colonel Bailey', for
fear that Julian 'exercised too great an influence on anyone he is
with'.[42] It was clear too that Julian's immediate superior in Cairo liked
neither Julian nor Bailey. Instead, Julian came up with an alternative
proposal. He had long maintained that the British should offer support
to Tito's Partisans in Yugoslavia, as well as to Mihailovic. He now suggested the formation of a joint Anglo-Yugoslav military staff in the
Middle East, answering both to the Yugoslav King and to the British
Commander-in-Chief. British liaison officers would be attached to
both camps in Yugoslavia, while Tito and Mihailovic would be invited
to send their own representation to Cairo. The intention was to prepare for a possible future landing by Allied forces in Yugoslavia and,
in the meantime, to try to achieve a cessation of hostilities between
the two rival factions.

King Peter in London welcomed the idea with enthusiasm, proposing that he should go out first to Cairo and then on to Yugoslavia
itself. He invited Julian to accompany him as his liaison officer.
Ministerial responsibility for SOE had, by now, passed from Hugh
Dalton into the hands of Lord 'Top' Selborne, the son of Leo's old
friend, the former High Commissioner in South Africa. Selborne
supported the King's proposal, but the Foreign Office once again
intervened to forbid Julian's accompanying him. The official reason
given was that Julian's proposal to support the Partisans proved that
he was too pro-Tito, a deeply ironic reason given the about-turn in
government policy that was then imminent. Indeed, just a few months

later it was decided to send a liaison officer to Tito in the form of Bill Deakin, a history don from Wadham College, Oxford. But there was still to be no role there for Julian.

With time on his hands in London, Julian decided that it would be a good opportunity to prepare for a post-war parliamentary career. Max Beaverbrook told him that there was a chance of a vacancy in Preston, then a two-Member constituency, because one of the two sitting Members 'could not stand Randolph Churchill as a bed-fellow'. The idea of joining his friend appealed to Julian, although Leo urged caution as Randolph had 'no stability or real staying power', and might 'easily do things which would only discredit anyone working closely with him'.[43] Instead, in April 1943 Julian applied for the vacant Aston constituency in Birmingham and, for several weeks, was a frequent visitor to the constituency, advised by some of his father's Birmingham friends and even attending a football match at Aston Villa in an attempt to find favour with the local selection com-mittee. For a while his prospects seemed good, although Leo reported that a 'glimpse of the Birmingham businessman Conservative has rather alarmed him',[44] but in the end he was deemed too young and inexperienced.

For the most part, the remainder of 1943 was a frustrating time for Julian. Selborne was known as an efficient minister, 'dealing resolutely with those in the high command of SOE whom he thought unfit for their tasks, sending them briskly into retirement or back to the departments that had seconded them to his'.[45] He had no such problem with Julian, telling Leo that he had been 'struck by his good judgement as well as by his brilliance'.[46] 'You cannot think how moved I was', replied Leo, 'to hear you speak as you did of Julian.' His illness had itself been 'the result of a very gallant performance', and had been directly attributed by his own doctors to the length of time spent submerged during 'Operation Bullseye'. Julian's 'moral and physical courage' were of 'a very high order', indeed he was 'all that one can wish in a son' and wanted only 'to be of use to his country'.[47] Selborne's view of Julian was shared by Chips Channon who, at the time, famously described Julian as 'the cleverest young man I have ever met'.[48]

When Bailey persisted with his request that Julian join him, Selborne agreed to overrule the objections of the Cairo office, so long as Julian was passed fit to undertake the necessary parachute jump. Julian regarded the medical as yet another device to prevent him going to Yugoslavia, a belief confirmed when Selborne told Leo apologetically that Julian had been passed as 'unfit to take the parachute course' because, in the doctor's opinion, 'any strenuous training of this character would be likely to exacerbate his lung condition.'[49] Julian was bitterly disappointed at 'losing his dreams of dropping into Yugoslavia and becoming a Lawrence of those parts',[50] but Selborne warned that 'life with Bailey would be very strenuous', and that the doctors felt that Julian might not even be 'yet strong enough for the preparatory course'.[51] Leo first demanded to see the medical certificate and then asked Sir Alexander Cadogan, the Permanent Under-Secretary at the Foreign Office, whether Julian might be able to join the Balkan section there.

In August King Peter was set to depart for Cairo, and again requested that Julian be allowed to accompany him, this time confronting Churchill personally. But the Foreign Office again refused and Leo angrily confronted Eden in person, finding him embarrassed and unsympathetic. The 'whole thing', observed Leo, 'looks like a disgraceful vendetta on the part of the Cairo gang based on nothing more than Julian's association with their predecessors.'[52] Selborne advised that Julian should, for the time being, give up any idea of returning to the Balkans and Leo turned instead to Wavell, whom he had recently appointed as Viceroy of India, to enquire whether there might be a space for Julian on his staff there. Wavell agreed that there would probably be an opening working for his Minister of State, and that he would be only too happy to accommodate Julian.

By September the situation had altered yet again. At dinner one night at Eaton Square, Julian met Brigadier Eddie Myers, who was returning to Greece for a further tour of duty and invited Julian to join him there, a proposal sanctioned by Selborne. When the Foreign Office once again vetoed the appointment, Selborne was furious and wrote to Eden demanding an explanation. Having 'known Julian since he was a boy', he regarded him 'as an exceptionally able and intelligent young man', who was well travelled in the Balkans and spoke the necessary languages. He described Julian's medical problems since his return from Cairo, and explained the history behind his earlier disagreements with Sir George Rendel in Belgrade, and Colonel Tamplin, his former SOE superior in Cairo, reminding Eden that he had himself been unimpressed by Tamplin's political judgement. It was vital, Selborne continued, that SOE should 'employ young men of intelligence who have some political background and training', and he was fed up with the Foreign Office's 'unfounded criticism of SOE'. Julian was 'admirably qualified' to support Myers in Greece, and he challenged Eden to own up as to whether 'there is any officer of SOE whose presence in any quarter of the world is an embarrassment to you'. If he was unable to do so, then Selborne hoped that SOE would be allowed to carry out its work unhindered, as it was 'vitally important that the policy of the Foreign Office should be carried out by men who are in fact capable of appreciating it'.

The letter was a ringing endorsement, both of Julian and of wider SOE policy, and Eden could only observe, somewhat lamely, that he had not objected to Julian being sent to Greece, 'only to not being consulted'.[53] He was, however, forced to climb down and Julian was given permission to accompany Myers, while Selborne advised him to 'profit by his past troubles and to temper enthusiasm and knowledge with discretion and tact.'[54] Leo was delighted by Selborne's unequivocal support, 'overwhelming in its confutation' of the Foreign Office, although he thought the 'whole thing almost had a Gestapo flavour' about it.[55] Before leaving for Cairo, Julian accompanied Leo to see Lloyd George at his home at Churt, and enjoyed a lengthy conversation with his old hero, in spite of his advancing years. 'Tell them to fight on and be worthy of their forefathers', was Lloyd George's message to the Greeks,[56] while at a dinner in honour of Wavell a few days later, Churchill took Julian on one side to wish him luck, adding 'with a smile, "Don't get rid of the King of Greece just yet".'[57]

When he arrived in Cairo, Julian was subjected to yet another medical, seeing both a lung specialist and a psychoanalyst to assess whether or not he was mentally fit for guerrilla warfare. Although he suspected a further plot against him, Selborne again soothed Leo's fears, assuring him that such an assessment was routine. Unfortunately for Julian, however, the situation in Greece had deteriorated sharply and it was decided that Myers's mission should not return there. Instead, it was proposed that Julian should be prepared to be sent into either Yugoslavia or Albania by boat, and he was enrolled on a three-week intelligence course at a training camp at Helwan, outside Cairo. Selborne reported back to Leo that Julian's final report had described him as a 'most intelligent and capable officer', with a 'firmer grasp of intelligence problems than many with much wider regimental experience'. He 'should do well in intelligence at higher levels.'[58]

In early December Churchill was back in Cairo, en route home from the Tehran Conference. Julian was one of a number of young officers invited to dinner at the British Embassy to celebrate the Prime Minister's birthday, along with Randolph Churchill, Fitzroy Maclean, Bill Deakin and George Jellicoe. They found themselves rubbing shoulders with the likes of Eden, Smuts and Cadogan, as well as Montgomery and Alexander. After dinner, large operational maps of the region were laid out in the Embassy drawing room and Churchill gathered the younger guests around him for a talk on Balkan affairs. It was evident to Deakin that this was to be a 'military occasion', and that they had all been summoned by the Prime Minister with the express intention of 'interrogating them in person on the situation'.[59]

The gathering lasted late into the night. Fitzroy Maclean, who had succeeded Deakin at Tito's mission, urged that the British should abandon Mihailovic and give exclusive support to Tito, advice which Churchill admitted he was likely to follow in the case of Yugoslavia, although the Government would maintain support for the King in Greece. When he then went round the table asking for further opinions, Julian nervously volunteered that it might be 'a bit awkward because Yugoslavia and Albania had a common border with Greece', but Churchill was having none of it. 'Well Julian, you may think I am being inconsistent,' he retorted angrily. 'That may be. But I still have some influence here and this is my policy.'[60] In spite of this crushing rejoinder, Churchill still found time to take Julian on one side at the end of the evening to wish him luck. Although he had 'backed the wrong horse in Greece', the Prime Minister hoped that he would 'ride home on the Yugoslav one'.[61] The following day, at Randolph's prompting, Julian called on Maclean. But there was to be no invitation to join him with Tito, and Julian did not ask. The interview was to mark the end of his wartime association with Yugoslavia.

▪ ▪ ▪

Julian was unemployed, had little prospect of seeing active service and was, by his own admission, deeply depressed. He spent Christmas 1943 in Jeddah, as a guest of King Ibn Saud, at the invitation of an old friend of Leo's, the Saudi Ambassador in London. But on his return to Cairo he was summoned to see the new head of the Albanian section of SOE, Philip Leake, who gave him the first piece of good news he had heard for some time. Unbeknown to Julian, his old school friend Billy McLean and David Smiley had visited Leo while they were on leave in London. Both had already served with the British mission in Albania, but had recently received the distressing news that the mission had been attacked, its commander, Brigadier 'Trotsky' Davies, wounded and taken prisoner by the Germans, and its remaining members forced to scatter, among them Alan Hare, another of Julian's old school friends. Winter conditions in the mountains were horrendous and Davies's Chief of Staff, Colonel Arthur Nicholls, had died a terrible and painful death from frostbite, later being awarded a posthumous George Cross. McLean and Smiley were to return to Albania to take control of the mission, and they wanted Julian to accompany them.

They rightly guessed that their team would be greatly strengthened by someone with political know-how, someone who could convince the disparate groups of Albanians to fight Germans rather than each other. Smiley knew that Julian 'had the political bug',[62] and Julian accepted Leake's invitation with alacrity, spending the next month preparing enthusiastically for the drop into Albania, taking a parachute training course and briefing himself fully on the political situation in Albania. After Italy's collapse in 1943, there had been a general uprising throughout the country, organised by two groups, similar in pattern to events in neighbouring Yugoslavia. In the north was a loose coalition of nationalist tribal leaders, led by his old friends from Belgrade, Abas Kupi and the Kryeziu brothers. The south of the country was largely controlled by the Communist resistance movement, the National Liberation Front, known as the LNC, which had been founded by another of Julian's Belgrade friends, Mustafa Djinishi, but was now under the command of Enver Hoxha. After the uprising the German High Command moved quickly to restore order, driving the resistance groups back into the mountains, and setting up a collaborationist government in Tirana. Now, however, with the increasing prospect of the Germans being driven out, the Albanians had again become more interested in fighting each other, in a battle for post-war supremacy, than the Germans. McLean's mission was charged with restoring British activity in Albania, encouraging the pro-Zogist forces of Abas Kupi to rise against the Germans, and to attempt some form of reconciliation between Kupi's movement and Hoxha's Partisans.

Julian, McLean and Smiley were transferred to Bari in Italy, where they bumped into Peter Kemp whom Julian had last seen in a trench outside Lérida during the Spanish Civil War, where he had fought for Franco in the Foreign Legion. He had since been with McLean and Smiley and was delighted to see them again, reasoning that 'the British Government would not send so powerful a mission to Kupi unless it intended to give them full support.'[63] Their first attempt to land in Albania had to be aborted when, after making the half-hour crossing of the Adriatic in a Dakota and successfully dropping their supplies over the first drop zone, the pilot searched in vain for their own target, while coming under increasingly accurate anti-aircraft fire, before deciding to head home. They later discovered that the officer in charge of their welcoming committee had panicked and failed to light the necessary signal fires, leading to the loss of all supplies. Two days later they found their drop zone, a broad open plateau at Bixha, but the pilot gave the order to jump too late and they landed instead in a rocky wood, on the side of a mountain a mile away. Julian was the last to jump, narrowly missing a pine tree and landing, fortunately for him, face down in deep, soft snow. That mattered little to him. He was, at last, engaged in an active operation behind enemy lines.

After spending the night and most of the next day with their welcoming party, a group of Zogist guerrillas, the three Englishmen set off on an eight-hour hike through the night, across the mountains, to meet up with Abas Kupi. On their arrival at the village where Davies had made his headquarters they heard for the first time the full story of his capture and Nicholls's death, but were relieved too to find a tired, but very much alive, Alan Hare, who was himself awarded the Military Cross a few weeks later. Abas Kupi soon arrived in the village, supported by a large *ceta*, or platoon, of his soldiers, 'wild and rugged men, corrugated with cartridge belts, and festooned with pistols, daggers, and hand grenades'. They wore 'black baggy Turkish breeches, braided homespun jackets of black or brown, with multi-coloured sashes wound above their waists, and white *fezes* or skull-caps on their heads'.[64] Sitting, cross-legged by the fire, Julian and McLean conferred with Kupi for several hours through an interpreter, and the illiterate tribesman soon grew fond of the three Englishmen, whom he liked to describe as '*Tre majora, dy per politike nji per lufte*' – three majors, two for politics and one for fighting.[65]

Julian was at last able to get down to business and discovered that Kupi was only too happy to help him to achieve the first of their tasks, namely the reorganisation of the British missions in the north of the country, which could be done secure in the knowledge that they could travel freely and operate in countryside which Kupi controlled. The prospect of possible future cooperation with the Communist LNC, however, presented more of a problem. The Partisans had become Kupi's principal enemies and, although he agreed to abide by any settlement imposed by the British, he doubted whether agreement could be reached with Hoxha. Finally, Julian enquired tactfully about Kupi's plans for fighting the Germans, to which he reacted indignantly, pointing to the very presence of the British mission, and to the sacrifices that he and his followers had already made, as proof of his commitment. However, as a show of faith by the British and evidence of Allied support, Julian should arrange for him to be sent arms.

A few days later Kupi invited Julian and McLean to accompany him on a tour of his local strongholds, while it was agreed that Smiley would stay behind to reorganise their headquarters, arrange for further drops of supplies from Bari and oversee the evacuation of the remaining wounded British soldiers. Although it was already May, it was still bitterly cold in the mountains, and snow lay on the ground, when Julian and McLean left with Kupi, guarded by over a hundred of his soldiers. But on the second day of the march, as they descended through the mountain mists and emerged into the sunlight, they saw for the first time the wide plains of the Mati valley, King Zog's homeland, spread out before them. Their progress was leisurely, Kupi insisting on travelling on foot and on parading his young English friends to his followers as an outward and visible demonstration of Allied support. They marched by day through rolling fields and leafy forests, making their way from village to village, where they would stop for the night, to be lavishly entertained as honoured guests in the home of the local chieftain.

On entering a house, tradition demanded that Julian and McLean remove their boots and surrender their rifles to the host. Having travelled in secret, their arrival was often the first that their host knew of their visit and, as custom demanded that he serve meat, it often took several hours for a sheep to be killed and the meal prepared. The Englishmen would be shown to the place of honour, sitting cross-legged on carpets or sheepskin rugs beside the fire, while Kupi and his senior followers would sit around them in a horseshoe. The assembled soldiers would then discuss politics or listen to a recitation of epic poems, recounting deeds of great Albanian bravery, to the accompaniment of a single stringed mandolin. Cigarettes would be rolled, a *mese* of onions, cheese and hard-boiled eggs served, washed down with *raki*, to the traditional toast *Tungyatyeta* – 'May your life be prolonged'. Dinner was finally served at a low, round table, the guests sitting on the floor sideways on to the table in crocodile formation, and later mattresses would be rolled out on the floor for the exhausted travellers to fall asleep.

Kupi's regal progress through the region was crowned with a gathering of all the Mati chiefs in honour of Julian and McLean. Although it was clear to Julian that they felt universal hatred for the Communists, Kupi surprised him by agreeing to a meeting with Hoxha if the British would arrange and supervise it. He would also resume military operations against the Germans if the British could secure an unambiguous order for him to do so from King Zog, and would themselves provide him with supplies and arms. Before leaving London, Smiley and McLean had obtained a letter of encouragement from Zog to Kupi, but the Foreign Office had refused to let them take it with them, a reluctance Smiley had originally attributed to a fear of offending the Americans. McLean now realised that the King's support was crucial, and made use of the direct line to the Foreign Secretary with which he had been provided. His message to Eden ended with the sombre warning that he believed there to be a very 'grave danger that without this measure of encouragement Abas Kupi will go the way of General Mihailovic'.[66]

While waiting for Eden's reply, Julian and McLean again left their headquarters to reconnoitre some of the areas they had not already visited with Kupi and to sound out other clan leaders. In Dibra they were disconcerted to discover that the local leader, Fikri Dine, was already in Tirana negotiating with the Germans, although they were assured that this was a purely short-term policy, designed to buy himself time in his struggle with the Communists. Like Kupi, he was waiting for orders from King Zog. Other clan leaders agreed to raise their tribes against the Germans, before Julian finally visited Kosovo where he was reunited with his old friend Said Kryeziu, who had initially been imprisoned by the Italians, but had later raised the flag of revolt against the Germans. When Julian and McLean returned to their camp on 8 June, they found Kupi waiting for them with news of the fall of Rome and the D-Day landings. Eden's reply to McLean, however, was less encouraging. The Foreign Office were still hesitating as to whether they wished to be beholden to King Zog, and Eden urged McLean to 'keep the pot boiling', a process, Julian 'ruefully reflected, which in politics, as in physics, leads to the eventual evaporation of the contents'.[67]

Kupi's offer to negotiate with the Partisans was taken seriously and Philip Leake himself parachuted into Hoxha's headquarters to secure agreement. But Hoxha flatly refused to work with Kupi and, tragically, Leake was killed in the course of his mission by a German air raid. Julian and McLean took Hoxha's refusal to negotiate as an indication that he was planning an imminent attack against Kupi and they warned their ally that he must now quickly gain favour with the Allies by attacking the Germans. Understandably, however, Kupi felt badly let down; there were to be no negotiations with Hoxha, there was no letter from Zog, and he was now being asked to fight without the arms he had requested. Meanwhile Smiley, a soldier of action, was becoming bored, and one day overheard McLean whispering to Julian that they must 'find him something to blow up'.[68] To everyone's surprise, Kupi agreed to accompany Smiley, with a *ceta* of his men, to blow up a local bridge, the Gyoles, one of the largest in Albania, on the main road from Scutari to Tirana. The operation was a total success, the bridge being completely destroyed and the road closed to German traffic for weeks.

Kupi was at last deemed to have recommenced hostilities and Julian signalled to Bari requesting that he should immediately be supplied with the necessary arms to equip as many as 10,000 men. When Bari promised that six aircraft-loads would be despatched shortly, by the end of June there was every prospect that most of northern Albania would rise in armed revolt and McLean called a meeting of clan leaders to organise the uprising. But the success of the congress was overshadowed by the news that Hoxha's troops had in the meantime attacked and overrun Kupi's headquarters and a full-scale civil war now appeared inevitable. Julian and McLean telegraphed Bari, asking that the British liaison officers attached to Hoxha should intervene to halt his advance, while Alan Hare was despatched to meet him face to face. But Bari's only reply was to parachute in, that same night, a Captain Victor Smith, whose job was to suggest an immediate armistice and to invite the two warring factions to send delegates to a peace conference in Italy. None of the three British officers thought much of Smith, whom they found to be amateurish and brisk, or his simplistic suggestion that all that was needed was to get the Albanian leaders back to Bari, where the Allies could then 'knock their heads together and make them see sense'. His boyish appearance – he was dressed in shorts and a thick pullover – led Smiley to christen him 'the boy scout'.[69]

Worse news soon followed. On the way back to their headquarters, they discovered that it too had been overrun by Hoxha's troops, and that their supplies had been looted and Hare and his wireless operator captured. Smith chose the moment casually to remark that the authorities in Bari had, behind their backs, accepted a proposal of Hoxha's that the LNC could 'take any British officers they might "meet" in Zogist territory under their "protection".'[70] McLean, Smiley and Julian accordingly decided that it was best to lie low in the forest for several days, in hiding from the Communist forces which were now searching for them. When they did eventually make it safely back to Zogist territory, they found that Kupi had mobilised 4,000 men and, within a few days, had succeeded in pushing Hoxha's forces back out of the Mati valley. Once again he asked Julian for help to wage war against the Germans, rather than his fellow countrymen. But British policy towards Albania was now in complete disarray. In June the minister responsible for SOE, Lord Selborne, had written to Leo praising Julian's early despatches from Albania, in which he had urged that Kupi and Hoxha be brought together. But Selborne admitted too that long-term support for one faction or the other was still 'under consideration by the Foreign Office', and that the Government would 'eventually have to decide which party we are to back at the expense of the other'.[71] By July Churchill was forced to write to Eden demanding, 'Let me have a note on this, showing which side we are on.'[72]

In fact, McLean's mission was fast losing the propaganda war in London and Bari. The head of SOE's mission attached to Hoxha, Colonel Alan Palmer, wrote to Anthony Eden, with whom he was on first name terms, warning him that he would 'no doubt be getting a blast of more right-wing sentiments soon' from Julian and McLean.[73] They, in turn, were aghast to discover, a few days later, that Bari was still dropping supplies and arms to the Partisans at the insistence of Palmer who had been convinced by Hoxha that Kupi was a traitor. Not only had Hoxha's successful offensive against Kupi been carried out with British arms and the advice of British officers, but one of them had sent a message to Bari stating that Julian, McLean and Smiley were 'working against partisans with collaborators'. Hoxha had accordingly given an ultimatum that they must leave the country within five days or 'hand themselves over to partisans for evacuation', failing which 'partisan patrols will be sent out to capture them and bring them back for trial by partisan military court'.[74]

Julian and McLean left Kupi's camp and went to stay for a few days at the farmhouse of Ihsan Toptani, a wealthy local landowner with strongly pro-British sympathies. Fikri Dine, whom Julian and Kupi had failed to see in Dibra on account of his negotiations with the Germans, had by now agreed to become Prime Minister in a collaborationist government. Toptani offered to act as an intermediary in an attempt to bring about a reconciliation between Kupi and Fikri Dine, but Julian would first have to accompany him into Tirana, the heart of the German presence in Albania. Dressed in one of his host's dark suits and armed with only a pistol and a bag of gold, Julian was duly driven into Tirana by Toptani's coachman, successfully negotiating several checkpoints, in spite of Julian's lack of either an identity card or any spoken Albanian. Their first stop was at Toptani's Tirana apartment, immediately opposite the local Gestapo headquarters, before going on to a meeting with Fikri Dine at a villa opposite the heavily guarded residence of the German Minister. Over lunch Julian tried to persuade Fikri Dine, and the other collaborationist nationalists, to rejoin the anti-German war effort, before he spent the afternoon casually strolling around Tirana, passing small groups of German officers, and taking the opportunity to inspect the Wehrmacht, Luftwaffe and Gestapo headquarters.

Julian's negotiations were successful. On 28 August Fikri Dine agreed to come over to Kupi's command, resigning as Prime Minister and leaving for his homeland in the north before the Germans could arrest him. But as news of his and Kupi's rapprochement with the British reached Hoxha, the Partisan leader reacted by issuing a further ultimatum demanding the withdrawal of McLean's mission, on the grounds that they were now working with 'Kupi and other traitors' against him. He no longer regarded them as Allied officers, but as 'agents of foreign reaction' and, unless they were withdrawn within five days, they would be captured and brought 'to trial before a *Partisan* court-martial'.[75] This demand proved too strong, even for the officers in Bari, who ordered Hoxha to withdraw the threat or face the immediate termination of all supplies and withdrawal of British officers. Hoxha claimed that he had been joking, and later referred to 'the wily officers McLean and Amery',[76] but Julian later discovered that they had indeed been tried, *in absentia*, by a people's court and sentenced to death. It was now more important than ever that they did not fall into Partisan hands.

Julian, McLean and Smiley were still to be involved in one further military engagement during their time in Albania when word reached them, through a German informer, that three battalions of troops were ready to desert from the German army. The soldiers were mostly Tajiks, Kazakhs and Uzbeks, who had earlier either been captured or had deserted from the Soviet army, and had then enlisted with the Germans for service in the occupied territories. Now it appeared that they were ready to mutiny again, and Julian sent a Turkish-speaking Albanian to urge them to kill their German officers and to come over to Kupi's camp. This they duly did, and a few days later Julian and McLean found some seventy of them, mainly Tajiks, roaming in the hills. Although their features were Mongolian, they wore German uniforms, from which they had torn the insignia, and carried Russian weapons. Communication was difficult as they spoke only a dialect of Persian, however Julian struck up an understanding with a young man called Achmet and it was agreed that the Tajiks would prove both their loyalty and fighting ability by joining an attack, with a force of a hundred and fifty Zogists, on a nearby German artillery headquarters.

The assault nearly had to be called off. Having reconnoitred the German camp the previous night, the Tajiks were left to rest for the day and to prepare for the operation that evening. However, during the day one of the Tajiks came forward to inform the British that they were unhappy with the manner in which their sergeant-major, or *Maréchal*, had treated them during their time under German command. Julian and McLean agreed that they would hear their complaint once they had finished their business with Kupi, but an hour later a gunshot rang out and Julian rushed to where the Tajiks were camped, to find them 'standing in a ring, singing and clapping their hands while the handsome Achmet danced a dance of victory round the corpse of the murdered *Maréchal*'.[77] There was considerable disquiet among the British contingent at this unfortunate turn of events, not least among the British NCOs, but it was decided that the only solution was to test the Tajiks in action as soon as possible to prevent further lawlessness.

That evening Julian, somewhat reluctantly, took command of the Tajik troops, while McLean led the force of over a hundred Zogists. Smiley was to give covering fire with machine guns. Julian's concern was understandable, but he decided that the best way to rouse the Tajik troops was to lead from the front, in spite of the knowledge that they had already murdered their Russian officers, their German officers, and their own sergeant-major. Their initial charge was notable only for Julian's own good fortune, when a bullet from a German machine gun grazed his chin. The injury was not serious, but it threw him to the ground, causing the Tajiks around him to pause momentarily. When he got up to continue the advance, they recovered their own momentum and attacked the German positions with gusto. McLean joined in from the other flank and the battle was soon over. Ten Germans lay dead and the rest had fled, while twelve Italians were captured. Before withdrawing, the Albanians and Tajiks looted what they could from the camp and burnt what was left.

News of the successful operation brought a further three companies over from the German lines, on this occasion Kazakhs. They arrived unannounced in the British camp one day, proudly showing off six ears, carefully wrapped in a handkerchief, as proof that they had murdered their German officers. Under Leo's influence, Julian had felt the lure of Central Asia since his schooldays and now 'by a freak of war, the day-dreams of childhood came true', as he 'rode at the head of a Turkoman horde.'[78] But while his newly assembled army carried out a number of successful raids over the next few weeks, the British found themselves increasingly caught in the tripartite fighting between Germans, Zogists and Partisans. And rather than the expected encouragement from Bari, in the shape of further drops of arms and supplies, after the success of the operation against the artillery base, they were shocked to receive orders that Smiley and McLean were to return to Italy, while Julian could stay behind with Kupi as a neutral observer. On no account, however, was he to encourage Kupi to fight, although, without further British support or arms, he could neither fight the

Germans nor defend himself against the Communists anyway. Julian and McLean contested the orders vigorously, but in vain.

McLean reluctantly proposed that he and Smiley should be evacuated by boat, but the SOE officers in Bari were keen to prove their good faith to Hoxha, and told McLean instead to hand himself and Smiley over to the Partisans for evacuation through the south of the country, a similar fate to that which had already befallen Alan Hare. Unknown to McLean, the officers in Bari had negotiated a military deal with Hoxha and they were now desperate to get his mission out of the country. Hoxha's intention was to parade the British officers as prisoners, but McLean refused to subject himself to such humiliation, and Bari grudgingly agreed to his demand. They steadfastly refused, however, to allow Kupi or any of his followers to accompany them for fear of offending the Communist leader. There followed an 'acrimonious exchange of signals with Bari', but the order to desert Kupi, their three interpreters and two Italians who had accompanied them throughout their mission, was reiterated. Smiley later recalled that the 'humiliation at such treachery', namely leaving behind the very people to whom they owed their lives, 'to the mercies of the Partisans, was intolerable'.[79]

For Julian and McLean, this was the final straw. At the risk of court-martial, they refused absolutely to abandon Kupi, and began instead to make plans for chartering an Albanian boat that would evacuate them all from the country together. A few days later they were joined by Kupi, by now a broken man, who had marched for twenty-seven hours with the last remnants of his forces to join them. McLean now sent a personal telegram to Eden, begging that they might be allowed to bring out Kupi, Said Kryeziu, and some of the others who had helped them. They later discovered that the officers in Bari had destroyed the message without sending it on to the Foreign Secretary, again to appease Hoxha. On the night of 24 October Smiley, with a number of other British officers, was evacuated by an Italian motor torpedo boat, which returned, two nights later, for Julian, McLean and their wireless operator. A British officer was sent with the boat to the embarkation point to ensure that Kupi remained behind. They also had to abandon the remaining hundred or so Turkoman troops and, most painfully of all, their three Albanian interpreters, to face almost certain death.

Back in Bari they were greeted with 'undisguised contempt'.[80] Denied the support that they had been promised, they felt utterly betrayed by the officers commanding the Albanian section. According to Smiley, most of them were 'either acknowledged Communists, like James Klugman, or unacknowledged ones such as John Eyre, who stood in the next election as a Communist'. Even the head of section, Eliot Watrous, had 'very left wing views'.[81] While this in itself was not a problem for the three young British officers, they realised that it had been hopeless from the outset to have tried to encourage support for Kupi, rather than Hoxha, in the face of such passionately held political beliefs. And they did object, most strongly, to being openly referred to as 'fascists' by Klugman and his colleagues. Having discovered that his telegram to Eden had been suppressed, McLean annoyed his antagonists still further by sending another, to which Eden replied, agreeing that Kupi should indeed be evacuated, although it was to be done 'without it appearing that H.M.G. have been involved in the operation',[82] so as to avoid further trouble with Hoxha. The officers in Bari stalled again, so Julian and McLean flew to Caserta, the Allied headquarters outside Naples, where they were received by the Resident Minister, Harold Macmillan, and General 'Jumbo' Wilson, the Supreme Allied Commander.

Macmillan and Wilson listened carefully to their story and agreed that Kupi should indeed be rescued, a decision Macmillan later admitted to taking 'without any authority', although he had 'never regretted doing so'.[83] When they returned to Bari Julian and McLean discovered that Kupi had eventually managed to charter his own boat anyway, and had escaped to Brindisi with his sons, and Ihsan Toptani and Said Kryeziu. Said's brother Gani had been arrested and, like almost all those nationalists who had opposed Hoxha, was later put to death. The Communist leader was furious at Kupi's escape and unsuccessfully demanded his return to face trial. Smiley, meanwhile, had managed to evacuate just two of the Turkoman soldiers with him, and they were now being held in an internment camp near Bari, facing repatriation to the Soviet Union and almost certain death. One morning Julian called at the camp and managed to secure permission to take them out to lunch in Bari, where he gave them each some money and turned them loose. One subsequently opened a café near Naples, and thereafter sent Julian a Christmas card every year for many years.

Julian was forced to watch on helplessly as Albania, like Yugoslavia, succumbed to oppressive Communist rule. He later argued that, although he accepted that the Partisans had been more effective in military terms than Kupi's forces, nevertheless the British Government should have 'taken a broader view of British interest than a simple order to "kill Germans".' Once it became clear that the Allies would win the war, what mattered most was 'who would take power in occupied countries after the Germans withdrew'. He believed that Albania could have easily been saved for the West and, worse still, that it was to the 'eternal dishonour' of SOE headquarters that Kupi and his followers were abandoned by the British. It has to be said that his views were robustly challenged in later life by another SOE officer, who served with Hoxha during 1943 and 1944. Sir Reginald Hibbert, who was to crown a career in the Diplomatic Service as British Ambassador in Paris, remained 'totally unmoved by Amery's outburst about Abas Kupi', who he considered had 'no right to any special claim'. Smiley, in turn, described Hibbert's remarks as 'revolting'.[84]

Whatever the merits of the case, Julian returned to London and was ultimately forced to conclude that his 'mission to Albania had ended in utter failure'.[85] However, the comparative lack of success of his own wartime involvement must have paled somewhat in the light of the news of his elder brother's experiences. Jack had spent the war years engaged in work of an altogether different nature.

CHAPTER TWENTY

On the Wrong Side of the Barricades

At the beginning of 1940 Jack was to be found in Portugal, dividing his time between Lisbon, where he stayed with friends of Leo and Bryddie, and the Hotel do Parque in Estoril. He was, as usual, desperately short of money, and pestered his father to arrange a bank transfer which would enable him to pay his way back to France. Leo, however, was more interested in corresponding 'on the subject of his moral duty to report for service'. In February Jack acquiesced, writing to Leo to ask for advice as to whether he should 'try to qualify for the Air Force or try to apply for the Intelligence Service in view of his knowledge of languages'.[1] Jack also claimed to have written to the Finnish delegation in Paris, offering to join one of the volunteer corps then being formed to fight for the Finns against Russia, but that he had never received a reply.

Jack's financial desperation is revealed in a letter, intercepted by British censors, which he wrote from Estoril, on 25 January, to Una, at their house in Cheltenham Terrace off the King's Road. Clearly she was still in touch with Jack, and had wired him asking if he could send her some money. He, however, was far more concerned with his own problems. 'Darling Toto,' he replied, 'far from being able to send any money to London I am most seriously perturbed as to what is going to happen to me.' He went on to give her careful instructions, in a letter riddled with spelling mistakes, as to how she should dispose of some diamonds in her possession whose value must have 'increased by over 25% since the outbreak of war'. It would be 'an absolute crime to lose this jewelry (*sic*) at the moment', and he suggested taking the diamonds to a Mr Nathan of Phillip Lane, whose sister 'used to be so often at Eaton Square', and who would 'certainly have friends in whose line of business that would be'.

Of greater interest to the MI5 officer on whose desk the intercepted letter later landed, was Jack's subsequent suggestion that the best thing would be for Una herself to take the diamonds to New York, where she could 'wear them in', and 'make at least £1,000 profit selling' them there. 'Please', he beseeched her, 'therefor (*sic*) give your undivided attention to this.' He knew that her powers of persuasion would be up to the job and his family would help her with any introductions she might need. She could keep any profit that she might make on the diamonds with his 'love and blessing' and, in the meantime, she was to stall his various creditors in London for as long as possible. 'I know perfectly well that I ought to be there to assist you and arrange everything,' he conceded, 'however that is impossible and I do beg you baby bear not to sit down and spend your time thinking how bad it is of me not being there because that is f-all good to anybody.' When he was 'in the money again', he promised that he would buy her 'some more ice to make up for what you have now to sell'. In the meantime, she should know 'how much I really love you', and he urged her to 'keep your chin up baby bear.'[2]

That Jack and Una were indeed engaged in some kind of smuggling operation, as MI5 later speculated, seems unlikely. A more plausible explanation is that these were diamonds which Jack had bought on credit or acquired by some other means, perhaps even those from Athens for which he had been arrested in Paris, and which he now urged Una to sell to bail him out of yet another financial crisis. Unbeknown to him, Una had moved from Cheltenham Terrace, not far down the road to 5 Chelsea Embankment, and the letter was returned to him unopened. He wrote back, clearly angry, accusing Una of being 'so bloody inefficient' that she couldn't get her letters forwarded to her new address and adding, for good measure, that she should 'smack the face of the bloody woman at Cheltenham Terrace at least.'[3] In the end, he seems to have found the money to leave Portugal, and he re-entered France on 6 March, by way of Spain, and returned to Paris.

Two weeks later, on 22 March, he saw Leo again in Paris, at first over lunch, before they spent the afternoon walking together in the Bois de Boulogne and enjoying a 'rather messy Russian dinner' at one of Leo's favourite restaurants. Jack told his father that he had made two return visits to Melilla before he had finally been paid the 'money owed him by the Spanish Government for his gun running performances three years' earlier. Having had no way of getting the money out of the country, he had entrusted it to an Argentine officer, who had agreed to meet him in Lisbon, where he would have been able to exchange it freely, but who, inevitably, had never turned up. Matters had been made worse still when his money and clothes had been stolen from his car in a Lisbon street, and he had got back to France only 'with the help of a film star friend in the clothes he stood up in'.[4] How much of this story was true, and how much of it Leo believed, we can only speculate.

Leo and Jack spent the next two days together in Paris, Leo remembering in particular their being involved in a car crash between Jack's car and a Parisian taxi. Jack told his father that he believed that 'the French army did not want to fight and would be very rapidly defeated'. Leo 'did not share this view', but instead repeated his urgent desire that Jack 'should in one form or another, political, intelligence, etc, join up'.[5] Jack agreed, on the condition that he might 'be allowed to join our forces directly in Paris without having to go home first', and Leo spent an afternoon making enquiries of the British Military Attaché in Paris as to whether or not this would be possible. Furthermore, Jack asked that his joining up be deferred until June, 'as he had secured a contract for the completion of three short films at Nice which would enable him to clear off his outstanding obligations.' On 25 March Leo saw Jack off to the south of France and returned home to London. It was to be the last time they would see each other for over five years.

It seems unlikely that Jack ever had any intention of joining up with the British forces in France, let alone of returning home. On his return to Nice, he obtained permission from the authorities of the Alpes-Maritimes region to remain in France at least until October and, in May, managed to convince his father that he had suffered a 'breakdown and was found to be suffering from tuberculosis, sufficiently serious to compel him to stop all work'.[6] He rented a cottage, La Pastorale, near the sanatorium in the village of Thorenc, near Grasse, in the hills north of Nice. And on the fall of France in June, Jack later claimed that he found himself 'virtually trapped in the Free zone',[7] successfully convincing his father that his poor health and the lack of travel facilities had precluded any attempt at escape, even though he owned a car of his own at the time. Leo acknowledged that he was 'now likely to be left isolated and perhaps completely stranded for some months'.[8] On 3 July, following a number of ultimatums, the British fleet in the Mediterranean sank the French fleet at Oran and Mers-el-Kébir off the Algerian coast, leading to the breakdown of diplomatic relations between Britain and France. Jack's position became still more uncertain and he quickly fired off a succession of telegrams to his father asking for money.

Leo was by now serving as Secretary of State for India and almost certainly had more important matters on his mind than his errant son's financial problems. Nevertheless, he reacted immediately to Jack's 'S.O.S.'. British interests in the south of France were now to become the responsibility of the American Consul in Nice, and Leo contacted the Foreign Office to ask them to make the necessary application for Jack's interests to be looked after in this way. He then organised a meeting at the Dorchester Hotel with the Swiss Minister in London, to discover whether money could be sent to Jack by way of Switzerland and whether it would be possible to get him out of France and into Switzerland where he could be looked after by friends. The Ambassador immediately contacted the Swiss Bank Corporation's office in London, who in turn instructed their Swiss headquarters to send Jack £100 and to do anything they could to facilitate his getting to Switzerland. The Ambassador promised that he, too, would do all he could to help.

It did not take Jack long to antagonise those who had been given responsibility for looking after British interests in Nice. Among those with whom he now came into contact was a Wilfred Brinkman, an English insurance assessor who before the war had been the local representative of his London-based insurance company, had subsequently remained in occupied France, and was now employed by the American Consulate to help to look after British nationals. The Swiss Minister in London had been true to his word and Brinkman soon found himself called in by the American Consul and instructed to deal with a telegram he had received 'requesting that Amery be taken to Switzerland, bearing in mind his medical condition'. Brinkman asked for help from another Englishman working in the American Consulate, one Alexander Ogilvie, who had worked before the war in an administrative role at the local hospital and would thus be able to help with what seemed to be a medical case. Between them they organised an ambulance to take Jack to Switzerland and arranged a visa for him with the local French authorities and the Swiss Consul. But, incredibly, once the arrangements were complete, Jack 'turned them down as he could not take his dog and lady friend with him'.[9]

Jack's new girlfriend was, as Una had been before her, a prostitute, this time by the name of Jeanine Barde. She had got to know Jack in Nice, although she came originally from the town of Bergerac, where she had a young daughter by a previous relationship who was looked after by Jeanine's parents. It is quite possible that Jack had become so attached to her that he refused to leave, and his wish to remain at all costs with his pet Pomeranian, Sammy, had already been used before as an excuse to his father to avoid returning to Britain. He therefore telegraphed Leo to say that he thought that it would be cheaper for him to remain in Thorenc, or even to go back to Portugal, than to travel to Switzerland. Leo's efforts to help him to escape from France had failed and it was to be the last opportunity Jack would have. In Belgrade Julian had heard the news of the armistice in France with more alarm than most. 'There's going to be a disaster,' he told Sandy Glen one evening as they listened to the radio. 'I know exactly what will happen, Jack will go over to the other side.'[10]

The telegram that Jack sent to Leo on 25 July, informing his father that he would be staying in France, was the first of several to come to the attention of the authorities, more specifically the 'Trading

With The Enemy' branch of the Board of Trade. For the next few months the department, based at its offices in Kingsway, was routinely to intercept the telegram traffic between Leo, Jack and the Swiss Bank Corporation's London office. Incredibly, one of Churchill's Cabinet ministers was, unbeknown to him, under investigation for trading with the enemy. The intercepting officer realised immediately the significance and sensitivity of what he was doing, carefully noting on the accompanying paperwork that the telegram was addressed to Leo and that the 'sender is probably his wayward son'. 'If he offends, we will have a go at a Minister' was the officer's conclusion, and the telegram was eventually forwarded to Leo, although he remarked at the delay in its reaching him. A fortnight later Jack cabled again, informing Leo that the American Consul was prepared to allow him fifty pounds a month from the British Relief Fund, considerably more than was usual, if his father would provide that amount by way of the Swiss Bank. That would enable him to live and to create a reserve to pay off his debts. The intercepting officer noted that 'this is the wayward son again', but acknowledged that he did not 'think we can do anything as it is officially recognised that this USA consul can help at his own risk'.[11]

The telegrams continued for several months. At the end of August Jack confirmed receipt of a further payment, but still asked Leo to send twenty-five pounds to a wounded French soldier in hospital in Southport, as his family had given Jack the equivalent amount in Nice. He had paid off his debts and was heading back to Thorenc. In September Jack was in touch again to complain that there had been problems in getting the money through from Switzerland, and asking Leo for 'confirmation that September money being sent'. He was pleased to say that his 'x-rays were slightly better'.[12] And in November the 'Trading With The Enemy' branch intercepted a telegram from the Swiss Bank's Basle office to London requesting that further funds be sent. This time, the controller of the department decided to take action, suggesting first that his officer telephone Leo's secretary to ask for an explanation. And later, writing to the Swiss Bank's headquarters at Byfleet in Surrey, he demanded an explanation of the movement of funds between London, Switzerland and Nice. In reply, Mr de Wolff, the manager of the bank's London branch, described Jack as a 'British subject', who had been living for some time at Thorenc 'for reasons of health'. His head office had endeavoured to 'make arrangements for his transfer to Switzerland' after the fall of France, but was now in touch with him in case 'he encounters any difficulties', and was currently dealing with a 'delay in the remittance of his monthly allowance'.

A further request for full details of all remittances and confirmation that none had been made since 10 July met with an abject apology from the bank, although their explanation sounds disingenuous. They had last asked the Basle office to send funds on 8 July, but their 'friends in Switzerland' had continued to send further payments subsequently. They now understood that those additional remittances were illegal since the breakdown of diplomatic relations with France. It appeared that 'regulations had been contravened in Basle', but an apology and an assurance that no further payments would be sent seemed to satisfy the Board of Trade.[13] Leo, at whose instigation, and with whose money the payments had been made, escaped censure, but he was now forced to halt the additional payments he had been making through Switzerland.

However, he appears to have quickly found an alternative channel through which to provide funds for Jack. 'I wonder whether I might trouble you to put a stamp on the enclosed letter and have it dropped into a letterbox for France,' he enquired of his old friend Sam Hoare, by now the British Ambassador in Madrid. Jack, he continued, 'whose lungs, I am sorry to say, are touched', had been forced to give up work and Leo admitted to finding it difficult to get money sent out to him. While telegrams were reasonably quick, letters were not, and it had occurred to him 'that a letter posted in Madrid might get through much quicker'. Either Hoare was taken in by this master-piece of understatement, or he understood only too well what he was being asked to do and thought nothing of it. He would, of course, send the letter on to Jack, 'and do anything else that I can for you in connection with him'. He even mused that his own job in Spain would be made easier by 'having some kind of semi-official British agent in non-occupied France', although given his knowledge of Jack's record it seems unlikely that he was proposing him for the position.[14]

In addition to the money from Leo which now reached Jack by way of Sam Hoare in Madrid, the American Consul in Nice also still had sufficient funds saved up to allow him to pay Jack more than the £10 a month relief grant to which he was officially entitled. This created a further source of resentment for the rest of the British community. Brinkman, who got to know Jack well, later recalled that he had 'considerable trouble with Amery over his relief allowance, as he expected to receive more than I was authorised to grant',[15] while an MI5 informant confirmed that Jack was 'loathed in Nice', because 'for some unknown reason he was allowed £20 a month instead of the usual £10.'[16] Brinkman also discovered that there was a 'traffic in sterling cheques', which 'apparently was being done in the Consulate' and which he traced back to Ogilvie. One day he noticed Jack 'walking in and out of the offices' of the local French police headquarters, 'showing he had a certain authority to do so'. When he asked an Inspector who he knew well what was the reason for this, the policeman claimed that, in fact, 'the cheques had been smuggled over the Spanish frontier' by Jack, using a 'British Diplomatic passport he held'.[17]

While no evidence remains of such a passport, the regular border crossings which we know Jack to have made throughout the 1930s, but of which there is no evidence in his own passport, suggest that such a claim may very well have been true. Whatever his involvement in the trafficking of cheques may have been, Jack made absolutely sure that he profited by it. Ogilvie later described how Jack had 'pestered him' to sell some dollars to a friend for the purpose of escaping to Spain, and had duly arranged for a meeting between them at Ogilvie's flat. The 'friend' turned out to be a policeman and Ogilvie was arrested for trafficking in stolen dollars. On arrival at the police station, Ogilvie made a statement admitting his guilt but, at the Inspector's request, left out Jack's name as he was told 'his father had such an important position it would save international complications.' Ogilvie later discovered that Jack had betrayed him to the police and had been paid 30 per cent of the money found at Ogilvie's flat as a reward. Ogilvie subsequently went to prison for six months.[18] Three years later, by which time Jack was in prison himself, Ogilvie was to write to him offering his 'forgiveness', in spite of Jack having 'ruined' him and his family, and the fact that they were 'still suffering, all through you'.[19]

In June 1941 Jack reacted to news of the German invasion of Russia with mixed emotions. On the one hand he already believed that 'Europe was in the greatest peril of a Communist invasion' which would 'sweep the whole continent', and that the 'Jewish race was mixed up and working hand in glove with Moscow'. He was therefore relieved that Germany had taken preventative action to 'spike the guns of the Communists in their world-wide revolutionary activities'. On the other hand, it came 'as a very great shock' to him that 'England and Soviet Russia had become allies'. So much so, that he thought that 'the people responsible in London were acting in a manner that no longer coincided with British Imperial interests.' Determined somehow to become involved, he decided to visit Vichy himself, in order to do what he could 'to create a situation whereby a united front of all nations might be organized against Russia'. But he was to be disappointed. He found that there was no intention there of 'carrying out any kind of Social Revolution', and that Vichy was an 'ultra-reactionary govern-ment; of priests, the worst type (in my opinion) of French industrialists and militarists'.

Jack's visit to Vichy had the unfortunate effect of raising his profile with the authorities there. 'If I did not take kindly to these people,' he admitted, 'they did not like me either, nor did they like [Jacques] Doriot.' In November, in retaliation for the arrest by the British of seven Vichy officials in Syria, Jack was among fourteen British passport-holders who were arrested in the unoccupied zone. On a 'frivolous pretext', he later complained, the police 'took me from my bed at 3 o'clock in the morning and threw me into jail at Val les Bains', an internment camp north of Avignon.[20] There he found himself rubbing shoulders with the former French Prime Minister, Paul Reynaud, and his former Minister of the Interior, Georges Mandel. It was during his brief internment in Val les Bains that he first came to the notice of MI6.

Two local MI6 agents, operating under the codename BAN-BANASTE, were interned with him and filed a report which was later passed on to MI5. The agents reported that Jack had 'sunk very low', and had acquired the 'habit of picking up in the streets the stub ends of cigarettes to smoke'. When the agents 'remonstrated with him', Jack replied indifferently 'that it did not matter as far as he was concerned as he was in an advanced state of TB'. He was also drinking heavily, often getting through 'a whole litre of gin or "fine", which he took to bed with him' in a single night. The BANBANASTE agents concluded that he was by now 'so dissipated and in such a bad state, both physically and morally', that he was not 'capable of doing harm to British interests'. They also remarked that Jack was allowed two visits a week from his 'mistress', Jeanine Barde, describing her 'as a "*morue*", i.e. a woman of the streets'. She was, they thought, 'a Frenchwoman of the worst type', who 'completely dominates him'. Jack did 'nothing without this woman's knowledge and consent' and it was thought significant that she was 'a frequent visitor to Vichy'.[21]

It was a commonly held view in Val les Bains that Jack 'was not one of them', and that he was, by now, on the Vichy payroll. He was released after a few weeks, supposedly thanks to the combined efforts of his old friend Jacques Doriot and Jeanine, to whom he now referred as Jeanine Amery-Barde. A further MI6 source reported that he was now to be found living at the Hotel de Noailles in Marseilles. The source regarded Jack 'with considerable suspicion', since the hotel was 'much frequented by members of the German Armistice Commission', and it seemed strange that he was 'able to stay at a hotel of this class on the £10 a month allowed to British subjects in France'.[22] From Marseilles, Jack moved to Grenoble, where he was required to reside under the terms of his release from internment. In February 1942, according to Leo, he 'appealed to the French authorities for repatriation to England in view of his state of health'. His application was 'refused, after a medical examination, by the Vichy authorities on the grounds that he might still be fit enough for "auxiliary service" '. From that moment, thought Leo, 'escape from France was no longer even a possibility.'[23] Leo's claim would appear to be borne out by a telegram from Jack, sent from Grenoble on 11 February: '*Commission medicale me considere bon service auxilliaire suis Grenoble hotel louver a part manque argent tout bien baisers*' – Medical commission consider me fit for auxiliary service . . . am at Hotel Louvre Grenoble . . . in spite of shortage of funds all well . . . kisses.[24]

Jack now found himself under virtual house arrest in Grenoble, desperately seeking a role as the war unfolded around him. It was not long before he found an opportunity to participate. On 3 March the RAF launched a bombing raid on the Renault works at Boulogne-Billancourt outside Paris. Three days later, under the heading '*Le fils d'un ancien ministre anglais proteste*', the *Petit Dauphinois*, a local newspaper in Grenoble, printed a letter from Jack. '*Je désire déclarer très haut – et je crois que cette pensée est partagée par nombre de mes compatriotes,*' protested Jack, '*que des opérations telles que le bombardement des quartiers ouvriers de Boulogne-Billancourt nous remplissent de tristesse et de honte . . .*' – I wish to assert most forcefully – and I believe that many of my fellow countrymen agree with me, that operations such as the bombing of the working-class district at Boulogne-Billancourt fills us with sadness and shame.'[25] Until the publication of this letter, Jack had been, in the words of one historian, 'little more than a shabby, disreputable and disturbed fantasist who had spent his adult life trading on his father's well-deserved reputation'. But by attacking his own government so openly and in such forthright terms in an enemy newspaper, 'he had crossed the Rubicon'.[26]

Whatever his motives for writing the letter, his behaviour soon came to the attention of British Intelligence who, for the first time, began to take an active interest in his movements. Desmond Orr, an MI5 officer working in Room 055 at the War Office, received a cutting of the article from MI6, along with the testimony of a local agent that Jack had been paid 10,000 francs. He duly submitted it to his superiors, with the accompanying comment that it 'should be sufficient to deter the young gentleman from ever again setting foot on British soil, or if he does, he should be assured of a reception at the hands of a firing squad'. The significance of Jack's behaviour must have been immediately obvious for, on the same day, another officer, Sydney Albert, sent a memo to his superior, a Captain Beaumont, confirming their earlier conversation 'about John Amery, son of the Secretary of State for India', about whom they continued to 'get detrimental reports'. A number of courses of action had been decided upon: to inform SIS what they already knew about Jack; to place his name on the Censor's Black List in an effort to find out with whom he was in contact in Britain; to find out from the Foreign Office what financial aid he was receiving and whether it might be stopped, thus forcing him to return home where he could 'do less harm'; and, finally, to alert the ports to keep a watch for him in case he did indeed return.[27] The following week another MI5 officer, Miss V. Gibson, wrote to SIS, informing them that Jack 'was living in the Grand Hotel d'Angleterre in Grenoble but is now back in Nice', and that he had been arrested 'once again for trafficking in stocks and shares'. In her opinion he was 'more of a crook than anything else', but she was 'considering putting him on the censorship list' to find out with whom he was in contact in Britain.[28]

Although completely unaware of the commotion his letter had caused within British Intelligence, Jack recognised that locally, at least, his 'little article' had 'brought down numerous letters of great displeasure' on his head. He was 'cut off from evryone (*sic*). Including England.' He therefore decided to pursue his theme further, and 'to attempt to talk to Dino Grandi, previously Italian Ambassador in London, to see if Italian diplomacy was not capable of organising an end to this kind of "civil war between the civilised when the barbarians were at the gate".'[29] Count Grandi was an old friend of Leo's and it is almost certain that Jack would have met him before the war at Eaton Square. Grandi was by now the Italian Minister of Justice, and Jack tried to contact him through the Italian Consul in Grenoble. Although he received no reply from Grandi, his high profile and increasingly eccentric behaviour, as well as his now public political views, had brought him to the attention of an altogether more significant authority for his purposes – the German Foreign Office. Accordingly, in August 1942 he was visited by Graf Ceschi, the German Armistice Commissioner for the Savoy region, together with Werner Plack, an official of the German Foreign Office.

The exact mechanism by which Jack was brought into direct contact with the German High Command will probably never be known. Three years later Leo did his best to put the most sympathetic interpretation possible on his son's actions. For several months, claimed

Leo, Jack had 'watched the struggle between Germany and Russia as one between forces both of which were enemies of his country, looking forward to the eventual exhaustion of both'. In his 'hopeless ignorance' of public opinion at home, he had assumed that the British Government would take the same view and 'find a convenient opportunity of making a compromise peace with Germany'. Doriot had then returned from a visit to the Russian front and had assured Jack that the 'Germans had shot their bolt in Russia', and that the only way to prevent 'Communist domination' of Europe was for Britain and Germany to come to terms. Through Doriot, Jack had been 'persuaded by a German emissary that Germany genuinely desired peace' and had believed the 'to us, fantastic notion', that even if the British Government rejected such a move, the 'British public could be brought round to it by propaganda.' Events at Stalingrad and El Alamein had, in Jack's eyes, confirmed Doriot's predictions and it was for that reason that he had agreed to go to Berlin.[30]

It is quite possible that, whatever his political motives, Jack was brought to the attention of the authorities in Berlin by Doriot, by way of his Nazi contacts in Paris. It is also possible that information about him, and his political views, had been passed on by officers, possibly agents, attached to the local Armistice Commission in the south of France. There seems to have been a good deal of confusion, even within the German Foreign Office itself. Dr Hesse, the official whose responsibility it subsequently became to look after Jack in Berlin, initially believed that he had been arrested by the German army during the early months of the war, on suspicion of being a 'British agent sent over to pry out military and political secrets', although he admitted that the corroborating material for this suggestion had been 'rather scanty'. In response to a request for further information from the Foreign Minister, Joachim von Ribbentrop, he advised that it might 'harm Anglo-German relations if the son of a British Cabinet Minister were executed for espionage without just cause', and suggested instead that he be 'brought to Berlin to see whether we could use him for any political purpose'. Both Ribbentrop and the Propaganda Ministry had apparently agreed.[31]

Whatever the real reasons behind his offer, Graf Ceschi, whom Jack claimed to have met in Vienna before the war, now suggested that he might like to go to Germany for exploratory talks. Jack was not immediately impressed. While he was undoubtedly attracted by the sense of self-importance that he would derive from such an adventure, he knew too that once he was removed from the relative safety of unoccupied France, he would be at the mercy of the Germans. He was sensible to be cautious, if only out of fear that details of his Jewish ancestry might be known to his proposed paymasters. On 12 May 1940, just a few days after the historic Norway debate in the House of Commons, German radio had run a feature about his father. Condemning the 'substantial atrocity' of 'killing little German children who were playing happily when death came down upon them', the announcer, possibly William Joyce – Lord Haw-Haw – had referred to the 'speech made by the half-Jew Leopold Amery'.[32] Whether or not those who now suggested that Jack should accompany them to Berlin were sufficiently well versed in their own propaganda, one can only speculate. Nevertheless, Jack asked for a 'formal guarantee' that he could subsequently 'return without let or hindrance', should the talks break down. While the German Foreign Office considered this request, Jack and Jeanine went to visit her family in Bergerac where, on 26 September 1942, Werner Plack returned to assure Jack that they would both enjoy safe passage to Berlin. 'He gave me the required assurances', recalled Jack, 'and we departed almost immediately.'[33]

Jack and Jeanine spent a few days in Paris, travelling under the names of Mr and Mrs Brown, before arriving in Berlin in early October, where he was to come under the control of Dr Fritz Hesse, the Foreign Office official responsible for British renegades. Hesse was a former Press Attaché at the German Embassy in London and had been 'a conduit for secret discussions between the British and German Governments right up until the outbreak of war'.[34] Therefore when Ribbentrop decided, in November 1939, to bring together the various sources of advice he received on British affairs into a single entity, and to create the so-called 'England Committee' within the Foreign Office, Hesse was the natural choice to act as the Committee's secretary and, later, as its chairman. At first the Committee's remit was to 'keep Ribbentrop generally advised on the question of how, when and [under] what circumstances peace could be brought about again with Britain'. Later on, as Ribbentrop and the Foreign Office began increasingly to encroach on territory which had hitherto been the exclusive domain of Goebbels, the Committee began 'to give advice on the general political line of propaganda'. In June 1940 the Committee's membership had been expanded to allow participants from various other departments to attend, including the Armed Forces and the Propaganda Ministry, as well as the regular attenders from within the Foreign Office. Hesse, by now the Committee's chairman, considered himself to be 'a sort of living dictionary', on hand to give either Hitler or Ribbentrop any information they might require 'on some aspect of British affairs, or some British personality'. He would be required also to give his views 'on the general trend of British public opinion'. Ribbentrop soon came to look on him as the absolute 'authority on how to get peace with Britain again'.

Jack and Jeanine had been accompanied on their journey to Berlin by Werner Plack, who had almost certainly suggested to Jack that he would be required to make broadcasts when he arrived. Plack had lived in America before the war, where he had met P. G. Wodehouse in Hollywood, and had subsequently been instrumental in persuading the writer to give the short series of radio talks which he had made in May 1941. Plack was now to be Jack's 'minder' too and, soon after their arrival in Berlin, he took him to see Hesse at the Foreign Office. By now Ribbentrop had already 'put the whole matter before the Führer' in an attempt to agree the precise line Jack would be required to take in his broadcasts. Hitler had approved of Ribbentrop's proposal that Jack should 'put over a kind of peace feeler through the agency of propaganda talks', and it was this suggestion that Hesse put to him when they met, albeit 'without telling him the full details, i.e. that the Führer was interested'.[35]

Jack listened carefully to Hesse's proposition and replied that, 'perfectly frankly', he was 'not interested in a German victory as such', but in 'a just peace where we could all get together against the real enemies of civilisation, and that the British Empire as it was intact must be a part of this and not a dependant of such a regroupment.' In agreeing to Hesse's ideas, Jack later claimed to have qualified his agreement by insisting that he be allowed to speak 'uncensored and uninterfered with in a special British hour on the radio'. Somewhat grandly, he also claimed to have demanded 'precise guarantees' concerning 'British Imperial territory', and an assurance that German policy remained as enshrined in the 'proposals of the German Chancellor to the British Government of July 1940'. Hesse gave his cautious approval, pointing out that Jack was 'asking a very great deal without giving any assurance of success' and that radio production lay in the hands of the Propaganda Ministry, who would ultimately make the final decision. Finally, he asked what Jack would require in the way of remuneration. The reply came as a surprise. 'I told him that far from wanting anything,' retorted Jack haughtily, 'I was not disposed to accept anything other than that he consider me as a guest having no resources of my own available.' Hesse was 'quite taken aback'.

Jack and Jeanine spent the next two weeks staying, away from the public gaze, at Plack's Berlin apartment, awaiting the result of Hesse's discussions on the matter with Ribbentrop. When the answer came, it was positive. Hesse informed him that he could now consider himself 'a guest of the Reich', that he might go wherever he pleased, and that he could now 'make on the Radio a series of weekly speeches which would be officially dissociated from the German senders and entirely uncensored'.[36] Jack's suggestion that the Germans should not pay him a salary, but should provide him with his expenses alone, had been a masterstroke. Hesse was 'ordered by Ribbentrop to cover his expenses and be as liberal as possible, as he thought that the son of a British Cabinet Minister should live at a certain scale'. Jack 'made liberal use of this arrangement',[37] a fact confirmed by another member of the England Committee, who observed that it was 'obvious from the way that he lived that he was allowed fairly unlimited expenses', and believed that Hesse had 'a special fund at his disposal for the purpose'.

That same member of the England Committee later recalled that 'it caused rather a sensation in Berlin when it was known that the son of a British Cabinet minister had volunteered to work for the Germans.'[38] Dr Reinhard Haferkorn, a university professor from Greifswald, had worked at the Foreign Office in Berlin since the outbreak of war, where he was now in charge of the English section of the *Rundfunkpolitische Abteilung*, the Foreign Broadcast Department. He was to be in charge of Jack's broadcasts. Haferkorn had already been responsible for most of the output, on the *Reichsrundfunk*'s 'Germany Calling' service, of the other British renegades in Berlin, most notably Norman Ballie-Stewart, the original 'Lord Haw-Haw' as identified by the *Daily Express* in September 1939, and William Joyce, who had subsequently inherited the title. Although Joyce's broadcasts were, by now, well known and widely listened to in Britain, Jack was scathing about the 'numerous other Englishmen in Berlin'. He complained that they had 'come to Germany on or before the declaration of war', and had subsequently 'adopted German nationality and considered themselves Germans'. As a result he believed that their 'views and outlook widely differed' from his own and that it was, in his opinion, 'quite insane to carry on as they did calling the British "the enemy" and so forth as was there (*sic*) custom'.[39]

Hesse and Jack now began work on the content of his talks. The propaganda value of having the son of a serving Cabinet minister broadcast from Berlin was, thought Hesse, inestimable. Although Joyce's talks were widely listened to in Britain, there is now general agreement that they were not taken particularly seriously, certainly not by the political elite. But Hesse correctly guessed that Jack would be listened to by at least one senior British politician, and it was therefore vitally important not to miss the opportunity to put across the desired message. They would 'put a lot of bad language into these talks to distract the ordinary people from understanding the real purpose of them', but if 'anyone of importance should listen to them in Britain he would infer that Germany was prepared to negotiate with Britain.' For that reason, there was to be 'no insult to Churchill' in the talks. Hesse duly 'suggested certain ideas' to Jack and 'asked him to submit me drafts', which he did.[40] Jack was sent to see Haferkorn to discuss the general content he was proposing and how the talks would fit in to Haferkorn's wider programme. The first broadcast was 'written and typed' by Jack himself, and then passed to Hesse, who in turn handed it on to Haferkorn for editing. It was decided that there were some aspects of the draft with which they disagreed, and Haferkorn then 'went over the manuscript' with Jack, and 'made certain suggestions to him, to which he agreed'. The finished version, together with a German translation, 'was then submitted to Ribbentrop, who took a personal interest in the matter and reserved his approval'.

Ribbentrop now gave the order for the broadcasts to go ahead. The time had come to bring Jack out of hiding and to announce his presence in Berlin to the world. Events moved quickly. He was first introduced to Eduard Dietze, the British-born head of the *Reichsrundfunk*'s English news service, in order to prepare a radio trailer promoting the talks. At the same time, the Propaganda Ministry's German News Service, Transocean, issued a press release. Three days later Jack went to the *Rundfunkhaus*, the headquarters of the radio station, to record his first talk under the watchful eye of Dr Haferkorn, who later recalled that Jack was so nervous that it was necessary for him 'to record this talk two or three times, before a suitable recording was made'.[41] Jack and Jeanine now moved to the Adlon Hotel in central Berlin and, when British-based news agencies got wind of Jack's presence there by way of Dietze's trailers, a reporter from the *Daily Mirror* confronted Leo in person on the doorstep of Eaton Square as to whether there was any truth in the allegations.

In London, on 17 November, Leo heard the 'unpleasant news from an American agency, afterwards confirmed by the Press Association', that Jack was indeed 'in Berlin, apparently staying at the Adlon'. What was worse, he appeared to have gone there 'by his own request before the Germans marched into unoccupied France'. More in hope than expectation, Leo tried to convince himself that the 'Gestapo had got hold of him and were bent on exploiting him in some way or other', possibly by 'trying to get him to say or do something foolish with the fear of the concentration camp over him.' He spoke to Brendan Bracken that evening, who 'promised to do what he could with the Press', but Leo knew that it was now too late to prevent the story becoming public. Ignorant of the degree to which Jack had brought about the situation himself, Leo resigned himself to hoping that his son would 'show some courage and that they give up the attempt to use him'.[42]

The following day Leo's worst fears were confirmed. Bracken had done his best, and most of the London papers had ignored the story, but *The Times* ran a short paragraph to the effect that 'so far as it has been possible to learn', Jack had indeed gone 'to Berlin at his own request some time before the German troops marched into the unoccupied zone'.[43] The *Daily Mirror* quoted from their snatched interview with Leo the previous day, highlighting in gruesome detail his ignorance as to Jack's true intentions. He had last heard of Jack 'through the Red Cross as an invalid', and it was 'just conceivable' that he had asked to go to Berlin 'for treatment for lung trouble'. He could 'not quite credit the German message', but nor could he confirm that Jack was still in the south of France 'because communication is still very difficult'.[44] The paper backed up its scoop with the assertion that not only was Jack in Berlin, he was there with the specific intention of broadcasting. And if Leo still had any lingering doubts as to his son's intentions, these were soon dispelled by the lead news story on the German News Service that morning. 'When John Amery heard in Berlin of the landings of Americans and British in Algiers and Morocco,' intoned the announcer, 'he decided to approach the Wilhelmstrasse with a request to be permitted to address his compatriots at home over the German wireless.' He had been in Berlin for three weeks, continued the Transocean story, and his 'presence there had been kept a dead secret'. At first, 'he wanted only to have talks and study conditions on the spot', but the 'attack on North Africa prompted him to come into the foreground'. His first broadcast would go out the following day.[45]

The irony of Jack laying the blame for his behaviour on the 'Operation Torch' landings in North Africa could not have been lost on Leo. He had himself 'urged this upon Winston in a memo'[46] the year before and, for several days, had closely followed the military progress in North Africa with his other Cabinet colleagues. Now he drew some comfort from those very colleagues. Beaverbrook called to commiserate. 'Thank you so much for what you said . . . and for what your papers have left unsaid,' replied Leo. 'I wish some of the other papers could have followed suit.'[47] And Churchill, on a visit with Leo to Harrow for the School Songs, assured him, perhaps with some personal feeling, that 'nobody could blame him for the aberrations of a grown up son.' Nevertheless, the truth was evident. As one colleague confirmed to him, the Germans were known to 'keep a whole bevy of people like Wodehouse, etc., at the Adlon Hotel to use for their wretched purposes', and they had now 'netted John to join them'. He could only hope that it would 'not be too awful', although 'the whole business was nearly unbearable.'[48]

Jack's first talk was aired twice during the evening of Thursday 19 November. Leo and Bryddie listened together to the first broadcast and were then joined by Julian, on his return from a dinner engagement, to listen again after midnight. The initial reaction of all three of them was one of confusion. They managed to convince themselves that it had not been Jack to whom they had been listening. His voice was 'low, soft and somewhat slurred', while what they had heard that evening was 'a hard, staccato voice by someone who had evidently done a good deal of speaking and broadcasting'. And, even if Jack had partly sympathised with the views expressed in the broadcast, 'the material and turn of phrase were also clearly not his.'[49] Leo telephoned Downing Street, leaving a message for Churchill assuring him that it had not been Jack on the radio at all, and reinforced the message the next morning with a letter to the Prime Minister. He had listened twice 'to what the German radio announced' as Jack's broadcast, and both he and Bryddie were 'convinced that it was not his voice but a voice of an entirely different character and that of a practised speaker and broadcaster'. The text had been 'the usual kind of anti-semitic diatribe put out by German propaganda headquarters to the effect that the Empire and our heritage are being vainly sacrificed for the benefit of the Jews and the Americans . . . I thought', concluded Leo, 'that you ought perhaps to know this.'[50]

While Leo, to some extent, and Bryddie in particular, remained in denial of Jack's treachery, the broadcast caused a good deal of interest in the press and within the innermost reaches of the British Security Service. While most of the broadcast had, indeed, been anti-Semitic 'incoherent drivel', a crucial passage in the middle of Jack's talk has subsequently been identified by at least one historian as a 'principal theme of Nazi propaganda aimed at Britain' at the time, namely Hitler's insistence that Germany was 'waging war, not on the British people, but on the small clique that rule them'. This passage 'was clearly the only part of Amery's speech which was inserted by the German Foreign Office', but its propaganda impact had been 'swamped by the sea of juvenile racism which surrounds it'.[51] At MI5 the same desk officer who had, a few months before, judged a firing squad to be suitable retribution for Jack's Grenoble article following the bombing of the Renault works, now took obvious pleasure in monitoring his output from Berlin. Warming to his earlier theme, he could not help wondering 'whether the influence of his unfortunate and much to be pitied father will save young Amery from the fate he so richly deserves'.[52]

Leo and Bryddie found themselves the object of widespread sympathy, especially among their friends and within political circles. And while one or two letters were received at Downing Street from the public, demanding Leo's resignation from the Cabinet, the majority of people shared the view of the Prime Minister that this was a personal tragedy, but not something for which Leo could be blamed. Julian, too, offered to resign his commission, an offer that was also turned down by his superiors at SOE. The day after Jack's first talk had gone out on British radio, Leo had an audience with the King, ostensibly to discuss generalities to do with India and, in particular, the appointment of the next Viceroy. However, he took the opportunity of broaching the subject of the previous night's broadcast and found that the King 'had just heard something, but was interested to hear the facts and very nice about it'. Other friends were 'very affectionate' and Leo was relieved to discover that, in spite of 'this slough of Despond', Jack's behaviour 'had rallied all [Leo's] friends to him in a wonderful way'.[53]

Only Beaverbrook seems to have shared Leo's original doubts as to the authenticity of the broadcasts. He had listened carefully, and had come to the conclusion that it had 'been done under some sort of duress'. 'The method of the broadcast' demonstrated that Jack had 'been driven to it by compulsion', and he did not see 'that anyone can resist compulsion if it is severe enough'.[54] But Leo soon had to accept the inevitable. He had 'more than once thought of a remark of old Clemenceau's', he wrote to Lady Milner, which she had once quoted to him about the wisdom of 'not having children'. They did not know what 'Jack had been cajoled or frightened into doing', but after his initial uncertainty that it had been Jack's voice, Leo now conceded that it would 'be futile to contradict' all the evidence.[55] Bryddie, on the other hand, remained firmly convinced of her son's absolute innocence. MI5 intercepted a letter she wrote at the time to a friend in Lisbon, who had looked after Jack during the time he had spent there. Jack, she believed, was now unfortunately 'in enemy hands'. She had listened 'very, very carefully', but she remained convinced that it was not his voice, nor did she 'believe him capable of writing the script'. He had endured a 'sad and horrid life', and she feared only 'to what use his father's honoured name will now be put'.[56]

After recording his first broadcast, and before transmission of the second, Jack was interviewed at the Adlon Hotel by a correspondent of the Transocean News Service. The published transcript provides the best possible proof of his brother Julian's assertion that he was indeed a 'congenital liar' who used to have 'difficulty telling the truth about the weather'.[57] 'This small, dark-haired man in [his] early thirties', who might well have been 'taken for a native of France' had, according to his interviewer, been proudly 'anti-Communist and anti-Semitic ever since he left Harrow'. Thanks to the 'Zionist leaders' he had met regularly at his father's house, he had had 'ample occasion to study the Jews', and had long since ceased to be surprised by newspaper accounts of the politics of Palestine when he realised that 'the British Press was virtually controlled by Jews.'

Throughout the rest of the article, every detail of his life up until that moment was inflated and exaggerated, each claim more ludicrous than the last, to satisfy his own sense of self-importance and, presumably, to justify his worth to his German hosts. He 'emphatically' denied that he had been 'fired from Eton school', but claimed that because of his high-profile 'anti-Communist and anti-Jewish attitude' he had been 'frequently shabbily attacked by the British press'. He had apparently visited Abyssinia, knew 'practically all the countries of

Europe', and had been in Madrid 'immediately after its liberation from the Red yoke'. He had 'rushed to Prague' in 1939 to witness the entry of German troops there, and had 'accompanied German panzers to Vienna in his Hispano-Suiza car'. During his stay in the south of France he had kept in contact with his family at home through the British Ambassador in Madrid, Sir Samuel Hoare, who had somehow become his godfather, while his single letter to the *Petit Dauphinois* had been transformed into a 'series of articles for the *Éclaireur de Nice*'. And while he harboured 'no political ambitions', when pressed he reluctantly conceded that he considered it his 'duty to tell the British people that they were not fighting for England as they believe'. Not content with destroying his own reputation, he dared claim that his father was happy that he was doing what he 'considers to be the right thing', and that indeed he had recently heard from him. 'You cannot expect an old man and Right Honourable like my father to find a way out of the old rut,' he asserted, 'but a large and growing number of young people in England are thinking the same way as myself.' Readers of the interview must have been relieved to find out that throughout it, 'his pet dog Sammy . . . was peacefully slumbering, curled up under his master's chair.'[58]

Over the next few weeks Jack recorded another nine talks for Hesse, each of them prepared in the same way as the first. Having written the first draft himself, he would pass on the text to Haferkorn for editing who, in turn, would seek final approval from Ribbentrop. But it soon became clear that neither party was happy with the arrangement. In among Jack's anti-Semitic and anti-Communist diatribes, Hesse continued to insist on 'camouflaging the political tendency' of the broadcasts. However, he was soon forced to admit that 'there was no response from Britain', while an unexpected complication was that 'the Japanese complained about the political tendency' of the talks.[59] Although Jack's broadcasts had aroused considerable interest within the confines of Whitehall, Hesse was correct in his assessment that they had made little impact on public opinion. The cause was twofold. While William Joyce was viewed as an accomplished broadcaster, Jack had little or no talent for either writing or broadcasting, and the majority of listeners considered his performances to be little more than 'screeching, incoherent rodomontades'.[60] According to contemporary Home Intelligence reports, his broadcasts for some reason aroused greatest comment in Scotland and Northern Ireland, while the most widely reported reactions were 'sympathy with his father, and condemnation of his anti-Jewish sentiments'.[61] The timing of the broadcasts was an additional problem. Jack complained to Hesse that it was 'absurd for me as an Englishman to talk about us all getting together if five minutes later from the same station another Englishman was to yell out abuse of my countrymen'.

After recording the first round of talks, Jack told Hesse that he 'desired to betake myself to Paris to talk these matters over with my French friends and to consider what next might be done under these circumstances'.[62] Hesse remembered events rather differently. He had, he claimed, sent Jack 'back to Paris, to have a good time and enjoy himself'.[63] Whatever the reason, by the time that the last of the seven talks that the Germans eventually decided to broadcast was aired on New Year's Eve 1942, Jack and Jeanine had already left Berlin for Paris. That same night, back at home in London, Leo was pondering the events of the past few weeks and his relationship with Jack. After so many years of provocation he had, at last, and with great regret, reached the fateful decision that there was now nothing more 'to be done but to shut one's mind to the degradation of it all and to steel oneself to going on as if he had never existed'.[64] The following week Leo called in on his solicitor and asked him to draw up new wills for himself and Bryddie, 'leaving Jack entirely out of the picture'. On 13 January 1943 Leo and Bryddie signed the new wills that left everything they owned to Julian after both of their deaths, thus disinheriting Jack for ever.[65]

On 17 November 1942 Jack and Jeanine booked themselves into the Hotel Bristol in Paris, supported no doubt by the almost unlimited expense account provided by Hesse at Ribbentrop's instigation. Jack had been a regular visitor to the hotel before the war, usually in the company of his father, who had stayed there during some of his visits to Paris. The hotel manager, M. Vidal, knew and admired Leo Amery and now had no trouble in recognising Jack, even when he booked in, once again, under the pseudonym John Brown. Vidal was to have ample opportunity to study Leo's son at close quarters during his frequent stays at the hotel over the next year and a half and, unsurprisingly, 'did not think highly' of Jack, believing that he was 'delicate and drank too much'.[66] The Bristol had already acquired a wartime reputation as a hotel for diplomats and, not only did it suffer no damage under German occupation, it was the only hotel in Paris which actually underwent restoration during the war. This standing was to attract accusations of collaboration against its owner after the war, but for Jack it provided the perfect milieu in which to mingle and to enjoy his newly acquired celebrity status.

Another resident at the time was P. G. Wodehouse, whom Jack had already befriended at the Adlon Hotel in Berlin. Wodehouse and his wife were to live at the Bristol for much of 1943 and 1944, during which time the writer received at least two substantial payments from the German Embassy. A discovery made after the liberation of Paris suggests not only that the two men became well known to each other, but that both may have been involved in giving more material aid to the Germans than has sometimes been supposed. In September 1944 Colonel Lord Victor Rothschild, by then in charge of SIS operations in Paris, wrote to Captain Guy Liddell at MI5 enclosing details of a discovery made by one of his agents, codenamed JIGGER, at the Hotel Lutetia, the former Paris headquarters of the Abwehr, the German Security Service. Not only had JIGGER found Jack's Abwehr identity card, number 1290, but he had also found evidence of meetings between Jack and a Captain Ameln of the Abwehr's *Zersetzung*, or 'decomposition', department. Furthermore, Jack had introduced Wodehouse to Ameln as a being a suitable recruit to carry out so-called decomposition work, and the writer had subsequently held a number of meetings with the German spy. While the full extent of Jack's, and indeed Wodehouse's, involvement with the Abwehr may never be known, such help would certainly have constituted a more serious charge against them both, and may help to explain Wodehouse's exile from Britain after the war.

Only once did Jack apparently face embarrassment, coming face to face in the lift with one of the hotel's most celebrated wartime customers. Mrs Dittenhofer, an American heiress in her own right who also happened to be married to a supermarket magnate, had divided her time before the war between Minnesota and her apartments at the Bristol and at Claridges in London, both rented by the year. Even when America had joined the war in the wake of the attack on Pearl Harbor, she had steadfastly refused to leave France and had been briefly interned outside Paris. Whether by bribery or by the sheer force of her personality, she had managed to secure her release from internment and had promptly booked herself back into a suite of rooms at the Bristol, where she was to stay for the remainder of the war. In 1934 her daughter had married the widowed Alfred Bossom, a parliamentary colleague of Leo's and a close friend of the Amery family. She knew Leo well and had met Jack on a number of occasions before the war, both in Paris and in London. While the precise details of their first meeting at the Bristol in 1943 are not recorded, she let it be known after the war that she had informed Jack, in no uncertain terms, what she thought of his behaviour.

▪ ▪ ▪

In Paris Jack quickly re-established himself in the company of Jacques Doriot and Marcel Déat, with whom he bemoaned the general lack of direction in Germany's war policy. 'We were very disturbed,' he complained bitterly. They saw themselves as 'partisans of a social revolution and of a getting together of all European nations', whereas the Germans 'were controlling Europe' and, rather than carrying out the hoped-for social revolution, 'were getting together with the reactionaries and what was worse the kind of people who were uniquely interested in getting rich quick at anybody's expense.' Inspired by his meetings with Doriot, he decided to return to Berlin, where he 'tackled Hesse again', and told him that it was now imperative to 'create a British anti-Bolshevik Legion however small'. 'If England saw that Europe was uniting against Bolshevism', promised Jack, 'she would come in as well.'[67]

It appears that Jack had first come up with the idea of an 'anti-Bolshevik Legion' of British volunteers, who would be engaged in fighting the Russians on the Eastern Front, in conversations with Doriot during his time in unoccupied France. In July 1941 Doriot had formed the Légion des Volontaires Français in Paris and Jack, enthused by the idea, had almost certainly suggested the idea of a similar British unit when he was first approached by the Germans in the summer of 1942. While Hesse had so far been primarily involved with Jack's propaganda broadcasts in Berlin, he admitted that on Jack's initial arrival there he had also 'received, through Ribbentrop, a direct order from the Führer to organise' a British Legion, as Hitler apparently 'thought it would have great propaganda value on the Eastern Front'. In spite of his personal reservations that such a unit could be made to work, Hesse duly obeyed orders and began to initiate plans for the recruitment and organisation of a British Legion, to be drawn from within the ranks of British prisoners of war in German camps. However, while the original idea might well have come from Jack, Hesse had not shared his view that he would himself be the best man to run the unit, and had recruited its leaders elsewhere. Jack, in the meantime, was 'kept in ignorance of what was really being done, as the whole affair of the British Free Corps was a first-class state secret'.

Unfortunately for Hesse, Jack 'frequently came back to the idea of creating such a body',[68] and he returned to Berlin in January 1943 unaware of Hesse's true plans. Instead, Hesse agreed with his suggestion that he should write a short book setting out his political ideas, and Jack duly settled down with Jeanine at the Kaiserhof Hotel to produce his masterpiece, *England Faces Europe*, in time for it to be published in Berlin in July 1943. The book is dismissed by one historian as a 'farrago of nonsense'.[69] In the words of another, it is 'an unedifying read, consisting of crude anti-Semitic insults dressed up in the high flown phrases of a semi-educated waster attempting to sound like a political commentator'. Nevertheless, it acts as 'a useful guide to the basic prejudices, hatreds and misconceptions that motivated' Jack at the time. Interestingly, the same historian describes Jack's political beliefs as 'an admixture of his father's progressive Imperialism, Jacques Doriot's Fascism and his own anti-Semitism'.[70] This judgement is confirmed by the diverse nature of the book's grandiose bibliography page, where Jack claims inspiration from, among other works, his father's *The Empire in the New Era*, Gibbon's *Decline and Fall of the Roman*

Empire, T. E. Lawrence's *The Seven Pillars of Wisdom* and, most fanciful of all, 'Secret State documents and information'.[71]

A German intelligence officer, Reinhard Spitzy, first met Jack and Jeanine on a train journey from Berlin to Paris in early 1943. He was asked by Jack's Foreign Office minders to look after the couple, and later described both the journey and his subsequent friendship with Jack in colourful detail. It was made clear to him that Jack was a 'real catch in propaganda terms', was 'valued extremely highly and was accordingly very heavily guarded'. Spitzy paints a portrait of Jack as a tormented man, 'frail, intelligent and typically English', a heavy drinker, who was prone to long bouts of depression. He was, at all times, determined to justify his behaviour on the grounds of his anti-Bolshevism, although he had 'no great affection for the Germans', and was 'rather half-hearted about the whole business'. Jeanine, on the other hand, was the life and soul of the party. A 'vivacious half-gypsy', she was an entertaining travelling companion, 'well-endowed, strikingly made up, outspoken and witty'. At Spitzy's request she sang, repeatedly, the French song 'Sur le Pont d'Avignon', which she 'trilled out with inimitable grace and ease'. Jack and Jeanine drank heavily throughout the journey and, from time to time, would retire to their sleeping compartment from where they would emerge after a short while, 'she evidently refreshed, he looking rather exhausted'.[72]

But a week after Jack handed in his manuscript at the end of March, disaster struck. 'On April the 7th to 8th', he recalled, 'my beloved friend and brave political revolutionary Jeanine Barde died.'[73] Behind this bland statement lies a bizarre story. Jack and Jeanine, known to Jack as 'Chicky', were well-known fixtures on the Berlin social scene, especially in the city's bars and clubs. They were regular visitors to the Foreign Press Circle, a bar on the Fasanenstrasse where the drink was heavily subsidised by the Ministry of Propaganda, and almost every contemporary statement about them at this time makes reference to their heavy drinking. They were often accompanied by Jack's minder Werner Plack, with whom they got drunk and who carried a ready supply of whisky for use when the bars were closed. Jeanine was considered eccentric by almost everyone who met her, while her appearance was also a frequent source of comment, as were her appalling table manners. Her heavily dyed black hair, dark eyes and plucked eyebrows were offset by thick red lipstick and nail varnish, all rounded off with copious amounts of imitation jewellery and an ankle bracelet. It was hardly surprising that the account of her death that did the rounds in Berlin at the time suggested that, having had a political quarrel with Jack at a party, she told him that she 'would rather die than live with him', whereupon he was supposed 'to have put some powder in her drink saying "Good luck to you", and the next morning she was dead'.[74]

The truth was more prosaic. Hesse later wrote up the report of an investigation carried out in Berlin by the Prosecutor-General of the Tribunal of the 1st Instance. During his interview, Jack agreed that they had both been drinking heavily at the Foreign Press Circle and claimed that, 'complaining of a headache', Jeanine had 'taken from her handbag a powder . . . carrying the inscription "Asciatine".' Having poured the powder into a glass of water, she 'said that she was going to poison herself', although Jack had thought the powder 'inoffensive' and had ignored the threat. Returning home to the Kaiserhof in the early hours of the morning, Jeanine had first collapsed at the tram stop, before Jack managed to get her home in a taxi where she 'was seized with a fit of vomiting', before he 'undressed her and put her into bed'. She had, by now, 'regained her calm and was breathing deeply', although Jack attributed that to her drunkenness; he took a sleeping pill himself and went to bed. When he woke at eleven o'clock the next morning, she was lying next to him, dead in her own vomit.

The German authorities were assiduous in carrying out a full autopsy on Jeanine's body, an examination of her blood-alcohol level and an analysis of the remaining powder. The 'results of the autopsy permitted the conclusion that death was due to the inhalation of stomach contents which had been vomited by the victim.' The concentration of alcohol in her blood was not, in itself, enough to have accounted for her death by alcohol poisoning alone, and 'all the organs examined revealed no other poison.' The expert conclusions of Professor Doktor Müller-Hess, Director of the Institute of Criminal and Legal Medicine at the University of Berlin, were, therefore, that Jeanine had died 'under the influence of alcohol, during the course of her sleep and as a result of her drunkenness'. She had been 'seized by a fit of vomiting and inhaled the material she had vomited'.

Jack was in the clear. His story had been believed and there 'was no evidence to support a criminal action'.[75] He does appear, however, to have been deeply shocked by what had happened. Although there is no evidence to suggest that he ever formally married her, a marriage which would have been bigamous anyway, he did refer to her through-out their relationship as his 'wife', while others preferred the more accurate description of her as his 'mistress'. His book, *England Faces Europe*, which was published later in the summer, contains a dedication to 'Jeanine, Who gave me the courage to go forward and without whose love nothing would ever have been undertaken, nothing ever accomplished. In gratitude.'[76] Jack accompanied her body back to Bergerac where, together with her parents and her seven-year-old daughter, he buried her. In a subsequent attempt at mitigation for the further acts of treachery he was about to commit, Jack later claimed that he was 'too distraught to pay any very great attention at the time'.[77]

After Jeanine's funeral he returned to Paris, where, however distraught he may have felt at her death, records at the Hotel Bristol reveal that just two weeks later he was staying there in the company of a new Parisian girlfriend, Michelle Thomas. It was during this stay in Paris that Jack committed what Leo was later to acknowledge was 'undoubtedly his most heinous offence' in British eyes, his 'attempt to create a British anti-Russian unit'.[78] Frustrated by Hesse's refusal to allow him a greater involvement in the British anti-Bolshevik Legion, on 20 April 1943 Jack decided to take matters into his own hands. With the help of the omnipresent Werner Plack, he visited the British internment camp at St Denis outside Paris in search of new recruits. Hesse knew nothing of the plan at the time and believed that Jack had 'blundered badly', enjoying 'no success whatever', while he had instigated 'a brawl at the camp, and numerous complaints about his and Plack's behaviour'. The visit had been 'quite unauthorised' and Hesse could only suppose that Jack and Plack were 'both almost continually under the influence of alcohol'.[79] MI5 officers were later able to secure numerous descriptions of the visit from angry internees.

Before Jack's arrival the German camp commandant had drawn up a list of some thirty-five internees, who were to be invited to meet Jack and hear his talk. The camp runner was then despatched to round them up, and each man was given a chit with his name on it to enable him to gain access to the visitors' hut, known as the T Hut because of its shape, where the meeting was to take place. Most of them apparently thought that they were to have a personal visit from a relative, but as word spread that something out of the ordinary was taking place, a number of internees forged their own chit and forced their way into the hut past the sentries outside. As the assembled crowd speculated among themselves as to why they had been summoned, Jack made a dramatic entrance with Plack, surrounded by about half-a-dozen members of the Gestapo in civilian clothes, several German officers in uniform, and the camp commandant. Jack himself was wearing a trench overcoat and a black trilby and, after making his way to the front of the crowd, he addressed his audience from a small stage.

He began by informing the internees that he was Leo's son and that he was there to recruit 'for a body known as the Legion of St George, which was a fighting force being formed in Berlin to take up arms against the Russians'. It already boasted '1500 volunteers which included three British aircraft and crews which had been flown to Germany by RAF deserters', and there were 'thousands of people in prison in Great Britain' who were 'only too anxious to join'. The Legion would be engaged solely on the Eastern Front against Russian forces and there 'was no question of volunteers being used against British troops'.[80] If any of those assembled wished to join, they would 'leave the camp immediately', and 'never come into it again'. They would have to 'wear German uniform', and would 'have German officers', but they would also be commanded by 'non-commissioned officers who are English or British'.[81] From the very outset the talk was ill-received and his audience subjected Jack to a barrage of hostile questions, none of which he answered to their satisfaction.

Unfortunately for Jack, matters now went from bad to worse. One of the internees at St Denis was his old sparring partner from the American Consulate in Nice, Wilfred Brinkman, who had been interned the month before, following the German occupation of the unoccupied zone. Brinkman was not on the original invitation list, but had heard rumours that the lecture was to take place and had already decided that he would do his best to break it up. Among his friends in St Denis were the Paris representatives of Tiffany's and Thomas Cook, both of whom claimed to have been swindled by Jack in the past, and to have it on absolute authority that Jack had been forced to leave London because of his involvement in the 'Mayfair Boys Cartier case'. As soon as Brinkman heard that Jack was in the camp, he forced his way into the meeting and began to heckle. He started by asking whether Jack recognised him, which he said he did, and then asked if he 'remembered his friend Ogilvie – which put him out of his coun-tenance'. He demanded to know what Jack was doing there, to which he received the same reply as had been given earlier, namely that he was 'explaining the advantages of joining in the fight against Bolshevism' by joining the Legion of St George, which already numbered 1,500 men recruited from prison camps and the three four-engined bombers which had flown over from England complete with their crews. To questions as to what would happen to any of the volunteers who were taken prisoner themselves, and what would be their fate once Britain had won the war, Jack was unable to provide answers. And when Brinkman asked if the assembled men realised 'that they would be traitors to their country, as [Jack] was', the meeting began to disintegrate, Jack promising that he would provide some literature that would further explain what he had been talking to them about.

As the other men filed out of the hut, Jack asked Brinkman to stay behind, suggesting that he 'seemed to misunderstand his position'. After a short argument about the true nature of Jack's past activities in Nice, he begged Brinkman 'not to mention in the camp anything that would appear derogatory to him'. Brinkman replied that that was precisely what he intended to do and, when Jack offered to shake his hand, ended the interview by replying that he was 'not in the habit of shaking hands with traitors'.[82] Outside the hut, mayhem ensued. Most of those who had attended were furious that they had been selected in the first place, imagining, correctly as it turned out, that their attendance would prejudice their position and reputation with their fellow detainees. By the end of the talk, a sizeable crowd had gathered outside the hut, and those who had been among the audience were roundly booed by their fellow inmates as they left. When Jack followed a few minutes later, he too was booed, while a few stones were thrown and isolated scuffles broke out. Jack seemed unperturbed, doffing his hat to the hecklers.

Most of those who had attended the meeting signed a statement objecting forcefully to their involvement, while the Camp Committee representing the interests of the internees posted a notice of protest on the camp's bulletin board that same afternoon. 'The Committee of this camp', they complained, 'wish to place on record that they had no prior knowledge of, nor were they invited to attend' the meeting that had been held that morning. Furthermore, they 'strongly resented the presence in the camp of Mr Amery', and had since 'advised the Camp Commandant' of the feeling 'of general disapproval of all internees'. The notice was signed by the Camp Secretary, G. D. Pugh, the Camp Adjutant, C. F. Hadkinson, and the Camp President, G. Fletcher.[83] How far their protest was genuine or merely a cover for their own connivance in Jack's visit is uncertain. According to the statements of other internees, Hadkinson, who was the Red Cross liaison officer, was thought to be a collaborator himself and 'had his own car, complete freedom and spoke fluent German', and was 'believed to go to a flat he owned in Paris' whenever he liked; Pugh was allowed to visit the Swiss Legation in Paris at any time to carry on his black market trading; while Fletcher was viewed as an 'errand boy of the Germans'.[84]

Whether genuine or not, the protests of the Camp Committee went unheeded. A selection of leaflets and posters advertising the Legion of St George was distributed around the camp and, a few days later, Jack and Plack returned to see what progress had been made and to interview any candidates who it was thought might be suitable targets for recruitment. Only two internees appear to have shown any interest in Jack's proposals, both apparently recruited by another internee with strong collaborationist tendencies, the camp's interpreter Oswald Job, already the object of widespread suspicion throughout the camp. Indeed, Job was later executed for treachery in 1944. Kenneth Berry, a sixteen-year-old merchant seaman from Cornwall, had left school at thirteen and gone to sea as a deck boy, only for his ship to be sunk in September 1940 and for him to be taken prisoner and interned at St Denis. 'Ill-educated and slightly dim-witted', Berry soon fell under the spell of Job who 'used him as a gopher around the camp, thus arousing the suspicion of other inmates and further isolating him'.[85] He had not been to Jack's original lecture, but was now taken to see him at a house nearby, where Jack was introduced to him as 'Mr John Amery, the Foreign Secretary of England'.[86] Jack offered him the chance to join the Legion and gave him a week to make up his mind.

Berry eventually agreed to join up, along with another young man, Jean Tunmer, who had previously been interned at Vittel and later claimed that he had only agreed to join as he thought it would provide a means of escape. Berry, on the other hand, apparently succumbed to the blandishments of Job who promised him a good time and a ready supply of food, clothes and women. Berry duly left the camp with Tunmer, Job and an elderly academic called George Logio, who was later to end up at the University of Sofia. Tunmer and Berry spent a few days living the high life at the former's flat in Montmartre, before Tunmer was taken away by two men in civilian clothes who called there one day. When Jack arrived at the flat later he was surprised to find that Tunmer had gone, and told Berry that it was no longer safe for him to remain there. He called the Gestapo and three officers came to remove Berry, who was kept in detention for about eight weeks. The sixteen-year-old Berry was to be the only real recruit for Jack's British Legion of St George, and even the MI5 officers who were later to have the job of prosecuting Jack, recognised that 'in view of the fanciful language' used by him in his recruiting efforts, 'he was bound to fail in his project'.[87]

Hesse now summoned Jack back to Berlin, well aware that during his stays in France he had 'caused constant trouble to the German authorities by his drunken habits and general activities', and fed up with the extortionate bills he had to pick up to fund Jack's lifestyle. Almost worse for the German propagandists, it was by now clear that 'no-one took him seriously'.[88] Nevertheless, it was important to find him something to do. At first he was offered the job of news editor for a new English language broadcasting service, Radio National, shortly to be launched by the German Foreign Office. Although Jack claimed that his appointment was blocked by William Joyce, the truth was that it soon became clear that he was neither up to the job, nor particularly keen to do it. In fact, all that Joyce had done was correctly to warn the authorities that Jack was 'irresponsible and that his playboy past would nullify his propaganda'.[89] Instead Jack set himself up in Berlin with Michelle Thomas, who he claimed to have married at the German Consulate in Paris on 4 October. If he did indeed go through some sort of marriage ceremony, based on the assumption that Jeanine's death had freed him from any previous alliance, then bigamy must be added to the charge sheet against him, since he had never been divorced from Una in the first place.

Jack now embarked on his secondary career on behalf of his German masters, that of celebrity lecturer and occasional broadcaster in the occupied territories. In November 1943 he spent five days in Belgrade at the invitation of General Milan Nedic, the leader of the pro-German Serbian government. During the visit, accompanied by Counsellor von Losch from the German Foreign Office, Jack was 'able to have numerous contacts with Serbian people both of the so-called aristocratic and merchant classes'. He had concentrated on those who were still 'neutral or else still hypnotised with the idea that their salvation would come from London'. His visit had, he boasted, come 'at a very opportune psychological moment, precisely when Mihailovic was being abandoned by the allies in favour of Tito'. With his usual arrogance and flimsy grasp of reality, he hoped that his visit 'may have added a little weight in the balance of the decisions that Mihailovic seems to be taking to collaborate with Germany now'.[90]

The highlight of his visit was a key-note speech at Belgrade University on 17 November. 'The ties between my family and Serbia date back far into the past,' he claimed, 'and in my childhood my father often used to tell me stories of Serbia's liberation from the Ottoman Empire. Thus it was fated that your country and your people should always have a special attraction for me.'[91] If Jack's analysis of his own role and importance was not wholly accurate, he had, nevertheless, correctly identified the contemporary tensions within Yugoslav politics. Yet he could not possibly have known at the time of the prominent role that had already been played, and was still to be played, by both his brother and his father on the opposite side of the political argument there; of Julian's time in Belgrade and his close association with opposition leaders; of his role in 'Operation Bullseye' in landing British liaison officers in Montenegro; of his conversation with Churchill, to take place just a month later in Cairo, discussing the relative merits of Tito and Mihailovic with the other young British officers involved in the region. And was Jack told in Belgrade about Leo's broadcasts to the Yugoslavs, urging them to take their lead from the heroes of the Battle of Kosovo and to rise up against their German masters?

Jack and Michelle returned to Berlin in time to be caught up in one of the worst Allied bombing raids of the war. He appears to have helped to try to extinguish the fires that destroyed the Kaiserhof Hotel, where they were staying, but later recorded only that he was 'granted a distinction for exceptional bravery in that affair', but lost most of his belongings.[92] They returned once again to Paris where Jack gave a speech, alongside Marcel Déat, on 29 December, remembered chiefly by one of those present for the passage in which he argued that 'the victory of the German armies was necessary in order that small children shall no longer be the victims of the Jews'.[93]

In January 1944 he visited Prague, and in February he was to be found in Norway, spending a fortnight there on a trip which he felt 'can only be described as most exceedingly satisfactory', and which 'caused a most extraordinary sensation'. He spoke in a number of towns, ending up in Oslo, and ascribed his great success to Norway's close relations with England and the fact that 'almost everybody speaks English'. He reported that he had given 'heart and courage to the members of Quisling's party', and had been praised by President Quisling himself for having been 'a great help to him and the friends of Germany'. He had left Norway 'in a storm of applause and enthusiasm such as I had not hoped for'.[94]

In March Jack and Michelle visited Belgium, where he spoke in Antwerp, Ghent and Brussels, a visit during which the only surviving photographs of him addressing a public meeting were taken. In April and May 1944 he embarked on a speaking tour of France, taking in Dijon, Lyon, Marseilles, Nice, Monte Carlo, Toulouse, Bordeaux, Poitiers, Nantes, Rennes, Rheims, Lille and Paris itself. A flavour of these rallies can be gauged from the description of one onlooker who attended the lecture in Lyon, at the Salle Molière, where Jack addressed an audience of some 300 people, including many German officers in uniform. After a short introduction in English, he spoke in fluent French for an hour while being filmed at the same time. The speech dealt with 'Bolshevism, Jews and slums in London', and praised the German army as the 'best in the world', ready for any invasion that might come. He launched a 'personal attack on Mr Churchill' – a far cry from Hesse's earlier caution – and reiterated that he could not agree with fighting the Russians. He 'spoke of the King in derisory terms as "Le Roi Bégayant" [the Stammering King] and of Roosevelt as the "Syphillitique Président" '. He finished by giving a Nazi salute and saying 'Heil Hitler'.[95]

In between these various trips around France, Jack also found time to broadcast on the radio and to try to resurrect his old contacts with the Wehrmacht-run version of the Legion of St George, now known as the British Free Corps. He met one of its senior officers, Thomas Cooper, at the Kaiserhof late in 1943, Cooper bringing with him both Berry and another officer, a New Zealander called Roy Courlander. Jack was desperate to achieve 'Fachführer rank', but Cooper reported that his 'reputation was so unsavoury that I did not want him anywhere near me or the Corps'.[96] When another Free Corps officer, John Brown, met Jack at the Adlon in June 1944, Jack first got drunk and then urged Brown to let him work with him to enlarge the Corps. Jack was furious that at first Brown seemed to have no idea who he was. Ironically, Jack could not even persuade the true traitors, who were already actually fighting alongside the German army, to let him join them. Perhaps it had something to do with Courlander's boast that Jack's 'connection with the unit was easily severed by pointing out to the SS that he was partly Jewish'.[97] Nevertheless, by and large he was happy with his lot. 'I have at last found my right place in this war', he reported to Hesse, and 'at last I am in something I understand and at which, I think I can claim, I excel.'[98]

Hesse, unfortunately for Jack, did not agree. He had received widespread reports from throughout Europe of Jack's heavy drinking and excessive extravagance. Spitzy recalled seeing him in the Foreign Press Club in 1944, 'absolutely paralytic and incapable of conducting a reasonable conversation'. It was clear that, since Jeanine's death, he had 'taken more and more to the bottle', and was 'plagued by increasingly dark depressions'. Jack's heavy drinking was treated almost 'as a state secret',[99] and he continued to be well looked after by his German masters, a fact that clearly rankled with the more accomplished, but less well-treated, Joyce, 'Lord Haw-Haw'. His working conditions were, throughout his time in Berlin, considerably worse than Jack's. 'If I were a quarter Yid, like Amery, I should be rolling in luxury', he mused, 'but I made the mistake of beginning as a National-Socialist. The Germans are a funny people.'[100]

Hesse decided that from now on Jack would play no further role of any substance in German plans and, in view of the impending invasion, should also 'leave France to the military'. Jack was 'grieved and surprised', sensing the hand of Ribbentrop behind the decision, but he returned to Berlin, as ordered. He moved to Gatow, a suburb of Berlin, from where he watched the drama of the unsuccessful attempt to assassinate Hitler unfold around him, and 'thought things pretty hopeless'. Apart from the odd broadcast on radio to let the world know of his existence, 'because it was being thought I was a prisoner of the Gestapo', he was largely unemployed and, at the end of September, leapt at an 'invitation from the Italian Government telling me that Mussolini wanted to see me'. A month later he met Mussolini at Lake Garda where 'contrary to what has often been said he was in good health and we talked for several hours.' Jack claimed that Mussolini, 'who had after all been responsible for organising the Peace of Munich', now 'felt himself capable of . . . obtaining the peace we had for long years been seeking.' Jack was apparently invited to help him and duly began a series of talks 'in Italian to the Italians over the Republican network', and gave speeches in Genoa, Turin and Milan. 'With Mussolini's gathering efforts', he reported, 'we seemed to be making some practical progress.'

Jack's 'progress' was briefly interrupted by what seems to have been a hoax message that he should go back to Berlin and, in the course of his visit, he attended the funeral of his old friend Jacques Doriot. He returned to see Mussolini in Milan in April 1945, but the military situation had become so dire that it was decided that they should take to the mountains along the Swiss border above Lake Como, where there would be a 'sufficient number of idealists who were willing to sacrifice a great deal', and would 'never surrender unconditionally or to the local Communists'. Mussolini went so far as to offer Jack a commission in his *Brigada Nera*, but this was a step too far, even for him, 'because such an acceptance might involve me firing on my fellow countrymen and this I was unwilling to do'. However, he agreed to accompany Mussolini and left Milan on the evening of 25 April. 'Two-thirds of the way along the autostrada to Como', Jack and Michelle were 'surrounded by partisans and made prisoner.'[101] 'They stopped me,' he complained disdainfully, 'dragged me out, stole my car', and then 'tore the fur coat off Michelle Thomas's – my wife's – back.'[102] It was to be the beginning of the end.

CHAPTER TWENTY-ONE

But I Am Your Son

During the two and a half years that Jack had spent touring occupied Europe in the pay of his German masters, MI5 officers on special secondment had, slowly but surely, been building the case against him from their temporary headquarters at the War Office in Parliament Street, Whitehall. Since he had first come to their attention, by writing to the *Petit Dauphinois* newspaper in Grenoble, they had monitored his broadcasts, taken first-hand witness statements from released British prisoners who he had tried to recruit to the Legion of St George, and used the extensive network of MI6 agents throughout Europe to trace his movements and monitor his lectures. Unbeknown to Jack himself and, indeed, it would seem, to his father and brother too, he had, by the time of his capture by Italian partisans in April 1945, become one of the most high-profile targets on the wanted list of British renegades. Interestingly, there is no evidence that either Leo or Julian used their respective Cabinet or SOE contacts even to make enquiries of the authorities as to Jack's status, or what progress was being made in his pursuit. One can only assume that they already understood the seriousness of his situation and had lost all hope of a happy outcome.

Jack's high-profile support for Mussolini in early 1945 ensured that, even before his capture, the advancing British troops were aware of his presence in Italy. On 16 April the 15th Army Group sent a telegram to Allied Forces Headquarters (AFHQ), informing them that Jack was likely to fall into partisan hands in the very near future and, 'in view of [the] record of Amery Junior, requesting guidance as to his treatment in case of capture'. AFHQ's immediate reply was that Jack's name appeared on the Central Security War Black List, and that he should be 'taken into the custody of the British authorities immediately'. He was, from now on, to be referred to by his MI5 codename, WARBLE 869.[1] Two days later MI5 was informed that his arrest was imminent and, on 29 April, Reuters put out a story on the wires that he was, indeed, in the hands of Italian partisans. On 1 May the partisans finally confirmed his capture in a statement: 'From the General Command of the Freedom Volunteer Corps: In the Novarese, a brigade of the Freedom Volunteers has arrested the British citizen John Amery – we repeat John Amery.' The 'General Command' had ordered that he was to be 'immediately transported to Milan to be handed over to the General Command' there.[2] In many ways Jack and Michelle had been lucky. Mussolini and his mistress Clara Petacci had been captured two days after Jack and shot by their captors on the way back to Milan. Jack and Michelle had, at least, escaped that fate and were now languishing in the San Vittore prison in Milan.

In London Leo greeted the news with dismay. The war in Europe was all but over, but in India the Viceroy, under Leo's instructions, was still locked in crucial negotiations that would determine the country's future. Two weeks before the news of Jack's arrest, Leo had been at a special Cabinet meeting, attended by the Dominion Prime Ministers, to discuss what action should be taken against alleged war criminals. Churchill had been 'dead against trying the Nazi leaders and all for just killing them outright', while Leo's old friend and Jack's godfather, John Simon, had 'pointed out that nothing short of some sort of trial would satisfy either the Americans or Stalin'. Leo had mused that 'Stalin enjoys trials and would no doubt secure from Hitler a lurid confession of his sins', but in the end he had supported a compromise solution, put forward by Cripps and Smuts, that there should be 'some formal arraignment',[3] with an opportunity for a written reply from the accused before any action was taken. He can hardly have failed to participate in such a debate without his mind wandering to the prospect of his own son's arrest and likely prosecution.

The day after Jack's arrest Leo went to see the Home Secretary, Herbert Morrison, to find out if there was 'any possibility of the wretched Jack's being tried out in Italy'. Morrison was 'doubtful though sympathetic'; indeed all his friends, recorded Leo, had 'been wonderful'.[4] The following day Morrison confirmed that it was inevitable that Jack would be brought home for trial, but that it would almost certainly take place after what now seemed likely to be an early general election. Leo accordingly offered to step down from any post-war reconstructed government but, once again, Churchill waved away the suggestion. On 23 May, two weeks after VE Day, and with the Labour Party refusing to preserve the coalition until after the defeat of Japan, Churchill tendered his government's formal resignation to the King and was invited to form a new government prior to a general election on 5 July. Two days later, on the very day that Jack came face to face with his British accusers in Italy for the first time, Churchill asked Leo to carry on at the India Office, flattering him that he was the only person who could deal adequately with the complex issues there.

On 3 May, MI5 sent a telegram to AFHQ, referring to recent press reports that Jack was now in Italian custody and urgently requesting that 'you take this man into British custody as soon as possible.'[5] The request was taken up by an enterprising young British officer, Captain Alan Whicker, in later years to become a celebrated television presenter and travel journalist. As an eighteen-year-old army officer, Whicker had joined the Army Film and Photo Unit, and had followed the Allied advance as it made its way through Italy. He had filmed at Anzio, met Montgomery and was now in Milan, having recently witnessed the surrender of the SS there. Now, with a nose for a good story, Whicker made his way to the local radio station, where he told them to broadcast an announcement asking for details of Jack's whereabouts. Within minutes he had received a message telling him which of the local prisons Jack was being held in, and he made his way there with an army sergeant and demanded that Jack be handed over. ' "Thank God you're here" said a very pale Amery when led into the Governor's office with his girlfriend, an appealing brunette in a dark trouser suit. "I thought they were going to shoot me." '[6] While they waited for the military police to arrive Whicker took some photographs and chatted with Jack, who once again insisted that he 'had never said anything against Britain', but 'was merely against the Russians'. Forty years later, Whicker was to muse that while he 'was proved wrong at that moment, subsequently, you might say he was proved right'.[7]

The photographs of Jack and Michelle being taken into custody were flashed around the world. On the morning of the Thanksgiving Service at St Paul's Cathedral, to celebrate the victory in Europe, Leo and Bryddie were horrified to see the 'awful picture of Jack in the *Sunday Express*', and it 'required courage to go at all' as 'poor B. dreaded it'.[8] Jack and Michelle were handed over to the Intelligence Corps and were sent first to Florence, and then on to 'R' Internee Camp at Terni, in northern Italy, where they were formally placed in military custody. MI5, meanwhile, had made arrangements for an interrogation team to fly out to Italy and, a few days later, Major Leonard Burt, a Scotland Yard detective on secondment to MI5 from the Murder Squad, travelled to Terni accompanied by a Captain Fish of the Intelligence Corps. They went first to the radio station in Milan where they confiscated twelve recording discs containing Jack's Italian broadcasts. Then, on 22 May, they arrived at the camp to interview Jack, to be greeted by him wearing 'a black shirt, black riding boots and greyish-green riding breeches'. Jack began by making a verbal statement, but when Burt suggested that it would be better in writing, he readily agreed, insisting 'I am a journalist. Give me a typewriter and paper, and I will type it out.' Burt requested that he 'embody the form of caution in his statement', which Jack duly did and began typing.[9]

Leonard Burt went on to have a long and distinguished post-war career in the police force, and Lord Victor Rothschild, who worked alongside him for MI5 during the war, described him as 'a brilliant and subtle interrogator' who enjoyed a 'reputation of being the most formidable sleuth in England'.[10] He was known for coaxing confessions out of his victims by putting them completely at ease and, in the case of Jack, he certainly enjoyed outstanding success. For two days Jack sat at his typewriter, producing an eleven-page statement in which he describes, with almost cheerful abandon, his activities over the past two years as broadcaster, recruiting sergeant and lecturer for his German masters. The apparent innocence of some of his concluding remarks is almost beguiling. He defied anyone to find in his speeches, on the 'radio or otherwise', in his 'conversations in private' and in anything he had written, 'one single word against my country'. His actions had been at all times 'anti-Bolshevik, guided by the certainty that Russia was a far greater danger to England than Germany as she stood at the end of 1942'. And, demonstrating a breathtaking ignorance of the seriousness of his situation, he suggested 'to the political and intelligence departments of His Majesty's Government' that, 'in some form or other I can still carry on my life's political work and render very considerable services to my country.'[11] Burt knew immediately that his statement was 'the full and complete case for the prosecution', and would be 'enough to hang him without a word from the Crown'.[12]

Jack chain-smoked throughout his interview with Burt and his mood fluctuated wildly. When he described how he had contracted tuberculosis and had been refused permission by the Vichy authorities to be repatriated to England, Burt 'felt sorry for him'. As Jack described how he could never forgive those authorities, nor indeed the British Government for siding with Russia during the war, Burt noted that his 'thin, handsome face flushed with fury'. And when he recalled his efforts to escape the censorship of his German masters he would bang the table, 'with one of those sudden bursts of fierceness which made him at once pathetic and attractive'.[13] Finally, to Burt's evident bemusement given the seriousness of the charges against him, he became obsessed with his missing possessions. The Italian colonel in command of the unit that had captured him 'undertook at the time to have returned my personal property that was seized by the partisans when they arrested me.' To date, he continued, 'of this nothing has so far been seen it consists of:

1 suit case (Important documents and personal effects)
1 overcoat
1 Fur coat and two silver foxes
A 20 liter petrol tin full
1 Lancia Aprilia motor car No. 78410 M1 C.D. I.'[14]

Burt was so taken by this bizarre request and, more probably, the prospect of finding incriminating diaries, that he actually travelled both to their headquarters in Milan and to Lake Como to seek out the partisans who had captured Jack and to try to track down these possessions. He managed to find nothing of importance, and was forced to conclude that they 'had helped themselves to the lot'.[15]

■ ■ ■

While Jack continued to languish in his internment camp in northern Italy, back home in London the world was preparing for a general election. Julian returned home on 2 June, having spent the last few months of the war in China, serving on the staff of General Carton de Wiart, Churchill's personal representative on the staff of Generalissimo Chiang Kai-shek. On his return from Albania he had pleaded with Lord Selborne to be allowed to continue his work for SOE, even though the war in Europe was apparently close to conclusion. He had suggested that he be sent to China to boost SOE's representation there and to see what could be done to prevent the 'uneasy truce between Chiang Kai-shek and Mao Tse-tung developing into a gigantic Far Eastern version of the struggle between Mihailovic and Tito or Abas Kupi and Enver Hoxha'. The opportunity to accompany General Carton, thanks to a chance meeting, naturally, at Eaton Square, made up Selborne's mind for him and Julian duly accompanied the General to China, by way of Cairo, Aden, Karachi, Kandy and Calcutta.

Julian's brief sojourn in China was not a success. He found the military and political situation there depressing in the extreme. The longstanding Japanese occupation of vast areas of the most developed parts of the country had left the government of Chiang Kai-shek with what little remained, while he soon realised that Chiang exercised limited authority, even over his own generals. Similarly, in spite of American efforts to achieve a long-term settlement between Chiang's ruling Kuomintang party and the Communist army of Mao Tse-tung, Julian could see little prospect of such an agreement being reached. His own efforts to act as a go-between were not welcomed by either side, while his time in China 'opened his eyes to another and more immediate threat', which was the 'unconcealed hostility of the United

States to European interests in the Far East'. It was, he thought, 'Washington's firm intention to break down the Colonial system throughout the Far East so as to open the area to American trade and investment.'[16] Worse still, they did not care how it was done. Although General Carton, who had a black patch over an empty eye socket, used to refer to Julian as his 'missing eye', in truth he struggled to find a role during these last six months of the war. SOE headquarters in London had subsequently, under American pressure, agreed to concentrate their efforts in South East Asia, leaving China to the United States, and it was with a sense of relief that Julian eventually decided to return home in time for the general election.

Looking back on his wartime service, Julian had good cause to feel satisfied. His war has been aptly described as 'distinguished if unconventional',[17] although the fact that he was the son of a famous father has led at least one historian to judge that he deliberately set out to avoid regular army service. But the accusation that he 'was allowed to swan around the Middle East solely because he was the son of a Cabinet Minister' is unfounded.[18] Perhaps it is true that he was overly romantic about his own role and, in spite of the frequent frustrations of time spent in London and Cairo, it is true that he looked back on the wartime years as a period of his life which he had largely enjoyed, in spite of the occasional danger and discomfort. However, throughout the war his only real desire was to get back into the action and to serve in a part of the world he understood politically. Likewise, there can be no doubting his bravery in the field, Billy McLean, with whom he served in Albania, supposedly saying that there 'was nobody better in battle than Julian'.[19] Denis Healey was later to describe him, appropriately enough given Leo's friendship with John Buchan, as 'nostalgic for the life of Richard Hannay',[20] and it is probably true to say that his military career, if 'not highly successful, was adventurous, and adventure was something he craved'.[21]

During one of his wartime stays in Cairo, in the autumn of 1943, Julian had been in the Mohammed Ali Club late one night when he ran into the Prime Minister's son, Randolph Churchill. Randolph, at the time one of the two Members of Parliament for Preston, told him, somewhat proudly, that his fellow Member so disapproved of him that he was not prepared to contest the seat again. Would Julian be interested in joining him? Randolph soon went off to join Fitzroy Maclean in Yugoslavia, while Julian left for Albania where, a few months later, he received a letter, by parachute drop, from the chairman of the Preston Conservative Association, confirming the invitation to stand as their candidate, alongside Randolph Churchill, at the next general election. The letter was already badly out of date but, with the help of his father, he managed to delay giving his decision until he next found himself in London.

However, in December 1944, having returned from Albania and in the midst of preparations for his trip to China, the decision could be put off no longer. He had 'first to decide whether to stand at the next election at all', so 'out of sympathy was he with much contemporary Conservative thinking.' What was more, his friends and family had warned him 'against the perils of trying to work in harness with Randolph', who was known to be 'quarrelsome, overbearing and selfish'. They all 'begged him to stand almost anywhere but Preston'.[22] Leo, while sharing the reservations of others about Randolph Churchill, tried hard to persuade Julian that the sooner he got into Parliament, the sooner he could influence the party's policies, but Julian remained uncertain where his true political loyalty really lay. In an effort to decide, he went to seek the advice of Hugh Dalton, his former chief at SOE and now a Labour minister, to whom he confessed that he did not 'think he agreed with the Conservative Party on most things'.[23] Nevertheless, two days before leaving for China, he made the journey to Preston for the first time and was duly adopted as their parliamentary candidate.

Julian had not been in Chungking long before Leo, at Winston Churchill's behest, was writing to urge him to come home to begin preparations for the general election. The Prime Minister was becoming increasingly agitated at the absence of both Julian and his own son Randolph. 'You must get Julian back soon,' he told Leo in April, conceding that, in spite of his exhortations, Randolph would only return 'if he isn't in a bad temper'.[24] On 30 April Churchill cabled Randolph in Rome, urging him to return and admitting that he was 'rather worried about Julian Amery being away in Chungking'.

Having repeated his request to Leo two weeks later, he again contacted Randolph, who was by now in Belgrade, reminding him that the time between an election being called and polling day would be short, and that 'very hard work will be required to educate the constituency.' He reinforced the urgency of the situation by reminding Randolph that Leo 'and others have telegraphed Julian Amery here pointing out that he should return at once'.[25]

Sure enough, by the time Julian arrived back from Chungking, Parliament had already been dissolved and the campaign was in full swing. The Prime Minister had decided to fight much of the election over the radio waves, wisely as Leo had thought at first. However, when he and Bryddie sat down to listen to Churchill's first broadcast, on 4 June, he was one of many thousands of electors who found themselves deeply disturbed by it. It was hardly surprising. In a speech which was to become notorious, Churchill attacked his former coalition partners for putting party before country by their withdrawal from the National Government and told voters that a Labour Government, if elected, 'would have to fall back on some kind of Gestapo, no doubt very humanely directed in the first instance'.[26] Churchill's wife, when she saw the 'odious and invidious reference to the Gestapo', is said to have begged him to delete the passage from the speech,[27] while Leo was 'greatly depressed by it'. He understood that many members of the armed forces returning home would have only one thing on their minds, and that the greatest stress should have been put on 'urgent measures of demobilisation and housing'. Instead, Churchill had 'jumped straight off his pedestal as world statesman to deliver a fantastical exaggerated onslaught on Socialism', and seemed determined to fight on the 'purely negative tack of the Socialist bogey'. Leo blamed Beaverbrook and Bracken, and thought back nostalgically, as 'a rather weary Sisyphus', to 1922 when the anti-Socialist agenda had been the very reason for his break with Lloyd George.[28] Julian, too, listened to the broadcast with dismay, although as he did so in the company of Randolph Churchill, who had seen, and apparently approved, the speech in advance, he did his best to conceal it. He was unhappy at 'the violence of Churchill's invective which seemed out of tune with the country's mood'[29] and, when he listened with his parents to Attlee's broadcast the following evening, Leo thought Julian 'considerably impressed' and feared that he 'had considerable searchings of heart as to whether he was really on the right side'.[30]

Julian and Randolph's campaign in Preston was colourful, to say the least. They drove up to the constituency in a 'large open car, lent to Randolph by King Peter of Yugoslavia' and with a boot filled with champagne, which set the tone for the rest of the campaign. Surprisingly, in spite of all earlier warnings, the two got on well. From Randolph's point of view, 'a more suitable partnership could hardly have been arranged'. Julian was a few years younger than Randolph, and his inexperience at campaigning 'made him, if not exactly pliable, at least receptive to his ideas'.[31] Julian, on the other hand, had liked Randolph since they had first met at the Oxford Union before the war, and he found that he had a 'lively intelligence, an astonishing memory and was a very stimulating companion'. He had feared an argument over the content of their election address, but instead found him 'very conciliatory', accepting several of Julian's more controversial suggestions.[32] Leo thought that they were a 'well-matched pair', Julian being the 'steadier and more thoughtful', Randolph the more obviously eloquent.[33]

Only once did they nearly come to blows, early on in the campaign. Julian had never spoken on a public platform before and, at their adoption meeting, when it came to his turn, he read out a carefully prepared, typewritten script word for word. To laughter from the audience, Randolph, forgetting that the microphone was still on, gruffly complimented him, 'Well, at least you can speak.' The following day, Julian prepared for his next speech in the same way and, just before he was due to perform, Randolph asked if he might see it. Taking the text from his pocket, Julian gave it to him, only to look on as Randolph 'tore it up, explaining that platform speeches were far more effective if made without notes'. They were in a crowded hotel bar, otherwise Julian would 'certainly have struck him'. But he learnt his lesson and, from then on throughout a long political career, 'spoke only from the briefest notes or from none at all'.[34] It was a story that Julian was fond of telling well into old age, and advice he was keen to pass on to novice politicians.

Among Randolph's more eccentric ideas to combat voter apathy was a proposal to hire two elephants, at considerable cost, from Manchester Zoo, on which he and Julian would parade through the streets of the constituency. Although Julian was broadly happy to support the venture, it was vetoed by their own rather staid Conservative Association, who decided that they did not 'like stunts in Preston'. Randolph told them that they were 'narrow-minded, middle-class provincials with no imagination and no guts', for which, not surprisingly, they never forgave him. Indeed, while he got on well with the electorate at large, Randolph had a natural gift for upsetting his own party workers. 'You know, Julian,' he once admitted, 'I ought never to be allowed out in private.'[35] Another innovation was a campaign song, to the tune of 'Lily of Laguna', which Randolph believed to be a Lancashire tune. The lyrics included such masterpieces as 'Churchill and Amery, we're backing Churchill and Amery, / They're the pair that Preston needs today', and 'Winston for Premier, we're backing Winston for Premier, / He's the one to make a Conference go, / He's the one who's known to Uncle Joe.'[36] The song was recorded, played in the streets and at meetings, while copies were distributed on the doorstep.

Julian enjoyed his first taste of campaigning. Writing to Lord Selborne in June, he told him that he and Randolph had enjoyed 'quite lively meetings', and that the local press had 'christened them the terrible twins'.[37] Towards the end of June Leo came to Preston to speak for them and addressed a crowd of 2,500 at the football stadium. It was the first time he had shared a platform with his son and the first time he had heard him speak. He was 'delighted with the vigour and effectiveness of his oratory' and thought that he had 'the makings of a really fine orator', in the mould of F. E. Smith.[38] A few days later came the climax of the campaign, a visit from the Prime Minister himself. Preston was to be his last stop on a gruelling, three-day tour of north-western constituencies. Julian and Randolph went to collect him from Blackburn, where they found him utterly exhausted. But he soon livened up as they drove into Preston, Churchill perched on the rear hood of an open-top car, waving and giving his trademark V-sign as they passed through the crowded streets. In the Town Hall square he addressed an audience of over 10,000 from the balcony of the Public Library, before collapsing exhausted into the back seat of his car to be taken home. Julian recalled that he paused only to launch into a violent diatribe against Herbert Morrison (who had attacked him in a speech the previous day), describing the former Home Secretary as 'that squealing pig'.[39]

Leo, meanwhile, had deliberately fought a low-key campaign in Birmingham, spending a good deal of time in other constituencies. He did, however, have the discomfort of an aggressive Communist candidate standing against him, 'the wretched [R. Palme] Dutt'. Like Leo, Dutt had been at Balliol, but there the similarity between them ended. For many years Dutt was one of the most senior members of the Communist Party of Great Britain and a staunch ideological adherent of Stalin. Throughout the campaign he harried Leo mercilessly at every opportunity. The spectre of Jack and his imprisonment also reared its ugly head from time to time. At one meeting Leo was barracked by a member of the audience demanding to know when Jack was to be brought to trial. It was, thought Leo, 'typical of the wonderful underlying sense of British fair play', that even the 'noisiest and most violent people at the back of the hall protested against this question'. It took a while for the commotion to calm down and 'to prevent angry ladies attacking the poor old boy'. Bryddie thought that 'he was going to have a stroke', so went and 'spoke to him and shook his hand'.[40] Julian, too, was subjected to occasional barracking about Jack, prompting one future colleague in the House of Commons to describe his campaign as among the 'bravest things he had ever done'.[41] By polling day, Julian and Randolph were convinced that they had won a handsome victory, while Leo in Birmingham was more cautious; his organisation had been poor, little campaign literature had been distributed and everywhere he looked there were posters of his Labour and Communist opponents. He feared the worst.

Four days later Leo's worries increased still further. Scotland Yard called to inform him that Jack had arrived back from Italy. It had taken some time for Major Burt to organise a return flight for them both from northern Italy and, even then, it had been a difficult few days. Burt had brought him first from Terni to Naples, where, for fear of him trying to escape, he had been forced to put Jack up in the local prison for the night. The next morning they finally took off for London, Jack travelling under the name of Mr Robinson, and dressed in his 'war paint – full Fascist uniform' of 'jack-boots and greenish-grey breeches and black shirt', even though Burt had especially bought a civilian suit for him. As they settled into their seats, Burt noticed that Jack was 'completely cocksure', repeating over and over again that everything he had done had been 'in the best interests of my country'.

On the journey home the Dakota developed engine trouble and they were forced to put down at the military airport in Marseilles. Burt and Jack took a short stroll around the airfield's perimeter, Jack 'eagerly' asking questions about the air raids that had hit London. 'I don't suppose for a moment they'll bring a charge against me,' he told Burt, 'but if they did, of course, my father would see that . . .' Burt interrupted Jack angrily, telling him not 'to bring your father's name into it', as Leo had already 'suffered enough'. Jack acquiesced and the talk returned to his favourite topic, the dangers of Communism, but the exchange provides an interesting insight into the aura of invincibility that Jack still believed enshrouded him. They arrived in London during the evening of 7 July and Jack was taken to spend the night at Bow Street Police Station where, the next morning, a Sunday, he was formally charged, by an Inspector Evan Jones, with high treason. Burt noticed that 'someone with stronger powers of persuasion' than his had coaxed him into a civilian suit, so that he no longer 'looked like an Albanian shepherd of the hills'.[42]

Bryddie wanted to go round to Bow Street immediately to see Jack, but Leo refused to let her go until he had been remanded to Brixton Prison on the Monday morning. He had shared the fears of Major Burt, sensing that Jack might be 'thinking of dramatising himself in a blackshirt'. However, in assessing Jack's future prospects, Leo demonstrated considerably poorer powers of prediction, appearing, unbelievably, to have shared his son's failure to understand the gravity of the charges facing him. 'Who knows,' he mused, 'the break in his life which he must now get may give him a new start, whereas otherwise he would have gone on drifting from one discreditable disaster to another.'[43] On Monday 8 July Jack was formally remanded at Bow

Street Magistrates' Court, to return to appear before the Chief Metropolitan Magistrate, Sir Bertrand Watson, when he returned from his holiday. Representing Jack was Mr Lickfold, of J. E. Lickfold and Sons of Woburn Square, a solicitor who had been highly recommended to Leo by various legal friends and who passed on to him Jack's first letter to his parents for three years, 'so naive and absurd as to make us laugh in spite of it all', and giving Leo serious cause to contemplate whether 'abnormality may not be the best defence'.[44]

Two days later Jack dropped a bombshell, suggesting an alternative line of defence to Lickfold; he claimed that during his time in Spain he had become a naturalised Spanish citizen, an action which would preclude him from being tried for treason by a British court. Leo was immediately sceptical, pointing out, as the prosecution were later to do also, that this was the first time he had mentioned it, even when it might have saved him from internment by the Vichy regime as a British subject. Much better, thought Leo, 'to plead his violent obsession against Communism and leave it at that'. John Simon called to offer his sympathy and, generously, to offer to act as a character witness for his godson. And over the next few days, all of the family except for Leo went regularly to visit Jack in Brixton. Bryddie found him 'quiet and affectionate', but came home in great distress. Leo, on the other hand, had 'long since lost all feeling in the matter'.[45] Julian, who later admitted that he would have killed Jack 'with his bare hands if he had met him during the war',[46] found him more reasonable and balanced than he had expected, and suggested that any notion of pleading abnormality should be quietly dropped. On the other hand, he thought that Jack's experiences had 'made a new man of him, broadened in outlook, even if fanatical, and calmly prepared to die for what he believes will generally be regarded as the right conclusion in a few years time'.[47]

Jack was also visited in Brixton by Una, the first time they had seen each other since the outbreak of war. She had long since moved from Cheltenham Terrace to Cobham, in Surrey, where she was living at Chico Cottage with a Miss Erica Marx, the daughter of a rich, naturalised German. This fact, and the hope that she might still be in touch with Jack, had led MI5 to keep a close watch on her movements throughout the war, but they had reluctantly decided that the only misdemeanour in which she and Miss Marx were involved was that they were 'Lesbians who resort at week-ends in the White Lion Hotel, Portsmouth Road.'[48] Una reported only that Jack was 'almost insane on the subject of Communism' and that, in spite of his being pleased to see her, he wanted her 'to divorce him as quickly as possible and at the same time to look after his French wife and her expected child'.[49] Jack appeared to think his request perfectly normal, while it was the first suggestion that the family had heard that Michelle might be pregnant.

▪ ▪ ▪

In the midst of these tribulations, Leo continued to carry out his ministerial duties and to keep a watchful eye on Wavell's progress in India. At Cabinet meetings Churchill remained confident of electoral victory, while the country waited for the overseas votes of the armed forces to be counted and the result to be announced. He was in ebullient form when he invited Leo and Bryddie, together with Randolph and Julian, down to Chartwell for lunch one weekend. Leo, as always, was quick to pass private judgement on the Prime Minister's home. The setting, he thought, was fine but the 'house itself was ugly', and a 'part of the valley had been disfigured by one of W.'s attempts to make a lake high up on a slope.' Nevertheless, he was full of admiration for all the walls that Churchill had famously built; he really was, he thought, 'a remarkable man'.[50]

Both Leo and Julian travelled north to their constituencies in time for the announcement of the election result on 26 July. Before they left, Lickfold took them both to the Brick Court chambers of Gerald Slade KC, who at the time was defending William Joyce on the same charge as that faced by Jack. He advised that, even if Julian was successful in Preston, the trial could be postponed for as long as was necessary for him to travel to Spain in search of the evidence that would prove Jack's Spanish citizenship. He also believed, although he made no attempt to substantiate his assertion, that the British public would be more sympathetic to Jack than they had been to Joyce. On returning to their constituencies, Leo and Julian discovered that they were both victims of the Labour landslide that had swept the country. In Preston the two Labour candidates had topped the poll by a wide margin, pushing Julian into fourth place, 5,168 votes behind the leading candidate, and bringing Randolph Churchill's short parliamentary career to an abrupt end – he had made just three speeches in the House of Commons and was never to return. They were bitterly disappointed, but took heart that they had done better than many others on a disastrous night for the Conservatives. Overall, Labour had a majority of 146 seats.

In Birmingham, Leo too was defeated, the new Labour Member gaining a majority of 5,634, although Leo took some solace at the Communist candidate, the 'wretched Dutt', losing his deposit. Almost all the other Birmingham constituencies had been lost too, and many of his fellow ministers had been defeated. Leo was now almost seventy-two years old and had represented the constituency in Parliament continuously for thirty-four years. In spite of it all, he could not 'help feeling amused and indeed cheered'. The events of the past few weeks would 'open a new chapter in one's life', and hopefully have a 'rejuvenating effect'. He was proud to hear news of Julian's 'very creditable defeat', even if it now meant that his dream of the two of them sitting side by side in the House of Commons was never to be realised. He was relieved too that the 'endless uphill battle' he had waged over India would be at an end, but was more than satisfied with the role he had played in safeguarding India's war effort. Above all, he would miss the constituency, where 'it had been a great thing to have my feet firmly planted among simple ordinary folk', who had taken Bryddie and himself 'just for what we were', and had supported them 'because they liked us and believed we were sincere'.[51]

Leo returned to London to face the further ordeal of Jack's first public court appearance. On 30 July he appeared at a pre-trial hearing before Sir Bertrand Watson at Bow Street, in a densely packed court. Described as being of 'no occupation' and 'no fixed address', Jack was charged that he had, between 22 June 1941 and 25 April 1945, 'being a person owing allegiance to the King, adhered to the King's enemies elsewhere than in the King's realm – to wit: in the German and Italian realms and in those parts of the Continent of Europe occupied or controlled by the King's enemies.' The charge was divided into eight counts, relating to his 'incitement' to others to join the Legion of St George, the speeches he had delivered throughout Europe and the broadcasts he had made from Berlin in December 1942. The statement he had typed for Major Burt at Terni was read out in open court, in all its dreadful detail, while a number of exhibits were produced, including posters and pamphlets, entitled 'British National Representation', which bore his name and which he had handed out at the camp at St Denis and elsewhere. A number of witnesses, already tracked down by MI5, appeared in person: Private Philip of the Black Watch, Royston Wood and the ubiquitous Wilfred Brinkman from St Denis; Georges Block, the commissioner of police in Antwerp who had attended Jack's lecture there, and Philippe Simcox who had done likewise in Lyon; and a BBC monitor confirmed his voice from the first of his Berlin broadcasts. (Jack's upper-class English drawl was remarked on by many of those he had met in France and Germany, in particular the manner in which he pronounced 'th' as 'f'.) Lickfold told the magistrate that Jack pleaded not guilty, and that he had a 'complete answer to the charge and that none of his activities had been directed against the British Empire'. On the contrary, 'he was now and always had been pro-British.'[52]

On 3 August Leo went to Buckingham Palace to hand over his seals of office to the King, who thanked him warmly for the work he had done at the India Office and privately 'murmured a few words of sympathy over our more domestic trouble'. Leo then welcomed his successor Pethick Lawrence to the department and, after briefing him for a short time, 'swapped chairs and then sent him off in my car'. Leo walked home, the emotion of giving up office leaving him momentarily short of breath, but feeling 'quietly content to close a chapter not of my choosing and certainly never easy with a Prime Minister who hated India'. That weekend he hired a car to take Bryddie and him to the country, 'a last little extravagance'.[53] Four days later, reflecting on the 'terrible' aftermath of Hiroshima, he remarked with some prescience that atomic power would have great 'creative possibilities when once it can be harnessed to the orderly creation of power', but that such an outcome was likely to be 'preceded by a whole generation in which only its destructive power is available'.[54]

Extraordinary as it might seem in modern times, Leo's first priority, at the age of seventy-one, was to find a constituency in order to return to the House of Commons, a goal which immediately ruled out acceptance of a hereditary peerage. Writing to 'Top' Selborne he admitted that he was 'not altogether sorry to close the Indian chapter and start a new one', and that he would 'presently begin to look around for an opportunity to get back into the House'. In the meantime, not for the first time, he still needed 'to earn a little money and contribute to public affairs by my pen'.[55] Churchill wrote with the news that he was to recommend Leo for a GCB, a Knight Grand Cross of the Order of the Bath, in the resignation Honours List. But Leo had 'no desire to be a knight or to share what is normally the honour of the head Civil Servant' and, without even discussing the matter with his wife, telephoned to decline the offer. Instead he asked that Bryddie should receive a GBE, and so become a Dame Grand Cross of the Order of the British Empire, for her wartime work as chairman of the Indian Comforts Fund, a charity devoted to the welfare of Indian troops and prisoners of war. For himself, Leo would rather become a Companion of Honour if anything, an Order whose membership is confined to the sovereign and sixty-five other members.

Bryddie was furious when she found out, arguing that he should have 'accepted nothing less than the House of Lords', but Leo was 'afraid of spoiling Julian's chances if Jack died childless'.[56] He was duly appointed a CH, alongside Clement Attlee and Jan Smuts, although the fact that there were no other GCBs on the list made him realise that Churchill had indeed intended his offer of one to Leo as a true personal compliment. Thanking Selborne for his letter of congratulation, he revealed that his true reason for accepting the CH was that it would allow him to re-enter the House of Commons 'under the style and designation by which my colleagues have known me',[57] while to Beaverbrook he confessed that he was still 'young and foolish enough to think that I may yet have another run for my money', and that he was only sorry not be twenty years younger.[58] Bryddie was awarded the Crown of India, one of the last occasions on which the Order was bestowed.

Leo moved quickly both to try to get back into the House and to restore various sources of income. He was invited back on to the boards of Goodyear and the Gloucester Wagon Company, while the newspaper magnate Lord Kemsley offered him £2,500 a year to become a consultant and occasional contributor to his newspapers, in particular the *Sunday Times*. At his first meeting at Conservative Central Office he was not unduly dispirited to be told that Churchill's immediate priority was to get back some of the younger Conservative Members who had lost their seats, and he was delighted at the success of Harold Macmillan, who secured the first by-election of the new Parliament in Bromley, just a month after losing his seat at Stockton. Leo also began work on the second volume of his non-political memoirs, *In the Rain and the Sun*, the sequel to *Days of Fresh Air* which had described his earlier mountaineering experiences.

Julian, meanwhile, had been told by SOE that they no longer had any peacetime need for his services, and he decided to take it upon himself to follow up Jack's claim to Spanish citizenship. Armed with a letter of introduction from the Spanish Ambassador in London, the Duke of Alba, he set out for Madrid in early September. His mission was doomed from the start. Jack's lawyers had been forced to request a delay in the court proceedings from the Director of Public Prosecutions, Theobald Mathew, in order to pursue their Spanish line of enquiry. In doing so, they had merely alerted both the DPP and MI5 to their likely line of defence. The officer at MI5 in charge of Jack's case, Colonel Cussen, in an apparent show of generosity, insisted that the Government and prosecuting authorities were 'most anxious that the defence should be given all proper facilities' to help Julian in his Spanish quest.[59] The resident SOE officer in Madrid, Squadron Leader Park, was briefed to help Julian wherever possible, including use of the British Embassy diplomatic bag to ensure speed of communication with Leo and the legal team. Julian was naturally delighted to have the help of a fellow SOE officer but, unknown to him, Park's true job was to spy on him and to assemble as much information as possible about his activities in Madrid, which he duly passed back to Cussen by way of SIS.

Initially Julian's search met with little success. He telegraphed home on a number of occasions asking for further clues, and at first Leo feared that it looked as if 'poor Julian has gone on rather a wild goose chase what between Jack's own flightiness and Spanish administrative chaos.'[60] SIS reported gleefully to Cussen that 'Amery frère has had no success in his mission'. But when Leo returned to see the Duke of Alba at the Spanish Embassy, he was rewarded with an introduction for Julian to two senior Spanish Generals, Blas Pérez and Muñoz Grandes, a development which caused considerable agitation at MI5. Between 1941 and 1943 Muñoz Grandes had commanded the notorious 'Blue Division', so-called because of their Falangist blue shirts, who had fought alongside the Germans against Russia on the Eastern Front. He was one of only seven foreigners ever to have been awarded an Iron Cross with Oak Leaves, with which he had been presented personally by Hitler in December 1942. He was, pointed out the SIS information, on the 'Russian War Criminal List', although in his native Spain he was regarded as a war hero. Julian's meetings with him in Madrid merely confirmed MI5's suspicions as to the seriousness of Jack's position.[61]

In London, on 18 September, William Joyce was found guilty and sentenced to death at the Old Bailey, the judge ruling that the act of 'holding and using a British passport certainly includes allegiance to the Crown outside this country'. Leo, who had never liked the idea of the proposed Spanish defence, and was torn between his patriotism and his desire to help Jack, thought that 'on general grounds of common sense' there was 'much to be said for the Judge's view', and that Julian was probably 'wasting his time'. He was also becoming increasingly concerned by the mounting costs associated with Jack's defence, and was forced to negotiate a new overdraft at the bank to pay the initial set of fees of £1,000. He wrote to Lickfold that he was 'prepared to pay whatever is necessary to give him a fair chance', but that he hoped that, in return, Lickfold and Slade would treat him 'with consideration both as to total amount and as to time of payment'.[62] Slade replied that he would be appealing Joyce's case and he still held out high hopes for defending Jack on the basis of his Spanish citizenship. Those hopes received a welcome boost a few days later when Jack, in answer to a number of further questions about his supposed Spanish citizenship, replied with a long and rambling letter to Leo 'containing all mind [*sic*] of information we have never had an inkling of before'. He claimed that his naturalisation had come about as a result of a specific request he had made at a time when, 'upset by King Edward's abdication, his own bankruptcy and his domestic disagreements, he was anxious to become permanently a Spanish citizen.' He claimed to have become a 'Lieutenant in the Spanish Army attached to the Italians', and to have been 'promoted to Captain and decorated for valour'.[63] The new information was sent out to Julian in Madrid.

Julian's precise movements and actions over the next three weeks will probably never be known. Having failed during the first few weeks of his stay to find any evidence of Jack's Spanish citizenship, he returned to London from Madrid in the middle of October, after a 'terrific hunt for clues', with 'a dozen sworn testimonies of people who met Jack during the Civil War'. Among the documents in his possession was a judicially authenticated certificate, which purported to show that Jack had become a member of the Spanish Legion on 15 March 1937. According to Leo Julian had subsequently, with the help of the Falangist writer Giménez Caballero, 'tracked down the actual entry in the register of one of the districts in Madrid', which provided 'conclusive evidence' that Jack had renounced his British nationality and taken Spanish citizenship on 19 March 1937. He claimed to have found an instruction from Ramón Serrano Súñer, then the Spanish Minister of the Interior and Franco's brother-in-law, 'declaring [Jack] a Spanish subject', which Julian had also had judicially certified as being an original. This, according to the lawyer at the Spanish Embassy in London, was 'conclusive evidence according to Spanish law'. The only remaining concern was as to whether Jack's action in having his passport extended to March 1943 by the American Consul in Nice, might bring him within British law for the broadcasts he had made at the end of 1942.

Julian had made some interesting acquaintances during his stay in Madrid. He had met the sister of Clara Petacci, Mussolini's mistress, who told him that on one occasion, when the Gestapo were threatening to arrest Jack for his criticisms of German foreign policy, Mussolini had offered to 'go to prison himself if John Amery was imprisoned'.

Right-wing opinion in Spain viewed Jack as 'a hero, a sort of Byron or Lord Holland prepared to go against the tide of feeling in his own country for what he thought was right'. But what amused both Leo and Julian most were the 'military testimonials to John's impeccable conduct while in the Spanish army'. Altogether, Julian had 'done a really remarkable piece of work'.[64] So concerned were the prosecution at the possible significance of Julian's discovery that the Director of Public Prosecutions, Theobald Mathew, decided to fly to Madrid himself in secret, accompanied by Cussen and Burt, in an effort to discredit the new evidence. He was further disturbed when he attempted to acquire the services of the leading Spanish lawyer in London, Rafael Valls of Brick Court, only to discover that he had already been retained by Leo. However, help was soon at hand for Mathew's case. It was at this stage that MI5 became aware of the contrary evidence that Jack appeared to have been at sea on the Dutch merchant ship the SS *Titus*, between 9 and 19 March 1937, bound from Lisbon to Genoa.

Another MI5 officer, Captain William Skardon, on secondment from Special Branch, was despatched to Amsterdam. Skardon had already tracked down much of the evidence against William Joyce, and was to achieve notoriety after the war as MI5's chief investigator and interrogator, known as the 'Head of the Watchers', extracting a confession from the Soviet spy Klaus Fuchs, and interviewing, among others, Kim Philby, Anthony Blunt and John Cairncross. Now, in October 1945, he managed to track down the logbook of the *Titus*, which clearly showed that Jack had been the only passenger on board during the period in question and that the ship had made no other stops en route, lying off the Algarve in bad weather for three days between the 12 and 14 March. The ship's chief engineer provided him with a sworn statement that no one could possibly have left the ship during the voyage.

In Madrid the British investigators too had met with success. They had at first been concerned to discover that Julian had indeed held meetings with both the Spanish Minister of Justice, apparently an ardent fascist, and Serrano Súñer, although no longer a minister, still an influential figure in Spanish legal circles thanks to his long career as a senior Falangist and confidant of Franco. However, it soon became clear that the relevant entries in the nationalisation register were not originals from 1937, but had been added in the past few weeks. Furthermore, it appeared that Julian and Serrano Súñer had paid two separate visits to a judge on 27 September and 15 October, with the express purpose of first inserting the entry relating to Jack, and then having it judicially certified. Major Henry Pakenham, the SIS officer in Madrid, wrote to his counterpart at MI5 that 'very strong suspicions exist that the whole conduct of Julian Amery's enquiries to assist his brother have involved conspiracy to manufacture evidence and documents.' If the defence of Spanish citizenship was to be used at Jack's trial, then 'ample evidence for the cross-examination of witnesses is available.'[65] Theobald Mathew was later to write to Sir David Petrie, the Director General of MI5, thanking him for the part his officers had played in the 'most difficult and delicate of all the treason cases, not excepting Joyce'. Cussen and Burt had dealt with an 'exceptionally difficult situation in Madrid . . . with outstanding success', not least in bringing about the 'successful demolition of the defendant's attempt to establish Spanish nationality'.[66]

Meanwhile, in spite of Joyce's failure in the Court of Appeal, Slade continued to advise that Jack's defence should concentrate on the question of nationality and the consequent misuse of a British passport, rather than trying to make out a case based on the issue of Jack's intent, or lack of it. Above all, he was keen to avoid putting Jack through a detailed cross-examination in the witness box. Both Slade, and Walter Monckton, who had briefly served as Solicitor General in the caretaker government, offered to take Jack's case to the Court of Appeal without a fee should it become necessary. On 23 November, while visiting Buckingham Palace to receive her Crown of India, Bryddie took her courage in her hands and spoke to the King about Jack, and was delighted when he thanked her for doing so and offered his sympathy. But three days later, and just two days before the trial was due to begin, Julian arrived home with bad news. He admitted to Leo that the certificates he had brought back from Spain had been 'prepared for the judge by [Serrano] Suner for the occasion', and 'did not copy the whole of the entry which gave the date of the entering'.

Not only had the prosecution now discovered this, but matters had been made worse by the fact that Serrano Súñer had become increasingly estranged from the Spanish Government and that the Ministry of the Interior now refused to support his story. After pondering the situation late into the night, Leo reluctantly decided that 'the whole Spanish nationality business had better be dropped'.[67]

The following morning, at Slade's chambers, the news was confirmed. The prosecution had written to Lickfold to tell him that the certificates presented by the defence had omitted to mention that they had been entered in the register only at the end of September that year, just two months earlier. Furthermore, the in-house lawyer at the Spanish Embassy had been summoned to a meeting later that afternoon with the legal adviser to the Crown Prosecutor of Spain, who had travelled over specifically to deal with the case himself. It was clear to Leo that the 'Spanish Government, presumably under some pressure from ours, had turned right round against Suner and those who helped Julian.' Pursuing the Spanish line of defence based on the discredited documents or, indeed, solely on Jack's word, would be hopeless. Similarly, defending on the basis of Jack's lack of intent would mean 'all the sorry evidence dragged out in detail and Jack cross-examined on every point'. While it was highly unlikely that a rendering of Jack's political views from the witness box would benefit him with either the jury or the judge, there was the very real danger that it would do untold damage to public opinion and thus adversely influence the Home Secretary in any subsequent appeal or plea for clemency. A straightforward guilty plea would 'create a better impression, especially contrasted with Joyce's shiftiness, and improve the chances of a reprieve'.

Julian, after all he had done, took the news very badly but reluctantly agreed with the decision. Later that afternoon, together with the lawyers, he visited his brother in Brixton to pass on the bad news, which Jack took 'very gallantly and gaily even and agreed with their conclusions'. He told Julian that he was inclined to say nothing at all, even when invited to do so by the judge at the end. Leo suggested that he should 'very briefly admit his guilt in law but make clear that his motive was against Bolshevism and not against his country'. That evening Leo took the chair at a dinner for defeated Conservative candidates from the general election and received a standing ovation when he rose to speak. It had been 'an anxious day'.[68]

Jack's trial was scheduled to take place on 28 November 1945, in Court One of the Central Criminal Court at the Old Bailey. The scene was later vividly described by Rebecca West, who was covering the trial for the *New Yorker* magazine. The prosecution was represented by Theobald Mathew and, as chief counsel, the Attorney General, Sir Hartley Shawcross, recently returned from the Nuremberg trials. It seemed to West 'quite certain' that the search for evidence of Jack's Spanish citizenship had been successful since, at the tables at the front of the court, Lickfold and Slade were accompanied 'by a number of trim and plump and florid young men who were said to be Spanish lawyers'. They, in turn, were joined by 'that famous figure of the courts, Mr Salzedo the interpreter', who introduced himself to his fellow countrymen 'not perfunctorily but as if they would presently be engaged in a considerable enterprise together'. Julian sat with them, said to be the 'principal witness for the defence', which West surmised could 'hardly be unless his search for evidence of John Amery's naturalization had been successful'.[69] In fact, the Spanish lawyers in court were there on behalf of the prosecution, in the event that Slade, in spite of Leo's warnings, had decided to pursue the Spanish line of defence anyway. Bryddie, too, had applied for a public seat in court.

By half-past ten, when the trial was due to begin, there was still no sign of the judge, the defendant or a jury to be sworn in. At eleven o'clock a court messenger approached Lickfold and Slade and there followed a 'fantastic moment when counsel, lifting their skirts, went into the dock and clattered down the steps to the cell below', where Jack was being held.[70] It was immediately obvious to everyone in the crowded court that something unexpected was happening. Twenty-five minutes later Slade and Lickfold came back into court, spoke briefly to Mathew and Shawcross, before the judge entered 'in shrivelled and eccentric majesty'. Sir Travers Humphreys, a veteran of a number of IRA trials, was in his late seventies and, thought West, 'as crisp as a fine winter night, with a fierce wit on his tongue and a fiercer wit on his face'. Jack was brought up into court, bowed to the judge, and nervously gripped the front of the dock, his 'small, bare hands very white and limp', looking neither left nor right, but directly at the judge. His skin was 'yellow and grooved round the small bones of his face by long exhaustion and fear and the immediate strain of the moment'. His face resembled 'the muzzle of a monkey',[71] while his 'long black hair, curling up at the back, was carefully brushed'. He was dressed in a 'brown overcoat and a black and yellow scarf which was knotted at his neck',[72] the scarf typical of the 'sort that used to be sold at the expensive shops on the Croisette at Cannes', while the weight of the overcoat 'was too much for the worn trifle of his body'. By his very appearance, thought West, 'he made the ultimate appeal against human justice'.[73]

The clerk read out the long indictment, the eight counts including one of broadcasting from Berlin, four of inciting David Philip, Royston Wood, Alfred Koerner and Wilfred Brinkman at St Denis, and three of addressing public meetings in Antwerp and France. Jack was described to the court as a 'politician'. Throughout the proceedings he appeared 'most of the time to have half a smile on his face', but as he listened intently to the charges against him, 'his brow puckered, the nervous smile left his face, and he stroked his chin with his forefinger.' He was then asked by the clerk to plead and, 'after a tense silence', he replied in a firm voice, 'I plead guilty to all counts.' A light murmur ran through the court and the judge leaned forward to point out to Slade that he never accepted a guilty plea on a capital charge unless he was absolutely sure that the accused 'thoroughly understood what he was doing and what the immediate result must be', and that he was 'in accord with his legal advisers in the course he was taking'.[74] Slade replied that he had, indeed, fully explained the position and its consequences to Jack.

West observed that the 'old judge's eyebrows and the corners of his mouth made a queer pattern' as he ordered that the plea be recorded. The clerk told Jack that he had been convicted of high treason and asked whether he had anything to say as to why judgement of death, in accordance with the law, should not be passed. Jack failed to reply, but when the judge repeated the question, Jack, in his 'well-bred and dying voice', replied 'No, thank you, sir.' It was clear, thought West, that Jack felt 'morally satisfied and that he was congratulating himself on having at the last, at the end of his muddled and frustrated existence, achieved an act of crystalline clarity.' The nervous smile returned to his face as Mr Justice Humphreys straightened his black cap and then addressed him directly. For a moment the judge 'seemed baffled', and there was a 'certain ineptness' in his remarks.[75] He had read the evidence in the case and had satisfied himself that Jack had known what he was doing and that he had done it 'intentionally and deliberately after you had received warning from more than one of your fellow countrymen that the course you were pursuing amounted to high treason. They called you a traitor and you heard them.' Yet Jack had continued on his chosen course, and he now stood before the court, 'a self-confessed traitor to your King and country'. Jack had, accordingly, 'forfeited the right to live'. Throughout these remarks Jack kept his eyes firmly fixed on the judge, in a show of 'complete composure'. As the sentence was read out he showed 'no signs of emotion', but 'bowed with dignity to the Judge and turned to walk down the stairs to the cells'. The entire proceedings had lasted just eight minutes.[76]

The news of Jack's guilty plea came as a 'bombshell' to William Joyce, already languishing in Wandsworth in the middle of his own, protracted appeal process. 'Whatever we may have said about the fellow in the past,' he conceded, 'he seems to have acted with courage on this occasion.' He presumed that Jack would petition the Home Secretary and wished him luck. Jack's conduct had been 'no more treasonable than that of the court-martial defendants who have not been condemned to death'.[77] Joyce was correct in his assumption. The campaign to have Jack's sentence commuted began almost immediately, and followed two distinct paths: on the one hand the more formal, legal attempts to have him declared medically insane and thus unfit for execution, and, on the other, the more straightforward pleas for clemency. On the evening of the trial Bryddie wrote the first of many letters she was to send to the new Home Secretary, James Chuter Ede, begging him, 'if it is possible, to have mercy on John'. In language that was to become familiar over the next few weeks, she pleaded with Ede that Jack had been 'so ill in the beginning and struggled with weakness and hunger',[78] but that now he had become 'so brave and utterly sincere'. He had pleaded guilty 'partly to save his father more misery', and had never meant to hurt England. 'I do believe', she concluded, 'that God is near and does help.'[79] Ede was clearly moved by her appeal and replied the next day that he understood and appreciated 'the motives which impelled you to write as you did about the responsibility which falls on me in respect of your son'. He only hoped that she and Leo, 'who was always so kind to me when we were colleagues, will believe that I shall give all the facts earnest consideration.'[80] Bryddie, who had written without Leo's knowledge, believed that his answer offered a gleam of hope. 'From my heart I thank you,' she replied. 'Your answer is my solace and I pray that there may stream forth the light of clemency over this dark world.'[81]

The morning after the trial Leo went to work on Jack's behalf. In spite of the 'anti-Franco obsession in Labour circles', it was agreed to ask the Spanish Ambassador to put in a word on Jack's behalf and to stress that his government's withdrawal of the naturalisation certificate did not imply hostility to Jack himself. But the best hope of reprieve lay in a request for a thorough medical examination. That afternoon Leo saw John Anderson, who had served as Home Secretary throughout the war, and was able to brief him with the 'precise details of the Statute of 1864 under which the Home Secretary is bound to appoint a medical tribunal and abide by its findings'. John Simon also called at Eaton Square, feeling 'rather gloomy', but still offering to help with the Home Secretary if he could.[82] On 30 November, almost four months after Jack arrived back in Britain, Sadie Rodney drove Leo to Wandsworth to visit him for the first time. Until then he had felt unable to face his elder son, who had 'made us all suffer so terribly', but Jack was still delighted to see him and insisted on discussing all the great political issues of the day. Leo found that he had 'grown into a real man and a personality', and was 'no longer a playboy'. But he also found in Jack's 'cheerful naturalness', echoes of Dr Wright's psychiatric diagnosis when Jack was fifteen of his inability to realise when he had done something wrong or to show remorse. Leo came away feeling that it 'would be a sad thing that he should be destroyed', especially when his most recent experiences, however much Leo disapproved of them, had 'made a man of him'.[83]

Lord Horder was an old friend of Leo's and a distinguished physician, who had numbered senior politicians and royalty, including both King George V and George VI, among his patients. He and Leo had first met over thirty years earlier, in May 1923, when Horder had cared for Bonar Law throughout his final illness and Leo had visited the ailing Prime Minister in Paris to urge him to carry on. Now Leo asked Horder to save his eldest son's life. Horder agreed to undertake an examination of Jack and, with the help of an eminent Wimpole Street psychiatrist, Dr Edward Glover, to compile a report into the state of Jack's mental health, which could be presented to the Home Secretary. Lickfold duly wrote to Ede's Parliamentary Under-Secretary, G. H. Oliver, informing him of the defence's intention to appeal against the sentence and to seek a reprieve, and asking for permission for Jack to undergo a mental examination with Horder and Glover. The request seems to have caught the Home Office by surprise, in particular the senior civil servant there, Sir Frank Newsam, the Permanent Under-Secretary. He recognised the 'desirability of giving the prisoner's friends the fullest opportunity to make any plea for mercy' which they might see fit, not least to avoid giving grounds for any 'suggestion that the SoS [Secretary of State] was unwilling to consider arguments in favour of a reprieve'.[84] But Oliver was still instructed to reply that a mental examination by anyone other than Home Office or prison doctors was out of the question.

Glover decided instead to construct his report around a series of interviews with as many people as he could identify who had known Jack at various stages of his unhappy life. With Leo's help he tracked down an impressive list of witnesses. He began by taking statements from Leo, Bryddie, Julian and Una, before interviewing Miss Irene Ironside from Jack's kindergarten, W. H. Barrett, one of his former housemasters at Harrow, and G. C. Nock, one of his post-Harrow tutors. He then assembled written evidence from Julian's former nurse Nanny Mead, Jack's headmaster at West Downs, Kenneth Tindall, two former Harrow Head Masters, Sir Cyril Norwood and Arthur Boissier, and two further former tutors, Kingsley Walton and Leander Jameson. In addition two doctors, Dr Maurice Wright and Dr Osmond, wrote reports on the findings they had reached when they had examined Jack as a teenager. Almost without exception, they all testified to Jack's history of abnormal behaviour and lack of moral responsibility. On 7 December Lickfold sent a dossier to the Home Secretary enclosing Glover's report, with a covering letter from Lord Horder. When Leo and Bryddie next visited Jack, he seemed 'quite interested in being examined for mental deficiency', pausing only to reflect that if he was indeed insane, 'he was obviously the last person to realise it'. At the same meeting Jack told his father that Mussolini had always spoken 'kindly of him', and had even suggested that had Leo been Foreign Secretary at the time of Munich, a 'rational peace' would have been more possible.[85]

Glover's report ran to several pages and drew on the impressive array of evidence which he had assembled in the short time that had been available to him. Above all, he had found that Jack was 'incapable of a normal appreciation of consequences', and was 'devoid of the moral sense by which normal people control their actions and utterances'. He began by listing Jack's symptoms as they had appeared to him, frequently confirmed by more than one witness, in the statements he had taken. Jack showed a history from early childhood of a 'complete absence of moral sense, guilt or remorse', and an 'equally persistent and unchanging negativism of thought and action'. His persistently 'bizarre' behaviour, including his 'delinquent conduct in childhood, adolescence and adult life', his 'pathological lying' and his 'abnormal sexual behaviour' were all symptomatic of long-term psychosis. His outbursts of unnatural excitement, violence, childhood neuroses such as bed-wetting and phobias, and his overly suspicious nature were also presented as evidence, as was his 'persistent tendency to grandiosity', his megalomania and his exhibitionism. Above all, he demonstrated a complete lack of 'social conscience and total insensitivity to the pain or injury caused to his family or friends'. Glover concluded that Jack was 'certainly a severe and long-standing case of psychopathic disorder of the type at one time called "moral insanity" or "moral imbecility".'[86]

Horder added his own conclusions to those of Dr Glover, agreeing that it was 'inescapable that John Amery has exhibited a psychopathic mentality all his life, of such a degree as to justify the term moral imbecility'.[87] Glover also sent his report to four fellow psychiatrists: Dr Rees, a former Director of Army Psychiatric services, Dr Hart of University College Hospital, Professor Henderson of Edinburgh University and Dr MacNiven, the Superintendent of the Royal Mental Hospital in Glasgow. All of them agreed with his diagnosis. And in an unusual move, Jack's counsel Gerald Slade and his junior Sidney Lamb wrote to the Home Secretary from their Brick Court chambers to add their own voice to the growing pleas that Jack be shown leniency. They admitted that they had not planned to put forward the plea of insanity at his trial, as they had feared that it would weaken the impact of their planned Spanish defence. However, they were 'satisfied that judged by any standard other than the now obsolete McNaghten rules', which were still used to assess claims of insanity, Jack was 'not, and never really has been, really sane'. They were now 'convinced that his case was one to which the provisions of the Criminal Lunatics Act, 1884, secs. 2 (1) and (4) should be applied', namely that he should be spared execution.[88]

For the first time Leo and Bryddie dared hope that something was at last going in Jack's favour, even if Glover's report did make disturbing reading. Although he found it painful to admit, Leo reluctantly conceded that had Jack not been his son and thus been regularly bailed out by him over the years, he would 'long ago have been shut up in an institution'. The evidence was 'overwhelming', and he did not see how the Home Office experts could disregard it. His mind was already beginning to turn to the prospect of a cure for Jack, even if it had to be carried out during a lengthy prison term. He could not see how 'petty traitors' such as Jack could be 'deserving of the same fate as those who butchered or tortured to death millions'.[89]

But the Home Secretary, and more particularly Sir Frank Newsam, remained unmoved. To date, Ede's only medical report on Jack was one that had been written by the doctor at Brixton prison, Dr Grierson, who had observed him since he had first been taken there on remand in July. Grierson remarked that Jack was an 'insignificant and weedy individual', who showed no sign of insanity, but a 'certain amount of nervousness which he tried to cover up'. He was 'untidy and not overclean', smoked innumerable cigarettes and was 'generally indolent'.[90] Newsam tried to persuade Ede that, in spite of the apparently superficial nature of this observation, it was sufficient to counter the reports of Lord Horder and Dr Glover, and that no further medical enquiry could be justified. But Ede was, by now, beginning to feel the overwhelming pressure of the decision that he was being asked to make. The press was speculating openly as to Jack's physical and mental condition, and a number of newspaper articles had appeared suggesting that he was in such an advanced state of tuberculosis that his sentence would inevitably be commuted to allow him to die peacefully within a few months anyway.

Ede received pleas for clemency from a wide variety of people and organisations. John Simon, himself a former Home Secretary and, more recently, Lord Chancellor, wrote to commiserate as to 'the personal burden of the Home Secretary in questions of reprieve'. As Jack's godfather he had known 'this miserable man' since early childhood, since when he had been 'cursed with a perverse twist of mind, obstinate and unresponsive'. Simon even regretted his own unsuccessful attempts 'to influence him', but concluded that Jack's mind was 'so impervious to normal considerations that he can only be regarded as mentally diseased', and should be spared accordingly.[91] Lady Carson, the widow of Leo's old Ulster Unionist friend, wrote asking that a 'little mercy' be extended to Jack; she had known him 'since he was a small boy and he has never been quite like other people.'[92] And Jack's former Head Master, Sir Cyril Norwood, by now the President of St John's College, Oxford, wrote a long, personal letter to Ede asking for clemency. Of the thousands of schoolboys he had known, Jack had been the most difficult. He had not lost his sense of moral responsibility, rather he had never had one in the first place. Jack had demonstrated a 'moral imbecility' and an accompanying lack of shame that had put him 'beyond the line where human weakness passes into abnormality'. Norwood admitted that he was himself a supporter of capital punishment, but could not agree that in the case of Jack 'justice demanded his death'.[93] Meanwhile Bryddie's brother Hamar Greenwood took advantage of sitting next to Clement Attlee at a Pilgrim's Trust dinner to suggest that it was 'time to leave off killing people for what are crimes of opinion and not of action'.[94]

On 10 December, just nine days before the date set for Jack's execution, Ede ordered that a statutory medical enquiry should be carried out by two Home Office appointed doctors, Dr Norwood East, the recently retired Medical Commissioner of Prisons, and Dr Hopwood, the Superintendent of Broadmoor. On 13 and 14 December they visited Wandsworth prison, where Jack had been held since being sentenced, to conduct their investigation under the Criminal Lunatics Act as Slade had earlier suggested. Over the two days they interviewed the Governor, Deputy Governor, Prison Chaplain, two medical officers, nine prison officers and the doctors from Brixton. They also interviewed Leo, Julian and Una, and were given access to all the documents that had already been submitted in the case. Leo took the opportunity of the interviews to talk at length with Una. She told Leo that Jack had always attributed his hatred of Communism to the suffering that had been inflicted on Leo by the Bolsheviks in Russia, from where he had supposedly narrowly escaped with his life. It was news to her that Leo had, in fact, never been near Russia, and that Jack had never been imprisoned on Ellis Island, as he had told her, let alone even crossed the Atlantic. She had always believed both stories, as she had many others, and now admitted to Leo that she doubted whether many of Jack's Spanish escapades were based on fact either.

On the evening of 14 December East and Hopwood visited the Home Office to deliver their findings in person to the Home Secretary, both verbally and in a written report. Their conclusions came as a considerable blow. While Jack was 'not insane according to the McNaghten ruling', they had no doubt whatsoever that he was indeed a 'moral defective', that he suffered from a 'condition of arrested or incomplete development of mind existing before the age of eighteen years', and should have therefore had 'care, supervision and control for the protection of others and himself'. There was no doubt in their minds that he was 'certifiable under the Mental Deficiency Acts', that he was of 'unsound mind', and that his 'defectiveness was so grossly abnormal' that they recommended that 'the question of commuting the capital sentence on medical grounds be favourably considered'.[95]

Ede was, understandably, appalled. Even his own department's expert doctors had now recommended that Jack's life should be spared. Leo took the opportunity to send a lengthy letter to him, seeking to explain, if not to justify, Jack's behaviour. Groups of his former constituents in Birmingham raised petitions appealing for clemency on the grounds of Leo's long and dedicated service to the country. And on 14 December the South African High Commissioner in London, Heaton Nicholls, telephoned Downing Street to pass on the contents of a cable he had received that day from his Prime Minister, Leo's friend of forty-five years, Jan Smuts. He was asked to 'convey to Mr Attlee a private and personal message' as soon as possible concerning 'the possible execution of Amery's son'. Smuts was familiar 'with similar cases in South Africa, in none of which execution had been inflicted, as the acts were more of an ideological than a criminal character'. He concluded that he was 'deeply moved by consideration for Amery and his wife, both of whom have deserved well of their country'.[96]

Newsam, however, remained unmoved. On 15 December, just four days before Jack was due to hang, he drafted two memorandums for the Home Secretary urging him to stand fast. He was firstly concerned that the Home Office doctors had recognised in their report that Jack's moral defects were so serious that it was 'not beyond the bounds of possibility that Amery might commit homicide'. As imprisonment for life was not a practical possibility, he questioned whether the Home Secretary should take the risk of any action which 'will sooner or later result in Amery's release'.[97] As one historian has subsequently observed, 'it must be somewhat unusual to justify executing a man for treason on the basis that he might, when released from prison, commit murder.'[98] Newsam then came to the crux of the entire issue. 'There is the further consideration', he warned, 'of the effect of a reprieve on public opinion.' Capital punishment in Britain was 'tolerated as a deterrent', because the 'man in the street believes that the law is administered without fear or favour'. If Jack were to be reprieved, 'it would be difficult to convince the ordinary man that Amery had not received exceptional and privileged treatment.'[99]

Leo spent three days keeping busy as best he could, reading Lucretius and closely following the proceedings in Parliament on the Washington Loan Agreements. He wrote to the editor of *The Times* enclosing a photograph of Jack for the newspaper's use, complaining that he and Bryddie had been 'made rather unhappy by an awful hangdog looking snapshot of him', which had been taken at the time of his capture 'after he had been hustled and knocked about by the partisans'.[100] Bryddie, too, waited anxiously with her sister Sadie as ever-present company, and kept herself occupied answering letters. 'The *Sunday Express* says today that Leo and I saw John yesterday for the final time,' she wrote to Beaverbrook. 'I think that might count against John. Surely Max, the punishment is out of all proportion to the crime?'[101]

On the morning of 17 December the family assembled at Lickfold's office and, after a long and agonising wait, they received final confirmation from Sir Frank Newsam. The Home Secretary had given the 'most careful and anxious consideration to all the circumstances of this case', but he very much regretted that he had 'failed to discover any sufficient reason to justify him in advising his Majesty to interfere with the due course of the law'.[102] Leo accepted the news with resignation. He thought the Home Secretary's refusal to consider the medical evidence 'inexcusable', but believed that the Government were 'determined to have at least one execution to satisfy what they believe to be public opinion and possibly with an eye on Russia and the Nuremberg trials'.[103] Smuts was told by Attlee, on the advice of Ede, that 'in this matter, I, as Prime Minister of the United Kingdom, have no locus standi.'[104]

Leo tried his best to rally one last show of support. At his encouragement Lord Horder asked for a personal meeting, as a fellow parliamentarian, with the Home Secretary to express his concerns. Jack's defence had been inadequate, the trial too short and subsequent medical examinations not nearly extensive enough. There had been no consultation with Jack himself and no 'lumbar puncture to see whether there were any evidence of syphilitic infection', as he had suffered in adolescence. Horder believed that Jack felt he was 'doing something magnificent in laying down his life'.[105] Other parliamentary friends also wrote to Ede, among them the Labour ministers Lord Pethick-Lawrence, Leo's successor at the India Office, and Viscount Stansgate. Former colleagues tabled questions in the House of Lords, while Clement Davies tried, but failed, to persuade the Speaker to accept an emergency question in the House of Commons, where the rules of procedure were more restricted. The Speaker told him privately that he would do anything for Leo, but could not do that. They had reached the end of the road. At Wandsworth Julian signed for Jack's few remaining possessions: a penknife, a key ring with a locket and medallion attached, a ring, a badge, a wallet and a lock of hair.

■ ■ ■

Jack had spent the past two weeks in Wandsworth, largely unconcerned as the frenetic efforts to save his life went on around him. In the immediate aftermath of his sentence, Michelle had cabled from Terni in Italy, where she was still being held in internment, begging to join him in London. 'I wish to come and see you immediately,' she pleaded. 'I am with you, I adore you.'[106] '*Ma vie*,' replied Jack, '*je fais tout le possible pour toi et moi ne désespères pas courage je t'adore, ton hibou*.'[107] Lickfold's request for permission for Michelle to come to England, with the assurance that she would stay at Eaton Square and be looked after by Jack's family, was initially met with suspicion by Colonel Cussen at MI5, not least because if Jack had indeed gone 'through any form of marriage to this lady, it would appear to have been bigamous'. A further complication was the rumour that she was pregnant, soon confirmed to be untrue, and the worry that the 'press would no doubt be all agog'.[108] However, Michelle duly arrived at Blackbushe aerodrome in Surrey on 13 December, and visited Jack with both Bryddie and Julian almost every day thereafter. The MI5 officer whose job it was to sit in on their meetings complained that they were conducted entirely in French. Leo and Bryddie immediately warmed to Michelle, although they did not relish the prospect of breaking the news to her that Jack was already married. She was 'good-looking, self-possessed and warm hearted',[109] thought Leo, and he only wished that Jack had met her sooner, in which case things might have turned out very differently.

On the afternoon of 18 December, the day before Jack's execution was scheduled to take place, Leo returned to the House of Commons for the first time since the election to hand-deliver a final plea for clemency to every member of the Cabinet. In the lobby he met his successor, the new Labour MP for Sparkbrook, who had defeated him at the polls just five months earlier and who now, in a touching gesture, offered to do all he could to help distribute the letters. From there, Leo went with Bryddie, Julian, Sadie and Michelle to see Jack at Wandsworth for the last time. For an hour Jack was 'full of charm and gaiety and whimsical humour and philosophic detachment'. He made arrangements with Michelle for disposing of some of his belongings and urged her to 'marry again as soon as she could find a nice man'. He joked that prison had reminded him of the similarities between the British and the Germans: 'cleanliness, good treatment, but inflexible regulations.' He spoke nostalgically of Italy, filled in some of the gaps of his wartime experiences and ended by declaring 'la vie est belle, but with no touch of sentimentality.' He said that he had enjoyed a full life during his last years, urged Julian to stand again at Preston, and his father to continue his efforts to get back into the House of Commons.

When the hour was up and it was time say goodbye, his family took turns to do so, Sadie first, then Bryddie. 'How lovely you look tonight,'[110] he told his mother. 'You must not be sad, darling mother at Destiny's call – so long as I answer it worthily.' Then he said goodbye to Michelle and to Leo, apologising for all the trouble he had caused during his life. 'No man ever had such a father as you have been to me,'[111] he said, to which Leo could only reply, 'I am so proud of your courage Johnny, you are so brave.' 'But I am your son,' replied Jack.[112] Finally, it was Julian's turn to say goodbye to the brother he had tried so hard to save. Leo thought it a 'happy and quite unforced' farewell, 'just a natural parting on the eve of a long voyage'. Their final hour together 'blotted out all memory of his many sad vagaries', and all talk of insanity seemed ridiculous. Jack was delighted that their efforts in that respect, at least, had failed. Leo would always remember him 'at his best as a man', and as the 'lovely elfin child of his earliest years'.

Back at Eaton Square Horder came to see Leo to complain about the meeting he had had that afternoon with Ede, which had 'disappointed and rather shocked him'. He thought that the Home Secretary was a 'small man shrinking from a big responsibility', while 'political reasons had prevented a fair consideration of the case'. Leo,

Bryddie, Julian and Michelle spent the evening together, writing last letters to Jack and sitting 'together very quietly'.[113] In Wandsworth Jack too wrote his last letters, shared a brandy with the prison Governor and chatted late into the night with his warder. At the Home Office, Newsam was appalled to discover at the last moment that the Governor, in apparent ignorance of the significance of the gesture, had given permission for Jack to wear a black shirt, riding breeches and boots at his execution. The consent was quickly withdrawn. Across London, at the Dorchester Hotel, many of Julian's friends gathered together for dinner in a curious show of solidarity. And late that evening, Julian and Michelle drove to Wandsworth in Sadie Rodney's car, to spend the night and following morning parked outside the prison in silent vigil, Julian paying his respects to Jack by dressing in full military uniform.

Shortly before nine o'clock the next morning Leo, Bryddie and Sadie assembled, with their long-serving family maids and butler, in their bedroom at Eaton Square. Leo told them about their last meeting with Jack the night before, read out a poem he had written and a few verses from Corinthians, before they all recited the Lord's Prayer together. At the same time, at Wandsworth prison, Jack was taken from his cell. He 'thanked the chaplain and warders for their kindness' and 'walked unassisted to his end.'[114] He was met by the executioner Albert Pierrepoint, and held out his hand. 'Mr Pierrepoint,' he said, 'I've always wanted to meet you, although not, of course, under these circumstances.' Pierrepoint shook his hand and led him into the execution chamber. He later claimed that, at the very end, Jack had been the 'the bravest man I ever met'.[115]

CHAPTER TWENTY-TWO

How Young He Began to Serve His Country, How Long Continued

The Amery family spent the days after Jack's execution trying to come to terms with the disaster that had befallen them. Leo dealt with the crisis in the best way he knew how, immersing himself in his work and in writing. Until now, he had followed the progress of the Washington Loan Agreement negotiations with frustration, unable to play an active role either inside or outside Parliament as he fought to save Jack's life. Now, on the very night of Jack's death, he sat down to reply to the many letters that he and Bryddie had already received from friends. 'All is over,' he wrote to Lady Milner. Jack had been 'gay and gallant to the last', and seemed to Leo 'not only to have become a real man, but also to have regained the charm and sweetness of his childhood days'. He had made 'no pose of being a martyr, but only as just one of the casualties of a world conflict of ideas', had 'remained convinced that he was serving his country in fighting Communism', and hoped that his 'conduct will be judged differently one day'. Lord Milner's widow, on receiving the letter, scrawled across the front that it was 'the most surprising letter' she had ever received.[1]

One of Leo's oldest friends, and a long-standing partner in the campaign for imperial preference, Sir Henry Page Croft, was astonished to receive a lengthy letter on economic affairs, written 'on the very day of John's execution'. Page Croft commented that Leo had been 'a wonderful father who even in his agony would not let up on

Empire affairs'.[2] Leo also wrote to Robert Barrington-Ward, the editor of *The Times*, enclosing the short poem he had composed on the way to see Jack at Wandsworth for the last time, and which he had recited when they parted:

> At end of wayward days he found a cause.
> 'Twas not his country's – Only time will tell
> If that defiance of our ancient laws
> Was treason . . . or foreknowledge. He sleeps well.

He asked that it might be printed as an anonymous obituary for Jack, but Barrington-Ward telephoned later to say that he feared its insertion would cause too much controversy.[3]

Leo was not wholly without bitterness, although he tried hard to suppress it. He reflected that the final decision to execute Jack had been, rightly or wrongly, a political one. Five days later, William Joyce followed him to the gallows at Wandsworth. Of the many who had broadcast from Berlin, they were to be the only two to be executed. 'By picking out certain men to be tried under the Act of 1351', which allowed of no other penalty but death, Leo thought that the prosecutors 'were bound to get a death sentence and no special reason for a reprieve.' Meanwhile, no soldier who had been 'tried by a military court [had been given a sentence of] more than fifteen years', while civilians tried under the Treachery Act had been sentenced to between one and five years in prison.[4] Rebecca West later claimed that, on the day of Jack's trial, the Attorney General, Sir Hartley Shawcross, 'did all he could to dissuade' Slade from allowing Jack to plead guilty, pointing out that 'the social climate would never permit such a concession', namely a reprieve, 'to one of the governing classes'.[5] In later life Shawcross strongly implied that he would have supported the commutation of Jack's sentence to life imprisonment, but that 'the Government rejected' the medical advice. 'I grieved for his family,' he recalled.[6]

Bryddie was, at first, inconsolable. Since the news of Jack's presence in Berlin had first been announced to the world, she had never been the same again. Barbara Pym recalled that Leo and Bryddie were frequently in the newspapers. 'Mrs Amery seems to spend her time attending memorial services', she observed, so much so that 'she must be dressed permanently in black'. It would be 'a nice role for a wife in a story'.[7] And Pym's portrayal of Bryddie in some of her later novels could easily have been based on Chips Channon's recollection of her at a wartime party, 'wandering sad-eyed, like a ghost'.[8] Now, after Jack's death, it was said of her that 'she never smiled again'.[9] Yet, like Leo, she too kept herself busy writing. She began by sending an open letter, entitled 'Christmas', to *The Times* and the *Manchester Guardian*. 'Now that my poor dear son has paid the penalty for his sincere if mistaken beliefs,' she wrote, 'may I, at this season of peace and goodwill, plead through you for the life of the few others who have been selected for trial under the Act of 1351?'[10] The *Manchester Guardian* published the letter, but the editor of *The Times*, Barrington-Ward, as he had with Leo's obituary poem, refused to publish it on the grounds that it 'would inevitably provoke controversy'.[11]

In a further exchange of letters with Barrington-Ward, Bryddie gave an extraordinary insight into the blinding power of the love she had felt for her elder son, and the burning sense of injustice that she endured following his execution. He had been 'such a radiant creature and so lovely in face and form'. He had been trapped in Vichy France through no fault of his own, had tried unsuccessfully to return on no less than three occasions, and had 'never worked to help Germany as others had, who had such light punishment'. During his final days, his 'courage throughout was superb', and he had been 'calm, sweet and selfless'. He had understood, as she had done, 'that they did not mean him to live', and she knew 'how out of all proportion his sentence was'. He had never been 'mean nor cruel, nor greedy in his short life', and had died 'with utter dignity and courage', which broke 'her heart with pride and longing for him'.[12] She wrote to Beaverbrook also, complaining that the *Daily Express* had once again published the 'untrue photograph' of Jack, and she enclosed one of her own for future use, urging him to 'destroy the dreadful Italian photograph'. But she thanked him too for the 'wonderful leader he had written' in support of Jack being spared the death penalty.[13]

In July 1944 Jack had drawn up a makeshift last will and testament in which he asked to be cremated, with no accompanying religious ceremony. His final wish was to be laid to rest alongside Jeanine Barde in Bergerac, but he had in fact been buried, in accordance with the law that applied to all executed prisoners, in an unmarked grave in unconsecrated ground within the confines of Wandsworth prison. Bryddie could not bear the fact that she was not allowed to grieve or to pray at his graveside, and she developed an obsession which she was to harbour for several years, and which was to have a profound effect on Julian. In June 1946 she asked the Home Office for permission to put flowers on Jack's grave, but was refused. The following spring she tried again, writing to Chuter Ede in person, begging him to let her 'visit my dear son's grave', promising that it would take 'no more than three minutes', and that 'there would be no scene'.[14] Again, her request was turned down. She wrote again in July, asking the Home Secretary to allow her 'just to put my hand on my darling son's grave',[15] and again in November, finally forcing Home Office officials into deciding that they must deal with the issue once and for all.

Unfortunately for them, there was a precedent to Bryddie's request, that of the traitor Roger Casement's sister, who had been allowed to visit his grave after his execution. But it was clear to the official in charge that 'this poor lady will not be content with one visit', that she would almost certainly ask to leave flowers again another time and, worst of all, that 'some reference might appear in the Press'.[16] Ede duly replied that he had 'given most sympathetic consideration' to her request, which he acknowledged 'must lie so close to your heart', but that he could not afford to set a precedent.[17] Bryddie's wish was never granted. The following year, in April 1948, she engaged a mutual friend to approach the chaplain at Wormwood Scrubs prison, who had been at Wandsworth at the time of Jack's execution and had sat with him during his final hours. The chaplain agreed reluctantly to her request to a meeting to discuss Jack, but the Home Office refused to allow it to take place. After this, Bryddie seems to have given up her efforts to visit Jack's grave. In old age Ede was to campaign for the abolition of the death penalty.

Leo, Bryddie and Julian spent Christmas of 1945 quietly, staying with the Rodneys in Sussex, although Bryddie became so upset during

the Christmas Day service in Tunbridge Wells that she had to leave
the church. On Boxing Day they left for Scotland, taking Michelle
with them, where they spent a few weeks, well away from the world, at
the invitation of the Duke of Westminster on his estate at Lochmore.
Looking back on 1945, Leo wrote only that he felt 'very much as if
the main chapter of my life has been closed'.[18] He used the time
in Scotland to write a number of letters which again provide a rare
insight into his family's feeling of pain, but also give an indication of
the sense of rapprochement which Leo himself had managed to
achieve with Jack at the end of his life. 'The poor boy met his fate with
cheerful courage,' he wrote to Bishop Palmer, 'never doubting that his
conduct may some day seem less unintelligible, and less unforgivable'
than it did at the time. He hoped that Jack would be judged 'as just a
casualty in a world revolution in which his sincere, if mistaken, convictions and the chapter of accidents, found him on the wrong side of
the barricades'.[19]

To Lionel Curtis in Oxford, Leo repeated the claim that Jack's
'earlier failings of temperament had been steadied by his absorption
in a cause', however 'wrong-headed and difficult to understand'. He
wrote too of the 'complete uplifting and ennobling of [Jack's] character in the face of death'. It had been a 'deep tragedy' for them all, but
had 'left that cleansing and calming of the spirit which the ancients
defined as the purpose of tragedy'. He and Bryddie hoped that
there might be the 'same cleansing effect on the public mind and an
end to the demand for public executions as the penalty for crimes of
opinion, however misguided'.[20] To 'Top' Selborne, Leo wrote that the
memories of Jack's last few days had 'blotted out in our minds earlier
failings and errors', and that they would remember only the 'courage,
cheerfulness and simple faith in which he met his fate'. Their last hour
together had been 'one of the happiest of our lives', and they had
parted in 'hope of reunion in some world, some time'.[21] And to Canon
Douglas, who had helped Jack in Athens in 1933, he again stressed
the 'courage and serenity with which at the end he faced the great
question mark of death', and Jack's 'love for those who were nearest
to him and from whom he had often felt estranged in the past'.

Leo also used the time to compose a short paper about Jack, which he subsequently had printed as a small booklet and privately circulated among his friends. The content of *John Amery: An Explanation* was drawn primarily from the statements he had already made in Jack's defence, both to the doctors he had appointed to save him from the gallows and to the Home Secretary. He believed that it 'stated the case for him fairly and without exaggeration'.[22] Jack had pleaded guilty, claimed Leo, 'in view of the legal advice that association with the Germans, even if confined to propaganda against the Russians, amounted under the Act of 1351 to adherence to the King's enemies'. He therefore had 'no possible defence in law for conduct for which he did not wish to apologize'. Jack had wished only to 'avoid the further distress to his family by uselessly prolonging proceedings', which had been widely recognised as 'a courageous and manly decision'. The paper also describes Jack's activities, both before and during the war, as Leo had understood them, not 'related as a justification for his conduct'. Rather he sought only to 'afford a coherent explanation of a course of action consistent with itself in its obsession with the Communist danger, and not incompatible, especially in one of his temperament and in his environment, with a sincere belief that he was acting in the best interest of his country'.[23]

While it is widely accepted that Jack was indeed violently anti-Communist, it is important to acknowledge too that not all historians have been prepared to accept Leo's explanation of his son's conduct at face value, or to believe that his behaviour was driven by anti-Communism alone. It is entirely possible that Jack inherited the basis for his anti-Communist views from his father, although he clearly expressed them in a greatly exaggerated style. Leo's antipathy to Communism was purely practical, and it is worth remembering that at the time of Munich he was one of only a handful of those MPs who were opposed to Chamberlain who ruled out absolutely any deal with Russia. It was a view that placed him at odds with most of his fellow dissidents, the Churchill group in particular. As late as 28 September 1938, Leo recorded in his diary that he was still hoping for a 'real European settlement' without Russia, and that, until the Czech crisis unfolded, he had always 'looked to Germany, France and Italy working together with our co-operation as forming the only basis of a satisfactory European system excluding Russia'.[24] In the words of one historian, this remark 'revealed all his anti-Communist, isolationist, and imperial preconceptions'.[25]

It has also been suggested that, in both his private and public explanations of Jack's conduct, Leo 'thoroughly failed to deal with the centrality of his son's antisemitism'.[26] An obvious possible motive for Leo's reluctance to confront this aspect of Jack's writing and broadcasting lies in his own Jewish ancestry. With the material currently available, it is impossible to ascertain whether or not Jack knew of his own Jewish roots, although it seems incredible to suppose that he had no idea whatsoever. If he did know, as seems most likely, then in the words of another historian, his 'anti-semitism must represent part of an oedipal revolt against his father'. Perhaps the shame of recognising that his son was a 'convinced and vicious anti-semite'[27] was too much, even for Leo, to bear.

If Leo was concerned with putting the best possible explanation on Jack's conduct, Bryddie had no such worries, believing that he had done very little wrong in the first place. Her post-war correspondence and behaviour reveal an increasing eccentricity when discussing Jack and a sense of denial apparently heightened by grief. Jack had been 'slender – with a delicate, really beautiful face and the large dark eyes of the Seeker for Truth'. He had 'grown through all his wild bit', and had become a 'rather wonderful person', no one doubting that he had found 'his faith in God' at the very end. And she would, 'for all eternity' be grateful for his 'sincerity, sweetness of nature and his superb courage'.[28] In April 1946 Leo and Bryddie spent a week in Athens, dining one night with Sir Patrick Reilly, who was later to serve as Harold Macmillan's Ambassador in Moscow and in Paris. As a fellow member of All Souls, Reilly already knew Leo well, but the dinner was an awkward affair. While Bryddie was, naturally, 'a very nice person', she was also 'obviously completely broken by the awful tragedy of her son, of whom she talks a lot . . . how good he was at languages and how he loved mountaineering'. It was, thought Reilly, all 'pretty embarrassing'.[29]

▪ ▪ ▪

Although he had failed to win a seat in Parliament at his first attempt, Julian was nevertheless re-adopted as the Conservative candidate for Preston in the summer of 1947. In the meantime he settled down during the post-war years to life as an author and, in 1948, he published *Sons of the Eagle*, a fast-moving and detailed account of his wartime experiences in Albania. He also began work on completing J. L. Garvin's extravagant official biography of Joseph Chamberlain, a formidable task. Garvin, the former editor of the *Observer* and an old friend of Leo's, had published the first three volumes between 1932 and 1934 but, on his death in 1947, the work still remained largely unfinished and Chamberlain's papers were in a state of considerable disorder. Julian published volume four to good reviews in June 1951, and went on eventually to publish volumes five and six in 1969.

In the late 1940s Julian was once again reunited with his former comrades in arms David Smiley and Billy McLean in an attempt to overthrow the regime of Enver Hoxha, the former Albanian partisan leader who now ruled his country. Both the British and American Governments had become increasingly concerned at the destabilising effect of Albania on the Balkan region. In October 1947 the United Nations General Assembly set up a committee to investigate the allegation that Greek Communist forces, then engaged in civil war in Greece, were being aided by Albania, Yugoslavia and Bulgaria. In the summer of 1948 Julian visited Greece and realised for the first time just how precarious was the position of the Greek Government. In his opinion the only way to defeat the Communist guerrilla movement was 'to strike at the safe harbours' that they enjoyed on the other side of their frontiers, 'either by hot pursuit . . . or by stirring up a guerrilla movement against the government providing the harbour'.[30]

In November 1948 the United Nations General Assembly passed a resolution confirming that the support given to the Greek rebels by Albania in particular 'endangers peace in the Balkans and is inconsistent with the purposes and principles of the Charter'. Writing in the London journal *Time and Tide*, Julian developed the theme more fully in an article provocatively entitled 'The Case for Retaliation'. 'The position of the Albanian state is particularly precarious,' he wrote. Since June 1948, when Stalin had expelled Tito from the Comintern,

Albania had been 'separated from the rest of the Comintern bloc by deviationist Yugoslavia'. The country was now 'desperately short of food', some of the old political outlaws were still hiding in the mountains, and the news of recent government purges suggested that the 'Albanian Communist Party was deeply divided between Stalinists and Titoists'. He continued that 'in the face of a popular revolt the regime would be hard put to defend itself, let alone to continue its support' for the Greek Communists. 'From the military point of view', Julian decided, 'retaliation has everything to commend it.' There was no reason to suppose that such action would lead to war. 'If Stalin wants war, there will be war', he concluded, but it was hardly likely that he would start it, 'just because, for once, he is given a taste of his own medicine'.[31]

Although he no longer had access to the higher echelons of government through an influential father, Julian nevertheless already had many friends of his own in senior political positions, and enjoyed the confidence of a number of his former SOE colleagues who had transferred across to SIS at the end of the war. His timing was perfect. The French Minister in Tirana, Guy Menant, who acted as a conduit for what little news reached the outside world from Albania, confirmed that 'the arrival on the frontier of sizeable numbers of allied troops would be the signal for a spontaneous uprising throughout Albania.'[32] The problem for the Government was how best to achieve such an outcome, given that the political climate of the day demanded that any action would have to be clandestine. A 'Cold War Sub-Committee' was set up within the Foreign Office to plan how best to achieve the relaxing of the 'Soviet hold on the orbit countries', and to help them to achieve ultimate independence by 'promoting civil discontent, internal confusion and possible strife in the satellite countries'. By the end of 1948 the Prime Minster, Clement Attlee, with the support of his Foreign Secretary, Ernest Bevin, had approved a small-scale military operation, to be carried out with both the encouragement and active involvement, in particular financial, of the Americans.

Julian had no problem morally justifying the course of action upon which they were to embark. As far as he was concerned, Stalin was trying to overthrow the pro-western government in Athens, and 'you can't apply the Marquess of Queensberry rules to one side and not the other'.[33] By the spring of 1949 preparations were well underway. Julian joined forces with Billy McLean to brief the relevant Foreign Office and SIS officials, while various leading Albanian exiles, who had known Julian and McLean during the war, were assembled in Rome. Julian's job would be to persuade the clans to put aside their differences and to form a united Albanian government-in-exile, which would enjoy the legitimacy needed to raise the small force of Albanian guerrilla fighters to carry out the action. Julian and McLean were considered to be the only two westerners capable of breaking down the existing barriers of mistrust among the various Albanian factions. Two further former colleagues from wartime Albania also became involved. Alan Hare was by now a serving officer with SIS, while David Smiley was recruited from his regiment in Germany, the Royal Horse Guards, to manage the military side of the operation. He was to set up and run a special training school in Malta for a hand-picked force of young Albanians, who would then be infiltrated into Albania by sea.

In May 1949 Julian, McLean and Hare flew to Athens where, with some difficulty, they managed to secure the agreement of the Greek Government to make use of Greek territory to launch the raids. Two weeks later the trio flew to Rome for discussions with the various Albanian exiles assembled there. Not only did they succeed in securing broad support for the operation, but they also, with the help of the Albanian leaders, soon identified thirty suitable young Albanians from the Italian refugee camps around Naples, who were subsequently smuggled into Malta to begin training at Smiley's secret camp. After returning to London to brief SIS officials and political friends, Julian again returned to Rome in June in an effort to get the various groups of Albanian exiles to cooperate in forming a representative Albanian Government after liberation. Since the war, royalists and republicans, Christians and Muslims, and northerners and southerners had been bitterly opposed to each other, even in exile. But after several days of intense negotiations, Julian and his team succeeded in getting agreement from the various factions to a political compromise and the creation of a national committee, along with the necessary individual appointments.

The final part of the political jigsaw was to persuade the exiled Albanian King Zog, now living in Alexandria, to support the plan. On 14 July Julian and McLean, accompanied by their American liaison representative Robert Low, flew to Egypt to be introduced to the King. The meeting started badly, McLean admitting that they 'rather blundered in, proud of having pulled off the Rome agreement', and assuming that the King would accept whatever ideas they put to him. But far from accepting the *fait accompli* with which he believed he was being presented, King Zog reacted angrily, demanding to know with what authority the agreement had been reached by the British and Americans behind his back, and refusing to acknowledge, let alone support, any Albanian government or leadership that did not have him at its head. The delegation left with their tails between their legs, but returned a few hours later, when Julian was given the task of trying to win back the King's support. 'Amery's performance was masterly,' recalled Low. 'I've never seen such diplomacy in my life. He was like Talleyrand.'[34] The trio eventually flew back to London having secured Zog's agreement that, while he would not give his support publicly, neither would he make known his concerns.

Julian's personal involvement with the operation was now largely at an end, but he closely followed the disastrous progress of the ensuing landings in Albania through to their eventual, well-documented conclusion several years later. On 28 September 1949 the first group of Albanian volunteers left Smiley's training camp in Malta by fishing boat, before transferring, three days later to a smaller boat off southern Italy. With Alan Hare monitoring their movements from a radio base on Corfu, the nine soldiers were put ashore by night at the same landing area as had been used to evacuate Julian and other SOE officers during the war. But when they finally made radio contact with Hare several days later, they reported that the Albanian authorities had clearly been expecting them, that three of their number had been killed, and the rest were now on the run. Hare ordered them to make their way to the Greek border, where they were at first arrested before being released into British custody. A similar fate befell other groups of armed Albanians put ashore in the same manner.

It was not until 1963, when Kim Philby defected to Moscow, that it finally transpired that, in the course of his role in Washington in 1949 as liaison officer coordinating combined CIA and SIS operations, Philby had been privy to full details of the Albanian landings. Unknown to the British, he had simply passed on full details of the operation to his Russian minders who had, in turn, alerted Hoxha's authorities. Although ignorant of his treachery at the time, the British and Americans ignored the losses suffered and, remarkably, continued to send further groups of agents into Albania, almost all of whom were killed or captured and sentenced to a lifetime in prison. Although Hoxha subsequently claimed that it was the 'wisdom, justice and the revolutionary vigilance of the Albanian people [which] brought about the ignominious failure of the plans of the foreign enemy',[35] there is nowadays no dispute that the operation failed thanks to one of Philby's most successful acts of treachery during his long career spying for Russia.

■ ■ ■

Over three years after leaving Parliament, at the age of seventy-five, Leo still continued to harbour the hope that a safe seat would be found for him to enable his return to active politics. 'I do think the Party owes me a reasonable seat,' he complained to Beaverbrook at the end of 1948, 'after thirty-four years of fighting a purely industrial one.' What he really wanted was a 'safe by-election' to give him another 'chance of joining the fight in Parliament'.[36] In the meantime, however, he was content to continue to play an active role within the voluntary ranks of the party, and he soon became a familiar face at Conservative gatherings, appearing and speaking every year without fail at the annual party conference. In doing so he quickly acquired a reputation for encouraging as his personal protégés many of the young Conservative politicians who went on to achieve high office in the 1960s and 1970s. He also continued to carry on an extensive correspondence with many senior politicians with whom he had served and who, in the case of Attlee, now governed the country.

Politically, Leo focused on a number of issues, some familiar over a lifetime of political work, others less so. He bitterly opposed the agreements reached over the American loan, believing that the accompanying conditions imposed by Washington were inimical to his long and passionately held belief in a policy of imperial preference. He continued also to take a close interest in Indian affairs, and was one of the first voices of any importance publicly to advocate an early relinquishment by Whitehall of control over India. It was, he told Attlee, a necessary step if an effective settlement was to be brought about between Congress and the Muslim League. And in February 1947 he loudly supported the announcement that a time limit would be set for the full transfer of power into Indian hands. When he visited Churchill one day at Chartwell, however, the topic of India was tactfully ignored, except when the former Prime Minister 'referred to that ass Wavell and that traitor Auchinleck'.[37]

Less predictably, Leo also became an ardent supporter of European union, writing to Churchill as early as November 1945 that there was 'only one way of limiting Russian demands and that is . . . build up some sort of European Union or Commonwealth that can hold its own . . . so long as Europe remains Balkanised European countries will be tempted to look to outside patrons in every quarrel and . . . in the end it will come to a final struggle between the patrons.'[38] A year later he expressed his delight that Churchill, in his celebrated speech at Zurich, had 'gone all out for the conception of a united Europe', flattering himself that Churchill had used a good deal of material from one of his own recent speeches, at London University, a copy of which Leo had sent him. He wrote to Churchill again, urging him to follow the speech up even more forcefully, and offering 'to help his campaign in any way I can'. He reflected that 'it would be interesting in this last chapter if Winston and I who have so consistently differed, when in the same government, now at last see eye to eye and work together.'[39]

Leo also pursued his interest in the Middle East during his twilight years, following closely developments in Palestine and the Suez Canal Zone. He visited the region in 1947, and again in 1950 accompanied by Julian, as a guest of President Weizmann, one of the first senior politicians to do so after the Jewish state's official recognition by Britain in 1949. Throughout the war years Leo had watched with horror as details of the Holocaust filtered back to London, and had recorded in June 1944 that Weizmann had brought him news of the 'monstrous German blackmailing offer to release a million Jews in return for ten thousand lorries and other equipment, failing which bargain they proposed to exterminate them'.[40] The poignancy of the news must have been enhanced by the knowledge that the majority of the Jews in question were Hungarian.

Now, in the post-war era, Leo found himself in bitter disagreement with the policy pursued by the British Government and by the Foreign Secretary, Ernest Bevin, in particular. While he supported American demands, unusually for him, for higher levels of Jewish immigration to be allowed into post-war Palestine, he refused – as he had throughout his own ministerial career – to allow his own Jewish ancestry to influence his own views in an unduly partisan fashion. Indeed he urged Weizmann to accept the partition of Palestine, and even went so far as to draw up carefully his own suggestions for what he believed would be a fair allocation of territory, to which he hoped both sides might ultimately agree. 'To my mind,' he wrote, 'acquiescence under protest by both would be much better than acceptance by either side.'[41] And with Jewish terrorism on the increase, he showed remarkable foresight when he wrote in 1948 that if the terrorists were 'eventually to get control of Israel and embark on a policy of wider conquest they may create an Arab resistance which may one day reverse the situation and cause the Zionist State to end like the Crusaders' Kingdom'.[42]

During the war years Leo had won recognition from a number of the bodies he had served so loyally for many years. He continued to play an active role as a Governor at Harrow until his death and, unlike some Governors who were considered 'iconic if not decorative', Leo was 'one of the most active and influential governors of the first half of the century'.[43] During the war, in spite of his duties as Secretary of State for India, he played a major role in ensuring the very survival of the school and, as Masters' Governor, successfully adjudicated over a potential rebellion by masters in 1942. He retained his strongest links, however, with Oxford, and was awarded a doctorate of civil law by the university and an honorary fellowship by Balliol. He had joined the Rhodes Trust in 1919, and had been instrumental in founding the Beit Scholarship, an award linked to Commonwealth Studies at Oxford. After some time spent as chairman of the Rhodes Trust, Leo continued as a member of the board until his death, rarely missing a meeting even during his years in Cabinet. When his old friend Jan Smuts died in 1950, he organised the Smuts Memorial Fund, which raised £152,000 to endow a professorship of Commonwealth History at Cambridge, for which he was awarded an honorary degree by that university also. And after almost thirty years as a Freemason, he continued to attend Masonic meetings after the war, having served as Grand Master of the Canada Lodge in 1942.

Leo had 'always regarded the Presidency of the AC [Alpine Club] and the Prime Ministership of the UK as the natural twin summits of ambition', and at the end of 1943 had been relieved 'to attain at any rate one of them'[44] when he was elected president of the Alpine Club, of which he had been a member since 1899. 'Public life is very much like mountaineering,' he once wrote. 'It needs determination and endurance. It needs judgement of what lies ahead and skill in dealing with each problem as you come to it. It needs, not least, a steady head on exposed summits. It has its long lower slopes, its dreary moraines, its long spells of bad weather. But it also has its keen delights, its glorious days, its summits of achievement. Above all, one enjoys it for its own sake, whether one gets to the summit or not.'[45] He also served as president of the Ski Club of Great Britain and, in 1946, he published the second volume of his non-political memoirs, *In the Rain and the Sun*, the sequel to *Days of Fresh Air*, the titles taken from a verse of Harrow's most famous school song. Indeed he wrote prolifically throughout his old age: in 1947 he published *Thoughts on the Constitution*, a collection of Chichele lectures he had given at All Souls the previous year, in 1948 *The Awakening*, in 1949 *Thought and Language*, based on his presidential address to the English Association and in 1954 *A Balanced Economy*. Finally, he wrote four substantial volumes of political memoirs, *My Political Life*, of which the first three were published to widespread acclaim between 1953 and 1955.

▪ ▪ ▪

In the spring of 1949 Julian had invited his old friend, Harold Macmillan's son Maurice, out to lunch, but when he had been unable to come had invited Maurice's sister Catherine instead. After visiting

Delphi in search of inspiration that summer, Julian proposed and the couple were married, as both sets of parents had been before them, at St Margaret's, Westminster, on 26 January 1950. Billy McLean, who had been adopted as Julian's running partner in Preston North in place of Randolph Churchill, was best man, and the honeymoon was curtailed to just three days in Paris, before Julian and Catherine embarked, as Leo and Bryddie had done forty years earlier, on a general election campaign. With help from both Leo and Harold Macmillan, this time Julian was elected with a majority of 938, although McLean just failed by fourteen votes. The Labour Government remained in power, but with its majority reduced to just six seats.

In his early years at Westminster, inspired no doubt by Leo, Julian was a strong supporter of Churchill's pro-European campaign. His maiden speech envisaged the possibility of a European army and, from 1950 until 1953, and again in 1956, he was a delegate to the Consultative Assembly of the Council of Europe, often travelling abroad with his new father-in-law, who found Julian a useful companion as he seemed to 'speak all languages and most dialects with useful and sufficient fluency'.[46] However, Macmillan was not so impressed by Julian's most prominent campaign during his early years in Parliament, after the Conservatives had been returned to power in 1951. The so-called Suez Group of some forty Conservative MPs, who were opposed to Eden's proposals to evacuate British troops from the Canal Zone, met for the first time at 112 Eaton Square on 5 October 1953, with Julian acting as secretary. Enoch Powell later recalled the 'colloquies, not to say cabals',[47] which Leo hosted at his home, while Macmillan, by now a Cabinet minister himself, merely commented of his son-in-law that he was 'able, but unduly influenced by his old father'.[48]

On 7 December 1951 Churchill drew Leo to one side at the annual School Songs at Harrow, and again offered him a seat in the House of Lords. He assured Leo that there would be reform of the Lords in due course, which would enable Julian to renounce a hereditary title if he should wish to remain in the Commons after his father's death. Leo was sufficiently interested to write a long letter the following day to Julian, who was in Strasbourg, 'balancing the pros and the cons'. But later that afternoon Harold Macmillan came to see Leo, and forcefully warned him that 'the advantage of going to the House of Lords could not outweigh the disadvantages to Julian'.[49] Macmillan was in fact privately appalled to hear that Leo was even considering the offer. 'It is a most selfish act,' he thought. 'He is 78 and will ruin poor Julian's life. No money; no career; and a peerage! Catherine is distraught.'

The following day Macmillan was relieved to hear that Leo had abandoned the idea after driving down to Hatfield for a lengthy talk with 'Bobbety' Salisbury, the senior Conservative in the House of Lords. However, Macmillan could still not quite get over the previous day's conversation. 'To ruin his son's life just for the chance of making a few more speeches to some bored noblemen!' he wrote. 'What folly!'[50] Leo had in fact completely misjudged Macmillan's likely reaction, and afterwards admitted to being relieved that his only interest was 'in Julian's success and not, as I thought it just possibly might have been, in seeing Catherine a viscountess'.[51] Bryddie, however, was bitterly disappointed at Leo's decision, believing that his work had never 'been sufficiently recognised and that this would have been a public recognition' and would have given Leo a 'fresh start'.[52] To Beaverbrook he joked that he had had to 'decline Winston's invitation to join your noble assembly in order not to queer Julian's pitch by dying at a moment when he just might be making his mark in the Commons'.[53] For the last few years of his life Leo joined the campaign for life peerages, which were finally introduced in 1958.

Far from his vigour being in any way abated during his final years, the fitness he had built up as a mountaineer remained with him until his death, with the exception of ever worsening deafness. 'I have given up up-hill climbing, except by funicular,' he wrote to Lionel Curtis in 1949, 'and even on the level I walk with sedateness befitting my years.' Yet in June that year he took Julian to the Rockies, 'giving him a look at Mt Amery (in order to inculcate a bit of filial respect)'.[54] And in response to a request from Curtis as how best to deal with heart trouble, Leo advised that, taking Churchill as his role model, he should 'cut out non-essential commitments . . . spend an occasional day in bed', and that 'speech making was the least tiring form of moderate exercise', as it 'expands the lungs and *mildly* exercises the brain!'[55]

Bryddie was not so lucky, suffering a stroke, although after their marriage Julian and Catherine moved into the upper floors of Eaton Square, thus ensuring that the Amery family remained as close-knit as they had always been.

Leo Amery died peacefully in his sleep at Eaton Square in the early hours of 16 September 1955, at the age of eighty-one. Harold Macmillan praised his 'fine record of devoted and sincere service', and his 'great dignity and nobility of mind'.[56] Bryddie was later fond of quoting one of Wavell's last statements before his own death, five years earlier, that Leo had 'the best brains in the country and the heart of a lion'.[57] Churchill, who had resigned the premiership just a few months earlier, was 'deeply grieved to hear of the death of my old friend Leo Amery. Statesman and man of letters, he was above all a great patriot. I mourn his loss.'[58] Leo was buried among his paternal ancestors in the peaceful, idyllic churchyard at Lustleigh, on Dartmoor, where Amerys had worshipped for many generations. His headstone records simply that he was a 'Statesman and Mountaineer'.

Epilogue

At a lunch given to mark his eightieth birthday in November 1953, Leo had finished his speech by quoting Bunyan: 'I give my sword to him that shall succeed me in my pilgrimage.'[1] Certainly Julian shared many of his father's political ideals, most notably his views on the Commonwealth, Britain's role at its centre, and the aspiration that Britain should be a major power in Europe. During the year after Leo's death, Julian fought what he considered to be the last great battle of the Commonwealth, that over Suez, loudly supporting military intervention in response to Nasser's nationalisation of the canal. When the use of force was subsequently abandoned, however, he failed to join many of his fellow members of the Suez Group who resigned the Conservative Whip, although in later years he claimed that his proudest moment in politics came when 'Nasser proved me right about the Suez Canal.'[2]

Although Julian never emulated his father by achieving Cabinet rank, he did go on to enjoy a distinguished political career over many years. In January 1957, when his father-in-law Harold Macmillan came to power, Julian was given his first junior ministerial post as Parliamentary Under-Secretary at the War Office and, in November 1958, he was transferred across to the same position at the Colonial Office where he found himself, ironically, forced to preside over the British withdrawal from Cyprus. Although on the surface such a policy flew in the face of his own opposition to the idea that Britain should dismantle any further her empire, he justified his position to his own satisfaction. For four months, until the end of June 1960, Julian lived in Cyprus and successfully concluded the interminable negotiations with Archbishop Makarios which secured the future of the British military bases after independence. During his time at the Colonial Office he also helped to bring stability to Oman with the Oman Treaty of 1958, and developed a close relationship with the countries of the Gulf and their rulers which was to grow ever stronger and to continue long into old age.

In October 1960 he was appointed Secretary of State for Air, became a Privy Counsellor, and two years later became Minister of Aviation. At that ministry he attracted perhaps the greatest controversy of his ministerial career by his enthusiastic advocacy of the Anglo-French project to build Concorde. In spite of the Government's poor relations with France after de Gaulle's Common Market veto, Julian entered into the discussions eagerly and subsequently reached agreement with the French over the joint development of the aircraft. In 1963 Julian did himself few favours with his support for Quintin Hogg's leadership campaign and, after the Conservative general election defeat of October 1964, he lost his front bench status under Ted Heath. Throughout this period, he was known as an influential supporter of Ian Smith's regime in Rhodesia and an outspoken leader of the backbench rebellion against sanctions. In March 1966 he lost his seat at Preston.

Out of Parliament, Julian returned to writing for a time and was able to finish the final two volumes of *The Life of Joseph Chamberlain*, but he was re-elected to Parliament for the constituency of Brighton Pavilion at a by-election in March 1969. Rather surprisingly, in view of his earlier rebellion over Rhodesia, after the general election of June 1970 Heath made him Minister of State for Public Building and Works and, soon after, Minister for Housing. In 1972 he moved to become Minister of State at the Foreign Office where, to his great delight, Julian found that he was to occupy his father's old office, the India Office. It was to be his last ministerial post. There was some talk during the Conservative leadership election of 1975 that Julian might put himself forward as a candidate, but in the end it was his old friend Hugh Fraser who stood unsuccessfully instead. And when the Conservatives returned to power in 1979 under Margaret Thatcher there was again some talk of Julian achieving high office, most notably in the spring of 1982 when, it has been suggested, the Prime Minister came close to appointing him Foreign Secretary following the resignation of Lord Carrington. But Julian had caused too much controversy over the years, in particular with his continued defiance of the party line over Rhodesia.

For the remainder of their lives, Julian and Catherine lived at Eaton Square with their four children and, until her death in February 1975 at the age of eighty-five, an increasingly frail Bryddie living upstairs. In November 1973 Julian held a dinner at Eaton Square to celebrate the hundredth anniversary of Leo's birth, attended, in the words of Isaiah Berlin, by 'some of those splendid pillars of the past, whose like, I suspect, we may never see again'.[3] Bryddie was too frail to join the party downstairs, but sent down a message to the effect that the house was 'full of Leo's spirit'. Julian, she believed, 'feels it and lives up to it as his dear father was his best friend'. Leo had 'served the nation well', while Jack had 'died bravely'.[4] Eaton Square was both a family home and, for the next eighteen years, while Julian sat on the back benches, an alternative Foreign Office, to which a never-ending procession of kings, oriental potentates, East European presidents, guerrilla fighters and intelligence officers from around the world beat a path. So too did many contemporary British politicians.

Julian was devastated when Catherine died before him in 1991, and he left the House of Commons at the general election of 1992, accepting the seat offered him in the House of Lords by John Major, as Baron Amery of Lustleigh. Before his own death four years later, Julian had just one more family duty to perform. Early in 1995 he invited the Home Secretary Michael Howard to lunch at Eaton Square. After the initial niceties had been observed, Julian quickly came to the real reason for the meeting. Would Howard give permission for Julian to have Jack's body exhumed from his unmarked grave at Wandsworth so that he could be properly buried with dignity elsewhere? So unusual, indeed in Howard's experience, so unique, was

Julian's request that the Home Secretary was temporarily lost for words. However, he returned to the Home Office after lunch and asked his officials to look into both the legality and feasibility of Julian's proposal.

The answer was that there was no legal impediment to Jack's exhumation, indeed William Joyce had been exhumed and reburied in Ireland in 1976. However, there was a practical problem, namely that another prisoner, a convicted murderer, had been hanged sometime after Jack and buried above him. The body could only be moved with the family's permission, but his wife and two children had gone away and, at first, no one could be found. However, eventually, after a long search, his next of kin were tracked down and gave their permission for the body to be moved and then reinterred. On 17 January 1996, Howard granted the licence allowing for Jack's exhumation and, a week later on 24 January, a leading firm of London undertakers disinterred Jack's body from its grave at Wandsworth, from where they took it to Mortlake crematorium for cremation. As he had always wanted, Jack's ashes were later scattered in the Dordogne region of France, almost certainly in the vicinity of Bergerac where his beloved Jeanine Barde had been buried in 1943.

Julian died peacefully at Eaton Square just a few months later, on 3 September 1996, and he was laid to rest alongside his wife and parents in the churchyard at Lustleigh. Although Jack had not been buried there with them, Julian died secure in the knowledge that he had fulfilled one last act of family love for his brother and his parents, especially Bryddie. After such a troubled life, Jack was at least now at peace fifty years after his own tragic death.

Notes

ABBREVIATIONS

Diaries I	Barnes, J., and Nicholson, D. (eds), *The Leo Amery Diaries 1869–1929*
Diaries II	Barnes, J., and Nicholson, D. (eds), *The Empire at Bay: The Leo Amery Diaries 1929–1945*
DOFA	Amery, L., *Days of Fresh Air*
LSA	Leopold Amery
MPL I	Amery, L., *My Political Life: Volume I, England Before the Storm 1896–1914*
MPL II	Amery, L., *My Political Life: Volume II, War and Peace 1914–1929*
MPL III	Amery, L., *My Political Life: Volume III, The Unforgiving Years 1929–1940*
TNL	Times Newspaper Limited

GOVERNMENT PAPERS AT THE PUBLIC RECORDS OFFICE

Board of Trade	BT
Cabinet	CAB
Colonial Office	CO

Central Criminal Court	CRIM
Foreign Office	FO
Home Office	HO
Special Operations Executive	HS
Central Office of Information	INF
Security Service	KV
Prime Minister	PREM
Prison Commission	PCOM
War Office	WO

PROLOGUE

1. HO 45/25773, Transcript of John Amery's Broadcast, 19 November 1942
2. MS Amery Diary, AMEL 7/36, 17 November 1942
3. KV 2/79, *Daily Mirror*, 18 November 1942
4. MS Amery Diary, AMEL 7/36, 18 November 1942
5. KV 2/79, Transocean Broadcast, 18 November 1942
6. MS Amery Diary, AMEL 7/36, 18 November 1942
7. HO 45/25773, *John Amery Speaks*
8. MS Amery Diary, AMEL 7/36, 19 November 1942
9. HO 45/25773, *John Amery Speaks*
10. MS Amery Diary, AMEL 7/36, 19 November 1942

CHAPTER ONE

1. Amery, C., *Notes on Forestry*
2. Rubinstein, W., *The Secret of Leopold Amery*, p. 177
3. Ibid., p. 176
4. Amery, L., *My Political Life: Volume I, England Before the Storm 1896–1914*, p. 28
5. Rubinstein, p. 180
6. Keay, J., *Eccentric Travellers*, p. 184
7. *MPL I*, pp. 28–9
8 Ibid., p. 32
9. Ibid., p. 33

10. Rubinstein, p. 181
11. *MPL I*, p. 35
12. Harrow School Broadsheets, December 1887 to April 1892
13. *MPL I*, p. 35
14. Amery, L., *Days of Fresh Air*, p. 21
15. Ibid., p. 20
16. Churchill, W., *My Early Life*, p. 31
17. Ibid., p. 32
18. *DOFA*, p. 21
19. Churchill, W., *My Early Life*, p. 32
20. Ball, S., *The Guardsmen: Harold Macmillan, Three Friends and the World They Made*, p. 214
21. *MPL I*, p. 47
22. Jones, J., *Balliol College: A History 1263–1939*, p. 221
23. *DOFA*, p. 34
24. *MPL I*, p. 52
25. *MPL I*, p. 69
26. Mackenzie, N., and J. (eds), *The Diary of Beatrice Webb: Volume II 1892–1905, 'All the Good Things of Life'*, p. 103
27. Ibid., p. 101
28. Simon, J., *Retrospect: The Memoirs of the Rt. Hon. Viscount Simon*, p. 37
29. MS Warden Anson 445, LSA to Anson, 10 December 1897
30. Dutton, D., *Simon: A Political Biography of Sir John Simon*, p. 9
31. *Memorial Addresses of All Souls College Oxford*, privately printed by Leopard's Head Press, 1989, p. 17
32. MS Warden Anson 446, LSA to Anson, 10 December 1897
33. MS Warden Anson 438, LSA to Anson, 29 December 1897
34. *Diaries I*, p. 25, LSA to Elisabeth Amery, 19 January 1898
35. *DOFA*, p. 70
36. MS Warden Anson, Salisbury to Anson, 13 February 1898
37 *DOFA*, p. 72

CHAPTER TWO

1. Repington, C., *The First World War 1914–1918, Volume II*, p. 499
2. *DOFA*, p. 74
3. Ibid., p. 75

4. Ibid., p. 76
5. Ibid., p. 79
6. Ibid., p. 81
7. *MPL I*, p. 84
8. *DOFA*, p. 91
9. Ibid., p. 96
10. Ibid., p. 99
11. MS Warden Anson 349, LSA to Anson, 18 October 1898
12. MS Warden Anson 466, LSA to Anson, 14 December 1898
13. *MPL I*, p. 89
14. Simon, p. 45
15. MS Simon 47/35, LSA to Simon, 20 March 1897
16. *MPL I*, p. 95
17. Ibid., p. 96
18. MS Warden Anson 295/296, LSA to Anson, 15 May 1899
19. *DOFA*, p. 121
20. Gollin, A., *Proconsul in Politics: A Study of Lord Milner in Opposition and in Power*, p. 123
21. *MPL I*, p. 101
22. Ibid., p. 104
23. Ibid., p. 106
24. *Diaries I*, p. 30, LSA to Elisabeth Amery, 6 October 1899
25. *MPL I*, p. 111
26. Churchill, W., *My Early Life*, p. 257
27. *DOFA*, p. 142
28. *Diaries I*, pp. 30–31, LSA to Chirol, 25 November 1899
29. *MPL I*, p. 122
30. Birkenhead, Lord, *Rudyard Kipling*, p. 206
31. TNL Archive, CMB/1, LSA to Moberley Bell, 28 March 1900
32. Ibid., 18 December 1899
33. *MPL I*, p. 150
34. Ibid., p. 152
35. Ibid., p. 154
36. Ibid., p. 156
37. Amery, L., *The Times History of the South African War: Volume II*, p. 32
38. Ibid., p. 34
39. Ibid., p. 41
40. *DOFA*, p. 161

41. TNL Archive, Manager's Letter Books 30/571, Moberley Bell to LSA, 11 April 1902

42. *MPL I*, p. 160

CHAPTER THREE

1. *MPL I*, p. 165
2. *DOFA*, p. 170
3. TNL Archive, Manager's Letter Books 31/306, Moberley Bell to LSA, 1 July 1902
4. TNL Archive, CMB/1, LSA to Moberley Bell, 15 September 1902
5. TNL Archive, Manager's Letter Books 32/147, Moberley Bell to LSA, 25 September 1902
6. *MPL I*, p. 192
7. Brett, M. (ed.), *The Journals and Letters of Viscount Esher, Volume I 1870–1903*, pp. 393–4
8. Mackenzie, N. (ed.), *The Letters of Sidney and Beatrice Webb, Volume II: Partnership 1892–1912*, p. 170
9. *MPL I*, p. 223
10. Lycett, A., *Rudyard Kipling*, p. 385
11. West, A., *H.G. Wells: Aspects of a Life*, p. 286
12. Wells, H.G., *Experiment in Autobiography: Volume II*, p. 762
13. Roberts, A., *Salisbury: Victorian Titan*, p. 783
14. Amery, J., *Joseph Chamberlain and the Tariff Reform Campaign: Volume V 1901–1903*, p. 191
15. *MPL I*, p. 238
16. *Sunday Times*, 7 February 1932
17. MS Maxse 451/693, LSA to Maxse, 20 September 1903
18. Amery, J., *Joseph Chamberlain and the Tariff Reform Campaign: Volume V 1901–1903*, p. 442
19. Smith, J., *John Buchan: A Biography*, p. 153
20. *MPL I*, p. 273
21. Gollin, A., *The Observer and J. L. Garvin, 1908–1914: A Study in Great Editorship*, p. 7
22. TNL Archive, Manager's Letter Books 40/253, Moberley Bell to LSA, 24 June 1905
23. *Diaries I*, pp. 51–2, Buckle to LSA, 28 June 1905

24. *MPL I*, pp. 277–8
25. *MPL I*, p. 290
26. MS Dawson 62/15, LSA to Dawson, 2 March 1906
27. *MPL I*, p. 291
28. Birkenhead, Lord, *F.E.: The Life of F.E. Smith, First Earl of Birkenhead*, p. 126
29. *Diaries I*, p. 55, Balfour to LSA, 30 July 1906
30. TNL Archive, Manager's Letter Books 50/814, Moberley Bell to LSA, 10 December 1908
31. *DOFA*, p. 223
32. Headlam, C. (ed.), *The Milner Papers, Volume II, South Africa 1899–1905*, p. 440
33. Gollin, A., *Proconsul in Politics: A Study of Lord Milner in Opposition and in Power*, p. 11
34. Marlowe, J., *Milner: Apostle of Empire*, p. 183
35. *MPL I*, p. 299
36. MS Maxse 457/513, LSA to Maxse, 21 April 1907
37. Young, K., *Arthur James Balfour: The Happy Life of the Politician, Prime Minister, Statesman and Philosopher, 1848–1930*, p. 263
38. *DOFA*, p. 251
39. MS Northcliffe, Add. 62157/147, LSA to Northcliffe, 8 May 1908
40. MS Balfour, Add. 49775/136, Balfour to LSA, 6 May 1908
41. Gollin, A., *Proconsul in Politics: A Study of Lord Milner in Opposition and in Power*, p. 163
42. *Diaries I*, p. 63, Moberley Bell to LSA, 3 February 1909
43. TNL Archive, Northcliffe Papers WDM/2/223, Grey to Northcliffe 28 July 1909
44. MS Northcliffe, Add. 62157/172, LSA to Northcliffe, 19 December 1911
45. MS Amery Diary, AMEL 7/8, 11 January 1909
46. Ibid., 9 January 1909
47. Ibid., 10 January 1909
48. *Diaries I*, p. 66, F. S. Oliver to LSA, 17 September 1909
49. Marlowe, p. 188
50. Dutton, D., *His Majesty's Loyal Opposition: The Unionist Party in Opposition 1905–1915*, p. 51
51. *DOFA*, p. 280
52. MS Northcliffe, Add. 62157/158, Northcliffe to LSA, 17 January 1910

53. MS Amery Diary, AMEL 7/9, 9 April 1910
54. *MPL I*, p. 345
55. MS Amery Diary, AMEL 7/9, 29 June 1910
56. Amery, J., *Approach March: A Venture in Autobiography*, p. 45
57. *Diaries I*, p. 71, Simon to Hamar Greenwood, 10 October 1910
58. *Diaries I*, p. 71, Milner to Bryddie, 27 October 1910
59. MS Milner dep. 37/120, Order of Service, 16 November 1910
60. *MPL I*, p. 362
61. *The Times*, 14 November 1910
62. Spender, J., and Asquith, C., *Life of Herbert Henry Asquith: Lord Oxford and Asquith, Volume I*, p. 297n
63. Nicolson, H., *King George the Fifth: His Life and Reign*, p. 138
64. MS Northcliffe, Add. 62157/160, Northcliffe to LSA, 29 November 1910
65. *MPL I*, p. 365
66. MS Northcliffe, Add. 62157/161, LSA to Northcliffe, 12 December 1910
67. *Diaries I*, p. 71, Joseph Chamberlain to LSA, 12 December 1910

CHAPTER FOUR

1. *MPL I*, p. 395
2. MS Amery Diary, AMEL 7/10, 23 November 1911
3. *MPL I*, p. 366
4. MS Amery Diary, AMEL 7/10, 14 February 1911
5. MS Bonar Law 18/6/146, LSA to Bonar Law, 16 December 1910
6. MS Amery Diary, AMEL 7/10, 27 February 1911
7. Ibid., 4 May 1911
8. *Diaries I*, p. 78, LSA to Bryddie, 21 April 1911
9. MS Amery Diary, AMEL 7/10, 17 May 1911
10. House of Commons, Official Report Volume 25, Col. 2076, 17 May 1911
11. *MPL I*, p. 375
12. Rose, K., *King George V*, p. 127
13. MS Amery Diary, AMEL 7/10, 10 August 1911
14. Rose, K., *King George V*, p. 130
15. MS Amery Diary, AMEL 7/10, 10 August 1911

16. MS Maxse 463/135, LSA to Maxse, 3 August 1911

17. Young, K., *Arthur James Balfour: The Happy Life of the Politician, Prime Minister, Statesman and Philosopher, 1848–1930*, p. 313

18. *MPL I*, p. 397

19. MS Cecil, Add. 51072/214, LSA to Cecil, 16 June 1912

20. *MPL I*, p. 414

21. MS Amery Diary, AMEL 7/11, 31 December 1912

22. MS Amery Diary, AMEL 7/12, 1 January 1913

23. *Diaries I*, p. 90, LSA to Sir Robert Borden, 6 January 1913

24. Blake, R., *The Unknown Prime Minister: The Life and Times of Andrew Bonar Law*, p. 48

25. *MPL I*, p. 417

26. Ibid., p. 422

27. MS Bonar Law 29/2/28, LSA to Bonar Law, 20 March 1913

28. Searle, G., *Corruption in British Politics, 1895–1930*, p. 178

29. MS Amery Diary, AMEL 7/11, 27 October 1912

30. Donaldson, F., *The Marconi Scandal*, p. 119

31. MS Amery Diary, AMEL 7/12, 25 March 1913

32. Hyde, H., *Lord Reading: The Life of Rufus Isaacs, First Marquess of Reading*, p. 147

33. Donaldson, p. 193

34. MS Amery Diary, AMEL 7/12, 27 March 1913

35. *MPL I*, p. 422

36. *Erskine May's Treatise on the Law, Privileges, Proceedings and Usage of Parliament*, 23rd Edition, Lexis Nexis Butterworths 2004, p. 8

37. Donaldson, p. 196

38. Searle, G., *Corruption in British Politics, 1895–1930*, p. 187

39. MS Maxse 469/486, LSA to Maxse, 9 January 1914

40. MS Cecil, Add. 51072/216, LSA to Cecil, 9 January 1914

41. Pound, R., and Harmsworth, G., *Northcliffe*, p. 441

42. MS Maxse 469/486, LSA to Maxse, 9 January 1914

43. *The Times*, 2 July 1913

44. *MPL I*, p. 424

45. MS Cecil Add. 51072/219, LSA to Cecil, 16 January 1914

46. *MPL I*, p. 441

47. Lycett, p. 440

48. Stewart, A., *The Ulster Crisis*, p. 135

49. *Diaries I*, p. 98, LSA to Neville Chamberlain, 16 January 1914

50. Add. Mss Eng. Hist c.689/5, Austen Chamberlain to LSA, 17 January 1914 (Additional Milner papers)

51. Add. Mss Eng. Hist c.689/9, Neville Chamberlain to LSA, 18 January 1914 (Additional Milner papers)

52. Add. Mss Eng. Hist c.689/10, Cecil to LSA, 18 January 1914 (Additional Milner papers)

53. Vincent, J. (ed.), *The Crawford Papers: The Journals of David Lindsay, Twenty-Seventh Earl of Crawford and Tenth Earl of Balcarres, 1871–1940* p. 323

54. Jalland, P., *The Liberals and Ireland: The Ulster Question in British Politics to 1914*, p. 218

55. *MPL I*, p. 443

56. Riddell, Lord, *More Pages From My Diary 1908–1914*, p. 203

57. Jalland, p. 219

58. Jackson, A., *Home Rule: An Irish History 1800–2000*, p. 130

59. MS Bonar Law 32/1/46, LSA to Bonar Law, 23 March 1914

60. House of Commons, Official Report Volume 60, Col. 246, 24 March 1914

61. Ibid., Col. 380, 25 March 14

62. *Diaries I*, p. 99, LSA to Bryddie, 21 April 1914

63. *MPL I*, p. 453

64. House of Commons, Official Report Volume 62, Col. 2204, 21 May 1914

65. Ibid., Cols 2213 and 2214, 21 May 1914

66. Blake, p. 211

67. Ramsden, J. (ed.), *Real Old Tory Politics: The Political Diaries of Sir Robert Sandars, Lord Bayford, 1910–1935*, p. 78

68. *MPL I*, p. 465

CHAPTER FIVE

1. Amery, L., *My Political Life: Volume II, War and Peace 1914–1929*, p. 15

2. Charmley, J., *Lord Lloyd and the Decline of the British Empire*, p. 33

3. MS Amery Diary, AMEL 7/12, 1 August 1914

4. Petrie, C., *The Life and Letters of the Right Honourable Sir Austen Chamberlain: Volume I*, p. 373

5. MS Amery Diary, AMEL 7/12, 2 August 1914

6. Wilson, K., *The Policy of the Entente: Essays on the Determinants of British Foreign Policy 1904–1914*, p. 138
7. *MPL II*, p. 20
8. Ibid., p. 22
9. MS Milner dep. 349/264, LSA to Milner, 1 November 1914
10. *MPL II*, p. 29
11. *MPL II*, p. 27
12. *Diaries I*, p. 110, Hamar Greenwood to Bryddie, 4 September 1914
13. Maurice, F. (ed.), *The Life of General Lord Rawlinson of Trent*, p. 106
14. *Diaries I*, p. 110, LSA to Bryddie, 17 October 1914
15. MS Selborne 92/253 and 254, LSA to Selborne, 11 December 1914
16. *MPL II*, p. 46
17. Ibid., p. 50
18. Ibid., p. 52
19. *Diaries I*, p. 112, LSA to Bryddie, 5 April 1915
20. *MPL II*, p. 54
21. *Diaries I*, pp. 112–13, LSA to Bryddie, 17 April 1915
22. MS Milner dep. 350/97–102, LSA to Milner, 27 April 1915
23. *MPL II*, p. 59
24. Ibid., p. 61
25. MS Bonar Law 50/3/9, Chamberlain to Bonar Law, 20 May 1915
26. *MPL II*, p. 66
27. *Diaries I*, p. 118, LSA to Bryddie, 18 June 1915
28. Ferguson, P., 'Fighting on All Fronts, Leo Amery and the First World War', *Essays in History: Volume XXXV*, p. 75
29. House of Commons, Official Report Volume 73, Cols 2421 and 2422, 28 July 1915
30. *Diaries I*, p. 123, Oliver to LSA, 23 July 1915
31. *Diaries I*, p. 125, Wilson to LSA, 22 October 1915
32. House of Commons, Official Report Volume 74, Col. 60, 15 September 1915
33. Ibid., Col. 801, 28 September 1915
34. *Diaries I*, p. 125, LSA to Bryddie, 30 September 1915
35. Self, R. (ed.), *The Neville Chamberlain Diary Letters, Volume I: The Making of a Politician, 1915–1920*, pp. 94, 98, 103
36. *Diaries I*, p. 124, LSA to Bryddie, 27 September 15
37. Searle, G., *Country Before Party: Coalition and the idea of 'National Government' in Modern Britain, 1885–1987*, p. 95

38. Gollin, A., *Proconsul in Politics: A Study of Lord Milner in Opposition and in Power*, p. 323

39. *MPL II*, p. 81

40. MS Lloyd George D/16/2/8, LSA to Lloyd George, 20 April 1916

41. Roskill, S., *Hankey, Man of Secrets: Volume I 1877–1918*, p. 270

42. Gollin, A., *Proconsul in Politics: A Study of Lord Milner in Opposition and in Power*, p. 342

43. Roskill, S., *Hankey, Man of Secrets: Volume I 1877–1918*, p. 270

44. *Diaries I*, p. 128, LSA to Bryddie, 21 March 1916

45. *MPL II*, p. 83

46. *Diaries I*, p. 131, LSA to Bryddie, 5 December 1916

47. MS Violet Milner 31/C117/12, LSA to Lady Edward Cecil, 12 December 1916

48. *Diaries I*, p. 132, Austen Chamberlain to Bryddie, 9 December 1916

CHAPTER SIX

1. *MPL II*, p. 92

2. Roskill, S., *Hankey, Man of Secrets: Volume I 1877–1918*, p. 349

3. MS Lloyd George F/23/1/2, Hankey to Lloyd George, 14 December 1916

4. Hankey, Lord, *The Supreme Command 1914–1918, Volume II*, p. 590

5. Middlemas, K. (ed.), *Thomas Jones: Whitehall Diary, Volume I 1916–1925*, p. 21

6. Roskill, S., *Hankey, Man of Secrets: Volume I 1877–1918*, p. 349

7. Ibid., pp. 352–3

8. *MPL II*, p. 94

9. Naylor, J., *A Man and an Institution: Sir Maurice Hankey, the Cabinet Secretariat and the Custody of Cabinet Secrecy*, p. 31

10. Grigg, J., *Lloyd George: From Peace to War 1912–1916*, p. 489

11. Self, R. (ed.), *The Neville Chamberlain Diary Letters, Volume I: The Making of a Politician, 1915–1920*, p. 185

12. Ferguson, p. 80

13. MS Amery Diary, AMEL 7/13, 20 April 1917

14. Ibid., 11 May 1917

15. *MPL II*, p. 92

16. MS Maxse 474/163, LSA to Maxse, 3 August 1917

17. *MPL II*, pp. 114–15

18. Weizmann, C., *Trial and Error*, p. 231

19. *MPL II*, p. 115

20. *Diaries I*, p. 170, LSA to Carson, 4 September 1917

21. Sanders, R., *The High Walls of Jerusalem*, p. 427

22. Reinharz, J., *Chaim Weizmann: The Making of a Statesman*, p. 116

23. *MPL II*, p. 118

24. Weisgal, M. (ed.), *The Letters and Papers of Chaim Weizmann: Volume VII, August 1914–November 1917*, pp. 505–6

25. MS Amery Diary, AMEL 7/13, 18 September 1917

26. *MPL II*, p. 117

27. Stein, L., *The Balfour Declaration*, p. 522n, LSA to Stein, 1 July 1952

28. Sanders, p. 593

29. Weizmann, p. 262

30. *The Times*, 2 November 1977

31. Weisgal, M. (ed.), *Chaim Weizmann: A Biography by Several Hands*, p. 163

32. MS Amery Diary, AMEL 7/13, 31 October 1917

33. Ibid., 14 November 1917

34. *MPL II*, p. 124

35. Ibid., p. 127

36. Callwell, C., *Field-Marshal Sir Henry Wilson: His Life and Diaries*, p. 32

37. Roskill, S., *Hankey, Man of Secrets: Volume I 1877–1918*, p. 464

38. MS Amery Diary, AMEL 7/13, 22 November 1917

39. Woodward, D., *Lloyd George and the Generals*, p. 221

40. MS Lloyd George F/2/1/36, Lloyd George to Bryddie, 16 April 1918

41. *MPL II*, p. 134

42. Roskill, S., *Hankey, Man of Secrets: Volume I 1877–1918*, p. 479

43. MS Amery Diary, AMEL 7/13, 12 January 1918

44. Ibid., 23 March 1918

45. Ibid., 28 March 1918

46. *Diaries I*, p. 213, LSA to Bryddie, 31 March 1918

47. *MPL II*, p. 149

48. MS Amery Diary, AMEL 7/13, 10 April 1918

49. Ibid., 3 July 1918

50. Roskill, S., *Hankey, Man of Secrets: Volume I 1877–1918*, p. 593

51. *MPL II*, p. 171

52. *Diaries I*, p. 241

53. MS Amery Diary, AMEL 7/13, 22 October 1918

54. Ibid., 8 November 1918
55. Dutton, D. (ed.), *Paris 1918: The War Diary of the British Ambassador, the 17th Earl of Derby*, p. 331
56. Beamish, H. (ed), *The Jews' Who's Who*, p. 75
57. *MPL II*, p. 175

CHAPTER SEVEN

1. *Harrow Memorials of the Great War, Volume III, 13 September 1915 to 3 July 1916*, Printed for Harrow School by Philip Lee Warner, 1919, p. 2
2. FO 383/426, Foreign Office memorandum, 23 August 1918
3. MS Amery Diary, AMEL 7/14, 29 July 1918
4. MS Amery Diary, AMEL 7/11, 14 March 1912
5. MS Leo Amery, AMEL 2/5/11, LSA to Garvin, 19 March 1912
6. MS Amery Diary, AMEL 7/11, 8 May 1912
7. HO 144/22823/227, report of Dr Edward Glover, 7 December 1945
8. MS Violet Milner 31/C116/1, Bryddie to Lady Edward Cecil, 10 April 1916
9. MS Violet Milner 31/C116/2, Bryddie to Lady Edward Cecil, 2 September 1916
10. HO 144/22823/242, statement of Miss Ironside, December 1945
11. MS Amery Diary, AMEL 7/13, 8 May 1917
12. MS Amery Diary, AMEL 7/14, 28 July 1918
13. HO 144/22823/235, statement of LSA, 14 December 1945
14. Ibid.
15. MS Amery Diary, AMEL 7/14, 8 January 1918
16. MS Amery Diary, AMEL 7/15, 27 March 1919
17. Ibid., 17 April 1919
18. HO/144/22823/228, report of Dr Edward Glover, 7 December 1945
19. HO 144/22823/269–271, Caroline Mead to Bryddie, December 1945
20. HO/144/22823/264, statement of K. B. Tindall, 1 December 1945
21. *Memories of the Tindall Era, 1922–1954*, by D. McClintock, published by Old West Downs Society
22. *Memories of the Helbert/Brymer Era, 1897–1922*, by Sir John Stephenson, published by Old West Downs Society
23. HO/144/22823/235, statement of LSA, 14 December 1945
24. MS Amery Diary, AMEL 7/17, 22 October 1923

25. HO/144/22823/264, statement of K. B. Tindall, 1 December 1945

26. *Memories of the Tindall Era, 1922–1954*, by Sir John Nelson, published by Old West Downs Society

27. MS Amery Diary, AMEL 7/17, 26 May 1923

28. MS Amery Diary, AMEL 7/19, 30 May 1925

29. HO/144/22823/235, statement of Leo Amery, 14 December 1945

30. MS Amery Diary, AMEL 7/17, 22 October 1923

31. HO/144/22823/265 and 266, statement of K. B. Tindall, 1 December 1945

32. Amery, L., *In the Rain and the Sun*, p. 213

33. MS Amery Diary, AMEL 7/17, 11 January 1923

CHAPTER EIGHT

1. MS Lloyd George F/2/1/33, LSA to Lloyd George, 27 December 1918

2. *MPL II*, p. 176

3. MS Amery Diary, AMEL 7/15, 9 January 1919

4. *The Times*, 11 January 1919

5. MS Amery Diary, AMEL 7/15, 2 February 1919

6. *MPL II*, p. 184

7. Ibid., p. 202

8. Amery, L., *In the Rain and the Sun*, p. 168

9. MS Milner dep. 47/5–9, LSA to Stamfordham, 17 January 1920

10. Amery, L., *In the Rain and the Sun*, p. 52

11. *Diaries I*, p. 269, Milner to LSA, 26 February 1921

12. *MPL II*, p. 212

13. *The Times*, 11 February 1922

14. *MPL II*, p. 224

15. Waley, S., *Edwin Montagu: A Memoir and an Account of his Visits to India*, p. 261

16. *MPL II*, p. 225

17. Middlemas, K., and Barnes, J., *Baldwin: A Biography*, p. 97

18. *MPL II*, p. 226

19. Ibid., p. 230

20. Hyde, H., *Baldwin: The Unexpected Prime Minister*, p. 91

21. *MPL II*, p. 231

22. MS Austen Chamberlain 32/3/3, LSA to Chamberlain, 21 January 1922
23. MS Austen Chamberlain 24/4/1, LSA to Chamberlain, 26 January 1922
24. MS Amery Diary, AMEL 7/16, 22 June 1922
25. Ibid., 23 June 1922
26. Blake, p. 441
27. MS Amery Diary, AMEL 7/16, 3 June 1922
28. *MPL II*, p. 232
29. Nicolson, H., *King George the Fifth: His Life and Reign*, pp. 512–13
30. MS Austen Chamberlain 5/1/251, Austen to Hilda Chamberlain, 20 November 1922
31. Middlemas, K., and Barnes, J., *Baldwin: A Biography*, p. 109
32. MS Amery Diary, AMEL 7/16, 3/8/22
33. Middlemas, K., and Barnes, J., *Baldwin: A Biography*, p. 109
34. MS Eng. Hist. d 432, memorandum by Sir Ernest Pollock
35. Winterton, Lord, *Orders of the Day*, p. 115
36. MS Austen Chamberlain 5/1/251, Austen to Hilda Chamberlain, 20 November 1922
37. MS Amery Diary, AMEL 7/16, 3 August 1922
38. *MPL II*, p. 234
39. MS Amery Diary, AMEL 7/16, 18 September 1922
40. Ronaldshay, Lord, *The Life of Lord Curzon: Volume III*, p. 307
41. Middlemas, K., and Barnes, J., *Baldwin: A Biography*, p. 113
42. MS Amery Diary, AMEL 7/16, 2 October 1922
43. *The Times*, 6 October 1922
44. Blake, p. 450
45. *MPL II*, p. 235
46. MS Austen Chamberlain 5/1/249, Austen to Ida Chamberlain, 24 September 1922
47. Blake, p. 451
48. Self, R. (ed.), *The Austen Chamberlain Diary Letters: The Correspondence of Sir Austen Chamberlain with his Sisters Hilda and Ida, 1916–1937*, p. 197
49. Blake, p. 451
50. MS Amery Diary, AMEL 7/16, 13 October 1922
51. *MPL II*, p. 235
52. Hyde, H., *Baldwin: The Unexpected Prime Minister*, p. 105
53. Ronaldshay, p. 314

54. MS Amery Diary, AMEL 7/16, 15 October 1922
55. Ibid., 16 October 1922
56. Ramsden, J. (ed.), *Real Old Tory Politics: The Political Diaries of Sir Robert Sanders, Lord Bayford, 1910–35*, p. 191
57. MS Austen Chamberlain 5/1/251, Austen to Hilda Chamberlain, 20 November 1922
58. MS Austen Chamberlain 33/2/69, Chamberlain to Bryddie, 16 October 1922
59. MS Austen Chamberlain 33/2/71, Bryddie to Chamberlain, 18 October 1922
60. *MPL II*, p. 237
61. Blake, p. 456
62. Rhodes James, R., *Memoirs of a Conservative: J.C.C. Davidson's Memoirs and Papers, 1910–37*, p. 125
63. Thorpe, D., *The Uncrowned Prime Ministers*, p. 73
64. Hyde, H., *Baldwin: The Unexpected Prime Minister*, p. 115
65. *MPL II*, p. 238
66. Rhodes James, R., *Memoirs of a Conservative: J.C.C. Davidson's Memoirs and Papers, 1910–37*, p. 127
67. Middlemas, K., and Barnes, J., *Baldwin: A Biography*, p. 122
68. Dutton, D., *Austen Chamberlain: Gentleman in Politics*, p. 197
69. MS Amery Diary, AMEL 7/16, 19 October 1922
70. Hyde, H., *Baldwin: The Unexpected Prime Minister*, p. 119
71. MS Amery Diary, AMEL 7/16, 19 October 22
72. Ibid., 20 October 1922
73. Beaverbrook, Lord, *The Decline and Fall of Lloyd George*, p. 212
74. MS Lloyd George F/31/2/74, LSA to Lloyd George, 19 October 1922
75. *MPL II*, p. 240
76. MS Lloyd George F/31/2/75, Lloyd George to LSA, 20 October 1922
77. *MPL II*, p. 240n
78. MS Austen Chamberlain 5/1/252, Austen to Ida Chamberlain, 21 November 1922
79. MS Austen Chamberlain 33/2/115, Chamberlain to LSA, 20 October 1922
80. *MPL II*, p. 244
81. Self, R. (ed.), *The Neville Chamberlain Diary Letters, Volume 2: The Reform Years, 1921–27*, p.104, Neville to Hilda Chamberlain, 26 March 1922,
82. Ibid., p.126, Neville to Hilda Chamberlain, 24 October 1922

83. MS Austen Chamberlain 5/1/250, Austen to Ida Chamberlain, 18 November 1922
84. *MPL II*, p. 245
85. Tyerman, C., *A History of Harrow School 1324–1991*, p. 309
86. Gilmour, D., *Curzon*, p. 555n

CHAPTER NINE

1. *MPL II*, p. 250
2. Ibid., p. 249
3. MS Amery Diary, AMEL 7/17, 27 January 1923
4. *MPL II*, p. 247
5. Blake, pp. 485–6
6. *Sunday Express*, 5 November 1922
7. MS Bonar Law 111/12/46, Curzon to Bonar Law, 14 December 1922
8. *MPL II*, p. 253
9. MS Amery Diary, AMEL 7/17, 18 May 1923
10. Blake, p. 513
11. MS Amery Diary, AMEL 7/17, 19 May 1923
12. Middlemas, K., and Barnes, J., *Baldwin: A Biography*, p. 165
13. Blake, p. 521
14. Middlemas, K., and Barnes, J., *Baldwin: A Biography*, p. 163
15. Middlemas, K. (ed.), *Thomas Jones, Whitehall Diary: Volume II 1926–1930*, p. 236
16. Rhodes James, R., *Memoirs of a Conservative: J.C.C. Davidson's Memoirs and Papers, 1910–37*, p. 151
17. Blake, p. 525
18. MS Amery Diary, AMEL 7/17, 21 May 1923
19. *MPL II*, p. 261
20. MS Amery Diary, AMEL 7/17, 24 May 1923 (Added in holograph in early 1950s)
21. Gilmour, p. 582
22. Blake, p. 527
23. Egremont, M., *Balfour: A Life of Arthur James Balfour*, p. 327
24. Thorpe, D. R., *The Uncrowned Prime Ministers*, p. 150
25. MS Amery Diary, AMEL 7/17, 22 May 1923
26. Ibid., 19 June 1923

27. Self, R. (ed.), *The Austen Chamberlain Diary Letters: The Correspondence of Sir Austen Chamberlain with his Sisters Hilda and Ida, 1916–1937*, p. 229, Austen to Ida Chamberlain, 22 June 1923

28. Self, R. (ed.), *The Neville Chamberlain Diary Letters, Volume 2: The Reform Years, 1921–27*, p. 169, Neville to Ida Chamberlain, 24 June 1923

29. Amery, L., *In the Rain and the Sun*, p. 62

30. MS Amery Diary, AMEL 7/17, 8 October 1923

31. Middlemas, K., and Barnes, J., *Baldwin: A Biography*, p. 212

32. Middlemas, K. (ed.), *Thomas Jones, Whitehall Diary: Volume II 1926–1930*, p. 305

33. MS Amery Diary, AMEL 7/17, 14 October 1923

34. Middlemas, K., and Barnes, J., *Baldwin: A Biography*, p. 212

35. Rhodes James, R., *Memoirs of a Conservative: J.C.C. Davidson's Memoirs and Papers, 1910–37*, p. 184

36. MS Austen Chamberlain 35/3/1, Chamberlain to LSA, 31 October 1923

37. MS Austen Chamberlain 35/3/2, LSA to Chamberlain, 1 November 1923

38. MS Amery Diary, AMEL 7/17, 10 November 1923

39. *MPL II*, p. 284

40. MS Amery Diary, AMEL 7/17, 8 December 1923

41. Ibid., 9 December 1923

42. House of Commons, Official Report Volume 169, Col. 609, 21 January 1924

43. Amery, J., *Approach March: A Venture in Autobiography*, p. 27

44. Churchill, R., *Lord Derby: King of Lancashire*, p. 563

45. MS Amery Diary, AMEL 7/18, 23 January 1924

46. Ibid., 6 February 1924

47. Ibid., 7 February 1924

48. Churchill, R., *Lord Derby: King of Lancashire*, p. 565

49. MS Austen Chamberlain, Austen to Ida Chamberlain, 9 February 1924

50. *MPL II*, p. 291

51. MS Austen Chamberlain 24/6/1, LSA to Chamberlain, 12 June 1924

52. Self, R. (ed.), *The Neville Chamberlain Diary Letters, Volume 2: The Reform Years, 1921–27*, p. 232, Neville to Ida Chamberlain, 22 June 1924

53. Ibid., p. 233

54. Middlemas, K., and Barnes, J., *Baldwin: A Biography*, p. 262

55. MS Amery Diary, AMEL 7/18, 24 February 1924

56. Ramsden, J., *The Age of Balfour and Baldwin, 1902–1940*, p. 191
57. MS Amery Diary, AMEL 7/18, 27 February 1924
58. *The Times*, 15 March 1924
59. Middlemas, K., and Barnes, J., *Baldwin: A Biography*, p. 263
60. House of Commons, Official Report Volume 172, Col. 594, 9 April 1924
61. MS Amery Diary, AMEL 7/18, 9 April 1924
62. *MPL II*, p. 294
63. Macmillan, H., *Winds of Change, 1914–1939*, p. 152
64. *MPL II*, p. 297
65. MS Amery Diary, AMEL 7/18, 29 October 1924
66. Middlemas, K., and Barnes, J., *Baldwin: A Biography*, p. 280
67. MS Amery Diary, AMEL 7/18, 5 November 1924
68. Middlemas, K. (ed.), *Thomas Jones, Whitehall Diary: Volume II 1926–1930*, p. 302
69. Stewart, G., *Burying Caesar: Churchill, Chamberlain and the Battle for the Tory Party*, p. 35
70. MS Amery Diary, AMEL 7/18, 5 November 1924

CHAPTER TEN

1. *MPL II*, p. 293
2. Amery, J., *Approach March: A Venture in Autobiography*, pp. 29–31
3. MS Amery Diary, AMEL 7/16, 14 May 1922
4. Ibid., 13 July 1922
5. MS Amery Diary, AMEL 7/18, 3 July 1924
6. Amery, L., *In the Rain and the Sun*, p. 93
7. Tyerman, p. 375
8. Ibid., p. 502
9. Gathorne-Hardy, J., *The Public School Phenomenon, 597–1977*, p. 302
10. Lycett Green, C. (ed.), *John Betjeman: Letters Volume II, 1952 to 1984*, p. 177 and p. 319
11. Tyerman, p. 481
12. Gathorne-Hardy, p. 302
13. Mack, E., *Public Schools and British Opinion Since 1860*, p. 447
14. Vickers, H., *Cecil Beaton: The Authorised Biography*, p. 23
15. Wansell, G., *Terence Rattigan*, pp. 27–8

16. Playfair, G., *My Father's Son*, p. 75
17. MS Amery Diary, AMEL 7/19, 4 October 1925
18. Harrow School Broadsheets, December 1925
19. HO 144/22823/236, statement of LSA, 14 December 1945
20. Playfair, p.104
21. Nehru, J., *An Autobiography*, pp. 17–18
22. Norwood, C., *The English Tradition of Education*, pp. 10–11 and p. 19
23. Tyerman, p. 446
24. Lunn, A., *The Harrovians*, p. 43 and p. 61
25. MS Amery Diary, AMEL 7/20, 21 February 1926
26. HO 144/22823/160, Boissier to LSA, 10 December 1945
27. MS Amery Diary, AMEL 7/20, 27 February 1926
28. Ibid., 22 March 1926
29. HO 144/22823/236, statement of LSA, 14 December 1945
30. Harrow Head Master's Punishment Book, 4 July 1926
31. MS Amery Diary, AMEL 7/20, 10 July 1926
32. Ibid., 24 July 1926
33. Amery, L., *In the Rain and the Sun*, p. 95
34. MS Amery Diary, AMEL 7/21, 1 January 1927
35. MS Amery Diary, AMEL 7/21, 25 January 1927
36. HO 144/22823/425, memorandum of Sir Cyril Norwood, 4 December 1945
37. HO 144/22823/258, memorandum of Dr Maurice Wright, 20 June 1945
38. HO 144/22823/160, Boissier to LSA, 10 December 1945
39. MS Amery Diary, AMEL 7/21, 16 February 1927
40. Ibid., 13 March 1927
41. HO 144/22823/249, Jameson to LSA, 4 December 1945
42. HO 144/22823/244, Jameson to LSA, 4 December 1945
43. HO 144/22823/250, Jameson to LSA, 4 December 1945
44. MS Amery Diary, AMEL 7/22, 13 March 1928
45. Ibid., 4 June 1928
46. Weale, A., *Patriot Traitors: Roger Casement, John Amery and the Real Meaning of Treason*, p. 106
47. HO 144/22823/252, statement of W.H. Barrett, December 1945
48. MS Amery Diary, AMEL 7/22, 6 June 1928
49. HO 144/22823/236, statement of LSA, 14 December 1945
50. HO 144/22823/160, Boissier to LSA, 10 December 1945

51. HO 144/22823/161, Walton to Julian, 8 December 1945
52. HO 144/22823/157, Walton to Julian, 9 December 1945
53. HO 144/22823/162, Walton to Julian, 8 December 1945
54. MS Amery Diary, AMEL 7/23, 3 March 1929
55. Ibid., 29 March 1929
56. HO 144/22823/236, statement of LSA, 14 December 1945
57. HO 144/22823/239, statement of G. Nock, December 1945
58. HO 144/22823/240, statement of G Nock, December 1945

CHAPTER ELEVEN

1. *MPL II*, p. 335
2. MS Amery Diary, AMEL 7/18, 21 November 1924
3. Dutton, D., *Austen Chamberlain: Gentleman in Politics*, pp. 232–3
4. MS Austen Chamberlain 52/240, Crowe to Chamberlain, 12 March 1925
5. Dutton, D., *Austen Chamberlain: Gentleman in Politics*, p. 254n
6. Roskill, S., *Hankey, Man of Secrets: Volume I 1877–1918*, p. 397
7. MS Amery Diary, AMEL 7/19, 28 December 1925
8. FO 800/258/587, LSA to Austen Chamberlain, 20 October 1925
9. *MPL II*, p. 310
10. Gertrude Bell Online Archive, Letters, 8 April 1925
11. Kisch, F., *Palestine Diary*, p. 177
12. MS Amery Diary, AMEL 7/19, 27 April 1925
13. Ibid., 3 September 1925
14. *MPL II*, p. 328
15. MS Amery Diary, AMEL 7/19, 4 August 1925
16. *MPL II*, p. 484
17. Ibid., p. 384
18. Amery, L., *Thoughts on the Constitution*, p. 128
19. Hall, H., *The Genesis of the Balfour Declaration of 1926*, Journal of Commonwealth Political Studies, Volume I 1961–1963, p. 187
20. *MPL II*, p. 389
21. *The Times,* 22 March 1930
22. Hall, p. 187
23. MS Austen Chamberlain 5/1/399, Austen to Ida Chamberlain, 7 November 1926

24. Roskill, S., *Hankey, Man of Secrets: Volume II 1919–1931*, p. 401 and p. 430 n5

25. MS Amery Diary, AMEL 7/20, 22 November 1926

26. *MPL II*, p. 400

27. MS Amery Diary, AMEL 7/21, 15 June 1927

28. Ibid., 12 April 1927

29. Dilks, D., *Neville Chamberlain: Volume I, Pioneering and Reform 1869–1929*, p. 517

30. Roskill, S., *Hankey, Man of Secrets: Volume II 1919–1931*, p. 473

31. MS Amery Diary, AMEL 7/21, 20 July 1927

32. MS Neville Chamberlain, diary 21 July 1927

33. MS Neville Chamberlain 7/2/33, LSA to Chamberlain, 20 July 1927

34. MS Amery Diary, AMEL 7/21, 10 August 1927

35. *MPL II*, p. 410

36. Ibid., p. 415

37. MS Amery Diary, AMEL 7/21, 1 September 1927

38. *MPL II*, p. 425

39. Ibid., p. 433

40. *MPL II*, p. 437, LSA to Baldwin, 19 November 1927

41. Ibid., p. 444

42. Ibid., p. 461

43. MS Amery Diary, AMEL 7/22, 20 January 1928

44. Amery, J., *Joseph Chamberlain and the Tariff Reform Campaign, Volume VI 1903–1968*, p. 1017

45. MS Amery Diary, AMEL 7/22, 3 February 1928

46. MS Baldwin, LSA to Baldwin, 22 March 1928

47. MS Amery Diary, AMEL 7/22, 7 May 1928

48. MS Maxse 480/120, LSA to Maxse, 6 July 1928

49. Self, R. (ed.), *The Neville Chamberlain Diary Letters, Volume III: The Heir Apparent, 1928–33*, p. 101, Neville to Hilda Chamberlain, 5 August 1928

50. MS Amery Diary, AMEL 7/22, 2 August 1928

51. Browning, R., *Men and Women: Volume I*, 'The Statue and the Bust', p. 164

52. MS Amery Diary, AMEL 7/22, 31 December 1928

53. Self, R. (ed.), *The Neville Chamberlain Diary Letters, Volume III: The Heir Apparent, 1928–33*, p. 114, Neville to Ida Chamberlain, 31 December 1928

54. MS Amery Diary, AMEL 7/23, 27 February 1929
55. Middlemas, K. (ed.), *Thomas Jones, Whitehall Diary: Volume II 1926–1930*, p. 180
56. Self, R. (ed.), *The Neville Chamberlain Diary Letters, Volume III: The Heir Apparent, 1928–33*, p. 132, Neville to Hilda Chamberlain, 12 April 1929
57. Steed, W., *The Real Stanley Baldwin*, pp. 106–7
58. MS Maxse 480/195, LSA to Maxse, 25 March 1929
59. *MPL II*, p. 499
60. MS Amery Diary, AMEL 7/23, 3 June 1929
61. Mackenzie, N., and J. (eds), *The Diary of Beatrice Webb, Volume III 1905–1924, 'The Power to Alter Things'*, p. 174

CHAPTER TWELVE

1. Summer Fields Archive, LSA to Bryddie, 10 March 1928
2. MS Amery Diary, AMEL 7/22, 17 March 1928
3. Day Lewis, C., *The Buried Day*, pp. 183–4
4. MS Amery Diary, AMEL 7/22, 31 March 1928
5. Usborne, R. (ed.), *A Century of Summer Fields*, p. 178
6. Amery, J., *Approach March: A Venture in Autobiography*, pp. 36–7
7. Summer Fields Archive, Julian to Bryddie, 5 May 1928
8. Ibid., 6 May 1928
9. MS Amery Diary, AMEL 7/22, 7 May 1928
10. Summer Fields Archive, Julian to Bryddie, 5 May 1928
11. Amery, J., *Approach March: A Venture in Autobiography*, p. 36
12. Summer Fields Archive, Dr Williams to LSA, 11 May 1928
13. Usborne, p. 238
14. Ibid., p. 186
15. Summer Fields Archive, Mrs Williams to Bryddie, 15 December 1928
16. Henderson, N., *Old Friends and Modern Instances*, p. 34
17. Usborne, p. 238
18. Aldridge, N., *Time to Spare?: A History of Summer Fields*, p. 115
19. Summer Fields Archive, Dr Williams to LSA, November 1928
20. Summer Fields Archive, Headmaster's Report, Summer 1928 and Christmas 1928
21. Summer Fields Archive, Mrs Williams to Bryddie, 6 May 1928
22. Amery, J., *Approach March: A Venture in Autobiography*, pp. 38–9

23. Usborne, p. 238
24. Amery, J., *Approach March: A Venture in Autobiography*, pp. 39–40
25. Strong, L., *Green Memory*, p. 197
26. Amery, J., *Approach March: A Venture in Autobiography*, p. 42
27. Henderson, p. 32
28. Nicolson, N., *Long Life: Memoirs*, p. 56
29. Usborne, p. 196
30. Macnee, P., *Blind in One Ear*, p. 44
31. Usborne, p. 196
32. Ibid., p. 212
33. Summer Fields Archive, *The Summer Fields Magazine, 1930–1933, Vol. I No. I*, p. 7
34. Ibid., *No. 2*, p. 39
35. Ibid., *No. 4*, p. 110
36. Ibid., *No. 4*, p. 111
37. Henderson, p. 32
38. Amery, J., *Approach March: A Venture in Autobiography*, p. 27
39. Henderson, p. 33
40. Usborne, p. 235
41. Summer Fields Archive, Julian to Bryddie, 23 February 1929
42. Ibid., 5 May 1929
43. Ibid., 7 June 1928
44. MS Amery Diary, AMEL 7/25, 16 March 1931
45. Ibid., 7 June 1931
46. Henderson, pp. 30–1
47. Amery, J., *Approach March: A Venture in Autobiography*, p. 45
48. MS Amery Diary, AMEL 7/24, 1 May 1930
49. Usborne, p. 235
50. Amery, L., *In the Rain and the Sun*, p. 188
51. Tyerman, p. 411
52. Amery, J., *Approach March: A Venture in Autobiography*, p. 47
53. Summer Fields Archive, A. F. Alington to Bryddie, 26 January 1932
54. Summer Fields Archive, A. F. Alington to Bryddie, 13 June 1932
55. Summer Fields Archive, A. F. Alington to Bryddie, 28 July 1932

CHAPTER THIRTEEN

1. Barnett, C., *The Collapse of British Power*, p. 129
2. Louis, W., *In the Name of God, Go!: Leo Amery and the British Empire in the Age of Churchill*, p. 26
3. Barnett, p. 130
4. Hyam, R., *The Failure of South African Expansion, 1908–1948*, p. 102
5. MS Baldwin 28/251–62, LSA to Baldwin, 10 April 1927
6. *Diaries I*, Introduction by Julian Amery, p. 22
7. *MPL II*, p. 502
8. Williamson, P., *National Crisis and National Government: British Politics, the Economy and Empire, 1926–1932*, p. 49
9. Middlemas, K. (ed.), *Thomas Jones, Whitehall Diary: Volume II 1926–1930*, p. 175
10. Dilks, D., *Neville Chamberlain: Volume I, Pioneering and Reform 1869–1929*, p. 440 and p. 500
11. Feiling, K., *The Life of Neville Chamberlain*, p. 165
12. Dilks, D., *Neville Chamberlain: Volume I, Pioneering and Reform 1869–1929*, p. 500
13. MS Austen Chamberlain 5/1/399, Austen to Ida Chamberlain, 7 November 1926
14. *MPL II*, p. 392
15. Thompson, R., *Churchill and Morton*, p. 188
16. Dilks, D., *Neville Chamberlain: Volume I, Pioneering and Reform 1869–1929*, p. 500
17. Vincent, p. 511 and p. 520
18. *Diaries I*, Introduction by Julian Amery, p. 21
19. Ball, S. (ed.), *Parliament and Politics in the Age of Baldwin and MacDonald: The Headlam Diaries, 1923–1935*, pp. 125–6
20. Middlemas, K. (ed.), *Thomas Jones, Whitehall Diary: Volume II 1926–1930*, p. 105
21. Louis, p. 104n, Curtis to Bryddie, 5 November 1934
22. Hyam, p. 102
23. MS Amery Diary, AMEL 7/23, 22 July 1929
24. Self, R. (ed.), *The Neville Chamberlain Diary Letters, Volume III: The Heir Apparent, 1928–33*, p. 149n
25. Self, R. (ed.), *The Austen Chamberlain Diary Letters: The Correspondence of*

Sir Austen Chamberlain with his Sisters Hilda and Ida, 1916–1937, p. 339, Austen to Hilda Chamberlain, 13 July 1929

26. Self, R. (ed.), *The Neville Chamberlain Diary Letters, Volume III: The Heir Apparent, 1928–33*, p.149, Neville to Ida Chamberlain, 13 July 1929

27. MS Amery Diary, AMEL 7/23, 11 July 1929

28. Self, R. (ed.), *The Neville Chamberlain Diary Letters, Volume III: The Heir Apparent, 1928–33*, p.149, Neville to Ida Chamberlain, 13 July 1929

29. Middlemas, K. (ed.), *Thomas Jones, Whitehall Diary: Volume II 1926–1930*, p. 197

30. MS Amery Diary, AMEL 7/23, 5 August 1929

31. Vansittart, Lord, *The Mist Procession: The Autobiography of Lord Vansittart*, p. 354

32. Rhodes James, R., *Churchill: A Study in Failure, 1900–1939*, p. 299

33. *MPL II*, p. 504

34. Vincent, p. 488 and p. 520

35. Amery, L., *In the Rain and the Sun*, p. 165

36. Ibid., p. 168

37. Ibid., p. 170

38. Ibid., p. 173

39. Ibid., p. 177

40. Amery, J., *Joseph Chamberlain and the Tariff Reform Campaign: Volume VI 1903–1968*, p.1020

41. Young, K. (ed.), *The Diaries of Sir Robert Bruce Lockhart: Volume I 1915–1938*, p. 98

42. MS Amery Diary, AMEL 7/23, 13 November 1929

43. Ibid., 31 December 1929

44. Amery, L., *My Political Life: Volume III, The Unforgiving Years 1929–1940*, p. 23

45. Middlemas, K. (ed.), *Thomas Jones, Whitehall Diary: Volume II 1926–1930*, p. 244

46. Self, R. (ed.), *The Neville Chamberlain Diary Letters, Volume III: The Heir Apparent, 1928–33*, p. 168, Neville to Hilda Chamberlain, 14 February 1930

47. *The Times*, 10 February 1930

48. Middlemas, K., and Barnes, J., *Baldwin: A Biography*, p. 562

49. Taylor, A., *Beaverbrook*, p. 282

50. MS Beaverbrook B/124, LSA to Beaverbrook, 19 February 1930

51. Middlemas, K., and Barnes, J., *Baldwin: A Biography*, p. 565

52. MS Amery Diary, AMEL 7/24, 3 March 1930
53. MS Beaverbrook B/124, LSA to Beaverbrook, 28 June 1930
54. Middlemas, K., and Barnes, J., *Baldwin: A Biography*, pp. 573–4
55. Churchill, R., *Lord Derby: King of Lancashire*, p. 582
56. Amery, L., *In the Rain and the Sun*, p. 182
57. MS Beaverbrook B/124, LSA to Beaverbrook 30 September 1930 and Beaverbrook to LSA 1 October 1930
58. MS Amery Diary, AMEL 7/24, 13 October 1930
59. Ibid., 6 November 1930
60. *MPL III*, p. 37
61. MS Amery Diary, AMEL 7/24, 31 December 1930
62. MS Amery Diary, AMEL 7/25, 30 January 1931
63. Macleod, I., *Neville Chamberlain*, p. 138
64. MS Austen Chamberlain 5/1/532, Austen to Ida Chamberlain, 28 February 1931
65. MS Amery Diary, AMEL 7/25, 25 March 1931
66. Amery, J., *Joseph Chamberlain and the Tariff Reform Campaign: Volume VI 1903–1968*, p. 1023
67. Amery, L., *In the Rain and the Sun*, Hutchinson 1946, p. 189
68. MS Amery Diary, AMEL 7/25, 23 August 1931
69. Cooper, D., *Old Men Forget*, p. 177
70. *MPL III*, p. 57
71. MS Amery Diary, AMEL 7/25, 25 August 1931
72. MS Maxse 480/332, LSA to Maxse, 26 August 1931
73. MS Amery Diary, AMEL 7/25, 7 September 1931
74. *MPL III*, p. 66
75. MS Austen Chamberlain 58/77, LSA to Chamberlain, 4 November 1931
76. MS Amery Diary, AMEL 7/25, 5 November 1931
77. Middlemas, K., and Barnes, J., *Baldwin: A Biography*, p. 655
78. MS Amery Diary, AMEL 7/25, 11 November 1931
79. Ibid., 22 November 1931
80. Barnes, J., and Nicholson, D. (eds), *The Empire at Bay: The Leo Amery Diaries 1929–1945*, Foreword by the Earl of Stockton, p. xi

CHAPTER FOURTEEN

1. Ball, S. (ed.), *Parliament and Politics in the Age of Baldwin and MacDonald: The Headlam Diaries, 1923–1935*, p. 224

2. Self, R. (ed.), *The Neville Chamberlain Diary Letters, Volume III: The Heir Apparent, 1928–33*, p. 299, Neville to Ida Chamberlain, 12 December 1931

3. MS Amery Diary, AMEL 7/26, 17 March 1932

4. Ibid., 6 July 1932

5. Ibid., 21 July 1932

6. Louis, p. 106

7. MS Amery Diary, AMEL 7/26, 17 August 1932

8. MS Neville Chamberlain 7/2/56, LSA to Chamberlain, 17 August 1932

9. *MPL III*, p. 86

10. Self, R. (ed.), *The Austen Chamberlain Diary Letters: The Correspondence of Sir Austen Chamberlain with his Sisters Hilda and Ida, 1916–1937*, p. 422, Austen to Hilda Chamberlain, 18 December, 1932

11. MS Amery Diary, AMEL 7/26, 12 September 1932

12. MS Violet Milner 31/C117/18, LSA to Lady Milner, 3 September, 1932

13. *MPL III*, p. 140

14. Ibid., pp. 144–5

15. House of Commons, Official Report Volume 280, Col. 377, 5 July 1933

16. MS Amery Diary, AMEL 7/26, 31 December 1932

17. House of Commons, Official Report Volume 285, Cols 81 and 84, 27 February 1933

18. *Diaries II*, p. 269

19. House of Commons, Official Report Volume 270, Col. 632, 10 November 1932

20. House of Commons, Official Report Volume 272, Cols 113 and 116, 23 November 1932

21. *MPL III*, p. 150

22. MS Amery Diary, AMEL 7/27, 14 March 1933

23. Ibid., 7 November 1933

24. House of Commons, Official Report Volume 281, Cols 105 and 106, 7 November 1933

25. MS Amery Diary, AMEL 7/24, 9 November 1930
26. *MPL III*, p. 99
27. Louis, p. 110n, Lloyd to LSA, 10 February 1931 and LSA to Lloyd 11 February 1931
28. *MPL III*, p. 99
29. Louis, p. 110
30. House of Commons, Official Report Volume 290, Cols 1736, 1737 and 1738, 13 June 1934
31. MS Amery Diary, AMEL 7/28, 13 June 1934
32. *MPL III*, p. 104
33. Templewood, Lord, *Nine Troubled Years*, p. 98
34. MS Amery Diary, AMEL 7/28, 15 June 1934
35. *MPL III*, p.109
36. MS Amery Diary, AMEL 7/28, 23 July 1934
37. MS Amery Diary, AMEL 7/29, 8 June 1935
38. MS Amery Diary, AMEL 7/26, 1 October 1932
39. MS Amery Diary, AMEL 7/27, 26 March 1933
40. Ibid., 10 October 1933
41. *MPL III*, p. 121
42. MS Amery Diary, AMEL 7/28, 14 May 1934
43. Ibid., 8 June 1934
44. MS Amery Diary, AMEL 7/29, 15 January 1935
45. *MPL III*, p. 127
46. Ibid., pp. 129–30
47. MS Amery Diary, AMEL 7/29, 13 August 1935
48. Amery, J., *Approach March: A Venture in Autobiography*, p. 62
49. Cowling, M., *The Impact of Hitler, British Politics and British Policy 1933–1940*, p. 121
50. Ibid., p. 122
51. *MPL III*, p. 170
52. MS Amery Diary, AMEL 7/29, 24 September 1935
53. *MPL III*, p. 175
54. MS Amery Diary, AMEL 7/29, 23 October 1935
55. Macleod, p. 184
56. MS Amery Diary, AMEL 7/30, 10 March 1936
57. MS Amery Diary, AMEL 7/29, 10 December 1935
58. Liddell Hart, B., *The Memoirs of Captain Liddell Hart: Volume I*, p. 319
59. MS Amery Diary, AMEL 7/30, 10 March 1936

60. *MPL III*, p.196
61. MS Amery Diary, AMEL 7/30, 13 March 1936
62. Ibid., 4 December 1936
63. Ibid., 7 December 1936
64. Ibid., 10 December 1936
65. Ibid., 11 December 1936
66. MS Neville Chamberlain 7/2/66, Chamberlain to LSA, 30 May 1937
67. MS Neville Chamberlain 7/2/67, LSA to Chamberlain, 4 June 1937

CHAPTER FIFTEEN

1. MS Amery Diary, AMEL 7/24, 22 November 1930
2. Ibid., 31 December 1930
3. HO 144/22823/237, statement of LSA, 14 December 1945
4. MS Amery Diary, AMEL 7/26, 20 January 1932
5. Amery, J., *Approach March: A Venture in Autobiography*, p. 65
6. MS Amery Diary, AMEL 7/25, 24 March 1931
7. KV 2/78, Special Branch report, 11 December 1942
8. HO 144/22823/253, statement of Una Wing, December 1945
9. MS Amery Diary, AMEL 7/26, 23 August 1932
10. Ibid., 7 September 1932
11. KV 2/78, Special Branch report, 11 December 1942
12. MS Amery Diary, AMEL 7/26, 8 September 1932
13. Ibid., 20 November 1932
14. Ibid., 31 December 1932
15. Self, R. (ed.), *The Neville Chamberlain Diary Letters, Volume III: The Heir Apparent, 1928–33*, p. 346, Neville to Ida Chamberlain, 12 September 1932
16. MS Amery Diary, AMEL 7/26, 31 December 1932
17. MS Amery Diary, AMEL 7/27, 5 February 1933
18. MS Simon 76/1, Bryddie to Simon, 2 March 1933
19. HO 144/22823/237, statement of LSA, 14 December 1945
20. MS Douglas 24/86, Nugent Hicks (Bishop of Lincoln) to Canon Douglas, 26 April 1933
21. MS Douglas 13/80, memorandum 4 May 1933
22. MS Amery Diary, AMEL 7/27, 19 May 1933
23. Ibid., 28 May 1933

24. Ibid., 30 May 1933
25. Ibid., 1 June 1933
26. MS Simon 76/184 and 185, Bryddie to Simon, 12 June 1933
27. MS Amery Diary, AMEL 7/27, 27 June 1933
28. HO 144/22823/254, statement of Una Wing, December 1945
29. HO 144/22823/253, statement of Una Wing, December 1945
30. HO 144/22823/235, statement of LSA, 14 December 1945
31. HO 144/22823/255, statement of Una Wing, December 1945
32. MS Amery Diary, AMEL 7/28, 1 June 1934
33. MS Amery Diary, AMEL 7/29, 2 September 1935
34. Ibid., 5 July 1935
35. MS Amery Diary, AMEL 7/30, 25 May 1936
36. MS Amery Diary, AMEL 7/29, 31 December 1935
37. HO 144/22823/215, LSA's 'Explanation' to the Home Secretary, 14 December 1945
38. HO 144/22823/238, statement of LSA, 14 December 1945
39. MS Amery Diary, AMEL 7/30, 15 October 1936
40. Weale, p. 119
41. MS Amery Diary, AMEL 7/30, 4 July 1936
42. KV 2/81 contains Jack's passport and a translation of all the stamps within it
43. KV 2/83 contains the log book of the *Titus*
44. Weale, p. 119
45. MS Amery Diary, AMEL 7/31, 25 March 1937
46. HO 144/22823/216, LSA's 'Explanation' to the Home Secretary, 14 December 1945
47. MS Amery Diary, AMEL 7/31, 9 September 1937
48. HO 144/22823/215, LSA's 'Explanation' to the Home Secretary, 14 December 1945
49. KV 2/81, statement of John Amery, 23 May 1945
50. MS Amery Diary, AMEL 7/33, 14 January 1939
51. HO 144/22823/215, LSA's 'Explanation' to the Home Secretary, 14 December 1945
52. Amery, J., *Approach March: A Venture in Autobiography*, p. 124
53. KV 2/78, Internal SIS memorandum, 23 June 1943

CHAPTER SIXTEEN

1. Summer Fields Archive, LSA to Julian, 2 August 1932
2. MS Amery Diary, AMEL 7/26, 22 September 1932
3. Amery, J., *Approach March: A Venture in Autobiography*, p. 49
4. Elliott, N., *Never Judge a Man by his Umbrella*, p. 33
5. Amery, J., *Approach March: A Venture in Autobiography*, p. 52
6. Ibid., p. 49
7. MS Amery Diary, AMEL 7/27, 21/5/33
8. Ibid., 6 June 1933
9. Matthew, H., and Harrison, B. (eds), *Oxford Dictionary of National Biography, Volume 18*, pp. 196–7
10. Amery, J., *Approach March: A Venture in Autobiography*, p. 50
11. Elliott, p.146
12. Amery, L., *In the Rain and the Sun*, p. 191
13. Amery, J., *Approach March: A Venture in Autobiography*, p. 58
14. Ibid., p. 57
15. MS Amery Diary, AMEL 7/31, 17 October 1937
16. MS Pym 103/66 and 67, diary 3 December 1937
17. MS Amery Diary, AMEL 7/31, 17 December 1937
18. MS Pym 147/1 and 2, Julian to Pym, 11 December 1937
19. Holt, H., *A Lot to Ask: A Life of Barbara Pym*, p. 74
20. MS Pym 147/5, Julian to Pym, February 1938
21. MS Pym 103/67 and 68, diary 25 February 1938
22. MS Pym 103/68, diary 26 February 1938
23. MS Pym 103/69 and 70, diary 2 March 1938
24. MS Pym 103/70, diary 3 March 1938
25. MS Pym 103/70 and 71, diary 5 March 1938
26. MS Pym 103/71 and 72, diary 11 March 1938
27. MS Amery Diary, AMEL 7/32, 19 March 1938
28. MS Pym 147/8 and 10, Julian to Pym, 19 March 1938
29. Holt, H. and Pym, H. (eds), *A Very Private Eye: The Diaries, Letters and Notebooks of Barbara Pym*, pp. 69–70
30. Amery, J., *Approach March: A Venture in Autobiography*, p. 89
31. Ibid., p. 92
32. MS Amery Diary, AMEL 7/32, 22 May 1938
33. Ibid., 8 May 1938

34. Holt, H. and Pym, H. (eds), *A Very Private Eye: The Diaries, Letters and Notebooks of Barbara Pym*, p. 73

35. MS Pym 147/12 and 13, Julian to Pym, 1 June 1938

36. MS Amery Diary, AMEL 7/32, 9 July 1938

37. Amery, J., *Approach March: A Venture in Autobiography*, p. 107

38. MS Amery Diary, AMEL 7/32, 24 October 1938

39. Amery, J., *Approach March: A Venture in Autobiography*, p. 113

40. MS Amery Diary, AMEL 7/33, 23 February 1939

41. Amery, J., *Approach March: A Venture in Autobiography*, pp. 110–11

42. Roberts, B., *Randolph: A Study of Churchill's Son*, p. 185

43. MS Amery Diary, AMEL 7/33, 27 April 1939

44. Churchill, W., *His Father's Son: The Life of Randolph Churchill*, p.166

45. Amery, J., *Approach March: A Venture in Autobiography*, p. 116 and p. 118

46. MS Pym 147/48, *Daily Express* 10 June 1939

47. MS Amery Diary, AMEL 7/33, 10 June 1939

48. Amery, J., *Approach March: A Venture in Autobiography*, pp. 119–120

49. MS Pym 147/15 and 16, Julian to Pym, 2 June 1939

50. Holt, H. and Pym, H. (eds), *A Very Private Eye: The Diaries, Letters and Notebooks of Barbara Pym*, pp. 91–2

51. Holt, H., *A Lot to Ask: A Life of Barbara Pym*, pp. 77–9

52. MS Pym 103/72, diary 27 March 1938

53. Pym, B., *Crampton Hodnet*, p. 13, p. 28, pp. 111–13, p. 118, p. 137 p. 201 and p. 211

54. Amery, J., *Approach March: A Venture in Autobiography*, p. 121

55. MS Amery Diary, AMEL 7/33, 4 July 1939

56. Ibid., 11 September 1939

57. Amery, J., *Approach March: A Venture in Autobiography*, p. 129

CHAPTER SEVENTEEN

1. MS Amery Diary, AMEL 7/32, 12 March 1938

2. *The Times*, 12 March 1938

3. House of Commons, Official Report Volume 333, Cols 85 and 86, 14 March 1938

4. *MPL III*, p. 239

5. MS Amery Diary, AMEL 7/32, 20 April 1938

6. *Diaries II*, p. 474 (Original in *New York Times*, 15 May 1938)

7. *MPL III*, p. 265
8. Thompson, N., *The Anti-Appeasers: Conservative Opposition to Appeasement in the 1930s*, p.167
9. Wheeler-Bennett, J., *Munich: Prologue to Tragedy*, p. 183
10. Eden, A., *The Reckoning*, p. 32
11. MS Amery Diary, AMEL 7/32, 14 September 1938
12. Feiling, p. 357 and p. 361
13. MS Neville Chamberlain 7/2/78, LSA to Chamberlain, 17 September 1938
14. MS Amery Diary, AMEL 7/32, 16 September 1938
15. Ibid., 19 September 1938
16. Feiling, p. 366
17. *MPL III*, p. 268
18. *Diaries II*, p. 483, LSA to Halifax, 24 September 1938
19. Roberts, A., *'The Holy Fox': A Biography of Lord Halifax*, pp. 113–14
20. Harvey, J. (ed.), *The Diplomatic Diaries of Oliver Harvey, 1937–1940*, p. 196
21. MS Amery Diary, AMEL 7/32, 25 September 1938
22. MS Neville Chamberlain 7/2/81, LSA to Chamberlain, 25 September 1938
23. Cowling, p. 227
24. *MPL III*, p. 274, LSA to William Hughes, 26 September 1938
25. *The Times*, 26 September 1938
26. MS Amery Diary, AMEL 7/32, 26 September 1938
27. Nicolson, N. (ed.), *Harold Nicolson: Diaries and Letters 1930–1939*, p. 367
28. *MPL III*, p. 278
29. Cooper, D., *Old Men Forget*, p. 239
30. Feiling, p. 372
31. MS Amery Diary, AMEL 7/32, 27 September 1938
32. Ibid., 28 September 1938
33. Gilbert, M., and Gott, R., *The Appeasers*, p. 174
34. Seton-Watson, R., *A History of the Czechs and Slovaks*, p. 367n
35. MS Amery Diary, AMEL 7/32, 30 September 1938
36. *MPL III*, p. 283
37. Thompson, N., *The Anti-Appeasers: Conservative Opposition to Appeasement in the 1930s*, p. 175
38. Boothby, R., *I Fight to Live*, p. 164
39. MS Amery Diary, AMEL 7/32, 27 September 1938

40. MS Emrys-Evans, Add. 58247/17, LSA to Emrys-Evans, 21 June 1954
41. MS Emrys-Evans, Add. 58247/22–23, Emrys-Evans to LSA, 1 July 1954
42. House of Commons, Official Report Volume 339, Col. 199, 4 October 1938
43. Nicolson, N. (ed.), *Harold Nicolson: Diaries and Letters 1930–1939*, pp. 375–6
44. MS Neville Chamberlain 7/2/82, LSA to Chamberlain, 6 October 1938
45. Thompson, N., p. 198 (House of Commons, Notice of Motions, 21 November 1938)
46. Cowling, p. 227
47. Thompson, N., p. 178
48. Nicolson, N. (ed.), *Harold Nicolson: Diaries and Letters 1930–1939*, pp. 377–8
49. Tree, R., *When the Moon was High: Memoirs of Peace and War 1897–1942*, p. 76
50. Crowson, N., *Facing Fascism: The Conservative Party and the European Dictators, 1935–1940*, p. 111
51. MS Selborne 87/129, LSA to Selborne, 12 October 1938
52. Amery, L., *In the Rain and the Sun*, p. 231
53. MS Beaverbrook C/7, LSA to Beaverbrook, 7 October 1938
54. *MPL III*, p. 305
55. Weizmann, p. 231
56. *MPL III*, p. 252
57. Ibid., p. 254
58. House of Commons, Official Report Volume 347, Cols 2004, 2013 and 2015, 22 May 1939
59. MS Amery Diary, AMEL 7/33, 23 May 1939
60. *MPL III*, p. 257
61. Nicolson, N. (ed.), *Harold Nicolson: Diaries and Letters 1930–1939*, p. 402
62. *MPL III*, p. 317
63. House of Commons, Official Report Volume 350, Cols 2494, 2495 and 2503, 2 August 1939
64. MS Emrys-Evans, Add 58247/2, LSA to Emrys-Evans, 5 September 1941
65. Rhodes James, R. (ed.), *Chips: The Diaries of Sir Henry Channon*, p. 212
66. *MPL III*, p. 324

67. Dalton, H., *The Fateful Years: Memoirs 1931–1945*, p. 264
68. *MPL III*, p. 324
69. MS Amery Diary, AMEL 7/33, 2 September 1939
70. Churchill, W., *The Second World War, Volume I: The Gathering Storm*, p. 318
71. Cameron Watt, D., *How War Came: The Immediate Origins of the Second World War, 1938–1939*, p. 579
72. Rhodes James, R., *Bob Boothby: A Portrait*, p. 231
73. Spears, E., *Assignment to Catastrophe, Volume I: Prelude to Dunkirk, July 1939–May 1940*, p. 21
74. Macmillan, H., *Winds of Change, 1914–1939*, p. 606
75. MS Amery Diary, AMEL 7/33, 2 September 1939
76. Cameron Watt, p. 593
77. Nicolson, N. (ed.), *Harold Nicolson: Diaries and Letters 1930–1939*, p. 421
78. MS Amery Diary, AMEL 7/33, 3 September 1939
79. MS Dawson 81/13, LSA to Dawson, 4 September 1939
80. MS Amery Diary, AMEL 7/33, 4 September 1939
81. *Diaries II*, p. 558
82. Ball, S., *The Guardsmen; Harold Macmillan, Three Friends, and the World They Made*, p. 201
83. Cowling, p. 376
84. Dalton, p. 276
85. Spears, p. 32
86. *MPL III*, p. 330
87. Ball, S., *The Guardsmen; Harold Macmillan, Three Friends, and the World They Made*, p. 205
88. MS Amery Diary, AMEL 7/34, 19 March 1940
89. Ibid., 16 March 1940
90. Nicolson, N. (ed.), *Harold Nicolson: Diaries and Letters 1930–1939*, p. 58
91. MS Emrys-Evans, Add. 58245/1, Salisbury to Emrys-Evans, 31 March 1940
92. Ramsden, J., *The Age of Balfour and Baldwin, 1902–1940*, p. 371
93. Ball, S., *The Guardsmen; Harold Macmillan, Three Friends, and the World They Made*, p. 208
94. Crowson, p. 173
95. MS Dawson 81/35, LSA to Dawson, 16 April 1940
96. MS Amery Diary, AMEL 7/34, 7 May 1940
97. *MPL III*, p. 359

98. House of Commons, Official Report Volume 360, Col. 1125, 7 May 1940

99. MS Amery Diary, AMEL 7/34, 7 May 1940

100. House of Commons, Official Report Volume 360, Cols 1141, 1146, 1149 and 1150, 7 May 1940

101. *MPL III*, p. 364

102. House of Commons, Official Report Volume 360, Col. 1150, 7 May 1940

103. Churchill, W., *The Second World War, Volume I: The Gathering Storm*, p. 521

104. MS Amery Diary, AMEL 7/34, 7 May 1940

105. Tree, p.113

106. Spears, p.120

107. Macmillan, H., *The Blast of War: 1939–1945*, pp. 69–72

108. Rhodes James, R., *Bob Boothby: A Portrait*, p. 244

109. *MPL III*, pp. 368–9

110. Macleod, p. 291

111. Pimlott, B. (ed.), *The Second World War Diary of Hugh Dalton: 1940–45*, p. 8

112. Roberts, A., *'The Holy Fox': A Biography of Lord Halifax*, p. 198

113. MS Amery Diary, AMEL 7/34, 9 May 1940

114. *MPL III*, p. 373

CHAPTER EIGHTEEN

1. Sanger, C., *Malcolm MacDonald: Bringing an End to Empire*, p.188

2. *MPL III*, p. 375

3. MS Amery Diary, AMEL 7/34, 13 May 1940

4. *MPL III*, p. 375

5. House of Commons, Official Report Volume 360, Col. 1502, 13 May 1940

6. Louis, p.123

7. MS Amery Diary, AMEL 7/34, 13 May 1940

8. Ibid., 28 May 1940

9. Pimlott, B. (ed.) *The Second World War Diary of Hugh Dalton: 1940–45*, p. 28

10. Macmillan, H., *The Blast of War: 1939–1945*, p. 196

11. MS Amery Diary, AMEL 7/34, 15 June 1940
12. Rhodes James, R., *Bob Boothby: A Portrait*, p. 259
13. Colville, J., *The Fringes of Power: Downing Street Diaries 1939–1955*, p. 164
14. *Diaries II*, p. 601
15. MS Amery Diary, AMEL 7/34, 18 June 1940
16. Colville, J., *The Fringes of Power: Downing Street Diaries 1939–1955*, p. 587
17. Rhodes James, R., *Bob Boothby: A Portrait*, p. 261
18. Ball, S., *The Guardsmen; Harold Macmillan, Three Friends, and the World They Made*, p. 220
19. Louis, pp.127–8
20. MS Amery Diary, AMEL 7/34, 2 June 1940
21. Gopal, S., *Jawaharlal Nehru: A Biography, Volume I 1889–1947*, p. 255
22. *Diaries II*, p. 607, LSA to Linlithgow, 13 June 1940 and 17 June 1940; Linlithgow to LSA, 1 July 1940 and 4 July 1940
23. Roberts, A., *'The Holy Fox': A Biography of Lord Halifax*, p. 245, LSA to Halifax, 12 July 1940
24. Louis, p. 131, Churchill to LSA and LSA to Churchill, 17 July 1940
25. *Diaries II*, p. 608, Linlithgow to LSA, 13 July 1940 and 15 July 1940
26. Louis, p. 132, Churchill to Linlithgow, 16 July 1940
27. MS Amery Diary, AMEL 7/34, 25 July 1940
28. Dilks, D. (ed.), *The Diaries of Sir Alexander Cadogan: 1938–1945*, p. 316
29. Colville, J., *The Fringes of Power: Downing Street Diaries 1939–1955*, p. 201
30. MS Amery Diary, AMEL 7/34, 25 July 1940
31. Colville, J., *The Fringes of Power: Downing Street Diaries 1939–1955*, p. 203
32. Roberts, A., *'The Holy Fox': A Biography of Lord Halifax*, p. 246
33. Colville, J., *Footprints in Time*, p. 93
34. Louis, p. 136, Churchill to LSA, 3 August 1940
35. *Diaries II*, p. 609, LSA to Linlithgow, 16 September 1940
36. Louis, p. 138, LSA to Linlithgow, 30 September 1940
37. Rizvi, G., *Linlithgow and India: A Study of British Policy and the Political Impasse in India, 1936–1943*, p.163
38. MS Amery Diary, AMEL 7/34, 13 September 1940
39. MS Amery Diary, AMEL 7/35, 11 October 1941
40. Ibid., 1 December 1941
41. Rizvi, p. 174, Linlithgow to LSA, 16 February 1942
42. Ibid., p. 177

43. Mansergh, N. and Lumby, E., (eds) *The Transfer of Power 1942–7, Volume I: The Cripps Mission January–April 1942*, p. 49, Linlithgow to LSA, 21 January 1942

44. *Diaries II*, p. 728

45. Mansergh, N. and Lumby, E., (eds) *The Transfer of Power 1942–7, Volume I: The Cripps Mission January–April 1942*, p. 75, Attlee to LSA, 24 January 1942

46. *Diaries II*, p. 729, Linlithgow to LSA, 16 February 1942

47. MS Amery Diary, AMEL 7/36, 26 February 1942

48. Ibid., 27 February 1942

49. Ibid., 4 March 1942

50. Rizvi, p. 184

51. *Diaries II*, p. 729, Draft for Volume IV of *My Political Life*

52. Mansergh, N. and Lumby, E., (eds) *The Transfer of Power 1942–7, Volume I: The Cripps Mission January–April 1942*, p. 390, LSA to Cripps, 9 March 1942

53. Hodson, H., *The Great Divide, Britain – India – Pakistan*, p. 98

54. *Diaries II*, p. 734

55. Gopal, p. 280

56. Mansergh, N. and Lumby, E., (eds) *The Transfer of Power 1942–7, Volume I: The Cripps Mission January–April 1942*, pp. 697–8, Linlithgow to LSA, 9 April 1942

57. MS Amery Diary, AMEL 7/36, 9 April 1942

58. Mansergh, N. and Lumby, E., (eds) *The Transfer of Power 1942–7, Volume I: The Cripps Mission January–April 1942*, p. 720, War Cabinet to Linlithgow, 9 March 1942

59. Hodson, H., *Autobiography*, Chapter VIII

60. Morris-Jones, W., 'Mansergh's *Transfer of Power, Volume II*', *Political Quarterly*, Volume 44, 1973, p. 94

61. MS Amery Diary, AMEL 7/36, 10 April 1942

62. Louis, p. 162, LSA to Linlithgow, 10 June 1942

63. *Diaries II*, p. 806, *Harijan*, 24 May 1942

64. Rizvi, p. 213

65. Mansergh, N. and Lumby, E., (eds), *The Transfer of Power 1942–7, Volume II: Quit India, 30 April–21 September 1942*, p. 376, LSA to Churchill, 13 July 1942

66. Rizvi, p. 215

67. MS Woolton 13/23, LSA to Woolton, 12 August 1942

68. Mansergh, N. and Lumby, E., (eds), *The Transfer of Power 1942–7, Volume II: Quit India, 30 April–21 September 1942*, p. 853, Linlithgow to Churchill, 31 August 1942

69. West, W. (ed.), *Orwell: The War Broadcasts*, p. 37

70. Mansergh, N. and Lumby, E., (eds), *The Transfer of Power 1942–7, Volume III: Reassertion of Authority, Gandhi's Fast and the Succession to the Viceroyalty, 21 September 1942–12 June 1943*, p. 451 and p. 453, LSA memorandum, 4 January 1943

71. MS Amery Diary, AMEL 7/37, 10 February 1943

72. Moon, P. (ed.), *Wavell: The Viceroy's Journal*, p. 461

73. MS Amery Diary, AMEL 7/37, 1 March 1943

74. Ibid., 5 March 1943

75. MS Amery Diary, AMEL 7/38, 9 May 1944

76. Louis, p. 167

77. Mansergh, N. and Lumby, E., (eds), *The Transfer of Power 1942–7, Volume III: Reassertion of Authority, Gandhi's Fast and the Succession to the Viceroyalty, 21 September 1942–12 June 1943*, pp. 327–9, LSA to Churchill and Churchill to LSA, 1 December 1942

78. MS Amery Diary, AMEL 7/36, 26 November 1942

79. MS Amery Diary, AMEL 7/37, 25 February 1943

80. Harvey, J. (ed.), *The War Diaries of Oliver Harvey 1941–1945*, p. 245

81. MS Amery Diary, AMEL 7/37, 22 April 1943

82. Thorpe, D. R., *Eden: The Life and Times of Anthony Eden, First Earl of Avon, 1897–1977*, pp. 285–6

83. Mansergh, N. and Lumby, E., (eds), *The Transfer of Power 1942–7, Volume III: Reassertion of Authority, Gandhi's Fast and the Succession to the Viceroyalty, 21 September 1942–12 June 1943*, p. 1048, LSA to Linlithgow, 8 June 1943

84. MS Amery Diary, AMEL 7/37, 28 June 1943

85. Moon, p.12 and p.14

86. Ibid., pp. 22–3

87. Morris-Jones, p. 96

88. Moon, p. 33, p.126, p.134 and p.135

89. Rhodes James, R. (ed.) *'Chips': The Diaries of Sir Henry Channon*, p. 396

90. MS Amery Diary, AMEL 7/38, 4 August 1944

91. Pimlott, B. (ed.), *The Second World War Diary of Hugh Dalton, 1940–45*, pp. 776–8

92. MS Amery Diary, AMEL 7/38, 6 November 1944

93. Ibid., 4 August 1944
94. Moon, p. 128

CHAPTER NINETEEN

1. MS Amery Diary, AMEL 7/33, 30 September 1939
2. FO 371/25037/8, Julian to Wardell, 1 April 1940
3. FO 371/25037/6, memorandum of R. Campbell, 4 April 1940
4. MS Lloyd George G/1/6/8, LSA to Lloyd George, 15 December 1939
5. MS Lloyd George G/1/6/11, Julian to Lloyd George, 12 February 1940
6. MS Lloyd George G/1/6/12, Julian to Lloyd George, 4 March 1940
7. FO 371/25031/196, Childs to Campbell, 5 January 1940
8. Amery, J., *Approach March: A Venture in Autobiography*, pp. 157–8
9. Author's conversation with Sir Alexander Glen, 27 January 2004
10. Amery, J., *Approach March: A Venture in Autobiography*, pp. 160–1
11. Glen, A., *Footholds Against a Whirlwind*, p. 56
12. Author's conversation with Sir Alexander Glen, 27 January 2004
13. Sweet-Escott, B., *Baker Street Irregular*, p. 60
14. Glen, p. 57
15. FO 954/24A, Lord Selborne to Anthony Eden, 4 October 1943
16. MS Amery Diary, AMEL 7/34, 13 October 1940
17. Ibid., 11 November 1940
18. Ibid., 16 July 1940
19. Amery, J., *Approach March: A Venture in Autobiography*, p. 212
20. MS Amery Diary, AMEL 7/34, 24 October 1940
21. Pimlott, B. (ed.), *The Second World War Diary of Hugh Dalton, 1940–45*, pp. 96–7 and p. 102
22. Amery, J., *Approach March: A Venture in Autobiography*, p. 214
23. MS Amery Diary, AMEL 7/34, 26 November 1940
24. Amery, J., *Approach March: A Venture in Autobiography*, p. 220
25. Ibid., p. 224
26. MS Amery Diary, AMEL 7/35, 11 May 1941
27. Ibid., 10 February 1941
28. Bassett, R., *Hitler's Spy Chief: The Wilhelm Canaris Mystery*, p. 212
29. MS Amery Diary, AMEL 7/35, 1 April 1941

30. Amery, J., *Approach March: A Venture in Autobiography*, p. 227
31. Pimlott, B. (ed.), *The Second World War Diary of Hugh Dalton, 1940–45*, p. 185
32. MS Amery Diary, AMEL 7/35, 27 October 1941
33. Deakin, F., *The Embattled Mountain*, p. 126n
34. MS Amery Diary, AMEL 7/36, 3 July 1942
35. MS Churchill, CHAR 20/55/30, memorandum to Churchill, 3 July 1942
36. Amery, J., *Approach March: A Venture in Autobiography*, p. 309
37. MS Amery Diary, AMEL 7/36, 3 July 1942
38. Danchev, A. and Todman, D. (eds), *War Diaries 1939–1945, Field Marshal Lord Alanbrooke*, pp. 276–7
39. Amery, J., *Approach March: A Venture in Autobiography*, p. 310
40. MS Amery Diary, AMEL 7/36, 3 July 1942
41. Rhodes James, R. (ed.), *'Chips': The Diaries of Sir Henry Channon*, p. 375
42. MS Amery Diary, AMEL 7/37, 17 March 1943
43. MS Amery Diary, AMEL 7/36, 14 October 1942
44. MS Amery Diary, AMEL 7/37, 11 April 1943
45. Matthew and Harrison (eds), *Volume 42*, p. 527
46. MS Amery Diary, AMEL 7/37, 24 March 1943
47. MS Eng. Hist. c1001/50, LSA to Selborne, 25 March 1943
48. Rhodes James, R. (ed.), *'Chips': The Diaries of Sir Henry Channon*, p. 335
49. HS 8/908, Selborne to LSA, 27 May 1943
50. MS Amery Diary, AMEL 7/37, 29 May 1943
51. MS Eng. Hist. c1001/52, Selborne to LSA, 29 May 1943
52. MS Amery Diary, AMEL 7/37, 18 May 1943
53. FO 954/24A, Selborne to Eden, 4 October 1943; Eden added his response in holograph on Selborne's original letter.
54. MS Eng. Hist. c1001/66, Selborne to LSA, 2 October 1943
55. MS Amery Diary, AMEL 7/37, 4 October 1943
56. Ibid., 3 October 1943
57. Amery, J., *Approach March: A Venture in Autobiography*, p. 268
58. HS 8/908, Selborne to LSA, 21 December 1943
59. Deakin, p. 261
60. Amery, J., 'Memories of Churchill and how he would have seen the world today', The Twelfth Crosby Kemper Lecture, p. 3
61. Amery, J., *Approach March: A Venture in Autobiography*, p. 270

62. Smiley, D., *Irregular Regular*, p. 101
63. Kemp, P., *No Colours or Crest*, p. 242
64. Amery, J., *Approach March: A Venture in Autobiography*, p. 337
65. Smiley, D., *Albanian Assignment*, p. 111
66. Fielding, X., *One Man in His Time: The Life of Lieutenant-Colonel NLD ('Billy') McLean DSO*, p. 46
67. Amery, J., *Approach March: A Venture in Autobiography*, p. 356
68. Smiley, D., *Albanian Assignment*, p. 121
69. Ibid., p. 125 and p. 127
70. Amery, J., *Approach March: A Venture in Autobiography*, p. 361
71. HS 8/908, Selborne to LSA, 2 June 1944
72. Halliday, J. (ed.), *The Artful Albanian: The Memoirs of Enver Hoxha*, p. 33
73. Barker, H., *British Policy in South-East Europe in the Second World War*, p. 183
74. Smiley, D., *Irregular Regular*, p. 107
75. Amery, J., *Sons of the Eagle: A Study in Guerilla War*, pp. 265–6
76. Halliday, p. 47
77. Amery, J., *Approach March: A Venture in Autobiography*, p. 379
78. Ibid., p. 383
79. Smiley, D., *Albanian Assignment*, p. 151
80. Kemp, p. 253
81. Smiley, D., *Irregular Regular*, p. 107
82. Barker, p. 182
83. Macmillan, H., *The Blast of War 1939–1945*, p. 690
84. Bethell, N., *The Great Betrayal: The Untold Story of Kim Philby's Biggest Coup*, p. 19 and p. 24
85. Amery, J., *Approach March: A Venture in Autobiography*, p. 405

CHAPTER TWENTY

1. HO 144/22823/216, LSA's 'Explanation' to the Home Secretary, 14 December 1945
2. KV 2/80, Jack to Una Wing, 25 January 1940
3. KV 2/80, Jack to Una Wing, 15 February 1940
4. MS Amery Diary, AMEL 7/34, 22 March 1940
5. KV 2/81, statement of John Amery, 'R' Internee Camp, Terni, Italy, 23 May 1945

6. HO 144/22823/216, LSA's 'Explanation' to the Home Secretary, 14 December 1945

7. KV 2/81, statement of John Amery, 23 May 1945

8. MS Amery Diary, AMEL 7/34, 14 June 1940

9. KV 2/81, statement of Wilfred Brinkman, 26 May 1945

10. Author's conversation with Sir Alexander Glen, 27 January 2004

11. BT 271/104, Jack to LSA, 25 July 1940

12. BT 271/104, Jack to LSA, 9 October 1940

13. BT 271/104, P. de Wolff to 'Trading With The Enemy' Branch, 28 October 1940 and 14 December 1940

14. MS Leo Amery, AMEL 2/1/31, LSA to Hoare, 23 October 1940 and Hoare to LSA, 29 October 1940

15. KV 2/81, statement of Wilfred Brinkman, 26 May 1945

16. KV 2/78, internal MI5 memorandum, 30 July 1942

17. KV 2/81, statement of Wilfred Brinkman, 26 May 1945

18. KV 2/81, statement of Alexander Ogilvie, 2 September 1945

19. HO 144/22823/366, Ogilvie to Jack, 5 December 1945

20. KV 2/81, statement of John Amery, 23 May 1945

21. KV 2/78, MI6 memorandum, 5 August 1942

22. Ibid., 22 February 1942

23. HO 144/22823/217, LSA's 'Explanation' to the Home Secretary, 14 December 1945

24. BT 271/104, Jack to LSA, 11 February 1941

25. KV 2/78, *Petit Dauphinois*, 6 March 1942

26. Weale, p. 140

27. KV 2/78, internal MI5 memorandum, 22 July 1942

28. KV 2/78, MI5 to SIS, 29 July 1942

29. KV 2/81, statement of John Amery, 23 May 1945

30. HO 144/22823/218, LSA's 'Explanation' to the Home Secretary, 14 December 1945

31. KV 2/81, statement of Dr Fritz Hesse, 17 September 1945

32. Doherty, M., *Nazi Wireless Propaganda, Lord Haw-Haw and British Public Opinion in the Second World War*, p. 15

33. KV 2/81, statement of John Amery, 23 May 1945

34. Weale, p. 145

35. KV 2/81, statement of Dr Fritz Hesse, 17 September 1945

36. KV 2/81, statement of John Amery, 23 May 1945

37. KV 2/81, statement of Dr Fritz Hesse, 17 September 1945

38. KV 2/826, statement of Dr Reinhard Haferkorn, 13 July 1945

39. KV 2/81, statement of John Amery, 23 May 1945

40. KV 2/81, statement of Dr Fritz Hesse, 17 September 1945

41. KV 2/826, statement of Dr Reinhard Haferkorn, 13 July 1945

42. MS Amery Diary, AMEL 7/36, 17 November 1942

43. *The Times*, 18 November 1942

44. KV 2/79, *Daily Mirror*, 18 November 1942

45. KV 2/79, Transocean broadcast, 18 November 1942

46. MS Amery Diary, AMEL 7/36, 8 November 1942

47. MS Beaverbrook C/7, LSA to Beaverbrook, 19 November 1942

48. MS Amery Diary, AMEL 7/36, 18 November 1942

49. Ibid., 19 November 1942

50. MS Churchill, CHAR 20/55/38, LSA to Churchill, 20 November 1942

51. Weale, pp. 161–2

52. KV 2/78, internal MI5 memorandum, 19 November 1942

53. MS Amery Diary, AMEL 7/36, 20 November 1942

54. MS Beaverbrook C/7, Beaverbrook to LSA, 29 December 1942

55. MS Violet Milner 31/C117/18, LSA to Lady Milner, 27 November 1942

56. KV 2/78, letter of Bryddie's, 21 December 1942

57. Author's conversation with Sir Alexander Glen, 27 January 2004

58. KV 2/78, Transocean interview, 25 November 1942

59. KV 2/81, statement of Dr Fritz Hesse, 17 September 1945

60. Bechhofer Roberts, C. (ed.), *The Trial of William Joyce*, p. 173

61. Doherty, p. 165

62. KV 2/81, statement of John Amery, 23 May 1945

63. KV 2/81, statement of Dr Fritz Hesse, 17 September 1945

64. MS Amery Diary, AMEL 7/36, 31 December 1942

65. MS Amery Diary, AMEL 7/37, 8 January 1943

66. KV 2/80, interview with M. Vidal of the Hotel Bristol

67. KV 2/81, statement of John Amery, 23 May 1945

68. KV 2/81, statement of Dr Fritz Hesse, 17 September 1945

69. Seth, R., *Jackals of the Reich: The Story of the British Free Corps*, p. 32

70. Weale, p. 190 and p. 194

71. KV 2/79, *England Faces Europe*, p. 100

72. Spitzy, R. (Translated from the German by G. Waddington), *How We Squandered the Reich*, pp. 353–4

73. KV 2/81, statement of John Amery, 23 May 1945
74. KV 2/80, statement of Helen Wies
75. KV 2/84, report of Dr Hesse on Jeanine's death
76. KV 2/79, *England Faces Europe*
77. KV 2/81, statement of John Amery, 23 May 1945
78. HO 144/22823/218, LSA's 'Explanation' to the Home Secretary, 14 December 1945
79. KV 2/81, statement of Dr Fritz Hesse, 17 September 1945
80. KV 2/79, statement of M. Keet, 18 December 1944
81. KV 2/79, statement of Royston Wood, 7 January 1945
82. KV 2/81, statement of Wilfred Brinkman, 26 May 1945
83. KV 2/79, Camp Committee Notice, 20 April 1943
84. KV 2/79, interrogation of Private E. Lee, 24 September 1944
85. Weale, p. 203
86. CRIM 1/485, statement of Kenneth Berry, 3 July 1945
87. KV 2/81, MI5 Report, *John Amery*, 23 June 1945
88. KV 2/81, statement of Dr Fritz Hesse, 17 September 1945
89. Cole, J., *Lord Haw-Haw – and William Joyce: The Full Story*, p. 207
90. KV 2/81, memorandum of John Amery for German Foreign Office following visit to Belgrade, 21 March 1944
91. KV 2/79, MI6 memorandum, 17 February 1945
92. KV 2/81, statement of John Amery, 23 May 1945
93. KV 2/80, MI5 report, 5 April 1945
94. KV 2/81, memorandum of John Amery for German Foreign Office following visit to Belgrade, 21 March 1944
95. KV 2/79, statement of Phillipe Simcox, 1 November 1944
96. KV 2/80, statement of Thomas Cooper, 23 May 1945
97. KV 2/80, MI5 report, 5 April 1945
98. KV 2/81, memorandum of John Amery for German Foreign Office following visit to Belgrade, 21 March 1944
99. Spitzy, pp. 355–6
100. Martland, P., *Lord Haw Haw: The English Voice of Nazi Germany*, p. 64
101. KV 2/81, statement of John Amery, 23 May 1945
102. Burt, L., *Commander Burt of Scotland Yard*, p. 5

CHAPTER TWENTY-ONE

1. WO 204/12601, exchange of telegrams between 15th Army Group and Allied Forces Headquarters (AFHQ), 16 April 1945

2. KV 2/80, statement of Italian partisans, 1 May 1945

3. MS Amery Diary, AMEL 7/39, 12 April 1945

4. Ibid., 2 May 1945

5. KV 2/80, MI5 to AFHQ, 3 May 1945

6. Whicker, A., *Within Whicker's World*, p. 45

7. *Evening Standard*, 4 September 1996

8. MS Amery Diary, AMEL 7/39, 13 May 1945

9. KV 2/81, statement of Major Leonard Burt

10. Burt, L., *Commander Burt of Scotland Yard*, Preface p. ix

11. KV 2/81, statement of John Amery, 23 May 1945

12. Burt, p. 5

13. Ibid., pp. 20–22

14. KV 2/81, statement of John Amery, 23 May 1945

15. Burt, p. 23

16. Amery, *Approach March: A Venture in Autobiography*, p. 409 and p. 418

17. Churchill, W., *His Father's Son: The Life of Randolph Churchill*, p. 267

18. Ball, S., *The Guardsmen; Harold Macmillan, Three Friends, and the World They Made*, p. 235

19. Private conversation with author

20. *The Oldie*, interview with Lord Amery, 27 November 1992

21. Matthew and Harrison (eds), *Volume 1*, p. 930

22. Amery, J., *Approach March: A Venture in Autobiography*, p. 432 and p. 441

23. Pimlott, B. (ed.) *The Second World War Diary of Hugh Dalton, 1940–45*, p. 821

24. MS Amery Diary, AMEL 7/39, 13 April 1945

25. Churchill, W., *His Father's Son: The Life of Randolph Churchill*, pp. 267–8

26. Roberts, B., *Randolph: A Study of Churchill's Son*, p. 282

27. Soames, M., *Clementine Churchill*, p. 382

28. MS Amery Diary, AMEL 7/39, 4 June 1945

29. Amery, J., *Approach March: A Venture in Autobiography*, p. 433

30. MS Amery Diary, AMEL 7/39, 5 June 1945

31. Roberts, B., *Randolph: A Study of Churchill's Son*, pp. 282–3

32. Amery, J., *Approach March: A Venture in Autobiography*, p. 441

33. MS Amery Diary, AMEL 7/39, 6 July 1945
34. Halle, K., *Randolph Churchill: The Young Pretender*, p. 195
35. Amery, J., *Approach March: A Venture in Autobiography*, p. 443
36. Churchill, W., *His Father's Son: The Life of Randolph Churchill*, p. 272
37. MS Eng. Hist. c1016/52, Julian to Selborne, 22 June 1945
38. MS Amery Diary, AMEL 7/39, 21 June 1945
39. Amery, J., *Approach March: A Venture in Autobiography*, p. 441
40. MS Amery Diary, AMEL 7/39, 29 June 1945
41. Author's conversation with Sir Clive Bossom, 17 November 2004
42. Burt, pp. 5–6
43. MS Amery Diary, AMEL 7/39, 8 July 1945
44. Ibid., 1 June 1945
45. Ibid., 9 July 1945
46. *The Oldie*, interview with Lord Amery, 27 November 1992
47. MS Amery Diary, AMEL 7/39, 13 July 1945
48. KV 2/78, Surrey Police report, 20 April 1944
49. MS Amery Diary, AMEL 7/39, 10 July 1945
50. Ibid., 15 July 1945
51. Ibid., 26 July 1945
52. *The Times*, 31 July 1945
53. MS Amery Diary, AMEL 7/39, 3 August 1945
54. Ibid., 7 August 1945
55. MS Eng. Hist. c1016/63, LSA to Selborne, 3 August 1945
56. MS Amery Diary, AMEL 7/39, 10 August 1945
57. MS Eng. Hist. c1016/64, LSA to Selborne, 20 August 1945
58. MS Beaverbrook C/7, LSA to Beaverbrook, 20 August 1945
59. KV 2/81, MI5 memorandum, 24 September 1945
60. MS Amery Diary, AMEL 7/39, 13 September 1945
61. KV 2/81, SIS to Cussen, 22 September 1945
62. MS Amery Diary, AMEL 7/39, 19 September 1945
63. Ibid., 24 September 1945
64. Ibid., 17 October 1945
65. HO 144/22822/71A, Major Pakenham to Major Hughes, 22 November 1945
66. KV 2/82, Mathew to Petrie, 4 December 1945
67. MS Amery Diary, AMEL 7/39, 26 November 1945
68. Ibid., 27 November 1945
69. West, R., *The Meaning of Treason*, p. 218

70. Burt, p. 27
71. West, R., *The Meaning of Treason*, pp. 219–20
72. *The Times*, 29 November 1945
73. West, R., *The Meaning of Treason*, p. 220
74. *The Times*, 29 November 1945
75. West, R., *The Meaning of Treason*, p. 222 and p. 225
76. *The Times*, 29 November 1945
77. Cole, p. 281
78. HO 144/22823/405, Bryddie to Ede, 28 November 1945
79. HO 144/22823/412 and 415, Bryddie to Ede, 30 November 1945
80. HO 144/22823/404, Ede to Bryddie, 29 November 1945
81. HO 144/22823/401 and 402, Bryddie to Ede, 1 December 1945
82. MS Amery Diary, AMEL 7/39, 29 November 1945
83. Ibid., 30 November 1945
84. HO 144/22823/353 and 354, Home Office memorandum by Sir Frank Newsam, 3 December 1945
85. MS Amery Diary, AMEL 7/39, 5 December 1945
86. HO 144/22823/224, 226 and 227, report of Dr Edward Glover, 7 December 1945
87. HO 144/22823/274, report of Lord Horder, 7 December 1945
88. HO 144/22823/395, Slade to Ede, 7 December 1945
89. MS Amery Diary, AMEL 7/39, 6 December 1945
90. HO 144/22823/274, report of Dr Grierson, 1 December 1945
91. HO 144/22823/399 and 400, Simon to Ede, 7 December 1945
92. HO 144/22823/408 and 409, Lady Carson to Ede, 3 December 1945
93. HO 144/22823/424 and 427, Norwood to Ede, 4 December 1945
94. MS Amery Diary, AMEL 7/39, 30 November 1945
95. HO 144/22823/352, Home Office report of Drs East and Hopwood, 14 December 1945
96. PREM 8/122, Smuts to Attlee, 14 December 1945
97. HO 144/22823/323, memorandum of Sir Frank Newsam, 15 December 1945
98. Weale, p. 243
99. HO 144/22823/323, memorandum of Sir Frank Newsam, 15 December 1945
100. TNL Archive, RBW/2, LSA to Barrington-Ward, 11 December 1945
101. MS Beaverbrook C/7, Bryddie to Beaverbrook, 9 December 1945
102. HO 144/22823/302, Newsam to Lickfold, 17 December 1945

103. MS Amery Diary, AMEL 7/39, 17 December 1945
104. PREM 8/122, Attlee to Smuts, 15 December 1945
105. HO 144/22823/292, Home Office minute of meeting between Ede and Horder, 18 December 1945
106. WO 204/12601, Michelle to Jack, 3 December 1945
107. KV 2/81, Jack to Michelle, undated
108. HO 144/22823/452 and 453, MI5 memorandum, 6 December 1945
109. MS Amery Diary, AMEL 7/39, 14 December 1945
110. Ibid., 18 December 1945
111. TNL Archive, RBW/2, Bryddie to Barrington-Ward, 2 January 1946
112. MS Douglas 24/93/g-i, Bryddie to Canon Douglas, 21 May 1946
113. MS Amery Diary, AMEL 7/39, 18 December 1945
114. MS Violet Milner 31/C117/19, LSA to Lady Milner, 19 December 1945
115. PCOM 9/1117

CHAPTER TWENTY-TWO

1. MS Violet Milner 31/C117/19, LSA to Lady Milner, 19 December 1945
2. MS Page Croft, CRFT 1/2/34, LSA to Page Croft, 18 December 1945
3. TNL Archive, RBW/2, LSA to Barrington-Ward, 19 December 1945
4. MS Amery Diary, AMEL 7/39, 18 December 1945
5. West, R., *The New Meaning of Treason*, p. 129
6. Shawcross, H., *Life Sentence: The Memoirs of Lord Shawcross*, p. 84
7. MS Pym 146/22, diary 20 February 1941
8. Rhodes James, R., *'Chips': The Diaries of Sir Henry Channon*, p. 377
9. Private conversation with the author
10. MS Violet Milner 31/C117/19, LSA to Lady Milner, enclosing press cutting from the *Manchester Guardian*, 25 December 1945
11. TNL Archive, RBW/2, Barrington-Ward to Bryddie, 23 December 1945
12. Ibid., Bryddie to Barrington-Ward, 2 January 1946
13. MS Beaverbrook C/7, Bryddie to Beaverbrook, 21 December 1945
14. HO 144/22823/21, Bryddie to Ede, 24 May 1947
15. HO 144/22823/18, Bryddie to Ede, 9 July 1947

16. HO 144/22823/13, Home Office memorandum, 10 November 1947
17. HO 144/22823/14, Ede to Bryddie, 22 November 1947
18. MS Amery Diary, AMEL 7/39, 31 December 1945
19. MS Palmer 3010/266, LSA to Palmer, January 1946
20. MS Curtis 32/4, LSA to Curtis, 2 January 1946
21. MS Eng. Hist. c 1016/78, LSA to Selborne, 3 January 1946
22. MS Douglas 24/93, LSA to Douglas, 17 May 1946
23. Amery, L., *John Amery: An Explanation*, privately published 1946, contained in MS Douglas 24/93
24. MS Amery Diary, AMEL 7/32, 28 September 1938
25. Thompson, N., *The Anti-Appeasers: Conservative Opposition to Appeasement in the 1930s*, p. 181
26. Copsey, N., 'John Amery: the antisemitism of the "perfect English gentleman"', *Patterns of Prejudice*, Volume 36, No. 2, p. 15
27. Rubinstein, p. 189
28. MS Douglas 24/93, Bryddie to Douglas, 21 May 1946
29. MS Eng. c 6920/122–123, Sir Patrick Reilly to Lady Florence Reilly, April 1946
30. Bethell, p. 34
31. *Time and Tide*, Volume 30, No. 4, 22 January 1949, p. 73
32. Bethell, p. 33
33. Ibid., p. 36 and p. 38
34. Fielding, p. 78
35. Halliday, p. 83
36. MS Beaverbrook C/8, LSA to Beaverbrook, 20 December 1948
37. MS Amery Diary, AMEL 7/40, 30 September 1946
38. *Diaries II*, p. 1059, LSA to Churchill, 12 November 1945
39. MS Amery Diary, AMEL 7/40, 19 September 1946
40. MS Amery Diary, AMEL 7/38, 5 June 1944
41. MS Amery Diary, AMEL 7/37, 7 September 1943
42. MS Amery Diary, AMEL 7/42, 17 September 1948
43. Tyerman, p. 424
44. MS Amery Diary, AMEL 7/37, 7 September 1943
45. *Alpine Journal*, Volume LVI, p. 11
46. Catterall, P. (ed.), *The Macmillan Diaries: The Cabinet Years, 1950–1957*, p. 75
47. *The Spectator*, 23 July 1988
48. Catterall, p. 342

49. MS Amery Diary, AMEL 7/45, 8 December 1951
50. Catterall, p. 123
51. MS Amery Diary, AMEL 7/45, 8 December 1951
52. Ibid., 9 December 1951
53. MS Beaverbrook C/8, LSA to Beaverbrook, 17 February 1953
54. MS Curtis 51/153, LSA to Curtis, 7 February 1949
55. MS Curtis 59/60, LSA to Curtis, 5 November 1949
56. Catterall, p. 477
57. MS Amery Diary, AMEL 7/44, 25 May 1950
58. *The Times*, 17 September 1955

EPILOGUE

1. MS Amery Diary, AMEL 7/47, 24 November 1953
2. *The Oldie*, interview with Lord Amery, 27 November 1992
3. Matthew and Harrison (eds), *Volume 1*, p. 936
4. MS Spears 1/6, Bryddie to Spears, 29 November 1973

Bibliography

MANUSCRIPT COLLECTIONS

Alpine Club Archive	
Julian Amery Papers	Churchill Archives Centre
Leo Amery Papers	Churchill Archives Centre
Anson Papers	All Souls College
Avon Papers	Birmingham University Library
Baldwin Papers	Cambridge University Library
Balfour Papers	British Library
Barrington-Ward Papers	Times Newspapers Limited Archive
Beaverbrook Papers	House of Lords Records Office
Bonar Law Papers	House of Lords Records Office
Cecil of Chelwood Papers	British Library
Austen Chamberlain Papers	Birmingham University Library
Joseph Chamberlain Papers	Birmingham University Library
Neville Chamberlain Papers	Birmingham University Library
Churchill (Chartwell) Papers	Churchill Archives Centre
Curtis Papers	Bodleian Library, Oxford
Davidson Papers	House of Lords Records Office
Dawson Papers	Bodleian Library, Oxford
Douglas Papers	Lambeth Palace Library
Emrys-Evans Papers	British Library
English History Papers	Bodleian Library, Oxford

Gwynne Papers	Bodleian Library, Oxford
Harrow School Archive	
Linlithgow Papers	India Office Library, British Library
Lloyd George Papers	House of Lords Records Office
Maxse Papers	West Sussex Records Office
Milner Papers	Bodleian Library, Oxford
Violet Milner Papers	Bodleian Library, Oxford
Moberley Bell Papers	Times Newspapers Limited Archive
Northcliffe Papers	British Library
Northcliffe Papers	Times Newspapers Limited Archive
Page Croft Papers	Churchill Archives Centre
Palmer Papers	Lambeth Palace Library
Pym Papers	Bodleian Library, Oxford
Reilly Papers	Bodleian Library, Oxford
Round Table Papers	Bodleian Library, Oxford
Selborne Papers	Bodleian Library, Oxford
Simon Papers	Bodleian Library, Oxford
Summer Fields School Archive	
Templewood Papers	Cambridge University Library
Woolton Papers	Bodleian Library, Oxford

PUBLISHED SOURCES

Adams, R., *Bonar Law*, John Murray, 1999

Aldridge, N., *Time to Spare?: A History of Summer Fields*, David Talboys Publications, 1989

Amery, C., *Notes on Forestry*, Trubner & Co., 1875

Amery, J., *Approach March: A Venture in Autobiography*, Hutchinson, 1973

——, *Joseph Chamberlain and the Tariff Reform Campaign: Volume V 1901–1903*, Macmillan, 1969

——, *Joseph Chamberlain and the Tariff Reform Campaign: Volume VI 1903–1968*, Macmillan, 1969

——, 'Memories of Churchill and how he would have seen the world today', The Twelfth Crosby Kemper Lecture, Westminster College, 1994

——, *Sons of the Eagle, A Study in Guerilla War*, Macmillan, 1948

Amery, L., *Days of Fresh Air*, Hutchinson, 1939

——, *In the Rain and the Sun*, Hutchinson, 1946

——, *My Political Life: Volume I, England Before the Storm 1896–1914*, Hutchinson, 1953

——, *My Political Life: Volume II, War and Peace 1914–1929*, Hutchinson, 1953

——, *My Political Life: Volume III, The Unforgiving Years 1929–1940*, Hutchinson, 1955

——, *The Empire in the New Era*, Arnold, 1928

——, *The Times History of the South African War: Volume II*, Sampson Low & Co., 1902

——, *Thoughts on the Constitution*, Oxford University Press, 1953

Ball, Simon, *The Guardsmen: Harold Macmillan, Three Friends, and the World They Made*, HarperCollins, 2004

Ball, Stuart, *Baldwin and the Conservative Party: The Crisis of 1929–1931*, Yale University Press, 1988

—— (ed.), *Parliament and Politics in the Age of Baldwin and MacDonald: The Headlam Diaries, 1923–1935*, Historians' Press, 1992

—— (ed.), *Parliament and Politics in the Age of Churchill and Attlee: The Headlam Diaries 1935–1951*, Cambridge University Press (for the Royal Historical Society), 1999

Barker, E., *British Policy in South-East Europe in the Second World War*, Macmillan, 1976

Barnes, J., and Nicholson, D. (eds), *The Leo Amery Diaries 1869–1929*, Hutchinson, 1980

—— (eds), *The Empire at Bay: The Leo Amery Diaries 1929–1945*, Hutchinson, 1988

Barnett, C., *The Collapse of British Power*, Eyre Methuen, 1972

Bassett, R., *Hitler's Spy Chief: The Wilhelm Canaris Mystery*, Weidenfeld & Nicolson, 2005

Beamish, H. (ed.), *The Jews' Who's Who*, London, 1919

Beaverbrook, Lord, *The Decline and Fall of Lloyd George*, Collins, 1963

Bechhofer Roberts, C. (ed.), *The Trial of William Joyce*, Jarrolds, 1946

Beckett, I. (ed.), *The Army and the Curragh Incident 1914*, The Bodley Head (for the Army Records Society), 1986

Bergmeier, H., and Lotz, R., *Hitler's Airwaves: The Inside Story of Nazi Radio Broadcasting and Propaganda Swing*, Yale University Press, 1997

Bethell, N., *The Great Betrayal: The Untold Story of Kim Philby's Biggest Coup*, Hodder & Stoughton, 1984

Birkenhead, Lord, *F.E.: The Life of F.E. Smith, First Earl of Birkenhead*, Eyre & Spottiswoode, 1959

——, *Rudyard Kipling*, Weidenfeld & Nicholson, 1978

Blake, R., *The Unknown Prime Minister: The Life and Times of Andrew Bonar Law*, Eyre & Spottiswoode, 1955

Boothby, R., *I Fight to Live*, Victor Gollancz, 1947

——, *Recollections of a Rebel*, Hutchinson, 1978

Brett, M. (ed.), *The Journals and Letters of Viscount Esher, Volume I 1870–1903*, Ivor Nicholson & Watson, 1934

Browning, R., *Men and Women: Volume I*, Chapman & Hall, 1855

Buchan, J., *Memory Hold-The-Door*, Hodder & Stoughton, 1950

Burt, L., *Commander Burt of Scotland Yard*, Heinemann, 1959

Callwell, C., *Field-Marshal Sir Henry Wilson: His Life and Diaries*, Cassell & Co., 1927

Cameron Watt, D., *How War Came: The Immediate Origins of the Second World War, 1938–1939*, Heinemann, 1989

Campbell, J., *F.E. Smith: First Earl of Birkenhead*, Jonathan Cape, 1983

Catterall, P. (ed.), *The Macmillan Diaries: The Cabinet Years, 1950–1957*, Macmillan, 2003

Charmley, J., *Churchill's Grand Alliance: The Anglo–American Special Relationship, 1940–1957*, Hodder & Stoughton, 1995

——, *Duff Cooper: The Authorized Biography*, Weidenfeld & Nicolson, 1986

——, *Lord Lloyd and the Decline of the British Empire*, Weidenfeld & Nicolson, 1987

Churchill, R., *Lord Derby: King of Lancashire*, Heinemann, 1959

Churchill, W., *My Early Life*, Thornton Butterworth, 1930

——, *The Second World War: Volume I, The Gathering Storm*, Cassell & Co., 1948

——, *The World Crisis: The Aftermath*, Thornton Butterworth, 1929

Churchill, W., *His Father's Son: The Life of Randolph Churchill*, Weidenfeld & Nicolson, 1996

Cole, J., *Lord Haw-Haw – and William Joyce: The Full Story*, Faber & Faber, 1964

Colville, J., *Footprints in Time*, Michael Russell, 1984

——, *The Fringes of Power: Downing Street Diaries 1939–1955*, Hodder & Stoughton, 1985

Cooper, D., *Old Men Forget*, Rupert Hart-Davis, 1953

Copsey, N., 'John Amery: the antisemitism of the "perfect English gentleman"', *Patterns of Prejudice*, Volume 36, No. 2, Institute for Jewish Policy Research, 2002

Cowling, M., *The Impact of Hitler, British politics and British Policy 1933–1940*, Cambridge University Press, 1975

Cross, J., *Sir Samuel Hoare: A Political Biography*, Jonathan Cape, 1977

Crowson, N., *Facing Fascism: The Conservative Party and the European Dictators, 1935–1940*, Routledge, 1997

Danchev, A. and Todman, D. (eds.), *War Diaries 1939–1945, Field Marshal Lord Alanbrooke*, Weidenfeld & Nicolson, 2001

Dalton, H., *The Fateful Years: Memoirs 1931–1945*, Frederick Muller, 1957

Davies, E., *Illyrian Adventure*, The Bodley Head, 1952

Day Lewis, C., *The Buried Day*, Chatto & Windus, 1960

Deakin, F., *The Embattled Mountain*, Oxford University Press, 1971

Dilks, D., *Neville Chamberlain: Volume One, Pioneering and Reform 1869–1929*, Cambridge University Press, 1984

—— (ed.), *The Diaries of Sir Alexander Cadogan, 1938–1945*, Cassell, 1971

Doherty, M., *Nazi Wireless Propaganda: Lord Haw-Haw and British Public Opinion in the Second World War*, Edinburgh University Press, 2000

Donaldson, F., *The Marconi Scandal*, Rupert Hart-Davis, 1962

Dutton, D., *Austen Chamberlain: Gentleman in Politics*, Ross Anderson Publications, 1985

——, *His Majesty's Loyal Opposition: The Unionist Party in Opposition 1905–1915*, Liverpool University Press, 1992

——, *Simon: A political biography of Sir John Simon*, Aurum Press, 1992

—— (ed.), *Paris 1918: The War Diary of the British Ambassador, The 17th Earl of Derby*, Liverpool University Press, 2001

Eden, A., *The Reckoning*, Cassell, 1965

Egremont, M., *Balfour: A Life of Arthur James Balfour*, Collins, 1980

Elliott, N., *Never Judge a Man by his Umbrella*, Michael Russell, 1991

Falk, S., *Qajar Paintings: Persian Oil Paintings of the 18th and 19th Centuries*, Faber, Sotheby Parke-Bernet Publications, 1972

Feiling, K., *The Life of Neville Chamberlain*, Macmillan, 1946

Ferguson, P., 'Fighting on All Fronts: Leo Amery and the First World War', *Essays in History*, Volume XXXV, University of Virginia, 1993

Fielding, X., *One Man in His Time: The Life of Lieutenant-Colonel NLD ('Billy') McLean DSO*, Macmillan, 1990

Foot, M., *H.G.: The History of Mr Wells*, Doubleday, 1995

Gathorne-Hardy, J., *The Public School Phenomenon, 597–1977*, Hodder & Stoughton, 1977

Gilbert, M., and Gott, R., *The Appeasers*, Weidenfeld & Nicolson, 1967

Gilmour, D., *Curzon*, John Murray, 1994

Glen, A., *Footholds Against a Whirlwind*, Hutchinson, 1975

Gollin, A., *Balfour's Burden: Anthony Balfour and Imperial Preference*, Anthony Blond, 1965

——, *The Observer and J. L. Garvin 1908–1914: A Study in Great Editorship*, Oxford University Press, 1960

——, *Proconsul in Politics: A Study of Lord Milner in Opposition and in Power*, Anthony Blond, 1964

Gopal, S., *Jawaharlal Nehru: A Biography, Volume I, 1889–1947*, Jonathan Cape, 1975

Griffiths, R., *Fellow Travellers of the Right: British Enthusiasts for Nazi Germany 1933–9*, Constable, 1980

Grigg, J., *Lloyd George: From Peace to War, 1912–1916*, Methuen, 1985

Hall, H. D., 'The Genesis of the Balfour Declaration of 1926', *Journal of Commonwealth Political Studies: Volume 1, 1961–1963*, Leicester University Press, 1963

Halle, K., *Randolph Churchill: The Young Pretender*, Heinemann, 1971

Halliday, J. (ed.), *The Artful Albanian: The Memoirs of Enver Hoxha*, Chatto & Windus, 1986

Halpérin, V., *Lord Milner and the Empire: The Evolution of British Imperialism*, Odhams Press, 1952 (Foreword by Leo Amery)

Hancock, W., *Smuts: The Sanguine Years 1870–1919*, Cambridge University Press, 1962

Hankey, Lord, *The Supreme Command 1914–1918, Volume II*, George Allen & Unwin, 1961

Harvey, J. (ed.), *The Diplomatic Diaries of Oliver Harvey, 1937–1940*, Collins, 1970

—— (ed.), *The War Diaries of Oliver Harvey*, Collins, 1978

Headlam, C. (ed.), *The Milner Papers: Volume II, South Africa 1899–1905*, Cassell, 1931

Henderson, N., *Old Friends and Modern Instances*, Profile Books, 2000

Hodson, H., *Autobiography*, Athelstane e-Books, 1999

——, *The Great Divide: Britain – India – Pakistan*, Hutchinson, 1969

Holt, H., *A Lot to Ask: A Life of Barbara Pym*, Macmillan, 1990

——, and Pym, H. (eds), *A Very Private Eye: The Diaries, Letters and Notebooks of Barbara Pym*, Macmillan, 1984

Hyam, R., *The Failure of South African Expansion, 1908–1948*, Macmillan, 1972

Hyde, H. M., *Baldwin: The Unexpected Prime Minister*, Hart-Davis, MacGibbon, 1973

——, *Lord Reading: The Life of Rufus Isaacs, First Marquess of Reading*, Heinemann, 1967

——, *Carson: The Life of Sir Edward Carson*, Heinemann, 1953

Ingham, K., *Jan Christiaan Smuts: The Conscience of a South African*, Weidenfeld & Nicolson, 1986

Jackson, A., *Home Rule: An Irish History 1800–2000*, Weidenfeld & Nicolson, 2003

Jalland, P., *The Liberals and Ireland: The Ulster Question in British Politics to 1914*, The Harvester Press, 1980

Jones, J., *Balliol College: A History 1263–1939*, Oxford University Press, 1988

Keay, J., *Eccentric Travellers*, John Murray, 1982

Kemp, P., *No Colours or Crest*, Cassell, 1958

Kisch, F., *Palestine Diary*, Victor Gollancz, 1938

Liddell Hart, B., *The Memoirs of Captain Liddell Hart, Volume I*, Cassell, 1965

Long, R., *Barbara Pym*, Ungar, 1986

Louis, W., *In the Name of God, Go!: Leo Amery and the British Empire in the Age of Churchill*, W. W. Norton, 1992

Lunn, A., *The Harrovians*, Methuen & Co., 1913

Lycett, A., *Rudyard Kipling*, Weidenfeld & Nicholson, 1999

Lycett Green, C. (ed.), *John Betjeman: Letters Volume II, 1952 to 1984*, Methuen, 1995

Mack, E., *Public Schools and British Opinion Since 1860*, Columbia University Press, 1941

Mackenzie, N. (ed.), *The Letters of Sidney and Beatrice Webb, Volume II: Partnership 1892–1912*, Cambridge University Press and London School of Economics, 1978

Mackenzie, N., and J. (eds), *The Diary of Beatrice Webb, Volume II: 1892–1905, 'All the Good Things of Life'*, Virago, 1983

—— (eds), *The Diary of Beatrice Webb, Volume III: 1905–1924, 'The Power to Alter Things'*, Virago, 1984

——, *The Time Traveller: The Life of H.G. Wells*, Weidenfeld & Nicolson, 1973

Maclean, F., *Eastern Approaches*, Jonathan Cape, 1949

Macleod, I., *Neville Chamberlain*, Frederick Muller Ltd, 1961

Macmillan, H., *Winds of Change, 1914–1939*, Macmillan, 1966

——, *The Blast of War, 1939–1945*, Macmillan, 1967

Macnee, P., *Blind in One Ear*, Harrap, 1988

Mansergh, N., and Lumby, E. (eds), *The Transfer of Power 1942–7, Volume I: The Cripps Mission, January–April 1942*, Her Majesty's Stationery Office, 1970

—— (eds), *The Transfer of Power 1942–7, Volume II: Quit India, 30 April–21 September 1942*, Her Majesty's Stationery Office, 1971

—— (eds), *The Transfer of Power 1942–7, Volume III: Reassertion of Authority, Gandhi's Fast and the Succession to the Viceroyalty, 21 September 1942–12 June 1943*, Her Majesty's Stationery Office, 1971

Marlowe, J., *Milner: Apostle of Empire*, Hamish Hamilton, 1976

Martland, P., *Lord Haw Haw: The English Voice of Nazi Germany*, The National Archives, 2003

Matthew, H., and Harrison, B. (eds), *Oxford Dictionary of National Biography*, Oxford University Press, 2004

Maurice, F. (ed.), *The Life of General Lord Rawlinson of Trent*, Cassell & Co, 1928

Middlemas, K. (ed.), *Thomas Jones, Whitehall Diary: Volume I 1916–1925*, Oxford University Press, 1969

—— (ed.), *Thomas Jones, Whitehall Diary: Volume II 1926–1930*, Oxford University Press, 1969

——, and Barnes, J., *Baldwin: A Biography*, Weidenfeld & Nicolson, 1969

Minney, R., *The Private Papers of Hore-Belisha*, Collins, 1960

Moon, P. (ed.), *Wavell: The Viceroy's Journal*, Oxford University Press, 1973

Moore, R., *Escape from Empire: The Attlee Government and the Indian Problem*, Clarendon Press, 1983

Morgan, K., *Consensus and Disunity: The Lloyd George Coalition Government 1918–1922*, Clarendon Press, 1979

Morris-Jones, W., 'Mansergh's *Transfer of Power, Volume II*', *Political Quarterly*, Volume XLIV, 1973

Naylor, J., *A Man and an Institution: Sir Maurice Hankey, the Cabinet Secretariat and the Custody of Cabinet Secrecy*, Cambridge University Press, 1984

Nehru, J., *An Autobiography*, John Lane, 1942

Nicolson, H., *King George the Fifth: His Life and Reign*, Constable, 1952

Nicolson, N. (ed.), *Harold Nicolson: Diaries and Letters 1930–1939*, Collins, 1966

——, *Long Life: Memoirs*, Weidenfeld & Nicolson, 1997

Norwood, C., *The English Tradition of Education*, John Murray, 1929

Page, B., Leitch, D., and Knightley, P., *Philby: The Spy who Betrayed a Generation*, Andre Deutsch, 1968

Parker, W., *Mackinder: Geography as an Aid to Statecraft*, Oxford University Press, 1982

Petrie, C., *The Life and Letters of The Right Honourable Sir Austen Chamberlain: Volume I*, Cassell & Co., 1939

Philby, K., *My Silent War*, Macgibbon & Kee, 1968

Pimlott, B., *Hugh Dalton*, Jonathan Cape, 1985

—— (ed), *The Second World War Diary of Hugh Dalton, 1940–45*, Jonathan Cape, 1986

Playfair, G., *My Father's Son*, Geoffrey Bles, 1937

Pollock, J., *Kitchener*, Constable, 2001

Pound, R., and Harmsworth, G., *Northcliffe*, Cassell, 1959

Pym, B., *Civil to Strangers, and other Writings*, Macmillan, 1987

——, *Crampton Hodnet*, Macmillan, 1985

Quayle, A., *A Time To Speak*, Barrie & Jenkins, 1990

Radice, L., *Beatrice and Sidney Webb: Fabian Socialists*, Macmillan, 1984

Ramsden, J., *The Age of Balfour and Baldwin, 1902–1940*, Longman, 1978

——, *The Age of Churchill and Eden, 1940–1957*, Longman, 1995

——, *An Appetite for Power: A History of the Conservative Party Since 1830*, HarperCollins, 1998

—— (ed.), *Real Old Tory Politics: The Political Diaries of Sir Robert Sanders, Lord Bayford, 1910–35*, The Historians' Press, 1984

Reinharz, J., *Chaim Weizmann: The Making of a Statesman*, Oxford University Press, 1993

Repington, C., *The First World War 1914–1918, Volume II*, Constable, 1920

Rhodes James, R., *Bob Boothby: A Portrait*, Hodder & Stoughton, 1991

——, *Churchill: A Study in Failure, 1900–1939*, Weidenfeld & Nicolson, 1970

——, *Memoirs of a Conservative: J.C.C. Davidson's Memoirs and Papers, 1910–37*, Weidenfeld & Nicolson, 1969

—— (ed.), *Chips: The Diaries of Sir Henry Channon*, Weidenfeld & Nicolson, 1967

Riddell, Lord, *More Pages From My Diary 1908–1914*, Country Life Ltd, 1934

Rizvi, G., *Linlithgow and India: A Study of British Policy and the Political Impasse in India, 1936–1943*, Royal Historical Society, 1978

Roberts, A., *'The Holy Fox': A Biography of Lord Halifax*, Weidenfeld & Nicolson, 1991

Roberts, A., *Salisbury: Victorian Titan*, Weidenfeld & Nicolson, 1999

Roberts, B., *Randolph: A Study of Churchill's Son*, Hamish Hamilton, 1984

Ronaldshay, Lord, *The Life of Lord Curzon: Volume III*, Ernest Benn, 1928

Rose, K., *King George V*, Weidenfeld & Nicolson, London, 1983

Rose, N., *Gentile Zionists: A Study in Anglo-Zionist Diplomacy, 1929–1939,* Cassell, 1973

Roskill, S., *Hankey, Man of Secrets: Volume I 1877–1918,* Collins, 1970

——, *Hankey, Man of Secrets: Volume II 1919–1931,* Collins, 1972

Rubinstein, W., 'The Secret of Leopold Amery', *Historical Research, Volume LXXIII,* Blackwells, 2000

Sanders, R., *The High Walls of Jerusalem,* Holt, Rinehart & Winston, 1983

Sanger, C., *Malcolm MacDonald: Bringing an End to Empire,* Liverpool University Press, 1995

Searle, G., *Corruption in British Politics, 1895–1930,* Clarendon Press, 1987

——, *Country Before Party: Coalition and the idea of ' National Government' in Modern Britain, 1885–1987,* Longman, 1995

——, *The Quest for National Efficiency: A Study in British Politics and Political Thought 1899–1914,* Blackwells, 1971

Self, R. (ed.), *The Neville Chamberlain Diary Letters, Volume I: The Making of a Politician, 1915–1920,* Ashgate, 2000

—— (ed.), *The Neville Chamberlain Diary Letters, Volume 2: The Reform Years, 1921–27,* Ashgate, 2000

—— (ed.), *The Neville Chamberlain Diary Letters, Volume 3: The Heir Apparent, 1928–33,* Ashgate, 2002

—— (ed.), *The Austen Chamberlain Diary Letters: The Correspondence of Sir Austen Chamberlain with his sisters Hilda and Ida, 1916–1937,* Cambridge University Press, 1995

Selwyn, F., *Hitler's Englishmen: The Crime of Lord Haw-Haw,* Routledge & Kegan Paul, 1987

Seth, R., *Jackals of the Reich: The Story of the British Free Corps,* New English Library, 1972

Seton-Watson, R., *A History of the Czechs and Slovaks,* Hutchinson, 1943

Shawcross, H., *Life Sentence: The Memoirs of Lord Shawcross,* Constable, 1995

Simon, J., *Retrospect: The Memoirs of the Rt. Hon. Viscount Simon,* Hutchinson, 1952

Smiley, D., *Albanian Assignment,* Chatto & Windus, 1984

——, *Irregular Regular,* Michael Russell, 1994

Smith, Janet, *John Buchan: A Biography,* Rupert Hart-Davis, 1965

Smith, Jeremy, *The Tories and Ireland 1910–1914: Conservative Party Politics and the Home Rule Crisis,* Irish Academic Press, 2000

Soames, M., *Clementine Churchill,* Cassell, 1979

Spears, E., *Assignment to Catastrophe, Volume I: Prelude to Dunkirk July 1939–May 1940*, William Heinemann, 1954

Spender, J., and Asquith, C., *Life of Herbert Henry Asquith: Lord Oxford and Asquith, Volume I*, Hutchinson, 1932

Spitzy, R. (Translated from the German by G. Waddington), *How We Squandered the Reich*, Michael Russell, 1997

Steed, W., *The Real Stanley Baldwin*, Nisbet & Co., 1930

Stein, L., *The Balfour Declaration*, Vallentine Mitchell, 1961

Stewart, A., *The Ulster Crisis*, Faber & Faber, 1967

Stewart, G., *Burying Caesar: Churchill, Chamberlain and the Battle for the Tory Party*, Weidenfeld & Nicolson, 1999

Strong, L., *Green Memory*, Methuen, 1961

Sweet-Escott, B., *Baker Street Irregular*, Methuen, 1965

Taylor, A., *Beaverbrook*, Hamish Hamilton, 1972

Templewood, Lord, *Nine Troubled Years*, Collins, 1954

Thompson, N., *The Anti-Appeasers: Conservative Opposition to Appeasement in the 1930s*, Oxford University Press, 1971

Thompson, R., *Churchill and Morton*, Hodder & Stoughton, 1976

Thorpe, D. R., *The Uncrowned Prime Ministers*, Darkhorse Publishing, 1980

——, *Eden: The Life and Times of Anthony Eden, First Earl of Avon, 1897–1977*, Chatto & Windus, 2003

Tree, R., *When the Moon was High: Memoirs of Peace and War 1897–1942*, Macmillan, 1975

Tyerman, C., *A History of Harrow School, 1324–1991*, Oxford University Press, 2000

Usborne, R. (ed.), *A Century of Summer Fields*, Methuen, 1964

Vansittart, Lord, *The Mist Procession: The Autobiography of Lord Vansittart*, Hutchinson, 1958

Vickers, H., *Cecil Beaton: The Authorised Biography*, Weidenfeld & Nicolson, 1985

Vincent, J. (ed.), *The Crawford Papers: The Journals of David Lindsay, Twenty-Seventh Earl of Crawford and Tenth Earl of Balcarres, 1871–1940*, Manchester University Press, 1984

Waley, S., *Edwin Montagu: A Memoir and an Account of his Visits to India*, Asia Publishing House, 1964

Wansell, G., *Terence Rattigan*, Fourth Estate, 1995

Weale, A., *Patriot Traitors: Roger Casement, John Amery and the Real Meaning of Treason*, Viking, 2001

Webb, B., *Our Partnership*, Longmans Green, 1948

Weisgal, M. (ed.), *The Letters and Papers of Chaim Weizmann, Volume VII: August 1914–November 1917*, Oxford University Press, 1975

—— (ed.), *Chaim Weizmann: A Biography by Several Hands*, Weidenfeld & Nicolson, 1963

Weizmann, C., *Trial and Error*, Hamish Hamilton, 1949

Wells, H.G., *Experiment in Autobiography: Volume II*, Victor Gollancz & The Cresset Press, 1934

——, *New Machiavelli, The Works of H.G. Wells*, T. Fisher Unwin, 1924–27

West, A., *H. G. Wells: Aspects of a Life*, Hutchinson, 1984

West, R., *The Meaning of Treason*, Second Edition, Macmillan, 1952

——, *The New Meaning of Treason*, Viking Press, 1964

West, W. (ed.), *Orwell: The War Broadcasts*, Duckworth, 1985

Wheeler-Bennett, J., *Munich: Prologue to Tragedy*, Macmillan, 1963

Whicker, A., *Within Whicker's World*, John Murray, 1994

Williamson, P., *National Crisis and National Government: British Politics, the Economy and Empire, 1926–1932*, Cambridge University Press, 1992

Wilson, K., *The Policy of the Entente: Essays on the Determinants of British Foreign Policy 1904–1914*, Cambridge University Press, 1985

Winterton, Lord, *Orders of the Day*, Cassell & Co., 1953

Woodward, D., *Lloyd George and the Generals*, University of Delaware Press, 1983

Wrench, J., *Geoffrey Dawson and Our Times*, Hutchinson, 1955

Young, K., *Arthur James Balfour: The Happy Life of the Politician, Prime Minister, Statesman and Philosopher, 1848–1930*, G. Bell, 1963

—— (ed.), *The Diaries of Sir Robert Bruce Lockhart: Volume 1 1915–1938*, Macmillan, 1973

Ziegler, P., *King Edward VIII*, Collins, 1990

Index